THE CHALLENGE OF POLITICS

The CHALLENGE *of* POLITICS

AN INTRODUCTION TO POLITICAL SCIENCE

Second Edition

Neal Riemer, Douglas W. Simon, Joseph Romance
Drew University

CQ PRESS

A Division of Congressional Quarterly Inc.
WASHINGTON, D.C.

CQ Press
1255 22nd Street, NW, Suite 400
Washington, DC 20037

Phone: 202-729-1900; toll-free, 1-866-427-7737 (1-866-4CQ-PRESS)

Web: www.cqpress.com

Copyright © 2006 by CQ Press, a division of Congressional Quarterly Inc.

Photo Credits:
Cover Photo: Courtesy of Art Resource
© 2000 Airphoto, Jim Wark: 423, 440
AP/Wide World Photos: 9, 16, 17, 23, 26, 33, 35, 48, 51, 57, 63, 79, 82, 88, 111, 148, 165, 170, 201, 214, 222, 255, 258, 263, 267, 276, 281, 310, 313, 318, 321, 322, 331, 332, 340, 349, 352, 360, 361, 369, 373, 380, 381, 383, 388, 390, 398, 405, 412, 430, 432
Courtesy of Art Resource: 123, 124, 128, 146, 154
Courtesy of Dr. Bruce Molnia, U.S. Geological Survey: 428 (left and right)
Courtesy of Prof. Donald F. M. Gerardi: 140
Courtesy of the National Archives: 218
Courtesy of the Thoreau Society: 27
Courtesy of Wan Kyun Rha Kim: 188
Courtesy of World Images News Services: 302
CQ file photo: 42, 169, 184, 186
Getty Images: 377
© Howard Davies/CORBIS: 419
Library of Congress: 20, 157, 187, 199, 205, 239
New Lanark Conservation Trust/www.newlanark.org: 175
North Wind Picture Archives: 134
Public domain/www.constitution.org: 135
Reproduced by kind permission of The Metropolitan Museum of Art, Catherine Lorillard Wolfe Collection, Wolfe Fund, 1931 (31.45): 39
Reuters: 93, 99, 108, 225, 236, 245, 290, 296, 358, 378, 413

Cover design: TGD Communications, Alexandria, VA

∞ The paper used in this publication exceeds the requirements of the American National Standard for Information Sciences—Permanence of Paper for Printed Library Materials, ANSI Z39.48-1992.

Printed and bound in the United States of America

10   09   08   07   06   1   2   3   4   5

Library of Congress Cataloging-in-Publication Data

Riemer, Neal
    The challenge of politics / Neal Riemer, Douglas W. Simon, Joseph Romance.—2nd ed.
    p. cm.
Includes bibliographical references and index.
    ISBN 1-933116-70-6 (alk. paper)
  1. Political science. I. Simon, Douglas W. II. Romance, Joseph, III. Title.
JA66.R498 2006
    320—dc22
                                                                                          2005037357

Brief Contents

Contents

Tables, Figures, Boxes, and Maps

TABLES

FIGURES

BOXES

MAPS

About the Authors

Neal Riemer was the Andrew V. Stout Professor of Political Philosophy at Drew University. After receiving a PhD from Harvard University, he taught at the Pennsylvania State University, the University of Wisconsin-Milwaukee, University of Innsbruck, Austria, and Drew University. His books include *Problems of American Government* (editor); *World Affairs: Problems and Prospects* (coauthor); *The Revival of Democratic Theory; The Democratic Experiment; The Future of the Democratic Revolution: Toward a More Prophetic Politics; New Thinking and Developments in International Politics: Opportunities and Dangers* (editor/coauthor); *Karl Marx and Prophetic Politics; James Madison: Creating the American Constitution; Creative Breakthroughs in Politics; Let Justice Roll: Prophetic Challenges in Religion, Politics, and Society* (editor/coauthor); and *Protection Against Genocide: Mission Impossible* (editor).

Douglas W. Simon is emeritus professor of political science at Drew University, where he specialized in international affairs, U.S. foreign policy, international organization, and national security. After receiving a BA from Willamette University, he served as an officer in U.S. air force intelligence, including a tour in Vietnam. Following his military service he earned a PhD at the University of Oregon. After arriving at Drew, Simon directed the university's Semester on the United Nations for fifteen years, served as convener of Drew's Masters in International Affairs Program, and later was department chair. In addition to *The Challenge of Politics,* he is coauthor of *New Thinking and Developments in International Politics: Opportunities and Dangers* and has contributed to such publications as the *Harvard Journal of World Affairs, East Asian Survey, Comparative Political Studies, International Studies Notes, Teaching Political Science,* and *Society.*

Joseph Romance is associate professor of political science at Drew University, teaching in the fields of American politics and political theory. He received a BA from the College of William and Mary and a PhD from Rutgers University. With Theodore Lowi and Gerald Pomper, he was coauthor of *A Republic of Parties: Debating the Two Party System* and is coauthor of and contributor to *Democracy and Excellence: Conflict or Concord?* Professor Romance is also the coeditor of *Democracy's Literature.* His articles and reviews have appeared in a number of journals, including *American Review of Politics, The Responsive Community, Perspectives on Political Science,* and *Newsday.* Romance has also contributed pieces to a number of edited volumes, including *Progressive Politics in the Global Age* and *Friends and Citizens.* He currently is working on a book about political foundings.

Preface

In this second edition of *The Challenge of Politics* we again advance a vision of political science that is sweeping in scope and integrative in nature. We believe that politics should be concerned with the creation of a humane, civilized society. For that reason, students of politics must not only work diligently to determine empirically what is and why, they must also make judgments as to which political systems and processes are most efficient and most humane.

We do not believe in a sharp distinction between classical and empirical theory in the pursuit of these goals. Instead, we strongly affirm students' need to appreciate the wisdom of classical theory as they address timeless questions: What is the good life? What is freedom? What is justice? When should citizens disobey their government? How do we balance individual rights and the broader interests of society? Throughout the text we constantly return to these and other fundamental questions.

We also welcome contemporary methods of investigating politics. For example, the ability to analyze data about what citizens and political actors think and do brings new dimension and depth to our understanding of what the good life is. Put simply, classical theory and the scientific method are never at war in this text. Knowing Plato's conception of the ideal just state, for instance, illuminates the kinds of political choices we make today as we think about war, economic efficiency and fairness, and the dangers of global pollution.

Further evidence of our desire to offer an integrative concept of political science is our belief that the four traditional fields of the discipline—political theory, American government, comparative politics, and international relations—can, and should, inform each other. When political science is taught in a compartmentalized fashion, as it frequently is, students may have difficulty seeing how the discipline's subfields interact as a whole. For example, controversies in American political parties can seem completely unrelated to the balance of power in international relations. Because we want students to see the whole of the political world, we focus on what constitutes a just and well-governed society. Students are motivated to see linkages between how governments work, how states interact, and how the great theorists of politics have shaped and influenced political actors.

This text puts forth the idea that all politics is about certain fundamental concepts. What are the political *values* that encourage a good political life? Can we develop a science of politics to help us understand the empirical realities of politics? Can we bring a high level of political prudence and wisdom to bear on public issues? Can we creatively address the future of politics? These are the concerns that form the bridges between the subfields of the discipline in *The Challenge of Politics*.

As we lead students to explore these questions, we remind them that politics is emphatically about choice and thinking about the possible. We give them the ability to make informed judgments about some of the most compelling public policy issues of our time: poverty, war and peace, human rights, and environmental degradation. In this way, we invite students to think about the future. How might a more just and civilized society come about? Can students of politics use their knowledge, reason, and innovation to develop creative breakthroughs in the way we govern ourselves as human beings?

ORGANIZATION

The Challenge of Politics is divided into four parts linked together by several common themes: political values, the science of politics, political wisdom, and the future of politics and political science.

Part 1 introduces students to the field of political science by focusing on the kinds of choices made by political actors. We use this approach because the element of choice is at the heart of politics and because we believe it is the most exciting way to engage students at the beginning. What is more compelling than to discover how giant political figures wrestled with political dilemmas, the resolution of which determined whether people lived or died? Chapters in this section also examine the tasks of political science and ask the critical question of just how scientific can political science be. Chapter 5 explores the physical, social, and cultural environments in which politics takes place, acknowledging that politics hardly occurs in a vacuum. For this edition we have added a more extensive discussion of religion and politics to this chapter, with particular emphasis on religious fundamentalism.

Part 2 explores the world of political philosophy and ideology. We give considerable attention to classical theory and the manner in which it illuminates our fundamental understanding of politics and the search for justice. In addition, we examine a number of modern ideologies, including liberal democracy, communism, and democratic socialism. In this edition of *Challenge,* we devote chapter 9 to an expanded discussion of dictatorship. While it is not widely considered an ideology, we believe it to be a significant challenge to other, more open, forms of government and as such deserving of attention. Examining these various forms of governance invites students to think about which values and ideas should take precedence over others. Is equality more important than freedom? Is democracy a better system than monarchy?

Part 3, Comparative and World Politics, examines political values and the problems that arise because of the gap between professed values and the actual behavior of political actors. This section is also concerned with the institutional context in which politics occurs. Why is this aspect of politics so important to students? In our judgment the reason is obvious. Tough political choices are shaped not merely by ideas but by the characteristics of the institutions of governance. How adequate and effective are these institutions of governance in seeking a just and humane society? Do they contribute to the political health of communities or to a more peaceful world? These are central questions that must be addressed by the student of politics. We assist this study by exploring the domestic political systems of a variety of countries, including discussions of their constitutions, voters, interest groups, political parties, media, legislatures, executives, bureaucracies, and courts. Later in the section is a chapter devoted exclusively to the world of international politics, within which we have updated and expanded our discussion of nongovernmental organizations and their growing importance in the world of foreign affairs. We conclude part 3 with a look at decision making in politics.

Part 4 invites students to apply the tools of the discipline to four critical public policy areas: war and peace, human rights, economic welfare, and the environment. We present a variety of approaches for dealing with these concerns. Some thought is devoted to considering which approaches offer the best opportunity for solving the most intractable policy problems. The chapters on public policy encourage students to articulate their own ethical values; to present and assess significant empirical findings relevant to the problems; and to balance ethical, empirical, and prudential concerns to reach sensible political judgments on important current problems. These chapters invite students to develop their own creative breakthroughs to solve these problems. In addition, part 4 is specifically designed to give instructors flexibility in the way they use the book. Each of the four policy chapters stands on its own; instructors can choose to have students read all four chapters or to assign chapters individually.

PEDAGOGY

We designed *The Challenge of Politics* to engage students' interest. Throughout this second edition students will find updated tables and graphs containing up-to-the minute data, as well as conceptual figures and maps that enhance the text. A wide array of photographs with substantive captions are incorporated throughout the text. In addition to traditional news and scenic photographs, we took considerable care to find photographs and portraits of important political theorists and personalities. For many students Plato, Machiavelli, Madison, Mill, Thoreau, and Marx are abstractions, merely names on a page. By presenting these images we hope that these figures will come alive.

Another feature of the book is the use of key questions at the beginning of most chapters. These questions are intended to get students thinking about some of the critical issues raised in each part of the book. Other features include an annotated list of suggested readings—a mixture of contemporary and classical works—at the end of each chapter as well as a list of key terms highlighted in the text and defined in an extensive glossary.

In addition to these text features, this new edition of *The Challenge of Politics* is accompanied by a redesigned Web site (www.cqpress.com/cs/challenge) composed of several elements: **chapter summaries** and **objectives**; **flashcards** to assist students in mastering key terms in the discipline; a **quiz section** with multiple-choice and true-false questions, an immediate grading feature, and the ability to e-mail results to instructors; **suggested readings** over and above those listed in the text; and **annotated Internet links** appropriate to each chapter. A test bank with multiple-choice, short-answer, and essay questions is available to instructors along with test generation software that allows instructors to customize exams, create various test forms (compatible with Blackboard and WebCT as well), and print out answer keys. And new to this edition, we created PowerPoint lecture slides to better assist professors in course planning.

Our hope is that after reading *The Challenge of Politics,* students will have gained a greater understanding and appreciation of the political world, perhaps even wanting to become active participants in the political arena themselves.

ACKNOWLEDGMENTS

Just as with the first edition of *The Challenge of Politics,* the entire staff at CQ Press has been a joy to work with. We would be hard pressed to find a group of people more professional, more responsive, and more helpful in getting this new edition into print. We are most appreciative to editorial assistant Anne Stewart, who was vital in photo research and acquisition. Production manager Paul Pressau and print buyer Margot Ziperman were instrumental in bringing *Challenge* to reality. Talia Greenberg did an absolutely superb job of copyediting, and we are deeply indebted to Lorna Notsch for her splendid work as production editor on this project. And, of course, we are thrilled once again to be associated with the fine leadership of Charisse Kiino, chief acquisitions editor for the College Division at CQ Press.

Our political science colleagues at Drew were once again most generous with their wise counsel: Catherine Keyser, Debra Liebowitz, Bill Messmer, Hans Morsink, Phil Mundo, and Paul Wice. We could not have a finer group of professional colleagues and friends.

Introduction

In *The Challenge of Politics* we seek to introduce you to the intriguing discipline of political science. We strongly believe that our unique and comprehensive approach can best equip you, the student of political science, to stay abreast of the ever changing, challenging world of politics, a world now beginning a new millennium. This is a world in which the paramount issues of peace/war, human rights/tyranny, prosperity/poverty, and ecological balance/malaise continue to dominate the political agenda.

Major changes and challenges demand the attention of students of political science. For example, the bitterly contested and close U.S. presidential election in 2004 and the continuation of the George W. Bush administration in Washington; the specter of terrorism after the September 11, 2001, attacks on the World Trade Center towers and the Pentagon, followed by major attacks in, among other places, Madrid in 2004 and London and Egypt in 2005; the global "war on terrorism" with major military efforts in Iraq and Afghanistan and the difficult task of nation-building in these countries; the ongoing struggle to balance the need for security and the maintenance of civil liberties as we fight terrorism; Russia's struggles under the leadership of what some believe is an increasingly authoritarian president; economic liberalization in China as the nation emerges as a growing economic power; and a host of other domestic and international struggles in Latin America, the Middle East, Africa, and Asia: all require us to reassess the strengths and weaknesses of liberal democracy in the United States. These changes and challenges require us to ponder the political, economic, and social evolution of such great powers as Russia and China; to evaluate prospects for peace in the Middle East and other conflict-ridden regions; and to assess the emergence of stable and rights-respecting regimes in the developing countries of the world.

As we seek to keep abreast of these developments, we need to keep our eyes focused on four key questions. These questions highlight the analytic framework of our unique and comprehensive approach to the study of politics and political science.

1. Can we as citizens and students articulate, and defend, a view of the good political life and its guiding **political values?**
2. Can we develop a **science of politics** to help us understand significant political phenomena—the empirical realities of politics?
3. Can we bring a high level of **political prudence or wisdom** to bear on judgments about politics and public issues?
4. Can citizens and students creatively address the **future of politics?**

These questions are difficult because vigorous debate still rages about the meaning of the good political life; about the very possibility of a science of politics; about the likelihood of making wise judgments; about the difficulties of linking the ethical, social scientific, and prudential concerns of political science; and about the future of politics. Despite the difficulty of the questions, asking them enables students of politics to explore political philosophy and ideology, major forms of government, and key public policy issues involving peace and war, prosperity and poverty, human rights and wrongs, and ecological balance and malaise. Why is that important? It is important because these are the critical belief systems and policy issues that directly affect people's lives—the way we choose our leaders, the way we govern ourselves, the way we treat each other as human beings inside and outside our country. We welcome the challenges of exploring these systems and issues, and hope that our approach will contribute to enlightened dialogue and creative debate.

POLITICAL VALUES

Addressing the first question of our framework, that of political values, we reaffirm our normative preference for politics as a civilizing enterprise, one that enables people in the political community to live better, to grow robustly in mind and spirit, and to find creative fulfillment. This normative preference has guided our choice of topics in this book. The theme of politics as a civilizing enterprise has also provided a standard for exploring the meaning of political health, a metaphor for the political community that is able to secure peace, protect human rights, enhance economic prosperity, and advance ecological balance—and thus facilitate creative individual realization within the framework of the common good.

To hold this perspective, however, does not mean ignoring the ugly fact that politics often is not a civilizing enterprise, that politics is sometimes a dirty and unpleasant business. Truth, honor, and decency are sometimes casualties in the world of politics. Appreciating the realities of politics clearly requires a keen understanding of war as well as peace, tyranny as well as freedom, injustice as well as justice, poverty as well as prosperity, ecological malaise as well as ecological well-being. Put simply, it remains important to see—and to seek to achieve—politics at its best, as well as to recognize how it can degenerate and function at its worst.

A SCIENCE OF POLITICS

The science of politics compels us to determine, as accurately and truthfully as possible, the objective reality of what goes on in the political arena. Students of politics are faced with the task of accurately assessing and understanding past, present, and emerging political realities. Understanding changing realms of domestic and international politics is an important, and often neglected, task.

Keeping abreast of the changing and challenging nature of politics is clearly an imperative of a realistic political science. However, change is not always unique or singular. Political science recognizes the enduring realities of the struggle for power. Current developments and contemporary changes are always best understood in the light of those enduring ethical, empirical, and prudential realities. It is also most important to appreciate that changes may pose dangers to be avoided as well as opportunities to be seized. Changes may, unpredictably, usher in the "best of times" or the "worst of times."

Strikingly, the changes and challenges outlined in this book all relate to the political values of peace, freedom, economic well-being, and ecological balance, and thus offer a way to link events across eras and regions, from the domestic realm to the international realm.

POLITICAL WISDOM

Political actors, as they seek to advance their values in the light of the realities of politics, will need to exercise wise political judgment as they respond to the striking changes that have taken place in recent years. The challenge of politics calls upon students and citizens to make wise decisions based on a combination of factors: thorough knowledge, deep understanding, rational thought, and a sense of compassion. Wisdom must be brought to bear in responding to the different character of the rivalries between the world's major powers since the end of the cold war, to the ongoing problems of liberal democracies, to the continuing plight of many developing countries, and to a host of other challenging political, economic, religious, scientific, and environmental developments.

THE FUTURE OF POLITICS AND POLITICAL SCIENCE

Attention to the preceding features of *The Challenge of Politics*—political values, the science of politics, and political wisdom—helps one to attend to future problems. Here we have in mind not only the immediate future but the long-range future as well. In the prophetic tradition we must carefully scrutinize the future as well as the past and the present. Political scientists need to be trained to employ futuristic scenarios, positive and negative, in order to critically assess the future of politics. Here students of political science are challenged to explore the future imaginatively. Consequently, we encourage you to utilize the analytical framework of the text (1) to probe the future of political values more clearly, fully, and critically; (2) to seek to grasp the emerging realities of politics more incisively, keenly, and astutely; and (3) to weigh the costs and benefits of future alternative judgments, policies, and actions more prudently, humanely, and practically in order to reach wise decisions.

Seeking to advance the critical exploration of the book's cardinal questions, each part will explore a key organizing question. In part one, "Rules of the Game"—our introduction to the field and study of political science—we ask this question: *How can we best understand politics and political science?* To stimulate interest about the nature and challenge of politics, chapters 1 and 2 utilize some dramatic "political games" to underscore crucial choices. Thus chapter 1 employs four cases drawn from history, literature, and political philosophy to focus on the players, stakes, rules, strategies, and tactics in the "game" of politics. Chapter 2 employs four memorable cases to emphasize the central role of choice in politics. Then after using these cases and choices to highlight goals, realities, and judgments in politics, we move on—in chapter 3—to outline the major tasks, fields, and controversies of political science in a more systematic way. Following naturally from that examination, chapter 4 explores one of the more critical questions about the discipline of political science: *Just how scientific can political science be?* Finally, in chapter 5, we emphasize how the larger physical, social, and cultural environment affects the discipline and its tasks.

Our guiding question in part two—"Political Philosophy and Ideology"—is: *How do political philosophy and ideology illuminate our understanding of politics?* In chapter 6 we discuss the contributions of the great political philosophers, and in chapters 7 and 8 we examine such political ideologies as liberal democracy, communism, and democratic socialism. In the final chapter in part two, chapter 9, we discuss a form of governance that poses a significant challenge to these ideologies (or belief systems), namely dictatorship, with emphasis on fascism.

In part three—"Comparative and World Politics"—we consider the question: *How far have we come in developing a fruitful science of politics?* In chapters 10–13 we focus on such significant empirical problems as the gap between the actual and professed values of political actors. We also explore which political patterns are successful in furthering cooperation, advancing accommodation, and handling conflicts in national and international politics. In chapter 14, on decision-making models in politics, we underscore the important reality that politics inescapably involves judgment and action—a topic that leads logically to a fuller exploration of public policy in part four.

In part four—"Political Judgment and Public Policy"—we focus on the question: *How can we sharpen our prudent judgment on key issues of public policy?* In order to probe this question we explore in chapters 15–18 a number of policy issues of global concern, such as the achievement of a peaceful world order, greater protection for human rights, economic well-being, and a sane ecological balance. The public policy chapters seek to encourage you to articulate your own ethical values, to present and assess significant empirical findings relevant to the problems at hand, and finally, to balance ethical, empirical, and prudential concerns in reaching sensible political judgments on important—and controversial—problems of the day, the decade, and the future.

In the conclusion, we ask: *How will we, in the twenty-first century, carry on the work of politics as a civilizing enterprise?* We will set forth some scenarios about the future of politics—scenarios involving the character of the political world in a new century. Our final chapter recognizes that you who read this book will be engaged in the politics of the twenty-first century. You will have to be prepared to take charge and to respond intelligently, effectively, and humanely to future political issues of this new century.

Part 1

RULES OF THE GAME

The chapters in part 1 seek to introduce you to politics and the discipline of political science and to provide you with a framework for a more complete exploration of the nature of politics and political science. They are designed to help you understand the political scientist's tasks, fields of study, and key controversies. You are invited to think critically about politics, especially about the extent to which politics functions as a civilizing activity. Are the tasks we discuss the tasks that political scientists ought to be performing? Do the traditional fields of study do justice to the discipline? The central question that each of these introductory chapters addresses is: *How can we best understand politics and political science?*

Chapters 1 and 2 begin by presenting some "games" that politicians play and by emphasizing the importance of choice. These games and choices highlight differing views of the good political life, of political realities, and of wise judgment. The metaphor of a game calls attention to these crucial features of politics: players, stakes, rules, and behavioral strategy and tactics. Four dramatic models illustrate the way power—a cardinal factor in politics—is used. These sample games are designed to help you think critically about ends and means in politics. These chapters also highlight the struggle for power in politics—that is, who gets what, when, how, and why. Our presentation builds on your commonsense understanding of power as strength and influence and on your appreciation of the military, political, economic, and ideological aspects of power.

Politics involves grappling with tough problems in an often difficult world. By focusing on four momentous choices in politics, chapter 2 again underscores the relationship among values, behavior, and judgment. These choices highlight the creative challenge involved in reaching wise decisions. Thoughtful investigation of these choices should stimulate you to probe political philosophy and ethics, comparative and world politics, and public policy in the succeeding parts of this book. Chapters 1 and 2 are designed to engage your interest and to prepare you for a somewhat more systematic presentation of our approach to political science and its main concern: politics.

Chapters 3 and 4 define political science and outline the conceptual framework for the entire book as well as address the critical question of just how scientific political science can be. Political scientists, we emphasize, explore the good political life, a science of politics, and wise judgment on public policy. Although these interests are evident in the traditional fields of political science, political scientists still argue about which of these concerns should be most prominent and about fitting them into a unified discipline.

Our exposition of the nature of political science assumes some familiarity with our suggested framework. Indeed, you could not have lived seventeen to twenty-one years or more without arriving at some views about the good political life, acquiring some understanding of political realities, and making some judgments about political actors, institutions, and policies. Chapters 3 and 4 build on this awareness.

Chapter 5, the final chapter in part one, explores how the larger physical, social, and cultural environment influences political values, behavior, and judgment. To understand problems in politics, people need to be aware, for example, of the geographic world they live in, the biological creatures they are, and the social communities they have built. The work of political scientists is thus informed by a variety of scholars, among them historians, economists, geographers, sociologists, anthropologists, psychologists, and physicists. Chapter 5 seeks to make students of political science very cognizant of the interdisciplinary setting of politics.

Chapter 1

GAMES POLITICIANS PLAY

At its best, politics can be a civilizing activity. It can preserve the peace, protect human rights, advance economic well-being, and encourage excellence in the arts and sciences. At its worst, however, politics—particularly for those on the losing side of the struggle for power—makes for war, tyranny, economic ruin, and barbarism. Even in democratic and constitutional countries, politics at its worst involves falsehood, deception, and meanness. In this chapter we explore politics at its best and at its worst by examining some classic models in history, literature, and political philosophy. These examples suggest certain patterns that we call "political games."

THE GAME OF POLITICS

Politics is a process, within or among political communities, whereby (1) public values are articulated, debated, and prescribed; (2) diverse political actors (individuals, interest groups, local or regional governments, and nations) cooperate and struggle for power to satisfy their vital needs, protect their fundamental interests, and advance their perceived desires; and (3) policy judgments are made and implemented. Although subject to certain constraints imposed by the larger environment, political actors are still remarkably free to shape their own destinies—for good or ill. They have a creative ability to respond to political problems in diverse ways. The political games we will analyze illustrate a variety of such responses. Your critical appraisal of these games should advance three of this book's central purposes:

- to deepen your critical appreciation of the good political life;
- to enhance your scientific understanding of politics;
- to develop your capacity for wise political judgment.

9

We chose the games that follow because they illustrate a wide range of political activity—physical annihilation, the Machiavellian struggle for power, the political strike, and nonviolent civil disobedience. These patterns illustrate various forms of power: military power, political cunning, the withholding of vital services, and the appeal to conscience. Although we do not include the wheeling and dealing of such constitutional games as "bargaining"—commonly referred to as the politics of accommodation—this pattern is treated frequently later in the book (for example, in chapters 2, 6, 7, 12, 13, and 15).

Elements of the Game

In this introductory chapter our guiding question is: *How can the metaphor of a game serve our understanding of politics?* The political games that we present are dramatic and educational. As drama they may entertain. As education they may enhance critical intelligence and shape political character and wise judgment. But can such a serious business as politics be called a game? We certainly do not mean to imply a frivolous pastime. We do, however, mean to suggest that all politics as contests have certain basic elements commonly found in other kinds of games. A game includes **players**—contestants who win or lose, who compete or cooperate in pursuit of certain goals, who exercise power or will, who enjoy or suffer. The **stakes** in the game are the goals that can be gained in victory or lost in defeat. The **rules** are the agreed-on procedures that must be followed if the game is to retain its identity; they regulate the conduct of the game. Finally, games entail **strategies and tactics**—plans of action, schemes of attack or defense, judgments that bring about victory or defeat.

Thus one way to look at politics is to see it as a gamelike struggle to fulfill certain purposes; to gain, keep, and use power; and to formulate public policy. By viewing politics in this way, we can better explore its key patterns, particularly with the help of the following questions:

- *Who are the players? Why do they play as they do? What are their strengths and weaknesses?* Answers to these questions can reveal the players' political values, behavior, and judgment.
- *What is the game about?* In politics the stakes may be life or death, freedom or slavery, peace or war. The issues may involve economic prosperity or poverty, order or disorder, civilization or barbarism. A given contest may take the form of an election. In a developing nation, independence and orderly growth may be at stake. Elsewhere the crucial issue may be economic growth, education, or crime. Or it may be increased opportunities for minorities. To explore such contests is to explore political ideals, behavior, and judgment.
- *How is the game ordered—if it is ordered?* Students of political games are vitally interested in what the rules permit and what limits and penalties they impose. Are the rules designed to advance order and fairness? Students of politics are particularly

concerned about the existence of an umpire to ensure that the rules are followed. Such considerations also require the student to explore ethical, empirical, and prudential questions.

- *Which strategies are wisest?* This question encourages students of political games to distinguish between strategy and tactics, to increase their capacity for wise judgment, and to explore the connections among policy, purpose, and power.

Unfortunately, the games politicians play are more complicated than football or chess. Unlike the contestants in such games, politicians involved in a given battle may not follow the same rules or even any discernible set of directions. If all the players do not follow the same rules, the players who have to respond to their opponents are at a serious disadvantage. This creates the kind of confusion and alarm that we call the Alice-in-Wonderland effect. When Alice plays croquet in Wonderland, she is not accustomed to using hedgehogs for croquet balls, flamingos for mallets, and soldiers for arches. Nor is she accustomed to a system in which the accused is first beheaded and then tried!

To compound the confusion created when there is no agreement on rules, politicians frequently shift from one game to another without warning. Consequently, a participant may not be aware of the decisive game—and its rules—until the contest is over. Politicians may also attempt to play several games simultaneously.

The Destruction-Accommodation-Conversion Continuum

Can we devise a scheme to help us understand the variety of political games? Several classifications are possible. Figure 1.1 offers a scheme in which the games are seen as ranging across a destruction-accommodation-conversion continuum. At one end of the con-

Figure 1.1 The Destruction-Accommodation-Conversion Continuum

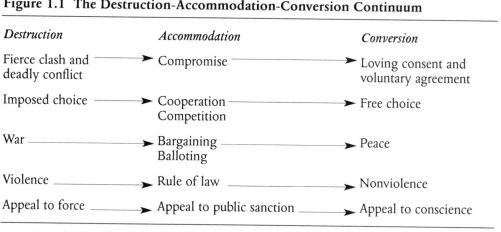

Destruction	*Accommodation*	*Conversion*
Fierce clash and deadly conflict →	Compromise	Loving consent and voluntary agreement
Imposed choice →	Cooperation / Competition	Free choice
War →	Bargaining / Balloting	Peace
Violence →	Rule of law	Nonviolence
Appeal to force →	Appeal to public sanction	Appeal to conscience

Source: Compiled by authors.

tinuum are games aimed at complete **destruction** of the opposing player. These games are marked by deadly conflict and war. Violence, including terrorism and torture, is prominent, and political, economic, psychological, and military instruments of force are used to exercise power.

Joseph Stalin's destruction of those he perceived as enemies within the Soviet Union is one infamous example of a game of destruction. Stalin came to power in the Soviet Union shortly after V. I. Lenin's death in 1924 and ruled with dictatorial power until his own death in 1953. Through his actions and policies, Stalin executed high-ranking political and military leaders and millions of other people suspected of disloyalty. Many people were killed outright; others died of starvation; still others died in prison camps. No one was allowed to stand in the way of his quest for absolute power.

Adolf Hitler also illustrates a twentieth-century pattern of destruction. He, too, killed high-ranking party members who had helped him come to power. He, too, destroyed all effective political opposition to his rule. His barbaric campaign of destruction led to murderous onslaughts against Germany's neighbors, to slave labor for millions forced to work for the Nazi war machine, to concentration camps and death for millions of Germans and other Europeans, and to the Holocaust (the systematic killing of six million Jews).

More recent examples of the destruction game can be found all around the world: in the genocidal slaughter in Cambodia (Kampuchea) in Southeast Asia, and in Rwanda and the Darfur region of Sudan in Africa; in the "ethnic cleansing" in Bosnia-Herzegovina, a former part of Yugoslavia, and in Kosovo, Serbia; and in the terrorism visited on New York City and Washington, D.C., with the total destruction of the World Trade Center towers and partial destruction of the Pentagon. Such destruction was a dreadful twentieth-century reality of politics at its worst, and now, it seems, it is a reality of the twenty-first century as well. Will this type of destruction continue in this century?

In the middle of the continuum are games of **accommodation**, marked by cooperation, bargaining, and balloting. This pattern of politics is characterized by free elections, a two-party or multiparty system, public debate, and constitutional action according to the rule of law. Games of accommodation predominate in liberal democracies and in democratic socialist regimes. However, variations on these games also occur in authoritarian regimes.

At the other end of the continuum are games characterized by the peaceful **conversion** of the opponent. This pattern of politics stresses voluntary agreement and emphasizes free choice. In this pattern even a majority decision may be ignored if the majority deviates from the claims of conscience. Love, conscience, and reason are the instruments employed in games of conversion. If games of destruction rely on arbitrary dictatorial edict and games of accommodation rely on constitutional majority rule, then games of conversion look to unanimous agreement. Players of the game of conversion—for example, religious groups such as the Society of Friends (Quakers)—may seek to exercise influence (a version of power), but such influence is based, they argue, on truth and love rather than on majority rule or physical force.

Thus the use of **power** to get political actors to do what they would not normally do ranges from overwhelming violence at the extreme pole of destruction to overwhelming charismatic, or spiritual, power—the free appeal, by word and deed, to the mind and heart—at the other pole of conversion. Political games, then, may involve fierce clashes and deadly conflicts, mild competition and pacific accommodation, or loving consent and freely given obedience.

Along the continuum, power may be used in many ways other than for destruction or conversion. Power may be used to balance, to seduce, or to support. For example, political actors may use the carrot or the stick to exercise influence: they may promise and deliver a host of benefits (money, goods and services, position, prestige), or they may threaten and retaliate with sanctions (the loss of benefits).

Political behavior is thus often a mixture of bullets and ballots, of arbitrary might and the rule of law, of bullying and encouraging. The character of the game depends significantly on the sanity of the players, the vital interests at stake, the status of rules and law, and judgments about wise policy and strategy.

Now we will turn to some dramatic games drawn from history, literature, and political theory. These moments illustrate the way the game of politics is played in all its variety.

WIPEOUT: THE POLITICS OF DESTRUCTION

Superficially, **wipeout** is a simple game. One player, insisting on total domination, encounters resistance and employs brute physical force to destroy an opponent. Wipeout exemplifies the ultimate use of force in the struggle for power. Of course, complications can occur because of the different ways in which power is used, the maneuvers that precede total destruction, the strange "logic" of a "reason of state" that "justifies" exterminating the opponent. The following classic model of wipeout will help explain some possible complications.

Athens and Melos

In his *History of the Peloponnesian War,* the Greek historian Thucydides presents the game with brilliant clarity.[1] The game unfolds at Melos, a Greek island caught in the midst of the savage war between two mortal political enemies: Athens and Sparta. Because the Melians will "not submit to the Athenians like the other islanders," they are forced into a confrontation. In the great struggle between Athens and Sparta for the mastery of greater Greece, the Melians at first remain neutral. But when the Athenians plunder Melian territory, the Melians assume "an attitude of open hostility." This leads to the brutal confrontation between the Athenians and the Melians.

Map 1.1 Ancient Greece

Initially, the Athenians seek to negotiate the capitulation of Melos without all-out war. They have overwhelming military power and want to press their advantage. Their message is loud and clear: Surrender or be wiped out! They attempt to win the Melians over by appealing to their self-interest. The safety and security—indeed, the very preservation— of Melos requires that the Melians submit to Athens. The Melians must accept the harsh realities of power politics. The Athenians candidly declare: "You know as well as we do that right, as the world goes, is only in question between equals in power. . . . The strong do what they can and the weak suffer what they must." Do not, they urge the Melians, rely on appeals to justice, the gods, or the Spartans. Such appeals will not be answered.

At a serious disadvantage in the contest, the Melians try desperately to shift the game's emphasis from power to **justice**. They plead for the "privilege of being allowed in danger to invoke what is fair and right." They appeal to the gods. They remind Athens of the power of Sparta. They warn Athens of potential dangers. They cling to the idea of heroic resistance: "To submit is to give ourselves over to despair, while action still preserves for us a hope that we may stand erect. . . . We will not in a moment deprive of freedom a city that has been inhabited these seven hundred years . . . and so we will try to save ourselves. Meanwhile we invite you to allow us to be friends to you and foes to neither party."

The Athenians reject the idea of a neutral Melos and reemphasize their earlier arguments. The neutrality of Melos would adversely affect Athenian power, and appeals to justice, the gods, and the Spartans will not be answered because gods and men respect power. "Of the gods we believe, and of men we know, that by a necessary law of their nature they rule wherever they can." The Spartans will aid the Melians only when Spartan self-interest is engaged and Spartan power can be mustered without grave risk. Unfortunately for Melos, Sparta's vital interests are not at stake, and its power is not great enough to warrant a challenge to Athens at Melos. And so the Athenians plead with the Melians: Do not be blind. Be prudent. Save yourselves. Do not be led by fear of disgrace into hopeless disaster. Do not hesitate to protect your country and its prosperity. Choose security, not war and ruin.

So the game is played. The Athenians seek domination without war but reserve the power to destroy their opponent. The Melians insist on freedom and independence even at the risk of war, and they hope for the best. Thus the debate over power and justice, over "reason of state" and enlightened self-interest, comes to an end. The war of words, which so candidly reveals the strategy and tactics of the players, ceases. Physical hostilities commence. The Athenians lay siege to the isle of Melos. Pushed beyond endurance, the Melians finally surrender. Thucydides writes that the Athenians "put to death all the grown men whom they took, and sold the children for slaves, and subsequently sent out five hundred colonists and inhabited the place themselves."

This sketch identifies the players, stakes, rules, and strategy of the game of wipeout. The opponents played for varied stakes. Athens sought to dominate Melos. For Melos there were three possible outcomes: (1) life and freedom, at best; (2) submission and domination if Melos agreed to accept Athens's terms; or (3) war, destruction, slavery, and death, at worst.

In examining this game, we discover that there were no agreed-on rules to protect the Melians. They sought in vain to persuade the Athenians to honor a code of justice and to respect the rules of neutrality. The Melians also failed to convince the Athenians to observe the rule that warns of the penalties for aggression. Such penalties may have to be paid when the aggressor's action engenders countervailing power or when the aggressor loses power.

The Athenians urged the Melians to accept the game of mastery. They urged the Melians to consider the penalties for failing to play the Athenian game: war, destruction, and death. They urged recognition of the rule that "justice" is the interest of the stronger party. Superior power, not abstract justice or sentimental good will, is what counts in politics. Athenian strategy was thus guided by Athens's need to protect its vital interests with superior strength. Such strength could normally convince an opponent, who sees self-preservation as the most vital interest, to back down. Melian strategy included an appeal to the gods, to justice, to the Spartans, and to Athenian self-interest.

The political game of wipeout was viciously played out in Cambodia during the mid-1970s, when more than one million people died at the hands of the radical Khmer Rouge. The landscape of this southeast Asian country is dotted with "killing fields" such as this one on the outskirts of the capital, Phnom Penh.

Relevance to Modern Politics

The pattern of purpose, power, and policy revealed by this game can be illustrated in a host of actions throughout history. We have already highlighted the destructive patterns of Stalin and Hitler. To their actions we can add thousands of other wipeouts, such as the conquests of native North and South Americans by Spaniards, Portuguese, Anglo-Americans, and French. Communist regimes in North Korea, China, and Cuba have also wiped out their political opponents, sometimes through murder, sometimes through imprisonment or exile. Fascist dictators such as Benito Mussolini in Italy and Francisco Franco in Spain did likewise. In recent history we have the brutality of Saddam Hussein in Iraq.

Genocide and **ethnic cleansing** are other forms of wipeout. Genocide is the systematic mass destruction of a national, ethnic, racial, or religious group and ethnic cleansing is the forceful displacement of a group from a given territory based on its religion, ethnicity, race, or nationality and may involve mass murder as well. In Cambodia (Kampuchea), from 1975 to 1978, the Khmer Rouge, led by Pol Pot, compiled one of the worst records of human rights violations in history as a result of a thorough and brutal attempt to restructure Cambodian society. More than one million people, out of a total population of approximately seven million, were killed or died under the Khmer Rouge's genocidal regime.[2] To this horror, we can add the genocide in Rwanda in 1994, in which members of the Hutu tribe killed nearly one million of their fellow Rwandans who were members of the Tutsi tribe. Ethnic cleansing in Bosnia and Serbia, also in the mid-1990s, and in the Darfur region of Sudan in the first decade of this century illustrate a contemporary pattern of wipeout.

Terrorism is another pattern of political wipeout. Defining the term is a very difficult and controversial task. Nonetheless, there is at least some agreement that terrorism is the use of violence against innocent civilians in order to achieve a political goal. But two issues make it difficult to get beyond this simple definition. The first issue is motive. There is an old cliché: "One man's terrorist is another man's freedom fighter." One view holds that terrorism is nothing more than a vicious criminal act and there is no excuse for the killing of innocent people. Others take the stand that terrorism can, at least to some degree, be a legitimate instrument to counter powerful government repression and other unjust policies. It is viewed by some as an act of liberation. The other controversy has to do with identifying the terrorists. Some people believe that the definition of terrorism should include acts of terror perpetrated by governments, not merely nongovernmental groups. With an understanding that these issues are not fully resolved, terrorism will be defined as the use of violence by nongovernmental groups against innocent civilians for the purpose of achieving political goals.

While in recent years much of our attention has been riveted on the September 11, 2001, attacks on the World Trade Center in New York City and the Pentagon in Washington, D.C., terrorism can be traced back two thousand years to groups like the Sicari and the Zealots, Jewish groups who fought against the Roman occupation of

Osama bin Laden, head of al Qaeda and architect of the 9/11 attacks on the United States, speaks from an undisclosed location in a televised image broadcast October 7, 2001, in which he praises God for the terrorist attacks and swears America "will never dream of security" until "the infidel's armies leave the land of Muhammad." The graphic at top right reads "Exclusive to al-Jazeera" (the all-Arabic television news channel). At bottom right is the station's logo. At top left is "Recorded," and at bottom left is "Urgent news." Born in Saudi Arabia, bin Laden seeks, among other things, to rid the Middle East of Western influence.

first-century Middle East. Another early religious terrorist group, the Assassins, operating in the eleventh century, found its origins in the Ismaili sect of Shia Islam. The Balkans, Russia, and Ireland were fertile grounds for terrorist organizations during the latter part of the nineteenth century. The United States was not immune from terrorism during this period, as evidenced by the violent activities of the Ku Klux Klan to fight Reconstruction after the Civil War. In the post–World War II period, terrorist methods were used by some, but not all, decolonization movements in Africa, the Middle East, and Asia.[3]

The modern era of international terrorism emerged primarily out of Europe and the Middle East with a variety of groups crossing national borders to carry out high-profile terrorist acts in order to maximize visibility for their cause. During the latter part of the 1960s and through the 1970s, groups such as the Palestine Liberation Organization, the Italian Red Brigades, and the West German Red Army faction carried out a large number of spectacular terrorist acts that involved airline skyjacking and kidnapping of high-profile hostages. Probably the most famous terrorist act prior to September 11 was the attack at the 1972 Olympic Games in Germany when the Palestinian group Black September seized and murdered eleven Israeli athletes.

Despite all the attention given to international terrorism, with the United States and other countries waging a war against terrorism, the actual frequency of terrorist incidents

Figure 1.2 Terrorist Attacks, 1982–2003

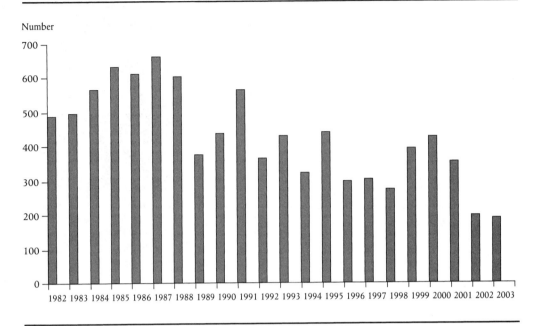

Number

Source: U.S. Department of State, *Patterns of Global Terrorism 2003, 2004*, www.state.gov.

is relatively low when compared to merely a few years ago. As Figure 1.2 notes, international terrorism reached near-epidemic levels during the latter half of the 1980s. In each of the years 1985, 1986, 1987, and 1988, the number of terrorist incidents exceeded six hundred. By 2003 that number had fallen to slightly more than two hundred per year. That is not to minimize the threat of this deadly game of wipeout. The September 11 attacks by al Qaeda operatives clearly demonstrate that a few incidents can kill thousands of people. And some worry that the sophistication of the attacks has grown in recent years.

To understand such political games is not to approve of them, any more than a doctor approves of disease. But in the body politic, as in medicine, diagnosis must precede prognosis. Only with a fuller, more critical understanding of purpose, power, and policy can we begin to explore what leads some political actors to engage in wipeout. We can then ask a crucial ethical question: What power should be exercised to protect a state's vital interests or a ruler's ideological commitments or positions? We can also ask an important empirical question: Is superior power (understood here as physical force) what counts in politics? And we can ask a troubling prudential question: Is it ever wise to sacrifice freedom to ensure self-preservation?

The relevance of these matters to modern politics is suggested by the following questions, which illustrate the problematic character of politics:

- In order to protect the lives of American soldiers and to bring World War II to a rapid end, was President Harry S. Truman justified in ordering the destruction of Hiroshima with the first atomic bomb?
- If the Allies had not mustered superior physical force against the Nazis and the Japanese in World War II, would Hitler and the Japanese warlords have triumphed, and with what consequences for freedom?
- Were the Japanese and the Germans wise to accept unconditional surrender—and at least a temporary loss of their freedom—to ensure their self-preservation?

These questions suggest the difficulties inherent in the struggle for power. Next we will examine another political game to illustrate the complexity of that struggle.

LION AND FOX: THE POLITICS OF THE NATION-STATE

We find the title of our second game in the work of Niccolò Machiavelli, a controversial student of Renaissance Italy.[4] The key players are the rulers of states. At stake are each state's vital interests: its unity, independence, freedom, security, power, and prosperity. The key rules in this game require leaders to behave realistically, to protect their community's vital interests, and to use both force and craft. Violation of the rules will incur severe penalties.

Machiavelli: The End Justifies the Means

If princes, or rulers, are to win amid the struggles for power that surround them, they must be adept at the "beastly" game of realistic politics. They cannot survive and prosper if they know or play only the higher human game of morality and law. They must know the game of **lion and fox**, played primarily with force and craft and, if necessary, unscrupulously. As Machiavelli puts it: "A prince being thus obliged to know well how to act as a beast must imitate the fox and the lion, for the lion cannot protect himself from traps, and the fox cannot defend himself from wolves. One must therefore be a fox to recognize traps, and a lion to frighten wolves."

Machiavelli holds that a prince is justified in playing the game of lion and fox because "in the actions of men, and especially of princes . . . the end justifies the means." "For," he writes, "where the very safety of the country depends upon the resolution to be taken, no considerations of justice or injustice, humanity or cruelty, nor of glory or of shame, should be allowed to prevail. But putting all other considerations aside, the only question should

Machiavelli is known as both a political thinker and practicing politician. In this painting Machiavelli is shown seated near Cesare Borgia—a true prince who was willing to use both force, like the lion, and cunning, like the fox, to achieve his goals. Machiavelli's most famous book, The Prince, *highlighted the abilities of men like Borgia to do whatever is necessary to achieve and maintain power. Painting by Faraffini, circa 1898.*

be, What course will save the life and liberty of the country?" When the occasion demands it, force and craft must be used boldly and shrewdly. On such occasions "good faith" and "integrity" can be sacrificed. The prince (as a lion or a fox) has only "to be a great feigner and dissembler." Machiavelli continues, "Thus it is well to seem merciful, faithful, humane, sincere, religious, and also to be so; but you must have the mind so disposed that when it is needful to be otherwise you may be able to change to the opposite qualities." Hence, "in order to maintain the state," a prince may be obliged "to act against faith, against charity, against humanity, and against religion."

Machiavelli outlines the general strategy of lion and fox with great candor. The prince must act "to secure himself against enemies, to gain friends, to conquer by force or fraud, to make himself beloved and feared by the people, [and] followed and reverenced by . . . [his] soldiers." With a keen regard for circumstances, he must act with Renaissance *virtù—* that is, with resolve and energy. Appreciative of dangers, the prince must be prepared to "destroy those who can injure him." With an eye to power, he must "maintain the friendship of kings and princes in such a way that they are glad to benefit him and fear to injure him." Recognizing the importance of the citizenry, the prince will win and keep widespread popular support and rely on a loyal citizen army. Above all, he will use muscle power and brainpower, severity and kindness, with discrimination and a shrewd regard for his ends and his power.

Machiavelli does not exclude the rule of law or the influence of traditional Christian morality. But he does assert that, in playing the game of lion and fox in a corrupt world, the prince who confuses what ought to be with what is will surely lose. "For how we live is so far removed from how we ought to live, that he who abandons what is done for what ought to be done, will rather learn to bring about his own ruin than his preservation."

The foregoing strategy is prominent in *The Prince,* which Machiavelli wrote as a textbook for statesmen who would establish a state in a world beset by corruption, quarrelsome groups, foreign interference, and external aggression. But even in *The Discourses,* his book on the internal and external affairs of Rome, Machiavelli insists that those who would rule a republic on the basis of good laws must also be concerned with good arms. Moreover, even in a republic, a high commitment to popular virtue, a balance of social classes, the constitutional competition of parties, and the sound exercise of public opinion must not make the republican ruler forget the beastly game of lion and fox.

Physical power, particularly military strength, is crucial in nation-state politics and must be used, when necessary, effectively. For Machiavelli, military power means a citizen army. Good soldiers are the "sinews of war." The prince must be skilled in the organization, discipline, and conduct of war. He must use power to eliminate actual enemies and to paralyze potential enemies. The prince must be wary of helping others to become powerful. He must avoid making common cause with someone more powerful than himself. He should always use shrewd judgment in exercising power—guarding against false hope, overexpansion, the "insolence of victory," empty threats, and "insulting words."

The prince must be a "ferocious lion" and an "astute fox." He must shrewdly consider the uses of power and the uses of love, fear, hate, cruelty, and magnanimity. Thus, to build a strong internal base for his power, a prudent prince should seek to maintain popular favor, satisfy popular needs, and reward merit and achievement. The prince must artfully seek "to be feared and loved." But since "it is difficult for the two to go together," if he has to choose, he will act on the assumption that "it is much safer to be feared than loved." Moreover, the "prince should make himself feared in such a way that if he does not gain love, he . . . avoids hatred." To this end, a prince should abstain "from interfering with the property of his citizens and subjects or with their women." If he has to take a life, let the reason be clear and the justification convincing.

If possible, villainy and hatred should be avoided, but sometimes circumstances require cruelty. Then, Machiavelli suggests, "the conqueror must arrange to commit all his cruelties at once, so as not to have to recur to them every day, and so as to be able, by not making fresh changes, to reassure people and win them over by benefitting them." Here Machiavelli makes his famous—or infamous—distinction between "well-committed" and "ill-committed" cruelties: "Well committed may be called those (if it be permissible to use the word well of evil) which are perpetuated for the need of securing one's self, and which afterwards are not persisted in, but are exchanged for measures as useful to the subjects as possible. Cruelties ill committed are those which, although at first few, increase rather than diminish with time." And, of course, the prince should let others handle his cruelties and unpopular duties while he bestows "favors."

Relevance to Modern Politics

Lion and fox is a difficult and dangerous game that is probably played more frequently throughout the world than most rulers (of liberal democracies as well as authoritarian regimes) are willing to admit. The high goals of classical political philosophy and modern constitutional morality are abandoned in this game. Machiavelli is willing to accept less than the best political life because justice is not possible for earthly political actors. In the battle between actual power and traditional morality, morality loses.

This game is notorious because of the candor with which Machiavelli laid bare its rules and its strategy. This notoriety should not obscure either the strengths or the weaknesses of the game. Machiavelli sought to achieve unity for Italy in the face of widespread popular corruption, dreadful internal divisions, and despised foreign domination. He held that the philosophy and tactics he advocated would achieve victory. He hoped, of course, that the outcome of the game would be a virtuous republic in which a divisive church, quarreling nobles, numerous principalities, and interfering foreign powers would not prevent the people from enjoying unity, liberty, prosperity, and strength.

But is it possible to find a great man—a Machiavellian prince—able to do the job? The problem haunted Machiavelli in Renaissance Italy:

> And as the reformation of the political condition of a state presupposes a good man, whilst the making of himself prince of a republic by violence naturally presupposes a bad one, it will consequently be exceedingly rare that a good man should be found willing to employ wicked means to become prince, even though his final object be good; or that a bad man, after having become prince, should be willing to labor for good ends, and that it should enter his mind to use for good purposes that authority which he has acquired by evil means.

The problem still haunts us today as we reflect on the careers of Napoleon, Otto von Bismarck, Stalin, Hitler, and hundreds of other national leaders, oppressive tyrants, and false messiahs.

It is a tribute to Machiavelli's genius that he understood so well what rulers of modern nation-states think they must do. They must protect the state's vital interests. They must be devoted, pragmatically, to success. They must maintain a love affair with power, particularly military power. They must not confuse what ought to be with what is. They must be prepared to operate as both lions and foxes.

Sometimes we may think that "lion and fox" describes only authoritarian rulers or such forceful and astute leaders as Bismarck, the "Iron Chancellor" of nineteenth-century Germany, whose use of military might and diplomatic cunning played a dominant role in unifying his country. Yet rulers of constitutional democracies also play lion and fox in foreign affairs. The Iran-contra scandal in the Reagan administration is one notorious illustration. This scandal involved secret efforts within the White House to violate federal law by selling arms to Iran to finance contra forces opposing Nicaragua's Sandinista government.

The game is also evident in U.S. domestic politics. For example, dirty tricks in political campaigns illustrate "foxy" politics in opera-

Although the game of the lion and the fox has many champions, it is a dangerous game to play. President Richard M. Nixon was forced from office in 1974 after the Watergate scandal tainted his administration and his part in the cover-up was discovered.

tion. The Watergate scandal is the best known because it reached into the office of the U.S. presidency itself. Watergate is the name given to a series of scandals in President Richard M. Nixon's administration. First, there was an attempted burglary of the Democratic Party's national headquarters at the Watergate office complex in Washington, D.C., June 1972. Two employees of President Nixon's reelection committee were involved, and Nixon's former attorney general was accused of approving the break-in. Then the president's top advisers, and allegedly Nixon himself, attempted to cover up the bungled burglary. A number of officials were convicted for their roles in the affair. On August 9, 1974, Richard Nixon resigned his presidency under threat of impeachment.

Leaders in other administrations have also been seen in a Machiavellian light. For example, James McGregor Burns titled his sympathetic study of Franklin D. Roosevelt *Roosevelt: The Lion and the Fox.*

Students of political science must ask critical questions about this game. Should we accept the doctrine that the end justifies the means—no matter what the end or the means? How realistic is Machiavelli's "realism"? Do Machiavellian realists miss important aspects of power because of their narrow understanding of power? Do such realists fail to see that short-range success does not necessarily secure long-range vital interests?

We now turn to another game, concerned with peace and an unorthodox means of achieving it.

STRIKE: THE POLITICS OF WITHDRAWAL

For our third game, we turn to the comedy of the dramatist Aristophanes. The geographic terrain is once again ancient Greece, and the background is once again the contest between Athens and Sparta.

Lysistrata: Make Love, Not War

The game is **strike**, as sketched with ribald delight in the play *Lysistrata.*[5] The women of Greece are pitted against the men of Greece. Peace or war is the issue. No orthodox set of rules seems to govern this game. But we do encounter a strategy in which one side seeks to paralyze the will and convince the mind of the other. Here in Aristophanes' bold and blunt play is the first women's strike for peace.

Lysistrata, the Athenian ringleader of the strike, and the other women of Greece are tired of war. They constitute one side in the game. The men of Greece, who have been fighting the Peloponnesian War for twenty-one years, constitute the other side. Lysistrata conceives a masterful plan to end the war. If all the Greek women on both sides of this protracted bloodletting will abstain from sexual relations with their men, then the men will be forced to sue for peace. The action is a strike, a true withholding action designed to make the soldiers on both sides see the profitlessness of war. The weapon to be employed is the power of sex.

The game reveals, with startling clarity, the strengths and weaknesses inherent in the game of strike. The strikers must be united and resolute. The activity withdrawn must be an indispensable one. Moreover, once victory is achieved, the strikers must be able to strike again if the other side reneges.

Initially, Lysistrata seeks to unite her forces. She gathers female leaders in Athens and proposes her strategy of total abstinence. There is murmuring in the ranks. Self-denial will affect the women as well as the men, and not all women are prepared to put peace before sex. Lysistrata must assure them that her strategy will be effective. She carries the argument and then moves to unite her forces by a solemn oath:

I will have nothing to do with my husband or my lover though he come to me in pitiable condition. I will stay in my house untouchable in my thinnest saffron silk and make him long for me. I will not give myself and if he constrains me I will be as cold as ice and never move.

Trouble, however, breaks out in the ranks that Lysistrata has assembled in the Acropolis, the citadel housing the Athenian treasury with which the war is financed. Many women find it too difficult to remain there. They lust after their men and seek to escape. Lysistrata urges them to hold out. "Of course you want your men. But don't you imagine that they want you just as much? . . . Just stick it out! A little patience, that's all, and our battle's won."

Aristophanes employs an encounter between Kinesias, an Athenian man, and his wife, Myrrhine, to illustrate the astute strategy in the game. "All afire with the flames of love," Kinesias approaches the group of women and asks for his wife. Lysistrata urges Myrrhine to employ her feminine power to force him to capitulate and give up war. "Oh then, get busy! Tease him! Undermine him! Wreck him! Give him everything—kissing, tickling, nudging, whatever you generally torture him with—give him everything except what we swore on the wine we would not give."

The dialogue between Kinesias and Myrrhine is an intimate and revealing account of one variety of feminine power in this game of strike. At the crucial moment when Kinesias hesitates about voting for peace, Myrrhine runs away. Kinesias, frustrated and tormented, is left to exclaim, "The agony!"

Meanwhile, the Spartan women have been successful with their part of the strike, and the Spartan men are ready to sue for peace. The strike is carried out successfully in all parts of Greece and brings peace to the land. The men of Greece wanted their women more than war. They are enjoined to return to their homes and henceforth make love, not war.

The play's ending has a modern ring. However, its feasibility, except in the imagination of a comic genius such as Aristophanes, remains to be tested. Quite clearly, enormous willpower on the part of a united womankind is mandatory. And it is by no means established that women have differed significantly from their men on the great issues of war and peace over the centuries. Nor is it clear that women have greater willpower than men.

Relevance to Modern Politics

The technique of the strike has, of course, been widely used in labor-management disputes, and it figures prominently in Marxist political strategy in capitalist countries. In the United States the strike has been a powerful weapon, employed by a wide range of workers to accomplish primarily economic objectives, such as higher wages, better working conditions, and increased benefits. The strike can be a potent weapon in strategic industries such as steel, coal, and railroads. If carried on long enough, strikes in key industries can bring a nation's economy to a halt. Certain local strikes also can have widespread consequences: a strike by garbage collectors in New York City, for example, could threaten public health. The withdrawal of important services—whether those of factory workers, teachers, telephone employees, or farmhands—can put great pressure on employers and government.

In some countries strikes have played a prominent role in attempts to bring down a government or alter its policies. For instance, in 2002 a business strike attempted to oust Venezuelan president Hugo Chavez. Although strikes in countries such as the United States are not intended to bring down a government, they have been used to exact concessions from government, and some have led to changes in public policy. For example, strikes in the auto industry in the mid-1930s led to the passage of the Wagner Act in 1935, which helped ensure labor's right to organize and bargain collectively.

In communist countries strikes have been rare. Nonetheless, the activities of the independent labor movement Solidarity in Poland in the 1980s led ultimately (despite repressive efforts) to a major upset of the Polish communist regime and to a presidential role for Solidarity's leader, Lech Walesa, in the Polish government of the 1990s. Even in the former

Venezuelan president Hugo Chavez was the target of massive strikes in December 2002 that effectively shut down all economic activity for a month. Chavez survived the crisis and remained in power as of late 2005.

Soviet Union, strikes (for example, by miners) sometimes led to concessions from the communist regime.

The use of the strike as a political weapon—as in the case of a "general strike" against a government in power or against particular policies of that government—is rare but not unknown in capitalist countries. The French writer Georges Sorel advocated the general strike as a way to bring about revolutionary change, but such strikes usually fail. Occasionally, student strikes (as in France in 1968 or in the United States during the Vietnam War) have put pressure on governments to change their policies. Such strikes are effective because they publicize issues, not because the students have withdrawn a vital service.

The political game of strike raises a number of ethical, empirical, and prudential questions. For example, should withdrawing vital services be considered a legitimate means of advancing a political objective? Do strikers have the ability to maintain unity to accomplish legitimate political objectives? Will strikers use their power on behalf of peace, human rights, and ecological health, as well as on behalf of economic prosperity?

CIVIL DISOBEDIENCE: THE POLITICS OF MORALITY

The game of **civil disobedience**, which was dramatized by the Greek tragedian Sophocles in *Antigone,* is well known to the modern world. Henry David Thoreau explored the game in a perceptive essay in the nineteenth century. Mohandas Gandhi made it popular in India—and the world—in the twentieth century. Norwegians and Danes used it tellingly against the Nazis in World War II. And Martin Luther King Jr. revealed its capabilities in the United States during his tragically brief but influential life. We have subtitled this game "the politics of morality" because the appeal to conscience, and thus to a higher law, is its central characteristic. In our examination we will use Thoreau's brilliant essay "On Civil Disobedience" as our model.[6]

Thoreau: "On Civil Disobedience"

Who are the players in Thoreau's game? His answer resounds across the years. On one side are people of conscience—people of superior morality and integrity, who are human beings first and subjects second. On the other side are those who lack moral vision or courage—governments, majorities, people blind to the higher law or lacking the courage of their convictions. Specifically for Thoreau, on one side are those who oppose slavery and war; on the other side are the federal and state governments and the spineless multitudes that follow them.

What are the stakes? Nothing less than the abolition of outrageous moral evil and the return to the commandments of the higher law. In Thoreau's case the evils are slavery and war, and the commandments are freedom and peace. Thoreau insists, "This people must cease to hold slaves" and cease to "make war on Mexico, though it cost them their existence as a people."

This 1856 photograph is one of the few of Henry David Thoreau. Thoreau, the author of a famous essay on civil disobedience, was a vigorous defender of the moral responsibility of individuals to challenge unjust laws. He had a tremendous influence on such later political actors as Mohandas Gandhi and Martin Luther King Jr.

The following rules apply to the people of conscience who play this game. First, the game must be peaceful. To employ violence is to break a cardinal rule. Second, the act of disobedience must be selectively aimed at an outrageous moral evil. The protest must not be an indiscriminate one against all authority. Third, those disobedient must be public, not secretive, in their actions. Fourth, the participants must be prepared to pay the price of their disobedience. Thus Thoreau peacefully went to jail rather than pay taxes to a government that supported slavery and fought the Mexican War. These rules hold only for those who engage in civil disobedience, not for their opponents.

What strategies and tactics guide the players? The disobedient must convert the ruling establishment by dramatizing the evil against which they protest. To do this they must mobilize the sleeping conscience of the political community and destroy support for a government that sanctions immoral acts. This they can do by (1) effectively rallying their own forces; (2) making moral partisans of the neutral and the indifferent; and (3) converting, or weakening the position of, the immoral ruling elite.

According to advocates of civil disobedience, this general strategy can be implemented when people of conscience cease to obey an unjust government. They do so by peacefully withdrawing their support "both in person and in property." They break the law rather than serve as agents of injustice. Some may, as in Thoreau's case, refuse to pay taxes and be put in jail. Here their purpose is to clog the courts and the jails. Consciences throughout the land will be aroused at the sight of just men and women in jail. A chain reaction will set in as conscientious citizens refuse allegiance to, and conscientious officers resign from, the unjust government. Such action will provide the friction essential for stopping the machinery of government. The ruling elite will be divided and thus weakened. When confronted with the possibility of keeping all just people in jail or of giving up war and slavery, the state will abandon its immoral acts. Blood need not be spilled. If it is, however, it will be spilled by a state that has superior physical strength but not superior moral strength. Thus moral strength will prevail. Civil disobedience is therefore not only desirable but also feasible.

Practitioners of civil disobedience are moral crusaders. To rally his own forces, Thoreau declares:

I know this well, that if one thousand, if one hundred, if ten men who I could name,— if ten honest men only,—ay, if one HONEST man, in this state of Massachusetts, ceasing to hold slaves, were actually to withdraw from this co-partnership, and be locked up in the county jail . . . it would be the abolition of slavery in America.

To rouse—indeed, to radicalize—the indifferent, Thoreau writes:

When a sixth of the population of a nation which has undertaken to be a refuge for liberty are slaves, and a whole country is unjustly overrun and conquered by a foreign army, and subjected to military law, I think that it is not too soon for honest men to rebel and revolutionize.

To induce neutral observers to join the cause of the righteous, Thoreau emphasizes several crucial arguments. Moral men and women cannot "recognize that political organization" as their government "which is the slaves' government also." They appreciate that under "a government which imprisons any unjustly, the true place for a just man is also a prison." To undercut the legitimacy of the immoral government, and to convert and weaken the ruling elite, Thoreau appeals to a higher law: "They only can force me who obey a higher law than I."

Thoreau is aware that his opponents will argue that he rejects democratic and constitutional politics. He knows that they will contend that civil disobedience illustrates a dogmatic, self-righteous position. He anticipates the criticism that civil disobedience is hostile to the normal give-and-take of democracy and constitutional compromise. Thoreau's critics will argue that he refuses to recognize that just and brave people may not agree about all moral issues in politics and that civil disobedience is incompatible with democratic accommodation and makes for anarchy.

Thoreau is ready to repel this counterattack. He insists that it is important to distinguish between minor and major matters in politics. Matters that present no serious moral problem can be handled by majority rule. However, fundamental matters such as slavery cannot be left to the ethical competence of majorities. He is not seeking to destroy all aspects of government. As a good citizen, he is quite prepared to pay his highway tax and to educate his fellow citizens. He is aware of the virtues of obedience to the law, of majority rule, of constitutional debate and decision. But a higher law may have to take precedence over civil law. A constitution that recognizes slavery and refuses even to receive petitions protesting slavery does not deserve respect. Thoreau does not "wish to quarrel" or "set myself up as better than my neighbors," and he seeks to obey the laws of the land. He concedes that "from a lower point of view, the Constitution, with all its faults, is very good; the laws and the courts are very respectable; even this State and this American government are, in many respects, very admirable, and rare things, to be thankful for." But from the vantage point of a higher law of justice, the Constitution fails.

So Thoreau elaborates the strategy and tactics of civil disobedience. The boldness, as well as the difficulty, of the game is underscored by his basic assumptions: the superior power of conscience in politics, agreement on what is righteous, and the establishment's ultimate benevolence. He assumes there will be no reactionary backlash and that disobedience will not be brutally repressed.

Relevance to Modern Politics

As we noted in discussing the game of lion and fox, Machiavelli challenged most of these assumptions. They are also impugned by the Athenians at Melos in the game of wipeout. Yet despite the objections of many people to Thoreau's assumptions, Martin Luther King Jr. used civil disobedience successfully in the civil rights movement of the 1960s. When employed according to Thoreau's rules, civil disobedience proved an effective weapon for advancing the rights of African Americans. Moreover, an accumulating literature highlights the success of civil disobedience against a wide variety of authoritarian regimes. Indeed, as we will see more fully in chapter 15, some scholars maintain that the only sane road to peace and human rights in the nuclear age is through nonviolent civilian defense.

Civil disobedience has also been employed in another highly controversial issue in American society—the morality, lawfulness, and wisdom of abortion. Antiabortion advocates have, for example, used civil disobedience in their protests against abortion clinics. This issue pits pro-choice advocates against pro-life advocates. The debate involves judgments on a number of troublesome moral and legal questions: whether a fetus is a person and therefore entitled to moral rights and legal protection; how much control a woman has over her own body; how to balance the competing needs of fetus, mother, and other parties; when a fetus is viable; and what to do about life-threatening pregnancies or those caused by rape or incest. Critical questions must be asked in evaluating civil disobedience. Should people rely mainly on civil disobedience to combat what they *believe* to be outrageous moral evils? What makes a moral evil outrageous? In the real world of politics, characterized by a struggle for power, is the risk of civil disobedience worth taking?

CONCLUSION

The games presented in this chapter are educational models. As such, they may help us to understand (1) the character of the major players in politics, (2) the stakes involved in key political games, (3) the rules of politics, and (4) influential strategies and tactics. These games may suggest other variations: for example, balance of power—the politics of equilibrium; class conflict—the politics of domination; stake-in-society—the politics of vested interests; bargaining—the politics of accommodation; miracle, mystery, and authority—the politics of benevolent authoritarianism.[7]

The games call attention to a number of important ethical, empirical, and prudential problems in politics. They highlight the clash between power and justice. They force us to look critically at "reason of state"—that rationale that prompts leaders of states to protect their nation's vital interests. They force us to ask whether a ruler must accept the "beastly" character of politics and function as both a ferocious lion and an astute fox to protect the state's vital interests. We must decide whether Machiavelli is right in holding that idealism will lead to ruin. The study of these games also entails a deeper look into the ethics and politics of political means. We have to decide if and when the strike is an effective and wise weapon, and whether civil disobedience is compatible with majority rule, democratic law, and other time-tested constitutional forms.

Today, we desperately need to clarify the purposes of politics, the uses of power, and the wisdom of policies. In recent years the ends of political life and the exercise of power have not been keenly criticized. The result has been failure to devise a prudent way to harness power for just and humane purposes. In chapter 2 we will investigate additional scenarios to focus on the problems of political choice.

SUGGESTED READINGS

The following novels and plays present a wide variety of additional games that politicians play.

Bolt, Robert. *A Man for All Seasons*. New York: Random House, 1966. Highlights the clash between loyalty to conscience (and God) and to king (and country). Also reveals the nobility—and weakness—of reliance on the law in the face of a powerful, determined, and unscrupulous ruler.

Dostoevsky, Fyodor. "The Legend of the Grand Inquisitor." Book 5, chap. 5, of *The Brothers Karamazov*. New York: Random House, Modern Library Edition, 1950. Contains the grand inquisitor's brilliant (if perverse) argument that a benevolent authoritarian ruler should relieve inadequate humans of the burden of freedom.

Kafka, Franz. *The Castle*. Trans. Willa and Edwin Muir. New York: Knopf, 1930. Addresses the individual's plight in the baffling world of bureaucracy.

[Klein, Joe]. *Primary Colors: A Novel about Politics*. New York: AOL Time Warner, 1996. The story of an ambitious, womanizing southern politician headed for the White House. Though the book is a work of fiction, its main character bears a remarkable similarity to a recent president of the United States.

Koestler, Arthur. *Darkness at Noon*. Trans. Daphne Hardy. New York: Macmillan, 1941. Illuminates the minds and politics of communist revolutionaries out of power and in power.

Lilla, Mark. *The Reckless Mind*. New York: New York Review of Books, 2001. A thoughtful account about why some political thinkers are attracted to extremely dangerous political ideas.

Orwell, George. *1984*. New York: New American Library, 1951. Another anti-utopian novel that throws light on the loss of freedom in a totalitarian society.

Shakespeare, William. *Richard III*, 1592; *Julius Caesar*, 1599; *Measure for Measure*, 1604; *Macbeth*, 1605; *Antony and Cleopatra*, 1606; *Coriolanus*, 1607. The games politicians play, as represented in the work of the greatest literary voice in the English language. Highlights political machinations involving the struggle for power and who gets what, when, and how.

Shaw, George Bernard. *Arms and the Man*, 1894; *The Devil's Disciple*, 1897; *Caesar and Cleopatra*, 1899; *Man and Superman*, 1905 (especially that section often produced separately as *Don Juan in Hell*); *Major Barbara*, 1905; *Saint Joan*, 1923. No one play can do justice to Shaw's witty socialist criticism of politics and society. And by all means read those magnificent lengthy prefaces, which are also great lectures on modern social science.

Skinner, B. F. *Walden Two*. New York: Macmillan, 1948. Portrays a genuinely utopian community based on scientific principles, especially stimulus, response, and positive reinforcement. Lots of cooperation and accommodation; hardly any conflict!

Sophocles. *Antigone* (c. 441 B.C.). A powerful play that illustrates the tragic clash between individual conscience (as informed by a higher law) and public order (as dictated by the need for stability and safety in the community).

Warren, Robert Penn. *All the King's Men*. New York: Harcourt, Brace, and World, 1946. Describes the rise and fall of a southern-style political boss.

GLOSSARY TERMS

Chapter 2

POLITICS
AND CHOICE

This chapter focuses on the challenging subject of politics and choice to underscore in yet another way the intimate connection among values, facts, and judgment. Four dramatic cases are used to illustrate the dimensions of choice in politics. These cases involve four crucial historical choices: (1) Socrates' choice not to flee Athens to avoid an unjust punishment, (2) James Madison's choice of a new political theory to guide the American Constitution of 1787 and the federal republic it created, (3) the choice by German citizens (and key leaders) of Adolf Hitler in 1932 and 1933, and (4) President John F. Kennedy's choice of a blockade to counter the Soviet Union's placement of offensive nuclear weapons in Cuba in the fall of 1962.

FOUR IMPORTANT THEMES

These cases illustrate that choices in politics can be tragic, creative, burdensome, and perilous. These examples enable us to see that it is not easy to choose what is right, to break through to a new political understanding, to bear the burden of freedom, or to select the least perilous alternative. As you read these cases, ask yourself what you would have done in each situation:

- What would you do if you had been lawfully sentenced to death on charges you knew were false and were then offered the opportunity to escape?
- Would you try a new, untested experiment in government in the face of conventional wisdom that suggested your experiment could never work?

- As a German citizen, would you have supported Adolf Hitler's Nazi Party in 1932 and 1933?
- As president of the United States, how would you have responded to the news that the Soviet Union had placed offensive nuclear missiles in Cuba?

Of course, these four cases do not exhaust the category of choices faced by political actors. However, these cases merit special attention because they invite critical thinking about four important themes in politics today.

Furthermore, these cases can help students begin to evaluate one of the most important choices of our time: the decision to invade Iraq in 2003. We do not believe that any firm conclusions can be drawn from this case because the outcome is still unknown. However, looking at the four examples that we will use in this chapter enables us to think carefully about the Bush administration's actions. Indeed, the decision to go to war can be viewed from many angles. Was President George W. Bush being prudent or reckless when he chose to take the war on terrorism to Iraq? Many Americans oppose the war. Should they engage in civil disobedience in their protests? Some soldiers also oppose the war. Should they act like Socrates and accept that their duty requires them to fight in a conflict they believe is wrong? Finally, does bringing the war on terrorism to Iraq and the attempt to foster democracy in a region where it is practically unknown an example of a creative breakthrough in political thought? Will we look back in ten years and marvel at the foresight of the decision as democracy sweeps not only Iraq but also the entire Middle East? Or, conversely, will we look back in a decade and say that this was a serious breakdown in wise political thinking? As we noted at the beginning of this paragraph, we cannot know the answers to these questions for years, possibly decades, to come. However, we can begin discussing them now and wait for empirical evidence to be gathered as we debate the first great political challenge of the twenty-first century.

The first case delves into *political obligation.* Why should we obey those who demand our allegiance in politics, particularly those who constitute our government?

The second case explores *creativity in politics.* Is it possible, in theory and practice, to achieve a new ethical, empirical, and prudential understanding of politics? More specifically, can we devise new ways to reconcile liberty and authority?

The third case explores the *responsible exercise of freedom*—whether citizens can respond sensibly to social, economic, and political crises. Are we strong enough to bear the burden of freedom? Are we mature enough to exercise freedom responsibly, or do we, under adverse conditions, abandon freedom for authoritarian rule?

The fourth case probes *power politics* in the nuclear age—the difficulty of working out sane, sound strategy and tactics. Can we avert situations that call for agonizing choices that might lead to nuclear war? In times of crisis can we choose courses of action that preserve our vital interests in peace, national security, and freedom?

Elaborating the Theme

Each case in this chapter develops one of these key themes, themes that recur throughout this book. Socrates, father of political philosophy in the West, initiates the critical examination of **political obligation.** His views present a counterargument to those advanced by Henry David Thoreau in chapter 1. And this debate persists whenever a government's legitimacy is called into question—by American students who protested the Vietnam War, resisted the draft, or left their country in the late 1960s and early 1970s; by Polish members of Solidarity who protested or resisted martial law in their country or fled to avoid tyranny in 1982; by South Africans opposed to apartheid from 1948 to 1989; by Chinese students in Tiananmen Square demonstrating for democratic reform in 1989; and by protesting Ukrainians who forced new presidential elections in their country after accusations of fraud and corruption in earlier elections. To explore the question of political obligation is to ask what makes a government legitimate—that is, what makes government lawful and entitled to obedience and respect.

Similarly, James Madison, father of the U.S. Constitution, merits our study. He is one of America's most important political theorists. His ideas help us understand the formation of the American federal republic, now the oldest constitutional democracy in the world—an experiment that is still unfinished.

A study of Madison's guiding theory illustrates **political creativity** at its best. The task of reconciling liberty and authority remains today. It is a problem common to all nations, whether they are rich or poor; developing or developed; liberal democracies, democratic socialist states, or communist states.

We focus on the fateful choices made by German citizens in 1932 and 1933 for several important reasons. Historically, we want to know more about the circumstances that permitted Hitler to attain power and to use that power to unleash World War II and its dreadful consequences. Who voted for Hitler and why? More generally, we want to know what produces **responsible citizenship** and leadership. Can people really govern themselves successfully,

In November 2004 thousands of Ukrainians staged mass rallies known as the "Orange Revolution," protesting the apparently rigged election of Leonid Kuchma. Weeks of demonstrations forced a new election that swept reformist Viktor Yuschenko into power.

particularly under adverse conditions? This question can be asked about authoritarian regimes on the left or the right, or about nations emerging from authoritarian rule (such as the republics of the former Soviet Union or the Eastern European nations now freed of communist domination; and Spain, the Philippines, and Chile, which have thrown off right-wing dictatorships). This question can also be asked about the struggling developing nations of the world and even about supposedly mature democratic regimes in times of crisis.

Finally, the Cuban missile crisis merits attention because it brilliantly illuminates key aspects of **power politics** in the nuclear age. In a world of nuclear weapons it is important to understand how in 1962 the leaders of the two military superpowers—the United States and the Soviet Union—responded to political crisis. When political actions reached the stage of big-power confrontation in the nuclear age, the fate of the entire globe was at stake. This chapter provides only a preliminary treatment of these four cases and the themes they illustrate; subsequent chapters will develop these matters more fully.

Values, Facts, and Judgment

By exploring these cases and the choices they involved, we discover the intimate relationship of values, facts, and judgment. For example, Socrates' choice is incomprehensible if we do not understand the high value he placed on his birth, education, and citizenship in the Greek *polis* (city-state). Of course, the unacceptable consequences of escape and life in exile also influenced his decision.

The second case shows that Madison's dedication to republican values of popular rule and basic rights, as well as to effective governance, clarified his quest for a breakthrough to our modern federal republic. His understanding of the seeming "facts"—that liberty is possible only in a small state or that a large country cannot be governed on republican principles—did not prevent him from challenging them and articulating a new empirical theory that enabled Americans to reconcile liberty and authority.

The third case depicts how adverse circumstances led Germans to seek a political change in order to give meaning to values such as order, strength, prestige, and prosperity. Many Germans supported Hitler because they sympathized with Nazi promises to help Germany overcome economic depression, avoid the alleged communist menace, and recover from defeat in World War I.

Finally, President Kennedy's choice also illustrates the close connection among values, facts, and judgment. His choice in the Cuban missile crisis was dictated by the value of national security; at the same time it was made agonizing by the danger of nuclear catastrophe if the Soviet Union refused to back down. Key facts—especially the military estimate that a "surgical" air strike could not guarantee the destruction of all Soviet missiles—led him to endorse a blockade, which permitted a firm response and gave the Soviet Union time to reconsider its bold gamble, yet held open more militant options if the Soviet Union refused to withdraw its offensive weapons.

Our key question in examining the four cases is: *How does political choice illustrate the intimate connection among values, facts, and judgment?*

SOCRATES AND THE MORAL LIFE: POLITICAL OBLIGATION IN ANCIENT ATHENS

The story of Socrates' life and teachings comes to us primarily in the writings of Plato, Socrates' devoted student. Here we focus on the very end of the great teacher's life.

Socrates' Choice

Socrates has been accused of corrupting the youth of Athens and of not believing in the gods. He vigorously denies both charges. He maintains that he is being falsely accused because of his relentless probing of ignorance and pretension among people of repute— particularly rhetoricians, poets, and artisans. This mission, ordained by God, has gotten him into trouble because those who pretend to be wise do not like having their folly exposed.

Socrates sees himself as a "gadfly"—"arousing," "persuading," "reproaching," "exhorting . . . to . . . virtue." He has tried to teach his students to put "virtue and wisdom" before their "private interests." He cannot hold his tongue because "this would be a disobedience to a divine command." And he cannot abandon his mission out of fear of death "or any other fear." He cannot give up teaching about the care of the soul. He has never yielded to injustice in either public or private life. His "only fear was the fear of doing an unrighteous or unholy thing." He has taught virtue for its own sake, not for the sake of money. He believes in a higher divinity: "Men of Athens, I honor and love you; but I shall obey God rather than you, and while I have life and strength I shall never cease from the practice and teaching of philosophy." [1]

When he is condemned to die by drinking hemlock, a poison, Socrates refuses to bargain for his life by asking for exile, a stiff fine, or imprisonment. He proposes as his proper punishment that which is his due—his maintenance at public expense! Why should he plead for his life when he cannot be sure that life is better than death? Imprisonment, as a punishment, is intolerable because it is a kind of slavery. He cannot pay a stiff fine because he has no money. Exile, too, is unthinkable: "What a life should I lead at my age, wandering from city to city, living in ever-changing exile, and always being driven out!" On the urging of his friends, he proposes a minuscule fine as punishment.

Socrates does not regret his defense—his "apology." He has avoided unrighteousness. He departs "condemned . . . to suffer the penalty of death." Those who have accused and condemned him to death are themselves "condemned by the truth to suffer the penalty of villainy and wrong."

Crito, one of Socrates' disciples, comes to him in jail with a proposal to bribe the guards and permit him to escape. Crito does not want to lose a dear friend, nor does he want people to think that he did not do enough to save his mentor's life. Appreciative of Socrates' sensibilities, Crito argues that Socrates should not play into the hands of his enemies. Crito points out that people will respect and love Socrates in exile, that he should not betray his own children, who need him for their education, and that escape will not be disgraceful. Crito knows that he has to make a strong argument to convince Socrates, for at his trial Socrates had already given signs that he would accept his punishment. Socrates had argued that he must always do what is right, that he cannot do anything "common or mean" in his hour of danger, that he would find exile unacceptable and unrewarding, particularly if he could not carry on his mission of critical inquiry, that his death was a meaningful choice, and that his oracle had opposed neither his behavior at the trial nor the verdict of his death.

Socrates responds to Crito's entreaty by arguing that the key question, "the only question . . . is . . . whether we shall do rightly either in escaping or in suffering others to aid in our escape." He cannot intentionally injure others; he cannot "render evil for evil to any one, whatever evil [he] may have suffered." In escaping, would he desert the just principles by which he has lived?

Socrates answers his cardinal question by imagining how those who speak for the "laws and the government" would answer it. He cannot be justified in escaping because that action would destroy the laws, the government, and the state. Athens cannot endure if its lawful decisions have no power, if individuals can set them aside at will. Socrates is indebted to his polis—his political community—for birth, for nurture and education, and for fulfillment in citizenship. By his life, growth, and fulfillment in the political community, he has undertaken a contractual agreement that he cannot now violate by escaping. He cannot disobey his parents, "the authors of his education," nor can he disavow his own agreement to obey the commands of the polis—especially when he has not been able to convince the political community that its commands are wrong. He must choose death over banishment; he could not be a "miserable slave," "running away and turning [his] back upon the compacts and agreements [he] made as a citizen." Having been born and having lived and enjoyed citizenship in the political community, Socrates cannot now repudiate that community.

Moreover, his escape would harm his friends and children and bring him no peace in exile. His friends would lose their property and citizenship and be driven into exile as well. Other good cities would view Socrates as an "enemy," a "subverter of the laws." And he would find no happiness in fleeing from "well-ordered cities and virtuous men." If he lived in disordered cities, could he, having turned his back on his own principles, talk of "virtue and justice and institutions and laws being the best things among men?" Would he deprive his children of Athenian citizenship?

And so Socrates concludes the argument he has made for law-abiding Athenians and against his escape. Law-abiding Athenians will say:

Socrates was executed in 399 B.C. by the Athenian authorities because of his incessant criticisms of Athenian democracy. Despite being condemned to death, he was unwilling to abandon his city or his friends. Socrates was willing to die for his beliefs, and thus, he offers an example of a man of principle and of civic loyalty. Jacques-Louis David, The Death of Socrates, *1787.*

Now you depart in innocence, a sufferer and not a doer of evil; a victim, not of the laws, but of men. But if you go forth, returning evil for evil, and injury for injury, breaking the covenants and agreements which you have made with us, and wronging those whom you ought least to wrong, that is to say, yourself, your friends, your country, and us, we shall be angry with you while you live, and our brothers, the laws in the world below, will receive you as an enemy; for they will know that you have done your best to destroy us.

Socrates' choice not to escape illuminates the problem of political obligation and the key question: Why should we obey the political community that makes claims on our allegiance? Socrates' answer is that because of the contribution that the political community makes to our life, growth, and fulfillment, we are required to obey its laws. He argues that if we cannot persuade the political community that its laws are wrong, we are obligated to obey them.

Questioning Socrates' Choice

Socrates' view, of course, is only one view of political obligation. Thoreau's position, discussed in chapter 1, represents another view. Thoreau argued that we have no obligation to obey a government that violates a higher law and engages in outrageously immoral action such as aggressive war or human slavery.

The American revolutionaries of 1776 articulated yet another position on political obligation. They held that when a government violates the trust that brought it into being, when it persistently violates the right to life, liberty, and the pursuit of happiness, and when it is not responsive to redress of grievances, the people have a right to revolt and overthrow such a government and establish a new one, based on their consent and dedicated to the protection of their rights. This position rests upon the premise that we owe obedience only to governments of our own making that protect our basic rights and, pursuant to our will, advance life, growth, and fulfillment.

Critical minds will raise questions for Socrates (held to be one of the wisest, most just, and best of human beings); for Thoreau (as we saw in chapter 1); and even for the authors of the American Declaration of Independence. For example, do we uncritically accept Socrates' statement that "whether in battle or in a court of law" we "must do" as our country orders? Do we accept that "punishment is to be endured in silence"? Even in battle, following orders is no legitimate excuse for violating international law or for committing war crimes, genocide, or other crimes against humanity. Moreover, is there no obligation to speak out against unjust punishment? Some would argue (as did Martin Luther King Jr. and many others—including Socrates—in a long tradition of obedience to a higher law) that to endure injustice in silence is to perpetuate injustice.

Even the theory of political obligation enshrined in the Declaration of Independence has its difficulties. How do we more precisely define those "unalienable rights" to life, liberty, and the pursuit of happiness that are to be protected by a government? What conditions justify our conclusion that government is destroying those rights? How do we understand the "consent of the governed" from which "just powers" derive?

African Americans were denied liberty, often life, and certainly the pursuit of happiness when they were enslaved in the United States and then treated as second-class citizens after emancipation. Even today they may not be treated with genuine equality in all respects. Women in the United States have also been fighting a long battle for genuine equality. Given this record of unequal treatment, do African Americans and women have the same obligation to obey the government as others? What about other mistreated minorities? In the wake of 9/11 many Muslim Americans have felt the sting of discrimination as the United States confronts terrorism that now springs from a small subset of Islam. If we extend our democratic theory of obligation—that is, obedience in return for fulfillment of basic rights—to include the right to education, a job, or adequate health care and housing, then the uneducated, the unemployed, the sick, and the homeless may have less of an obligation to obey the government than the educated, wealthy, and well housed. This theory of obligation certainly provides food for thought.

These critical inquiries are disquieting, but they make us see that our judgment about obligation cannot be separated from our evaluation of whether a government is legitimate, whether it honors our rights, and whether it is truly based on the consent of the governed. Depending on their values and their assessment of the facts, different observers may reach different conclusions about political obligation. The young Americans who refused to fight in Vietnam had a different sense of obligation than those who did. African Americans who refused to accept racial segregation in buses, restaurants, movie theaters, and schools had a different sense of obligation than did those who went along with "separate but equal" legislation.

Clearly, an individual's respect for his or her political community—and responsibility to the government—can be interpreted in different ways, and these interpretations are closely related to how the interpreter balances values, ascertains circumstances, and weighs alternatives. James Madison and the constitutional reformers of 1787, for example, felt obligated to disobey the instructions from their states to simply amend the flawed Articles of Confederation that had governed the nation since 1781. In the very interest of improving the young republican union, they drafted a constitution with striking new powers. They undertook what some people consider to be a contradiction in terms—a "peaceful revolution."

MADISON, THE NEW REPUBLIC, AND FEDERAL THEORY: THE STRUGGLE FOR A CREATIVE BREAKTHROUGH IN MODERN POLITICS

James Madison's choice in 1787 was not as simple as Socrates'. Madison's choice represents a theoretical and practical response to a more complicated problem. Between 1776 and 1783, the Americans had fought a revolution to achieve independence as a new nation. But could the new nation hold together? Could the Articles of Confederation, adopted in 1781, cope with four major difficulties that plagued the infant republic: disunion, large size, faction, and the antirepublican danger?[2] Would it be enough to patch the Articles of Confederation? Or was a more fundamental change required? And how far should radical reform go?[3]

The Problem: Reconciling Liberty and Authority

These questions led Madison to formulate his key problem as follows: How can we reconcile liberty and authority in a large state? This problem would dominate Madison's thinking throughout his life. It certainly dominated his thoughts and actions in 1787–1788 as he battled to draft and win support for a new constitution. It also influenced key decisions he made in the 1790s in his fight against rich, powerful forces that were unsympathetic to popular interests and to a more generous protection of democratic rights. And, finally, it dominated Madison's thinking and writing in the late 1820s and mid-1830s as he fought the growing forces of nullification and secession. These forces held that a state

James Madison, one of the authors of the U.S. Constitution and the fourth president of the United States, was famous for his ability to rethink how republican governments work. Before Madison, it was believed that republics could exist only in small political communities—geographically large and culturally diverse communities like the current United States were inconceivable.

could nullify an act of the national government and could even secede from the Union that was the United States. (As we will see, these battles in the 1790s and later also throw considerable light on the meaning of political obligation.)

Madison's values and the facts of American geography significantly shaped his problem. Madison was strongly committed to popular government and human freedom in a new and large American nation that required power and authority for survival. Madison's problem was most troublesome because the conventional wisdom— the evidence of history, the testimony of political theorists, the judgment of the political science of his day—declared that it was impossible to reconcile liberty and authority in a large state.

According to conventional wisdom, republican government (based on self-government and liberty) was possible only in a small political community—for example, a city-state such as Athens, Florence, Venice, or Geneva. Moreover, according to the conventional wisdom, a large state could be governed only by a monarch or a despot—rulers incompatible with self-government and liberty. How, then, were Americans to deal with this dilemma? Could American republicans have the best of two seemingly contradictory worlds? Could they have self-government and liberty in a republic and also enjoy legitimate power, order, and security in a country as large as the United States?

Other politicians had refused to face up to the problem because they believed it to be insoluble. Patrick Henry and the other Anti-Federalists, who were opposed to the new constitution of 1787, argued that republican government is possible only in a small political community. They did not lift their sights beyond the loose political alliance of the Articles of Confederation. They rejected the possibility—and the desirability—of a greatly strengthened central government. On the other side of the political spectrum, men like Alexander Hamilton, who supported the movement for a new and stronger constitution, initially maintained that only an empire or a strong central government based on the British model could hold together a political community as large as the new American nation. Confederations, they insisted, were notoriously weak, unstable, and detrimental to the interests of justice. Thus, while Henry and his friends argued that great strength in a central government jeopardized republican self-government and republican liberty, Hamilton and his friends held that in the small political community, **faction** prevailed and jeopardized both the public good and a strong national union.

Neither Henry nor Hamilton challenged the accepted political science of his day or perceived that the traditional understanding of how to reconcile liberty and authority (in the large expanse of the new United States) had to be reexamined. Only Madison challenged the conventional wisdom and was bold enough to look at the problem in a new light and to ask if a new political theory—that of a federal republic—suggested a way out.

Madison's Solution

Madison's theory of the **extensive republic** constituted a **creative breakthrough** in political thought because he proposed that Americans could work out a new synthesis. They could have liberty, self-government, and justice at the local level of state government and also have a powerful central government able to protect the common interests of the whole Union—but only by adopting the model of the new constitution of 1787. This new federal model allowed the states to control their local affairs while giving the new central government authority in matters concerning all members of the Union. For good measure, the new federal republic operated to control the effects of faction. The Constitution created a central authority—the new federal government—that rested more legitimately on popular consent and the Union's component states, yet possessed greater strength than any confederation in history.

The features of the American federal republic are well known today, but in 1787 they constituted a creative breakthrough in governmental theory and practice. The federal republic had such unique features as the division and sharing of powers among Congress, the president, and the Supreme Court; constitutional limitations on national and state governments; a national government with significant powers operating directly on the people; and a strong chief executive. The breakthroughs, moreover, occurred on three fronts.

Ethically, Madison's theory (particularly as fully developed in the 1790s) included broadened concepts of liberty, self-government, pluralist democracy, and the good political life. More specifically, Madison advocated modern principles of religious liberty; freedom of speech, press, and assembly, and other constitutional protections of liberty; an explicit acceptance of interests, parties, and public opinion in the process of self-government; and a more enlightened idea of popular rule, governmental power, and national union.

Empirically, Madison's theory of the extensive republic was designed to explain how Americans could enjoy the best (and escape the worst) of two worlds: how they could enjoy liberty without fear of anarchy and the adverse effects of faction, and how they could enjoy authority without fear of tyranny and the adverse effects of an overly powerful central government. The political community's large size plus its diversity and multiplicity of interests would inhibit the negative aspects of faction and thus ensure greater success for the public good. The existence of many different interests in the geographically large political community—farmers, merchants, bankers, and workers—would make it difficult for any one interest to achieve power and work against the public interest.

Representation would also filter the evil effects of faction. People would not determine policy in one great mass meeting (where they might easily be inflamed by demagogues). Rather, they would select leaders to represent them. Presumably, these leaders would be chosen because of their virtue, character, and intelligence, and they would, in turn, meet with other comparably chosen representatives to make law. This process would make it difficult for factional interests—interests opposed to the public good—to prevail.

Constitutional limitations on power and the separation of powers were "auxiliary precautions" that would help reconcile liberty and authority in the new republic. Congress would have broad, but not unlimited, powers to tax and spend, to regulate interstate commerce, and to attend to other designated objectives. But a wide range of powers would remain with the states. Moreover, the power given to the central government would not be concentrated in one organ or person; rather, it would be divided among Congress, the president, and the Supreme Court.

In addition, as Madison was to emphasize in the 1790s (in his battle against the alleged plutocratic, antirepublican policies of the Hamiltonian-led Federalist Party), a loyal republican and constitutional opposition party would guard against tyranny at the center. Several factors would protect against the evils of monarchy, plutocracy, and tyranny in the central government and against antirepublicanism and anarchy in the component states: (1) the constitutional operation of majority rule; (2) a sound public opinion, based upon a free press; (3) a healthy two-party system; (4) the federal judiciary; and (5) wise statesmanship that could distinguish between usurpation, abuse, and unwise use of constitutional power. Given the assumptions of this theory, the central government could safely exercise generous and necessary republican power.

Prudentially, Madison's theory constituted sound political judgment on a number of crucial matters, not only in 1787, but in the 1790s and later in the 1820s and 1830s. In 1787 Madison saw the need to strengthen the powers of the central government. He wisely insisted on a new federal system that would do a better job of reconciling liberty and authority. He refused to listen to those naysayers who denied the possibility of republican government in an extensive country. And he was willing to settle for a central government that was not as strong as he had wanted because he perceived that the Constitution of 1787 was at least a major step in the right direction. Guided by his political theory, Madison articulated key features of the new federal republic in Philadelphia in 1787 and defended the Constitution effectively in *The Federalist* and at the Virginia Ratifying Convention. After the adoption of the Constitution in 1789, he authored the Bill of Rights and supported other key legislation to shore up the Constitution. In the 1790s he led a constitutional opposition party when he became unhappy with the Alien and Sedition Acts and other Federalist legislation. Finally, at the end of his long life, he defended the Union against the advocates of nullification and secession.

Madison took issue with the Sedition Act because it labeled as seditious (stirring up discontent, resistance, or rebellion against the government in power) any hard-hitting criticism, in speech or publication, of the government. For Madison, such criticism was essential to republican government—government based on popular consent and the protection of basic rights. Indeed, Madison maintained, criticism was an obligation of good citizenship.

Nullification and secession were different matters. The Union would be destroyed if single states could nullify national legislation or withdraw from the Union at will. Either action would mean the end of republican government. Nullification and secession could only lead to tyranny and anarchy. Such actions would defeat the creative endeavor to reconcile liberty and authority in a large political community. States had an obligation to abide by majority rule in the national government and to use the U.S. Constitution to seek necessary changes.

Continuing Efforts to Reconcile Liberty and Authority

Madison's republican and federal theory of 1787 constituted a generally successful guide to prudent action throughout his lifetime. His theory demonstrated that Americans could wisely reconcile liberty and authority in a large state. When Americans deviated from this theory, they encountered grave difficulties. The most serious was the Civil War, perhaps the worst difficulty that can occur within a political community. Madison's theory illustrates great creativity in politics; the American Civil War represents the failure of politics as a civilizing activity.

The search for new approaches to such persistent problems as the reconciliation of liberty and authority continues, and it occurs all over the globe. This search is apparent in the countries that made up the former Soviet Union. Comparable efforts to reconcile liberty and authority are going on in other central and Eastern European countries as they painfully attempt to achieve constitutional democracy.

Many developing countries in Asia, Africa, and Latin America also struggle to reconcile liberty and authority, often under adverse circumstances. Such struggles can be seen in Cambodia (Kampuchea), the Democratic Republic of the Congo, El Salvador, Indonesia, Lebanon, Liberia, Nicaragua, the Philippines, Sierra Leone, and South Africa. Many of these countries have suffered the agonies of civil war or acute internal discord.

Will troubled countries be successful in their efforts to reconcile liberty and authority? Can they achieve breakthroughs in politics comparable to Madison's? Such breakthroughs are rare, but the Madisonian example does hold out hope for such countries, and it may stimulate political scientists in their search for creative breakthroughs in politics.

We now turn to another case, which illuminates the burden of choice under adverse circumstances. If Socrates' decision illustrates the tragedy of choice and Madison's illustrates the creative opportunity of choice, then the decision of German citizens in 1932–1933 highlights the burden and disastrous consequences of choice.

THE GERMAN CITIZEN AND THE NAZI REGIME: CAN MODERN CITIZENS BEAR THE BURDEN OF FREEDOM?

Choice presupposes **freedom.** And freedom, to be most defensible, requires responsible judgment. When "the times are out of joint," responsible judgment is not easy. Does the average citizen, especially under difficult circumstances, have the common sense, virtue, wisdom, and strength to choose responsibly? Can we trust the people to make the right choices?

Plato, Socrates' greatest pupil, would have answered no. After all, the people had condemned his beloved teacher to death. Aristotle, Plato's greatest pupil, was also suspicious of Greek democracy, which he understood as rule by the people in their own selfish interest. He argued that only in a polity (which we translate as a constitutional democracy) would popular rule be safe. A polity, he maintained, would be most secure when it rested upon a strong, virtuous, well-educated, prosperous middle class. But what happens when such a middle class does not exist?

Suspicion of the people has endured. In the nineteenth century, Alexis de Tocqueville saw democracy as providential and inevitable. The United States, he felt, illustrated the future. Yet he worried about democratic despotism. Given a favorable Old World inheritance, a favorable New World environment, and creative statesmanship (illustrated, for example, in the work of people such as James Madison and other Founders), the United States might make democracy work. But what of countries that lacked these favorable conditions?

John Stuart Mill, in nineteenth-century Great Britain, also worried about the tyranny of the majority. However, he maintained that a sound constitutional, representative government—with excellent political and intellectual leadership—could preserve liberty. His fundamental confidence, despite misgivings, was reinforced by a long tradition of British liberty and by Britain's relative stability and prosperity in the nineteenth century. But, again, how would democracy work in the absence of favorable circumstances?

In the case at hand—Germany in 1932–1933—we will focus primarily on the voters who chose the Nazi Party and Adolf Hitler. What circumstances led to their choice? How many, in fact, supported the Nazis and why? We will also ask what other choices—by leaders, voters, and even anti-Nazi forces—contributed to Hitler's triumph. Our treatment will again underscore the interrelationship of values, facts, and judgment.

The Situation in Germany

First, we must examine the adverse circumstances that existed in Germany at the time. From 1919 to 1932 Germany struggled to make democracy work under the least favorable conditions. In Germany, unlike in Great Britain or the United States, constitutional democracy had not put down firm roots before World War I. The new German republic—

known as the Weimar Republic because its constitution had been proclaimed in the city of Weimar in 1919—was ushered into the world under severe difficulties. Germany had lost World War I (1914–1918), during which 1,744,000 of its soldiers had been killed and 225,000 of its civilians had died. Economic distress was rampant. The Weimar Republic struggled in the early and mid-1920s to cope with postwar reparations, inflation, and depression. Its modest successes after 1925 were seriously jeopardized by the Great Depression, which began in 1928. Bad times affected almost every segment of German society: industry, small business, labor, agriculture, and civil service. In a nation of 60 million, 6 to 8 million were unemployed. Farmers revolted; small business owners and craftspeople feared destruction.

From the beginning, enemies on the left and the right sought to overthrow the infant republic. The attacks intensified in the early 1930s. Nationalists, National Socialists (Nazis), and reactionary liberals attacked from the right. Communists attacked from the left. And the center (the Weimar coalition of the Social Democrats, which was a center-left party, the Catholic Center Party, and the Democratic Party) did not hold together. The Democratic Party disintegrated. The Catholic Center Party governed ineffectively in the crucial years from 1930 to 1932. And as one historian noted, the Social Democrats and Communists "devoted far more energy to fighting each other than to the struggle against the growing threat of National Socialism." [4] The Nazis played on the fear of communism and falsely accused the Social Democrats of being responsible for the defeat of 1918, the Treaty of Versailles, inflation, and other German ills. The Nazis condemned the ineffectiveness of the center parties.

Hitler shrewdly took advantage of Germany's disarray to encourage the German people to escape from responsible freedom to a regime of miracle, mystery, and authority. He promised miraculous results that would endure for a thousand years. The German people had only to follow his authority to see the payoff in jobs for unemployed workers, profits for suffering industrialists, self-respect for an alienated middle class, and power and prestige for a defeated army. The people were not, however, to inquire closely into the mystery whereby the Nazis would accomplish the miracle of the thousand-year Reich.

How many Germans actively supported the Nazis? And how did this support contribute to Hitler's ascent to power? In 1928 only 2.6 percent of the total vote went to the Nazi Party. This figure rose to 18.3 percent in 1930 and to a high of 37.3 percent in the first 1932 election. In the second 1932 election, which was the last free election under the Weimar Republic, the Nazi vote actually fell to 33.1 percent. However, because the left was split (the left-of-center Social Democrats receiving 20.4 percent and the Communists 16.85 percent of the vote), the Nazis emerged with the single largest party vote. The Catholic Center Party had maintained its percentage (16.2), but the other middle-class parties had disintegrated. Even after January 30, 1933, when Hitler was appointed chancellor, the Nazi vote in the spring 1933 election came to 43.9 percent, not a clear majority.[5]

The political and economic chaos of the 1920s and 1930s made some people believe that individual freedom of expression was dangerous. Adolf Hitler's appeal was based in part on the rejection of intellectual freedom and cultural diversity. Here members of the Nazi Youth are shown burning books in Salzburg, Austria, on April 30, 1938.

Hitler's appeal was reflected in the first 1932 (April) presidential election, when he polled 11,339,446 votes, or 30.1 percent. Paul von Hindenburg, Germany's leading general in World War I, received 18,657,497 votes, or 49.6 percent. The Communist Party candidate, Ernst Thaelmann, received 13.2 percent, and Theodore Duesterberg, a right-wing candidate, 6.8 percent. On the second ballot in 1932, candidates received the following percentages of votes: Hindenburg, 53.0 percent; Hitler, 36.8 percent; and Thaelmann, 10.2 percent.[6]

The rise of the Nazis led President Hindenburg, at the urging of right-wing, conservative advisers—especially his former chancellor, Franz von Papen—to offer Hitler the chancellorship. (The chancellor in Weimar Germany was the equivalent of the British prime minister.) Hindenburg and Papen believed that a cabinet of conservatives would be able to control the policies that Hitler would sell to the country through his party and its propaganda machine. This decision proved to be a fateful mistake.

But how had Nazi strength increased to the point that President Hindenburg and his advisers felt it necessary to bring Hitler in as chancellor? Why did people vote for the Nazis? The choice of Hitler was fateful; it doomed German democracy, brought on World War II, made the Holocaust possible, and split Germany into two parts from 1945 to 1990.

"The ideal-typical Nazi voter," wrote Seymour Martin Lipset in *Political Man,* "was a middle-class self-employed Protestant who lived either on a farm or in a small community, and who had previously voted for a centrist or regionalist political party strongly opposed to the power and influence of big business and big labor."[7] Obviously, those who voted for the Nazis had other common characteristics as well. The Nazis drew some support from every large group of voters. They had success with the middle-class unemployed and with conservative and nationalist voters on Germany's eastern borders. The Nazis also received above-average support from male voters and from younger voters. In general, however, according to Lipset, Nazi votes came "disproportionately from the ranks of the center and liberal parties rather than from the conservatives."

The Nazis were weakest among laborers, residents of big cities, Catholics, women, and older voters. Lipset noted: "With the exception of a few isolated individuals, German big business gave Nazism little financial support or other encouragement until it had risen to the status of a major party. . . . On the whole, however, this group remained loyal to the conservative parties, and many gave no money to the Nazis until after the party won power." [8]

So the heart of Nazi strength was the middle class: small businessmen, small farmers, the self-employed, white-collar workers, civil servants, and inhabitants of small towns. These voters were hostile to big industry, big cities, big unions, and big banks, as well as to the Versailles treaty, Communists, and Jews. Nazi supporters felt threatened by a loss of their status, by liberal values, and by economic depression.[9] They were threatened by key developments of modern society. As David Schoenbaum has noted in *Hitler's Social Revolution,* the Nazis drew on a longing for security, a common hostility to the existing order, and a universal desire for change.[10]

It is extremely important to emphasize that the middle class was not alone in its inability to bear the burden of responsible choice. Choices made by other segments of the German population also paved the way for Hitler. For example, there was the conservatives' disastrous decision to persuade Hindenburg to offer Hitler the chancellorship, as well as the poor policy choices of the Catholic Center Party and its leader, Heinrich Bruning, chancellor from 1930 to 1932. Bruning's deflationary policies (designed to decrease the amount of money in circulation, with a resultant increase in the value of money and a fall in prices) were very unpopular. Many scholars believe that his attempts to govern by decree undermined German democracy. In addition, the Social Democrats were unable to devise a strategy to stop Hitler. German Communists made fateful choices to work against the Social Democrats and thus divided working-class support for the Weimar Republic. Moreover, some army generals (Erich Ludendorff is the most notorious) supported the Nazis early on; others, closing their eyes to Nazi domestic politics and dreaming of the rebirth of German military power, gave their allegiance to Hitler after he became chancellor and then president. Industrialists, fearful of bolshevism and disorder and longing for profits and prosperity through armament sales, also decided, early or late, to support the Nazis. Thus, in one way or another, many Germans proved unable to exercise freedom responsibly.

Lessons of the Nazi Experience

The Nazi experience illuminates the problem of political obligation and the failure of creativity in politics as well as the difficulty of bearing the burden of freedom under adverse conditions. Too few people in Germany were dedicated strongly enough to the Weimar Republic and to democratic values. The Nazi right and the Communist left clearly sought the demise of liberal democracy in Germany. The parties committed to the Weimar Republic—especially the Social Democrats and the Catholic Center—were uncreative and ineffective. Unquestionably, unsettled social and economic conditions led to the poor political decisions that jeopardized German democracy. The Communists hoped that they would come to power with the collapse of the Weimar Republic. The Nazis used the fear of communism to rally support for their cause. Democratic forces were unable to unite effectively and rally the majority of Germans to their side.

The Nazi experience raises the following question: Which values, which circumstances, and which leadership judgments make the responsible exercise of freedom possible—and probable? This question is particularly troubling in many developing nations, especially the younger countries of Asia and Africa. People there may despair of finding democratic solutions for internal strife, poverty, unemployment, and loss of international respect, and may look for authoritarian rulers and solutions. They, too, may seek escape to a regime of "miracle, mystery, and authority."

Comparable difficulties also face many Latin American countries. These nations have longer histories of independence but often lack the social, economic, and political conditions that make for successful democratic and constitutional government. The record of the new regimes in Eastern Europe and the former Soviet Union is a mixed one. Some, like Poland and the Czech Republic, appear to being making successful transitions to democracy, while Russia's democratic record is less clear. Is it possible for such countries to create conditions of peace, human rights, prosperity, and self-esteem that will ease the burden of freedom and facilitate democratic, constitutional, and humane governance?

We now turn to critical decision making in another period of crisis.

JOHN F. KENNEDY AND THE CUBAN MISSILE CRISIS: THE PERILS OF CHOICE IN THE NUCLEAR AGE

On Tuesday, October 16, 1962, at 8:45 A.M., McGeorge Bundy, the special assistant for national security affairs, informed President John F. Kennedy: "Mr. President, there is now hard photographic evidence . . . that the Russians have offensive missiles in Cuba."[11] This disturbing news presented Kennedy with the most difficult choice of his presidency.

He convened a small group of top-level advisers to help him decide on an appropriate response. The news was especially troubling because the Soviet Union had previously stated that it would not place offensive nuclear weapons in Cuba and that any weapons supplied to Cuba were defensive. Despite Soviet insistence, there had been rumors and charges that the Soviets were "up to something" unusual in Cuba. And in late August the Central Intelligence Agency had reported that "something new and different" was under way. What did those late-summer Soviet shipments to Cuba indicate?

Although in early September the president did not have hard evidence of offensive weapons in Cuba, he had warned that the "gravest issues would arise" if such evidence were found. At his September 13 press conference, he had declared that new Soviet shipments to Cuba did not constitute a serious threat, but he warned that if Cuba were to "become an offensive military base of significant capacity for the Soviet Union, then this country will do whatever must be done to protect its own security and that of its allies." With evidence of the missiles' arrival, Kennedy felt betrayed. He felt as if his efforts to work toward a more peaceful world had been compromised.

Considering the Alternatives

The Executive Committee of the National Security Council—or ExCom, as the president's group of advisers came to be known—met at 11:45 that Tuesday morning to consider a response. They explored six major alternatives. The United States could (1) do nothing, (2) engage in diplomacy, (3) secretly approach Castro, (4) blockade Cuba, (5) launch a surgical air attack, or (6) invade Cuba. ExCom operated with the knowledge that the Soviet missiles would be on their launch pads and ready for firing within ten days.

"On the first Tuesday morning the choice for a moment seemed to lie between the air strike or acquiescence—and the president had made clear that acquiescence was impossible," historian Arthur M. Schlesinger observed. The argument for doing nothing was based on the view that the Soviets' ability to strike the United States from Cuba made little difference, given America's vulnerability to missiles already stationed in the Soviet Union. Doing nothing would prevent escalation and avert the danger of overreaction and an eventual nuclear catastrophe. Playing it cool would deprive Nikita Khrushchev, the Soviet leader, of any political advantage from his bold stroke.

Opponents of this alternative raised a number of serious objections. Doing nothing would permit the Soviet Union to double its missile capability, to outflank the U.S. early warning system, and to reverse the strategic balance by installing yet more missiles on a base ninety miles from the American coast. Politically, the "do nothing" option would undermine U.S. credibility and resolve in the eyes of the world by making the United States appear weak.

Diplomatic approaches—through the United Nations (UN), through the Organization of American States, or directly or indirectly to Khrushchev—required time, and the United States did not have much time. The Soviets could stall or veto action

During the Cuban missile crisis of October 1962, U.S. attorney general Robert Kennedy (left), confers with his brother, President John F. Kennedy, at the White House. Robert Kennedy chaired the ExCom committee whose work was crucial in helping the president arrive at what is widely considered one of the most critical decisions of the twentieth century—how to get Soviet missiles out of Cuba without triggering a nuclear war.

in the United Nations. While diplomats talked, the missiles would become operational. Approaches to Khrushchev might lead to an unsatisfactory deal in the midst of a threatening crisis. A secret approach to Castro overlooked the vital fact that the missiles belonged to the Soviet Union and that the key decision to withdraw them was the Soviets' alone.

So the president was initially drawn to the possibility of a surgical strike, an air attack confined to the missile bases. But was there no choice between bombing and doing nothing? If successful, an air strike would eliminate the threat to the United States. But could it be successful? Military leaders at the Pentagon concluded that a surgical strike would still leave Cuban airfields and Soviet aircraft operational. Moreover, the Pentagon could not guarantee that the U.S. Air Force could destroy all the missiles. A limited strike might expose the United States to nuclear retaliation. It would be prudent, militarily, to opt for a large strike to eliminate all sources of danger. So the surgical strike might have to be replaced by a massive strike; but this could lead to loss of Soviet lives and, perhaps, to Soviet retaliation in the divided city of Berlin or in Turkey, where American strategic forces were deployed. Moreover, could the president of the United States, with his memory of Pearl Harbor, order a surprise attack? Was the elimination of the missiles and of Castro worth the cost of a massive strike?

Kennedy's Latin American advisers warned that a massive strike would kill thousands of innocent Cubans and do great permanent damage to the United States in the eyes of Latin Americans. His European advisers warned that the world would regard a surprise attack as an excessive response. And if the Soviets moved against Berlin, the United States would be blamed and might have to fight under disadvantageous circumstances.

An invasion was also risky because U.S. troops would be confronting about twenty thousand Soviet troops in the first direct conflict between the forces of the world's two great superpowers. Would such an invasion guarantee a Soviet move against Berlin? Would it bring the world closer to World War III?

On the next day, Wednesday, Secretary of Defense Robert McNamara argued strongly on behalf of another alternative: a blockade, which would provide a middle course between doing nothing and engaging in a massive attack. The blockade would require Khrushchev to respond to a firm but not excessive step; he could avoid a military clash by keeping his ships away. The blockade would set up a confrontation in an advantageous location—the Caribbean. This alternative kept open other options, such as diplomacy or other military action, and it averted the confrontation that brought one's "adversary to the choice of either a humiliating defeat or a nuclear war," as President Kennedy noted.

But there were objections to the blockade. A blockade was an act of war and might be deemed a violation of the UN charter or of international law. Even more seriously, would the blockade bring enough pressure on Khrushchev to remove the missiles already in Cuba? Would it stop work on the bases? Opponents of the blockade maintained that it would lead to a Soviet counterblockade of Berlin and to confrontation with the Soviet

Union: if Soviet ships did not stop, the United States would have to fire the first shot, and this might invite Soviet retaliation.

On Thursday evening, President Kennedy met with ExCom. According to Schlesinger's account, the president was leaning toward the blockade:

> He was evidently attracted by the idea of the blockade. It avoided war, preserved flexibility and offered Khrushchev time to reconsider his actions. It could be carried out within the framework of the Organization of American States and the Rio Treaty. Since it could be extended to nonmilitary items as occasion required, it could become an instrument of steadily intensifying pressure. It would avoid the shock effect of a surprise attack, which would hurt us politically through the world and might provoke Moscow to an insensate response against Berlin or the United States itself. If it worked, the Russians could retreat with dignity. If it did not work, the Americans retained the option of military action. In short, the blockade, by enabling us to proceed one step at a time, gave us control over the future. Kennedy accordingly directed that preparations be made to put the weapons blockade into effect on Monday morning.[12]

Making the Choice

The debate between advocates of the blockade and those of the air strike persisted until the formal meeting of the National Security Council on Saturday. After hearing both arguments again, Kennedy endorsed the blockade. But before making his decision final, he wanted one last talk with the Air Force Tactical Air Command to satisfy himself that a surgical strike was not feasible. This meeting was held Sunday morning. The air force spokesman told the president that the air strike would have to be massive, and even then it would not guarantee the destruction of all Soviet missiles. The president had been worried that the blockade would not remove the missiles; now it was clear that an air attack could not guarantee that result either.

On Monday, October 22, at 7:30 P.M., President Kennedy addressed the nation (which had known nothing of the crisis that had engaged ExCom since October 16) and set forth his choice. He emphasized that the Soviet missile bases provided the Soviet Union with "a nuclear strike capability against the Western Hemisphere." Soviet action constituted "a deliberately provocative and unjustified change . . . which cannot be accepted by this country, if our courage and our commitments are ever to be trusted again by either friend or foe." The nuclear threat to Americans had to be eliminated. The president then indicated that he had imposed a "quarantine" on all offensive military equipment under shipment to Cuba. Cuba would be kept under intensive surveillance. The president also declared that any missile launched from Cuba would be regarded as an attack by the Soviet Union on the United States and would elicit immediate retaliatory response upon the Soviet Union. He called for a meeting of the Organization of American States to consider the threat to the security of the American hemisphere and for an emergency meeting of the UN Security Council to consider the threat to world peace. Kennedy also appealed to Khrushchev "to abandon the course of world domination, and to join in an historic effort to end the perilous arms race and to transform the history of man."

So the basic choice was made. But before the crisis was over, Kennedy would have to make other key choices: to interpret the blockade flexibly (rather than rigidly) to give the Soviets time to respond to a peaceful solution, and to use diplomacy (rather than force) to accomplish his objective of removing the missiles. By Thursday Adlai Stevenson, the U.S. ambassador to the United Nations, had effectively destroyed the Soviet argument that the missiles were defensive. Within the Security Council chamber, the following extraordinary exchange took place between Stevenson and Valerian Zorin, the Soviet ambassador to the United Nations:

STEVENSON: "Do you, Ambassador Zorin, deny that the U.S.S.R. has placed and is placing medium- and intermediate-range missiles and sites in Cuba? . . . Don't wait for the translation!"

ZORIN: "I am not in an American courtroom, sir, and I do not wish to answer a question put to me in the manner in which a prosecutor does—"

STEVENSON: "You are in the courtroom of world opinion right now, and you can answer yes or no. You have denied that they exist, and I want to know whether I have understood you correctly."

ZORIN: "Please continue your statement. . . . You will receive your answer in due course."

STEVENSON: "I am prepared to wait for my answer until hell freezes over, if that is your decision. I am also prepared to present the evidence in this room." [13]

Stevenson then presented the aerial photographs that revealed Soviet nuclear installations. The Soviets then probed for a deal, and the Americans responded favorably. The Soviets would remove their missiles under UN inspection, and the United States would promise publicly not to invade Cuba. On Friday, October 26, Khrushchev cabled Kennedy: "If the President and Government of the United States were to give assurances that the U.S.A. itself would not participate in an attack on Cuba and would restrain others from this kind of act, if you would recall your fleet, this would immediately change everything." [14] Kennedy responded by indicating that as soon as work stopped on the missile sites and the offensive weapons were rendered inoperable, a settlement along Khrushchev's lines was in order. U.S. attorney general Robert Kennedy, in delivering his brother's message to the Soviet ambassador to the United States, Anatoly Dobrynin, indicated that unless the United States received assurances within twenty-four hours, it would take military action by Tuesday.

Saturday night was a disturbing night for President Kennedy as he waited for Khrushchev's reply. At 9 A.M., Sunday, October 28, Khrushchev's response came in. Work would stop on the missile sites: the arms "which you described as offensive" would be crated and returned to the Soviet Union. Negotiations would start at the UN.

And so the two-week crisis—perhaps the closest we have come to World War III—ended. President Kennedy's choices in the Cuban missile crisis underscore the dangers and difficulties of achieving national security in the nuclear age. Presidential choices have become more potent for good or ill. Presidents are forced to recognize that the stakes are higher and that their actions affect the vital interests of not only the United States but all humankind. These same thoughts must have troubled the Soviet leaders. This recognition may explain the relative prudence both superpowers demonstrated in respecting each other's vital interests, in achieving arms reduction and arms control agreements, and in limiting the spread of nuclear weapons. Later chapters, particularly chapters 13 and 15, examine how prudent such policies actually are.

CONCLUSION

Our brief examination of these four cases makes clear that wise choices in politics rest on sound values, accurate understanding of political phenomena, and astute judgment. These components are very closely connected. The four cases also emphasize the importance of addressing the problem of political obligation, striving for creative political breakthroughs, learning to bear the burden of freedom, and responding wisely to the perils of decision making in the nuclear age.

Succeeding chapters reveal a host of other choices. Many of them are less momentous and less dramatic than those examined in this chapter. Some are more modest personal choices. All, however, reveal the intimate connection among values, facts, and judgments. A number of decision-making models are, for example, more fully explored in chapter 14. And the public policy chapters in part 4 illustrate at greater length what contributes to sound judgment on four major issues.

SUGGESTED READINGS

Allen, Reginald A. *Socrates and Legal Obligation.* Minneapolis: University of Minnesota Press, 1980. Helpful for those who want to explore more fully the pros and cons of Socrates' choice in Plato's *Apology* and *Crito.*

Allison, Graham T., and Philip Zelikow. *Essence of Decision: Explaining the Cuban Missile Crisis.* 2nd ed. New York: Longman, 1999. A brilliant analysis of a crucial choice, and a penetrating exploration of decision making in general.

Brinton, Crane. *The Anatomy of Revolution.* 1938. Rev. ed. New York: Vintage Books, 1965. Illuminates judgment and choice in four successful revolutions.

Browning, Christopher. *Ordinary Men.* New York: HarperCollins, 1992. Examines the lives of members of a German police unit involved in the Holocaust.

Fromm, Erich. *Escape from Freedom.* New York: Avon, 1965. Explores the factors in the modern world that created the "burden" of freedom and choice and tempted modern people (especially the Germans) to succumb to Nazism.

Gosnell, Harold F. *Truman's Crises: A Political Biography.* Westport, Conn.: Greenwood Press, 1980. Deals with a number of critical presidential decisions at the end of World War II and in the crucial post–World War II years, including the decision to drop the atomic bomb at Hiroshima.

Hamilton, Alexander, John Jay, and James Madison. *The Federalist.* 1787–1788. Cleveland: World, 1961. Persuasive arguments on behalf of the choice of the new federal constitution of 1787. Unrivaled in its influence on the fateful choice more than two hundred years ago.

Kershaw, Ian. *The Nazi Dictatorship: Problems and Perspectives of Interpretation.* 2nd ed. London: Edward Arnold, 1989. Chapter 1 deals with "Historians and the Problem of Explaining Nazism."

Riemer, Neal. *Creative Breakthroughs in Politics.* Westport, Conn.: Praeger, 1996. Explores two genuine and two spurious historical breakthroughs, one contemporary breakthrough still in progress (European Union), and a future breakthrough (protection against genocide).

———. *James Madison: Creating the American Constitution.* Washington, D.C.: Congressional Quarterly, 1986. Highlights Madison's choices as a nationalist, Federalist, empirical political scientist, and democrat. Underscores Madison's theory as a creative breakthrough in politics.

Riesman, David, Norman Glazer, and Reuel Denney. *The Lonely Crowd.* New Haven: Yale University Press, 1950. People are tradition directed, other directed, and inner directed. Underscores the difficulties of rational and ethical choice in the modern world.

Stone, I. F. *The Trial of Socrates.* Boston: Little, Brown, 1988. A wonderfully refreshing account by a great journalist. Much more sympathetic to those who tried Socrates and more critical of Socrates than most accounts.

GLOSSARY TERMS

creative breakthrough (p. 43)
extensive republic (p. 43)
faction (p. 43)
freedom (p. 46)
political creativity (p. 35)
political obligation (p. 35)
power politics (p. 36)
responsible citizenship (p. 35)

Chapter 3

POLITICAL SCIENCE

Components, Tasks, and Controversies

How can we usefully define the discipline of political science? This basic question is addressed specifically in this chapter and is also explored throughout the book. We begin with a brief discussion of the basic organizational structure of the discipline followed by analysis of three subjects of great interest to political scientists: political philosophy and ethics, the empirical and behavioral study of politics, and public policy.[1] These subjects concern:

1. the good political life and the underlying ethical principles of politics;
2. a science of politics and an understanding of significant empirical phenomena (facts, circumstances, experiences);
3. political wisdom and judgment in the arena of citizenship and public policy;
4. and—because the first three concerns are interrelated—the integration of ethics, science, and statesmanship.

THE BASIC STRUCTURE OF POLITICAL SCIENCE

The discipline of political science in the United States is traditionally divided into four subfields:

1. **American Government and Politics.** This is the study of how the system of governance in the United States works. At all levels of governance—local, state, and national—how do we select our leaders and representatives? How are major public policies developed and decided upon? Traditionally, there have been a large number of areas of inquiry subsumed under the American subfield. These include but are

not restricted to public administration, public policy, political economy, presidential elections, judicial behavior, legislative behavior, and state and local government.

2. **International Relations.** This is the study of how countries and other major actors in the international system interact with each other. Some of the more important questions that political scientists working in this area address include: Why do countries go to war? Why and how do countries make peace? How do we deal with issues such as global poverty, environmental degradation, terrorism, and nuclear proliferation? As in the case in the American field, there are a large number of specialized fields, including foreign policy, international organization, international law, international political economy, national security, diplomacy, and war and peace studies.

3. **Comparative Politics.** This is the study of political and governance processes in countries around the world. It is a huge field that includes not only the study of specific governments but topics such as ethnic politics, democratization, feminist studies, and economic and political development.

4. **Political Theory or Political Philosophy.** This is the one subfield that in many ways bridges the other three subfields of the discipline. At its core it involves the study of fundamental questions about governance: What should be the relationship be between government and the governed? What constitutes legitimate government? Are there fundamental political rights and freedoms? Is one form of government preferable to another? Under what circumstances is the overthrow of a government justified? In the broader sense, political theory is concerned with the idea of justice. It is in this subfield of the discipline that great attention is paid to the most influential political thinkers in history, such as Plato, Socrates, Machiavelli, Hobbes, Augustine, Aquinas, Rousseau, Burke, Mill, and Marx.

It is important to note that these four subfields are not mutually exclusive. How does one understand American foreign policy without some knowledge of American government? Is the study of energy policy exclusively an international or a domestic concern? The federal budget of the United States mandates consideration of a number of questions that clearly fall under the area of international relations—foreign aid allocations, the size and shape of the military, funds to fight terrorism, etc.

Beyond the basic organization of the discipline, we note that political scientists who favor the more traditional approaches to their discipline tend to stress the importance of ethics, history, law, constitutions, formal institutions, and citizenship. Other political scientists stress scientific methodology and human behavior. They usually draw on psychology, sociology, economics, and mathematics in their investigations. Sometimes they combine political science and a related discipline to form a subfield such as political economy.

The controversies between approaches have centered on arguments about these emphases. Less traditional political scientists have argued that instead of focusing on questions about the good life and wise public policy, political science should be made a rigorous empirical science like physics or biology; in recent years the discipline has drawn extensively from the field of economics. Other political scientists counter that such moves are false to the nature of politics, which is inevitably concerned with both the good political life and wise action in the political arena.

To highlight another emphasis, radical political scientists have attacked the empirically oriented students of politics for being not only narrowly scientific but also conservative. They argue that empiricists focus too narrowly on dominant power relationships and ignore the poor, the weak, and the maltreated. Empirical political scientists tend to accept what is normal as what should be. Radical political scientists, who may be Marxists, critical social theorists, feminists, or postmodernists, are generally unhappy with the status quo.

Controversies such as these suggest the wisdom of a broader approach. They indicate that any definition of political science that rules out political philosophy and ethics, empirical and behavioral studies, or public policy is inadequate. With this warning in mind, we can attempt a tentative definition of the field: *Political science is a field of study characterized by a search for critical understanding of (1) the good political life, (2) significant empirical observations, and (3) wise political and policy judgments.* **Political science** is thus concerned with the search for meaningful knowledge of the interrelated ethical, empirical, and prudential components of that community concerned with the public life.

The central activity of the political community is, of course, politics. *Politics is a process within or between political communities whereby (1) public values are articulated, debated, and prescribed; (2) diverse political actors (individuals, interest groups, local or regional governments, nations, international organizations) cooperate and struggle for power in order to satisfy their vital needs, protect their fundamental interests, and advance their perceived desires; and (3) public policy judgments are made and authoritative actions on crucial public problems are taken.* Let us now try to clarify these definitions by addressing the components of political science and the tasks they suggest.

THE THREE MAJOR COMPONENTS OF POLITICAL SCIENCE

Three interrelated components of the study of politics shape the political scientist's major tasks (see Table 3.1). By major components we mean the major concerns or parts of political science: ethical, empirical, and prudential. Throughout history, political scientists have been concerned with the study of the good political life, political institutions, behavior, and wise judgment. Until recently, these emphases were linked. In the post–World War II period, some political scientists argued that these components should be separated for study. Others, however, continued to insist on integrating these concerns.

Table 3.1 Three Major Components of Political Science

Component	Main Focus	Main Question	Foundation
Ethical	Political values	What ought to be?	Philosophy
Empirical	Political phenomena	What is (what has been, what will be)?	Science
Prudential	Political judgment	What can be?	Public policy

Source: Compiled by authors.

The Ethical Component

The student of politics is concerned with worthy political values, or **ethics,** with *what ought to be* in politics. Every community adheres to certain values, is inspired by certain purposes, is dedicated to certain goals, and is committed to certain conceptions of the good life. Critical examination of these norms is a central concern of the political scientist as an ethical theorist or political philosopher. For example, the Preamble to the U.S. Constitution expresses the cardinal values of the American political community: "We, the people of the United States, in order to form a more perfect Union, establish justice, insure domestic tranquility, provide for the common defense, promote the general welfare, and secure the blessings of liberty to ourselves and our posterity, do ordain and establish this Constitution for the United States of America." Other constitutions contain similar statements of goals, purposes, and values.

But what do these values mean? This is a question the political scientist cannot avoid; it is a starting point for her or his critical investigation. Although there is widespread agreement at a very general level on such values as life, liberty, peace, justice, and economic well-being, the specific meaning of these concepts in particular circumstances—and their harmony with one another—remains a source of great controversy. Indeed, most political battles center on the meaning given to these values.

Thus critically examined values provide a *standard for judgment* in politics. This standard permits one to say that a domestic law is good or bad, that a foreign policy is morally right or wrong, or that the action of a governmental official, politician, or interest group is desirable or undesirable.

The Empirical Component

Political scientists are also concerned with understanding political phenomena—political realities—in the community: events and their causes, conditions of well-being, patterns of conflict and accommodation, institutions, and public policies. In short, political scientists are concerned with political **empiricism**—*what has been, what is, and what will be.* As social scientists, they investigate empirically significant problems related to politics, such as the causes of war and the conditions that make for peace, the factors influencing democratic or undemocratic rule, and the circumstances connected with justice or injustice within a political community. Political scientists are also interested in the behavior of key political actors (such as the president, Congress, and the Supreme Court) and in the role of political parties, the media, and interest groups in the political process.

To investigate these questions we rely primarily on the methods of empirical science: observation, description, measurement, inductive generalization, explanation, deductive reasoning, continued testing, correction, corroboration, and carefully qualified prediction. Empirical investigations are designed to discover who rules and who benefits in politics and why. Indeed, one famous shorthand definition of the empirical approach to political science is found in the title of Harold Lasswell's influential book *Politics: Who Gets What, When, How.*

Empirical evidence is used to test hypotheses and to arrive at supportable generalizations. Do businesspeople or farmers or factory workers get the biggest "breaks" from income tax legislation in the United States? Is it really true that the "strong do what they can and the weak suffer what they must" in international politics? Is there an "iron law of oligarchy" at work in politics as well as in large organizations—a "law" that states that a minority of insiders runs the show? In their empirical investigations, political scientists explore these and other questions to arrive at meaningful, coherent, and objectively testable generalizations.

The Prudential Component

Political scientists are also concerned with political **prudence**—*what can be,* that is, with workable public policies and a host of practical judgments. The prudential component refers to wise judgment about the practical tasks of politics.[2] How can a political candidate gain enough votes to win an election? How can a nation's leaders most wisely deal with their actual or potential enemies? What actions can a citizen take to influence public officials? How can a nation grapple with problems such as nuclear disarmament, violations of human rights, poverty, unemployment, pollution, crime, drugs, and debilitating diseases such as AIDS? Formulating answers to such questions requires practical judgment, or good sense.

Wise practical judgment must be exercised in making or carrying out public policy and in deciding disputes under the law. But legislators, executives, and judges are not the only political actors who make judgments. Prominent party officials, powerful interest group leaders, and influential members of the media also make key judgments. And beyond even these important decision makers, a variety of economic, social, religious, and educational groups and scores of individuals influence public policy in major or minor ways. Citizens voting in the election booth are making practical judgments. Furthermore, millions of ordinary people are involved in the process of making judgments as they read newspaper stories, listen to political news on their televisions or radios, peruse the Internet, hear political candidates, and contribute to or work in political campaigns.

We will postpone consideration of how these components interrelate until we have examined the four major tasks they suggest.

THE FOUR MAJOR TASKS OF POLITICAL SCIENCE

The major tasks of political science follow logically from an acceptance of the major components of the discipline we have just examined:

1. the concern for what is right or wrong in politics leads, initially, to the task of ethical recommendation;
2. the concern for political phenomena—facts, circumstances, experiences—leads to the task of empirical understanding;
3. the concern for what can sensibly be done leads to the task of prudential, or wise, judgment or action;
4. and—because the first three tasks suggest it—the theoretical integration of these ethical, empirical, and prudential concerns.

Let us now examine each task in turn.

Ethical Recommendation

Political scientists have the important (and admittedly controversial) task of recommending what actions leaders of state, citizens, and all others involved in politics ought to take. They prescribe standards and make critical appraisals that assist political actors in pursuing the good political life. This task also helps political scientists address problems of legitimacy and obligation in politics: for example, which governments or actions are legitimate and therefore entitled to public consent, and which political rights and responsibilities citizens are obliged to honor.

Political philosophers have been concerned about the ideal regime and the best practical political community since the birth of systematic philosophy with Socrates, Plato, and Aristotle in ancient Greece. But what is "best" calls for critical examination. The definitions of key political values—whether justice or the common good or liberty or order or equality or fraternity—are not self-evident. People in politics dispute the meaning of these values. Moreover, the relationship of one value to another—for example, of justice to order, of liberty to equality—cries out for analysis.

In carrying out such a study, political scientists as political philosophers are not completely divorced from the world as it is and as it can be. Their ethical analysis must be compatible with real people, as they now are or as they can sanely become in a real world. Thus political scientists cannot sensibly recommend political values that are biologically and physically impossible or socially and politically perilous.

Yet political scientists as philosophers are, if not completely unlimited, significantly free to let their imaginations soar. They can raise their ethical sights to discover possibilities undreamed of by pedestrian political actors following the unexamined routes or the bureaucratic ruts carved out by tradition. Political scientists are free to articulate political ideas far removed from the current system. They can voice better ways for handling the business of the political community.

Public demonstrations are one way that American citizens can express their views on what politics they believe the government should or should not pursue. As the war in Iraq dragged on and U.S. casualties mounted, more and more Americans became disenchanted with the policy. Some engaged in public protests, although, as of the middle of 2005, the demonstrations were not nearly as large as those against the Vietnam War thirty-five to forty years before.

They can, for example, imagine a world without war and political communities wherein social and economic justice prevails and policies ensure economic well-being for all. They can conceive of a global physical environment in ecological balance, of a world where disastrous diseases, such as AIDS, have been successfully overcome. In more concrete terms, they can imagine the reduction and eventual elimination of nuclear arms, poverty, and torture. They can conceive of good jobs for all persons capable of working, financial security for the aged and the ill, pure water, and the end of racism and debilitating disease.

Critical analysis of values goes beyond a keen appraisal of standards that ought to guide political actors. It includes criticism of actual behavior, institutions, and policies in the light of these standards. Is a given country, for example, engaged in a war? Is it oppressing its own people? Is the U.S. presidency, or the Chinese leadership, tyrannically powerful? Is the United States taking appropriate action to curb terrorism, enhance employment, extend health care, reform the welfare system, ensure educational opportunity, and protect the environment?

Finally, such critical analysis involves examination of sensible alternatives for the future. Can the proliferation of nuclear weapons be avoided? How should that be accomplished? In the near future should the number of nuclear weapons be reduced to zero?

As political scientists analyze the protection of human rights, we can ask whether "quiet diplomacy" works best or whether violators should face publicity and strong sanctions.

Disturbingly, answers depend on whether the violators of human rights are powerful nations such as China or weak nations and whether they are "friends" or "foes."

And how should Americans criticize alternatives as they seek to overcome poverty? Should the poor lift themselves by their own bootstraps? Or should the rich nations (mostly located in the Northern Hemisphere) help the poor nations (mostly located in the Southern Hemisphere)? Or should Americans favor a more complex set of policies—self-help, governmental assistance, and salutary international policies of trade and aid?

And how should Americans respond to the ecological alternatives and disastrous diseases facing the world? Should science and technology be relied on to overcome the dwindling supplies of oil and other precious nonrenewable resources? Or should the focus be prudently managing natural resources to achieve a "steady-state" society? And how can we successfully prevent and treat the disastrous diseases?

These questions underscore the connections among ethical recommendation, empirical understanding, and prudential judgment.

Empirical Understanding

Political scientists seek to understand how political actors carry out their business. What really goes on in politics—and why? Here political scientists are concerned with political realities, with what can be scientifically observed, described, confirmed, and explained. Their interest is what has been, is, and will be the case in politics. But they seek more than just the bare facts; they seek comprehensive knowledge. Although they may begin with description, they hope to end with explanation. A number of important empirical questions challenge the political scientist:

- How indeed does the larger environment of politics—the geographic world we human beings live in, our biological endowment, our economic resources and activity, our historical memory, our religious beliefs, our scientific and technological achievements, our social mores—influence our political values, patterns of conflict and accommodation, and decision making?
- Are people's political values rooted in universal human needs or merely the result of a particular culture?
- Do citizens, as creative political actors, make wise decisions?
- Why do some political communities succeed better than others at satisfying such values as security, liberty, justice, and welfare?

In attending to these and comparable questions, empirical political scientists attempt to develop a general theory that will aid their efforts to order and explain the complex data of politics. As they develop their theories, they follow, as much as possible, the elements of scientific investigation. Thus they try to examine the data systematically and critically and to develop fruitful generalizations. Such generalizations enhance the ability of political scientists to grasp connections in the world of political phenomena and even (sometimes) to predict future political events.

This, of course, is an ideal portrayal of the empirical task. In fact, political science is far from reaching this ideal. Nonetheless, the empirically oriented political scientist strives to explain how and why political actors (1) formulate political values; (2) accommodate diverse interests and umpire the struggle for power; and (3) exercise judgment (wisely or foolishly) in grappling with problems, making decisions, and administering public policy. Thus the empirically oriented political scientist is concerned with values and judgment as well as with actual behavior.

Prudential Judgment

Political scientists also must provide sensible guidance in political life. This means employing practical wisdom and making decisions in concrete situations. Political scientists may use this capability when they exercise power themselves as politicians or administrators; when they advise leaders of state, legislators, and party officials; when they work as teachers or scholars; or when they function as ordinary citizens.

Initially, political scientists need to be clearheaded about the values—such as peace, prosperity, human rights, or clean air—they seek to preserve. Second, they need to recognize the factors that threaten (or advance) these values. Third, they must identify and debate alternative policies addressed to these problems. Finally, they need to decide on the most desirable and feasible policy. Part 4 of this book explores these matters in greater depth.

The task of prudential judgment rests on, but differs from, the tasks of ethical recommendation and empirical understanding. Of course, judgment must be guided by critically examined values (for example, respect for human life and human rights) and must recognize the limitations and opportunities of political reality. Yet prudential judgment differs in important ways from the other tasks.

In contrast to political scientists who make ethical recommendations, those engaged in making wise judgments are limited by the constraints of politics as the art of the possible. They must tailor their judgments to fit a real, rather than an ideal, world. But political scientists do not have to be timid or rigidly conservative. Bold, imaginative judgments that are nonetheless prudent are possible, even though they often have to be made under urgent circumstances. Nonetheless, there always remains a tension in politics between the ethically ideal and the politically feasible.

Although feasibility requires political scientists, when exercising prudent judgment, to respect reality, they are only concerned with that reality as it helps them judge present and future behavior, consequences, and alternatives. Such judgments are not fully scientific because they go beyond knowledge of what is, to what can be, to practical wisdom. Practical wisdom calls for judgment in action—judgment that must usually be made in the absence of complete scientific knowledge. Thus the judgmental process is not fully scientific, and it entails more than science. Science is, however, indispensable in politics.

Ethical and empirical components are integrally connected with prudent judgments. The interrelationship of these three components brings us now to a fourth task, theoretical integration.

Theoretical Integration

Although political scientists may specialize in any one of the three realms we have discussed—ethical, empirical, or prudential—they must still appreciate how these components interrelate in a unified and coherent discipline. Table 3.2 presents one view of their interrelationship.

For example, in this framework, on the issue of ecological health, political philosophers concerned with ethics would ask: Should ecological health be a cardinal value in the political community? Empirical political scientists would ask: Does such a condition of ecological health actually exist? And students of public policy would ask: Is ecological health a value that nations can practically achieve?

Other ties among the components of political science are apparent. Indeed, the history of political science and the very nature of politics call for a unified discipline. The great political philosophers—the first creative political scientists—were very concerned with the relationship of ethics to politics. They also saw that politics embraced both empirical understanding and prudent judgment.

Moreover, as we have tried to emphasize, the nature of politics forbids the separation of tasks. Values guide empirical investigation and inform prudent judgment in public policy. Political values make little sense unless they are in accord with actual (or potential)

Table 3.2 Interrelationship of the Three Major Components of Political Science

Component	Political Values	Political Phenomena	Political Judgment
Ethical	Which political values should exist?	How should political actors behave?	Which public policies should prevail?
Empirical	Which values actually exist in the political community?	How do political actors actually behave?	Which public policies actually exist?
Prudential	Which values can wisely exist in the political community?	How can political actors wisely behave?	Which public policies can be formulated and sensibly implemented?

Source: Compiled by authors.

Figure 3.1 Tying Together the Components of Political Science

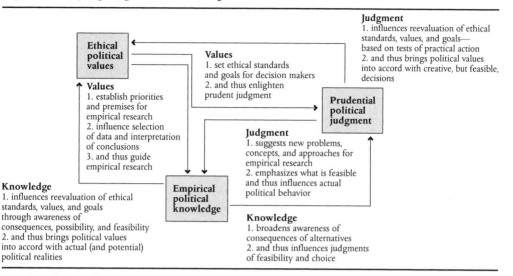

Source: Compiled by authors.

political realities and with creative, but feasible, political decisions. Judgments as to what is feasible influence actual behavior. And judgment is not only informed by the values that motivate political actors but also qualified by the realities of political phenomena. Thus political science is fruitful because political scientists, at the highest level of political theory, grapple critically with the interrelationship among (1) articulated political values, (2) empirical data and theory on the actual behavior of political actors (individuals, interests, political communities), and (3) the creative judgments required in statesmanship. In the political life of the real community, these three components, although partially separable in logic and distinguishable for purposes of specialized research, cannot be treated in isolation. Figure 3.1 illustrates this point.

Some additional illustrations will help clarify this interrelationship. Concern for the value of human survival has led inexorably to an appreciation of the disastrous consequences of nuclear war and to a search for prudent ways of controlling and eventually eliminating nuclear weapons. Heightened awareness of the meaning of equality in the United States has led to empirical investigation of racial discrimination, poverty, and sexism, as well as to measures to reduce inequalities: a civil rights act, a "war on poverty," and affirmative action programs. Some programs helped, others worked imperfectly, and still others backfired—that is, they often resulted in protests against such policies as "forced busing," "forced integration," or "reverse discrimination." These consequences sometimes led to a reconsideration of the methods used to fight inequality and of the meaning of equality, and thus to new empirical research.[3]

Political Health as an Example of Theoretical Integration. So the tasks of ethical recommendation, empirical understanding, and prudential judgment stimulate political scientists to envisage an ambitious fourth task: integration in the discipline. Such theoretical integration might come with an old or new concept, such as the idea of political health or well-being. The concept of **political health** encourages integration because it enables political scientists to address the three major concerns—ethical, empirical, and prudential.

There are several ways political scientists could explore political health. First, they could do so as a norm or a standard of the good life. Theoretically, it is possible to define health in politics as peace and peaceful constitutional change, security, liberty, democratic governance, political and social justice, economic prosperity, and ecological balance.

Second, political scientists could investigate political health in a scientific fashion. Are political communities healthy? Why or why not? What evidence supports an empirical conclusion about their well-being? Here we emphasize that political scientists can move beyond symptoms of political well-being or malaise to empirical generalizations and theories about the healthy political community.

Third, political scientists—guided by an ethical norm and aided by social scientific knowledge—could engage in healing by addressing themselves to wise actions, policies, and judgments designed to maximize political health. They are encouraged as teachers, political advisers, citizens, governmental leaders, or administrators to put their knowledge to work as best they can.

To summarize, the task of theoretical integration involves developing a general theory (say, of political health) that harmoniously relates the discipline's ethical, empirical, and prudential components and ties together its traditional (and nontraditional) fields of study. Ambitious? Yes. Impossible? No, but very difficult!

Historical Theories of Integration. The linkage of political values, social scientific knowledge, and wise action has been noted by key political philosophers such as Plato, Aristotle, James Madison, and Karl Marx, as well as by twentieth-century political scientists. In ancient Greece, Plato saw no sharp division between fact and value, or between these two and practical wisdom. For Plato, the good was true, and practical wisdom involved approximating the good as closely as circumstances permitted. Aristotle took a somewhat different position but argued on behalf of the intimate linkage between ethics and politics; he saw prudence—or practical wisdom—as depending on a good goal pursued sensibly in the light of existing realities.

In the late eighteenth century James Madison, as noted in chapter 2, clearly saw the importance of making republican values central in his thinking. He also recognized that he must advance those republican values in the light of America's realities—a nation of large size with diverse interests. Prudence dictated the concept of an "extensive republic"—the present U.S. federal republic—as a wise solution to the problem of reconciling republican liberty and size.

Modern Approaches. In the mid-twentieth century David Easton used the phrase "political system" in his highly influential 1953 book by that name, to underscore his commitment to understanding the whole domain of political science. And although his major concern was scientific unity, he understood that ethical values underlie the scientific enterprise and that knowledge cannot be easily separated from action. Karl Deutsch, another prominent twentieth-century political scientist, wrote:

> We need a cumulative political science where knowledge will grow and clearly improve in scope, amount, and quality, as it has done in so many other fields of human knowledge. Such a cumulative knowledge of what can and what cannot be done in politics under specific conditions should open the way to more effective applications of political science in the service of freedom and peace, within countries and among them.[4]

Other modern political scientists press more frankly for a *holistic* approach, which calls for an appreciation of the whole: concern for the survival of all people on earth, social and political justice, economic interdependence in a global community, and environmental quality of life. They are joined by an array of humanists, who argue that the earth is an interrelated global community and who never worry about separating their ethical beliefs from their empirical observations about the world or from their judgments about wise public policy.

Practical Applications. Political scientists in all the traditional fields undertake the four tasks we have outlined. At first glance, this may not seem to be the case. To the superficial observer, ethical recommendation may seem more immediately visible in the field of political theory, empirical understanding more apparent in comparative politics and American politics, and prudential judgment more central in international politics and in public administration and public policy. However, a more thorough examination of the fields reveals that the ethical and prudential approaches are never much below the surface in comparative politics or American politics. Moreover, international politics, public administration, and public policy are clearly guided by ethical norms and must rest on a sound foundation of empirical understanding. And, of course, political theory presupposes both a firm appreciation of political reality and appropriate attention to wise judgment.

The traditional fields of political science—and the several approaches in these fields—are explored more fully later in this book. Political theory is explored in part 2. Comparative politics, American politics, and international politics are explored in parts 3 and 4. Before turning to the fuller exploration of problems in these fields, we must point out that not all political scientists agree on the approach outlined in the previous pages. Controversy persists on the legitimate subject matter of political science, on proper methodology for the discipline, and on approaches to be taken in the several fields of political science.

CONTINUING CONTROVERSIES IN
POLITICAL SCIENCE

Controversies center on the priority to be given to (1) the quest for the good political life, (2) the search for a science of politics, (3) guidance for citizens and leaders of state, and (4) the importance of a unified discipline that can do justice to politics. Moreover, political scientists remain divided on key questions within each area of emphasis.

The Quest for the Good Political Life

Should the ethical quest for the good political life be guided by a philosophical, religious, or scientific concern for the highest truth? Or should it be led by a quest for the most acceptable opinion? Are philosophical reason, religious revelation, historical experience, human needs, or societal preference the keys to unlock the mysteries of the good political life?

Some political scientists argue that only ethical reasoning can help determine standards for what is right or wrong. Others contend that such norms and standards derive from religious faith and divine revelation as expressed, for example, in the Ten Commandments. Many look to human needs as the root of cardinal values. They insist that human beings elevate their needs for food, shelter, sex, expression, companionship, and fulfillment into preferred values and then into human rights—the rights to life, liberty, property, and so on. Finally, some political scientists maintain that society strongly influences, if not dictates, the ways in which the good political life is understood.

The Need for Standards. Leo Strauss, a profound student of classical political philosophy, argued that the quest for the "best political order" must be central in politics. Politics, he maintained, inevitably requires "approval and disapproval," "choice and rejection," and "praise and blame." Neutrality is impossible; political matters inevitably "raise a claim to men's obedience, allegiance, decision or judgment." Inescapably, citizens judge political affairs "in terms of goodness or badness, of justice or injustice." Since judgment requires a standard for judgment, and since sound judgment requires sound standards of judgment, citizens seek the best standard for the good political life. Only with such a standard of excellence, of virtue, of the best political order can political leaders umpire the "controversies between groups struggling for power within the political community." Here the tie between ethics and statesmanship becomes explicit. A standard of excellence is necessary if a leader is "to manage well the affairs of his political community as a whole." [5]

Political science, Strauss pointed out, originally meant the skill, art, prudence, and practical wisdom of the excellent leader of state. Such a leader could only shape sound public policy if he or she were knowledgeable about sound political standards and possessed prudential skill. Policies recommended by the philosopher-statesman are normally "a compromise between what he would wish and what circumstances permit. To effect that compromise intelligently, he must first know what . . . would be most desirable in itself." After that, the leader tries prudently to bridge the gap between what is most desirable in itself and what is possible in given circumstances. Those "scientists" and "historicists" who deny the possibility or desirability or primacy of the quest for the good political life, Strauss argued, are the enemies of a true political science.

Robert Dahl, an outstanding and sophisticated empirical political scientist, also addressed the relationship of ethics to politics. He asked: Can the study of politics be ethically neutral? Should it be? He presented the "value-fact" controversy as seen by empirically oriented political scientists and their opponents. This controversy revolves around the question of whether "ought," or value, propositions differ fundamentally from "is," or empirical (factual), propositions. Empirical theorists, Dahl wrote, hold that a "substantial and important aspect of politics is purely empirical, and that this empirical aspect of politics can be analyzed (in principle at least) neutrally and objectively." And so the battle is joined. Dahl attempted to find common ground between the conflicting schools and to explain and defend the position of a sophisticated empirical political science.[6]

Ethics Versus Positivism. Like Strauss, John H. Hallowell defended the primacy of the ethical approach to politics and attacked positivistic—or empirical—political science. **Positivism** is a philosophy that holds that human beings can know only that which is based on positive, observable, scientific facts, on data derived from sense experience. "Positivism . . . the dominant and most influential perspective within American political science today . . . is reflected in contemporary political science in what has come to be called the behavioral approach to political phenomena." Hallowell was disturbed by two theoretically inconsistent characteristics of this approach: on one hand, "an attempt to avoid all normative judgment," and on the other, a dangerous "conception of politics as a science of social perfection." Hallowell endorsed Thomism (the political philosophy of Thomas Aquinas) as a sound tradition for politics because it "combines the wisdom of the Greeks with the revelation of Christ." Politics is given meaning by a divine order and a natural law that "man can participate in because he is a rational being." Politics "is good only to the extent that it assists human beings to realize their potentialities as persons who belong ultimately to God."[7]

British political theorist Alfred Cobban took his cues from the tradition of political theory as it culminated in the ethics of the Enlightenment. Cobban was disturbed by the fact that political theory was not employed to clarify and prescribe political values in the interest of a sane and humane politics. If such politics is to survive, he said, the political theorist must be concerned primarily with what ought to be, with ethical political preferences, with condemnation, support, or justification of existing institutions, with persuasion on behalf of political change where needed, and with appraisal of and influence on actual political problems. Such activity can help guard against the monstrous cruelty and brutality of modern politics. Genuine public discussion of "the rights and wrongs" of political behavior can reintroduce the sense of ethical purpose and rational direction that Cobban saw as absent. Without this ethical concern, empirical political science would remain a "device, invented by university teachers, for avoiding that dangerous subject politics, without achieving science." [8]

The Search for a Science of Politics

Should the search for an empirical science of politics be based on the models of the physical and biological sciences—or on some other model? Does an empirical science wisely or unwisely stress empirical theory, precise language, quantifiable findings, rigorous investigation, careful verification, and the unity of all the social and behavioral sciences? Some behavioral political scientists maintain that we will progress in political science only if we recognize that our primary business is to state and test hypotheses about relationships in the world of sense experience. Others may even argue that at the highest level (following the model of physics), political scientists should seek the political science equivalent of Albert Einstein's famous formula $E = mc^2$, a result of his special theory of relativity. Still other political scientists contend that we should follow a biological model, guided by a political science equivalent of Louis Pasteur's germ theory of disease, to explain health or illness in the body politic. All empirical political scientists do not agree on these models. Clearly, we are far from masterful empirical breakthroughs in political science. Quarrels persist on models and methodology, even as empirical political scientists agree in emphasizing the importance of scientific investigation as a way to proceed.

The Behavioralist Approach. The search for an empirical science of politics in modern America has been closely associated with the behavioral emphasis in the discipline. While there continue to be debates about how best to approach the study of politics, many of the most important debates on the subject occurred in the 1960s between behavioralists and their critics. These debates continue to shape, to a significant degree, the field of political science. And although not all behavioralists agree, they do seem to share—as David Easton, a leading empirical theorist, pointed out in 1965—a common goal: "a science of politics modeled after the methodological assumptions of the natural sciences." Easton identified eight "intellectual foundation stones" of **behaviorialism**:

1. a belief in *regularities,* "discoverable uniformities in political behavior" that "can be expressed in generalizations or theories with explanatory and predictive value";
2. a commitment to *verification* of such generalizations through testing;
3. an experimental attitude toward *techniques,* with the goal of obtaining ever more rigorous means for observing, recording, and analyzing behavior;
4. an emphasis on *quantification* where possible, relevant, and meaningful;

5. a sophisticated attitude toward *values* and especially a recognition that ethical "valuation and empirical explanation involve two different kinds of propositions that, for the sake of clarity, should be kept analytically distinct";

6. a stress on *systemization,* on the importance of theory in research and in the development of a "coherent and orderly body of knowledge";

7. an acknowledgment of the primacy of *pure science,* as against applied science or practical problem solving; and

8. an acceptance of *integration* of the social sciences and the value of interdisciplinary fertilization.

Easton emphasized not only the importance of a unifying empirical theory but also of empirical "units of analysis." These units of analysis provide frameworks for empirical investigation. They are the concepts—such as power, group, decision, structure and function, message, and system—that can help political scientists make sense out of the otherwise bewildering data of politics.[9]

The controversy between the behavioralists and their opponents involves a number of points. The more radical behavioralists criticize traditional political scientists for not pushing their discipline toward "a science capable of prediction and explanation." Many behavioralists criticize traditionalists for not limiting political science to a study of "phenomena which can actually be observed" and for not pushing quantification more rigorously. The behavioralists also fault the traditionalists for using unsophisticated methods, for not being interdisciplinary, and for not seeking overarching generalizations about politics. Behavioralists also tend to dismiss the legitimacy of the task of ethical recommendation. They hold that the "truth or falsity of values . . . cannot be established scientifically" and that values "are beyond the scope of legitimate inquiry." They also tend to reject as illegitimate political scientists' engagement in political reform.[10]

Beyond Behavioralism. Behavioralism has been criticized from a number of perspectives. One such perspective is commonly called rational choice or "rat choice." While behavioralism emphasizes the scientific method and uses the natural sciences as a model, rational choice is inspired by economics. Put simply, rational choice models provide conclusions about how politics works that follow deductively from a set of simple assumptions about political actors, such as voters, elected officials, and government administrators.[11] The assumptions are that political actors are rational and choose the most efficient means in reaching whatever ends they seek. In many ways this may seem obvious; however, rational choice is significantly different from behavioralism. Behavioralism typically requires political scientists to observe the world and then offer theories about politics. Much emphasis is placed on quantifying political actions. Rational choice, at least in its purist form, requires only a clear theory about what motivates people and an assumption that people are rational in fulfilling those desires; from the theory and this assumption simple logic can generate interesting hypotheses about how politics works.

Hans J. Morgenthau, a refugee from Nazi Germany and an influential student of politics, asked: "What, then, ought a political science be like, which does justice both to its scientific pretense and to its subject matter?" Such a political science will profit from the "valuable insights" of philosophical traditions other than the dominant positivism of contemporary political science. It will appreciate that although these insights are not rigorously scientific, they do illuminate a scientific understanding of politics. Such a political science will maintain "ties with the Western tradition of political thought, its concerns, its accumulation of wisdom and knowledge." It will recognize the identity of political theory and political science. It will hold that a "scientific theory is a system of empirically verifiable, general truths sought for their own sake." Political science will also communicate an "objective and general truth about matters political," a truth that holds "regardless of time and place." Such a political science will be guided by a theory whose purpose, of course, "is to bring order and meaning to a mass of phenomena." Contemporary political scientists will wisely recognize that their task is "to reformulate the perennial truths of politics" in the "light of contemporary experience." Even at the almost certain risk of being controversial, political scientists must grapple with the burning problems and great political issues of society. Here the relevance of political science to statesmanship becomes clear. A "theory of politics presents not only a guide to understanding but also an ideal for action." It maps the political scene "in order to show the shortest and safest road to a given objective." [12]

Helpful Guidance for Leaders of State and Citizens

Is prudential guidance for leaders of state and other political actors influenced primarily by practical wisdom? Is sound judgment based on good character, significant intelligence, common sense, and political intuition? Those concerned with wise judgment and action in politics may concede that there are no scientific answers to the problems that baffle them in politics, yet they seek to enhance the capacity to decide how, for example, to avert devastating wars, to protect human rights, to enhance prosperity, and to guard against ecological disasters. They know that a conscious appreciation of key values and realities is crucial in this endeavor.

Take the issue of poverty and welfare reform in the United States. It is relatively easy to affirm the value of a decent income, decent housing, decent health, decent diet, and decent education for all Americans. It is also relatively easy to identify the poor and those on welfare (the elderly poor, the severely disabled, poor and jobless women and their dependent children, poor and jobless men); the working poor; and the homeless who are destitute and not on welfare. But it is considerably more difficult, although not beyond current capability, to determine why people are poor and why, in some respects, the welfare system fails. It is also difficult to know which rational policies will turn things around.

Is the key to sensible welfare reform private sector or community service jobs for those men and women now on welfare who are capable of working, plus an income tax credit for the working poor, plus appropriate health insurance and day care for working mothers and their children? Or is it better education and job training? Is it more generous welfare benefits, or perhaps the abolition of the entire welfare system? Will the costs and benefits of the choices turn out to be politically feasible?[13] Clearly, assessing alternatives is central to sound judgment, even though no one can be absolutely sure which alternatives will be the wisest or which specific qualities make for sound judgment.

The senior author of this book, in *The Revival of Democratic Theory*, attempted to remedy the neglect of prudence by highlighting its special role in politics. He defined prudence as "practical wisdom or that sound judgment which requires conscious and rational adaptation of means to ends." The ends must be proper ends, or else the judgment is not prudent but simply clever, narrowly expedient, or basely pragmatic. Prudence requires the ability to judge what is appropriate in a specific situation. It is not to be confused with timidity, priggishness, overcautiousness, weakness, or paralysis. Prudence involves deliberation, awareness of consequences, and appreciation of the relationship of means to ends. Moreover, prudence requires the ability to act in a real world to meet real problems and the strength to make decisions in a morally ambiguous world, where there are only proximate solutions to insoluble problems; prudence can provide a bridge between what ought to be and what is. Most important, prudence may enable the political scientist to focus on fundamental political problems as they are currently illustrated in public policy.[14]

In his important article "Political Science and Prevision," French political scientist Bertrand de Jouvenal illustrated in more detail the role of the political scientist in providing prudent guidance for leaders of state. He saw the political scientist as "a teacher of public men in activity." Guidance for leaders of state requires, above all, foresight. The political scientist, he argued, "must therefore develop that skill in himself, and in his pupils, and offer it to statesmen he has to advise." [15]

Harold Lasswell also sought to bring political science to bear on problems facing decision makers in politics. The problem-solving approach, he wrote, "poses five intellectual tasks"—clarifying goals, ascertaining trends, identifying conditioning factors, noting projections, and posing policy alternatives. Political scientists have concentrated on one or more of these tasks throughout the history of their discipline. They will undoubtedly continue to do so as they grapple with unprecedented and far-reaching challenges in the future. Moreover, they will do so in performing their professional roles as teachers, researchers, advisers, managers, and leaders.

Their contribution to what we have loosely referred to as statesmanship and public policy can be more accurately understood in connection with their involvement in every phase of the decision-making process. The phases of this process, as seen by Lasswell, include: (1) intelligence (political information), (2) recommendation (promotion of policy), (3) prescription (articulation of official norms), (4) invocation (provisional conformity to policy),

(5) application ("final" administration of policy), (6) appraisal (assessment of goal, strategy, and results), and (7) termination (settlement of expectations and claims).[16]

Toward a Unified Discipline of Political Science

So the vital questions recur: Is political science to be viewed primarily in terms of ethics? Or science? Or statesmanship? Some political scientists emphasize politics as the quest for the good political life. Others stress the search for an empirical science of politics. Still others underscore the importance of prudential guidance for leaders of state. But even if we agree on one focus or another, we must still explore the brand of ethics, the kind of science, and the pattern of leadership involved.

Moreover, we still need to know how the three major components of political science are related to one another in a unified discipline. We need to integrate what ought to be, what is, and what can be. We still need to search for a more systematic theory for the discipline's major emphases and its traditional fields: American politics, political philosophy, comparative politics, international politics, public administration, and public policy. This theory would relate political norms, empirical generalizations, and public judgments. It would reconcile philosophy, science, and public policy without withdrawing from politics, distorting political phenomena, or making faulty efforts to bridge the gap between aspiration and reality.

David Easton, an early leader of the post–World War II behavioral revolution in political science, advocated greater harmony in the discipline. In "The New Revolution in Political Science," Easton outlined a "post-behavioral revolution" to help political scientists integrate their tasks. This revolution would move beyond the important work of behavioral political scientists. Easton called attention to the postbehavioralists' plea for the "constructive development of values" as a key part of "the study of politics." Postbehavioralists also call for realistic and substantively meaningful empirical research—a political science that will "reach out to the real needs of mankind in a time of crisis." They are, finally, endorsing the need "to protect the humane values of civilization" by taking responsible action "in reshaping society" and by fulfilling their "special obligation" to put their "knowledge to work." [17]

In this account of the postbehavioral revolution, Easton saw a clear relationship between the ethical, empirical, and prudential components of the discipline. The postbehavioralists modestly endorsed the legitimacy of the four major tasks of the discipline. But, clearly, their perspective by no means dominates the field.

Legitimate doubts, difficulties, and dangers will be encountered in this integrative effort, but these problems do not rule out either the desirability or the possibility of using political health as an integrative concept. This concept will be explored throughout this book.[18]

CONCLUSION

Despite the continuing debate about the scope, substance, and methodology of political science, we can confidently affirm the reality of three central concerns: (1) an ethical concern for the good political life, for the best political community; (2) a scientific concern for empirical theory, generalization, and explanation relevant to the business of the political community; and (3) a prudential concern for judgment, decision making, public policy, and action. With somewhat less confidence, we can also affirm a fourth concern—a theoretical concern for the integration of the normative, empirical, and prudential components that constitute the leading threads in the design of a complete political science. Each of these concerns underscores significant problems, suggests appropriate methodologies, and leads to fruitful responses, which we explore in succeeding chapters.

SUGGESTED READINGS

Almond, Gabriel A. *A Discipline Divided: Schools and Sects in Political Science.* Newbury Park, Calif.: Sage Publications, 1989. Sees some schools of political science ("soft-left," "soft-right," "hard-left," "hard-right") as separate ideological and methodological tables, each with its own conception of political science. Insists that the "overwhelming majority of political scientists" are in the center—"liberal" and moderate in ideology, and eclectic and open to conviction in methodology.

Ball, Terence, James Farr, and Russell L. Hanson, eds. *Political Innovation and Conceptual Change.* Cambridge: Cambridge University Press, 1989. Essays explore a number of key concepts: constitution, democracy, state, representation, party, public interest, citizenship, public opinion, rights, property, and revolution.

Bluhm, William T. *Theories of the Political System: Classics of Political Thought and Modern Political Analysis.* 3rd ed. Englewood Cliffs, N.J.: Prentice Hall, 1978. A stimulating effort to compare certain "classical" political philosophers and their modern analogues.

Crotty, William, ed. *Political Science: Looking to the Future.* 4 vols. Evanston: Northwestern University Press, 1991. (Vol. l: *The Theory and Practice of Political Science.* Vol. 2: *Comparative Politics, Policy, and International Relations.* Vol. 3: *Political Behavior.* Vol. 4: *American Institutions.*) Highlights issues, concepts, methodologies, changes, and concerns.

Downs, Anthony. *An Economic Theory of Democracy.* New York: Longman, 1997. Considered the classic statement on rational choice applied to the study of politics.

Easton, David. *A Systems Analysis of Political Life.* New York: Wiley, 1965. Develops the systems approach, which sees the political system embedded in an environment, receiving input (demands and supports), and delivering output (decisions and actions).

Katznelson, Ira, ed. *Political Science: The State of the Discipline, Centennial Edition.* New York: W. W. Norton & Company, 2002. Series of essays that avoids the traditional subfields of the discipline but instead focuses on the state, democracy, agency, and inquiry.

Lasswell, Harold D. *Politics: Who Gets What, When, How.* New York: Meridian, 1965. One of the most popular definitions of politics by one of America's most creative and versatile political scientists.

Morgenthau, Hans J. *Politics among Nations: The Struggle for Power and Peace.* 6th ed. Revised by Kenneth Thompson. New York: McGraw, 1985. A prominent "realist," Morgenthau debunks moralists and cynics alike, emphasizes the importance of protecting the national interest in the struggle for power, and favors the use of diplomacy to obtain peace through accommodation.

Ricci, David M. *The Tragedy of Political Science: Politics, Scholarship, and Democracy.* New Haven: Yale University Press, 1984. Argues that the tragedy of political science lies in the conflict between a commitment to science and a commitment to the good, wise, democratic life.

Riemer, Neal. *Creative Breakthroughs in Politics.* Westport, Conn.: Praeger, 1996. Examines several historical breakthroughs (Roger Williams and religious liberty; James Madison and the federal republic); two spurious breakthroughs (John C. Calhoun and protection of minority rights and Karl Marx and universal human emancipation); a contemporary breakthrough-in-progress (European Union); and a proposed future breakthrough (protection against genocide).

———. *The Future of the Democratic Revolution: Toward a More Prophetic Politics.* New York: Praeger, 1984. Analyzes the strengths and weaknesses of Machiavellian politics, utopian politics, and liberal democratic politics, and argues on behalf of the desirability and feasibility of a model of prophetic politics.

———. *The Revival of Democratic Theory.* New York: Appleton-Century-Crofts, 1962. Analyzes the decline of democratic theory and suggests a case for its revival. Argues that political theory must clarify political values, illuminate empirical political reality, facilitate prudent guidance in politics, and unify the discipline of political science.

GLOSSARY TERMS

behavioralism (p. 72)
empiricism (p. 61)
ethics (p. 60)
political health (p. 68)
political science (p. 59)
positivism (p. 71)
prudence (p. 61)

Chapter 4

THE SCIENTIFIC ENTERPRISE

The guiding question in this chapter is *To what extent and how best can scientific method be used to better understand politics?* This question is generated by more than curiosity about the word *science* in the term *political science.* It originates in what was called the **behavioral revolution** in the social sciences, including political science. The behavioral revolution was a post–World War II movement in the social sciences to apply scientific methodology to the study of complex human behavior. It had a particularly profound impact on political science. Proponents of behavioral methodology asserted that we must be more objective in our inquiry. To buttress that objectivity, the use of quantifiable data and mathematical analysis was encouraged. The controversy between the behavioralists and those political scientists who preferred using more traditional methods of inquiry reached a fever pitch in the 1960s. Since that time, divisions within the discipline of political science have calmed down. But it was an important chapter in the history of political inquiry, and a short discussion of what we learned is important.

The central question raised in this chapter requires us to define science, to identify the common features of the scientific enterprise, and to assess its strengths and weaknesses. In general we argue that the appropriate research strategy for political science depends on the character of the problem being investigated. A sensible research strategy thus calls for a fourfold approach: (1) identifying the significant problem, (2) articulating a guiding hypothesis to answer the problem, (3) obtaining evidence to test the guiding hypothesis, and (4) validating and explaining the fuller significance of the hypothesis and the findings on which it rests.

The most fruitful research strategy seeks to place scientific work in a theoretical framework that demonstrates how the part relates to the whole. At its best the research will be genuinely comparative. Such a research strategy is oriented toward the future and is as predictive as the subject matter permits. This strategy takes into account the tie between values and scientific research and the tie between scientific research and practical political action designed to maximize preferred values.

In subsequent chapters in parts 3 and 4 we also will explore the various ways in which students of politics obtain evidence to support their empirical hypotheses.

SCIENCE AS A CRITICAL AND SYSTEMATIC SEARCH

Most philosophers of science view **science** as a critical and systematic search for knowledge. Jacob Bronowski called science a "search for order within the facts." It is, he said, "an activity of putting order into our experience." And the ordering is systematic.[1]

Similarly, philosopher and logician Irving M. Copi underscored science as a search for systematic relationships of particular events. The scientist, he wrote, "seeks more than a mere record of . . . phenomena; he strives to understand them. To this end he seeks to formulate general laws that state the patterns of all such occurrences and the systematic relationship between them. The scientist is engaged in a search for the natural laws according to which all particular events occur and the fundamental principles which underlie them."[2]

Karl R. Popper, another philosopher of science, emphasized the quest for truth rather than the possession of absolutely certain knowledge. "The wrong view of science betrays itself in the craving to be right; for it is not his possession of knowledge, or irrefutable truth, that makes the man of science, but his persistent and recklessly critical quest for truth." Science, Popper wrote, "never pursues the illusory aim of making its answers final. . . . Its advance is, rather, towards an infinite yet attainable aim: that of ever discovering new, deeper, and more general problems, and of subjecting our ever tentative answers to ever renewed and ever more rigorous tests."[3]

Is there a right approach to scientific searching? Clearly, as Aristotle recognized long ago, there are many methods in the many sciences. And one would be foolish indeed to insist that the method of any one science (say, physics) is necessarily the method that can successfully be used in all sciences, including the social sciences. And the social sciences, because they deal with people, differ in certain aspects from sciences that deal with inanimate objects or nonhuman animals. For instance, social scientists may have an advantage in understanding their subjects—other human beings—that physical scientists do not have with their subjects; on the other hand, there may be a distinct challenge in being human while studying other humans. Nonetheless, we can think of **scientific method** in the singular as meaning some pattern of reasoning common to all empirical sciences. Such a pattern of reasoning may hold for the social sciences in general and for political science in particular.

COMMON FEATURES OF THE SCIENTIFIC ENTERPRISE

In their problem solving, in their quest for order, and in their search for more comprehensive knowledge to enhance understanding, all scientists use some common methods:

1. Scientists have to identify the problem to be investigated. The problem must be formulated clearly and precisely and must be susceptible to empirical investigation.
2. Scientists try to shape an initial **hypothesis**, a tentative assertion usually attempting to explain a cause and effect, to guide their empirical and logical investigation of the problem.
3. Scientists must obtain and organize data in order to test the hypothesis.
4. Scientists must test (and retest) the validity of their hypothesis. Do the data support the hypothesis, the assertion being made?

In the next section we will expand on these four common features.

Problem Identification

Empirical scientists speculate or investigate because they are puzzled or troubled about a problem. The problem, then, creates an initial sensitivity, or primary orientation, that leads to an effort to articulate the trouble, to get at its root. Identification of the problem is the first step in the scientific procedure. It is the first effort to see which questions need to be asked and answered if the problem is to be "solved," the difficulty overcome, the uncertainty cleared up. Some of the troubling questions in political science include:

- Why is there war, terrorism, political injustice, poverty, or ecological imbalance?
- What are the necessary and sufficient conditions of peace, justice, prosperity, and ecological health?
- How do we account for cruelty, intolerance, vulgarity, or mediocrity in social, cultural, and political life?
- What are the necessary and sufficient conditions of excellence in the community?

These certainly are big questions. But they provide a framework for posing and exploring more manageable problems. Thus students of politics can focus on a specific war such as World War II, the Vietnam War, one of the two recent wars in Iraq, or America's war on terrorism. Focus can center on a specific peaceful arrangement such as the Camp David accords between Israel and Egypt, the Oslo accords between Israel and the Palestinians, or the Dayton accords on Bosnia. Or they can concentrate on specific instances of injustice, whether it be Hitler's savage treatment of the Jews, Joseph Stalin's liquidation of the kulaks

On July 8, 1972, a South Vietnamese plane accidently dropped napalm on South Vietnamese soldiers and civilians. Kim Phuc (center), her siblings, and her cousins were among those burned. Such terrible human costs of war lead political scientists to investigate one of the great questions of human experience: Why is there war?

(well-off peasants), or America's mistreatment of minorities. Why certain societies (such as Sweden) score higher on a democratic and constitutional index than others (such as Argentina) also can be explored.

Even these topics may be too big and may have to be formulated more clearly and narrowly, the components reduced to manageable size. Put simply, it is important not to bite off too big a chunk in trying to identify the problem; to do so is to invite intellectual indigestion.

The ability to formulate a problem calls for curiosity, appreciation of facts that have no presently acceptable explanation, recognition of a difficulty that demands clarification, and appreciation of a mystery that begs for a solution. This is a creative ability. Only when we are able to formulate an answerable question can we make progress in dealing with a problem. As Karl Popper pointed out, "It is we who always formulate the questions to be put to nature; it is we who try again and again to put these questions so as to elicit a clear-cut 'yes' or 'no' (for nature does not give an answer unless pressed for it)." [4] The significant problem, clearly formulated, provides a focus for worthwhile scientific investigation.

Hypothesis Articulation

Once the problem has been identified, there is a target to shoot at, a goal to achieve. How do we explain a particular phenomenon? Why did the war break out? Why does the poverty persist? Why did the election come out the way it did? Answering these kinds of questions takes the form of a tentative explanatory assertion, a hypothesis. The tentative hypothesis asserts that a set of conditions, events, or factors or a situation results in another condition or situation. In other words, the tentative hypothesis asserts cause and effect. The tentative hypothesis is a powerful tool for focusing intelligence, directing vision, and relating data to the problem. If the tentative hypothesis is sound, it is a great aid. Even if it is not sound, it offers a chance to explore and exclude an initially persuasive possibility.

To illustrate the task of articulating a hypothesis, we will formulate some tentative hypotheses. For simplicity, we offer two contrasting examples. In reality, numerous hypotheses could be proposed and explored for each issue.

1. *Problem:* Why did World War II occur? Tentative hypothesis: World War II was caused by the aggressive, nationalistic ambition of Germany to dominate Europe and of Japan to dominate Asia. Alternative tentative hypothesis: World War II was caused by the stubborn refusal of the Allies—Britain, France, the Soviet Union, and the United States—to allow Germany and Japan a more generous "place in the sun" in Europe and Asia.

2. *Problem:* Why was Stalin's treatment of Russian kulaks so brutal? Tentative hypothesis: Stalin believed that communism in the Soviet Union could not be achieved unless farms were taken away from their owners to make way for collectivization (the merger of a number of farm households or villages working under state control, effectively ending private family farming); farmers, such as the kulaks, who opposed Stalin's will had to be destroyed or repressed to ensure the triumph of communism. Alternative tentative hypothesis: the treatment of the kulaks was a result of Stalin's paranoid personality and perceived need to obliterate political opposition.

3. *Problem:* Why is the United States rich and India poor? Tentative hypothesis: a number of factors account for America's affluence and India's poverty—(a) the United States has a relatively small population and abundant resources, whereas India has a large population and meager resources; (b) the United States has been an independent nation for more than two hundred years, whereas India, before 1949, was an exploited colony of another country; (c) the United States has a more favorable geography than India; and (d) America's religious and social system is more attuned to the production of wealth than India's. Alternative tentative hypothesis: the United States profits from capitalistic imperialism; India is a victim of it.

4. *Problem:* What causes ecological imbalance all over the world? Tentative hypothesis: a materialistic, hedonistic, egoistic, and profit-driven philosophy of growth accounts for worldwide ecological imbalance. Alternative tentative hypothesis: the Martians are to blame for ecological imbalance.

Articulating a useful hypothesis in scientific investigation is vitally important, according to a number of students of science. W. C. Kneale declared that the "all-important act in scientific discovery is the finding of a hypothesis that will survive testing." A hypothesis such as "the Martians are to blame for ecological imbalance" would never survive testing, even if it managed to be formulated. That "World War II was caused by the aggressive, nationalistic ambition of Germany to dominate Europe and of Japan to dominate Asia" may survive testing.

A hypothesis is a point of view designed to address a problem and to make data meaningful and testable. The point of view is crucial because, as the great English biologist Charles Darwin emphasized, "all observation must be for or against some view, if it is to be of service." The hypothesis provides direction and guidance. Undirected, unguided observation is fruitless.

Although there is no textbook rule or clear-cut method for formulating hypotheses, there are criteria in addition to that of testability for determining the worth and acceptability of a tentative hypothesis. These criteria include relevance, compatibility with previously well-established hypotheses, predictive or explanatory power, and simplicity. These criteria supplement, but by no means replace, testability. The hypothesis that "the United States profits from capitalistic imperialism; India is a victim of it" is simple, may be compatible with previous hypotheses, has predictive power, and may be relevant, especially for India; it may not, however, survive testing.

Before evidence can be gathered, one must know as precisely as possible what is being sought. Thus key terms in the problem and hypothesis must be clearly defined. For example, in our problem and hypothesis about World War II, we would need to know the meanings of *aggressive, nationalistic ambition,* and *dominate.* These words must have an operational meaning, so that empirical evidence can be used to confirm or disprove the hypothesis that the "aggressive, nationalistic ambition of Germany to dominate Europe and of Japan to dominate Asia" caused World War II. The word *caused* would also have to be carefully defined. Unless the terms are clear the hypothesis will be too ambiguous and imprecise to accurately reflect reality. Too often in debating political matters, people mistake causation for correlation. Sometimes events happen at the same time, yet are unrelated.

Reliable Data Collection

The next systematic step is to obtain, organize, and focus the relevant data. The data must be coherent, accurate, and usefully related to the hypothesis and problem. Thus we need a scheme for knowing what data to obtain, how to classify them, and what instruments to use to gather them. The scheme, classification, and instruments will depend on the specific problem being investigated.

Data make testing possible. Scientists seek data that will corroborate their hypotheses. Debate still rages on the correct way to test and verify, but it is clear that data are indispensable no matter what procedure is followed. The data must be relevant to the hypothesis; they must be able to prove the empirical proposition true or false. The data must be accurate. They must add up or fit together as a meaningful pattern.

To understand the causes of World War II, for example, we would seek evidence, in word and deed, of Germany's and Japan's aggressive, nationalistic ambition or, alternatively, of the stubborn refusal of Britain, France, the Soviet Union, and the United States to allow Germany and Japan a "place in the sun." To understand Stalin's unjust treatment of his own people, we would seek evidence of his conviction that communism in the Soviet Union could not be achieved without collectivization and that collectivization could not be a voluntary and peaceful process or, alternatively, that Stalin acted not in accordance with communist principles but out of his own paranoia. To understand prosperity and poverty in the United States and India, we would need evidence concerning population and resources in both countries, the history of each as a colony and as an independent nation, and information on their geography and their religious and social systems. To understand ecological imbalance, we would seek evidence of conscious or unconscious decisions that led to dangerous levels of pollution, population wildly in excess of resources, and profligate waste and misuse of resources.

There are many types of data (such as historical, economic, voting, and public opinion). For some time now students of politics have sought to use quantifiable data. That, of course, is not always possible. Some political phenomena are not conducive to numerical measurement. Regardless, as stated above, the data should lead the investigator either to verify a hypothesis or prove it false. The data may also lead an investigator to modify the tentative hypothesis and statement of the problem or to substitute a new and different hypothesis. This, in turn, would lead to the gathering of additional data to establish or disprove the new hypothesis.

Hypothesis Validation and Scientific Explanation

After testing and critical examination, the tentative hypothesis is either established more firmly or rejected. This step involves **validation** or corroboration to determine a fit between hypothesis and evidence. Does the hypothesis help solve the problem, overcome the difficulty, clear up the uncertainty? The hypothesis must take into account what needs to be accounted for.

After full investigation, for example, do we attribute World War II to the aggressive, nationalistic ambition of Germany and Japan, or to the stubborn refusal of Britain, France, the Soviet Union, and the United States to allow Germany and Japan a "place in the sun," or to some other hypothesis, perhaps the clash of capitalistic and imperialistic rivals, or maybe sunspots? Was Stalin's understanding of communism or his paranoid personality responsible for the unjust treatment of so many Soviet citizens under his rule? Do prosperity and poverty depend not on a single factor, such as "capitalistic imperialism," but on a conjunction of circumstances: population, resources, geography, and economic and social philosophy? Is ecological imbalance understandable only in terms of a materialistic, hedonistic, egotistic philosophy of growth that characterizes the United States as well as China, India as well as Brazil, and Japan as well as Egypt?

The validation of hypotheses is closely linked to scientific explanation. We want to validate an immediate hypothesis (about World War II or Stalin's injustices, for instance). But we also want to see how the mature hypothesis fits into a larger pattern, a more complete and satisfactory story. Hence we ask, does aggressive, nationalistic ambition also explain World War I? All war? And why does this aggressive ambition exist? Is it rooted in the sovereign nation-state system? Or in the aggressive nature of people? We also want to know whether it is a rigid ideology that explains injustice in China or Iraq or what was once Yugoslavia as well as in Stalin's Soviet Union or Hitler's Germany. Or is the deeper explanation to be found in pathological leaders or a repressive economic system? Similarly, we want to know whether ecological imbalance is rooted in an intrinsic need for growth characteristic of modern capitalism and socialism.

Explanation is the process of fitting pieces of the puzzle together, determining how the pieces relate to each other and also how the immediate problem relates to the larger, puzzling configuration. World War II is one major configuration. How does it fit into the larger pattern of conflict and accommodation? Are sovereign nation-states key factors in major wars? Communism is one ideology. Is there something about rigid ideologies that makes for injustice? Is economic prosperity the result of luck or design? Is ecological imbalance characteristic only of the modern impulse to dominate nature? As we explore topics such as war, totalitarian ideology, economic prosperity, and economic imbalance, we must ask large questions such as these to find a full explanation.

Explanation expands our scientific power enormously, enabling us to connect links in a chain and to extend the chain. This extension involves expanding the hypothesis to gain the maximum value. Explanation may pull together ideas and evidence not previously linked. It may throw unexpected light on additional problems. It can considerably extend the range of knowledge and illuminate further hypotheses. In all these ways explanation clarifies the initial problem and hypothesis.

Let us use the analogy of a mystery story. The explanation of the mystery—what was the crime, who did it, and how—may throw light on other unsolved crimes. In another analogy, solving the mystery of a disease that has strangely afflicted one person will explain the same ailment in others. At the beginning of the search for causes of disease, scientists discovered that certain germs caused chicken cholera and anthrax in animals. With the germ theory, or explanation, accepted, the scientists went on to search for other germs responsible for other diseases.

Significant problems in the social sciences—war, injustice, and poverty—are more complicated than most in the physical sciences. Single-factor explanations—for instance, the sovereign nation-state, capitalism, or ideology—are rightly suspect most of the time. And yet bold and seemingly outrageous hypotheses—such as certain Marxist hypotheses— may illuminate problems. And so too may hypotheses about the sovereign nation-state, falsely messianic ideologies, and the growth mania that afflicts communist and capitalist countries alike.

Fruitful hypotheses and explanations solve significant problems and account for a wide range of puzzling circumstances. At the highest and most fruitful level these hypotheses serve as building blocks for the development of grander **theory**—a larger body of principles offered to explain phenomena. So empirical scientists move from hunch to tentative hypothesis to theory. In this way they try to move from opinion to knowledge, from the less systematic to the more systematic, from scattered knowledge to more reliable architectonic (systematic) understanding. They seek, by their more systematic and critical searching, to expand the boundaries of humanity's understanding as widely as possible.

Problem solving is their primary function. Their objective in performing this function is to attain the broadest and most reliable knowledge and understanding.

THE STRENGTHS AND WEAKNESSES OF THE SCIENTIFIC ENTERPRISE

Properly used, the common features of the scientific enterprise can greatly help the investigator in politics. But we should not expect too much of the scientific enterprise, and we need to be aware of certain dangers that may befall the scientific investigator in politics.

Strengths of the Scientific Enterprise

There is value in a systematic, rational, and critical scientific approach. Such a pursuit seeks to define the empirical problem clearly, so that it can be investigated with the help of relevant evidence. There is value in responding to the empirical problem by framing a tentative hypothesis that can be tested. There is value in moving beyond hunch to evidence, beyond opinion to knowledge; there is value in bringing relevant evidence, particularly quantitative data, to bear on a tentative hypothesis. And there is value in validating a hypothesis, obtaining a sensible explanation of a "why" or a "how" question, and fitting the pieces of a puzzle together in a more coherent whole. The scientific enterprise facilitates problem solving. It helps students of politics to be more directed, more economical, more logical, and more searching. It helps them manage their problems.

Weaknesses of the Scientific Enterprise

Students of politics make a serious mistake, however, if they expect too much of the scientific enterprise and if they succumb to certain dangers that sometimes affect the scientific investigator. For example, empirical political scientists may think that all problems in politics are empirical; that all empirical problems can be easily solved; that even difficult problems can be solved if enough money and effort are poured into the search for a solution; and finally that politics is ultimately reducible to the objective investigation at the level of, say, physics, biology, or mathematics.

As we noted in chapter 3 and will emphasize throughout part 2, politics contains ethical problems as well as empirical ones. And, as we stressed in chapter 3 and will reemphasize in part 4, politics contains prudential problems as well. We are concerned with questions about the good political life and wise public policy as well as with strictly empirical questions. Moreover, not all empirical problems can be easily solved. Many important empirical problems are exceedingly difficult. Solutions to such big problems as "why war?" or "why injustice?" or "why poverty?" are not easily found. The empirical problems that can be successfully dealt with are generally much more modest.

Furthermore, it is not clear that even large expenditures of money and effort can solve difficult empirical problems. Governments in most industrial societies still struggle to achieve economic stability, as this involves, for example, the problem of avoiding periodic recessions, maintaining high levels of employment and income without inflation, and taming (as in the United States) budget and trade deficits.

Finally, although political science may wisely borrow some methods from the physical or biological sciences, the fruitfulness of such borrowing is limited. For example, students of politics cannot experiment with political actors in the same controlled way that physicists or chemists can experiment with atoms and molecules, or biologists with bacteria or DNA. Fruitful empirical generalizations are rare in political science. Master generalizations such as Einstein's $E = mc^2$ do not exist in politics.

In addition, a number of dangers face the empirical political scientist. One is the ant complex. This is the danger of what David Easton has called "hyperfactualism"—collecting data for their own sake, as the ant piles up bits of dirt in big mounds.[5] This is the danger of operating without a guiding empirical theory that gives direction and meaning to the collection of data.

A second danger is the spider complex. This is the danger of sterile theoretical speculation, of spinning grand empirical theories divorced from fertile interaction with reality. It is the danger of the armchair theorist who develops grand ideas about empirical reality but is unwilling to relate theory to evidence, to test theory in the real world.

Abraham Kaplan, following Francis Bacon, prefers the bee syndrome to the ant or spider complex. "Bacon himself characterizes the scientist as being neither wholly speculative and like the spider spinning his web from his own substance, nor wholly empirical and like an ant collecting data into a heap, but like the bee feeding on the nectar it gathers, digesting it, and so transmuting it into the purest honey."[6]

A third danger is that of the law of the instrument. This is the danger of becoming so fascinated with a newly discovered tool—greatly useful on a particular problem or in a par-

Billions of dollars have been spent by the U.S. government to attack poverty. While enormous progress has been made, pockets of severe inner city poverty still exist in places like Camden, New Jersey. Once again, an example that empirical problems are not always easily solved by the expenditures of large sums of money.

ticular area—that one insists upon using it on all problems and in all areas. The popularity of survey research—an instrument of great help in a particular area of research—may illustrate this danger. Survey research greatly illuminates certain problems, particularly in the realm of public opinion, but its usefulness may be nil, or decidedly limited, in other important empirical questions, such as why the Soviet Union decided to withdraw offensive missiles from Cuba.

A fourth danger is that of focusing on the status quo—currently dominant actors, institutions, or ideas. This peril exists because of the visibility and influence of powerful political actors, institutions, and ideas. It is easier to explore what is familiar. It is more difficult to deal with the invisible or less visible, the unimportant or less powerful. Thus it is relatively easy for the empirical political scientist to ignore the invisible poor, impotent minorities, and the unorganized. The danger is that preoccupation with the dominant forces of the status quo leads to neglect of other important forces in politics, forces whose potential is recognized only when a riot occurs or when a revolution overthrows the regime in power. Then empirical political scientists who have been preoccupied with the status quo are surprised by the dramatic development. This danger can also lead the empirical political scientist to ignore the gap between an ethical ideal and political (and social and economic) reality, to neglect the empirical exploration of the process of social change (whether development or decay), and to miss the emerging realities of the future. The failure of almost all political scientists to predict the collapse of the Soviet Union—and the demise of communism there—is a most dramatic illustration of the danger of focusing on the status quo.

A fifth danger is triviality, that is, choosing to investigate inconsequential problems. Such problems are often chosen because they are easy to handle. The trick in empirical research is to select a meaningful but manageable problem. Striking a balance takes considerable judgment, but guarding against the danger of triviality will help strike that wise balance.

Assessment of the Scientific Enterprise

Science does not require perfect understanding or demand a specific, elegant, hypothetical-deductive model. It does not insist on an architectonic, all-encompassing general theory. Nor does it invariably stipulate a controlled experiment or even prediction or mathematically precise laws. Science requires only a search for greater understanding, with the help of whatever tools will advance that understanding.

On balance, the behavioral revolution in political science—which placed great emphasis on the scientific approach—has strengthened empirical political science. When divorced from the status quo bias that has sometimes characterized it, when carried on in a more critical spirit to address significant problems of war and peace, injustice and justice, poverty and prosperity, the behavioral revolution can show that the quest for a science of politics is compatible with the good political life.

The empirical aspects of political science must be investigated with the best scientific tools available, with the understanding that investigation is subject to the limitations and constraints imposed by the nature of empirical phenomena in politics. The search can be only as rigorous and objective as the problem permits. The complexity of political phenomena, "the multiplicity, interaction, and the elusiveness of key variables in politics," makes a scientific effort difficult but not impossible. Human freedom does not make it impossible to study human regularities and even to scientifically attempt to account for creativity, surprises, and departures from regularity.

In science, investigators rely on sensory data, but they are not limited to one preconceived empirical model in their efforts to understand political phenomena. Quantification is a tool to be employed on significant empirical problems and pushed far as the subject matter will permit. Empirical political scientists can dream of an architectonic general theory, even though it may not seem presently attainable, if the quest for such a theory is fruitful and does not discourage more modest, middle-range, empirical theory or more modest generalizations.

Moreover, empirical political research can focus on problems of great ethical importance. Why are some political communities more successful than others in achieving a peaceful, just, prosperous, constitutional order? Do answers to this question also throw light on peace, justice, prosperity, and democracy in the emergent global community? Although these are big questions, they can be broken down into smaller, more manageable problems involving, for example, the exploration of certain operative ideals in certain countries, certain patterns of conflict and accommodation, and certain public policy decisions.

Empirical research on the burning practical issues of the day is most important. But students of politics must always realize that fundamental empirical research (which may not seem immediately relevant) may have an important payoff for momentous practical problems. The question of the triviality of empirical research must be raised, but not always because of a concern for immediate practical payoff. The question may be raised out of concern for a genuinely fruitful understanding of politics. So a balance must be struck between a concentration on the practical and the manageable, on one hand, and the fundamental and the significant, on the other. The most fruitful empirical research would be simultaneously fundamental and practical, significant and manageable.

It cannot be successfully argued that empirical political science is intrinsically characterized by conservatism, a fear of popular democracy, and an avoidance of vital political issues, even though some empirical research may reveal these characteristics. However, empirical political scientists who focus only on what is (and ignore what has been, and what will or can be) may be status quo oriented. Empirical political scientists who want to do justice to politics as a dynamic activity, and to political actors as both products and shapers of evolution, cannot ignore change. Within the framework of this critical assessment, "unafraid of politics and convinced that politics can be a civilizing activ-

THE SCIENTIFIC ENTERPRISE   91

ity," empirical political scientists can proudly hold as their motto: "The more science at its best, the better."

CONCLUSION

In this brief chapter we have argued that an appropriate research strategy depends on the character of the empirical problem to be investigated. This suggests the great importance of clarifying and stating the problem. The significant problem will then suggest to creative and imaginative students of politics which approach to take. There is no rigid, dogmatic formula for the right scientific approach to every empirical problem. Given the diversity of empirical problems, there will be diverse strategies and diverse methods.

Empirical theory of one kind or another will guide empirical political scientists. Their theory may be modest or ambitious. It may rest on an age-old formulation of politics as a struggle for power in which political actors seek to protect their vital interests or on the pluralist formula of public policy as a result of group pressures. It may rest on a Marxist concept of class struggle or on a more complex systems theory. To be most fruitful, however, empirical theory must link up with ethical theory and with prudential theory. That is, the search for an empirical science of politics must be related to the quest for the good political life and to wise public policy.

SUGGESTED READINGS

Almond, Gabriel A. *A Discipline Divided: Schools and Sects in Political Science.* Newbury Park, Calif.: Sage Publications, 1989. An assessment by a keen student of comparative politics. Chapter 1 specifically deals with political science as a science.

Crotty, William, ed. *Political Science: Looking to the Future.* Vol. 1: *The Theory and Practice of Political Science.* Evanston: Northwestern University Press, 1991. See, particularly, the illuminating articles by Donald M. Freeman, "The Making of a Discipline"; J. Donald Moon, "Pluralism and Progress in the Study of Politics"; and Terrence Ball, "Whither Political Theory."

Davis, James W. *Terms of Inquiry: On the Theory and Practice of Political Science.* Baltimore: Johns Hopkins University Press, 2005. Addresses the problem of the increasing inaccessibility of and dissatisfaction with social science research based on scientific method.

Easton, David. *The Political System: An Inquiry into the State of Political Science.* New York: Knopf, 1953. A highly influential attempt to direct work in political science toward a more self-conscious, systematic, and empirical theory. Easton's own follow-up work is found in *A Framework for Political Analysis* (Englewood Cliffs, N.J.: Prentice Hall, 1965) and *A Systems Analysis of Political Life* (New York: Wiley, 1965). Long on system, framework, and classification; short on rich, empirical generalization and theory.

Kuhn, Thomas. *The Structure of Scientific Revolutions.* 2nd ed. Chicago: University of Chicago Press, 1970. Enormously influential in the social sciences. Stresses the importance of the new paradigm, or model, that helped scientists break through to a hypothesis that could overcome the puzzles of normal science (the accepted way of understanding).

Pollock, Philip H., III. *The Essentials of Political Analysis.* 2nd ed. Washington, D.C.: CQ Press, 2005. Thorough and readable text on empirical research techniques in the field of political science.

Popper, Karl R. *The Logic of Scientific Discovery.* London: Hutchinson, 1968. Stresses the critical quest for truth as the distinguishing characteristic of the scientist. For Popper's adverse criticism of the "science" of Plato, Hegel, and Marx, see *The Open Society and Its Enemies* (Princeton: Princeton University Press, 1945).

Ricci, David M. *The Tragedy of Political Science: Politics, Scholarship, and Democracy.* New Haven: Yale University Press, 1984. Sees a conflict between science and commitment to the good, wise, democratic life.

GLOSSARY TERMS

behavioral revolution (p. 79)
explanation (p. 86)
hypothesis (p. 81)
science (p. 80)
scientific method (p. 80)
theory (p. 86)
validation (p. 85)

Chapter 5

THE PHYSICAL, SOCIAL, AND CULTURAL ENVIRONMENT OF POLITICS

Politics is a creative, but not a completely autonomous, activity. Although political actors are free to make choices in order to fulfill their values, they must make these choices in an environment not entirely of their own choosing. Politics—and political decisions—can be understood only in terms of the physical, social, and cultural environment in which a community is embedded.

PROPOSITIONS AND CHALLENGES

The key question in this chapter is: *How does the larger environment influence politics and political science?* Let us first consider some important propositions that may help us to understand the impact of the physical, social, and cultural environment on politics.

1. The *physical coexistence* of all political communities on a single globe in the nuclear and biochemical weapons age means that we must learn to live together sensibly or we may die together horribly.
2. Our *biological nature* and destiny should inspire respect for our common humanity—our fundamental equality—and the importance of maximizing cooperation, halting dangerous aggression, and minimizing the conflicts that threaten our biological existence.
3. *Human needs* such as security, acceptance, and recognition suggest the origins of values that provide common purposes, goals, and standards for politics.
4. The *reduction of distance* between people as a result of the communication and transportation revolutions has enhanced *global interdependence* and cooperative patterns of behavior—political, economic, and scientific.

5. Human *vulnerability to common disasters*—military, physical, and ecological—underscores the need for global agreements to avert war, famine, disease, and ecological damage.

6. The rapid *exhaustion of nonrenewable resources and the growth of population* beyond what existing resources can support highlight the need for political policies that encourage prudent growth of population and management of resources.

7. The *growth of cities* and their suburbs calls attention to a host of problems—inadequate housing, unemployment, poverty, faulty transportation, crime, and disease—and thus to the need for prudent policy to maintain our cities as healthy, vital, and manageable centers of modern civilization.

8. Modern *economic life*—involving industrialization, gaps between rich and poor, periodic recession, and worker alienation—requires policies to ensure full employment, an equitable distribution of income, and a host of services to protect workers and consumers.

9. The worldwide **revolution of rising expectations**, especially in the developing nations, is significantly influenced by modern ideology and technology; this revolution bespeaks the need for wise political balance between hope and possibility.

These propositions highlight a number of political challenges:

1. The very survival of humanity is threatened by weapons of mass destruction. The challenge is to figure out how to control the spread of and ultimately eliminate these weapons—nuclear, biological, and chemical—brought into existence by science, technology, and political decisions. This problem has become even more urgent as the war on terrorism develops.

2. A healthy ecological balance is vital; both ecological and political disaster can result from upsetting this balance. The challenge is to move away from policies that threaten disasters and toward prudent management of resources, population, and polluting industries and activities without sacrificing a decent standard of living, human integrity, or employment and profits.

3. Current political behavior is based on historical patterns of behavior. The challenge is to keep what is best from our past while endorsing change to meet new conditions—changes that help us, for example, to turn away from racism, sexism, or poverty through peaceful, constitutional effort.

4. Dominant economic systems have often shaped politics, law, and the distribution of wealth. The challenge is to ensure that the economic system—whether capitalism, socialism, or a combination—serves human needs at the least cost to freedom.

5. Politics can be understood in terms of conflict and cooperation among economic, social, ethnic, religious, and political groups. Most often it is their struggle for power that determines who gets what, when, and how. The challenge is to umpire this struggle in ways compatible with the public interest.

6. Human beings have biological, psychological, and social needs that must be satisfied. Politics can be understood as the effort to work out patterns to meet these needs. These needs suggest values—goals, purposes, policies—in politics and point to action. The challenge is to ensure that the proper patterns are developed.
7. The challenge in connection with a wide range of scientific and technological developments (space exploration, DNA mapping, new communication modes) is clear: How can public policy wisely harness the powers of science and technology for beneficial human ends?
8. In the cultural domain, concerned with the development and refinement of thought, spirit, literature, art, and taste, the challenge is to develop the creative imagination in all realms to foster a guiding vision of human excellence.

In exploring the physical, social, and cultural environment of politics, this chapter sketches some of the factual background to these propositions and challenges. Our treatment must be selective, while also emphasizing the interdisciplinary setting of politics.

Students of politics must appreciate this interdisciplinary setting because political science is only one of many social sciences, and the social sciences themselves constitute only one division of human knowledge and experience. In our treatment of the larger environment of politics, we cannot completely separate the physical and social aspects from the cultural aspects. Anthropology embraces all three worlds—physical, social, and cultural in the larger sense (embodying the concepts, habits, skills, arts, instruments, and institutions of a given people in a given period). Ecology can be considered as a branch of biology that deals with the relations between living organisms and their environments or as a branch of sociology (human ecology) that deals with the relations between human beings and their environment. Human biology cannot be discussed in isolation from important societal considerations. The religious setting of politics is both cultural and social. History can be viewed as both a social science and a branch of the humanities. Science and technology are usually located in the physical domain, yet they are products of human society, and they illustrate culture at work.

THE PHYSICAL WORLD WE LIVE IN

The physical sciences call attention to limits, capabilities, dangers, and opportunities in politics. For example, they stimulate us to ask about the **carrying capacity** of the planet (that is, how large a population the earth's resources can support). They provide information that enables students of politics to grapple more intelligently with problems.

To the best of current knowledge, Earth is the only habitable planet in our solar system. As far as we know, we are the only intelligent beings in the universe, although some astronomers speculate that there must be other planets capable of sustaining creatures like ourselves. Presently, we are the dominant species on a 4.5-billion-year-old planet in one modest-size solar system of a larger universe whose gigantic dimensions we can barely imagine. We speculate that we have achieved our position as *Homo sapiens*—the knowledgeable human being—after 3.5 billion years of organic evolution, 2 million years of human evolution, and only 5,000 years of historical experience.

The Population Tidal Wave

Currently, our planet supports nearly 6.5 billion people, distributed unevenly. Population estimates for 2025 run to approximately 9 billion. This population tidal wave is of relatively recent origin. The rapid escalation began with the Industrial Revolution at the end of the eighteenth century, and the population doubled in the twentieth century. This increase poses momentous problems for politics. It requires study of the correlation between a burgeoning population and other significant developments, such as the opening up of new lands in the Americas and revolutions in industry, transportation, medicine, and agriculture. Figure 5.1 illustrates population growth and its correlation with a number of key events, including those such as war, famine, and disease that decreased population or slowed growth. Information about national populations, when combined with other data (population density, arable land, material resources, economic resourcefulness, political skill) tells a great deal about nations' political problems, strengths and weaknesses, and potential power.

As Table 5.1 demonstrates, over half of the world's population (3.6 billion) is found in Asia, with China being the most populous country at slightly more than 1 billion people.

Figure 5.1 Ten Centuries of World Population Growth

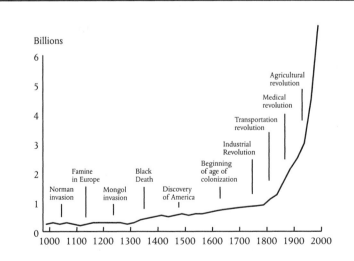

Source: Updated from a report from the Agency for International Development, *War on Hunger,* 8, no. 1:5, 1974.

Table 5.1 World Population Distribution and Projections (in millions)

	Year	
Region	*2000*	*2025*
Africa	905	1,937
Asia	3,905	5,217
Latin America and Caribbean	561	783
Oceania	33	48
North America	331	438
Europe	728	632
Total	6,465	9,076

Source: United Nations, Economic and Social Affairs, *World Population Prospects 2004, Revision* ESA/ WP.193 (New York: United Nations Publications, 2005), 17.

In contrast, North America, which includes the United States, Canada, Bermuda, Greenland, and Saint-Pierre et Miquelon, with a combined population slightly in excess of 331 million, constitutes only 5 percent of the world's total population. It is especially significant that 80 percent of the world's population lives in the less-developed countries.[1]

Finite Resources

The problems for a growing population on a finite earth with **finite resources** are compounded by the fact that not all land can produce food. For example, approximately 29 percent of the planet's surface is land, but 40 percent of this land is desert or frigid wasteland. Moreover, 33 percent is pasture, forest, marsh, and mountain. Additional amounts must be subtracted for urban areas, leaving only about 10 percent of the earth's land for producing crops. And of that potential agricultural land, only about 43 percent is in use.

As Table 5.2 reveals, some countries (for example, Canada, Argentina, Kyrgyzstan, and the United States) have a more favorable population/land ratio than others. Yet this information must be examined with care. Some countries with favorable population/land ratios are not well developed (such as Kyrgyzstan), while some countries with unfavorable ratios are (such as Japan). This fact suggests that factors other than population and land are important and that we can learn a great deal about the nation's politics and policies by examining such factors.

The United Kingdom and Japan used their human and natural resources to industrialize and to establish global trading networks. Britain's historical devotion to the policy of free trade and freedom of the seas and its long-standing position as a great sea

Table 5.2 Population per Square Mile, 2003

Country	Population
Canada	9
Argentina	37
Kyrgyzstan	65
United States	82
Egypt	194
Germany	609
United Kingdom	644
Japan	835
India	914
Bangladesh	2,678
Singapore	17,751

Source: Department of Commerce, *Statistical Abstract of the United States, 2004–2005* (Washington, D.C.: U.S. Government Printing Office, 2005), 841–843.

power are intimately connected to its need to import food and raw materials and export finished industrial products. Japan's historical development as a great power, from its opening to the West in the nineteenth century through its defeat in World War II, is closely connected to its unfavorable population/land ratio, its need for raw materials for industry, and its need to import food, as well as to the skill and energy of its people. However, both the United Kingdom and Japan remain vulnerable to a cutoff of food, raw materials, and international trade.

The United States is more favorably endowed, and this is unquestionably a source of its political strength. Yet even the United States may suffer if foreign crude oil cannot be imported cheaply. In 1970 the United States imported approximately 483 million barrels of crude oil. Thirty-four years later, in 2004, the amount was in excess of 3.7 billion barrels. As China and India continue to develop economically, the issue of oil consumption will only grow more acute.

Asian nations are among the most disadvantaged in terms of balance between population and food. And many countries may not be as fortunate as Japan in achieving a healthy economy in spite of this disadvantage. Although large populations can be a source of political strength, they can contribute to political weakness when nations cannot feed their people because food supplies are inadequate, food cannot be imported, distribution is faulty, or the people have no money. These conditions can lead to economic and political crisis.

A good distribution system and prudent management of other natural resources clearly enhance a nation's strength. Saudi Arabia, for example, was a poor desert country before oil was discovered there. Now oil figures prominently in its economic and political power. The location of key resources (for example, water for irrigation, oil, natural gas, coal, and iron ore) tells a great deal about the raw materials of economic, and thus political, power. The locations of some key mineral resources are shown in Table 5.3.

Favorable natural endowments may create difficulties as well as advantages in politics. For example, more powerful nations may covet the natural wealth of weak nations. In the past this situation led to imperialism and colonialism as European countries sought to conquer and colonize Africa, Asia, and North and South America. Today, richly endowed countries such as Nigeria, Saudi Arabia, and Venezuela may have trouble absorbing and sensibly using their oil wealth. The wisest use of such wealth requires considerable economic and political skill.

Critical finite resources are not confined to valuable minerals or petroleum.

The importation of crude oil is vital to many countries, particularly key economies in the industrialized world like the United States, Japan, and the countries of Western Europe. Although these countries import from all over the world, the Middle East has the largest known reserves of petroleum in the ground, making the region of great strategic interest.

Access to safe drinking water is increasingly being viewed as a critical resource. Some experts believe that as many as fifty countries are running out of water, and the prospects for interstate conflict over this valuable resource are increasing.[2]

Finally, as will be discussed in chapter 18, there is serious concern about humanity's relationship to its global home. In a number of ways we may be irreparably damaging the planet. The ozone layer, which protects the earth from ultraviolet rays, is being destroyed by the release of harmful man-made gases. Massive industrialization is causing the planet to warm at an alarming rate, threatening coastal regions over the next century. Each day about 140 plant and animal species become extinct, never to be seen again. Forests are vanishing at an annual rate of approximately seventeen million hectares, an area slightly larger than Malaysia, Norway, or Vietnam. The degradation of the environment is critically important.

Table 5.3 Leading Producers of Major Resources, 2001

Metals		Nonmetallic Minerals	
Aluminum	Russia, China, United States	Nitrogen in ammonia	China, United States, India
Bauxite	Australia, Guinea, United States	Phosphate rock	United States, Morocco, W. Sahara
Chromite	South Africa, Kazakhstan, India		
Copper	Chile, United States, Indonesia	Salt	Canada, China
Gold	South Africa, United States, Australia	Sulfur	Canada, United States, Russia
Iron ore	China, Brazil, Australia	**Mineral Fuels**	
Lead	Australia, China, United States	Coal	China, United States, India
Nickel	Russia, Australia, Canada	Natural gas, dry	Russia, United States, Canada
Tin	China, India, Peru	Natural gas, liquid	United States, Saudi Arabia, Canada
		Petroleum crude	Saudi Arabia, Russia, United States

Source: Department of Commerce, *Statistical Abstract of the United States, 2004–2005* (Washington, D.C.: U.S. Government Printing Office, 2005), 865.

THE BIOLOGICAL, PHYSIOLOGICAL, PSYCHOLOGICAL, AND SOCIAL CREATURES WE ARE

Our human nature significantly influences our political values, behavior, and judgments. Many political values are rooted in human needs. We do not have to believe that biology is destiny to recognize that cooperation and conflict may have some relation to our human endowment. And certainly many political actors have decided (foolishly, in the authors' view) that inequality, whether racial or sexual, is somehow rooted in our genes.

Human beings are highly developed primates with four unique species characteristics—large brain size, upright posture, longevity, and thought. These characteristics have permitted human beings to develop a complex language, to reason, and to make ingenious tools. Human beings have been able to develop a system of communication, gain mastery of their environment, and reshape the natural world.

Human Needs

Although human beings can restructure the natural world, human needs (biological, physiological, psychological, social, and cultural) significantly influence their economic and social life and thus their politics.[3] People need to survive, grow, and develop mentally and socially. To survive, they must satisfy certain material needs, such as physiological needs for air, sleep, water, food, and shelter. Heterosexual intercourse is normally necessary to produce children and perpetuate the species. People also need safety and security.

Human beings also have certain social needs: belonging, love, affection, and acceptance. They also must have self-esteem and esteem from others. Deficiencies here can impair both life and development. In addition, people have ethical and cultural needs—a need for love, truth, and service, for justice and perfection, and for aesthetics and meaningfulness. The legitimate satisfaction of these varying needs makes life, growth, and development possible. Satisfying these needs calls for considerable social and political cooperation, which has been richly documented in sociobiology, anthropology, and history.

Cooperation Versus Conflict

How, then, do we explain conflict, aggression, and war? Are conflict and cooperation rooted in our biological nature? Some students of human biology, ethology (the study of animal behavior), and anthropology argue that human beings are aggressive by nature and that war is one outcome of such aggression. They maintain that war could not have existed for hundreds of thousands of years if it did not have roots in our very genetic code. For example, two of the better-known ethologists, Konrad Lorenz and Robert Ardrey, on the basis of their studies of animal behavior, have posited instinctual human aggression.[4] However, most biologists, anthropologists, and social psychologists think otherwise. Social psychologists such as Leonard Berkowitz contend that human aggression is learned behavior.[5]

Perhaps Julian S. Huxley best summed up the argument against instinctual aggressiveness when he maintained that "human nature . . . contains no specific war instinct, as does the nature of harvester ants." Huxley wrote:

> There is in man's make-up a general aggressive tendency, but this, like all other human urges, is not a specific and unvarying instinct; it can be molded into the most varied forms. It can be canalized into competitive sports, as in our own society, or as when certain Filipino tribes were induced to substitute football for headhunting. It can be sublimated into non-competitive sport, like mountain climbing, or into higher types of activity altogether, like exploration or research or social crusades.[6]

However, even if war is not the expression of a biological imperative, it remains, wrote Huxley, an ugly and devastating reality for humankind, especially for political leaders. He emphasizes that war is "a biological problem of the broadest scope, for on its abolition may depend life's ability to continue the progress which it has slowly but steadily achieved through more than a thousand million years. . . . War is not inevitable for man." But what is imperative is a politics "to make war less likely." [7]

Racism and Sexism

Political battles over slavery, racism, and sexism also require an understanding of human beings as biological creatures. In human history, slavery has been justified on the ground that some people are slaves by nature. This view has been thoroughly discredited, but slavery still exists in a few regions of the developing world, as it did in some American states through the middle of the nineteenth century.

Moreover, racial differences, particularly skin color, remain the actual basis for discrimination over most of the world. **Racism**—the belief that certain races are inferior—explains the brutal treatment of Native Americans by the Spanish, the English, and other Americans, and of Africans and Asians by Anglo-Saxons, Portuguese, Belgians, and French. And, of course, racial doctrines based on false science dominated the Nazi regime and guided its extermination of European Jews.

Although racial discrimination, segregation, and persecution have been repudiated by enlightened public opinion, racism remains a fact of social and political life throughout the world and a continuing problem for public policy. In the United States, for example, immigration policy has historically been prejudiced against Asians and Africans (and even against Caucasians from eastern and southeastern Europe). Battles continue to be fought in American politics over measures to overcome racial discrimination against African Americans, Hispanics, and Native Americans. Arguments continue to rage about such public policies as affirmative action programs to ensure equality in employment and in educational opportunities.

Sexism, usually understood as the doctrine of male superiority and the practice of male dominance, is a worldwide phenomenon. Women have been overwhelmingly subjected to unequal treatment before the law, in economic life, and in politics and society. Only in the twentieth century and in liberal democratic and socialist countries have women achieved legal and political equality in theory. However, many of these gains, such as the right to vote in the United States and Great Britain, came only after protracted political battles. But even in advanced liberal nations, de facto (actual) discrimination against women persists in the job market, in political life, and in social affairs. In the United States, for example, the political impact of women's fight for equality is dramatized by the controversial, ill-fated struggle to ratify an equal rights amendment to the Constitution during the late 1970s and early 1980s. In politics and in society women have been fighting to overcome the still widespread social conviction, rooted in a narrow view of biology (and religion), that "a woman's place is in the home."

Human biological, psychological, and social characteristics thus strongly influence the development of social communities. In examining these communities we pay particular attention to how they respond to human needs, especially in politics; to how politics affects human tendencies to cooperate and clash; and to political efforts to deal with inequality and equality.

THE SOCIAL COMMUNITIES WE HAVE BUILT

How are the social communities we have built a response to our biological needs and the physical world? How are these communities influenced by psychological needs, by methods of earning a living and carrying out our economic relations, by developments in science and technology, and by historical memory? Throughout our analysis we will emphasize the ways in which the social environment influences politics.

The Sociopsychological Setting of Politics

Material, social, and cultural needs shape values, behavior, and judgment in society and in politics. Social psychologists say these needs include "a frame of orientation and devotion," a sense of roots and of unity, a feeling of "effectiveness," a capacity for "excitation and stimulation," and a guiding "character structure." [8] According to Erich Fromm, these needs can be satisfied in many ways; different political systems represent different modes of satisfaction.

For example, Fromm notes that the "need for an object of devotion can be answered by devotion to God, love, and truth—or by idolatry of destructive idols." The adulation of Adolf Hitler was the worship of a destructive idol. Other needs can also be answered in different ways. Thus the "need for relatedness can be answered by love and kindness—or by dependence, sadism, masochism, destructiveness, and narcissism." Nazism again illustrates a flawed political response. "The need for unity and rootedness can be answered by the passions for solidarity, brotherliness, love, and mystical experience—or by drunkenness, drug addiction, and depersonalization." Drunkenness and drug addiction are clearly social matters that call for a public policy response.

"The need for effectiveness can be answered by love, productive work—or by sadism and destructiveness." The former response enhances political trust and economic prosperity; the latter wreaks havoc in the political community. "The need for stimulation and excitation can be answered by productive interest in man, nature, art, ideas—or by a greedy pursuit of ever-changing pleasures." A thoughtless, pleasure-loving society—heedless of future dangers—bodes ill for ecological and political well-being.

Moreover, the guiding character structure can be principled or unscrupulous, cooperative or combative, altruistic or selfish, democratic or authoritarian. Unscrupulous, combative, selfish, authoritarian people may create political communities that lack agreement on fundamental human rights and are thus prone to exploitation, domination, and war.

Human character can be positively influenced by historical tradition and by coherent inner principles. Vibrant and functional political communities are held together by healthy political traditions and principles that merit widespread community agreement and by thoughtful discussion about what those principles mean. However, if people are thoughtlessly directed by tradition, they may not be able to adapt politically. For example, ruling aristocrats who are unwilling to alter their ways may invite disaster for themselves by refusing to admit the middle class into political rule. In turn, the middle class may invite a comparable disaster by refusing to admit the working class. The same risk is taken by whites unwilling to admit African Americans or by men unwilling to admit women.

The Economic Environment of Politics

People's methods of earning a living have always crucially influenced political life. Moreover, the larger economic relationships of society have an enormous impact on politics and public policy. People seek to protect their economic interests, and this leads almost inevitably to politics. The economic influence on politics has been demonstrated by a number of perceptive observers. Aristotle, for example, saw politics in ancient Greece in terms of the struggle between the few rich and the many poor, with the poor often battling to secure a more equitable distribution of wealth and the rich battling to secure their larger slice of wealth and power.

In seventeenth-century England, James Harrington argued that political power rests upon economic power; specifically, he maintained that political power is influenced by the distribution of land. Harrington held that if one man is the sole landlord or if he dominates the people, the result is "absolute monarchy." If a few—the nobility or the nobility and the clergy—own the land or dominate the people, the result is a mixed monarchy, or what we call an aristocracy. But where the people are the landlords or there is a wide distribution of land, the outcome is a commonwealth, a republic, a government of laws and not of men. Although Harrington's understanding of economic power was somewhat limited, he nonetheless perceived that military and political power were clearly related to ownership of land, an important component of economic power in his day.

The importance of economics to politics was almost a political truism at the birth of the American republic. America's Founders understood that British economic policy had triggered the American Revolution. James Madison, the key author of the U.S. Constitution, held that "the principal task of modern legislation" was to regulate key interests—those with and those without property, creditors, debtors, manufacturers, merchants, and bankers.

Karl Marx, in nineteenth-century Europe, articulated an even more sweeping view. He held that a society's economic structure, especially its system of economic production, was the real foundation upon which the political superstructure and other aspects of the superstructure—such as religion, art, and ethics—rested. For Marx, the power of the ruling class came from its control of economic life. In the nineteenth century this ruling class was the bourgeoisie (the property owners and capitalists in general). As Marx described it: "The executive of the modern state is but a committee for managing the common affairs of the whole bourgeoisie."

Table 5.4 The Development Gap: Developing and Developed Nations, 2002

	Low-Income Developing Countries (64 countries)	High-Income Developed Countries (41 countries)
Undernourished people[a]	24%	<1%
Life expectancy at birth[b]	59.1 years	78.3 years
Adult literacy[c]	63.6%	100%
Gross domestic product[d]	$2,149	$28,741

Source: United Nations Development Program, *Human Development Report 2004* (New York: Oxford University Press, 2004).

Note: Low-income developing countries are those with a gross national product (GNP) per capita of $735 or less per year. High-income developed countries have a GNP per capita of $9,076 or more in 2002.

[a] Percentage of total population, 1999–2001.

[b] Average in years, 2002.

[c] Percentage literate age fifteen and above, 2002.

[d] GDP per capita in $US, 2002.

A political scientist need not be a Marxist to recognize the influence of economics. This influence manifests itself in the varying ways that powerful economic interests (for example, farmers, workers, and industrialists) seek to shape public policy at home and abroad through favorable legislative, administrative, or judicial decisions. Such interests, of course, may favor inaction as well as action in the political sphere.

Economics, as well as biology, throws light on equality and inequality, values always at the heart of the struggle for power that is politics. Some nations are rich and developed and others are poor and developing, or less developed—a gap dramatically illustrated by Table 5.4. Of course, great disparities exist not only between countries but within countries as well. The rich-poor gap, within and between nations, is an actual and potential source of troublesome conflict and a major challenge to political leaders. Poverty has political consequences. These problems arise from nations' attempts to feed their people; accumulate capital for development; balance needs for defense against those for development and consumers; and, in general, respond to their people's aspirations for a better life. Under certain circumstances, poverty can lead to riots. By intensifying a sense of injustice, poverty can make poor people and those attracted to their cause more sympathetic to radical political ideologies and solutions.

Economic and related social problems are particularly acute in less-developed countries. The lack of nutritious food, pure water, good health care, and adequate income seriously threatens human life and decency in many of these countries. In addition, rapid

Table 5.5 Urbanization in the Developing World (in millions)

City	*1975*	*2000*	*2005*	*2015*
Bombay, India	7.3	16.1	18.3	22.6
Delhi, India	4.4	12.4	15.3	20.9
Mexico City, Mexico	10.0	18.1	19.0	20.6
São Paulo, Brazil	9.6	17.1	18.3	19.9
Jakarta, Indonesia	4.8	11.0	13.2	17.5
Karachi, Pakistan	3.0	10.0	11.8	16.2
Cairo, Egypt	6.4	10.7	11.2	13.1
Manila, Philippines	5.0	9.9	10.6	12.6

Source: United Nations Department of Economic and Social Affairs/Population Division, *World Urbanization Prospects: The 2003 Prospects: The 2003 Revision* ESA/WP.190 (New York: United Nations Publications, 2004), 121–123.

urban growth creates economic, social, and political problems by straining the economies and exerting extreme pressure for jobs, decent food, water, health care, and housing for millions of often unprepared urban dwellers. Table 5.5 illustrates the recent and projected rapid urbanization of some cities in developing countries.

Our consideration of the economic environment of politics has already overlapped its sociological setting, which is the subject of the next section.

The Sociological Setting of Politics

Economic interests are not the only powerful influences in society and therefore in politics. Other groups—social, ethnic, racial, and religious—are also at work, and their efforts to protect their vital interests also impinge on politics. Indeed, all these groups are central to politics, because public policy often results from their activities. But how else do noneconomic groups influence society? Let us first look at the role of religion in politics.

Religion and Politics. Since the Protestant Reformation in the sixteenth century, battles between Roman Catholics and Protestants in Western Europe have divided nations and led to civil wars. Religious persecution was a factor in the settlement of North America. The multiplicity and diversity of religious groups in the United States made for religious freedom. Yet, despite separation of church and state, religious groups have exerted much political influence. For example, they influenced the movement to abolish slavery, although northern and southern churches split along regional lines. Protestants, especially Methodists, were active in the Anti-Saloon League, which worked successfully for the 1919 Prohibition amendment to the Constitution, which outlawed the manufacture, sale, or transportation of liquor in the United States. The Catholic Church has taken a strong stand against abortion and on behalf of protecting the needy. American Jews are strongly pro-Israel. Conflicts between Protestants and Catholics in Northern Ireland continue to trouble that part of the British Isles. Israeli and Islamic claims on the city of Jerusalem add a religious dimension to complicated nationalistic and political rivalries in the Middle East.

One of the more important recent developments in the area of religion and politics has been the growing influence of religious fundamentalism. Islamic fundamentalists have received a great deal of attention in this area, along with the rise of the Christian right in the United States—subjects we will deal with shortly. But it is important to note that religious fundamentalism is not confined to these two high-profile cases. For example, fundamentalist Hindus and Sikhs and Theravada Buddhists have had a profound influence on the political fabric of India and Sri Lanka. Latin America has seen the growth of a significant number of Pentecostal communities as well.

Defining religious fundamentalism is a difficult task. Each religion has its own unique ideological, cultural, organizational, and historical characteristics. Nevertheless, with some caution, we can define religious fundamentalism as a movement to uphold, defend, and/or preserve age-old religious traditions and values. In the modern context, fundamentalists adopt new methods, organizational structures, and policies to accomplish their goals. It is here that we see the interface between religious fundamentalism and the world of politics. For a fundamentalist activist, it is not enough "to be merely a conservative or traditionalist in these threatening times." [9] Fundamentalists view modernity as a serious threat to traditional values and the acquisition of political power as an important means to preserve traditional religious practices and values. Space does not permit a comprehensive discussion of all religious fundamentalist movements and their activities, so we will narrow our discussion to two movements, one domestic and one international: the rise of the Christian right in the United States and Islamic fundamentalism in many countries throughout the world. While each possesses certain characteristics common to fundamentalist movements, we must emphasize that they also have striking differences—differences that should be noted as we consider their respective influences on politics.

The 1973 U.S. Supreme Court decision *Roe v. Wade,* which effectively legalized abortion, was instrumental in galvanizing a coalition of evangelical leaders to move beyond their pulpits and into action at virtually every level of American politics. Through various organizations such as the Moral Majority (renamed the Liberty Federation), the Religious Roundtable, and the Christian Voice, these leaders and their followers began to seriously challenge what they saw as an erosion of traditional values. They actively supported conservative candidates for political office and lobbied for action to reverse a variety of societal trends they found objectionable, such as growth in the pornography business,

In February 1979 the Ayatollah Khomeini returned to Iran after fourteen years in exile. Here he is shown a few minutes before the plane took off from Paris. Once in Tehran he proceeded to establish an Islamic republic governed by Islamic theology, with Muslim clerics holding the most powerful government offices.

banning of prayer in schools, moves to allow euthanasia, wider acceptance of homosexuality, genetic research that could lead to human cloning, sex education in public schools, the taxing of private Christian schools, and, of course, the legalization of abortion.

The evangelical leaders and their followers do not constitute the entire Christian right, but they can be seen as a vanguard of the movement. There are a significant number of nonevangelical Christians who at the very least are sympathetic to the political goals of the evangelicals but may not be as politically active. Determining the size of this movement has been difficult. Polling data and conservative Christian book sales indicate that the hardcore Christian right may number no more than two hundred thousand. But as Grant Wacker of Duke University's Divinity School notes, "fellow travelers, people who explicitly identify themselves as partisans of the religious right, ranged from ten to fifteen million. Sympathizers who might be mobilized over a specific issue such as abortion or gun control may have enlisted thirty-five million." [10] The Christian right now constitutes a major force within the Republican Party. In both the 2000 and 2004 presidential elections, evangelical Protestants accounted for about 23 percent of the electorate, and in 2004 78 percent of them voted for George W. Bush. They are active not only in supporting conservative political candidates at all levels, but also in lobbying for specific legislation and in pushing for the appointment of conservatives to federal judgeships and other high-ranking appointed positions in government.

While Islamic fundamentalists have been active for decades in various political arenas around the world, the event that brought the movement to new heights of attention was the Iranian revolution of 1979 that toppled the shah of Iran. The revolution was inspired by the strong-minded Shiite Islamic leader, the Ayatollah Khomeini, who, as the seizure of power became imminent, returned triumphant from years in exile in Paris. The ayatollah established an Islamic republic in which powerful clerics dominated the government and the conservative values and practices of Islam became the basis of governance. The Iranian revolution energized the Islamic fundamentalist movements around the world. Fundamentalists made aborted attempts to seize power in countries like Egypt and Algeria but succeeded in Afghanistan, where the Taliban—a very conservative militia that enforced a strict Islamic code of behavior—ruled from 1996 until 2002. Although out of power, it remains a force in Afghanistan. Where full seizure of power did not appear feasible, Islamic fundamentalist movements sought at least to expand their influence in places like Malaysia, Indonesia, and the Philippines. Some of these movements have been accompanied by considerable violence, in some cases originating from factions within the movements themselves and in others resulting from brutal repressive campaigns initiated by governing officials within these countries. But it is important to note that Islamic fundamentalists are not universally violent. In the wake of violent acts carried out by groups such as Hezbollah, Hammas, and al Qaeda, there has been the unfortunate tendency to equate Islamic fundamentalism with terrorism. In truth, terrorists who use violent methods to further their political agendas constitute a distinct minority of the Islamic fundamentalist movements. While Western culture does not see eye to eye with such Islamic fundamentalist beliefs as those involving the role of women in society, and there is a great deal of mutual distrust and hostile rhetoric, it is also true that many of the movements are characterized by a genuine sense of social conscience and community as evidenced by the construction of thousands of schools, hospitals, orphanages, and health clinics throughout the Muslim world.

Race, Ethnicity, and Politics. Race and ethnicity also figure prominently in politics. Battles over slavery, emancipation, reconstruction, integration, and affirmative action have characterized U.S. politics. Discrimination against various ethnic groups—Irish, Chinese, Japanese, Jews, Italians, Poles, Hispanics—has echoed and reechoed throughout American history.

Ethnic minorities in political communities create both dangers and opportunities. The dangers are usually most prominent. The dominant ethnic majority often finds the ethnic minority a thorn in its side; the ethnic minority, which often subscribes to a different religion and may also speak a different language than the dominant majority, seeks to preserve its ways and enhance its power. Thus a significant percentage of French-speaking Canadians, particularly in the province of Quebec, do not want to be absorbed into an Anglo-Saxon Canada. Their desire for power in Quebec—and perhaps for independence from the rest of Canada—is a thorny problem for Canadians. Sizable Muslim populations in India, Kurds in Iran and Iraq, Arabs in Israel, Chinese in Malaysia, Basques in Spain, and Ibos in Nigeria pose comparable problems. Lithuanians, Latvians, Estonians, Georgians, and Ukrainians—once part of the Soviet Union—finally gained their independence and statehood, but now, ironically, Russians are ethnic minorities in the newly independent states. Moreover, Russia faces national and ethnic tensions amounting to regional civil wars in such parts of Russia as Chechnya. In the former state of Yugoslavia, violent conflict erupted among Serbs, Croats, Bosnian Muslims, and Kosovars of Albanian heritage, creating the worst warfare in Europe since World War II.

Countries often overlook the positive opportunities that ethnic minorities offer. The key opportunity is to fashion a successful multiethnic society where groups can preserve their customs, characteristics, languages, and religions in a diverse and pluralistic society; where political power can be shared; and where social trust can ensure peace and constitutionality. Despite its sometimes deplorable historical record with many ethnic groups, the United States has attempted to seize this opportunity with its diverse cultural fabric, including the Irish, Jews, Hispanics, Asians, and American Africans. But a truly multiethnic society is more often myth than reality.

Class and Politics. Although anti-Marxists claim it is a myth, the influence of **class** on politics is a reality that students of politics and students of sociology must critically explore. Marxists make class struggle, which for them is rooted in economics, the key to their analysis of society and politics. They see a working class and a capitalist class (owners of the means of production and exchange) competing for power. This struggle, Marxists believe, has universal application: it can be seen at work in both developed and developing countries. A study of class struggle identifies the forces contending for power; their basic interests; their values; their economic, social, and political behavior; and their contending public policies.

Some Marxists have even used class analysis to critically analyze communist countries such as the former Soviet Union or Yugoslavia. For example, they have criticized the emergence in such countries of a "new class" of elite rulers in defiance of the orthodox Marxist view of a classless society. Indeed, the 1989 dismantling of Communist power in Eastern Europe revealed that Communist officials in country after country had lived isolated lives of privilege while the economies they were charged with running collapsed around them.

Some social scientists maintain that class analysis is limited—that it focuses too sharply on one factor. Other social scientists argue that class analysis has been largely neglected. Nevertheless, it should be clear that the Marxist approach to class is only one of several, albeit one of the most powerful.

The Scientific and Technological Environment of Politics

Modern science and technology have significantly affected the world we live in. They have facilitated industrialization and urbanization. They have brought people and goods closer together through rapid transportation and communication. They have increased our economic interdependence. They have led to the development of modern machinery and fertilizers that enable a tiny farm population in a developed country to produce enough food for a huge nation. Through modern medicine, science and technology have assured the growth of population. Most dramatically, they have intensified war's destructive powers, particularly the power of nuclear weapons. As science and technology have altered our world, they have created problems for politics—just as they have helped policymakers solve problems. A number of key problems cannot even be understood without the help of scientists. For example, scientists warn that the planet can sustain only a certain level of population with current resources. But scientists also offer potential solutions, such as holding open the possibility that key ecological problems can be dealt with by developing solar power, prudently limiting population, and increasing the food supply.

The advance of scientific knowledge and technology has had paradoxical results for society and politics. On the one hand, science and technology have encouraged democratic achievements and a revolution of rising expectations. The burst of scientific accomplishments in the nineteenth and twentieth centuries coincided with the advent of liberal democracy in the Western world and with significant efforts to overcome backbreaking handwork, illiteracy, disease, and famine. On the other hand, science and technology have made pos-

Although technology has provided many benefits, it also has a dark side. This is nowhere more dramatically reflected than in the quest by countries to build and deploy weapons of mass destruction. The awesome destructive power of these weapons was demonstrated by the dropping of the atomic bomb on Hiroshima, Japan, on September 8, 1945. Tens of thousands of people perished, and virtually all the houses and buildings in the city were leveled, with the exception of this movie theater.

sible the totalitarian state and the potential suicide of the human race through nuclear holocaust. Those scientific advances also coincided with an often virulent nationalism and with dreadful patterns of exploitation, mind control, degradation, and death.

Political leaders have to guard against the pride—the hubris—and the conceit that scientific mastery can create a technological fix for all our problems. As indicated above, technological advances can just as often be used destructively as positively. The atomic bomb can kill as well as protect. Missiles can destroy cities as well as help unravel the mysteries of the solar system. Nuclear plants create dangerous radioactivity even while providing an alternative to expensive oil. Gene splicing (recombinant DNA) can unleash new, virulent microbes or lead to a cure for cancer. Modern drugs can be used to brainwash dissidents in a totalitarian state and to relieve heart attacks. Modern methods of communication may increase the ability of a dictator or an authoritarian state to control thought, yet they may also permit oppressed people to acquire outside information. New electronic toys may dull our critical senses or open up avenues of excellence in the arts, education, sports, and politics. Clearly, science and technology create problems that impinge directly on politics and call for difficult decisions to balance benefits and risks. These problems have become an inevitable part of the social and political environment.

The Historical Setting of Politics

An old adage holds that "political science without history has no root; history without political science has no fruit." Historical roots nourish the societal tree and its political fruits. Historical memory, for example, plays a vital role in social and political communities. A nation's **prescriptive constitution**—that is, its traditional way of conducting social, economic, and political business—originates in a community's history. That history shapes key principles: respect for private property or a belief in public ownership, a belief in separation of church and state or their connection, a primary emphasis on liberty or on equality. These principles often become associated with national patriotism and generate powerful emotions that influence political values and behavior.

Our current social and political environment is an inheritance. To understand that historical inheritance is to understand key forces still influencing the present. Alexis de Tocqueville, the French author of a perceptive nineteenth-century study of the United States, *Democracy in America* (1835, 1840), understood this point well. In seeking to explain American society and politics, he called attention to several important factors. He noted the significance of a unique American history, relatively free of aristocracy and feudalism. He stressed the value of an Anglo-Saxon inheritance of constitutional liberty and a sound religious tradition. And he thoroughly appreciated the strategic worth of a bountiful land removed from Europe by three thousand miles of ocean. These factors, Tocqueville argued, made it easier for creative statesmen to advance democracy and equality in the United States. In contrast to the French in 1789, Americans in 1776 did not have to concentrate great power in a central government to overthrow a monarchy, a nobility, and an established Church in order to ensure equality and freedom. Americans, Tocqueville contended, had been "born equal." They had already established vital institutions of freedom. This history, he argued, moved Americans toward a more egalitarian democracy. They faced challenges to freedom, but their history promoted the success of their democratic experiment.

The study of history helps students of political science appreciate both change and continuity in politics. Traditions persist, but change and revolution may also occur. Both peaceful change and more violent transformation may be part of a nation's heritage and may influence its politics. Today, for example, the United States, France, and the United Kingdom are devoted to peaceful constitutional change, but each experienced important revolutions that significantly affected its current politics. The ideological forebearers of today's political conservatives were often political radicals.

History shows that nations wax and wane in power. Empires rise and fall, as do civilizations. These are the truisms of history; yet they may stimulate us, as students of politics, to ask about the dynamics of social and political change. For example, does the study of history help us understand the nature of revolution in general and of specific revolutions? Historian Crane Brinton's *Anatomy of Revolution* points toward certain stages that apply to successful democratic revolutions other than the four he studied (the English

Civil War in the seventeenth century, the American and French Revolutions in the late eighteenth century, and the Russian Revolution in the twentieth century). Brinton saw revolution characterized by (1) economic difficulties and the desertion of the intellectuals from existing values; (2) a failure on the part of the existing government to maintain its legitimacy, affirm its power, and crush the rebels; (3) the achievement of power by the revolutionaries, with the moderates initially in power; (4) the displacement of the moderates by more radical revolutionaries who undertake a reign of terror; and then (5) a return to more normal, and perhaps even reactionary, behavior after the fires of revolution die down. Not all scholars agree with Brinton, but his investigation stimulates questions about how such historical studies can illuminate past and present revolutions.[11]

History also shows that views of peoples and nations change over time. So, too, does the **civic culture**—the set of attitudes toward citizenship and politics that helps sustain a democratic, stable, and effective nation. Germany is a good case in point. There was no state called Germany before the nineteenth century. As late as the eighteenth century, or even the early nineteenth, German-speaking people were often viewed as easygoing, pacific, and sometimes ignorant and uncultured. They lived in a number of separate states in central Europe. However, by the late nineteenth century, under Prussian domination, a German state had emerged, and Germans were frequently looked on as energetic, militant, intelligent, and cultured. Then with Hitler's dictatorship (1933–1945) still another transformation took place. German leaders and many German people were characterized as savage, brutal, and sadistic.

After World War II the Federal Republic of Germany (West Germany) emerged, strongly committed to constitutional democracy. But German citizens did not yet illustrate civic culture at its best. German voters seemed "relatively passive," politically detached, and cynical; hostility between the supporters of West Germany's two largest parties was high and not "tempered by any general social norms of trust and confidence." In 1963 Gabriel A. Almond and Sidney Verba, two students of civic culture, attempted to explain the attitudes of German citizens by noting Germany's "bitter and traumatic political history," its terrible disillusionment with Nazi politics, and "the intense commitment to political movements that characterized Germany under Weimar (the Weimar Republic, after the end of World War I and before the advent of Hitler) and the Nazi era." [12]

Yet in a follow-up study on West Germans and civic culture published in 1980, David P. Conradt demonstrated how more recent history had changed West German attitudes, indicating that the portrait of the West German political culture painted only a decade and a half earlier had "changed in every important respect." By the mid-1970s, Conradt observed, "Germans had greater feelings of trust in government and were more supportive of their political system than mass publics in Britain." (In 1963 Almond and Verba had found the United States and Britain to be exemplars of the civic culture.) Conradt held that the Almond-Verba study was a "dated . . . snapshot of a political culture being remade." Conradt saw signs of a healthy, vital, democratic order and concluded that four historical events accounted for these key changes among West German voters: (1) post-war socialization, (2) the absence of any credible alternative to liberal democracy, (3) post-war socioeconomic modernization, and (4) system performance.[13]

The historical setting of politics thus enables us to see how tradition influences polit-ical values, behavior, and judgment and to understand political problems. Our study of history helps us, as students of politics, to appreciate both continuity and change.

THE CULTURAL UNIVERSE WE HAVE CREATED

In politics, as in other arenas of human endeavor, a people without a vision will perish. This vision of a life to lead—of the good, the true, and the beautiful—comes to all peo-ple, including political actors, from a part of our culture understood here as high cul-ture. We distinguish high culture to emphasize the development and refinement of thought, spirit, literature, art, and taste. Thus our concern is with how philosophy, reli-gion, literature, and art provide insights into human life and creativity. These disciplines call attention to the larger meaning of our world. They underscore the complexity and ambiguity of politics and the wide range and subtlety of human behavior. High culture depicts both the joy and the despair of judgment in human and political life and adds a rich texture to the fabric of societal life and to politics.

The Culture of the Enlightenment

Culturally and politically, Westerners are still the children of the **Enlightenment**—the way of thought and life that emerged most clearly in the late eighteenth century, the cen-tury of the American and French Revolutions. Despite the cataclysmic events of the twen-tieth century, most Westerners still share the outlook of the Enlightenment—a strong commitment to freedom, reason, and progress. We still condemn the follies and barbar-ities of an oppressive and ignorant past characterized by religious intolerance, violations of due process of law, and a rigid class structure. Westerners also look forward to the earthly emancipation of all human beings. The outlook of the Enlightenment has shaped the political philosophy of liberal democracy, democratic socialism, and communism. And despite the hold of traditional cultures in developing countries, this outlook has influ-enced the viewpoint of intellectuals and leaders in most Asian and African nations.

But the culture of the Enlightenment is not without its critics, who assail it as naive and unrealistic and who point out the shortcomings of faith in reason, freedom, and progress. The culture of the Enlightenment, they argue, has refused to face up to human irra-tionality, the denial of freedom, and political retrogression. The critics call attention, for example, to the decline of belief in eternal truths such as liberty, equality, and fraternity. Looking especially to modern totalitarian regimes, they note that the tradition of civil-ity has been badly wounded in the modern world. They emphasize that the prerequisites for a genuinely democratic society are weak even in developed nations and often non-existent in others. These critics underscore the failures of both liberalism and communism, pointing out that neither old nor new nations can overcome strife, hatred, poverty, and ignorance. The dreadful years of instability, war, authoritarianism, and totalitarianism of the twentieth century should refute those who continue to believe in progress, ever upward and onward. And now in the early years of the twenty-first century we are faced with the specter of global terrorism. Indeed, there are terrorists who are appalled by the Enlightenment beliefs in freedom and progress. Unrelenting in their attack, the critics insist that the easy faith of the Enlightenment cannot be sustained in the light of the disillusioning lessons of modern psychology, which reveal our irrational and childish urges, or in the light of the disheartening data about political behavior and institutions that expose incredible greed, venality, and flagrant abuse of power.

Striking a Cultural Balance

Yet overall, political thinkers seem to be striking a balance between the adulation of Enlightenment culture and harsh criticism of it. That balance has produced a much more sober and prudent—yet still affirmative—assessment of reason, freedom, and progress than previously existed. In striking that balance, these political thinkers have become conscious of the need to limit the power of political actors, including those with good intentions. They have come to see the dangers that people may face even from those who would usher in a just and peaceful world. The new balance is leading to a keener assessment of citizens' political capabilities—what we can and cannot do—and it is challenging us to seize real opportunities for greater control of our destiny. For example, we may not be able to end all conflicts in human affairs, perhaps not even all warfare, but we may be able to abolish nuclear warfare. Similarly, we cannot eliminate all violations of civil liberties, but we may significantly reduce flagrant and persistent violations, especially genocide. It may be utopian to believe that we can rid the world of poverty and disease, but we can overcome chronic hunger and starvation, and we can prevent a good many afflictions. Overcoming all pollution may be out of the question, but cleaner air and purer water are attainable.

Some students of religion maintain that religion may play a key role in striking a cultural balance. Are they correct? And what can we say about the way in which religion, as a vital part of our culture, influences politics?

Students of religion and politics argue that too often the religious influences on politics are overlooked. They emphasize that our basic philosophy, our deepest aspirations, and our daily commitments have been vitally affected by religion. Often religious tradition—whether we are orthodox believers, deists, agnostics, or atheists—has shaped our ideas and practices with regard to birth, education, marriage, and death. Students of religion insist that religion influences our understanding of love, compassion, faith, righteousness, charity, and friendship, as well as our notions of peace, liberty, equality, fraternity, and justice. Certainly, they maintain, Judeo-Christian religious conceptions—whether of the covenant or of the biblical commandments—have influenced ideas of constitution and law in the Western world. A comparable account of Islam and other great religions would reveal the political importance of those religious outlooks. For good or ill, the world's great religions have provided a vision for society and politics.

Culture shapes and is shaped by politics. On one hand, religion, literature, and art can influence our political values and behavior. On the other hand, what happens in politics and in society is expressed in religion, literature, and art. These forms thus reveal the creative imagination at work and show integration and disintegration, harmony and alienation, peace and war—among nations, within society, and in the human mind. We can profitably turn to great literary figures—Sophocles, Aristophanes, Dante, Cervantes, Shakespeare, Goethe, Dostoevsky, and Tolstoy—for deeper understanding of people, politics, and society. Novelists such as Charles Dickens, Emile Zola, Charlotte and Emily Brontë, George Eliot, John Steinbeck, Sinclair Lewis, and Virginia Woolf have successfully popularized a host of social issues.

Great religious leaders and some students of religion have also profoundly influenced politics. A few examples include Moses, Jesus, Saint Paul, Confucius, and Mohammed; reforming popes such as John XXIII and John Paul II; inspiring women such as Mother Teresa; great religious leaders from the developing world such as Mohandas Gandhi; influential black religious leaders such as Martin Luther King Jr.; and modern students of religion, society, and politics such as Reinhold Niebuhr. Of course, the creators of great world religions stand in a class by themselves, as do the great Protestant reformers Martin Luther and John Calvin. Yet the interpretation of religion—and its impact on politics—goes on.

The reforms set in motion by Pope John XXIII breathed new life and vitality into the Catholic Church and helped address a number of religious, social, and political issues. Martin Luther King Jr. helped lead African Americans into a new day of freedom. Reinhold Niebuhr developed a position of political **realism** that influenced the thinking of a generation of U.S. social scientists.

Niebuhr's Political Realism

Niebuhr emphasized that social scientists must recognize that the morality of the individual will not operate in larger social organizations, especially nations. He called attention to the will to dominate as well as the will to achieve a good life. He underscored the importance of the need for power to cope with power. He criticized naive liberals and pacifists who ignored the dark side of human nature—evil, pride, and irrationality.

For domestic affairs, Niebuhr advocated a tough-minded liberalism that was sympathetic to the rights of working people in general and to African Americans and other disadvantaged minorities, and to the need for government regulation of capitalistic abuses. In foreign affairs he saw the need to resist Nazi power in Europe and to contain communist expansionism after World War II. At the end of his life, he again endorsed the civil rights movement and opposed America's ill-fated intervention in Vietnam.

Niebuhr constantly reminded his readers of his religious perspective—informed by St. Augustine—that insisted that there can be no perfect justice in this world; in politics there are only proximate solutions to insoluble problems. Yet, within these limitations, Niebuhr urged that people fight valiantly to achieve significant reforms in society and politics.

Along with creative intellectuals in the social and physical sciences, culturally creative individuals see the possibility of creative breakthroughs to a new ethical understanding of the good political life, to a new empirical understanding of what really goes on in politics, and to a new prudential understanding of what can and cannot be done in the domain of public policy. These breakthroughs point toward a vision of diversity in human life. They emphasize that the good life in politics must be carried beyond peace, civil liberty, social justice, and ecological balance to a vision of human excellence in all domains. By advancing such a vision of excellence, a society's culture encourages politicians to view their calling as a civilizing enterprise.

CONCLUSION

Politics and political science cannot be understood in a vacuum. The activity that is politics and the discipline that is political science exist in a larger world and are affected by a larger environment. In important ways, that larger environment—physical, social, cultural—influences political values, behavior, and judgment and sets the stage on which the political play proceeds. The larger environment calls attention to limits, capabilities, dangers, and opportunities that are the central concerns of those who study politics.

We gain a fuller appreciation of the larger environment of politics from other academic disciplines, ranging from history and physics to literature and art. These disciplines shed considerable light on the political scientist's four major tasks: ethical recommendation, empirical understanding, prudent judgment, and theoretical integration. These disciplines suggest theories, generalizations, models, methods, and insights that help students of politics address their own significant problems.

For purposes of specialization, we have separated political science from the other social sciences, yet this division is arbitrary and often severs connections that cannot be cut off in the real world. Academic disciplines overlap, just as politics overlaps economics and other human activities. As we come to understand the interdisciplinary setting of politics, we can also understand the importance of focusing on our public life and values, on the struggle for power and patterns of accommodation in the political community, and on public policy judgments.

SUGGESTED READINGS

Barber, Benjamin. *Jihad vs. McWorld.* New York: Times Books, 1995. A thought-provoking book positing conflict between two powerful forces—an integrative capitalist global economy and the return of fragmentary ethnic and religious movements.

Brown, Lester R. *State of the World 2005.* New York: Norton, 2005. Annual volume containing informative articles on the ecological state of the planet.

Diamond, Jared. *Guns, Germs, and Steel: The Fate of Human Societies.* New York: Norton, 1998. Diamond offers reasons why the Europeans have been in such an advantageous position in the world for so long. A major factor in his thesis is geography.

Friedman, Thomas. *The Lexus and the Olive Tree: Understanding Globalization.* Rev. ed. New York: Farrar, Straus, and Giroux, 2000. Eminently readable and basically optimistic description of the globalization process and its potential problems.

———. *The World Is Flat: A Brief History of the Twenty-First Century.* New York: Farrar, Straus & Giroux, 2005. Friedman's continuing commentary on the state of an increasingly globalized world in the post-9/11 era.

Harrison, Lawrence E., and Samuel P. Huntington, eds. *Culture Matters: How Values Shape Human Progress.* New York: Basic Books, 2000. This book argues persuasively that culture does indeed matter in virtually all key areas of human life.

Kaplan, Robert. *The Coming Anarchy: Shattering the Dreams of the Post Cold War.* New York: Random House, 2000. A very grim yet fascinating view of the global political environment now and in the future.

Landes, David. *The Wealth and Poverty of Nations.* New York: Norton, 1998. Argues that the key to understanding why there is a gap between rich and poor countries is to be found in the Industrial Revolution. For Landes, cultural values are an important factor.

Maslow, Abraham. *Motivation and Personality.* 3rd ed. New York: Addison-Wesley, 1987. Maslow developed a highly influential hierarchy-of-needs argument that throws a great deal of light on political values and behavior. See also his *The Farther Reaches of Human Nature*, 3rd ed. (New York: Arkana, 1993); and *The Farthest Reaches of Human Nature* (New York: Peter Smith, 1977).

Poulsen, Thomas. *Nations and States: A Geographic Background to World Affairs.* Englewood Cliffs, N.J.: Prentice Hall, 1995. Excellent and very thorough text on political geography.

Riemer, Neal, ed. *Let Justice Roll: Prophetic Challenges in Religion, Politics, and Society.* Lanham, Md.: Rowman and Littlefield, 1996. Explores the biblical roots, historical development, and contemporary relevance of the prophetic in the domains of religion, politics, and society. Brings to bear on contemporary problems the insights and understanding—ethical, empirical, and prudential—of the prophetic mode.

United Nations Development Programme. *Human Development Report 2005, International Cooperation at a Crossroads: Aid, Trade, and Security in an Unequal World.* New York: Oxford University Press, 2005. Produced annually, this is an excellent narrative and statistical summary of the conditions under which human beings around the world live.

Wallis, Jim. *God's Politics: Why the Right Gets It Wrong and the Left Doesn't Get It.* San Francisco: Harper San Francisco, 2005. An interesting take on religion and politics in America that criticizes both political parties.

Yergin, Daniel. *The Prize: The Epic Quest for Oil, Money, and Power.* New York: Simon and Schuster, 1991. Pulitzer Prize–winning history of oil and its role in international politics. Sweeping in scope and very readable.

GLOSSARY TERMS

carrying capacity (p. 95)
civic culture (p. 113)
class (p. 110)
Enlightenment (p. 114)
finite resources (p. 97)
prescriptive constitution (p. 112)
racism (p. 102)
realism (p. 116)
revolution of rising expectations (p. 94)
sexism (p. 102)

Part 2

POLITICAL PHILOSOPHY AND IDEOLOGY

The four chapters that constitute part 2 begin a fuller exploration of the ethical task in political science. Our guiding question is: *How do political philosophy and ideology illuminate our understanding of politics?* By political philosophy we mean a critically examined understanding of the values, realities, and judgments of politics—an understanding that is essential to the search for excellence and fulfillment in a just community. By political ideology we mean those beliefs, or ideals, that in a very practical way guide political actors in a given community and the justification of those guiding beliefs.

Chapter 6 presents the contributions of some outstanding Western political philosophers to the difficult quest for the good political life and a fuller understanding of politics. Although there is more to political philosophy than the quest for the good political life, there is justification for focusing, at least initially, on this pursuit. It leads to a conscious appreciation of the importance of ethical standards for politics, dictates an empirical search for the necessary and sufficient conditions of the good political life, and encourages students of politics to search for wise public policies.

Questions of the good life are central to politics because answering them leads to the establishment of critical standards. These standards then make it possible to say that a value, a political actor, an institution, an action, or a policy is good or bad; that a judgment is wise or foolish.

Moreover, these questions lead to a critical examination of the great political issues. Here we must confront the nature of human beings, the character of community, and the meaning of human destiny. We must probe frequent conflicts between justice and power, liberty and authority, and individual interest and the public interest. We must ask about the relationship between means and ends, higher law and human law, and personal aspirations and the common good. Intrigued by the elusive character of the good life, we seek to understand the constitutional order, a nation's vital interests, and political obligation, and we try to assess the reality of human fulfillment and the pros and cons of evolutionary versus revolutionary change. In brief, we seek to uncover the meaning—and the necessary and sufficient conditions—of political health.

The brief review in chapter 6 of how outstanding Western political philosophers have responded to fundamental issues will help you assess the strengths and weaknesses of liberal democracy, democratic socialism, communism, and other alternative outlooks. Chapters 7, 8, and 9 focus on a number of these contemporary ideologies and also on past, present, and future challenges to those dominant belief systems.

Chapter 6

THE QUEST FOR THE GOOD POLITICAL LIFE

The inquiry that will guide us in this chapter is: *How have the great political philosophers contributed to the difficult quest for the good political life and a fuller understanding of politics?* Our selective examination will address (1) the problem that prompted their explorations of the good life, (2) their "solutions" and their arguments on behalf of their positions, and (3) the heritage they bequeathed to us. Although this brief treatment cannot do full justice to the richness, complexity, and subtlety of these philosophers' thoughts, it may open the door to deeper study. We encourage you to read further the works of the authors you find interesting.

CLASSICAL GREEK THOUGHT: THE SEARCH FOR POLITICAL EXCELLENCE

Socrates, one of the world's most creative and stimulating teachers, founded Greek political philosophy. Although he wrote nothing down, he did employ the dialogue, a question-and-answer technique, and sought to explore the nature of the good, the true, and the beautiful. Socrates placed the Greek ideal of *arete,* or excellence, which the Greeks sought to fulfill in all fields of human activity, at the center of thinking and action in the political community. He gathered around him a number of pupils, the most brilliant of whom was Plato, and through relentless examination probed the character of moral life, which was for him the heart of both human and communal life. Socrates' passion for excellence in the political community—a concern that required him to articulate an ethical standard, probe political behavior, and seek the wise course of action—remained a central motif in the political philosophy of Plato and Aristotle.

Plato: Justice as the Harmony of Classes and Rule by Philosopher-Kings

Plato's problem in his classic work *The Republic* can be stated simply: What is justice? Plato seeks to rationalize, spiritualize, and universalize the ideal life for the **polis**, the Greek city-state.[1] He seeks to establish the polis on sound principles, suffuse it with excellence, and help it endure. Justice, Plato argues, is the harmonious ordering of the functional classes in the polis: philosophers ruling, soldiers defending, and farmers and artisans providing the necessary food, clothing, and utensils for everyday life. In this fashion, the wise would rule, the brave would defend, and those with basic appetites and talents would sustain the polis with their labor. Plato believes that the philosopher-kings should order the life of the polis in accordance with a vision of the good that their superior intellect allows them to perceive. This intellect permits them to grasp the truth of reality. Because

Plato and Aristotle were both committed to understanding how to live the "good life" and examining how politics makes this possible. Despite their shared concerns and close relationship—Aristotle was a student of Plato—the two offered very different conceptions of politics. The more practical Aristotle criticized Plato's theories as too utopian. This depiction of the two philosophers is a detail from Raphael's early-sixteenth-century fresco, the School of Athens, *in the Vatican Museums. Plato (left) points upward, while Aristotle gestures toward the ground.*

of this intelligence—ensured by education and strengthened by the critical examination of ideas—they would govern wisely and ensure excellence. And because each class would do that which it is best endowed by nature to do, each class would receive its due. Conflict would be overcome; justice, or harmony, would prevail.

Plato's preference for the good, for the enduring truth that lies beyond mere appearances, for excellence, for the rational, for the order that is justice, is very clear. In one bold stroke he solves the problem of the clash between justice and power by making the just powerful. Philosophers are entitled to their power because of their knowledge of the good and the supreme truth. Justice cannot be the interest of the stronger, because might does not make right. Justice cannot be expediency, because it must rest on something more enduring than immediate satisfaction or personal advantage. That deeper truth—the idea of the good—provides the proper standard in politics. That truth is illuminated by Plato's theory of ideas, which holds that ideas—the true "forms"—are the true realities. To grasp these forms we must get past our earthly perceptions of reality, which are actually a debased version of a higher truth. It takes great discipline and learning to see past everyday life to this higher truth—the reality of beauty and justice. And, naturally, those in touch with the higher truth—those who have ascended the ladder of truth to grasp the idea of the good—may wisely guide others in political life.

To the extent that other forms of government move away from the harmony of classes and the rule by philosopher-kings, they are deficient. Plato identifies these deficient forms of government as timocracy, oligarchy, democracy, and tyranny. They reveal what the good political life is not. They represent a falling away from **aristocracy**, which is government by the best. **Timocracy** is government by people of honor and ambition. As aristocracy degenerates into timocracy, so timocracy degenerates into **oligarchy**—government by the rich and lovers of money (what we would call plutocracy). Oligarchy, in turn, degenerates into what Plato calls **democracy**, government by the many poor. Democracy emerges "after the poor have conquered their [oligarchic] opponents." Democracy is based on everyone's having "an equal share of freedom and power." Democracy, however, is also unstable. It degenerates into tyranny when democratic people, preoccupied with "liberty and equality," lose a sense of law and order, a sense of discrimination, and turn to a "champion" to protect them against the rich. **Tyranny**, the lawless rule of one individual, is the worst form of government and receives Plato's harshest criticism.

Plato's critics have attacked him as an enemy of the open society, hostile to democracy, a proponent of censorship, and an advocate of a rigid class society. His supporters have defended his commitment to rule by wise people (including women), his affirmation of a standard of a good life as a guide in politics, his dedication to reasoned examination of arguments, and his insistence on moving from opinion to knowledge. Among his critics is his most illustrious student, Aristotle, who, despite differences with Plato, remained indebted to his teacher for many of his own ideas.

Aristotle: Constitutional Government and Rule by the Middle Class

Aristotle criticizes key features of Plato's *Republic* as unrealistic, especially his advocacy of communism for his class of philosopher-kings. Plato favored this system because public ownership would remove a real source of contention—conflicts over private property—among the members of this class. Aristotle thinks such a system of communism is unrealistic and incompatible with human nature.

Aristotle seeks to adjust Plato's severely aristocratic principles to the actualities of life in Greek political communities. But even as he does so, he endorses the need to understand the ideal regime, to relate ethics to politics, and to come as close to the best regime as human nature and political experience permit. Aristotle never loses sight of the anthropological principles holding that the family, the economy, and the local village come into existence to satisfy the bare necessities of life and that the polis then goes on to make the good life possible. The fulfillment of human beings in the political community remains a basic principle. To help guide you in understanding his preferences, Table 6.1 presents Aristotle's famous classification of governments. Note that Aristotle classified regimes according to the number who ruled—the one, the few, the many—and the goals of those rulers—ruling for the sake of all or ruling for the sake of oneself or one's class.

Table 6.1 Aristotle's Classification of Governments

Number Ruling	Rule in Accord with the Common Good	Rule Motivated by Individual or Class Self-Interest
One	Monarchy (government by a virtuous ruler)	Tyranny (government by one lawless person)
The few	Aristocracy (government by the virtuous few)	Oligarchy (government by the rich and noble)
The many	Polity (constitutional government— a mixture of democracy and oligarchy)	Democracy (government by the poor and free)

Which form of government provides the best practicable good life? Aristotle's answer is the **polity**, or constitutional government—a mixture of democracy and oligarchy. Such a government would rest most securely on a well-educated, reasonably virtuous, sufficiently wealthy, moderate middle class. The middle class is more likely to represent a "golden mean" between poverty and riches. It would not be envied by the poor or feared by the rich. Members of this class would be interested in politics and good government but would not be overly ambitious. Moreover, the middle class would be able to maintain the rule of law and justice.

Just because Aristotle prefers polity does not mean that he believes it is the best choice. In fact, he personally favors monarchy and then aristocracy, but acknowledges polity's practicality. All three of these forms of government—polity, monarchy, and aristocracy— are preferable to what he considers the three perverted forms of government: democracy (the most tolerable), oligarchy (a little better than tyranny), and tyranny (the worst of all).

Aristotle recognizes that "the best is often unattainable, and there the true legislator and statesman ought to be acquainted, not only with (1) that which is best in the abstract, but also with (2) that which is best relative to circumstances." [2] Given what is relative to circumstances in Greece, Aristotle favors the polity, in which the middle class is dominant, because such a government would be well administered, would prevent extremism in politics, would be freer of "factions and dissensions," and would be reasonably stable. Aristotle still hopes, however, that his polity would approach his ideal state as closely as circumstances permit. The polis should be small but not too small. Its territory and resources should permit its citizens to live liberally and with abundant leisure. Citizens should be educated, dedicated to wisdom and virtue, and active in the life of the polis.

The Aristotelian heritage is the mixed constitution, respectful of the common good and the rule of law, aristocratic in the best sense but willing to come to terms with the legitimate claims of the many poor and the few rich. Yet Aristotle's clear bias against "mechanics" and "tradesmen" and farmers, his justification of slavery, and his exclusion of women from the political process lead modern democrats to challenge those aspects of his heritage.

CHRISTIANITY AND THE GOOD POLITICAL LIFE

As we pointed out in chapter 5, religion has significantly influenced our understanding of human values, behavior, and judgment. When Christianity became tolerated in the Roman Empire early in the fourth century, its impact was widely felt in the Western world. Christianity's influence grew as it became the empire's favored religion.

Augustine: Incomplete Worldly Peace, Order, and Justice

How does the concept of the City of God help us understand the good political life on earth? Augustine (354–430) wrote *The City of God* to defend Christianity against the charge, leveled by pagan Romans, that Christianity caused the fall of Rome in A.D. 410. He denies the charge, arguing that Roman vice, not Christian virtue, was responsible. In the course of his argument, Augustine writes of two cities—the City of God (the heavenly city) and the City of Man (the earthly city)—that provide two influential standards for judgment, one positive and one negative.

The heavenly city is formed "by the love of God," whereas the earthly city is formed "by the love of self, even to the contempt of God." [3] The City of God is the kingdom of Christ. In this kingdom, composed of the elect, people live according to God in the hope of everlasting happiness. Perfect love, peace, justice, freedom, and fulfillment are possible only in the immortal life of the heavenly city.

The earthly city is the kingdom of Satan. In this city, made up of the damned, people live according to human appetites and seek earthly happiness. Perfect love, peace, justice, freedom, and fulfillment are not possible in this world; indeed, the earthly city is characterized by conflict, injustice, and war. It is a hell on earth.

Augustine maintains that the City of God is not coextensive with the earthly church, even though the church may represent the heavenly city. Church leaders and church members are not necessarily among the elect. Similarly, the earthly city cannot be absolutely equated with Rome or any actual state. Some members of actual states are also citizens of the heavenly city; they are pilgrims sojourning on earth while awaiting heavenly salvation. On the whole, although the two cities are commingled in any historical state, any actual political community is closer to the City of Man than to the City of God.

Human history will reveal the clash between the two cities and the ultimate triumph of the City of God. That triumph will not take place in this world but in the heavenly one hereafter. The best regime, as the City of God, will emerge only after the end of history. From God's creation of the world and of people, through the Fall (people's turning away

St. Augustine is remembered for several important theological works, including The City of God, *his epic defense of Christianity. This influential book, written in the early fifth century, attempts to explain the Christian understanding of history and how it relates to the political world. Augustine does not reject the importance of the political world, although in his view politics will always be less important than spiritual matters. His concern for the maintenance of peace makes him an important contributor to the idea of political realism. This fresco by Botticelli (1480) in Florence's Chiesa di Ognissanti portrays Augustine, shown here in his studio, as a man of letters and learning.*

from God) and the advent of Christ (offering hope for salvation in God's grace), to the ultimate triumph of the City of God, we can discern God's providence.

But how does this outlook clarify our understanding of the good political life? Augustine's philosophy of history, his idea of human nature, and his view of the two mystical cities lead to a very modest view of the good political life on earth. Perfection is out of the question. True love—of God and of neighbor—must be professed but cannot be perfectly fulfilled. Justice—which means giving God his due—cannot be realized completely in this world. The Christian commonwealth, in which the one true God is recognized, is Augustine's ideal regime, but it is possible only in the immortal, heavenly city, not in any earthly community. Similarly, perfect peace is not possible on earth. The good political life in any community is inevitably incomplete. Human nature after the Fall reveals self-love, cupidity, domination, and concupiscence (fleshly lust). Egotism, pride, and lust for money and power lead to dissatisfaction, strife, misery, and war. Even the elect who are intermingled with the damned in this world cannot fully escape the evil consequences of the world of flesh.

According to Augustine's perspective, the best that people in any earthly political community can hope for is an incomplete, although still beneficial, peace and order. The state and its rulers are God's instruments to maintain peace and justice. The political and legal order must restrain human appetites and passions—especially the lust for riches and power—and guide behavior through law and punishment. Political authority is a gift from God to fallen human beings. Even evil rulers must be seen as divinely appointed instruments to govern people after the Fall. Subjects must obey the powers that be. The state's coercive powers are necessary to restrain prideful appetites and conflicts among sinful human beings. Rulers should be resisted only if they command what God's ordinances forbid, and even then resisters must accept punishment.

Citizens in the political community—including the elect on pilgrimage to the heavenly city—see the value of even this incomplete peace, order, and justice. They see the value of law and of ensuring the necessities of human life. Augustine does not ignore the worth of such temporal blessings as health, material possessions, honor, friends, home, and family, but he insists that they are always subordinate to those of the heavenly city.

Augustine leaves a heritage of political realism. Given the nature of human beings—their pride, egotism, cupidity, and lust for power—our efforts to achieve perfect peace or justice in this world cannot succeed. Nevertheless, in our need for peace, order, security, and justice—however incomplete—we can look to government to help maintain a minimum level of civilization. But is Augustine's realism too pessimistic? And can his optimistic faith in God's providence be interpreted differently? Another Christian perspective on politics may provide answers.

Thomas Aquinas: Constitution, Law, Common Good, and Reason

Thomas Aquinas (1225–1274) is more optimistic about the good political life on earth than is Augustine. He views the political community (and its possibilities for human fulfillment) more positively. Aquinas, like Augustine, endorses the surpassing importance of eternal salvation and other key Christian concepts, but he is more inclined to see the political community as an arena for human development. Following Aristotle, Aquinas holds that society and government are natural and arise out of human needs. The political community is necessary to fulfill humanity's nature.

> Life in a community . . . enables man . . . to achieve a plenitude of life; not merely to exist, but to live fully, with all that is necessary to well-being. In this sense the political community, of which man forms a part, assists him not merely to obtain material comforts, such as are produced by the many diverse industries of a state, but also spiritual well-being.[4]

Of course, complete spiritual fulfillment is possible only through eternal salvation beyond this mortal life. But the church must do preparatory work in this world, in partnership with the state. Church and state play complementary roles in advancing human fulfillment. The church is primarily concerned with ordering religious life; the state deals with secular life. Both operate within a framework of law: eternal law, natural law, human law, and divine law. For Thomas Aquinas, **law** is "an ordinance of reason for the common good, promulgated by him who has the care of the community." [5]

Eternal law refers to the reason of God ("God's grand design") by which the universe and all things in it are governed. As rational creatures, human beings are able to participate in eternal law through the light of natural reason and to discern what is good and what is evil. Thus **natural law** is that part of the eternal law known through reason. **Human law** is the application, in specific circumstances, of natural law in our earthly affairs. **Divine law**, revealed by God and found in the Scriptures, helps human beings understand natural law while guiding them toward their supernatural end.

The good political life calls for peace, right action, and life-sustaining necessities. According to Aquinas:

> Therefore to establish the good life for a multitude, three things are required: first, that the multitude should be brought into the unity of peace; secondly, that the multitude, having been united by the bond of peace, should be directed to good action . . . ; thirdly, that through the care of the ruler there should be provided a sufficient supply of the necessaries for good living.[6]

Adherence to virtue, the common good, a constitutional regime, and the reign of law would lead to peace, right action, and life-sustaining goods. Thomas Aquinas's ideal political regime is monarchy, which requires virtue in rulers and ruled. His best practicable regime is a mixture of monarchy, aristocracy, and democracy. This regime combines a preeminently virtuous ruler, a virtuous governing elite under the ruler, and shared rule. Aquinas holds that "a government of this kind is shared by all, both because all are eligible to govern and because the rulers are chosen by all." This form of mixed government is "the best form of polity." As Aquinas points out in *Summa Theologica,* it is "partly kingdom, since there is one at the head of all; partly aristocracy, in so far as a number of persons are set in authority; partly democracy, i.e., government by the people, in so far as the rulers can be chosen from the people and the people have the right to choose their rulers."

Constitution, law, common good, and reason are inseparable in Aquinas's conception of the good political life. Those who exercise power must do so constitutionally—within limits ordained by law. Such law—whether natural, divine, or human—protects against the arbitrary use of power. Rulers are thus bound up in a system of law. Power is justified only insofar as it serves the common good. Authority is legitimate because it is reasonable and right. Aquinas defines law as "an ordinance of reason for the common good, promulgated by him who has the care of the community." Thus unlawful rulers are rebels against God's divine system. In extreme cases, when constitutional redress has been tried and has failed, tyrants can be resisted.

For Aquinas, then, the true end for a human being in the political community is a happy and virtuous life. Such a life contributes to the heavenly life. In a partnership guided by the spiritual leadership of the church, church and state can work together toward human fulfillment in this world and in the next.

Aquinas's synthesis of faith and reason, of Christianity and Aristotle, becomes a mighty medieval resource for modern constitutionalism. His belief in a higher law, a common good, the power of reason, and the importance of earthly (as well as heavenly) fulfillment reinforces efforts to overcome arbitrary power and to make government limited and responsible. His appreciation of the need, in politics, to apply sound principles to specific circumstances ensures his continued appeal to the modern mind. Critics of the "Angelic

Doctor" (as Aquinas is known) question what remains of his political philosophy if one lacks his faith in God and his belief in reason. Such skepticism, they argue, undermines the constitutional system Aquinas has created. Niccolò Machiavelli lacked Thomas Aquinas's faith and subscribed to another line of reasoning in quest of a virtuous republic.

THE RENAISSANCE: NICCOLÒ MACHIAVELLI AND THE QUEST FOR A VIRTUOUS REPUBLIC

Machiavelli marks a sharp break from the earlier thinking epitomized by Aquinas; however, it is difficult to understand Machiavelli without a few words about Renaissance politics in his country. During the late fifteenth and early sixteenth centuries, Italy was divided among a number of often-warring states. The papacy was both a religious and a political power. France dominated parts of Italy. Moreover, the Renaissance gave birth to a new secular spirit, which manifested itself in creative activity in literature, art, and architecture and bubbled over into politics, calling traditional religious views into question and inviting bold leaders to demonstrate their talents. Machiavelli, an experienced and resourceful Florentine civil servant, was unquestionably influenced by the energetic mood of the Renaissance as he endeavored to articulate a creative approach to politics.

Machiavelli's thought is paradoxical, and at times confusing, because he had two great political goals. He was first concerned with how to achieve national unity in an Italy characterized by a corrupt people, foreign domination, and internal division caused by the Catholic Church and quarreling nobles. This question elicited his "lion and fox" philosophy, discussed in chapter 1. The second problem that Machiavelli addressed—how to maintain a virtuous republic—is often overlooked, but it can help us understand his conception of the good political life.

Machiavelli is convinced that the political community's vital interests—liberty, independence, self-government, unity, security, power, prosperity, and glory—can best be protected, once national unity has been achieved, in a virtuous republic. His virtuous republic is characterized by civic virtue and by Renaissance *virtù* (energy, will), not by the Christian love of God or by the Greek devotion to justice. Although Machiavelli questions the existence of an ultimate standard that people of reason or faith can know and that might guide them in politics, he still affirms a view of political ends and means that can sensibly guide republics. For a political community to succeed in protecting its vital interests in a virtuous republic, certain elements must be present:

1. A republican government, one that gives the people a significant role in governing themselves, requires a *virtuous people*. They must possess civic virtue: probity, integrity, love of liberty, patriotism, concern for the political community, trustworthiness, and

good sense. A virtuous people must be intelligent, confident about public affairs, disciplined, and concerned about the welfare of the republic.

2. A *mixed and balanced constitution* is Machiavelli's preferred constitution. The equilibrium is to be political, economic, and social. The people will exercise control in policymaking and share governance with nobles under a wise ruler. The balance of people and nobles will contribute to the public good, prevent domination by a single interest, limit power, and keep political actors responsive.

3. *Good laws* are crucial to good republican government. A government under good laws will be stable and prudent. A prince might be superior in making laws, but "the people are superior in maintaining" the laws.

4. *Public opinion and popular participation* are crucial in maintaining the virtuous republic. Freedom to debate and to propose measures for the public good is most important. It "cannot be wrong to defend one's opinions with arguments founded upon reason, without employing force or authority." Elections give people the chance to choose good, capable rulers and to keep those who hold office responsible. Debate and elections allow grievances to be aired and conflicts to be settled peacefully.

5. Machiavelli also believes that the *existence of and competition between parties* makes for republican liberty. In republican Rome, he notes, "all the laws that are favorable to liberty result from the opposition of these parties . . . the nobles and the people . . . to each other."

6. Again and again, Machiavelli endorses the value of a *citizen army* for maintaining a republic. People who fight for their own country, government, security, family, and property will be a reliable bulwark for the republic. When they share power in the republic, they will stoutly defend it.

7. Machiavelli sees the need for *strong and wise leadership,* provided by a public-spirited elite and a virtuous ruler. This leadership will enlighten and guide public opinion. The ruler will be a person of energy, resolve, foresight, and courage, who—along with the elite—will enhance governmental competence and executive vigor.[7]

Machiavelli's republican heritage has often been overlooked by those scandalized by his more notorious call for a "lion and fox" prince. Yet, directly and indirectly, his republican vision has influenced modern liberal democratic societies, especially through his argument for a virtuous people, a balanced and mixed constitution, liberty under law, the competition of parties, and creative leadership. Machiavelli's skepticism about absolute truth (whether classical or Christian), his realistic observation of politics, and his Renaissance commitment to will (energetic activity and hard work) can contribute to toleration, pluralism, and wise and bold efforts to protect our vital interests as best we can in this nonheavenly city. But are the people virtuous enough to govern themselves? Thomas Hobbes, the next political philosopher to be discussed—and the first one in modern political thought—did not think so.

MODERN POLITICAL THOUGHT

We may consider the seventeenth century as the beginning of modernity in political thought. It was then that key modern themes, especially constitutionalism, individualism, and sovereignty, were sounded by philosophers and affirmed in practice. These themes gained even more prominence in succeeding centuries. Constitutional ideas, of course, precede modern times, yet their effective practice had to wait until the late seventeenth century (when Britain's Glorious Revolution of 1688–1689 occurred) and the eighteenth century (when the American and French Revolutions took place).

Thomas Hobbes: The Need for a Supreme Sovereign Leader

The English philosopher Thomas Hobbes, born in the momentous year (1588) that the Spanish Armada invaded the British Isles, experienced the troubled birth pangs of modern constitutionalism. He lived through a civil war (1642–1648); the execution of Charles I (1649); Britain's experiment with a republican government (the commonwealth of 1649–1653); the protectorate of Oliver Cromwell (1653–1658), a military dictatorship; and the restoration of the monarchy with Charles II in 1660. Hobbes died in 1679, a decade before Britain's Glorious Revolution. Little wonder that he was driven to ask: How can one obtain peace and maintain civilization in a troubled time? This question recurs throughout human history and politics. Certainly it was Hobbes's central problem in mid-seventeenth-century England, wracked as it was by civil war.

To appreciate Hobbes's response, we have to understand what disturbs him. He is deeply upset by civil war and the disorder it creates. His image for the unhappy condition of humankind is that of a state of nature, a state prior to society and government, wherein people lived "without a common power to keep them all in awe." Such a state of nature was a state of war, "of every man . . . against every man." Human beings are selfish, self-seeking, materialistic animals. It is no wonder, then, that Hobbes believes in the state of nature:

> There is no place for Industry; because the fruit thereof is uncertain; and consequently no Culture of the Earth, no Navigation, nor use of the commodities that may be imported by Sea; no commodious Building; no Instruments of moving, and removing such things as require much force; no Knowledge of the face of the earth; no account of Time; no Arts; no Letters; no Society; and which is worst of all, continual feare, and danger of violent death; And the life of man, solitary, poore, nasty, brutish, and short.[8]

In such a world, which lacks sovereign authority, the "notions of Right and Wrong, Justice and Injustice have there no place."

By contrast, the good political life calls for peace and a sovereign power, a "Mortall God." Only such a sovereign can maintain peace and order, law and justice. Only such

Thomas Hobbes's concern about the need for peace and order made him a defender of a great and powerful centralized authority, which he called the Leviathan. The front page of his famous book, Leviathan *(1651), included a fanciful image of a giant walking the land. A close look shows that the Leviathan is made up of numerous little people. In pictorial fashion, Hobbes says that the individual must give up political power to the sovereign. In return, all can prosper.*

a sovereign can ensure a civilization of industry, agriculture, science, arts, letters, and commodious living. But how can one move from the state of nature into civilized society under the protection of a sovereign power? Hobbes's answer is a particular kind of social contract that people can make because they possess reason, which urges them to seek peace and their own self-preservation. Consequently, they contract with each other to give the sovereign the power to make law, ensure justice, and advance civilization.

However, this sovereign is not limited by the people, who have contracted with each other (but not with the sovereign) to grant supreme power. Moreover, Hobbes's sovereign is not limited by divine law—since the sovereign determines the meaning of divine law. The sovereign is also not limited by natural law—because the reason of natural law led to the social contract in the first place. Nor is the sovereign limited by civil law, which is the sovereign's own command. Finally, the sovereign is not limited by common law, or custom, since the sovereign assents to common law by his or her silence and also determines the civil law that overrides the common law. Hobbes's logic here is based on the principle that to limit the sovereign is to limit the ability to maintain the very peace and order that the people contracted to obtain.

Of course, the sovereign's common sense will ensure that property and liberty are respected, but only within a framework of peace and order. Beyond the maintenance of peace and order, justice, and national defense, the sovereign need not choose to exercise power. People, therefore, are at liberty "to buy and sell, and otherwise contract with one another; to choose their own aboad [abode], their own diet, their own trade of life, and [to] institute [rear] their children as they themselves see fit."

Hobbes's sovereign may be one person, a monarch (Hobbes's personal preference), or a parliament. What is crucial is not the form of government, but that there be a sovereign power to overcome the "perpetuall war" of "masterlesse men," which jeopardizes security, property, justice, and civilization.

The Hobbesian heritage is mixed. Supporters interested in peace, law, and order understand the logic of a supreme authority that can overcome the war "of every man . . . against every man," which can also be the war of every nation against every nation. They further understand the logic of giving power to an agreed-on authority to protect people from their own self-destructive appetites and egoistic liberties. Others, however, are not convinced. They object to Hobbes's unlimited sovereign power and—like John Locke, our next political philosopher—call for another kind of contract to reach most of Hobbes's objectives. Locke sees more virtue and a different kind of reason in people.

John Locke: Popular, Limited, Responsible, Representative Government

If Hobbes saw the need for a sovereign—a "Leviathan," a "Mortall God"—to maintain peace and order, John Locke (1632–1704) worried about the absence of limitations on sovereign authority. Hobbes wrote during the turmoil of the British civil war in the mid-seventeenth century, whereas Locke's world was characterized by the monarch's constitutional violations of liberty toward the end of the seventeenth century. Is it possible to reconcile liberty and authority? Can one devise a political system to give sovereign author-

ity legitimate power without sacrificing constitutional liberty? Locke's answer was yes, but only if one opts for a governmental system that is popular, limited, responsible, and representative.[9]

Locke holds that people in the state of nature (a presocietal state) enjoy certain natural, inalienable rights, especially those to life, liberty, and property. However, these rights are not fully secure. Unfortunately, there is in the state of nature no common superior person, no common judge, no common executive. There is no established, settled, known rule based on common consent; no known and impartial judge to decide disputes; and no fair, impartial organ to execute the laws. Consequently, people—possessing reason and good will—recognize the desirability of moving out of the insecure and inconvenient state of nature into a state of civil society where they can enjoy their inalienable rights more fully. They do this by means of a **social contract** whereby any number of people (capable of abiding by majority rule) unanimously unite to effect their common purposes. They thus establish a society

Like Hobbes, John Locke was concerned about the need for peace and order in society. However, he also feared tyranny and believed in the necessity of protecting individual rights, in particular, the right to property. Locke, who was born in the shadow of a church, also was a proponent of religious tolerance.

and a body politic. They create governmental organs to make law, resolve disputes, and execute the law. The common legislative and executive power is thus directed toward peace, safety, and the public good.

The government is therefore based on *popular consent.* The legislature is the supreme power in the commonwealth because the people consent, via the contract, to put trust in the legislature. The government is *limited* by the very nature of the contract. Neither the legislature nor the king can act arbitrarily. Both are required to act within constitutional limits. The legislature, for example, cannot take a person's property without that person's consent or the consent of his or her representatives. The king cannot hinder the legislature from assembling or acting freely pursuant to its constitutional powers. The government is to be *responsible* to the people. It must honor the terms of the social contract that empowers it, terms that obligate it to protect life, liberty, and property. Moreover, the government is *representative;* the people are to judge whether their representatives in the legislature (parliament) and their executive (king) act in accord with their trust.

Revolution is the people's ultimate weapon if government becomes tyrannical and violates the social contract—if it arbitrarily deprives people of life, liberty, and property. The people will, of course, invoke this right of revolution only when the government's violation of its trust is clear to a majority and persists, and when all other constitutional attempts to redress grievances have been tried and have failed.

Locke has been both hailed and condemned as the father of liberal democracy. His supporters argue that liberal democracy rests on the constitutional protection of life, liberty, and property by a government that is limited, representative, popular, and responsible. They maintain that Locke has successfully reconciled liberty and authority. Locke's critics attack the conservative implications of his defense of property, because it leads to inequality of wealth and power. Among Locke's critics is Jean-Jacques Rousseau.

Jean-Jacques Rousseau: Popular Sovereignty through the General Will

Jean-Jacques Rousseau (1712–1778) criticizes Locke's political philosophy. Rousseau continues to probe the problem of political obligation and to seek a more democratic solution. He asks: What principles of political right make government legitimate, "men being taken as they are and laws as they might be"? [10] "The problem," as he sees it, "is to find a form of association which will defend and protect with the whole common force the person and goods of each associate, and in which each, while uniting himself with all, may still obey himself alone, and remain as free, as before." Rousseau's solution is yet another version of the social contract: a unanimous agreement to associate under the **general will**. "Each of us puts his person and all his power under the supreme direction of the general will, and, in our corporate capacity, we receive each member as an indivisible part of the whole." This social contract also removes people from an inconvenient and inadequate state of nature (where they enjoy only natural liberty) and creates a moral civil society—with a unity, identity, life, and will of its own. In this society people have civil and moral liberty and better opportunity to fulfill themselves. The general will that guides their development is the constant will—the best, long-range will—of the sovereign people; it is the public good or public interest; and it is always right. In this way sovereign authority becomes: (1) *legitimate* because it is based on unanimous agreement, not on force; (2) *equitable* because it is common to all; (3) *useful* because sovereign authority can have no other object than the common good; and (4) *stable* because it is guaranteed by the public force and supreme power in the political community.

According to Rousseau, the general will works to the public advantage and is the public's best long-range interest. The general will does not include selfish private interests. It resides in the majority, yet it is not necessarily identical with majority rule. It may be found by counting votes, yet it is not found simply in counting votes. It is the true will of all the people. The people are sovereign under the direction of the general will. Sovereignty is inalienable and indivisible, and it cannot be represented. Thus the people cannot be separated from their sovereign power and they cannot allow representatives to make policy on their behalf. The sovereign people control their government's policy and personnel, its form, and its membership. The government merely executes the people's will. In this way the people remain free because obedience to self-prescribed law is liberty. Thus Rousseau "rediscovers" the democratic political community and its role in advancing the fuller civil and moral liberty of those in the community. Only such a community is capable of the good political life.

Rousseau's political philosophy, too, has its proponents and opponents. Democrats applaud his endorsement of popular sovereignty and a fuller democracy. Advocates of the common good praise his conception of the general will as an idea that can transcend selfish, shortsighted interest and can bind us together in recognition of a public interest that makes fulfillment possible. Libertarians, on the other hand, worry about Rousseau's argument that we can be "forced to be free," that we can be required, under law, to do what is right. They see Rousseau as opening the door to dictatorship or to "totalitarian democracy." Political realists doubt whether Rousseau's concept of direct democracy is either desirable or feasible. Still others wonder if the good political life can be based on so nebulous a standard as the "general will." Edmund Burke, although he had a strong sense of community, did not share Rousseau's radical outlook.

Edmund Burke: Prescriptive Constitutional Government

Edmund Burke (1729–1797) asks whether a prescriptive or historical constitution, prudently interpreted, is the best means to a sane balance that will preserve the right values, principles, and institutions for the political community.[11] This is Burke's central question in the last quarter of the eighteenth century, a period that witnessed the outbreak of two great democratic revolutions—the American Revolution in 1775 and the French

Revolution in 1789. Burke's "Old Whig" answer is a resounding yes. But to understand his answer (and his support of the American colonists, his hostility to the French Revolution, and his mixed attitude toward reform in Britain), it is necessary to understand what he means by (1) "prescriptive constitution," (2) "balance," (3) "political community," and (4) "prudence."

1. By prescriptive constitution Burke means a constitution—or way of political life—that is the historical choice of successive generations, the successful inheritance of those who have gone before, and the embodiment of the wisdom of the species over time. Such a prescriptive constitution has passed the "solid test of long experience." The British Constitution is one such constitution, which Burke sees as a fortress of genuine natural rights. Justice, private property, instruction in life, and consolation in death are the rights of human beings in and under a prescriptive constitution. Burke contrasts such real rights with the theoretical, abstract rights, such as liberty, equality, and fraternity, delineated in the French Declaration of the Rights of Man. These abstract rights of man did not take sound tradition into account. They ignored other values in society—peace and order, morality and religion, civil and social manners, the need for a police power and for an effective and well-distributed revenue.

2. Burke sees the British Constitution as a **balance of principles**—monarchic, aristocratic, and democratic. He sees the British Constitution as "a monarchy directed by laws," balanced by an aristocracy (which encompassed the nation's great hereditary wealth, dignity, and leadership), and controlled by the democracy, the "people at large" (in the House of Commons). Burke sees the British Constitution as a successful attempt "to unite private and public liberty with public force, order, peace, justice, and above all, the institutions formed for bestowing permanence and stability" on the nation through the ages. Balance, of course, does not rule out necessary change. Indeed, the British Constitution is based on the principle of progressive inclusion of all politically minded people in the life of the state and on the enlargement of liberty. Only radical innovation is to be avoided.

3. Burke views the state—the *political community*—as a high and noble association. It is not to be seen as temporary, perishable, or crassly utilitarian. Such a state deserves to be approached with reverence; even its defects should be viewed with awe and caution. "It is a partnership in all science; a partnership in all art; a partnership in every virtue, and in all perfection." The state is "a partnership not only between those who are living, but between those who are living, those who are dead, and those who are to be born." [12]

4. But the people must interpret the prescriptive constitution prudently if they wish to achieve the good political life. *Prudence* means giving attention to sound principles as well as to circumstances. The people must understand political actualities

thoroughly and avoid dogmatic, abstract theorizing. They must exercise foresight. Although they reject radical innovations, prudent people see the need for sensible change. In the case of the American colonies, for example, Burke is convinced that the abstract principle of parliamentary supremacy should not prevent Britain from conceding autonomous home rule to the colonies, thereby creating practical independence within the British Empire. This wise course of action is suggested by both his interpretation of the British Constitution and specific circumstances: the Atlantic Ocean that separates Britain from its American colonies; a flourishing Anglo-American trade; and America's "fierce spirit of liberty" (rooted in British notions of liberty, in popular colonial governments, and in the colonialists' "republican religion"). On the other hand, Burke opposes the French Revolution because he thinks the French revolutionaries are extremists in rejecting the old French Constitution and in ignoring the mandate of prudent statesmanship—to combine "an ability to improve" with a "disposition to preserve."

Burke can be viewed as the father of enlightened constitutional conservatism or an opponent of radical democracy. He makes a powerful case for the prescriptive constitution and for prudent statesmanship. His criticism of radical democratic theory is hard hitting. However, his political philosophy may seem too respectful of the status quo, not sufficiently aware of the need for more fundamental and speedy change in the interest of constitutional equality, fraternity, and liberty. A political philosopher more open to change was John Stuart Mill.

John Stuart Mill: Utilitarianism and Liberty

What principles of liberty and authority best guide the individual's and society's quests for happiness through fulfillment? The answer of John Stuart Mill (1806–1873) provides one influential response. Mill bases his liberal political philosophy on several assertions.

Despite recognizing the weaknesses of **utilitarianism**, Mill still adheres to the "creed which accepts as the foundation of morals 'utility' or the 'greatest happiness principle.' " This creed "holds that actions are right in proportion as they tend to promote happiness; wrong as they tend to produce the reverse of happiness. By happiness is intended pleasure and the absence of pain; by unhappiness, pain and the privation of pleasure." [13]

However, Mill insists on a noble interpretation of the utilitarian standard. He recognizes a hierarchy of pleasures and absorbs traditional concepts of justice and virtue. According to Mill, "pleasures of the intellect, of the feeling and imagination, and of the moral sentiments" rate more highly than mere sensation or "the animal appetites": "It is better to be a human being dissatisfied than a pig satisfied; better to be Socrates dissatisfied than a fool satisfied." Superior pleasures should be determined on the basis of the "decided preference" of knowledgeable people of taste and discernment. Mill clearly prefers the

John Stuart Mill was one of the great defenders of individual freedom, and his most famous work, On Liberty, *was published in 1859. Mill, who was also an early feminist, wrote a defense of women's rights in* The Subjection of Women *(1869). He always maintained that many of his ideas came from his wife, Harriet Taylor.*

pleasures of the cultivated mind interested in science, art, poetry, history, and social science. He sees humankind as slowly progressing in its battle against evils of life such as indigence, disease, unkindness, and worthlessness. He sees a harmony between the individual's interest and the public interest. He is convinced that the utilitarian standard will, in time, discredit the false "aristocracies of color, race, and sex," as it has already discredited the "injustice and tyranny" of slavery and serfdom.

Mill endorses representative, constitutional government because of the way it melds liberty and authority. Such a government would permit popular control of the legislature, legislative (or parliamentary) control of the executive, and strong and skilled executive leadership. Mill favors as much popular participation as possible. "But since all cannot, in a community exceeding a single small town, participate personally in any but some very minor portions of the public business, it follows that the ideal type of a perfect government must be representative." [14] The educated and publicly spirited minority should be given a prominent voice in Parliament through a system of proportional representation and plural voting.

Liberty, for Mill, is the means to happiness through fulfillment. In *On Liberty* Mill explores the nature and limits of power—particularly the power that society can legitimately exercise over the individual. His key principle is "that the sole end for which mankind are warranted, individually or collectively, in interfering with the liberty of action of any of their number is self-protection." Mill maintains that "the only purpose for which power can be rightfully exercised over any member of a civilized community, against his will, is to prevent harm to others." Mill is not convinced that an individual's "own good, either physical or moral," is a sufficient reason for interfering with his or her liberty. In brief, a person is to be free in connection with his or her "self-regarding action." Society can interfere only when the individual's action is harmfully "other-regarding." Consequently, Mill defines the sphere of human liberty as that sphere wherein society, as distinct from the individual, has only an indirect interest. He singles out three fields of human liberty: (a) "the inward domain of consciousness" (liberty of belief, thought, and feeling, and freedom of speech, press, and opinion); (b) "liberty of tastes and pursuits"; and (c) "liberty of combinations" (or associations).

Mill seeks a **modified laissez-faire political economy** that is compatible with liberty, the satisfaction of human needs, and the advancement of individual and social happiness. He opposes monopoly and dislikes governmental interference. But he is not blind to the need for sensible regulation of industry to protect workers' health, safety, and welfare. (Here Mill partly opens the door to the modern welfare state.) In successive editions of *On Political Economy,* he becomes more willing to modify a strict laissez-faire economic system. He moves toward allowing workers greater voice and control, especially through cooperative ventures. (Here he opens the door slightly to a modest variety of democratic socialism.)

Mill is by no means a radical democrat. He opposes giving the suffrage to the "poorest and rudest class of labourers." Nonetheless, in *The Subjection of Women* (strongly influenced by his wife, Harriet Taylor Mill), he writes a powerful essay on behalf of greater freedom for women. Indeed, Mill can fairly be called one of the most eloquent nineteenth-century sponsors of women's liberation. He argues that happiness for individual women cannot be achieved unless they are given greater opportunity, recognition, suffrage, and equal education—in a word, true equality. The happiness of society depends on women being more fully admitted into the life of the nation. Mill emphatically insists "that the principle which regulates the existing social relations between the two sexes—the legal subordination of one sex to the other—is wrong in itself, and now one of the chief hindrances to human improvement; and that it ought to be replaced by a principle of perfect equality, admitting no power or privilege on the one side, nor disability on the other." [15]

Modern liberal democracy embodies a great many of Mill's principles: his powerful argument on behalf of liberty of thought and discussion, his utilitarian concern for happiness, his preference for representative government, his growing attention to the welfare of workers, and his bold advocacy of women's liberation. Yet his political philosophy still provokes a number of disturbing questions. Is utilitarianism strong enough to protect constitutional democracy, human liberty, and the least free? Is Mill's position too elitist, too aristocratic for the modern world? Does he really come to grips with worker alienation and capitalist abuses? For more radical ideas about liberty and emancipation, we turn to Karl Marx.

Karl Marx: Universal Human Emancipation via Communism

How can universal human emancipation be achieved? This is the radical question posed by Karl Marx (1813–1883).[16] His answer is no less radical: via the proletarian—or communist—revolution. Marx's philosophy will be explored in greater depth in chapter 8; however, it is appropriate to briefly summarize the key points of his views about politics in this chapter because Marx is an important contributor to debates about what the good life means.

First, Marx has a vision for humanity that values human freedom. Freedom will not be complete until the most alienated and oppressed—the workers—have overthrown "all the conditions" that keep people "abased, enslaved, abandoned, contemptible." Marx, in *The Economic and Philosophic Manuscripts,* sees this problem as arising from people's estrangement from what they produce, from their work; this contributes to most people's alienation from their own humanity and their fellow human beings. His vision of the good life is predicated on liberating people from oppression and letting them work on endeavors they want to work on.

Second, Marx believes that this challenge is best overcome by understanding the economic conditions of society. Thus he spends an enormous amount of time analyzing capitalism and explaining how it exploits workers—leading to their alienation and limiting human freedom. Capitalists control the means of production, and furthermore, the state, religion, law, and ethics all reflect the values and beliefs of those capitalists who control the world. If the world is viewed in this light, political equality and economic equality become central goals in creating a world in which human beings are free.

Finally, although Marx is persuaded that capitalism's own weaknesses—its lust for profits at the expense of the worker and its vulnerability to economic crisis—create the conditions for its inevitable downfall, to achieve the good communist society, a revolutionary reconstruction of society is necessary. (Capitalism also contributes to this process by creating the working class that will eventually rise up in revolution.) The old bourgeois capitalist order must be destroyed and replaced by a communist order based on worker control of the means of production and exchange. There will be a revolution that occurs in stages: first, the revolutionary overthrow of capitalism; then, the interim "democratic" dictatorship of the proletariat; next, the stage of socialism; and finally, communism. Peaceful reform is not likely to achieve communism. Marx says relatively little about what communism will look like; however, we can get some glimpse of what it means and appreciate its radical egalitarianism by recalling the communist motto: "From each according to his ability, to each according to his needs."

Marx's contribution to modern political thought was to systematically analyze the transformative power of capitalism; provide a compelling vision of an egalitarian society, a theory of history that emphasized materialism; and develop an alluring theory of revolutionary action. To his critics, Marx fails to understand human nature and is too utopian in his call for a classless society. Many others fault his materialist theory of life—saying such a theory places too much emphasis on the economic and physical forces that shape our lives and fails to appreciate the transcendent—God, spirit—in history. Still others believe that Marx failed to appreciate capitalism's ability to adapt to new conditions, and they reject Marx's emphasis on a violent revolution to achieve a better society.

CONTEMPORARY POLITICAL PHILOSOPHY

Contemporary political philosophy, as it becomes intertwined with political ideology, is examined more fully in the following chapters. Here only a few preliminary observations are in order.

First, contemporary political philosophy can only be understood as an outgrowth of the great tradition that we have attempted to sample in the preceding pages. Contemporary political philosophers are deeply versed in the classic tradition. In addressing modern problems and circumstances, they draw inspiration from that tradition. In doing so they often attempt to present a vision of the good political life that, as we have tried to suggest, must deal with political actualities and prudential judgments as well as with ideals.

Second, the great tradition of political philosophy has clearly influenced not only political philosophers but also those who are called political scientists. William T. Bluhm has persuasively argued that "the classic theories furnish the foundations of nearly all the work which is being done today in the field of politics, work which is as vital and varied as the constellation of the classics." [17]

Third, even the analytical political philosophers, some of whom have given up the search for the good political life, continue the dialogue on a good political life. Even as they reject key aspects of the great tradition, they articulate their own conception of a good political life, a position that may owe much to the insights of certain political philosophers. They may, for example, reject Plato or Aquinas and yet accept Burke or Mill.

Fourth, new and creative voices in political philosophy must always be heard. Political philosophers may try to retain the best in the classical and modern tradition while they address the unique problems of the twenty-first century. Indeed, many argue that political philosophy is exactly this ongoing dialogue between our understanding of past thinkers and our ability to think creatively about new problems and challenges.

The great political philosophers most often wrote in the heat of crisis. Creative political philosophy was born out of real difficulties faced by real political actors and communities. As we assess the contemporary scene, we should be open to the creative work of today's political philosophers and their efforts to address our difficult problems in the light of a great tradition.

CONCLUSION

And so we return to our guiding question in this chapter: How have the great political philosophers contributed to the difficult quest for the good life and a fuller understanding of politics? They offer critically examined visions of the good life. They force us, whether we agree or disagree, to confront political ideals, political actualities, and prudent judgments. They require us to think through the standards we would employ: justice, the common good, order, happiness, individual fulfillment, liberty, equality, and fraternity. These political standards are also significant for empirical inquiry. They lead us to examine the use and abuse of power, the proper functioning of institutions, and the consequences of operative ideals. They encourage us to give normative meaning to empirical measurements so that, by assessing relevant facts, we can determine whether we are politically healthy. In this way we can sensibly appraise data about war and peace, poverty and prosperity, slavery and freedom, and inequality and equality. Finally, determining standards for the good political life leads to prudent judgment, which is what we also call political wisdom. Means can be truly prudent only if they are humanely and rationally calculated to achieve good ends. Guided by critically understood standards of the good political life, we can assess the character of political behavior, politics, and institutions and determine whether they are wise or foolish, feasible or infeasible. The political philosopher, in exploring the good political life, thus facilitates the political scientist's three major tasks—normative recommendation, empirical inquiry, and prudential judgment.

SUGGESTED READINGS

To explore the contributions of the great political philosophers to the good life and to a fuller understanding of politics, there is absolutely no substitute for reading their original writings. They have endured for good reasons. Also see:

Arendt, Hannah. *The Human Condition.* Chicago: University of Chicago Press, 1958. A thoughtful attempt to analyze how people work and act together politically. Suffused with reflections about many of the writers discussed in this chapter.

Barker, Ernest. *Principles of Social and Political Theory.* Oxford: Oxford University Press, 1956. Argues on behalf of justice as the concept that balances liberty, equality, and fraternity. Mature reflections of a distinguished student of political thought.

Bernstein, Richard J. *The Restructuring of Social and Political Theory.* New York: Harcourt Brace Jovanovich, 1976. Maintains, in agreement with Jürgen Habermas, that the primary task of "critical theory" today "is the reconciliation of the classical aim of politics—to enable human beings to live good and just lives in a political community—with the modern demand of social thought, which is to achieve scientific knowledge of the workings of society."

Brecht, Arnold. *Political Theory: The Foundations of Twentieth-Century Political Thought.* Princeton: Princeton University Press, 1959. Holds that scientific political theory can contribute to the defense of the good life, enlarge our knowledge of politics, and deepen our "wisdom-of-action" in political affairs. But it cannot establish the absolute validity of ultimate standards.

Dworkin, Ronald. *Sovereign Virtue: The Theory and Practice of Equality.* Cambridge: Harvard University Press, 2000. Well-known and respected political and legal theorist's interpretation of the importance of equality in a democratic and liberal state.

Flathman, Richard, ed. *Concepts in Social and Political Theory.* New York: Macmillan, 1973. A helpful, intelligent introduction to the analytic, linguistic, and conceptual approach to political and social philosophy.

Kaus, Mickey. *The End of Equality.* New York: Basic Books, New Republic Books, 1992. Provides a journalist's view of the need to conceptualize equality.

Rawls, John. *A Theory of Justice.* Cambridge: Harvard University Press, 1971. A highly influential argument on behalf of justice as fairness.

Riemer, Neal. *Creative Breakthroughs in Politics.* Westport, Conn.: Praeger, 1996. Explores two genuine historical breakthroughs (Roger Williams and James Madison), two spurious breakthroughs (John C.

Calhoun and Karl Marx), a contemporary breakthrough still in progress (European Union), and a proposed future breakthrough.

Sabine, George. *A History of Political Theory.* New York: Holt, 1937. A balanced, critical, and humane history, even though written from the perspective of "social relativism."

Tinder, Glenn. *The Political Meaning of Christianity: An Interpretation.* Baton Rouge: Louisiana State University Press, 1989. Concerned with Christianity's contribution to civility via the exaltation of the individual, agape, prophetic hope, liberty, and social transformation.

Wolin, Sheldon. *Politics and Vision.* Boston: Little, Brown, 2004. An influential look at the great tradition of political theory and its relevance to our contemporary concerns.

GLOSSARY TERMS

aristocracy (p. 125)
balance of principles (p. 138)
democracy (p. 125)
divine law (p. 129)
eternal law (p. 129)
general will (p. 136)
human law (p. 129)
law (p. 129)
modified laissez-faire political economy (p. 141)
natural law (p. 129)
oligarchy (p. 125)
polis (p. 124)
polity (p. 126)
social contract (p. 135)
timocracy (p. 125)
tyranny (p. 125)
utilitarianism (p. 139)

Chapter 7

LIBERAL
DEMOCRACY

Beginning with this chapter and the following chapter, we will identify and try to clarify the major ideologies that have traditionally dominated contemporary politics—liberal democracy, democratic socialism, and communism. We thus shift from the classical political philosophers and their conceptions of the good political life to modern politics and its guiding views of the good life in the contemporary world. **Political ideologies** are the beliefs and practices that guide political actors in political communities. These ideologies reflect the underlying vision of political actors, and studying the ideals that inspire political leaders often illuminates political practice. These ideals—of course—are not always fully achieved, but they help explain the purposes, principles, and rules of politics. By studying ideologies we thus pay attention to what political actors say they ought to do as well as to what they actually do. In addition to identifying and clarifying ideologies, we will address the strengths and weaknesses of political ideologies such as liberal democracy, democratic socialism, and communism by considering the ideals of the good life advanced by the great political philosophers discussed in earlier chapters.

Chapters 7 through 9 will thus help readers (1) critically explore the good political life in contemporary politics; (2) locate themselves on the modern political spectrum (left, center, or right; radical, liberal, conservative, or reactionary); (3) understand the reasons for their political positions; and (4) set the stage, through a critical exploration of the meaning of the good political life, for the fuller analysis of comparative politics in part 3 and for the more thorough considerations of public policy in part 4.

The central question in this chapter is, *What are the strengths and weaknesses of liberal democracy?* We will focus primarily on the United States. This chapter is divided into four sections: discussion of the main ideas that define liberal democracy; analysis of its historical roots; discussion of its strengths and weaknesses; and assessment of its current liberal and conservative variations in the United States.

TOWARD A DEFINITION OF LIBERAL DEMOCRACY

Although the ideal of **liberal democracy** is open to continued reinterpretation, there are a number of continuing themes that animate this ideology. As you can see in the name, liberal democracy embodies two great ideals.[1] The *democratic* ingredients in liberal democracy include popular rule, freedom, and equality. These ideals are complex and open to continued debate about what they mean. For instance, the call for greater popular participation in politics remains a persistent cry of radical liberal democrats—although it is highly unlikely that Americans will abandon representative government and move toward any form of **direct democracy** (as embodied in the New England town meeting of the seventeenth century), where citizens vote directly on matters of public policy.

The *liberal* ingredients in liberal democracy include constitutionalism, protection of basic rights—including the right of private property—political and economic competition, and free choice both at the ballot box and in the marketplace. But, as we shall see, **liberalism** in the United States has changed from a **laissez-faire** position (where government has relatively little interference in the economy) to one that favors government intervention in the interest of public welfare, social justice, and fair play. The U.S. Constitution has been interpreted to permit these changes. Of course, liberalism has always recognized a common good. What has often been at issue is the meaning of that common good and the means to achieve it.

Combining these two ideals helps us see the guiding liberal democratic vision. Such a vision calls for the freest and fullest possible realization of individual freedom within the framework of the common good. Individuals must have the opportunity, within justifiable limitations, to develop the best in themselves. The Preamble to the Constitution captures many of the objectives of a liberal democracy when it states that the United States will "establish justice, insure domestic tranquility, provide for the common defense, promote the general welfare, and secure the blessings of liberty." The liberal democratic vision is not a single vision; it is a pluralistic vision providing for justice as well as order and for the general welfare as well as liberty. Because many persons, groups, and interests seek fulfillment, a balance must be struck in a highly diverse political community.

The most influential school of liberal democratic thought in contemporary America—the **pluralist school**—maintains that this balance can best be achieved through a constitutional system of representative democracy, with the help of skillful leaders and resourceful political parties, with the recognition that a rough approximation of the public interest emerges from the clash of contending interests, and in accord with policies that advance the general welfare.

THE IDEALS OF LIBERAL DEMOCRACY

Liberal democrats want their political ideals to be reflected in actual political practice. They endorse pluralism because society includes many interests seeking to protect and advance themselves. The struggles of these contending interests constitute the raw material of politics. Struggles are inevitable because they are rooted in liberty and diversity. Government regulates these struggles on behalf of freedom and the common good.

But, liberal democrats insist, government itself must be controlled and politics kept honest, and the struggle for power must be kept within bounds. This struggle must be consistent with justice, domestic tranquility, the common defense, the general welfare, and liberty—it must be civilized. Politics contributes to this civilizing process, which, at its best, allows fuller individual realization. The civilizing process requires decent rules and decent results in politics. Contending interests must accommodate each other. Basic human needs must be satisfied, and there must be opportunities for social, economic, aesthetic, and spiritual enrichment. To advance their vision, liberal democrats support the following operative ideals.

Popular Government. Popular rule requires that the people make political judgments. They must be free to debate and to select among competing leaders, parties, and broad policies. To make choices, the people must enjoy civil liberties that permit them to evaluate how the government operates. They must be able, especially, to assess the character and performance of parties and political leaders. Thus the liberal democratic system is committed to **civil liberties** and universal suffrage. The system is also committed to an informed and vigilant public opinion, to a diligent and responsible press, to a plurality of contending interests able to articulate their claims, and to competitive parties. Such elements protect the people's vital interests and help fulfill their needs and aspirations.

Iraqis queue to vote at a polling station in Az Zubayr, Southern Iraq, on January 30, 2005. They were among roughly 8.3 million Iraqis who turned out for their first democratic election in nearly half a century. While not without its flaws, many nevertheless considered the election a remarkable achievement—especially in light of a violent insurgency movement that tried to disrupt the process by stirring up the deep ethnic divisions that plague the country.

Rights-Respecting Government. Basic democratic rights are both political and nonpolitical. As we have seen, freedom of speech, press, and assembly, as well as the right to vote, are clearly political and are intimately related to popular rule. People cannot shape public policy unless they can speak, read, and write about public issues; assemble and organize in political parties or other interest groups; and exert political pressure through the vote. They need these rights to rule indirectly and to control the government.

Other freedoms and basic rights are nonpolitical, but they are equally vital to liberal democracy. These religious, cultural, economic, and social rights include, for example, the right to worship according to the dictates of conscience; the right to think one's own thoughts; the right to express one's intellectual, artistic, and scientific ideas; the right to own property; the right to find a job of one's choice; and the right to marry and have children. There is, then, a realm of activity that must be beyond governmental reach and should be safeguarded by a constitutional government that grants, prohibits, and restricts power.

Constitutional Government. In the liberal democrat's preferred system of constitutional politics, power is granted to government, but it is also limited. Thus the constitutional rules of the game establish what government can and cannot do and how those with power are to act.

Some powers, such as the powers to tax, to spend on behalf of the general welfare, and to regulate commerce, may be expressly granted. Other powers may be granted if necessary and proper to carry out expressly granted power. Limits on governmental power—explicit prohibitions—exclude government from entering areas such as religion and thought. But even when exercising its legitimate powers, government cannot act arbitrarily; it must follow due process to ensure the protection of life, liberty, and property.

Moreover, because of the fear of unrestrained and arbitrary power in the United States, power is divided and shared. The American ideal of constitutional government puts the concept of balance to work in several ways: (1) a balance of governmental organs (in the national government)—two branches of Congress, a president, a Supreme Court; (2) a balance of geographical units (ensured by federalism)—the national government, the fifty states, and the District of Columbia; and (3) a balance of social, economic, and political forces.

Representative Government. Liberal democrats favor **representative government** because they believe it is the realistic way for the people to govern. Extensive direct democracy—citizens voting directly about policy—is not feasible. In a democratic and constitutional system, the electorate usually chooses representatives with the organizing help of political parties. Government leadership is determined, directly or indirectly, by majority or plurality decision.

But what does representative government really mean in liberal democratic theory? Liberal democrats do not agree on the meaning. They answer the question of who the representative should—and can wisely—represent in at least two ways.[2] Each position illustrates an aspect of the liberal democratic theory of representation, and each position creates difficulties. Some liberal democrats believe that representatives should be delegates, democratically representing primarily (if not solely) the will of the majority of the people who elected them. Other liberal democrats object. They argue that it is not easy to know the will of the majority. They also contend that elections rest on powerful political and economic interests in the constituency rather than on the hard-to-recognize and transient majority. Furthermore, there are those liberal democrats who look on representatives as trustees who, once elected, act on behalf of the higher interests of the whole political community (past, present, and future), following their perception of the nation's good. But some critics, objecting to this view, hold that representatives are elected by the people and should represent the people and not their own consciences; others say the representatives are elected as members of a political party and should represent the party and not their own conceptions of the public interest. Of course, these concepts of representation simplify politics quite a bit. Various other forces are always at work when politicians make their decisions. For instance, many liberal democrats argue that representatives should be partisans fulfilling a party platform; however, party platforms may be vague and not fully understood by citizens. Many liberal democrats admit that representatives are politicians who must constantly balance many conflicting claims on their judgment.

Responsible Government. Responsibility in a liberal democracy also has several interrelated meanings:

1. Liberal democratic government should be accountable to the people from whom it derives its power. More accurately, in the United States the government must be answerable to the electorate or a majority or plurality within the electorate. (By way of contrast, in Great Britain the government is directly answerable to a majority party or a coalition of parties in the House of Commons and is indirectly answerable to an electoral majority or plurality in the country.)
2. Liberal democratic government should be responsible to the political party that puts candidates and choices before the people, helps elect a president, ensures a majority in Congress, and in general facilitates decision making and public policy.
3. Liberal democratic government should be responsible to the Constitution and to the laws and regulations made under the Constitution. Government may be called to account if it violates its own operating rules.
4. Liberal democratic government should be answerable to an authority higher than the people or the Constitution. Government may be answerable to God, to natural law, or to conscience (as it reflects a higher authority).
5. Finally, those in government—whether the president, members of Congress, members of the Supreme Court, or millions of bureaucrats—should be responsible to

professional standards of conduct and administration established by their peers, past and present, in and out of government.

In liberal democratic politics the effort is made to ensure governmental responsibility to "rules of the game" through various means of accountability: elections, public opinion, a free press, party discipline, interest group pressures, an independent judiciary, legislative and administrative investigation, impeachment, and administrative supervision.

General Welfare Government. Modern government in the United States is clearly committed to the idea of advancing the general welfare. As a liberal democratic operative ideal, this means that minimal needs—safety, civil liberties, income, food, housing, health, education—should be satisfied through the democratic process and in a caring and compassionate community. The liberal democratic nation stands ready to protect these needs, indirectly and directly, when private organs (the family, the church, and charitable organizations) and state and local governments cannot do so. Debate rages, however, on the desirable extent and character of such help.

We should be able to use the foregoing operative ideals to determine whether a nation is a liberal democracy. Affirmative answers to the following questions will characterize a liberal democracy:

1. Do most people really have the opportunity, by means of genuinely free elections, to select the people and policies that will govern the nation? Is the government truly based on the consent of the governed?
2. Do the people enjoy the right to speak, write, publish, and assemble freely in order to criticize the government, parties, and leaders in power?
3. Is there at least one independent opposition political party or coalition that is realistically able to supplant the governing leadership if, in a free election, the people turn the incumbents out?
4. Do the people enjoy the right to worship as their consciences dictate, participate in religious or spiritual life through a free organization (church, synagogue, mosque, or meeting) of their own choice, and pay allegiance to a higher power than the secular state? Do they have the right to refrain from worship?
5. Are people protected against the kind of arbitrary and unreasonable action by government that would deprive them of life, liberty, and property without **due process** of law? (Due process is here understood to forbid two kinds of governmental action: action such as the systematic destruction of a religious group, race, or class, or spuriously "legal" action such as a trial based on false evidence or coerced confession. The first action should be beyond the power of government in a liberal democracy. The second is flawed because false evidence and coerced confessions violate proper legal conduct.)

6. Is the state's role limited to certain legitimate and necessary public functions, or does the state dominate the cultural and social life of the community? Is the state, for example, forbidden to dictate which books to read, which plays to see, which radio and television programs to tune in, and which clubs and organizations to join?

7. Is the state prevented from becoming so economically powerful that it not only controls the modes of production and exchange (and the livelihood of all citizens) but also uses its economic power to nullify political freedom and dominate other aspects of society such as church, press, and education?

8. Is the state willing and able, if necessary, to enhance the physical and environmental safety of its citizens, guard their civil liberties, ensure their minimal income, assist the unemployed, feed and house the needy, enhance health care, and facilitate education? (In other words, is the state willing to advance its people's minimal welfare needs?)

Where did this list of liberal democratic ideals come from? In the following section, we will examine the sources; in doing so, we will be in a better position to understand the complexity of these liberal democratic ideals and see how variations are possible.

THE SOURCES OF LIBERAL DEMOCRACY

Political ideologies have a historical life and development, and political ideals and their implementation are significantly influenced by events. Contemporary conceptions of the good life did not emerge full blown. Many strands have entered into the political ideology known as liberal democracy. Although its roots—in theory and practice—are old, its flowering (despite great growth in the late eighteenth and nineteenth centuries) is a mid-twentieth-century phenomenon.

The Greek Heritage of Democracy. The word *democracy* comes from the Greek words *demos,* meaning "the people," and *krateia,* meaning "rule" or "government." Hence, democracy means "the people's rule." Aristotle understood democracy as government by the many poor, who governed in their own class interest and favored freedom and equality. Democracy meant the rule of the less wealthy and less educated citizen-masses in contrast to that of the plutocratic and aristocratic classes. But democracy in the Greek sense was not constitutional in the modern sense: it lacked effective and regularized restraints on those who wielded power. Moreover, Greek democracy excluded women and slaves from the suffrage. Nonetheless, the Greek democratic ideal did eventually stimulate the imagination of Western Europe. Pericles, a popular Athenian leader, in his great "Funeral Oration," gave a famous accounting of what democracy means when he said it included equal justice, excellence, opportunity, public reverence for the laws, citizen involvement in public affairs, and sound democratic judgment. Although Athenian democracy was incomplete, and some would say unstable, Pericles' conception perpetuated a noble ideal.

Christian Theology and Roman Republicanism. By insisting on absolute freedom to worship God, Christians began a development that was to culminate, first theoretically and later practically, in constitutional protections against governmental interference with religious worship and in constitutional limitations on arbitrary political power. At first, Christians worried about their right to worship God. However, over centuries this led to a general belief that all people had a right to worship God as they saw fit. People must be free to worship God. Moreover, all men and women are equal under God; they are brothers and sisters under a common deity. Both Christian theology and Stoic philosophy emphasized equality, another concept crucial to liberal democracy. Of course, Christianity's attitude toward women has varied in its accepted practices. Yet, at its heart, Christianity emphasized the equality of all people before God. However, it took a long time for moral equality to become translated into political, social, and economic equality. Slavery characterized the Roman period and was, we must remember, not abolished in the United States until 1865.

The Romans made a twofold contribution. They helped keep alive, at least in theory, the concept of **popular sovereignty** (republican, or popular, rule), and they broadened the concept of citizenship. For the Greeks, all foreigners were barbarians and were excluded from citizenship. The Romans, however, eventually extended citizenship, which brought with it the protection of Roman law, to all who came within the jurisdiction of their empire, whether Roman, Greek, Christian, or Jewish.

Medieval Europe. Constitutional ideas, crucial to the evolution of liberal democracy, were current in medieval political theory. Almost all theorists contended that political rule must be just and in the interest of the people. No earthly ruler was absolute. The theorists insisted that princes (rulers) follow the precepts of a higher law: God's law or natural (moral) law, which could be known by humans possessed of "right reason." Of course, political practice in the medieval world fell considerably short of modern canons of democratic and constitutional governance.

The Protestant Reformation. Martin Luther and John Calvin, the great Protestant reformers, were not modern liberal democrats. In most respects they shared a medieval Christian outlook about politics. Although they believed in a higher law, they still took a dim view of popular resistance to political tyrants. Nonetheless, their revolt against the Roman Catholic Church, and some of their ideas, set the political and intellectual scene for the emergence of constitutional ideas crucial to liberal democracy. Of special importance were Luther's idea of the freedom of individuals to find God on their own and

Calvin's concept of the legitimacy, in very limited cases, of resistance to political rulers by certain magistrates.

The American Republic: The First Great Democratic Experiment. The American Revolution ushered in the world's first large modern republic. Building on Lockean constitutional principles (see chapter 6), on colonial experience in self-government, and on a physical environment that favored widespread possession of property, the Americans made important contributions to the eventual development of liberal democracy. Americans also drew on the republican tradition. As noted above, this tradition has roots that stretch back to Rome and was an important aspect of the work of such writers as Niccolò Machiavelli (see chapter 6) and James Harrington (see chapter 5). *Republicanism* was a highly contested term, but it always included some notion of constitutional rule by the many. Despite the property qualifications (actually relatively modest) that prevailed in most states in 1787 and the fact that African Americans, Native Americans, and women were excluded from the ballot and denied other freedoms, the Americans affirmed their general belief in popular rule and the protection of basic rights.

Both the logic of republican, or democratic, theory and the pressure of disenfranchised groups contributed to a growing movement to enlarge the suffrage and expand basic freedoms. In time the commitment to **liberty** and **equality** made slavery an anomaly, revealed the racist treatment of Native Americans, and highlighted sexist discrimination against women. In addition, it underscored the exploitation of workers, the often perilous economic situation of farmers, and the miserable lot of the poor. Of course, battles had to be fought to expand popular rule and human freedom, but almost all were fought to fulfill the American people's understanding of a democratic constitution.

One of the great—and controversial—events that contributed to the rise of liberal democracy was the French Revolution. In this famous painting, Liberty Leading the People *(1830),* the French artist Eugène Delacroix captures the intensity and romantic ideals of an entire nation united in an effort to overthrow tyranny. The painting, now hanging in the Louvre, was hidden soon after it was painted, for fear that it would stir up public unrest.

The French Revolution of 1789 and Liberal Democracy in Europe. Although the British had pioneered constitutional and representative government, it was the French Revolution of 1789 that most dramatically challenged political absolutism and popularized democratic ideas throughout the European continent. The inspiring motto of the French Revolution, "Liberty, Equality, Fraternity," became the political watchword of European liberal democracy in the nineteenth century.

Nationalism—above all a powerful sense of group identity and loyalty—and liberalism joined in a powerful movement against absolutist governments. For a number of countries this led to national independence, greater political freedom, and more popular rule. Increasingly, more liberal laws and constitutions (guaranteeing basic rights, enfranchising more groups, and providing for greater popular control of government) were secured. However, setbacks for liberal democracy (Napoleon's dictatorship in France, the defeat of liberal forces in the several revolutions of 1848, and battles against such "iron" chancellors as Germany's Otto von Bismarck) emphasized that liberal democratic forces on the European continent were incomplete and shaky.

In addition to its contribution to democracy, the emergence of nationalism in the late eighteenth century added a psychological dimension to the way political scientists label countries, namely as **nation-states**. As indicated above, nationalism is a sense of group identity, of belonging. In contrast, **state** is a legal term for the entity we know as a country, requiring people, territory, government, and acceptance by the international community.

LIBERALISM, CAPITALISM, AND DEMOCRACY

The rise of the nation-state, at least in Europe, led to the spreading of ideas about democracy, constitutional government, and the liberal ideal of individual rights. Of course, liberal democracy had its critics, but the nineteenth century witnessed the continuing intermingling and spread of these ideas. This occurred first in Europe and then throughout the rest of the world.

Liberalism began as a movement for political, economic, social, and cultural freedom. It was strongly endorsed by the growing middle class and its allies, because such freedom protected and advanced their vital interests. These interests included a stronger role in government; safeguards for religion, speech, press, assembly, and due process; freedom from adverse governmental actions in the economic domain (that is, governmental monopolies, economic regulations, and restrictions); and the opportunity for freer choices in politics, economics, and society.

The French Revolution symbolized the triumph of the middle class—the bourgeoisie—over a royal monarchy, a feudal aristocracy, and an established church. The French Revolution was not only a political triumph of republicanism over monarchy and of more genuinely constitutional government over autocracy; it was also an economic triumph of the middle class over the feudal aristocracy. Further, the revolution was a social triumph of the middle class and its allies among peasants and workers over feudal and church privilege. It was also a cultural and intellectual triumph of largely middle-class writers, artists, and thinkers over monarchical and religious censorship and oppression.

The concurrence of the American and French Revolutions with the Industrial Revolution and the emergence of **capitalism** is not accidental. The year 1776 saw both the American Declaration of Independence and the publication of *The Wealth of Nations*. Written by Scottish economist Adam Smith, *The Wealth of Nations* became the inspiration for the nineteenth- century liberal policy of restricting governmental interference in economic matters. The new capitalists favored a hands-off policy in the economy, except where it would benefit their enterprise. They wanted governmental policy to favor private enterprise.

The links between liberalism and capitalism, and between liberalism and democracy, are a little clearer than the connection between democracy and capitalism. For example, liberalism and capitalism share a common interest in economic freedom. Similarly, liberalism and democracy share a common interest in freedom, including economic freedom. Of course, capitalists and other members of the middle class share a democratic interest in popular rule and the protection of basic rights, especially when suffrage is limited to people of property and when governmental policy does not interfere with capitalistic enterprise. However, an expanded franchise may lead to policies that protect workers and their needs, and such policies may cut into the power and profits of capitalists. Moreover, capitalists and democrats may disagree on which basic rights to protect and how to protect them. Especially in the United States, middle-class liberals dedicated to freedom, including economic freedom, may join with working-class men and women to fight capitalistic abuses that threaten freedom and jeopardize the fulfillment of human needs.

However, we cannot deny that modern democracy emerged and grew up alongside the economic system of capitalism. Moreover, private ownership of the means of production and exchange, a market economy, economic competition, and consumer sovereignty in the marketplace still command widespread popular support in the United States. Historically, there can be little doubt that liberal democracy—committed to each person's political, economic, social, and cultural freedom—forged ahead with the growth of an essentially capitalistic middle class. Certainly in Europe, the new middle class used liberal democratic principles to gain greater economic, political, and social powers at the expense of absolutist governments and feudal aristocracies. In the United States, where there was no significant feudal aristocracy to overthrow and where the abundant riches of the frontier beckoned, free and enterprising Americans welcomed the opportunities to advance their economic status in a political economy free of government's interfering hand.

As liberalism, democracy, and capitalism began to interact, the ideal of liberal democracy began to evolve. Many of the debates over the past hundred years have involved the question of how political regimes balance, in a practical way, market pressures (capitalism), the rule of the people (democracy), and the desire for individual freedom (liberalism).

The Changing Character of Liberalism

Liberalism changed significantly between the nineteenth and twentieth centuries. Many nineteenth-century liberals, originally committed to a very limited government, began to believe in the wisdom of more government intervention in economic and social life. Such liberals made this shift in pragmatic response to capitalistic abuses that hurt farmers, small businesspeople, workers, and consumers. Those people who were hurt protested private monopolies, unfair trade practices, tight money, low farm prices, low wages, bad working conditions, and adulterated food. These protests were heard particularly in bad economic times. Legislation to regulate trusts and railroads came at the federal level as early as 1887. Other important

The Works Progress Administration (WPA) was part of President Franklin D. Roosevelt's New Deal program to put to work those unemployed during the Great Depression of the 1930s. It also marked an unprecedented degree of government activism that changed the way liberalism was understood in the United States. Here WPA workers construct a playground on Chicago's South Side.

legislation—involving, for example, banks and impure food and drugs—came after the turn of the twentieth century. The new twentieth-century liberalism did not fully emerge, however, until the advent of the New Deal, a program initiated by President Franklin D. Roosevelt to fight the Great Depression of the 1930s.

The New Deal ushered in a government strongly dedicated to the general welfare. Government attempted to stabilize prices, provide jobs, stimulate the economy, regulate banking, strengthen labor's right to organize and bargain collectively, provide for unemployment compensation, ensure a fair minimum wage, guarantee a decent retirement income via Social Security, and provide cheaper electric power. In succeeding decades these reforms opened doors to more reforms in education, health, and housing; provided more generously for those in need; ensured the right to vote for African Americans; enhanced cultural opportunities; and protected the environment.

The Changing Character of Democracy

Democracy in the United States has changed significantly in the past two hundred years. Although the American founders saw themselves as republicans, they did not extend the right to vote to poor white men, to women, or to most blacks, slave or free. And slavery persisted until the Civil War. Americans adhered in theory to what we today call democratic principles: rule by the people, through majority decision, in a representative and constitutional system that protects individual and group rights and the freedoms of both majority and minority. But in practice their conception of popular rule and basic rights—although remarkably advanced for its day—was not democratic by modern standards.

Although the old fear of democracy as rule by the many poor and ignorant (the classic Greek model, as in Aristotle) remained, the republican-democratic demand that suffrage be extended could not be denied. Moreover, the word *democracy* began to replace republicanism as the key concept characterizing the American republic. In 1835, when Alexis de Tocqueville searched for a title for his perceptive study of the young United States, he chose *Democracy in America*. Abraham Lincoln also recognized democracy as popular government in his memorable phrase in the Gettysburg Address: "government of the people, by the people, and for the people."

Yet the wider use of the term *democracy* and a truly universal suffrage had to await the twentieth century. *Democracy* gained great popularity and prestige in the United States and throughout the world early in the century thanks to President Woodrow Wilson (1913–1921). This began with Wilson's reforms of the U.S. government but was extended by his efforts to characterize World War I as a war to defend democracy. Practical and legal obstacles to universal suffrage, however, were not fully overcome until fairly late in the century. American women did gain the right to vote with the passage of the Nineteenth Amendment in 1920: "The right of citizens of the United States to vote shall not be denied or abridged by the United States or by any state on account of sex." But limitations on the right of African Americans to vote persisted into the 1960s. And the poll tax was not outlawed in federal elections until the passage of the Twenty-fourth Amendment in 1964. (A poll tax is a fixed amount for all adults, and its payment is usually a requirement for voting.)

As people—regardless of sex, race, or property holdings—acquired the right to vote, they also theoretically gained the power to protect their needs and their welfare within a constitutional system. They have not used this power to destroy constitutional government, the rule of law, minority rights, or private property, as conservative critics of democracy feared. Instead they have used their political power to address the content of legislation. They have become increasingly concerned with social and economic laws to advance the fuller life of the many.

With these roots and this evolution in mind, we are in a better position to outline and understand the operative ideals of liberal democracy in the United States today.

VARIATIONS ON THE LIBERAL DEMOCRATIC THEME

Despite the great variety of groups that populate the American political landscape, most Americans are liberal democrats. This may sound odd to many readers; however, despite the important differences in the United States between what we call liberals and conservatives, or between Democrats and Republicans, the average American politician and

Figure 7.1 Issue Dimensions and Ideological Categories

		Government intervention in economic affairs	
		For	*Against*
Expansion of personal freedoms	*For*	Liberal	Libertarian
	Against	Populist	Conservative

Source: William S. Maddox and Stuart A. Lilie, *Beyond Liberal and Conservative: Reassessing the Political Spectrum* (Washington, D.C.: Cato Institute, 1984), 5.

citizen adheres to the major ideals we have outlined—popular, constitutional, rights-respecting, and responsible government, and even the concept of government dedicated to the general welfare. Of course, they may interpret these ideals differently. One way of looking at American politics is to divide it into four groups: **liberals, conservatives, populists**, and **libertarians**.[3] Each of these groups emphasizes a different aspect of the liberal democratic tradition. Thus American liberals see themselves as more tolerant, generous, willing to experiment, and progressive than conservatives. American conservatives see themselves as more respectful of traditional values and institutions (private property and enterprise, family, church, and established governmental authority) than liberals; they may favor liberty over equality on some issues (for example, affirmative action) when these two ideals clash; they see themselves as preserving responsible initiative, a richly textured community life, and standards of excellence in a world driven toward uniformity, novelty, and crass materialism. American populists generally tend to favor government intervention in economic affairs and may oppose expansion of some "liberal" personal freedoms. American libertarians rather consistently oppose government intervention in economic affairs and favor expansion of personal freedoms. This fourfold classification may bring liberals and populists together on some issues of pro-government action in the economic realm, and conservatives and libertarians together on some issues of antigovernment action in the economic realm. It may also bring liberals and libertarians together on some issues of personal liberty, and conservatives and populists together on some issues of personal and social morality. Figure 7.1 highlights the cardinal features of this fourfold classification.

So American liberals, conservatives, populists, and libertarians differ on how to safeguard democratic ideals and the guiding vision of human realization in the American republic. They differ, especially, on three interrelated points: (1) their concern for the least free, (2) their view of the role of government, and (3) their attitude toward change. We will concentrate here on the perspectives of American liberals and American conservatives, indicating where they agree or disagree with populists and libertarians.

We should note, though, that American politics is driven by the two-party system. Obviously, there will be difficulties in fitting four major versions of liberal democracy into only two parties. The Democratic Party is now the home of most liberals and the Republican Party can count on the loyalty of most conservatives. However, when we consider populists and libertarians, the alliances and party loyalties become more complicated.

American Liberals

First, American liberals in general favor a greater concern for the least free and the least powerful in society—poor people, ethnic minorities, women, working people, small farmers, small-business owners, and consumers. Like populists, they seek to expand popular power and overcome abuses of economic, social, and political power. American liberals seek to end oppression, injustice, poverty, and inequality. Libertarians, by contrast, are concerned with protecting individual freedom of both the rich and poor.

Second, American liberals are willing to employ the power of government, especially the national government, to seek changes on behalf of fair play for the least free and the least powerful. Populists, too, favor government action to protect groups such as farmers, workers, or small investors from what they deem the unjust or oppressive action of such powerful economic forces as industrial corporations and banks. American liberals and populists favor broader measures to advance the general welfare. Libertarians are generally opposed to government intervention in economic and social affairs.

Third, American liberals are more favorably disposed to political, economic, and social change to accomplish the objectives mentioned in the preceding paragraphs. They are not afraid to alter the status quo to permit a liberal democratic society to live up to its own ideals. On some economic issues, populists may share with liberals this more favorable attitude to change. Libertarians, as we have noted, take a dim view of governmental changes affecting the lives of people.

American Conservatives

First, while many American conservatives are genuinely concerned about the most needy in society, they are deeply skeptical of the ability of government—particularly the federal government—to solve the problems associated with poverty. They often believe that such programs are wasteful and inefficient. They also may make more distinctions than liberals between who is deserving of help and who may, through their own actions, not be worthy of government aid.

Second, American conservatives generally endorse a laissez-faire position; they are opposed to adverse government interference in their economic, political, and social affairs.

Libertarians, more consistently than conservatives, hold to a laissez-faire position. Conservatives do not object when government acts to support private enterprise and profit, which they see as crucial to freedom and prosperity. But conservatives are suspicious of intervention on behalf of the least free (whether in the form of school busing to overcome segregation or of affirmative action programs, which conservatives see as reverse discrimination). Conservatives normally favor a strong defense establishment and a balanced budget.

Third, American conservatives seek to maintain the existing economic, political, and social scheme of things. They are reluctant to abandon that which is known—tried and true and of proven value. They may, however, endorse changes that favor traditional values and institutions. Libertarians take a more consistent position in opposing government economic and social regulations affecting individual or corporate freedom.

AN ASSESSMENT OF LIBERAL DEMOCRACY

Liberal democracy, as we have seen, has different variations. Furthermore, it has critics on both the left and the right. In this section, we evaluate the strengths and weaknesses of liberal democracy.

The Defense of Liberal Democracy

Liberal democracy's defenders argue that its guiding vision and ideals enable Americans to achieve a greater measure of civilized life, healthy growth, and creative fulfillment than is possible under any other political ideology. They maintain that more people enjoy more freedom, equality, and prosperity under liberal democratic regimes. A liberal democracy has three key advantages or strengths that make it appealing.[4]

First, it is remarkably adaptive to changing circumstances and it shows a willingness to change and evolve. Democracy's defenders acknowledge its historic and contemporary shortcomings but point out that over time the United States moved successfully toward universal suffrage, freed the slaves, and checked plutocratic abuses of economic and political power. Despite severe trials, democratic institutions demonstrated a remarkable ability to cope with great difficulties. For example, Americans were able to respond to the worst effects of the Great Depression by shaping a state judiciously balanced between liberty and equality, freedom and security.

Second, a liberal democracy is able to effectively respond to the worst examples of tyranny and the abuse of power, so prevalent in the twentieth century. Responding to friendly critics such as Reinhold Niebuhr, who urged liberals to face the harsh realities of evil and power, Americans learned to mobilize countervailing power against abusive forces at home and abroad. For example, laborers formed unions to protect their interests. Demonstrating the organizational ability of a free people in an open society, the

United States mobilized to defeat German fascism and Japanese militarism in World War II, a mighty feat of skill and courage. Then with great imagination, the United States helped Western Europe and Japan recover from the ravages of war with remarkable speed. America's foreign policy achievements included leadership in establishing the United Nations, the Marshall Plan to reconstruct war-torn Europe, and the North Atlantic Treaty Organization to protect Western Europe against Soviet aggression.

Finally, a liberal democracy is realistic about politics, and this creates a stable regime. To many students of politics, there is a danger that politics can become messianic—that in the search for the good life unrealistic expectations about what human beings can be and achieve are created. Liberal democracy is not prone to such thinking. The recognition of the rich diversity of life and the acceptance that individuals must be as free as possible to develop themselves as they see fit encourages a tolerance of many perspectives about life and politics. Politically this results in a pluralistic system that values the representation of many interests, balancing those interests and fostering compromise between competing political forces.

To its defenders, liberal democracy is a great historical achievement, a landmark in the evolution of human civilization. It has largely worked out the rules of the political game to strike a proper balance between individual freedom and the common good. It legitimizes government power but provides effective restraints on the exercise of that power to protect individual rights. Government is responsible to the people's representatives, and these representatives are responsive to the people. Liberal democratic politics avoids the worst features of both "lion and fox" and utopian politics, while realistically safeguarding vital community interests.

The Attack on Liberal Democracy: Left and Right

Radical, democratic, communitarian, and socialist critics on the left contend that American liberal democracy has failed to fulfill its own promise. These critics are concerned that not enough people participate in the modern democratic state. They protest that individuals are not really free but rather are confined in an exploitive economic and social system characterized by inequality that is nourished by racism and sexism and magnified by a lack of genuine concern for the least free. While seeking to protect and expand civil liberties, these critics advocate using the state's powers to advance greater social and economic justice. They are worried about the harmful consequences of a still largely laissez-faire economy and the persistence of the "vandal ideology of liberalism" (an ideology of reckless waste) and the "theory of possessive individualism" (a theory of selfish individualism).[5] They argue that Americans worship private property, profits, and free enterprise at the expense of a healthy society, a meaningful community, and the common good. They emphasize that the United States is an affluent, largely white, democratic nation-state in a globe that is poor, mostly nonwhite, and either unprepared for or hostile to liberal democracy.

Aristocratic, individualistic, and capitalist critics on the right worry that liberal democracy has degenerated into mobocracy, serfdom, and socialism. They worry about the threat to such liberal democratic principles as representative democracy and equality of opportunity. They see dangers in participatory democracy: the decline of prudent judgment, submission to the ignorant, and loss of quality. They worry about replacing equality of opportunity with a doctrine of equality of results, about reverse discrimination and other programs of preferential treatment. They worry, too, about the triumph of vulgarity, meanness, and mediocrity in our social and cultural lives. They bemoan the loss of individual moral character and responsibility. They fear that the state's growing bureaucratic power to regulate economic affairs will undermine private property and enterprise as bastions of freedom. These critics deplore governmental controls and the encroachment of centralized state power. They favor limited government and are happiest when governmental power is in their hands and is used only to advance their purposes. They are traditionally opposed to big spending for welfare, unless it is their own welfare.

Certain weaknesses in liberal democracy, according to other critics, need attention and correction: (1) a faulty ethical vision; (2) a deficient empirical understanding; and (3) a timid prudential assessment. These critics do not share the more accepting "realistic" perspective of those pluralists set forth above.

Faulty Ethical Vision. Ethically, according to these critics, the vision of liberal democratic politics is faulty. The liberal democratic understanding of American politics has historically excluded Native Americans, African Americans, women, and the poor. Recent efforts to correct this faulty vision are incomplete. Although working people have fared reasonably well, Americans have never forthrightly faced the problem of worker alienation and democratic direction of the economy. Unemployment continues to plague too high a percentage of the working force, with the unemployment rate among African Americans double or triple the figure for adult whites. As a people, Americans have been wasteful with their natural resources of land, water, timber, and minerals, and have demonstrated a shocking disregard for ecological health. Americans may have limited the tyrannical power of government, but they have not seriously questioned abuse of human and natural resources. Americans have not adequately protected against the "vandal" aspects of liberal ideology.

For the critics, the American sense of responsibility for the least free, for the environment, and for the future is weak. Politicians have too frequently been the rich and the powerful. They have lacked concern for the quality of the American union, for a just and caring community. Proponents of liberal democracy have been complacent in appraising it. Americans have been too tolerant of existing evils and have lacked a firm conviction of a common good that would ensure a more desirable political order.

So liberal democratic politics today suffers from a too easy acceptance of the status quo and the prescriptive constitution. Americans too often act as if they have reached the pinnacle of wise political evolution. They tend to accept the rhetoric of liberal democratic ideals as reality and to close their eyes to ugly truths. Those who support liberal democratic politics may forget to dream. Unless prodded, liberal democratic politicians may lose a passionate and imaginative commitment to a better future.

Deficient Empirical Understanding. Empirically, the ideology of liberal democracy is deficient. It has refused to examine how ethics, economics, and ecology influence politics. It has not properly studied how group pressures affect public policy. It has been blind to the reckless and wasteful aspects of liberalism. By focusing too sharply on the status quo, it has neglected the weak, the poor, and the oppressed. It has ignored underlying forces that will become dominant. It has overlooked new possibilities. It has never fully explored the relationship between a capitalistic economic system and a democratic order. Its commitment to incremental change has prevented more radical criticism. It has often failed to acknowledge the gulf between the principles and the practice of liberal democracy.

A powerful existing system often conceals important political forces, seemingly invisible forces that do not come to our attention except in periods of crisis, riot, and revolution. To miss the underlying forces of today that will dominate tomorrow is to miss future possibilities and actualities. This deficient empirical understanding is manifested in a wrongheaded view of change. Politics is too often seen in terms of balance and hence in terms of maintaining the status quo. Politics based on progressive change does not allow for radical and rapid change—the kind that may sometimes be needed to handle some crucial contemporary problems.

These generalizations come to life most dramatically in the neglect of African Americans, women, and the poor in an often racist, sexist, and blindly affluent society. Liberal democratic politics also seems congenitally unable to promote satisfaction and creativity in work—human beings' most basic life activity.

Timid Prudential Assessment. Prudentially, liberal democratic ideology is too timid. It is often wrongly conservative instead of rightly conservative; for example, it preserves racism and sexism and prefers property rights to human rights. It is often too hesitant. Liberal democrats are often unwilling to try bold new economic, social, and political experiments. Too frequently they prefer stability to change, the known to the unknown. They may, for example, have waited too long to clean up the environment and to revive mass transportation. Guided by a timid ideology, liberal democrats have been too slow to attack admitted evils such as the drug problem, homelessness, and AIDS.

Liberal democratic politicians may lack the passion and the vision to act wisely. They may be wrongly convinced that most of the ways ordained by the prescriptive Constitution are sound for the present and future. Consequently, they will be unreceptive to creative political breakthroughs that could, for example, significantly reduce crime, drug abuse, pollution, and cancer, and assure adequate employment, health care, and housing for all Americans.

Unfortunately, the motto of the liberal democratic politician— "to get along one must go along"—often transforms genuine prudence into weak-kneed timidity and makes bold political action impossible. And so a desirable tension between what ought to be and what is—one that nourishes courageous judgment in politics—disappears. Modern "realistic" revisions of liberal democratic ideology have hastened the disappearance of this tension. These revisions mistakenly reflect a lack of faith in the intelligence and capability of the common people, in the pos-

In the wake of the July 2005 bombings of the London transit system, New York City police began random searches of bags of passengers entering the city's subway system. Some question whether such searches were a violation of their civil liberties.

sibility of identifying a common good, and in more radical alternatives to the status quo. These revisions call for democratic elitism (leadership by an elite responsible to competing political parties), acceptance of the approximate justice in a public policy hammered out by contending interests, and a complacent appreciation of life in a welfare state.

There are good reasons to critically analyze these revisions. For example, the judgment of what David Halberstam called the "best and the brightest" turned out to be defective in the Vietnam War.[6] The governing elite's temptation to guard state security by fair means or foul reveals a failure of leadership. Vietnam, the Watergate and Iran-contra scandals, and the foolish coddling of Iraq before the Persian Gulf War in 1991 illustrate the persistence of questionable "lion and fox" politics in the liberal democratic state.

Seeing public policy as a result of group pressures frequently leads politicians to endorse the order imposed by the powerful. Such an order may benefit the powerful— whether corporations or labor organizations—but does it benefit weaker forces in society? We must ask how it helps the larger public made up of unorganized consumers.

These critical inquiries suggest a need for the bolder judgments that are the very stuff of creative breakthroughs in politics. We are challenged to explore those judgments that might enhance the vitality of liberal democratic politics.

CONCLUSION

In our presentation of liberal democracy we deliberately stressed the importance of democratic and constitutional principles. Constitutional principles preceded the liberal democratic state and were incorporated into its politics. These principles will, and must, endure in any future democratic political order.

One of the hallmarks of democratic liberalism is its ability to adapt. Groups that were once excluded from politics, such as African Americans, women, and workers, have used constitutional and democratic principles on their own behalf. Moreover, they may use such principles on behalf of a common good that transcends all classes—capitalist or working class, white or African American, male or female. Historically, excluded groups have broadened both constitutionalism and democracy by demanding inclusion. In spite of being self-interested, these claims enhanced society's understanding of the common good, of legitimate human interests and needs, and of the linkage between democratic power and constitutional protection.

Of course, as we have seen, liberal democracies can be criticized for being overly cautious in expanding democracy at times and a bit too complacent about the inequities created by capitalism. However, at their best, liberal democracies have avoided the horrible excesses of so many other ideologies that captured the imaginations of people in the twentieth century. Thus the liberal democracies avoided the disastrous policies that were pursued by fascists such as Adolf Hitler or communists such as Joseph Stalin.

Probably one of the greatest challenges facing liberal democracies in the twenty-first century is how to continue balancing freedom and equality. Certainly liberal democracies are wedded to the idea of personal freedom, and this is most powerfully expressed in the freedom allowed by the free market. Yet this very freedom can lead to remarkable levels of economic inequality. At the same time, any effort to alleviate this disparity (through the redistribution of wealth, for instance) can be attacked, particularly by the conservative and libertarian variations of the ideology, as restricting liberty and creating an overly powerful government. This challenge, somewhat successfully met in the past, will remain a persistent problem in the coming years. And, if liberal democrats fail in this task, the call for a more egalitarian politics will emerge with renewed vigor.

SUGGESTED READINGS

Dahl, Robert. *On Democracy*. New Haven: Yale University Press, 1998. An excellent introduction to the key concepts and challenges of the ideal of democracy. Deftly explores the economic questions that pervade recent discussions about the development of democracy.

Galston, William. *Liberal Purposes: Goods, Virtues, and Diversity in the Liberal State*. New York: Cambridge University Press, 1992. A thoughtful defense of liberalism.

Glassman, Ronald M. *Democracy and Equality: Theories and Programs for the Modern World*. New York: Praeger, 1989. Argues that achievement of democracy and equality requires Americans to build on—but find correctives for—liberal democracy. Finds correctives for liberal democracy and capitalism in Aristotle, John Maynard Keynes, and John Rawls.

Hartz, Louis. *The Liberal Tradition in America*. New York: Harcourt, Brace, 1955. Building on Alexis de Tocqueville's brilliant *Democracy in America* (1835, 1840), Hartz emphasizes why and how the United States has avoided the extremes of left and right and adhered most often to the vital center.

Lowi, Theodore J. *The End of the Republican Era*. Norman: University of Oklahoma Press, 1995. A provocative exploration of the "End of Liberalism," the "Republican Era," the "Conservative Era," the "End of Conservatism," and "Restoring the Liberal Republic." See also Lowi's earlier *The End of Liberalism* (New York: Knopf, 1969)—a critique of interest group liberalism and a plea for the rule of law—and Theodore J. Lowi and Benjamin Ginsberg, *Embattled Democracy: Politics and Policy in the Clinton Era* (New York: Norton, 1995).

Maddox, William S., and Stuart A. Lilie. *Beyond Liberal and Conservative: Reassessing the Political Spectrum*. Washington, D.C.: Cato Institute, 1984. Convincingly argues on behalf of broadening the ideological categories of liberal democracy to provide room for populists and libertarians as well as liberals and conservatives, with each group defined by its views on government intervention in economic affairs and expansion of personal freedoms.

Niebuhr, Reinhold. *The Children of Light and the Children of Darkness*. New York: Scribner's, 1944. An unflattering critique of soft-headed idealists, moralists, and pacifists, and a resounding defense of democratic realism. Provocative.

Parenti, Michael. *Democracy for the Few*. New York: St. Martin's Press, 1988. A sharp, hard-hitting criticism of American politics and society as benefiting primarily the rich and the powerful, the greedy rather than the needy.

Riemer, Neal. *The Future of the Democratic Revolution: Toward a More Prophetic Politics*. New York: Praeger, 1984. Chapter 4 assesses the strengths and weaknesses of liberal democracy from the perspective of a model of prophetic politics.

———. *The Revival of Democratic Theory*. New York: Appleton-Century-Crofts, 1962. Bases his case for a reinvigorated democratic theory on eight orienting concepts: political theory as a prudent guide to action; individual realization within the framework of the common good; sensible dimensions of maneuver; the prudential logic of realization; democratic and constitutional accommodation; majority rule; pluralistic and conditional obligation; and constant rescrutiny of democracy's well-calculated risks.

Slater, Philip. *A Dream Deferred: America's Discontent and the Search for a New Democratic Ideal*. Boston: Beacon Press, 1991. Contends that the democratic megaculture requires the complete rout of authoritarianism—military, political, economic, social, religious, educational, medical, and psychological.

Spitz, David. *Patterns of Anti-Democratic Thought*. New York: Macmillan, 1949. A keenly reasoned defense of democracy against a wide variety of critics.

Zakaria, Fareed. *The Future of Freedom* New York: Norton, 2003. Argues that democracy is not always a good thing—that it depends on the right circumstances for it to flourish and not decline into a kind of authoritarianism.

GLOSSARY TERMS

capitalism (p. 156)

civil liberties (p. 148)

conservatives (p. 159)

direct democracy (p. 147)

due process (p. 151)

equality (p. 154)

laissez-faire (p. 147)

liberals (p. 159)

liberal democracy (p. 147)

liberalism (p. 147)

libertarians (p. 159)

liberty (p. 154)

nationalism (p. 155)

nation-state (p. 155)

pluralist school (p. 147)

political ideologies (p. 146)

popular sovereignty (p. 153)

populists (p. 159)

representative government (p. 149)

republicanism (p. 154)

state (p. 155)

Chapter 8

DEMOCRATIC SOCIALISM AND COMMUNISM

Ideologies of the Left

As the twenty-first century dawned, it appeared that liberal democracies had won the day. The ideology that underpins those democracies, which we explored in chapter 7, had many converts and champions, particularly in the United States and Western Europe. The fall of the Soviet Union indicated that the appeal of communism was waning.[1] Many countries in Eastern Europe adopted some form of democracy and initiated market reforms that might lead to a capitalist system so familiar to Americans.

However, the story of recent politics is much more complicated. A number of countries, such as China, Cuba, North Korea, and Vietnam, still maintain an allegiance to some form of communism. Even more numerous are the nations that hesitate to embrace all the ideals of liberal democracy, particularly that of a free market. Despite the current popularity of liberalism and democracy, there continues to be a vibrant leftist tradition that offers a powerful critique of liberalism in nations such as France, Greece, Finland, Belgium, and the United Kingdom. Furthermore, the left offers its own version of the good life and how to achieve that life with a different set of government institutions and an alternative arrangement of the economic sphere.

Students of politics need to be aware that the triumph of liberal democracy is neither all encompassing nor necessarily permanent. Change is a constant in the political world, where great transformation of politics can occur with little warning, a truth clearly illustrated by the dramatic—and generally unpredicted—collapse of the Soviet Union in 1991. As stated earlier, a powerful critique of the liberal democratic tradition continues to exist. What unites these critics, from moderate socialists to traditional communists, is the importance of **egalitarianism** as a political goal. Whereas liberal democrats believe that personal freedom is the most important basis for the good political society, many other people believe that equality should be the starting point (and ending point) of any theory of politics. No matter how breathtaking the changes in politics we have witnessed in the past fifteen years, the call for human equality remains compelling to many. The debate, among those on the left, is how best to achieve this egalitarianism and whether human freedom is sacrificed in reaching the left's goal of economic and social equality.

In this chapter we explore the ideologies of the left: namely, democratic socialism and communism. Although the two are related and share some common history and, at times, a common set of ideals, they are distinct ideologies, with important differences, that need to be examined individually. Therefore this chapter will be divided into three sections. First, we will define democratic socialism, describe its intellectual sources, and offer an assessment of its strengths and weaknesses. Next, we will provide the same analysis of communism. Finally, we will consider the recent changes in democratic socialism and communism and offer some thoughts about the future of each ideology. The central questions that readers need to think about in this chapter are, *In what ways do the ideologies of the left offer a powerful criticism of liberal democracy? How are democratic socialism and communism different from each other and from liberal democracy? In what ways do these three ideologies share similar goals and beliefs?*

Gerhard Schroeder bids farewell to party delegates during his last speech as Democratic Socialist chancellor of Germany November 14, 2005. Schroeder had found his position weakening with, among other problems, a significant decline in party membership from roughly one million in 1976 to six hundred thousand in 2005.

DEMOCRATIC SOCIALISM

One of the oldest egalitarian political theories is called democratic socialism. While this theory is not spoken of frequently in the United States, it has played an important part in the political tradition of Europe.

Toward a Definition of Democratic Socialism

Democratic socialism, as the term clearly indicates, combines democracy and socialism. But because there are many varieties of both democracy and socialism, it is not an easy term to define. In fact, democratic socialism combines several ideas. *Politically,* it involves a commitment to popular, constitutional rule and the protection of basic rights. *Economically,* it involves an equitable distribution of the community's wealth. To ensure this equitable distribution, democratic socialists maintain, key aspects of economic life must be publicly owned or socially controlled. Democratic socialists are especially concerned that workers have a voice in their economic (and political and social) destiny and that human needs (particularly those of the least free) are adequately satisfied. *Socially,* democratic socialism involves the belief that all human beings, in a cooperative community, should have the opportunity to fulfill their good and creative potential.

The Ideals of Democratic Socialism

In their pursuit of social justice, democratic socialists believe that a society must be organized in such a way that all people can develop their basic human potential. In achieving such a society, there are six key ideals that underlie democratic socialist thinking:

1. *Adherence to the main tenets of liberal democracy.* These tenets include such concepts as popular rule and protection of basic rights. Thus democratic socialists fully accept the principles of parliamentary government, majority decision making, and peaceful constitutional change. However, they go beyond these democratic and liberal ideals; traditionally, democratic socialists have sought to advance the cause of economic democracy, and this goal requires strengthening trade unions, passing laws to protect labor, advancing worker voice and control in industry, and encouraging cooperative societies. There is, however, no unanimous, single policy to expand economic democracy. In a fundamental sense, the extension of social democracy involves a continuing battle against social privilege, whether related to a snobbish and limiting educational system or to social inequalities produced by unearned wealth.

2. *A belief in public ownership.* Democratic socialists believe that public ownership of key aspects of the economy is essential to public well-being. The rationale for the common ownership of the means of production, distribution, and exchange is that there should be collective enjoyment of the fruits of labor. The case is strongest for those industries at the commanding heights of the economy. Furthermore, industries that are monopolies—public utilities such as railroads or electric companies—should be nationalized to serve the community. And private industries that have been inefficient and failed to meet public needs (the coal industry in the United Kingdom, for instance) should be nationalized.

3. *Mixed economy.* There is a strong belief that the economy should be controlled both privately and publicly—a **mixed economy**. This includes governmental intervention in, and regulation and control of, the economy on behalf of employment, economic productivity, and prosperity; decent conditions of work; and a more equitable sharing of the common wealth.

4. *An extensive welfare state.* Democratic socialism insists upon an extensive **welfare state**, one that provides social services to ensure a better family life, health, and housing; protection against unemployment; and security in old age. There is a strong belief that the state should protect citizens from cradle to grave and the realities of poverty must be addressed by any legitimate government.

5. *A global perspective.* Democratic socialism champions its ideals for all human beings. Thus democratic socialists speak of a unity of all workers around the globe, of freedom from imperialism and colonialism, and of world peace. Attempting to establish unity across political borders can, however, generate many problems because the demands of socialism can easily come into conflict with the appeal of nationalism.

6. *A belief in the centrality of equality.* Democracy, public ownership of the means of production, government regulation, the welfare state, and international unity and peace are designed to enhance the quality of life in a more cooperative community. Democratic socialists are thus concerned with greater equality of individuals on the one hand and greater quality of life on the other. These socialist ideas have roots in the egalitarian, libertarian, and aesthetic traditions of socialism. The socialists attack privilege, favor greater intellectual and moral freedom, and have sought to overcome social barriers and to bring people closer together.

THE SOURCES OF DEMOCRATIC SOCIALISM

Where did these six ideals come from? How did they evolve? We explore these questions below, though our review of democratic socialism's roots and evolution is selective. It emphasizes how modern democratic socialism drew on the early liberal democratic and socialist traditions for its own synthesis. In highlighting democratic socialism's fundamental aspects, we will draw particularly on its religious, utopian, Marxist, revisionist, Fabian, trade unionist, and reformist roots. We will focus especially on how these ideas contributed to social justice, democracy, public ownership, and the cooperative commonwealth. And we will show how these influences contributed to a growing criticism of the capitalist, industrial order and a demand for a new order that would be both democratic and socialist.

We must keep in mind that democratic socialism is the product of ideas and economic, social, and political developments that created an environment receptive to these new ideas. Capitalism and modern industrialism, in particular, created the setting for democratic socialism. Capitalism was sympathetic to liberal democracy and to greater economic, political, and social freedom for the middle class. Capitalism and industrialism helped by creating the modern working class and trade unions. The lot of workers in modern industrial societies produced many critics, often inspired by the French Revolution and its ideal of extending freedom and equality to all, whose attacks on capitalism significantly shaped intellectual and political opinion and opened people to socialist ideas. The advance of suffrage, made inevitable by liberal democracy, gave workers and their allies political leverage. The institutions of liberal democracy made it possible for democratic socialists—in time and after many hard-fought battles—to take over the reins of political power. Thus a number of forces converged to develop a philosophy of democratic socialism. Events (such as the French Revolution and the Industrial Revolution), the development of institutions (such as trade unions and democratic reforms to government), and new ideas (from the thinkers listed below) all contributed to the rise of a new ideology.

What follows are some of the key intellectual and historical sources for democratic socialist thinking.

Religious Roots

The Judaic-Christian prophetic tradition is one source of democratic socialism's ethical ideal. The prophetic emphasis on justice and peace sustained the vision of human beings of integrity joined in a cooperative community where care for the least free—the poor, widows, and orphans—fulfilled God's commandments. This emphasis, reinforced by the primitive communalism of early Christianity, has echoed throughout the history of Christianity. It was reflected in the conviction, widespread during the Middle Ages, that covetousness and greed led to evil, and that common ownership was ideally preferable to private ownership, which led to conflict, exploitation, and inequality. Religious influences manifested themselves, for example, in the work of Christian socialists such as Charles Kingsley and British Labour Party leaders such as George Lansbury and Clement Atlee. "Socialism," Lansbury wrote in 1934, "which means love, cooperation, and brotherhood in every department of human affairs, is the only outward expression of a Christian's faith."

As religious nonconformists in Great Britain sought religious freedom from the established church, so they sought greater political freedom from the government. They cherished freedom of conscience, which most often meant freedom to challenge dominant political, economic, and social arrangements. This democratic emphasis emerged in Great Britain as early as the seventeenth century, during the civil war between the Parliamentarians and the supporters of the crown. In attacking the crown, the supporters of Parliament began to articulate key democratic and egalitarian ideas. In the seventeenth century as well, the Levellers—who were really radical middle-class democrats—articulated the fundamental argument for universal suffrage (for males, that is) that the Chartists (nineteenth-century political reformers) and others battling for the vote were to repeat in later centuries. As John Lilburne, a leader of the Levellers, put it, people were "by nature all equal and alike in power, dignity, and majesty," and consequently civil authority was to be exercised by "mutual agreement and consent." Although this may sound like common sense to many contemporary Americans, in the seventeenth century it represented a radical demand for social equality.

The modern welfare state has deep roots in the Judaic-Christian tradition's concern for the poor and the needy, its preference for a more cooperative commonwealth, its insistence on fair and just economic rules, and its belief in dignified human life. It should, therefore, not be too surprising that nonconformists, such as the Diggers (or "true-Levellers"), would surface in Britain's seventeenth-century civil war to advocate a primitive communism. Their most prominent spokesperson, Gerrard Winstanley, understood the law of nature as a communal right to the means of subsistence: individuals had an equal right to use and enjoy the earth and its fruits. People should be free to draw upon the common land and the common produce according to their needs. These compassionate and egalitarian ideas continued to find expression in those individuals in the Judaic-Christian religious tradition with a socialist orientation.

The religious socialists consistently held up a vision of brotherhood and sisterhood: all human beings were equal before God. They sought a society in which the gospel principles of love could be more fully realized. They preached cooperation and opposed conflict. They worked to elevate the spiritual character of social life. They emphasized humanity's obligation to the least free. They took seriously the social gospel and envisioned a socialist society that would fulfill their religious vision of a genuine community.

Utopian Roots

The term **utopia** has come to stand for the perfect political and social order. Utopians have always cherished the concepts of justice and communal life and have valued education and cooperation. The **utopian socialists** (who wrote in the middle of the nineteenth century) stressed cooperation and underscored the possibilities of using education to change the social and economic environment. Frequently, the utopian socialists concentrated on building self-sufficient communities, divorced from the political mainstream. Although the utopians often called for elite leadership to create such communities, democratic principles frequently prevailed in the communities themselves. The comte de Saint-Simon (Claude Henri de Rouvroy), Robert Owen, and Charles Fourier represent the variety of influential utopian socialists.

Although it is by no means clear that Saint-Simon was a utopian, a socialist, or a democrat, his ideas about the emerging industrial society did influence socialism. He emphasized that "industry cannot be fully efficient, nor its products justly distributed, unless it is socially controlled." Saint-Simon had an uncanny insight into the future of the new industrial society and a "vision of the good society," a social order administered by working industrialists, scientists, and engineers, all in the service, not of the state, but of "the most numerous and the poorest classes." [2] He favored leadership by an industrial elite to advance the cause of the masses.

In *A New View of Society* (1813), Robert Owen looked to a cooperative and integrated agricultural-industrial community to overcome the evils of modern industrial society. Owen favored "villages of cooperation" as models for the new social order. Such planned villages would relieve unemployment by enabling the unemployed to grow their own food. Industrial production, as well as farming, would be communal. Owen's communities would eliminate the squalor of modern industrialism, and good working conditions would prevail.

Owen's ideas stimulated his followers to raise a number of questions important for socialism—for example, whether human nature was compatible with the egalitarian system Owen was trying to establish in his model factory community. They also asked, "Why are working people poor and wretched?" and "Is the laborer entitled to the whole produce of his labor?"

Owen was a remarkable socialist pioneer with a tremendous faith in the power of education and reform. As early as 1834 he tried, without suc-

Located near Glasgow, Scotland, New Lanark was purchased by Robert Owen in 1799. Owen expanded the public buildings, banned child labor, and incorporated employee-friendly policies. The complex was a living reflection of Owen's contribution to the development of democratic socialist thought.

cess, to form a national trade union organization, an "attempt to assemble the entire working class under socialist leadership." He saw his Grand National Union as the means to socialize the economy. Owen also fathered the cooperative movement in Britain—the idea of mutually owned stores selling industrial goods for the benefit of their members. In addition, Owen emphasized the importance of education in shaping people and society. The cardinal premise of his social philosophy was the right environment. "Any general character," he wrote, "from the best to the worst, from the most ignorant to the most enlightened, may be given to any community, even to the world at large, by the application of the proper means; which means are to a great extent at the command and under the control, or easily made so, of those who possess the government of nations." [3]

Another communal model was offered by Saint-Simon's French countryman Charles Fourier. Fourier favored a small agricultural community (the *phalanstere,* in French)— voluntary, self-sufficient, combining a "minimum of public regulation with a maximum of individual freedom." [4] His community was a model for Brook Farm, an American nineteenth-century utopian experiment, and anticipated the 1960s commune in the United States. Fourier would guarantee everyone a livelihood. In his communal association the harmonious economy blended with the harmonious society. Fourier also expressed a number of themes that came to characterize modern democratic socialism. He sought to create a working and living environment free from coercion and arbitrary conventions. His writings illustrate a strong humanitarian, profeminist concern and a strong feeling for society's outcasts.

Marxist Roots

We will discuss Karl Marx's views in greater detail later in this chapter. However, we should note that Marx drew on earlier socialist thinkers in developing his political philosophy, and he, in turn, influenced later socialists. In general, Marx's ethical concerns—for universal freedom, peace and harmony, a more genuine community, and rich human development—were widely shared by all socialists. He also provided socialists with a powerful systematic analysis of how capitalism worked.

There are a number of areas, however, where Marx's views diverged from, or caused problems with, democratic socialism. First, Marx differed from many other socialists in his attempt to establish a more rational, comprehensive, and scientific framework for socialism. Second, and more disturbing to many democratic socialists, Marx's commitment to democracy is questionable. Can socialism be achieved peacefully and by democratic, constitutional means? Marx was ambiguous on this point. At times, he did seem to believe that some countries (many of the advanced industrial nations of western Europe, for instance) could achieve socialism democratically. However, he never ruled out a violent revolution by the majority against a capitalist minority. He was also vague or silent on the question of minority rights for those who opposed socialist rule. For example, he never clearly addressed the question of socialists being voted out of office in a free election. Apparently, these matters did not bother Marx because he held that the state (as a coercive organ) would wither away and a classless society would emerge under communism.

Revisionist Roots

The **revisionists** shared Marx's general outlook but differed with his economic and political diagnosis. They felt Marx had to be revised in order to advance socialist goals. This section focuses on one important revisionist, the German Eduard Bernstein (1850–1932). Bernstein was a social democrat who spent many years of exile in England and whose views reflect the pragmatic and constitutional British tradition and a devotion to ethical concerns that modified his appreciation of the economic and political ideas of Marx.[5]

Ideals had an important role to play in socialism. For Bernstein, socialism was not inevitable, but it was supremely desirable; ethically it was inspired by Immanuel Kant, as eloquently expressed in the second categorical imperative: "Act so as to treat man, in your own person as well as in that of anyone else, always as an end, never merely as a means." Bernstein's ethical position reflects a break with Marx's materialistic outlook.

Politically, Bernstein broke sharply with the revolutionary Marxists. He opted clearly for the peaceful, evolutionary path to socialism and rejected the dictatorship of the proletariat as a barbaric idea incompatible with democracy. He accepted the constitutional rules of the game of liberal democracy, although he differed with liberal democrats on how far a democratic state could intervene in the economy. Democracy—understood as popular rule and protection of basic rights—was crucial to Bernstein's political philosophy. Universal suffrage for workers was so crucial that Bernstein was willing to endorse using a general strike to obtain the ballot or guard it against attack. However, once real political democracy had been obtained, the political strike would become obsolete. Bernstein's political strategy rested on building a broad coalition of Socialist Party members, trade unions, cooperatives, and radical members of the bourgeoisie. Such a broad electoral base had to rest on democratic principles, class cooperation, and mutual trust.

Bernstein also took issue with the Marxist view that the state was purely repressive. He held that under democratic auspices the state was capable of great accomplishments on behalf of working people. Bernstein would use a democratic suffrage to gain control of the state and then employ its powers for democratic and socialist ends. This led him to conclude that the "withering away of the state" was a foolish, utopian idea that was unlikely to happen.

Economically, Bernstein adopted a philosophy that called for the coexistence of socialism and capitalism in a mixed economy, not for capitalism's complete destruction. The evidence had not persuaded Bernstein, as it had Marx, that capitalism was going to die, that the middle class was disappearing, and that the workers' lot was becoming ever more miserable. He noted the rising standard of living of many people and recognized the continued vitality and viability of capitalism—its economic strengths, changing character, and susceptibility to democratic reform. Bernstein wanted a more genuine socialist society, but he was content to move gradually toward public ownership and control of the commanding heights of the economy; to favor a mixed economy (partly public, partly private); to endorse government regulation where public ownership was not feasible; and to accept what we today call a welfare state, one that provides key social services for its citizens. Bernstein rejected the complete socialist revolution that meant the abolition of private property and the total destruction of the social privileges and the economic, political, and military power of the bourgeoisie. He thus opted for the reformist posture of class cooperation on the peaceful road to socialism. Greater social and economic equality would come with key social policies such as nationalization of basic industries, social insurance, better housing, and food programs.

Fabian Roots

The Fabian Society, which came into being in 1883, grew out of an ethical society called the Fellowship of the True Life. The **Fabians** represented a group of intellectuals committed to the gradual achievement of socialism. The term *Fabians* derives from the name of the Roman general Fabius, who opposed Hannibal. The society's numbers included luminaries such as George Bernard Shaw and H. G. Wells, and also social scientists such as Sidney and Beatrice Webb. The Fabians were strongly motivated to overcome the injustices of modern industrial society. This ethical indignation unquestionably motivated their criticism of capitalism. Their critique uncovered a host of problems involving working people and the maldistribution of wealth and social services.

Whereas the revisionists sought to revise Marx in a more liberal direction, the Fabians sought to revise British liberalism in a more radical, socialist direction. Convinced of the importance of constitutional and parliamentary government, the Fabians advocated a moderate, pragmatic, nondoctrinaire variety of socialism to be achieved gradually. There was no need for violent revolution. The Fabians sought to educate and persuade the leaders of the British middle and upper classes and to provide intellectual leadership for the emerging British Labour Party, which was founded in 1901. They sought practical solutions for practical problems—public control of municipal transport, decent labor conditions in laundries, health regulations in the milk industry, and liquor licensing. They constituted an influential lobby on behalf of social reform and planning. Municipal socialism would lead to government ownership of basic industries. Specific social and economic reforms would create a climate of opinion for broader reforms. Fabians called for reform of the educational system to eliminate social privilege and overcome social inequality. They would build new towns with better housing and amenities for workers.

Trade Union Roots

Democratic socialism is, of course, impossible without popular support. Working people provided the bulk of that mass support. In Britain the political role of workers and trade unions had received a setback with the defeat of the Chartist movement (1838–1848) for universal suffrage and other reforms. Leaders of the working class turned away from political action and began building a strong trade union movement. They did not return to politics until the founding of the Independent Labour Party in 1893. One student of British socialism, Anthony Crosland, has emphasized the importance of the generous ideals of brotherhood, fellowship, service, and altruism in the Independent Labour Party, which anticipated the modern British Labour Party.[6] Members were concerned with working people at the economic bottom of society. This concern for social justice appealed strongly to members of the labor movement. A similar concern, in addition to economic self-interest, motivated the millions of workers who joined trade unions and labor parties in other European countries.

As noted above, the present British Labour Party was formed in 1901. With strong trade union support, it began building an electoral following, though it did not adopt a clearly socialist ideology until 1918. In succeeding decades it came to challenge, and then replace, the Liberal Party as the country's second major party. Trade unions remain a major source of strength of democratic socialism in Great Britain. Their battles for economic, political, and social reform have been central to democratic socialism.

Reformist Roots

No account of the roots and evolution of democratic socialism would be adequate if it ignored a miscellaneous group of reformers—from Jeremy Bentham and John Stuart Mill to R. H. Tawney, John Maynard Keynes, and William H. Beveridge—whose ideas and actions helped set the stage for democratic and socialist victories. Some reformers protested the adverse consequences of the Industrial Revolution, particularly the dreadful working conditions that workers endured. A number of reformers maintained that laborers produced value and were not getting their fair share of what they created. Some protested inequities in the way wealth was obtained and distributed. Many reformers pressed for universal suffrage. Others advocated governmental intervention in the economy to counter depression. Reformers called for social services on behalf of the needy and emphasized the importance of a better quality of life for all. They helped to radicalize elements of the middle class and to unite them with working-class people.

DEMOCRATIC SOCIALISM AS POLITICAL IDEOLOGY: PRO AND CON

To its proponents, democratic socialism constitutes a brave attempt to advance social justice for those traditionally left behind in a free society. To its detractors, it is a failed utopian theory that would lead to economic crisis.

Criticism of Democratic Socialism

Critics insist that democratic socialism is a contradiction in terms. Socialism, they maintain, gives the government too much power, and such great power is the enemy of liberty. In particular, governmental limitations on private enterprise destroy freedom.

Critics also argue that socialism is inefficient. In socialized enterprises production is bound to lag, and services are likely to deteriorate as the generally overregulated economy crushes incentive, daring, and flexibility, stifling the innovative spirit of capitalism. Socialism is bound to fail because it kills the goose (capitalism) that lays the golden egg (a prosperous economy). In addition, by interfering in the market economy, socialism does not allow full consumer choice in the marketplace. The policies advocated by social democrats, critics charge, would often lead to massive government deficits and create a government bloated with bureaucracy. Finally, democratic socialists have not been able to overcome many of the problems of modern industrial society: economic recession, unemployment, troublesome inflation, and declining productivity.

Orthodox communists, and some very left-wing democratic socialists, attack mainstream democratic socialism because they contend that by coexisting with capitalists, democratic socialists failed to carry out the revolution. Socialist values can only be achieved if capitalist power—economic, political, and social—is destroyed. Under democratic socialism workers cannot be emancipated, the fruits of collective labor cannot be fairly shared, and bourgeois power, values, and policies will still prevail. Although there is much debate on this last point between socialists and communists, many of them believe that some market reforms are compatible with the socialist ideal—a position China appears to be taking with its recent reforms.

The Defense of Democratic Socialism

To its defenders, democratic socialism remains compelling in the twenty-first century because the new global economy, whatever its appeal, still appears to create political and economic inequalities between people (and nations). Social democracy places equality at the center of political discussion and insists that a just society address the problems created by great inequalities of wealth—both in the name of democratic equality and in the fervent belief that the dignity of citizens requires a more equal distribution of wealth.

Pragmatically, defenders of democratic socialism argue that it offers a sane middle ground between capitalism and communism. Under democratic socialism, they insist, freedom and economic well-being can come together. They note that democratic socialist programs have overcome the worst abuses of an unregulated capitalism, have transferred wealth to workers and the needy, and have made life more attractive for the mass of people.

COMMUNISM

While democratic socialism represents a strong critique of liberalism and the capitalist tradition, there are still stronger criticisms of the capitalist system. These are most powerfully embodied in the theory of communism.

Toward a Definition of Communism

Although communism shares with democratic socialism a powerful critique of capitalism and a stirring call for equality, it is a distinct political ideology, with its own diagnosis of what ails society and its own solution for achieving a better, healthier society. Communism is, in many ways, an ancient ideal that received its modern definition from Karl Marx. **Communism** in the modern context means that all people share equally in controlling the production and exchange of things of economic and social value. This ideology demands the end of private wealth and insists on the public ownership of property and the means of production. Communism insists that the exploitation of human beings must end and that freedom must be universally achieved. In this section, we provide a brief overview of the main ideals that animate communism.

The Ideals of Communism

Theoretically, communism is a vision of a better world. Communist doctrine envisions an earthly paradise in which peace, abundance, community, and fulfillment prevail for all people, regardless of race, color, or sex. Communists claim to stand for freedom as opposed to "slavery"—that is, wage servitude, political oppression, and social subjugation—and promise justice on earth to the exploited and the abused. Communism, with its vision of a cooperative and altruistic community struggling against an individualistic doctrine of profit making, appeals most pointedly to the oppressed workers, the **proletariat**.

Communism predicts the eventual rise and triumph of the proletariat, which will not only usher in a classless and conflictless society within a nation but also overcome hostility between nations. Such a society will ensure economic abundance and individual development and realize the ultimate egalitarian principle in the communist motto: "From each according to his ability; to each according to his needs." In this sense, communism is a humanistic philosophy.[7]

Communism is also a philosophy of history. Communism purports to explain rationally the evolution and structure of human society. It describes historical development in terms of clashing material forces related to how people earn a living and conduct their economic activities. Communist philosophy emphasizes that human ideas and behavior are significantly influenced by the material environment. Communism sees history as moving toward a classless society in which the means of production, distribution, and exchange will be owned by the community. Between the revolution, which abolishes the capitalist order, and this final communist society lies a transitional period, known as the dictatorship of the proletariat—rule (which may sometimes be coercive) by the overwhelming majority of workers in their own interest. In the final communist community, the state (understood as an instrument of coercion and oppression) will disappear.

Marx's conception of history is based on three factors: (1) materialism, (2) class struggle, and (3) dialectical change.

1. **Materialism.** For Marx, "life involves before everything else eating and drinking, a habitation, clothing and many other things." History, therefore, requires the production of the means to satisfy these material needs.[8] The economic structure of society, which is shaped by the prevailing mode of production (industrial society, for instance), constitutes the society's real foundation, upon which the superstructure of law, politics, ethics, religion, philosophy, ideology, and art is built. All these institutions are simply a reflection of the underlying economic forces at work in history.
2. **Class struggle.** History is dynamic, and this dynamism is the result of economic conflict, according to Marx and Friedrich Engels, a German industrialist who frequently collaborated with Marx. Both saw all history as the result of class struggles.

Earlier, the struggle was between "freeman and slave, patrician and plebian, lord and serf, guild master and journeyman, in a word, oppressor and oppressed." In the modern period the struggle is between the bourgeoisie (the oppressor) and the proletariat (the oppressed). Here **bourgeoisie** refers to the class of modern capitalists, owners of the means of social production and employers of wage labor. The proletariat—the class of modern wage laborers having no means of production of their own—are reduced to selling their labor power in order to live.[9] Communists believe that just as feudalism collapsed and was replaced by capitalism, so capitalism will break down and be replaced by communism.

3. **Dialectical change.** While Marx never employed the rigid dialectal formula of "thesis," "antithesis," and "synthesis" to explain the movement of history, he did underscore the importance of contradictions in a given economic system (whether feudalism or capitalism) that generate change in that system. For example, the contradictions or challenges that led to the breakdown of feudalism involved new inventions and discoveries that stimulated commercial and industrial production (capitalism) and made individual workshops and the guild economy obsolete. Capitalism produces its own contradictions. Marx emphasized two of them: First, capitalism creates a large class of exploited workers whose labor makes profits for capitalists; these workers become conscious of their exploitation, band together, and eventually overthrow their exploiters. Second, capitalism operates in a faulty, uneven way because it produces periodic catastrophic depressions.

Communism is, additionally, a critique of capitalism and imperialism and a justification of the new communist order and the "new person" who will live under it. Communism condemns the exploitation of workers that is allegedly inherent in a system of private ownership and exchange. It views capitalism and imperialism as inseparable phenomena of the modern world, and it castigates what it contends are the consequences of capitalism and imperialism: the misery of workers, colonialism, and war.[10] Communism offers a new order based on worker control of the means of production, the satisfaction of real human needs, and an altruistic pattern of cooperation and development. It has been particularly appealing to radical leaders in poor, formerly colonial nations that seek a rapid path to modernization.

Finally, communism is a strategy of revolutionary action for overthrowing capitalist society and enabling the world's workers to establish the inevitable communist society. This is one of the most controversial aspects of communist thought. How does change occur? As we will see, Marx certainly thought that the point of his political ideas was to effect change in society. But how could such change be advanced? Would it require violent means? In classical Marxist theory, the communist revolution would occur in three stages: First, the overthrow of capitalism; second, the revolutionary **dictatorship of the proletariat;** and, finally, communism. Capitalism would give birth to the proletarian revolution only after capitalistic society had developed the material conditions necessary to sustain the revolution. A feudal society could not jump to a communist economy without passing through the capitalist stage.

Workers prepare for the revolution by understanding the march of history (from feudalism to capitalism to communism), their own exploitation under capitalism, the weakness of capitalism, and the nature of the class struggle. Workers begin by organizing and unionizing, working with progressive democratic forces, arming themselves, and adopting an independent and militant stance on revolution. They must never lose sight of the ultimate goal of overthrowing capitalism, and they must be wary of being deceived by utopian socialists and liberal reformers, who offer false hopes and no real societal change. The communist revolution must be permanent—it cannot merely patch up the bourgeois order; it must give workers control of production and put state power in the hands of the proletariat.

In 1872 Marx said that in advanced bourgeois democratic countries, such as the United States and England, workers might be able to "attain their goal by peaceful means." But, he added, "in most countries on the Continent the lever of our revolution must be force." [11] Communists, Marx and Engels claimed, will be the leaders in this class struggle, since they have "the advantage of clearly understanding the line of march, the conditions, and the ultimate general results of the proletariat movement." However, Marx and Engels also specifically asserted that communists should "not form a separate party opposed to other working-class parties." It was this ambiguity about the role of the party that allowed V. I. Lenin to maintain that, left alone, workers would never advance beyond a trade union consciousness, would never become truly communistic. Lenin argued, as we shall see, for a much more elite party to lead the revolution, and he was quite fervent in justifying violent revolution and the dictatorial use of state power to reach the ends that Marx advocated.

THE SOURCES OF COMMUNISM

Communism is clearly identified with several big thinkers and political actors. In the following section, we will look at the ideas of Karl Marx, Vladimir I. Lenin, Joseph Stalin, and Mao Zedong.

Karl Marx: Master Theoretician

V. I. Lenin, in his essay "The Three Sources and Three Component Parts of Marxism," noted that Germany made Karl Marx a philosopher, France made him a socialist revolutionary, and England made him a political economist.[12] What Lenin neglected to add was that the Enlightenment—which informed German philosophy, French revolutionary theory, and British political economy—made Marx a prophet of the new communist world.

The Enlightenment was a complex and influential movement that dominated Western thought in the eighteenth century, the century of the American and French Revolutions.

Karl Marx was one of the most dominant thinkers of the nineteenth century. His varied writings have influenced both democratic socialism and modern communism. Even after the fall of the Soviet Union, Marx's theories about the inequalities generated by capitalism continue to sway political thought.

Many of the *philosophes*—the enlightened ones—condemned the follies and barbarities of an oppressive and ignorant past and looked forward to the emancipation of humanity. Believing in reason, freedom, and progress, they appealed to reasonable people, extolled liberty, and hailed the march of humankind toward a better world. Marx attempted to carry the Enlightenment to what he thought was its logical conclusion: real freedom for all, which for him meant freedom in a classless, communist society.

Marx derived important philosophical ideas from two German philosophers, Georg Hegel and Ludwig Feuerbach. As noted earlier, Marx did not slavishly adopt the rigid Hegelian formula of thesis, antithesis, and synthesis. But he did borrow the general concept of the dialectic (or clash of ideas) for interpreting historical evolution. According to Hegel, the principal clue to historical development lay in the clash of opposing ideas. Marx was impressed with Hegel's concept of the dialectic but disagreed about the opposing forces. Hegel had argued that ideas were the opposing forces, but Marx concluded that material forces—economic classes—rather than ideas explained evolution in history.

From Feuerbach, Marx derived a philosophic materialism (a belief that matter is the ultimate reality) and a radical critique of religion. Both ideas helped him formulate communism. Marx agreed with Feuerbach that religion was an illusion that prevented human beings from focusing on their needs in this world. He also agreed that the critique of religion led to a critique of society. But, Marx held, Feuerbach's materialism was inadequate. One had to move beyond an understanding of the material world to an effort to change that world. As Marx said in his critique of Feuerbach, "The philosophers have only interpreted the world, in various ways; the point, however, is to change it." [13] It was true, as materialist doctrine held, "that men are products of [material] circumstances," but materialists forget "that it is men who change circumstances." The interrelation of objective, material forces and of human thought and action troubled Marx and those who followed him.

Marx drew heavily on French socialist literature, revolutionary theory, and experience. He was influenced by French social philosophers such as Saint-Simon and by such theorists of the French Revolution as Augustine Thierry, whom Marx regarded as the father of the class struggle in French historical writing. These French thinkers were disturbed about what the capitalist economy was doing, particularly to workers. [14]

Marx also was influenced by the French revolutions of 1789, 1848, and 1871. He saw the revolution of 1789 as the triumph of the French bourgeoisie; the revolution of 1848 as the failure of the bourgeoisie when they had to choose between liberty and property, family, and order; and the revolution of 1871—the short-lived workers' commune in Paris—as a model of the workers' revolution and the dictatorship of the proletariat. Never satisfied with mere intellectualizing, Marx sought to grasp the relationship between theory and practice in order to change the world in a communist direction.

Marx's stay in England and his wide reading of such British political economists as Adam Smith and David Ricardo made him a well-informed political economist. Friedrich Engels's firsthand study of British labor conditions, published in 1845 as *Conditions of the Working Class in England,* stimulated Marx's interest in the actual working of industrialism in the most advanced capitalistic country in the world. Marx spent long hours in the library of the British Museum in order to explore and document ideas about capitalism that he had begun to develop (1857–1858) in a vast outline called the *Grundriss,* or *Foundations of the Critique of Political Economy.* A part of this research was published as *Das Kapital,* or *Capital,* in three volumes.

V. I. Lenin: Master Revolutionary Strategist and Tactician

Lenin's modifications of Marxist doctrine became fundamental parts of communist strategy and tactics in his home country of Russia.[15] Lenin's contributions must be viewed in the context of that politically autocratic, economically backward state. Marx had generally assumed that bourgeois capitalism would prepare the way for the communist revolution, and thus he expected the triumph of communism to begin in western Europe. In tsarist Russia, the bourgeoisie were weak and the industrial proletariat few, especially compared to the peasantry. But World War I offered Lenin a unique opportunity. Losses on the battlefield and widespread discontent on farms and in factories made Russia ripe for revolution. Lenin took advantage of this discontent, winning allies among the peasants and adopting a revolutionary interpretation of Marx. The autocratic and repressive environment of tsarist Russia unquestionably made Lenin's communist strategy sharply revolutionary, conspiratorial, and dictatorial instead of evolutionary, open, and democratic.

In February (or March) 1917 rebels successfully overthrew the tsar, Nicholas II.[16] He abdicated and was replaced by a provisional government interested in establishing liberal, democratic institutions. Eight months later, when the time seemed ripe, the Lenin-led communists overthrew the provisional government and seized power (the October Revolution). A shrewd politician, Lenin promised peace to soldiers, jobs to city workers, and land to peasant farmers.

Lenin was not afraid to adapt Marx to the revolutionary circumstances of Russia. He used the Communist Party to lead the revolution, and he used a minority (party and industrial workers) to lead the majority (who were peasants and not communists).[17] Once in power, Lenin did not hesitate to slow up nationalization and encourage small capitalistic

Lenin was both a powerful political thinker and a gifted practical politician. He is known for his attempt to bring Marxism to Russia—a country that strict Marxist theory said was not ready yet. In this image, note Stalin standing behind and to the left of Lenin.

undertakings in agriculture and retail trade when the speed of the communist experiment threatened the regime's existence.

Lenin had argued in his 1902 publication *What Is to Be Done?* that the Communist Party had to lead the revolution. Only such a revolutionary party—equipped with "an advanced revolutionary theory"—could educate and lead the masses to victory. Arguing that such a party had to be united, ideologically homogeneous, limited in membership, and disciplined, Lenin advocated the principle of "democratic centralism," which called for intraparty democracy at the top level of leadership and subordination of the lower levels of the party to that elite. Lenin, thus, accepted a one-party state in which that party monopolized all political power.

Lenin also believed that violent revolution was justified. While such ideas can be seen in Marx's writings, Lenin was much more explicit about the need for such violence. He argued that there can be no liberation of the oppressed proletarian class unless the workers destroy the apparatus of state power built and operated by the ruling class. He insisted that bourgeois state power must be smashed, not merely taken over. He attacked the supporters of gradual reform, who maintained that it was possible to evolve peacefully to socialism. The state, as a repressive agency, however, still had to be used temporarily (now by the proletariat) to wipe out all vestiges of capitalism. During this dictatorship of the proletariat, the liquidation of the bourgeois state and society would continue until completed. Private ownership of the means of production would be abolished, and thus the old exploitation of the worker would end with the public ownership of the means of production. There were other changes that had to occur along with these economic ones: armed citizens had to replace the standing army and police, and the old administrative machinery had to be replaced by a new one, drawn from the people. Thus Lenin disagreed with the anarchists, who maintained that, with the overthrow of the bourgeois state, coercive power would cease to exist.

Furthermore, during this period—economically the period of socialism—all vestiges of bourgeois society would not immediately disappear. Since socialism could not instantly create an economy of abundance, goods would continue to be distributed according to the amount of work each person did. The socialist motto is "From each according to his ability; to each according to his work." This is significantly different from the equality embodied in the communist motto, "From each according to his ability; to each according to his needs." However, it was this theorizing about the revolutionary and transitionary period of socialism that marked a key difference between Marx and Lenin.

Joseph Stalin: Master Builder of Soviet Power

If "Leninism is Marxism in the epoch of imperialism and of the proletarian revolution" (as Stalin once remarked), Stalinism is Leninism in the epoch of the building of Soviet power. Lenin had appreciated the importance of consolidating the Bolshevik revolution in Russia. Thus Stalin could cite Lenin's actions to justify his own emphasis on "socialism in one country" when he was accused of giving up on world revolution and of assuming that the Soviet Union could survive in a world without immediate communist revolutions in the advanced industrial nations.

As Lenin built upon and altered Marx, so Stalin built upon and altered Lenin. He took from Marx and Lenin those ideas that harmonized with his program and his sense of Russian and world realities, and he abandoned ideas that did not fit.[18] In so doing, Stalin made two important, and controversial, modifications to communism:

1. *Socialism in one country.* Despite his attention to the success of the Russian Revolution, Lenin assumed that the communist revolution in the Soviet Union would be secured by communist revolutions in the advanced industrial countries of Europe. By the time of Lenin's death in 1924, it was evident that communism was not emerging in other countries. Against Leon Trotsky, Stalin argued that socialism had to be built in one country, the Soviet Union, by that country's own efforts, despite its lack of industrial

Joseph Stalin ruled the Soviet Union from 1928 until his death in 1953. Although he oversaw the nation's rise to a modern industrial and military power, he governed principally by terror.

maturity. In theory, Stalin supported world revolution, but practically he emphasized socialism's development in the Soviet Union.

2. *The power of the soviet state to build socialism.* In several five-year plans Stalin accel-
   erated industrialization and placed the demands of heavy industry ahead of the production of consumer goods. He defended his use of state power by arguing that the
   mightiest and strongest form of state power must be developed "in order to prepare
   the conditions for the withering away of state power" and that the state cannot
   wither away as long the Soviet Union is "surrounded by the capitalist world [and]
   is subject to the menace of foreign military attack." Stalin's tyrannical dictatorship
   led to a brutal reign of terror through party purges, phony show trials, mass executions and internments, and the general suppression of all dissent. To his critics,
   he is the prime example of a totalitarian leader.

Mao Zedong: Founder of Chinese Communism

Mao's main contribution to communism stems from his view of how to achieve power in
China and from his concept of the continuing revolution. His primary goal was a united,
strong, prosperous, and egalitarian China.[19] He was guided by these objectives: China
not only had to repel foreign invaders (such as Japan in World War II) but also had to defeat
reactionary forces (such as the Nationalist forces of Chiang Kai-shek and China's warlords)
that oppressed and divided the country. China had to be strong to prevent future humil-
iation by foreign powers, had to move out of poverty and into a modern prosperous economy, and had to achieve a more
egalitarian society. These objectives,
Mao held, could only be achieved
by a communism adapted to China's
history and conditions.

*Although influenced by Marx and Lenin, Mao Zedong offered significant mod-
ifications to communist theories. In this 1951 painting by Luo Gong Liu, the
founder of the Chinese Communist Party speaks in front of portraits of his two
communist role models.*

Although Lenin recognized the
need to forge an alliance between
urban workers and rural peasants,
he was sufficiently within the orthodox Marxist tradition to rely on
the urban proletariat to make the
Soviet revolution. Such a strategy
did not make sense to Mao Zedong.
China's economy, Mao recognized,
was even more agricultural than
that of the Soviet Union. The urban
workers' movement in China was
small. Moreover, Chinese National-

ist leader Chiang Kai-shek had crushed the power of the Chinese communists in the cities at an early stage. Consequently, Mao held that Chinese communists had to build their strength among the peasants and in the countryside of northwest China rather than in the cities and among industrial workers. Aided by the Japanese attack on China before and during World War II, which weakened Chiang Kai-shek's Nationalist regime, Mao and the Chinese communists proceeded—after World War II was over—from their rural base to conquer the cities by military might. Mao successfully used guerrilla warfare to maintain his strength until he could muster superior force against the Nationalist regime.

Although the Chinese communists took over the economy when they seized power in 1949, they did not immediately expropriate all private property. Subsequently, however, following Mao's philosophy of the continuing communist revolution, the government moved to exert greater control over the economy, to collectivize agriculture, and to industrialize.

One important ideological difference from classical Marxian theory emerged as Mao began the transition to communism. Mao sought to abbreviate the period of socialism and move more rapidly toward communism (in the Great Leap Forward, launched in 1958) by introducing communes—economic and governmental units for both agricultural and nonagricultural work—a policy ultimately doomed to failure.

Later, in 1966–1969, Mao attempted a Cultural Revolution to renew revolutionary vigor, speed up the revolutionary process, avoid bureaucracy, and enhance egalitarianism. The Cultural Revolution illustrates his theory of continuing the revolution under the dictatorship of the people. The Cultural Revolution—which had catastrophic political, economic, and social results—was Mao's effort to continue the communist revolution by resolving the contradictions that he saw in Chinese society: for example, the contradiction between tradition and modernity, between town and country. The revolution was seen as an effort, by societal upheaval and renewal, to move toward an egalitarian, classless society. It was characterized by direct popular action, attempted radical communist changes, and attacks on allegedly corrupt power holders. The Cultural Revolution sought periodic shakeups to ensure that communism would stay true to its developmental goals.[20]

COMMUNISM AS A POLITICAL IDEOLOGY AND PHILOSOPHY: PRO AND CON

Communism is one of the most controversial theories of politics. In this section, we will review arguments in its favor as well as its failings.

Criticism of Communism

Communism, as a set of ideas, has been attacked as utopian in theory and totalitarian and Machiavellian (that is, committed to a strategy of "lion and fox") in practice. Moreover, communism's critics argue that it has failed not only as a political and social system but also as an economic system because it cannot produce goods efficiently and abundantly. Finally, it is attacked for its failure to appreciate capitalism's adaptive power, and thus critics seriously contend that communism is not a scientific theory of society. These critics find confirmation in the theory and practice of Marxism-Leninism-Stalinism and in the failure of communism in the Soviet Union.

1. Communism is *utopian* because it rests, theoretically, on the unrealistic premise of a classless, conflictless society. No such harmonious society is possible, given human fallibility, liberty, and diversity. The quest for a society that will achieve universal freedom, abundance, and virtue and will banish alienation is a utopian dream. This dream led communists, in the now defunct Soviet Union, to try the impossible and to be willing (especially, but not exclusively, under Stalin) to pay a terrible price in human freedom and sacrifice to achieve their goals. People in China and other communist countries continue to pay a heavy price for communism's unrealistic aspirations.

2. Communist theory contains elements that can lead to a *totalitarian* dictatorship or severely repressive *authoritarian* rule. Marx's division of the world into an oppressed proletariat and an oppressive capitalist class is the first step toward totalitarian or authoritarian rule. The historical communist commitment to a (generally) violent revolution to overthrow capitalism and establish a dictatorship of the proletariat is an important second step. Lenin's emphasis on the crucial role of the Communist Party is a third step. The momentum of the communist revolution then moves from the dictatorship of the proletariat to the dictatorship of the party (with Lenin) to the dictatorship of the party leadership (the Politburo) to the dictatorship of the key party leader (Stalin). Moreover, given the fear of internal and external enemies, and the herculean job of building socialism, the growth and use of state power seem inevitable. The communist theory on the dictatorship of the proletariat has been significantly influenced by the Soviet and especially the Stalinist example. Millions of lives were lost during the Soviet Union's dictatorship of the proletariat, which was really Stalin's personal dictatorship. The list of Stalin's victims is endless and includes not only capitalists, but liberals, democratic socialists, peasants, and even loyal communists as well. It is easy to blame these excesses on a cruel, despotic, and paranoid Stalin. However, the theory of the dictatorship of the proletariat itself cannot be exempt from criticism, especially as it leads to highly centralized control of the state by the Politburo and, ultimately, one person.

    And so the **totalitarian** state emerges (a) resting on a comprehensive ideology (which has illuminated the true course of history); (b) based on a single party, with top leadership resting ultimately in one person—the dictator; (c) using the state's coercive powers, including terror, secret police, purges, assassinations, and slave-labor camps to accomplish the party leader's purposes; (d) enjoying a monopoly of weapons; (e) taking full advantage of a communications monopoly; and (f) employing a centrally directed economy to carry out plans for development. Although the Soviet Union—after Stalin—and China today cannot be called fully totalitarian, the Soviet Union—except perhaps in its very last year—was clearly **authoritarian**. China is so today.

To accomplish their central objective—the worldwide triumph of communism—communists, whether in Russia, China, or elsewhere, will not hesitate to use both craft and force. They are able to zig and zag to accomplish their central objective, leading critics to contend that communism is Machiavellian. For example, communists will play the game of peaceful coexistence until they are ready to seize power—either peacefully if they can or violently if they must. Marx and Lenin were so strongly convinced of the evils of capitalism that they were willing to pay the price of violent revolution, despite the serious moral objections to the tremendous costs of such action. Communists are equally willing to use violence to maintain power. The Soviet Union, for instance, did not hesitate to forcefully put down the "liberal" communist revolution against rigid rule in Hungary in 1956; or to send tanks into Prague in 1968 to overthrow the Dubček government when it sought to develop a more democratic, open variety of communism; or to invade Afghanistan in 1979 to prop up a troubled and faltering communist regime.

3. The *failure of communism as a political, economic, and social system* is clear. This failure is illustrated by the collapse of communism in the Soviet Union and by the disintegration of the Soviet Union itself. The repudiation in free elections of authoritarian Communist rulers and regimes in Eastern Europe is additional evidence of communism's failure. The attempt by Chinese rulers to liberalize their economy is further evidence that communist economic ideas do not work. Moreover, political discontent with China's authoritarian political system—as illustrated by the 1989 protest in Beijing's Tiananmen Square—indicates that many Chinese long for greater freedom.

4. *Communism has underestimated the ability of capitalism* to adapt to changing circumstances. In the past, communists have been critical of capitalism because values such as peace, freedom, justice, and prosperity were not being fulfilled for the great majority of people. This claim seems less valid today for advanced industrial liberal democracies. In fact, workers in liberal democratic nations have significantly improved their lives. Even if the communist criticism of capitalistic and imperialist abuses is morally justified, it is by no means clear that this ideology offers a realistic way to alleviate the problems of capitalism. Capitalism has not withered away and died. It has, in fact, demonstrated a tenacious staying power.

The Defense of Communism

Communism's beleaguered defenders still maintain that it is a liberating revolutionary philosophy, truly democratic and peaceful, guided by consistent principles, and able to reform itself. They also believe that the history of communism is a great deal more complex than its critics allow.

1. Communism—its true believers insist—remains a *liberating* philosophy. As Marx pointed out, communism stands for universal human emancipation. In advanced countries where capitalism is overthrown, workers will finally gain control of their economic, social, and political lives and be able to satisfy their needs in the realms of work, education, health, housing, and culture.[21] In new nations, as Lenin anticipated, former colonial subjects will manage their own destinies and, by following the socialist path of development, will lift themselves into the modern world.

2. Communism is committed to *democratic, peaceful* policies. Communism is democratic in that it seeks rule by the overwhelming majority of workers in their own interest. The dictatorship of the proletariat is democratic (the majority exercises power) as opposed to the undemocratic dictatorship of the bourgeoisie (the minority acts in the interest of capitalist exploiters). The use of force and violence in the communist revolution depends on the resistance of those who oppose it.

3. Wise *consistent Marxist-Leninist principles* can still guide communist theory and practice. According to communists, these principles make it clear that the communist victory is inevitable but that circumstances must be considered in moving toward that victory. These circumstances include, for example, a country's stage of economic, social, and political development. Communists maintain that in light of the dangers of nuclear war, peaceful coexistence is the only sane policy. Peaceful coexistence does not, however, bar ideological, economic, and political competition.

4. We should appreciate the *tremendous strides* that were accomplished in many sectors of society economically in the Soviet Union. For all his faults, Stalin presided over a country that made incredible advances in industrialization, achieved an impressive record in scientific accomplishments, and made advances in areas such as education (where illiteracy was virtually eliminated), medical care, and housing. All this was accomplished in a largely hostile international environment. Even if, in many areas, standards of living fell short of those enjoyed by Americans, we should consider what was accomplished in light of the backward economic conditions that the Soviet Union had inherited from tsarist Russia.

5. The *reform* possibilities of communism, its true believers maintain, were tragically cut short in Mikhail Gorbachev's Soviet Union. China, however, as it liberalizes its economy, demonstrates the viability of communist reform.

6. Finally, because *no nation has yet moved to a mature stage of communism,* it is difficult to compare theory to actual practice. Marx thought it foolish to describe the details of a full-fledged future communist society. So he did not address problems of freedom, integration, abundance, and community. Marx apparently believed these matters would take care of themselves because society would be based on worker control of the means of exchange, because workers would achieve communist abundance, and because workers would make the leap from the realm of necessity to the realm of freedom. At worst, Marx's deficiency in not spelling out a democratic theory of mature communism is merely an example of naïveté. He was wrong to trust the people to work out the details of a fair and free communist society.

THE RECENT PAST AND FUTURE OF DEMOCRATIC SOCIALISM AND COMMUNISM

The ideologies of democratic socialism and communism have had a tremendous effect on the day-to-day politics of many nations. In this section, we discuss the history and future of these two bodies of thought.

Democratic Socialism

Although it is the case that democratic socialism and communism as political systems have never been adopted in America, their ideas exert an influence in the United States as well as in Europe and elsewhere. Furthermore, if Americans are uncomfortable with the labels of socialism and communism, the values of social justice, greater democracy, a mixed economy, a welfare state, a cooperative community, international freedom, unity, and peace nevertheless have a deep hold on modern citizens in America. The democratic socialist commitment to democracy links it to liberal democracy. Its commitment to public ownership links it, in part, to communism. From the perspective of a liberal democrat attuned to capitalism, democratic socialists go too far in the economic sphere; from the perspective of orthodox communists, democratic socialists do not go far enough. But have democratic socialists struck the right middle ground in their understanding of the good political life?

We must emphasize that it took a long time to bring together democratic socialist ideas and mass electoral support. Even though, by 1914, socialism had become an important political force on the European continent, no democratic socialist party came to power until after World War I. Even after World War I the prospects for democratic socialism were grim in the major European powers. (However, we should note that Sweden, while not considered a major power, nevertheless provides a striking example of social democratic success. The Swedish Socialist Party came to power in the 1930s and initiated major reforms concerning social security, equal opportunity, full employment, and national health insurance.) In Europe's larger countries democratic socialism is predominantly a post–World War II phenomenon. Given the democratic socialists' relatively short tenure in power, it is often difficult to compare their professed values with their actual behavior. In general, however, democratic socialists have remained true to political democracy. They have modestly moved in the direction of greater social justice and a more equitable distribution of wealth. They seem to have accepted a socialist version of the welfare state and the mixed economy and to have backed away from more complete nationalization or public ownership. Through educational reform, they have attempted to enlarge opportunities for the less privileged. But they have not been able to overcome (though they have managed to alleviate) a number of key economic problems of modern industrial society: periodic recession or depression, persistent unemployment (particularly among people at the low end of the economic and social ladder), and worker alienation. The golden dream of industrial democracy in a cooperative society has not been fulfilled. Nor have dreams of international freedom, unity, and peace. Yet democratic socialists have unquestionably made life better for working people and the needy. They have helped to tame and harness modern capitalism. And they have kept the costs reasonable.

Nonetheless, democratic socialists still face a dilemma in fulfilling their historic mission. If they are too radical, they will frighten off the middle-class support they need for gaining and wielding power. If they are too conservative, their philosophy and programs will be indistinguishable from those of their political rivals. One of the recent developments in European politics (and to a degree American politics) is the rise of "third way" politics. This movement tries to capture many of the ideals of democratic socialism, particularly its commitment to education and its effort to soften the hard edges of capitalism, while at the same time harnessing the creative and productive forces of capitalism. Tony Blair, who became prime minister of the United Kingdom in 1997, has often been seen as representing this new kind of politics, but it remains to be seen just how successful or widespread this synthesis will be.

Moreover, democratic socialists face the same problem that liberal democrats face: how to deal with an industrial society characterized by periodic recession, serious unemployment, painful disparities of income (particularly between the rich and the poor), worker alienation, environmental pollution, urban malaise, crime, and shoddy materialistic values. Democratic socialists must still develop effective, humane ways to advance social justice, democracy, the satisfaction of human needs, a cooperative community, and human excellence.

Communism

The history of communism encompasses many countries, but we will focus on the two most significant cases—the Soviet Union and China.

The Soviet Union. The story of communism, and its future, is even more interesting. Even before Mikhail Gorbachev came to power as general secretary of the Communist Party in 1985, Nikita Khrushchev, who led the Soviet Union from 1958 to 1963, made efforts to reform the communist system. As early as 1956 Khrushchev confronted Stalin's terrorist rule and Stalin's "cult of personality," a phenomenon that makes a "particular leader a hero and miracle worker." He also worried about the advent of nuclear weapons. Khrushchev was cheered by the existence of communist states outside the Soviet Union and the emergence of new nations from among the former colonies of the great powers. In facing up to these developments, Khrushchev attempted to "liberalize" the Soviet Union in various ways, to reject the idea of the "fatal inevitability of war," to highlight "the emergence of socialism from the confines of one country and its transformation into a world system," and to emphasize the possibility of peaceful, parliamentary socialism and communism in the new states of the formerly colonial world as well as in the capitalist world. Gorbachev attempted to follow through on many of these points.

Gorbachev's "new thinking" rested on policies of *glasnost* (openness) and *perestroika* (restructuring) designed to achieve—at home and abroad—something akin to communism with a human face. Gorbachev also stressed the importance of *uskorenie*—the acceleration of reforms in the communist system. There is little doubt that Soviet domestic and foreign policies underwent a significant change between 1985 and 1990. Domestically, Gorbachev sought to move the Soviet Union toward greater respect for the rule of law and other basic freedoms, to reform the distressed economy by opting for "market socialism" (away from a centralized, command economy and toward a decentralized market economy), and to reinvigorate the Communist Party as well as political, economic, and social life in general. In foreign policy, Gorbachev sought to end the cold war, to reduce arms, to allow the formerly communist regimes of Eastern Europe to go their own ways, and to bring the Soviet Union into a common European home.[22]

Ironically, Gorbachev's efforts at reform placed him in the position of the sorcerer's apprentice, who could not stop the actions he had started. The loss of Soviet preeminence in the international communist movement, the end of Soviet dominance in Eastern Europe, a failing and seriously flawed agricultural and industrial economy, and greater freedom for Soviet citizens all contributed to the unraveling of both communism and the Soviet state itself. By the 1990s the Soviet Union had collapsed, and Russia was under the leadership of Boris Yeltsin, the former mayor of Moscow. For roughly a decade, Yeltsin served as president of the new Russian Republic as it made its transition to democracy and a free market economy. Yeltsin was followed in the year 2000 by Vladimir Putin (Edinstvo Party), a relatively young, energetic, and highly organized graduate of the State University in St. Petersburg. On his rise to power, Putin served as an officer in the KGB, the Soviet Union's foreign intelligence service. Many now worry that Putin is weakening the elements of democracy in Russia today.

China. After Mao's death in 1976, and under the leadership of Deng Xiaoping, efforts were made to accept the realities of a market economy and to bring China into a more modern, free, and open world. Deng Xiaoping continued to adhere to the famous four principles of Chinese communism: the socialist way, dictatorship of the proletariat, leadership of the Communist Party, and what was called Marxism–Leninism–Mao Zedong thought. But Deng interpreted these principles pragmatically so that they would not interfere with his ideas for the Four Modernizations: in agriculture, industry, science, and defense. Revolutionary class struggle could not be allowed to interfere with sensible economic reform. The Communist Party, of course, would retain control of policy; however, China would move toward a less centralized, less collectivistic, and less bureaucratic communism.

Deng's position would keep China focused on a central point: economic development. The country would persevere in economic reform and open up to the outside world. Economic reform meant "maintaining the system of private agriculture that replaced collective farms, dismantling central planning generally in favor of private entrepreneurship and the market, and fully integrating China into the global economy." [23]

The limits to modernization, and to certain democratic trends in China, were highlighted in 1989 by the Chinese regime's response to the remarkable pro-democracy student demonstrations in Tiananmen Square in Beijing. After tolerating the demonstrations for nearly a month, the Chinese government brutally crushed them and then conducted a campaign of arrests and repression designed to punish the pro-democracy movement and its supporters. Economic reform did not mean political reform in the liberal democratic tradition, and China's future remains problematic. What is particularly uncertain is whether China can modernize economically while resisting political reform (and freedom) and while keeping the Communist Party as the only center of political power.

CONCLUSION

Many former communists have resurrected political careers in Germany, Poland, and elsewhere in Europe. We should not be surprised by this phenomenon. Democratic socialism and communism remain important political forces. They will remain so as long as economic and social conditions create significant inequalities. The demand for some kind of egalitarian politics will not disappear, although it might appear under different names and in different guises. No matter what name it appears under, we can be sure that traditions of criticism developed by socialists and communists will contribute to any new ideology devoted to making people politically equal.

SUGGESTED READINGS

Bronner, Stephen. *Socialism Unbound.* 3rd ed. New York: Routledge, 1990. A thoughtful defense of the Marxist tradition.

Cole, G. D. H. *A History of Socialist Thought.* 5 vols. New York: St. Martin's Press, 1953–1960. The richest, most comprehensive account of the roots and evolution of socialism.

Gay, Peter. *The Dilemma of Democratic Socialism: Eduard Bernstein's Challenge to Marx.* New York: Collier-Macmillan, 1962. An illuminating study of one of the most important revisionists and democratic socialists.

Gorbachev, Mikhail. *Perestroika: New Thinking for Our Country and the World.* New York: Harper and Row, 1988. Recommended for the remarkable thought of this extraordinary, if tragically flawed, Soviet leader.

Kolakowski, Leszek. *Main Currents of Marxism.* 3 vols. New York: Oxford University Press, 1978. Vol. 1 *(The Founders)* explores Marxism's origins and other socialist ideas, along with the writings of Marx and Engels. Vol. 2 *(The Golden Age)* deals with Marxists such as Karl Kautsky, Rosa Luxemburg, Eduard Bernstein, Jean Jaures, Georges Sorel, George V. Plekhanov, and V. I. Lenin. Vol. 3 *(The Breakdown)* treats the evolution of Marxism from the mid-1920s to the mid-1970s and Joseph Stalin, Leon Trotsky, Gyorgy Lukacs, and key figures in the Frankfurt School—Herbert Marcuse and Ernest Bloch. A very rich history and analysis by a Polish scholar sympathetic to Marxist humanism.

Maass, Alan. *The Case for Socialism.* Chicago: Haymarket Books, 2005. Makes the case that the rise of socialism is still possible in the world today.

McLellan, David. *Karl Marx: His Life and Thought.* New York: Harper and Row, 1973. The fuller authoritative biography. Contains good summaries of Marx's writings.

Pipes, Richard. *Communism: A History.* New York: Modern Library, 2001. A highly critical history of the rise and fall of modern communism from the time of Marx and Engels through the Russian Revolution to the ultimate collapse of the Soviet Union.

Remnick, David. *Lenin's Tomb.* New York: Random House, 1994. A thoughtful and literate account of the collapse of the Soviet Union.

Riemer, Neal. *Karl Marx and Prophetic Politics.* New York: Praeger, 1987. Assesses Marx according to the standard of prophetic politics.

Schram, Stuart R. *The Thought of Mao Tse-tung.* Cambridge: Cambridge University Press, 1989. A balanced, scholarly presentation and assessment of Mao's developing ideas.

Terrill, Ross. *China in Our Time.* New York: Simon and Schuster, 1992. A revealing account of China under Mao and Deng. Notes that although communism as an idea may be dying, the Communist Party is growing stronger.

Tucker, Robert C., ed. *The Marx-Engels Reader.* 2nd ed. New York: Norton, 1978. An excellent, handy collection. See also Tucker's helpful *The Lenin Anthology* (New York: Norton, 1975); and his comparable collection of Stalin's key writings.

GLOSSARY TERMS

authoritarian (p. 191)
bourgeoisie (p. 182)
class struggle (p. 181)

communism (p. 180)
democratic socialism (p. 170)
dialectal change (p. 182)
dictatorship of the proletariat (p. 182)
egalitarianism (p. 169)
Fabians (p. 177)
materialism (p. 181)
mixed economy (p. 171)
proletariat (p. 181)
revisionists (p. 176)
totalitarian (p. 190)
utopia (p. 174)
utopian socialists (p. 174)
welfare state (p. 171)

Chapter 9

TOWARD A GENERAL UNDERSTANDING OF DICTATORSHIP AND AUTHORITARIAN STATES

In the previous chapters of part 2, we have explored the good political life. We have reviewed the perspectives of the great political philosophers on the great issues of politics and examined such political ideologies as liberal democracy, communism, and democratic socialism.

In this chapter we address some challenges to the dominant political ideologies in the democratic and communist worlds. We look at dictatorships and authoritarian regimes. Furthermore, in discussing such states in general we will also turn to one extended case study. Thus we turn to a past challenge, fascism, and its most virulent form, Nazism. The central question for this chapter is, *What kinds of challenges do dictatorships and authoritarian regimes pose to liberal democracies and democratic socialist regimes?*

A **dictatorship** is a form of government in which power is centralized under the control of a single person or possibly a small group of people.[1] There is no separation of power in any meaningful sense—such as the division of power in the United States among the presidency, Congress, and the courts—and there is, in a "perfectly" functioning dictatorship, no way to limit the dictator's rule. It may be very difficult to achieve such tremendous power, and one might argue that there is a continuum on which we could place dictatorships. At one end of the spectrum is the case of a dictator limited by the need to work with the military, respect business leaders, or deal with some powerful national institution. In Spain, for instance, from the late 1930s until 1975 the country was ruled by Francisco Franco, who in some ways aligned himself with the Roman Catholic Church in a connection that both bolstered and limited his ability to rule. Dictatorships can also be limited by the very fact that a group is ruling collectively. If there are several leaders sharing power they will need to develop some procedures for how they come to a decision.[2] Thus during the French Revolution, France was ruled for a time by the Committee of Twelve. However, even this limit on power does not spring from the people or some other institution; it is merely a procedural issue that must be resolved by a group of dictators. On the far extreme are places like North Korea, where there appear to be few limits on what Kim Jong Il may do in his country. In this sense dictatorships should be distinguished from traditional monarchies that frequently have to work with some form of legislature; the justification for the dictator's rule centers on the person or persons in question and does not derive authority from dynastic principle.[3]

Unlike the other ideologies discussed in the previous three chapters, dictatorships do not necessarily reflect any fully developed set of political ideas beyond simply concentrating power, although such ideologies can develop. Dictatorships often arise from some society-wide crisis that may or may not encourage the development of a complex set of ideas to justify their rule. Thus dictatorships can be found in countries like North Korea, which is officially communist. In reality it appears that North Korea is a dictatorship that borders on being a cult of one man. Many also point to Cuba under Fidel Castro as a dictatorship, although officially Cuba considers itself a communist nation. According to these examples, dictatorships appear to be largely associated with communist and left-leaning countries. Yet in South America for much of the twentieth century there were a number of dictatorships associated with right-wing political forces that were, to a large extent, friendly to capitalism. This was true of Augusto Pinochet's rule of Chile from 1973 through 1989.

Some dictatorships do develop a set of ideas designed to vindicate their ruler and the ruling party, if there is one. As we will see later in the chapter, Nazi Germany under Adolf Hitler developed a version of fascism that, while reprehensible, offered a worldview that competed with liberal democracy, socialism, and communism. This does not mean that the Nazi ideology was rational or even coherent; however, it offered what passed as an explanation for what the Nazis were doing and a racial ideology that was pseudo-scientific. Also, in Italy under Benito Mussolini, fascism developed a rather extensive ideology to validate itself. However, as these diverse examples illustrate, it is hard to describe one ideology that explains the beliefs that justify all dictatorships. In this chapter we are exploring a different phenomenon than we did, for instance, in the case of liberal democracies in the previous chapters. The regimes we will discuss in this chapter do not have such unifying principles as the **rule of law** or the belief in freedom and equality that unite Western Europe and the United States.

We should note that the concept of dictatorship is a very old one that has gone through various permutations through the centuries. The concept first developed in Ancient Rome and did not have the pejorative connotation it suffers from today. These days dictatorships are seen as extraconstitutional rule that either forgoes any accountability that constitutions impose on political rulers or governs under a constitution that is such a pliable document that, for all practical purposes, it is a pretense. However, in Rome the dictator was part of an existing and legitimate practice of politics. Dictators were appointed by the Senate and confirmed by the Comitia Curiata, which was a popular assembly of Rome.[4] Such constitutional leaders were appointed in times of crisis when it was believed that power needed to be centralized and decisive leadership was necessary. The Roman dictator did have immense powers, but for only a limited and proscribed time—although over time the institution of dictatorship became corrupted and the ruling time limit meaningless. These restrictions were not normally known in dictatorships of the past hundred years, although various European countries in the twentieth century have had in their constitutions various procedures for the establishing emergency powers under the direction of the executive. This was most notable in Germany before World War II.

In thinking about politics and political ideology we must consider not only what the good life looks like and how to achieve a healthy political system; we must face up to the possible perversions of a political system. In this chapter we will explore the darker side of politics. In so doing, we invite students to think about the cautionary tales that history presents us. There is nothing to guarantee that liberal democracies will predominate in the future. Although they do appear to be ascendant today, that was not the case only sixty-five years ago. It is important for us to realize that dramatic change can occur quite quickly and "out of the blue." Thus students should face the unpleasant past so as to learn about the danger signs that may help them develop an appreciation of a healthy political society.

Current or recent examples of dictatorships include North Korea under Kim Jong Il, Iraq controlled by Saddam Hussein, Zimbabwe under Robert Mugabe, and Uzbekistan ruled by Islam A. Karimov. We could add to the list a number of places where a tendency toward dictatorship seems to be appearing. Some commentators, for instance, worry that Russian president Vladimir Putin, although popularly elected, is becoming increasingly dictatorial. And we should note that although many dictatorships are reviled, they are also often quite popular for some length of time. Since they often emerge during times of crisis, the people often welcome the strong leadership that seems to create stability and stop

Islam A. Karimov, president of Uzbekistan since the country's independence in 1991, has become increasingly authoritarian in his rule, with numerous human rights groups condemning his regime.

chaos. There is ample evidence that Hitler enjoyed widespread, although certainly not universal, support for his rule. Many have also claimed that Joseph Stalin was similarly popular in the Soviet Union. We must hasten to add, however, that since dictators have such extensive powers they are frequently able to manipulate the mass media and control their self-image in such a way as to virtually "brainwash" the populace. In many cases they are known to eliminate any possible opposition or even any negative history that might be known about them. Thus the official line taught in school, seen on television, or heard on the radio is that the leader or leaders are right and have always been right. The powers of a modern American president to "spin" a story pale in comparison to the ability of a dictator to control how his regime is perceived by the general populace. A literary example of this phenomenon can be found in George Orwell's cautionary novel *1984*. The main character, Winston Smith, has a job rewriting history and destroying documents that might reflect inconsistencies and failures of Oceania's leaders. Even though this example is found in a piece of fiction, similar things occurred with great frequency under Stalin and Hitler.

Dictatorships are frequently used as examples of authoritarian regimes. In fact, they may be perfect examples of such regimes. Authoritarian states are ones in which the rulers impose values on society regardless of what the people may want, there are few to no limits on the rulers' powers, and the people do not consent to this form of politics.[5] There are many different types of authoritarian states, and some have been described as tyrannical, fascist, and totalitarian, to name just a few. In earlier times dictatorships were sometimes called despotic. Some political scientists make subtle and nuanced distinctions between all of these terms, while others use them fairly interchangeably. For instance, one frequently made, important distinction is that **authoritarianism** and **totalitarianism** are two different forms of government. The authoritarian wants to have political power but might let other spheres of life be relatively untouched by his rule. For instance, the business community might enjoy freedom to operate as long as it does not challenge the ruler. However, in totalitarian regimes some argue that all aspects of life are rigidly controlled by the rulers. In some sense there might be a virtual eradication of private life and thought in the name of the state—an overpowering state, as desired by the rulers.

There have been few thinkers who defend the idea of dictatorships or authoritarianism. In the nineteenth century the French thinker and diplomat Joseph de Maistre justified such harsh rule in the name of stability and tradition. He was also skeptical of reason alone in making good politics. In one of his dialogues de Maistre wrote:

Before anything else, I should like to suggest to you that authority should be Fundamental ground for decision. Human reason is manifestly incapable of Guiding man, for few can reason well, and no one can reason well on every Subject, so that is it in general wise to start from authority. . . .[6]

In the twentieth century Carl Schmitt, a German legal theorist, defended a similar set of political ideas. In times of crisis he advocated giving extensive powers to the government: to centralize power and suspend the nation's constitution. He was sometimes called the philosopher of Nazi Germany. However, for the most part the idea of dictatorship and authoritarianism has relatively few modern defenders, particularly in the West.

One of the more interesting questions that face students of politics is whether certain ideologies are likely to encourage the development of a dictatorship or encourage authoritarian politics. Thus some have argued that Marxism led naturally to the paranoid and dangerous rule of Stalin in the Soviet Union. The need to transform society to create Marx's egalitarian politics requires concentrating great powers in the state and the Communist Party. In so doing, opposition is silenced and eventually, maybe quite quickly, a dictator will emerge. A second position argues that Stalinist Russia, with its cult of Stalin, is a perversion of what Karl Marx taught: that there were unique and specific historical reasons that made Russia an unlikely place for making Marx's ideas work, and that Marxism might succeed in countries with different cultures and histories. A third position is that Lenin and Stalin were dictators whose development of a revolutionary Communist Party to create a Marxist state led to an authoritarian society; however, much of what Marx taught can be salvaged from his apparent connection with the Soviet Union. Thus a new kind of Marxism could be created that does not lead down the path to the bleak Soviet state.

Despite the variety of dictatorships discussed so far, we would like to take a closer look at one such regime. In this example we use Nazi Germany as a case study of one of the most horrific dictatorships ever developed. However, we must caution students that this is only one case study and that not all authoritarian regimes practice the sorts of policies of the Nazis. The centrality of racism to Nazism is not always a major aspect of the dictatorial state.

THE NAZI VARIETY OF FASCISM

Fascism, particularly as the Nazis practiced it before and during World War II, was an enormously destructive ideology, involving not only the physical destruction of people and property, but the devastation of human dignity as well. Yet this horrifying ideology, which has appeared in various forms throughout history, clearly constituted one of the major political ideologies of the twentieth century.

Toward an Understanding of Nazi Germany and Fascism

Fascism is the general term used to describe a totalitarian or authoritarian political ideology characterized by dictatorial leadership; an oppressive one-party system; glorification of the nation-state and its people; aggressive militarism; and political, economic, and social policies designed (allegedly) to overcome the weaknesses of liberal democracy, the threat of anarchy, and the fear of communism.[7] The term *fascism* first came into prominence when used by the Fascist Party, organized by Benito Mussolini, which ruled Italy from 1922 until Mussolini's defeat in World War II. **Nazism**, as we shall see in this chapter, is the particularly virulent racist, anti-Semitic, militantly aggressive variety of fascism that characterized Germany under Adolf Hitler's dictatorship.

Why study Nazism—a dead, discredited political ideology that held sway only from 1933 to 1945? There are several reasons. First, Nazism threatened to annihilate the very fabric of modern civilization. For twelve nightmarish years German power, guided by the insane Nazi ideology, was a mortal enemy of peace, social and political justice, human rights, economic well-being, and human decency. Hitler's Germany aggressively attacked its neighbors and brought on World War II, with its enormous costs in death and destruction. The Nazis barbarically exterminated millions of innocent Jews and others in the Holocaust. And they opened the door to repressive Soviet communist power in Eastern Europe.

Second, Nazism posed a mortal challenge to liberal democracy, democratic socialism, and communism. For twelve years it destroyed those outlooks in Germany, in all areas under its control, and almost throughout Europe. How could this have come about? And what lessons can be learned from a critical examination of Nazism?

Third, a study of Nazism may shed light on neofascism and right-wing authoritarianism. Although it does not presently appear that Nazism could regain control of a major state in the contemporary world, before 1933 (when Hitler became chancellor of Germany) many thoughtful, civilized people believed that something like Nazism could not arise in the first place. Elements of fascism, and of Nazism, still remain, and there are many who still admire Hitler. Neo-Nazis have blatantly attacked and even killed "foreigners" in Germany. Particular targets have been nonwhite immigrant workers. Outbursts of anti-Semitism still mar a number of European countries. In the United States there is a small but definite neo-Nazi movement. Moreover, authoritarian regimes on the right side of the political spectrum still prevail in the world. Thus a study of Nazism may illuminate the political ideology of right-wing groups and regimes that play an important role in modern politics.

The Operative Ideals of Nazism

Nazism never gave its followers a rational, comprehensive political ideology. The Nazis were opportunistic and shifted ground in the course of their struggle to gain power, so it is not easy to compile a list of consistent Nazi principles. Yet many of the ideas expressed in Hitler's book, *Mein Kampf* (My Struggle), were put into practice—with catastrophic effect. Thus we can identify six major operative ideals around which to organize our presentation of Nazi principles and behavior. With modifications and exceptions, these operative ideals also hold for fascism in general.

1. *The glorification of the authoritarian nation-state.* The Nazis articulated a mystical concept of the nation-state; for them the German state embodied the good political life. The state expressed the unity, community, power, superiority, virtue, and civilization of the German people. The success of the German nation-state exemplified the survival of the fittest. Only through such a state could the German people find fulfillment. The motto *Deutschland über alles*—"Germany above all else"—expressed this belief.

2. *Strong dictatorial leadership.* The Nazis in Germany, like the Fascists in Italy, emphatically endorsed the principle of elite leadership, embodied in a single authoritarian party and culminating in der Führer, or "the Leader." (In Italy Mussolini was Il Duce, "the Chief" or "the Leader.") This idea illustrates the perverse fulfillment of the great man theory. The Nazis emphasized the importance of the leadership principle *(Führerprinzip)*, by which the right goals, principles, direction, and discipline could be achieved. All looked to der Führer, who embodied the rightful will of the nation. All Germans had to give their obedience to Hitler. The subleadership of the Nazi elite could, in turn, demand obedience from those under their orders.

3. *Racial superiority and anti-Semitism.* The Nazis made racial superiority and **anti-Semitism**—and their monstrous consequence, genocide—into a fanatical dogma. Although the Nazis had scientific trouble in identifying the Aryans, or Nordics, who were to be the superior people *(Volk)*, they never doubted that the Jews were inferior. Hitler's talk about the destruction of the Jews and the virulent anti-Semitism of the Nazis were at first translated into a denial of rights. German citizens of Jewish faith and sometimes merely of Jewish ancestry were dismissed from government jobs, teaching, and other professions. Their property was taken away. Then the Nazis went further than a denial of rights. Synagogues were destroyed, and Jews were arrested and imprisoned in concentration camps. In time, the anti-Semitic campaign was extended to all countries that came under Nazi control in World War II and resulted in the dreadful "final solution" of the "Jewish question"—the Holocaust, the extermination of six million Jews. Other so-called inferior groups—gypsies, the mentally ill, homosexuals—were

Fascist dictators Benito Mussolini of Italy (right) and Adolf Hitler of Nazi Germany (left) at a military review in Venice, June 14–16, 1934. Both men committed ruthless acts against those they perceived as enemies. However, Hitler's treatment of Jews and other groups was especially heinous.

also treated barbarically. The objective of Nazi ideology and policy was a "pure" German people—tall, blond, and blue-eyed—who would dominate Europe militarily, politically, economically, and culturally.

4. *Enforcement of conformity at home.* To pursue their objective of a dominant German *Volk*—free of Jewish, communist, liberal, and cosmopolitan "corruptions"—the Nazis required conformity to Nazi political, economic, and social ideology within Germany. The Nazis used both craft and force, carrot and stick, in their efforts to control key aspects of German life.

5. *Totalitarianism.* Total political, economic, and cultural domination, totalitarianism was a primary objective. Only one political party, the Nazi Party, was to operate in Germany. Other parties were abolished. Political opponents were killed, jailed, or driven into exile. Opposing political ideas—in the press, schools, trade unions, the military, and business—were suppressed. Elections became endorsements of der Führer's will. No independent source of political power—in religion, among labor unions, in the military, or in the business community—was tolerated.

6. *Imperialism, war, and destruction.* The Nazi commitment to struggle against enemies also found expression in Hitler's imperialist policies before and during World War II, policies that brought great destruction to Europe. The Nazis sought revenge for the lands they had lost in World War I (such as Alsace-Lorraine) and "redemption" of ethnic Germans in Austria, Czechoslovakia, and elsewhere. They also sought *Lebensraum*—"living space"—to the east of Germany. Only military might could achieve these objectives, a military might forged by a cleansed, united, and strong German nation under the resolute leadership of der Führer. Fantastic successes included remilitarization of the Rhineland in 1936; *Anschluss* (union) with Austria in 1938; the Munich Pact (1938) and dismemberment of Czechoslovakia in 1939; and the German-Soviet nonaggression pact of 1939. These successes were followed by World War II and incredibly rapid military successes: the defeat of Poland, the overrunning of Holland and Belgium, the capitulation of France, and initial victories in Russia.

The destruction wrought by the Nazis in Poland, Holland, Belgium, France, England, the former Soviet Union, and the Balkan states is hard to believe. Even harder to fathom is the genocidal murdering of Jews that went on in towns and cities that came under German domination, and the even more systematic extermination that occurred in the Nazi death camps, a horror revealed to the world when the camps were overrun by Allied troops in 1945.[8]

The Sources of Nazism

Nazism was not a coherent, comprehensive, rational ideology. There was no political philosopher for the Nazis as there was a Marx for communists or a John Locke, James

Madison, or John Stuart Mill for liberal democrats or an Eduard Bernstein for democratic socialists. Moreover, as noted above, the Nazis were highly opportunistic and did not hesitate to shift their principles or stance on policies. Nonetheless, key ideas did influence their outlook and behavior, and these ideas have roots and an evolution.

The Racial and Anti-Semitic Roots. Belief in racial superiority is a major root of Nazi ideology. This belief is expressed in several ways and finds its most murderous manifestation in anti-Semitism. German philosopher Johann Gottlieb Fichte (1762–1814), in his *Address to the German People* (1808), preached the superiority of the Germans in an effort to awaken their nationalistic instincts. A Frenchman, Count Joseph Arthur Gobineau (1816–1882), argued on behalf of the supremacy of the white race (and of the Teutons within that race). An Englishman, Houston Stewart Chamberlain (1855–1927), conceived the folk-nation, the German nation, "destined to triumph because of its superior genetic gifts." [9] Not only are certain races considered superior (the white race), but other races are considered inferior. And, of course, there is a hierarchy within the white race, with Germans at the top and (depending on the writer) groups such as the Slavs at the bottom.

The Elitist and Leadership Roots. The call for a truthful and righteous leader has, of course, deep roots in the Judaic-Christian tradition and in Greek philosophy. But the Judaic-Christian tradition also warned against false prophets and false messiahs, and while Aristotle and Plato spoke warily of monarchy, they were also concerned about the corruption of leaders. Nonetheless, the cry for an elite leadership continued to echo in European and German thought. Johann Gottfried von Herder (1744–1803) saw the Germans as the ruling elite in Europe. The influential German philosopher Georg Hegel (1770–1831) was impressed by Napoleon and other "world historical" individuals. Friedrich Nietzsche (1844–1900) looked to a race of supermen. And the social Darwinists (who applied Charles Darwin's ideas about the struggle for existence to society and politics) envisioned the leader as an example of the survival of the fittest. It is, of course, a mistake to see Nietzsche, Hegel, or other elitists as Nazis; often their ideas were misconstrued or misused. Nonetheless, their contributions to the mythology of an elite and of a leader remain part of a falsely aristocratic heritage from which fascism, especially Nazism, drew.

The Totalitarian Roots. Although the idea of a state that promotes its own engulfing claims against the freedom of the individual has older roots (elements of a closed society are found in a limited way, for example, in Plato's *Republic*), it was the rise of the modern nation-state that facilitated the totalitarian state. This does not mean that the advent of the nation-state *caused* totalitarianism, only that the nation-state's existence has made it easier to impose the level of control necessary for totalitarianism to arise. The nation-state, with its high percentage of like-minded citizens (intense nationalism) in a well-delineated territory and a central government, is well suited for the exercise of control. In addition, the rise of the totalitarian state, as approximated in Nazi Germany, was further facilitated by the advent of modern means of controlling mind and body, particularly mass communication and sophisticated propaganda techniques. When total control, physical and mental, is achieved, the totalitarian state becomes a reality.

The concept of sovereignty also facilitated (but did not cause) the rise of totalitarianism. Our modern understanding of sovereign state power was first crystallized by the Frenchman Jean Bodin (1530–1596), who defined sovereignty as supreme power over all, unrestrained by law.[10] Bodin saw in sovereignty a weapon to protect nations against civil war. Englishman Thomas Hobbes, in his *Leviathan* (1651), also saw no theoretical or practical limits on sovereign power. Neither man, of course, advocated a modern totalitarian state, but both underscored the cry for order that made the masterful sovereign state so appealing. All those who exalt the state, who fight against an open society, and who would limit reason and freedom make the totalitarian state possible.

The Nationalist Roots. Nationalism, a strong sense of cultural belonging and group loyalty, can be used for good or evil. In the nineteenth century, nationalism was mainly a movement for national freedom and independence; it was an effort to achieve political, economic, and social freedom. However, as ultranationalism—nationalistic feelings carried to extreme levels—it can become divorced from freedom. Ultranationalism leads to the denial of freedom for minority ethnic groups within a nation or to aggression against other nations. Those who preach ultranationalist ideas such as "my country right or wrong" help prepare the way for fascism. Clearly, not all nationalists were, or are, fascists, but all fascists are nationalists. The Nazis fed on national pride and honor. They fed on the resentment that grew out of Germany's defeat in World War I and its national weakness in the 1920s. They fed on the passion to vindicate German strength and respect.

The Socialist Roots. The Nazis called themselves National Socialists. Benito Mussolini (1883–1945) was a socialist before becoming a fascist and Italy's dictator (1922–1945). Sir Oswald Mosley (1896–1980) in England and Marcel Déat (1894–1955) in France were also socialists who turned to fascism. Jacques Doriot (1898–1945) was a leading member of the French Communist Party before leaving it to join the French fascists. Clearly, there was considerable hostility to capitalism among fascists, and this made them partially sympathetic to some socialist ideas. It would be a mistake to associate Nazism with the highly ethical socialism of a highly ethical thinker such as Eduard Bernstein.

One aspect of socialism that appealed to fascists was the power socialism promised to the state. As early as 1920 the infant Nazi Party included a number of statements of intent that might generally be regarded as impeccably socialist in origin. Among these were the nationalization of major industries and industrial combines; the abolition of unearned income, profiteering, and speculation; the provision of equal opportunity in education and employment; the institution of workers' shops; acknowledgment of the right to work; and encouragement of work in the communal interest. The fact that the Nazis did not deliver on these early party planks is less important than the fact that their initial bias was hostile to big business and its abuses and that the Nazis deliberately sought to appeal to workers.

The Militarist Roots. The glorification of the military and of military virtues has clear roots in German history, particularly Prussian history. This glorification placed a halo over war. Thus University of Berlin professor of history Heinrich von Treitschke (1834–1896) wrote that although the "superficial observer" saw war as "brutal and inhumane," it was really a "moral force," justified by "the great patriotic idea." The literary philosopher Nietzsche wrote, "Ye have heard men say: Blessed be the peacemakers; but I say unto you: Blessed are the warmakers, for they shall be called, if not the children of Jahwe, the children of Odin, who is greater than Jahwe." And "Do ye say that a good cause halloweth even war? I say to you a good war halloweth any cause." And the official organ of the German army declared in 1932, "War has become a form of existence with equal rights with peace. Every human and social activity is justified only if it helps prepare for war."

The Autarkic Roots. The economic theories of Nazism spring from **autarky**, a doctrine of self-sufficiency that calls for protecting a nation against interfering economic activity by other nations. Autarky favors protectionism rather than free trade. It calls for national regulation to ensure prosperity, access to vital resources, and a strong army. Power must be concentrated in the hands of the state to help it achieve self-sufficiency.

The Roots of the Might Makes Right Doctrine. Long before the Nazis came to power, the ideological forerunners of Nazism maintained that concepts such as natural law, natural rights, and morality were irrelevant. According to Paul M. Hayes, the "search for the heroic leader, militarist glory and economic autarchy left no place for individual rights or free will." [11] As we saw in chapter 6, Machiavelli opened the door for immoral actions in defense of the state. This idea was later echoed by Prussian king Frederick the Great (1712–1786) in his frankly expressed philosophy of machtpolitik—the politics of might or power politics. Frederick the Great and Machiavelli were political actors who defended what they saw as political necessity; however, during the nineteenth century various historians and philosophers offered intellectual justifications for this kind of rationalization. Heinrich von Treitschke was attracted to Machiavelli's doctrine of the need to sacrifice right and virtue in the interest of national power.[12] Later Nietzsche, though no Nazi and not an anti-Semite, articulated the idea of the "will to power" and rule of the strong, which the Nazis found so attractive.[13] Some of these ideas were also repeated by the German historian Oswald Spengler (1880–1936) in his epic work, *The Decline of the West*.[14] We should make clear, though, that none of these men were Nazis; however, their ideas were later appropriated by the Nazis to various degrees.

A Critique of Nazism

There can be no rational, humane defense of Nazism. But we are still puzzled by its operative ideals. How could this Nazi vision of the "good" political life—and the behavior that flowed from this vision—have dominated Germany for even twelve years? This disturbing question forces reflection on the choice (explored in chapter 2) that Germans made in 1933 and raises other questions. Was Nazism unique? Or do the forces and circumstances that produced Nazism in Germany—and fascist regimes in Italy and elsewhere—still exist? Can Nazism happen again? What lessons in political philosophy and ideology can be drawn from the nightmarish Nazi experience?

Of course, humanity can forthrightly reject the key Nazi operative ideals. Yet we still have nation-states, and there is a demand for strong leadership. Attitudes of racial superiority and anti-Semitism still persist. They may not retain quite the virulent form they took in Nazism, but they are here. How should these ideas be dealt with in today's world? What form will they take in the twenty-first century?

Of course, many people in many nations seek to use the nation-state to achieve freedom and a sense of community. They seek decent, humane, constitutional rulers. They say they fight against attitudes of racial superiority and anti-Semitism and against imperialism, war, and destruction. But what is the actual record? And, in this fight, is the right political philosophy being followed?

Today, Germany (reunited in 1990) and Italy have democratic and constitutional governments. So does Japan, World War II's other fascist and militaristic regime, which tried to dominate East Asia. It seems unlikely that fascism or militarism will ever again seriously influence the policies of these countries. However, repressive authoritarian regimes are still very much alive in some Middle Eastern, Asian, and African nations. They demonstrate the inability of liberal democracy and of democratic socialism to take hold in unfavorable circumstances. In some countries, right-wing regimes feed on a political or economic crisis and the call for a strong leader. Military leaders sometimes seem to be the only ones capable of maintaining "law and order." Many of these countries have no tradition of constitutional government or respect for political parties and civil rights. This suggests that there may still be breeding grounds for some variety of fascism, if not the seemingly unique, virulent Nazi strain.

CONCLUSION

Fascism—especially its most virulent form, Nazism—seriously challenged liberal democracy, communism, and democratic socialism. The defeat of fascism and militarism in World War II does not, however, mean that challenges to dominant political philosophies and ideologies have disappeared. Right-wing authoritarian regimes still function in many parts of the world. No society is immune to authoritarian political practices. Societies in crisis are particularly vulnerable. Economic depression or threats to physical safety have too often led countries to seek security in the simple appeal of authoritarianism.

Let us now move from the world of political philosophy and ideology in part 2 to the more empirical world of actual governance in part 3. We will examine first the degree to which political values actually guide behavior and second how human beings politically organize themselves. This section will serve as a final preparation for our later consideration of major public policy issues that students of politics and politicians alike must grapple with.

SUGGESTED READINGS

Bracher, Karl D. *The German Dictatorship*. New York: Praeger, 1970. An authoritative account of the internal and external Nazi record of domination, aggression, and war.

Burleigh, Michael. *The Third Reich*. New York: Hill and Wang, 2000. An extensive study of the development of Nazi Germany.

Goldhagen, Daniel J. *Hitler's Willing Executioners: Ordinary Germans and the Holocaust*. New York: Knopf, 1996. A powerful and provocative account of the murderous role of many ordinary Germans, infected by a diabolical anti-Semitic mind-set that characterized so many in Nazi Germany, in the nefarious execution of the Nazis' "final solution."

Johnson, Eric A. *Nazi Terror: The Gestapo, Jews, and Ordinary Germans*. New York: Basic Books, 1999. A scholarly, balanced, valuable contribution to our understanding of Nazi terror and key aspects of the genocidal undertaking in Germany.

Maistre, Joseph de. *The Works of Joseph de Maistre*, trans. Jack Lively. New York: Macmillan, 1965. An extensive collection of the philosopher's works.

Moore, Barrington. *Social Origins of Dictatorship and Democracy*. Reprint ed. Boston: Beacon Press, 1993. Classic study of governmental forms, including dictatorship.

Paxton, Robert. *The Anatomy of Fascism*. New York: Knopf, 2004. A historical study of fascism in both Germany and Italy.

Pfaff, William. *The Bullet's Song: Romantic Violence and Utopia*. New York: Simon and Schuster, 2004. Study of several thinkers who supported fascism. Expands beyond the topic of fascism.

Riemer, Neal, ed. *Let Justice Roll: Prophetic Challenges in Religion, Politics, and Society*. Lanham, Md.: Rowman and Littlefield, 1996.

GLOSSARY TERMS

anti-Semitism (p. 205)
autarky (p. 209)
authoritarianism (p. 202)
dictatorship (p. 199)
fascism (p. 203)
Nazism (p. 204)
rule of law (p. 200)
totalitarianism (p. 202)

Part 3

COMPARATIVE AND WORLD POLITICS

In part 3 we begin to examine the actual political process. Chapters 10 through 14 investigate three important areas: the political values of political actors; patterns of political cooperation, accommodation, and conflict; and decision making in politics. Chapter 10 is specifically concerned with the gap between professed values and actual values. Chapters 11, 12, and 13 focus on how current political patterns in the United States and other countries and in the broader international community protect security, liberty, justice, and welfare. Chapter 14 explores some models of decision making and provides a foundation for the examination of specific public policy concerns undertaken in part 4 of the book.

Chapter 10

THE POLITICAL VALUES OF POLITICAL ACTORS

The preceding four chapters have dealt with political philosophical questions about what the good life looks like. We have also investigated the main ideologies that animate contemporary politics—liberal democracy, democratic socialism, and communism. However, in considering the meaning of the good life or political ideologies, students of politics might immediately wonder if this is all merely talk. Just because theorists of liberal democracy say they value justice and believe in individual freedom does not necessarily mean that countries professing to be liberal democracies practice what they preach.

The fact that Karl Marx wrote about freedom, equality, and the idea of human development does not mean communist states actually further those ideals. Even if democratic socialists claim that they can combine the advantages of democracy with the ideals of socialism, it does not necessarily follow that politicians who claim to be democratic socialists bring that philosophy to bear on their day-to-day actions. Therefore the questions we focus on in this chapter are, *How do the actual political values of political actors compare with civilized values such as peace, liberty, justice, and welfare? What do the professed values of political actors really mean? Can political actors harmonize different, sometimes competing, values? Finally, how do the values of political leaders differ from those held by common citizens?*

These questions might sound rather simple to answer; however, that is not the case. They force us to consider the practical world of politics and how that world interacts with the world of ideals. The last question, in particular, forces us to evaluate the practice of democracy itself.

SOME KEY TERMS DEFINED

To get a better grip on how to approach the question of values we must define the following key terms: *political values, goal, principle, policy,* and *political actor.* The first of these terms, **political values**, refers to the important beliefs about what goals, principles, and policies are worthwhile in public affairs.

The second term, a **goal**, means an objective. It may be peace, security, and order—or war, domination, and power. It may be liberty, equality, justice, and fraternity—or slavery, subordination, tyranny, and enmity. The goal may be a fair return on national investment and international respect—or rampant profit and national self-righteousness. The goal may be democratic and constitutional government—or oligarchic or dictatorial/authoritarian rule. The goal may be economic prosperity for all—or affluence for the few. It may be a healthy environment—or a highly productive society that ignores ecological health. The goal may be a creative, robust quality of life—or mediocrity.

A **principle** is a basic truth or belief that is used as a basis of reasoning or as a guide to behavior. It may be peaceful change (reliance upon ballots rather than bullets)—or violent change (bullets). The principle may be freedom of speech for all—or freedom only for the elite. Principles actually at work in political communities often illustrate compromises among competing ideas.

A **policy** is a course, or general plan, of action. It may be balance of power, balance of terror, or unilateral disarmament. The policy may be universal suffrage—or suffrage limited to rich, well-educated males. It may be a progressive income tax or a sales tax, a public standard for clean air and pure water, or a hands-off policy on environmental issues.

Goals, principles, and policies (which sometimes overlap) often function as norms. They help determine whether certain standards are being met. Consequently, they serve as important guideposts in politics and, as such, merit careful study.

A **political actor** is an individual or a group that expresses and shapes public values, struggles for power, and decides issues of public policy. Governmental, economic, social, and military elites are political actors as well. Political parties, a wide range of interest groups, and agencies of the mass media—newspapers, television networks, and newsmagazines—are political actors. Individual citizens—letter writers, demonstrators, and voters—are political actors.

In a broader sense, political communities themselves are actors. Nation-states constitute one important form of actor in the international system. The United Nations is another type of political community. The subdivisions of nation-states are also political actors: for example, each of America's fifty states, 3,043 counties, and nearly 87,000 local governments is a political actor. A number of regional and functional organizations—for example, the European Union—are political actors. And so, increasingly, are the multinational corporations.

This incredibly diverse array of political actors has led students of politics to wrestle with what is sometimes referred to as the "level of analysis problem." [1] In attempting to understand international relations, for instance, is it more appropriate to concentrate on *national governments* as the primary actors or on the *decision makers* who lead the governments? Or should one concentrate on the *international system* itself and its patterns of military, economic, and political interaction among governments, international organizations, and nongovernmental organizations? In other words, must one operate on a global level to really understand what is going on?

In our exploration of the values of political actors in this chapter, we limit our analysis to what we consider to be some of the most important values—national values, popular (citizen) values, and interest group and class values. A helpful theoretical orientation always advances a sound empirical analysis. Such a theoretical orientation uses a meaningful hypothesis addressed to the empirical questions. Our rough-and-ready guiding hypothesis is fourfold. First, the political values of political actors are rooted in their vital needs, fundamental interests, and perceived desires. Second, the struggle over political values is conditioned by the differing interpretations of needs, interests, and desires by diverse political actors and by the historical distribution of power. These factors make for both conflict and consensus in politics.

Third, the world of politics frequently contains serious gaps between professed values and actual behavior. The gaps exist because political actors—nation-states, governing elites, powerful interests, and citizens themselves—are unable to break out of parochial, rigidly ideological patterns of thought and behavior. Because human resources and capabilities are limited, it is often difficult to narrow these gaps. And, as we have seen in the former Yugoslavia, ancient, historical forces (long-held, ethnic grievances) can impose one set of demands on political actors that can come into conflict with other professed values.

Fourth, although prediction is hazardous, the future will probably include a major constitutional and democratic struggle between what we might call broad values and narrow values. This struggle will manifest itself in several ways. There will be a contest between broader global or regional human needs and narrower, parochial national interests. There also will be a contest between broad, truly fundamental community interests and narrower, selfish group and individual desires. Finally, there will be a contest between vital individual and local interests and oppressive, centralized interests and desires. This struggle will most certainly require a realistic understanding of vital needs, of compatible fundamental interests, and of modest and prudent desires.

THE VALUES OF NATIONS AS POLITICAL ACTORS

Nations (more accurately, national leaders, ruling elites, or governing parties) generally profess and often seek to protect the national interest in foreign affairs and the public interest in domestic affairs. They generally interpret the **national interest** as the vital needs and fundamental interests of the nation as a whole. This would include such concerns as security, liberty, justice, and welfare, all of which are essential to the independence, prosperity, and power of the nation-state.[2] Related to the idea of the national interest is the idea of the **public interest**, which is supposed to be the interest of the entire community and which presumably transcends the selfish interests of individuals or groups. Public interest presumably expresses the best long-range interests of the nation.[3]

There is considerable historical evidence that many leaders of national governments value survival, security, safety, peace, territorial integrity, defense, prosperity, independence, and power. They value their freedom, their capacity to govern themselves, their control of their own destiny, and their enjoyment of the rights—at home and abroad—that make freedom meaningful. They seek a measure of justice at home and, sometimes, abroad. They profess, at least in most nations, to favor equality before the law, due process of law, and an equitable distribution of wealth. They favor the principle of equal treatment of sovereign nations in the world community and respect for international law and procedure. They profess to care about the welfare of their citizens at home and the afflicted abroad. They often favor policies to enhance national economic well-being through growth, production, full employment, decent farm prices, and satisfactory business profits. They support policies that enhance social well-being through literacy, adequate food and housing, and good health and nutrition. They endorse stable institutions and organizations as a way to ensure political well-being.

But—in the critical and truth-seeking tradition of political science—we must probe more deeply. What more specific meaning—in deed as well as in word—do those who exercise power on behalf of nations give to their values? Are such terms as the *national interest* and the *public interest* idealistic myths? Are they cover-ups for naked national power or for dominant elites? Are vital national needs really vital? For whom? And are there serious gaps between civilized (and often professed) values and the actual values revealed in national behavior?

Let us now investigate these key national values articulated by many leaders throughout the world. We can, of course, present only a modest part of the evidence that bears on our questions and might sustain our hypothesis. But such evidence may at least suggest the larger empirical task required for a more rewarding understanding of nations' political values.

Security and Peace

The leaders of most nations say they believe in security and peace. Yet the history of the twentieth century and early years of the twenty-first are littered with violent conflict—interstate wars, revolutions, assassinations, rebellions, wars of national liberation, ethnic conflict, terrorism, and genocide. While definitions of war vary slightly from study to study, data indicate that over the past ten to fifteen years, somewhere between thirty and forty

What caused World War II? Although several reasons have been advanced, there is little doubt that fundamental democratic values were at stake as the Allies fought Nazi Germany, fascist Italy, and militarist Japan.

wars were raging at any given point in time.[4] The ongoing cost of this behavior is enormous. Though estimates on deaths directly attributable to warfare vary, Zbigniew Brzezinski, in his book *Out of Control: Global Turmoil on the Eve of the Twenty-First Century*, puts the total for the twentieth century at roughly 87.5 million dead—33.5 million combatants and 54 million civilians.[5]

There is a sarcastic adage in international relations that says, "All wars are fought in self-defense." Has each nation engaged only in just wars, defending itself against aggressive opponents and protecting its security against real attack? Or have at least some, using the pretext of protecting their vital interests, attacked and jeopardized the security of other, peace-loving countries? Do wars, or defense preparations, actually serve to protect a nation's security?

Scholars will quarrel about answers to these questions. Evaluations are difficult because there is no agreement on the key terms used in discussions of these matters. For example, there is no common definition of *just war, defensive war,* or *aggressive war,* or of *vital interests* or *security.* Also there is no consensus on the meaning, value, and cost of *adequate defense.* The enormous tension and distrustful atmosphere of the cold war provided a powerful driving force for the building of conventional and nuclear arsenals in the years following World War II. More recently, the dangers of terrorism and nuclear proliferation have complicated the question of security even further. At this point, it is too early to tell how the need to deal with these phenomena will finally affect demands of national security, but in the coming years we can be certain that ensuring security and peace will become even more complex.

There can, however, be little quarrel about the following points: (1) There is a serious gap between talk of peace and the reality of war. (2) Different nations often hold incompatible conceptions of national security. (3) Sometimes nations counter power with power in order to protect vital national interests. (4) National defense expenditures are huge and distort other priorities. (5) The machinery for peace and peaceful change is inadequate.

Adolf Hitler talked of peace but did not hesitate to launch World War II by attacking Poland, then the Low Countries and France, then Britain, and then the Soviet Union. Was Germany's security threatened by the people it attacked? The Soviet Union professed, at its inception in the early twentieth century and in the decades that followed, to be a peace-loving state that respected the national integrity of its neighbors. Yet in 1956 the

Soviets invaded Hungary to put down a revolt against the rigid communist regime that ruled the country. In 1968 the Soviet Union invaded another communist neighbor, Czechoslovakia, to turn back an attempt to liberalize the regime there. In late 1979 the Soviet Union invaded Afghanistan, presumably to defend a recently installed communist regime against alleged internal and external enemies. In these cases the Kremlin's interpretation of the Soviet Union's national security and national interest clashed with its alleged peace-loving and freedom-loving pretensions, and perhaps with the national and security interests of most people in Hungary, Czechoslovakia, and Afghanistan.

The United States, too, professes to be a peace-loving nation, yet it became involved in a bloody, destructive, and expensive war in Vietnam between 1965 and 1973. Was our action in Vietnam, like our military resistance to Germany and Japan in World War II, based on protecting the legitimate security interests of the United States? More recently, some Americans began to seriously question why the United States invaded Iraq in 2003. With few links between al Qaeda and Iraq, and with the failure to find any weapons of mass destruction, was U.S. national security directly threatened enough to warrant the invasion? Supporters of American action reply with an unequivocal "yes." Saddam Hussein was a brutal dictator and a dangerous and destabilizing force in a region critical to U.S. security. This debate is likely to persist for years regardless of the outcome of postwar reconstruction and democratization efforts in Iraq.

Clashing conceptions of national security highlight international relations. In the 1930s and 1940s Japan's "co-prosperity sphere"—as envisaged by Japan, a bloc of Asian nations led by Japan and free of Western powers—clashed with the national security interests of China, Britain, France, and the United States and led directly to the Japanese attack on Pearl Harbor on December 7, 1941. In 1956, presumably to protect their strategic security interests—although at Egypt's expense—Britain and France, with Israel's help, seized control of the Suez Canal after Egyptian president Gamal Abdel Nasser had nationalized the waterway. Israel has resisted the establishment of a Palestinian state on the west bank of the Jordan River because of fears about Arab military forces being close enough to Israel's cities to jeopardize security. Obviously, neither the Egyptians nor the Palestinians agree with these assessments of national security. Whose interpretation is correct?

Recent debates among political scientists have focused on the nature of ethnic and cultural conflicts that persist, sometimes with greater vigor, with the end of the cold war. In *The Clash of Civilizations*, Harvard University's Samuel P. Huntington argues that with the fall of communism different civilizations—Western, Islamic, Latin American, among others—will come into conflict. These civilizations represent great blocs of countries with similar cultural, religious, and political histories. While there is a great deal of controversy about Huntington's theory, it is a provocative argument about the way to view peace and conflict since the end of the cold war.[6] His argument highlights the intersection of values, culture, and security. He posits that different civilizations have different values, springing out of different cultural histories. While that is an interesting hypothesis in and of itself, it leads

directly, according to Huntington, to a clash of civilizations as they try to protect themselves. Diverse values, thus, become the source of clashing security concerns.

The discussion in this section does not necessarily prove that all official government
policies on military spending are wrong and that the critics are right. We should, however, be leery of automatically accepting what governments profess. The national value of
security and peace is subject to differing interpretations. We should be sensitive to the
price that is often paid to achieve national security. And we should be aware of the gap
that so often exists between professed, civilized values and the actual values expressed
through behavior.

Liberty, Human Rights, and Democracy

Most nations profess a commitment to liberty, human rights, and democracy. In fact, with
the collapse of the Soviet Union, the world seemed to witness a spectacular rise in the
number of democracies. But how do all of these self-proclaimed democracies perform?
This is a rather difficult question to answer because just what constitutes a democracy is
open to debate. However, if we accept that democracies must have freedom of expression,
free elections, and the ability to gather alternative sources of information, the number
of democracies has indeed increased in the past few years. We should also note, though,
that countries might achieve some level of democracy, but not complete democracy.[7] Various scholars have tried to create different scales on which countries can be arrayed. Freedom House has developed a means of ranking countries into three categories—Free,
Partly Free, and Not Free—and their recent rankings are shown in Table 10.1.

This table tells us a number of things. First, there are more democracies than ever
before. Second, many countries profess to be democracies and yet are not quite living
up to the high standards that democracy demands. Thus students of politics must continue to investigate the gap between rhetoric and reality. For example, in 1975 the Soviet
Union, the United States, and thirty-three other governments signed the Helsinki Pact,
which included provisions for respecting human rights. But did the Soviet Union act in
accord with its signature? The record reveals the Soviet Union was a place where dis-
senters were imprisoned, confined to mental hospitals, exiled within Russia, and forced
into foreign exile. Soviet citizens were not allowed the right of free emigration, and the
free flow of information was impeded. Between 1975 and 1987 Soviet behavior was
not consistent with the principles professed in the Helsinki Pact.

Historically, the U.S. record on human rights, although considerably better than that
of many other countries, has by no means been exemplary. FBI actions at home and CIA
actions both abroad and, more disturbingly, at home have been criticized by civil rights
groups, the press, congressional committees, and governmental commissions. The FBI made
illegal wiretaps particularly in the 1950s and 1960s. In the mid-1960s and early 1970s,
the CIA worked covertly in Chile to influence a presidential election and to overthrow a
democratic government led by Salvador Allende Gossens. In the wake of the terrorist

Table 10.1 Countries Rated by Degree of Freedom, 2004

Combined Average Ratings: Independent Countries

FREE	Poland	Benin	Paraguay	Kuwait	Qatar
1.0	Portugal	Ghana	Seychelles	Liberia	Russia
Andorra	San Marino	Guyana	Solomon Islands	Tonga	Rwanda
Australia	Slovakia	Lithuania	Honduras	Burkina Faso	Tajikistan
Austria	Slovenia	Mali	Niger	Congo	Togo
Bahamas	Spain	Mexico	Papua New Guinea	(Brazzaville)	Tunisia
Barbados	Sweden	Mongolia	Sri Lanka	Morocco	
Belgium	Switzerland	Samoa	Trinidad and	Singapore	**6.0**
Canada	Tuvalu	Sao Tome and	Tabago	Uganda	Cameroon
Cape Verde	United Kingdom	Principe	Turkey		Congo (Kinshasa)
Chile	United States	Vanuatu		**5.0**	Cote d'Ivoire
Costa Rica	Uruguay		**3.5**	Bahrain	Iran
Cyprus		**2.5**	Bosnia-	Burundi	Iraq
Czech Republic	**1.5**	Brazil	Herzegovina	Djibouti	Swaziland
Denmark	Belize	El Salvador	Fiji	Ethiopia	United Arab
Dominica	Bulgaria	India	Georgia	Nepal	Emirates
Estonia	Greece	Jamaica	Indonesia	Yemen	
Finland	Grenada	Lesotho	Moldova		**6.5**
France	Japan	Namibia	Mozambique	**NOT FREE**	Belarus
Germany	Latvia	Peru	Sierra Leone		China
Hungary	Monaco	Philippines	Tanzania	**5.5**	Equatorial Guinea
Iceland	Panama	Romania	Ukraine	Afghanistan	Eritrea
Ireland	St. Kitts and Nevis	Senegal	Venezuela	Algeria	Haiti
Italy	St. Lucia	Seria and		Angola	Laos
Kiribati	St. Vincent and	Montenegro	**4.0**	Azerbaijan	Somalia
Liechtenstein	Grenadines	Thailand	Bangladesh	Bhutan	Uzbekistan
Luxembourg	South Africa		Colombia	Brunei	Vietnam
Malta	South Korea		Comoros	Cambodia	Zimbabwe
Marshall Islands	Suriname	**PARTLY FREE**	The Gambia	Central African	
Mauritius	Taiwan		Guinea-Bissau	Republic	**7.0**
Micronesia		**3.0**	Malawi	Chad	Burma
Nauru	**2.0**	Albania	Malaysia	Egypt	Cuba
Netherlands	Antigua and	Bolivia	Nigeria	Guinea	Libya
New Zealand	Barbados	East Timor	Zambia	Kyrgyzstan	North Korea
Norway	Argentina	Ecuador		Lebanon	Saudi Arabia
Palau	Botswana	Kenya	**4.5**	Maldives	Sudan
	Croatia	Macedonia	Armenia	Mauritania	Syria
	Dominican	Madagascar	Gabon	Oman	Turkmenistan
	Republic	Nicaragua	Jordan	Pakistan	

Source: Freedom House, *Freedom in the World: The Annual Survey of Political Rights and Civil Liberties, 2004* (New York: Freedom House, 2004).

Note: The freedom rating is based on real-world situations caused by state and nongovernmental factors, instead of governmental intentions or legislation. Governments are not rated per se, but rather the rights and freedoms enjoyed in each country or territory. Two checklists are used—one for questions regarding political rights and one for civil liberties—and countries and territories are given a numerical rating for each checklist. The two ratings are then averaged and used to assign an overall status of "Free," "Partly Free," or "Not Free." A detailed explanation of the methodology for establishing the ratings can be found at www.freedomhouse.org.

A young Chinese demonstrator stands alone in front of a tank column in Tiananmen Square on June 5, 1989. This man was pulled away from the tanks. Hundreds of others, however, were eventually killed or wounded at the square. Still others were later executed or imprisoned as the pro-democracy demonstration was crushed.

attacks on September 11, 2001, civil libertarians in the United States have become increasingly worried about actions taken by the U.S. Justice Department in detaining legal and illegal immigrants. And in June 2005 Amnesty International released a report highly critical of the treatment and prolonged detention of Muslim prisoners at the U.S. military base in Guantánamo Bay, Cuba. Although the concerns about security are real and justified, there are those citizens who are equally worried that demands for safety will override the fundamental belief most Americans have in basic individual rights and freedoms.[8]

A comparable gap between rhetoric and reality exists in many developing countries. The annual *Country Reports on Human Rights Practices* by the U.S. State Department, testimony before congressional committees, and documented records of such groups as Amnesty International illustrate this gap. The records of such countries as Cambodia (Kampuchea), Iraq, North Korea, and Uganda have been shocking. And that of the People's Republic of China has been horrendous, particularly during the Cultural Revolution in the late 1960s. As political and economic reform movements swept through the communist world in the 1980s, there was considerable hope that basic human rights and principles of democracy would be part of the Chinese reform movement. Tragically, a stated respect for human rights by the Chinese government lost all meaning as hundreds of students were either shot or crushed under the treads of tanks at Tiananmen Square in Beijing in June 1989 during a peaceful demonstration for democracy. A wave of trials, executions, and long imprisonments followed the defeat of the democratic movement. What most of these examples have in common is the belief, cited by many governments, that national security justifies violations of liberty, human rights, and the democratic process.

Justice, Equality, and Liberty

Justice, understood roughly as "fairness," involves balancing liberty and equality. But justice is perceived in different ways by different nations and by different groups within

Table 10.2 Income Concentrated in Wealthiest 10 Percent of Population, 2004

Country	Share of Income
Norway	23.4%
Australia	25.4
Netherlands	25.1
United States	29.9
Spain	25.2
Philippines	36.3
Peru	37.2
Tunisia	31.5
Bolivia	32.0
Nicaragua	45.0
Swaziland	50.2
Nigeria	40.8
Angola	42.2
Central African Republic	47.7

Source: United Nations Development Program, *Human Development Report, 2004* (New York: Oxford University Press, 2004), 143–146.

Note: Countries are listed in rank order of development, high to low, using the Human Development Index.

nations. Developed nations, and the more affluent citizens in all nations, may understand justice in terms of liberty, including the liberty to pursue wealth and protect property. In contrast, communist and developing countries, and the poor in many nations, may understand justice in terms of equality, particularly as signifying a fair share of the national wealth.

Thus there are many ways to measure a nation's commitment to justice, or fairness. One way is to examine the division of the national "pie"—that is, the way in which income is actually distributed within a nation. Table 10.2 indicates the extent to which overall national income was distributed within a variety of countries, developed and developing. The data represent the distribution of total disposable household income accruing to the wealthiest 10 percent of each country's population.

What is evident from these data is that, in general, the higher the development level, the more equitable the distribution of income within the society. However, even among developed countries, there are significant variations. The United States tends to have a greater gap between the rich and poor than other Western liberal democracies. A number of factors may contribute to the more skewed distribution of income in the developing world and in the United States. In some cases, consciously designed policies ensure that a small elite retains a higher percentage of wealth. These policies are frequently the result of values held by elites—in the United States, for instance, many elites (as well as common citizens) tend to believe that the state should not engage in an aggressive redistribution of wealth. But other factors—such as limited resources, capabilities, and power structures—may also be relevant. In addition, the larger pie in more affluent countries permits larger slices to be offered to all parts of the population.

The issue of justice and equality goes to the very heart of what values political elites hold. In particular, justice addresses the question of how to balance competing values. For instance, Americans believe in equality as well as individual freedom. It is quite possible that the demands of personal freedom—which might require a limited state that allows people to do what they want—will come into conflict with the ideal of equality—which might call for the state to limit concentrations of wealth.

Welfare and Economic Well-Being

Most nations endorse (at least in their rhetoric) the **welfare** and **economic well-being** of their people.[9] But what do the national governing elites mean by welfare and by economic well-being, and how successful are nations in advancing them? In general, the terms refer to people's needs for employment, income, food, housing, health, and literacy. Richer, industrial, developed nations have a much easier time satisfying these needs. They tend to allocate substantially more for education and health combined than they do for their military. This is not the case for the developing world, where the relative commitment to spending in education and health is more closely aligned to defense spending. Consequently, in poorer countries, military spending tends to more seriously detract from money allocated for welfare and economic well-being (for example schools, hospitals, and social welfare programs). Additionally, there is evidence that in poorer countries increases in military spending are associated with slowdowns in economic growth.

Global military spending increased sharply over 1995–2004, after having experienced a decline in the immediate post–cold war years 1990–1995. No region of the world was immune from these increases, but an encouraging trend occurred among some of the poorest countries, where significant reductions in military spending and increases in health and, to a lesser degree, education took place. Of the twenty-four poor countries for which data are available, sixteen, or 66 percent, reduced their military expenditures between 1990 and 2002. At the same time, seventeen, or 71 percent, increased their spending on health. A little less encouraging, yet positive, was the increase in spending on education among 37.5 percent of the poorest countries.

POPULAR VALUES

So far, we have investigated values from a national perspective. Furthermore, in considering what values nations claim to support, and in thinking about how they may, from time to time, fail to live up to their ideals, we have focused on the actions of elites. However, we also need to consider what citizens believe. In thinking about this, there are four main questions that we must take into account. First, what shapes the values of citizens? Second, what are those actual values? Third, how do they vary from country to country and within countries? Finally, is there a divide between the values espoused by elites and those espoused by average citizens? Related to this last question is the democratic concern about whether elites should follow public opinion and respect the basic values of the typical citizen.

There is considerable evidence that the values of the people who make up political communities are rooted in, and correlated with, a hierarchy of human needs: for sustenance and safety; for belonging and esteem; and for intellectual, aesthetic, and social fulfillment. This proposition is associated with the work of social psychologist Abraham H. Maslow (see chapter 5, Suggested Readings). A number of social scientists have tried to test Maslow's ideas. In two of the most famous attempts, Ronald Inglehart and Hadley Cantril found a great deal of empirical evidence supporting Maslow's hypothesis in their public opinion surveys.[10]

Most nations seek to ensure the economic well-being of their citizens. Some countries perpetually battle the odds. Bangladesh is one of the poorest countries in the world. The nation struggles to balance an enormous population, few natural resources, and debilitating weather. Here flood victims wait for food and fresh water in Bangladesh's northern Rajshahi district in September 1998.

Cantril's research found that a decent standard of living, a happy family life, and health ranked high among popular hopes.[11] Economic, family, and health concerns ranked high among popular leaders. Not surprisingly, war loomed large as a major fear among countries that had experienced it. Similarly, political instability was a major fear among

Figure 10.1 Public Preferences on Federal Spending, 2005

Mean billions cut or increased

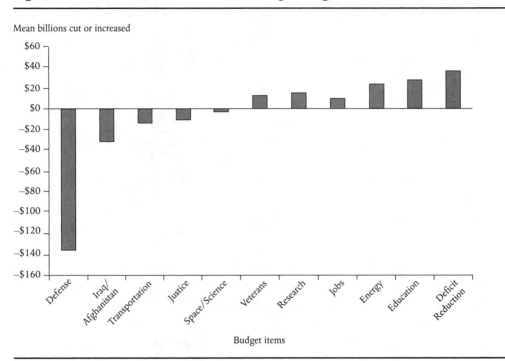

Budget items

Source: University of Maryland, Program on International Policy Attitudes (PIPA), *The Federal Budget: The Public's Priorities,* March 7, 2005, 5.

people whose countries had experienced major disorders. Inglehart's study found that, with some exceptions, the "priorities of Western publics correspond to a Maslovian model." [12]

However, that is only part of the story. Another important issue in thinking about popular values is whether, among citizens of a given society, there is broad consensus or significant disagreements about certain basic values. For example, party positions, electoral outcomes, and public opinion surveys in all Western democracies demonstrate that the main features of the modern welfare state—for example, unemployment compensation, old-age pensions, health care, and housing support—are here to stay. Similarly, most Western democracies are clearly committed to maintaining economic stability (in employment and prices) and to safeguarding law and order. Figure 10.1 reflects the results of a fascinating exercise conducted by the Program on International Policy Attitudes (PIPA) in 2005. The data clearly illustrate the wide support enjoyed by many of the government spending programs. They also show that in some fields, such as veterans' benefits, research, jobs, energy, and education, many Americans would like the government to spend even

Table 10.3 Views on Increasing or Cutting Spending on Government Service, 1990–2000 (in percentages)

Position	Party	1990	1992	1994	1996	1998	2000
Favor More	Democrats	47	39	35	38	45	51
Spending On	Independents	32	37	30	22	46	41
Services	Republicans	26	19	19	17	30	21
Favor Less	Democrats	17	14	22	18	19	8
Spending On	Independents	16	17	24	20	20	15
Services	Republicans	33	43	54	51	39	37
(N)		(1,962)	(2,438)	(1,773)	(1,711)	(1,281)	(1,980)

Source: Data are from the Research Center and the Center for Political Studies of the Institute for Social Research at the University of Michigan, National Election Study, www.umich.edu/~nes/.

more money than it currently does. We should note that sharp disagreements can exist between voters. In the United States, Republicans and Democrats differ substantially on such issues as government spending. (See Table 10.3.)

In the first decade of the twenty-first century, particularly after the 2000 and 2004 presidential elections, a phenomenon known as **culture wars** was elevated in the public consciousness. Stimulated in part by the increased political activism of the Christian right (see chapter 5), the American public seemed to be sharply divided over an array of values reflected in various positions on key public policy issues such as abortion, gay marriage, prayer in public schools, euthanasia, genetic research, and sex education. The division was epitomized by the "red" state and "blue" state analysis of the 2004 election. Through the heartland of America, a swath of "red" states was taken by incumbent George W. Bush while his opponent, John Kerry, took the predominantly "blue" states of the northeast and West Coast. But the blue and red labels stood for more than the Democratic and Republican Parties, or even the simple liberal and conservative designations. These colors were symbols of a deep culture war that had enveloped the United States, a battle for the soul of the country. Was this an accurate analysis of what was going on? Given second and third looks, many political analysts are not so sure. There is no question that there is a degree of liberal and conservative division among the electorate. But Morris Fiorina, Samuel J. Abrams, and Jeremy C. Pope assert that a politically polarized America is a myth, or at the very least grossly exaggerated. Political parties, individual politicians, and elements in the media perpetuate the notion of extreme polarization for their own ends. The reality is that most Americans are centrists, although there is evidence that at the elite level such bitter divisions do exist.[13]

One of the common objections to following too closely the values of typical citizens is that their views are fickle and uninformed. Many public surveys confirm that citizens are remarkably ignorant of basic political facts. Thus surveys of Americans show that people do not know who their congressional representative is, how many senators each state has, and who is chief justice of the United States.[14] When you take this ignorance and combine it with an apparent inconsistency of beliefs—citizens apparently change their views about public policy frequently and without reason—skeptics of democracy are bound to discount the importance of popular values.[15] However, recent work concerning American politics tends to find that inconsistency among voters is much less prevalent than we originally thought. Benjamin Page and Robert Shapiro, in their book *The Rational Public,* show how basic policy preferences of Americans, from the 1940s to the 1990s, are remarkably consistent and not subject to irrational changes. That said, consistent views do not necessarily translate into a culture war.

Of course, just because public opinion about key policies and support for certain basic values are stable does not mean there are no changes over time. For example, from 1965 to 1973 American public opinion turned against involvement in the war in Vietnam. Similarly, between 2003 and 2005 public support for America's war in Iraq declined significantly. Over a longer period, comparable or greater changes have taken place on other issues—changes supercharged with meaning for liberty, justice, and welfare. For example, U.S. values have changed significantly regarding race relations (attitudes toward African Americans), religious relations (attitudes toward Catholics and Jews), gender relations (attitudes toward women), and labor-management relations.

As we noted earlier regarding welfare, Western democratic publics and legislators have historically agreed about the main outlines of the welfare state, although more recent conservative governments (for example, former prime minister Margaret Thatcher's government in Britain and former president Ronald Reagan's administration in the United States) have begun movements to cut back or reform the welfare state. During the summer of 1996, President Bill Clinton, who had campaigned on the pledge to change welfare as we know it and had previously vetoed two Republican welfare bills as too harsh, finally signed into law sweeping welfare reform legislation largely sponsored by Republican lawmakers. In addition to significant changes in welfare benefits, the law called for greater emphasis being placed on getting welfare recipients off the welfare rolls and back to work. Finally, the federal government began divesting itself of some of its responsibility for welfare and giving greater responsibility to the fifty state governments.

We have little evidence on public opinion for most communist and developing countries. From 1917 in the Soviet Union and from the late 1940s in Eastern Europe to the recent collapse of communism in these regions, there were no elections involving competing parties to indicate popular responses to governing parties. Because of the lack of electoral history and general chaos in some of these systems, it may still be too early to make anything more than preliminary assessments. The peoples of the former Soviet Union and Eastern Europe are struggling with campaign and electoral processes they find unfamiliar. Slowly but surely, however, electoral processes began to take hold during the 1990s. The 1996 presidential election in Russia was hotly fought by those who constituted the winning majority in support of Boris Yeltsin and the reform movement, and by those who campaigned vigorously on behalf of the losing, but significant, minority who supported Gennadi Zyuganov, the Communist leader. In March 2000 another successful election was held, and Vladimir Putin, of the Edinstvo Party, was elected president. By 2005, however, serious questions were being raised about just how democratic the Putin regime really was. For example, increasing state intervention into the national media and use of the justice system to harass opponents of the government were disturbing trends.

Recent events in Eastern Europe and the former Soviet Union indicate a profound difference between the long-held values of government officials and values held by the people. For years Communist officials extolled the virtues of the economic systems they led. They publicly justified invasions of Hungary, Czechoslovakia, and Afghanistan. Centrally planned and administered policies were designed to provide adequate food, shelter, and medical care for all citizens. When the Eastern European economies collapsed and the Soviet system faced severe self-criticism under glasnost, the differences between the elite and the people became glaring. To varying degrees, domestic policies in all these states had failed to provide adequate food, housing, and medical care. The people were bitter; they felt betrayed. Hungarians and Czechoslovakians obviously resented the Soviet invasions of 1956 and 1968. It is clear now that many Soviet citizens saw the 1979 invasion of Afghanistan as immoral, destructive, and wasteful, despite years of official pronouncements about its necessity.

INTEREST GROUPS AND CLASS VALUES

Many political scientists are skeptical about national and popular values and about such notions as the national and the public interest. Such views, some critics contend, are too idealistic or too fuzzy. Instead, they see politics as a tug-of-war among competing interests. Or, to express it differently, they see public policy as the result of group pressures. Consequently, political scientists emphasize the importance of understanding the values and behavior of powerful interest groups in the political community. **Interest groups** usually comprise members of the public who organize and attempt to shape public policy on issues of concern to them.[16]

Other social scientists, those influenced by the egalitarian ideas of Marxism or socialism, call special attention to the interests held by each of the various classes, especially workers and capitalists. These social scientists emphasize the crucial political role played by **class values**. They, too, see key interests struggling for power, working to implement their values in laws, administrative policies, and court decisions. But these political scientists identify the key interests as classes. They see bourgeois politics in terms of conflict between the working class and the capitalist class. Communists see politics in communist countries in terms of a classless society. Other social scientists, however, have not been so sure and have seen subtle class conflicts persisting. They have also noted struggles among interest groups.

What interest group and class values operate in highly industrialized, communist, and developing countries? How do interests and classes agree and disagree? And is there a gap between actual values and the ideal values often associated with the public interest?

Interest Groups

Almost all modern political communities contain interest groups—economic, religious, ethnic, racial, professional, and reformist—seeking to protect their vital needs and fundamental interests. For example, labor unions seek to protect their right to organize and bargain collectively and to obtain full employment at good wages under good working conditions. Business and industrial groups seek to maintain a good profit margin. Farm groups seek higher farm prices.

Religious groups insist on religious freedom and a climate of opinion and public policies compatible with their objectives. Ethnic groups (which are sometimes also sectional groups) seek to preserve their heritage, including their language, customs, and way of life. Racial groups seek protection against an oppressive majority—protection in employment, housing, voting, and education. Professional groups (doctors, lawyers, journalists) seek to protect their independence, integrity, freedom, and profits.

A multitude of reform groups work to advance their special concerns. They fight for or against gun control, for or against national health insurance; they fight to protect the environment; they fight for amnesty for political prisoners. American students are familiar with many such interest groups: NRA (National Rifle Association), AFL-CIO (American Federation of Labor–Congress of Industrial Organizations), NAM (National Association of Manufacturers), the U.S. Chamber of Commerce, the National Council of Churches of Christ, the Anti-Defamation League of B'nai B'rith, NAACP (National Association for the Advancement of Colored People), the Sierra Club, Planned Parenthood, and the National Right to Life Committee.

Assessing the role that interest groups play in developing countries is difficult, given the wide range of economic and political systems. In older developing nations (for example, those in Latin America), interest groups are generally well established. Trade unions, in particular, have been extremely powerful in places such as Chile and Argentina. Roman Catholic liberation theologians and priests working in the rural and poverty-stricken areas of Latin America have become influential in recent decades. In more recently independent countries (for example, those in Africa), interest groups are present but are not always mature or possessed of a strong sense of history. They and their values become more apparent in times of political crisis, particularly when their actions produce dramatic change.

Because government, party, and public are so closely tied in communist countries, non-governmental interest groups have been less visible. Yet students of the communist political systems argue that governing party professionals, security police, military officers, industrial managers, economists, writers, scientists, educators, and jurists function the way that interest groups do in most developed nations, even though these people are very closely tied to the government.[17]

Class Values

In noncommunist countries, are values based on class? Do capitalists in bourgeois societies value private property, profits, and prestige, and act to enhance these values? Do workers value control of the means of production and exchange, a democratic political order able to satisfy their vital needs, cooperative production, and equitable enjoyment of community wealth? Do the values of capitalists and workers conflict in bourgeois societies?

Public opinion surveys, election statistics, and other studies throw some light on these questions. The evidence supports some aspects of class analysis but invalidates others. Most European countries are highly class conscious, but the United States tends to identify with the large, all-embracing middle class. Like the United States, Mexico is only moderately class conscious. But workers and lower-paid groups in Britain, France, Germany, and Italy tend to "vote for working-class Labour, Socialist, and Communist parties, while middle-class and professional people are more likely to vote for liberal and conservative parties."[18] Class values are more prominent in countries with strong social democratic parties (for example, Britain and Germany). Yet in Britain there is a sizable number of working-class Tories (Conservative Party members), and in Germany a sizable contingent of workers supports the more conservative Christian Democratic Party.

The power of class values in European countries was put to one dramatic test in World War I. In general, socialist parties, which expressed class values, had opposed the war because they interpreted it as a capitalist war; they endorsed the brotherhood of workers across national lines. Yet when push came to shove in 1914, German, French, and English workers forgot their class values of peace and international brotherhood, jumped on the nationalist bandwagons, and supported their countries' war efforts with great patriotism, courage, and sacrifice.

Proponents of class analysis sometimes explain the working class's lack of devotion to class values by invoking Marx's doctrine of "false consciousness." They argue that workers have been brainwashed by dominant capitalist values and have thus acquired bourgeois values that do not serve the vital needs and fundamental interests of the working class. However, critics of class analysis maintain that workers are not a monolithic class united by their common economic exploitation; although they will press pragmatically for their vital interests, they do not subscribe to wholesale socialism.

What about capitalists as a class? If workers do not neatly fit into a rigid class scheme, do capitalists? There is abundant evidence—in words, votes, and deeds—that capitalists try to protect the institution of private property, their profits, their power, and their prestige. But it would be a mistake to conclude that all capitalists agree on a common "class line." Although they may all want to protect private property and enterprise and to enhance their profits and influence, they differ about how to achieve those ends.

Moreover, in advanced industrial and democratic countries, capitalists accept a degree of government intervention in the economic sphere that their laissez-faire ancestors would have considered intolerable. Such an acceptance has, of course, resulted from considerable struggle: economic organization and strikes, political organization and reform leadership, and social education. Capitalists have, often reluctantly, but sometimes in their own self-interest, accepted economic reforms designed to satisfy not just the interests of workers but also the interests of small business owners, farmers, and consumers in general.

CONCLUSION

Our guiding hypothesis helps us understand the political values of political actors. We know that the values of nations, citizens, and interest groups are rooted in their vital needs, fundamental interests, and perceived desires. But to really understand political values we must precisely define such values as security, liberty, justice, and welfare. And we must ask critical questions. Security, liberty, justice, and welfare for whom? At what price?

General agreement about fundamental needs and interests holds all political communities together and enhances politics as a civilizing process. People do not have to agree on all fundamentals (say, on religion and economics), but they must know how to disagree in a civilized way. Sharp disagreements within and between political communities on needs, interests, and desires challenge politics as a civilizing process. Can humane and peaceful patterns of accommodation be worked out? Or must conflicts lead to violence, lawlessness, civil war, and international war?

The empirical political scientist must recognize that serious gaps exist between civilized (and often professed) national values and actual national values as measured by behavior. Perhaps not surprisingly, nations often do not practice what they preach about peace, human rights, justice, or welfare. These values are often sacrificed to distorted conceptions of national security and sovereignty, to falsely messianic ideologies, and to short-sighted self-interest.

If political scientists wish to put empirical science to work on behalf of politics as a civilizing process, they must more fully address the following questions about key values:

1. About peace: Are nation-states really dedicated—in thought and deed—to the values of peace and peaceful change? How can political scientists attack the root causes

of conflicts over vital needs and fundamental interests? Which breakthroughs in goals, principles, and policies will bring about a free, just, and peaceful world?

2. About liberty: Do the peoples of all political communities enjoy fundamental human rights and the power to govern their own lives? Why or why not? Which breakthroughs in goals, principles, and policies are required to achieve fuller human rights and democratic governance throughout the globe?

3. About justice: Do the goals, principles, and policies of justice really prevail within and between political communities? Why? Why not? Which breakthroughs in goals, principles, and policies are called for if a fuller approximating of human rights and democratic governance is to be achieved throughout the globe?

4. About welfare: How well off, economically and socially, are the peoples of the world? What accounts for their level of well-being? Which goals, principles, and policies can sensibly be pursued to satisfy basic economic and social needs and to create the conditions for more satisfying lives?

Our investigation of values invites both hopeful and fearful forecasts. Individual values are correlated with a hierarchy of needs, and it becomes obvious why such values are firmly grounded in human biology, psychology, and sociology. Thus such fundamental values cannot be so easily ignored by governing elites who fear satisfaction of the people's needs as a threat to their own income, power, or status. In all likelihood, sustenance and security needs, which rank high even in more advanced industrial societies, will preserve welfare policies in all political communities. Despite recent assaults on the welfare state in the United States, there is a wide consensus about the goal of fostering the citizenry's welfare. The debate largely centers on the means to reach this laudable goal. But our investigation also underscores the tragic folly of policies that force nations to choose between guns and butter—to skew other urgent national priorities in favor of armaments even though their limited resources are badly needed for food, clothing, shelter, and education.

There is evidence that more affluent, better-educated people in all systems are more attuned to the social value of belonging and to intellectual and artistic values. It should be possible for such people to transcend the narrow nationalist commitments so frequently associated with war, as well as the materialist concerns that threaten the ecological environment. This prospect is less promising, however, in the poorer countries of the developing world, where basic needs are not fulfilled and where nationalism remains a potent, and often valuable, force for social cohesion.

The spread of affluence in the closing decade of the twentieth century and the new century may be limited (in rich and poor countries alike) by ecological problems: a population out of balance with resources (particularly in poorer, developing countries), the depletion of such nonrenewable resources as oil, and the social costs of pollution. Here the empirical political scientist must ask disturbing questions. If the cornucopia (abundant land, water, and resources) becomes exhausted, will support for a more generous community and for human development disappear? Will tensions increase within and between nations? Will potentially serious conflicts leading to revolution and war be exacerbated?

The critical student of politics must also ask tough questions about interest groups and classes. If public policy results from powerful group pressures, what does this mean for the peace, liberty, justice, and welfare of the less powerful (for example, the poor, minorities, and women)? Will their vital needs and fundamental interests be neglected? Or will changes favorable to them only be slowly paced or come in small increments?

As we critically explore the values of political actors, we become aware of political well-being in communities around the globe. We understand such well-being as a particular cluster of values: security and peace; liberty, human rights, and democracy; justice and equality; economic and social welfare. We may also ask what accounts for such political well-being. A fuller account requires an exploration of patterns of cooperation, accommodation, and conflict in politics. These patterns within nations are discussed in chapter 11.

SUGGESTED READINGS

Almond, Gabriel A., and Sidney Verba. *The Civic Culture: Political Attitudes and Democracy in Five Nations.* Boston: Little, Brown, 1965. Explores the cluster of values that sustain an effective and stable democratic policy. For a valuable criticism and update of the five countries studied (Britain, Italy, Mexico, the United States, and West Germany), see Almond and Verba, eds., *The Civic Culture Revisited* (Newbury Park, Calif.: Sage Publications, 1989).

Cantril, Hadley. *The Pattern of Human Concerns.* New Brunswick: Rutgers University Press, 1965. Uses global interviews—and sample survey techniques—to identify popular values. Provides basis for cross-national comparisons. Finds common demands rooted in values of self-preservation, security, order, opportunity for development, and integrity.

Cigler, Allan J., and Burdett A. Loomis, eds. *Interest Group Politics.* 6th ed. Washington, D.C.: CQ Press, 2002. An informative and varied group of up-to-date essays on various kinds of interest groups, including both domestic and foreign lobbying efforts.

Fiorina, Morris, Samuel J. Abrams, and Jeremy C. Pope. *Culture War? The Myth of a Polarized America.* New York: Longman, 2004. A serious critique of the notion that the American public is deeply polarized as a manifestation of a great cultural divide. To the contrary, most Americans are centrists or moderates.

Huntington, Samuel P. *The Clash of Civilizations and the Remaking of World Order.* New York: Simon and Schuster, 1996. A provocative look at the post–cold war era, with an emphasis on the potential for cultural conflict.

Inglehart, Ronald. *The Silent Revolution: Changing Values and Political Styles among Western Publics.* Princeton: Princeton University Press, 1977. Sees the values of Western publics shifting from "an overwhelming emphasis on material well-being and physical security toward a greater emphasis on the quality of life." Provides empirical support for Abraham H. Maslow's hierarchy of needs hypothesis. Thought provoking. Also see Inglehart's *Culture Shift in Advanced Industrial Societies* (Princeton: Princeton University Press, 1990).

Maslow, Abraham H. *Toward a Psychology of Being*. 3rd ed. New York: Wiley, 1998; and *Motivation and Personality*. 3rd ed. New York: Addison-Wesley, 1987. Maslow's influential views of the relationship between needs and values and his famous hierarchy of needs. For a keen and penetrating analysis of the concept of human needs, see Patricia Springborg, *The Problem of Human Needs and the Critique of Civilization* (London: Allen and Unwin, 1981).

Page, Benjamin, and Robert Shapiro. *The Rational Public*. Chicago: University of Chicago Press, 1992. A superb account of American public opinion from 1940 to 1990. The authors make a strong case that public opinion is more reasonable and consistent than many other critics of democracy allow.

Stimson, James A. *Tides of Consent: How Public Opinion Shapes American Politics*. New York: Cambridge University Press, 2004. Thoughtful and well-written analysis of American public opinion, with some emphasis on opinions that reside below the polling data.

GLOSSARY TERMS

class values (p. 229)
culture wars (p. 227)
economic well-being (p. 224)
goal (p. 215)
interest groups (p. 229)
national interest (p. 216)
policy (p. 215)
political actor (p. 215)
political values (p. 215)
principle (p. 215)
public interest (p. 217)
welfare (p. 224)

Chapter 11

NATIONAL POLITICS: CULTURE, CONSTITUTIONS, CITIZENS

In chapter 10 we were concerned with the political values of political actors. These values call attention to the purposes of politics; the vital needs and fundamental interests of political actors; and such objectives as security, liberty, justice, and welfare. But we did not explore the patterns that political actors follow to satisfy these values. These patterns will be the subject of our inquiry in this chapter and in chapter 12.

As we noted in chapter 10, the needs, interests, and desires of the various political actors do not always mesh. Different people interpret security, liberty, justice, and welfare in different ways. They struggle for power to determine who gets what, when, where, and how. These facts of political life prompt students of politics to ask, How, in the absence of unanimity as a regular condition in politics, do political actors achieve their values? How do they cooperate for common ends? Work out accommodation among competing interests? Handle conflicts when accommodation fails? Political actors must cooperate because if they do not, civilized politics and effective government are impossible. Political actors also must accommodate competing interests, because if they do not, priorities cannot be established and decisions made. Moreover, political actors must handle conflicts prudently, or the community may be torn apart by strife too difficult to moderate.

Accommodation involves both governmental and nongovernmental actors. Since government is one major instrument to help citizens achieve their purposes, citizens must make sure that government does what they want it to do. And because government is so powerful, citizens must make sure that it does not abuse its power—that it remains subject to their control. These ethical and empirical considerations point toward the significant empirical problem we explore in this and the following chapter: *Given that politics is a struggle for purpose and power, which political patterns further cooperation, advance accommo-*

dation, and handle conflicts in domestic politics? We define successful cooperation in terms of maximizing willing cooperation, humane accommodation, and peaceful resolution of conflicts, and also in terms of the ability to maximize security, liberty, justice, and welfare.

PATTERNS FOR COOPERATION, ACCOMMODATION, AND CONFLICT RESOLUTION

Although we cannot definitively resolve this important but complex problem, we may use the key question itself to explore patterns of politics, with a particular focus on industrialized democratic countries. Our hypothesis in chapters 11 and 12 is that successful patterns for furthering cooperation, advancing accommodation, and handling conflicts in politics require the following:

1. Agreement on certain constitutional fundamentals to facilitate consensus and trust. Without a certain amount of consensus, no political community can carry on its business. Without a certain amount of trust, orderly procedures for discussion and decision would be impossible. Agreement on fundamentals involves accepted rules of the constitutional game (on voting; freedom of speech, press, and assembly; majority decision; due process of law) that enable political actors to civilize the struggle for power. Some political cultures are more effective at reaching agreement on fundamentals by making it easier to educate and socialize citizens in sound rules of the political game.

2. Meaningful opportunities for expressing needs, interests, and desires to direct us to **interest articulation.** Political actors must be able to express themselves, to articulate their needs, interests, and desires. They may do this in a number of ways: by voting, speaking out in public forums, working for a political party, joining interest groups, using the mass media, and contacting their elected representatives. Such opportunities facilitate cooperation and accommodation in responsive political systems. Citizens who take advantage of such opportunities are often more knowledgeable about politics and better educated than nonparticipants.

3. Sound mechanisms for selecting priorities involving what some political scientists call **interest aggregation**, by which political actors build support for certain proposals and not for others. Some needs and interests are more important than others. Political actors usually find it necessary to work with others to advance the ideas that they believe merit support. Political leaders and parties play key roles in building support for political priorities, but they do not have a monopoly on this enterprise.

4. Concern with acceptable ways of legitimating public policy choices, which means articulating, and agreeing on, principles and mechanisms of political obligation. Why do people obey those officials who make law and execute public policy? Why, for example, in the United States do citizens accept the result of an election, a law

passed by Congress, a decision of the Supreme Court, or a presidential initiative in foreign affairs? Why do people go along with a majority decision? The answer is simple. Without agreement on ideas and ways to obtain approval of the exercise of political power, the struggle for power could easily get out of hand; politics would quickly disappear; and lawlessness, disorder, and civil war would ensue.

5. A government that can maintain freedom, law, and order; raise and spend revenue on behalf of agreed-on public purposes; and ensure the provision of necessary services and benefits. If government cannot modestly fulfill its own objectives—say, of security, liberty, justice, and welfare—it is in deep trouble. Political patterns cannot succeed unless they advance effective governance.

6. Regular and effective controls on government. There must be constitutional mechanisms to ensure that government is a wise and limited servant, not a tyrannical master.

We will explore our hypothesis by focusing on political culture, constitutional arrangements, and the role of nongovernmental actors. Throughout our analysis we will be concerned with whether the political patterns we have examined are voluntary or imposed, humane or barbaric, peaceful or violent.

POLITICAL CULTURE AND THE FRAMING OF POLITICS

One way of exploring how political regimes function is to investigate the idea of political culture. **Political culture** refers to the distinguishing attitudes, habits, and behavior patterns that characterize a political community—the ethos of a place. Students of politics can observe important distinctions between what values and beliefs are central to a given society. The ethos of a country may be peaceful or warlike, tolerant or intolerant; it may be altruistic or selfish, trustful or suspicious, cooperative or competitive. The dominant ethos may be genuinely egalitarian or racist and sexist. The people may be cultured, literate, and active in politics, or they may be uncultured, uneducated, and uninvolved. We do not mean to suggest that all people within a given society agree about politics or even agree with all the traditions and customs of their culture. However, societies have a dominant set of characteristics that enjoy widespread support. In the United States, for instance, there is a great emphasis placed on individual freedom. Other cultures may be more concerned with collective equality or less enamored with the very idea of personal freedom.

A political community's culture is significantly influenced by a number of factors. These include the larger environment, as we saw in chapter 5. The climate, kinds of natural resources, and population all affect political culture. A nation's historical experience and memory clearly shape its culture, as do its language, religion, literature, art, and social mores. Economics (how people earn a living) and geography (especially the prevalence and distribution of resources) also influence the cultural ethos. Science and technology influence how political business is conducted. These influences in the broader culture dictate certain patterns of cooperation and accommodation, and they set in motion certain conflicts, which politics must moderate or resolve.

Why Is Political Culture Important?

Some examples may help illustrate the importance of the political culture. For instance, in the United States the acceptance of slavery in the southern states and the development of an industrial and agricultural economy based on free labor in the northern and western states created tension and conflict between the South and the North and West. The outcome was a dreadful civil war—the worst fate that can afflict domestic politics. But although slavery in the United States made for conflict, the fact that Americans have been a people of plenty—and have lived in a spacious land of abundant resources—has undoubtedly taken the edge off class conflict and made it easier to achieve accommodation in politics. The Civil War and its aftermath also illustrate the way in which political cultures can change and evolve over time.

Russia and the Soviet Union offer another example. Tsarist Russia lacked a tradition of natural law (or higher law), meaningful representative government, and effective local democracy. The despotism of the tsars unquestionably stimulated cruel and conspiratorial responses by the Russian Bolsheviks as they sought to overthrow this despotism and build a heroic communist society. Finally in the late 1980s and early 1990s, forces arose to challenge the centralized power of the Soviet Communist Party. But even as late as 2005, during the postcommunist era, the Russian government under Vladimir Putin continued to struggle to preserve new democratic patterns. As economic challenges and ethnic conflict continue to frustrate many in Russia, forces of authoritarianism threaten its fragile democracy.

In India, religious, social, geographic, and economic differences have made cooperation and accommodation in politics

Black Americans participated in the Northern forces during the American Civil War, inspired by the promise of an end to slavery. Their efforts helped win the war for the Union; however, they were treated far from equally. The black soldiers in this photograph, taken at City Point, Virginia, are clothed in cast-off federal uniforms. Black soldiers such as these were also forbidden to carry arms for the first two years of the war.

difficult. After World War II old British India was divided into a primarily Muslim Pakistan and a Hindu India. Despite this political division, differences between Muslims and Hindus have caused great tension in modern India, both between Pakistan and India and within India itself. Kashmir, which is populated largely by Muslims, remains an Indian state and is a source of chronic conflict. Throughout the 1990s and continuing until the present, religious differences led to violence in the region. Caste differences—with Brahmins at the top and "untouchables" at the bottom of the social and economic scale—also militate against cooperation in the spirit of equality. India's religious and social system makes reform urgent and yet extraordinarily difficult. On the other hand, Mohandas Gandhi's philosophy of nonviolence and democracy has encouraged peaceful resolution of disputes and the maintenance of traditions such as village industry—much to the dismay of those Indian revolutionaries who believe that the country will not become free and prosperous without a radical, even violent, revolution to usher in a new social and economic system.

A nation's broader culture makes an important contribution to successful (or unsuccessful) patterns of political accommodation. Indeed, the other factors that will be examined—expression of needs and interests, selection of priorities, legitimation of public choices, effective governance, and controls on government—flow from the broader cultural framework.

Agreement on the Fundamentals of Political Culture

The cultural framework is important because it provides the fundamental agreement—and therefore the trust—without which politics cannot advance as a civilizing process. It provides sound rules for the political game. This agreement on fundamentals does not require agreement on all aspects of life. All citizens need not belong to the same religion or speak the same language. They do not have to have the same economic, political, or social views. Homogeneous (similar) values may contribute to political trust, but heterogeneous (diverse) values do not necessarily lead to civil war. What is crucial is that there is enough agreement on enough fundamentals to hold the political community together. And there must also be agreement on how to disagree.

Thus Americans may be Protestants, Catholics, Jews, Muslims, atheists, or agnostics. They may be capitalists, socialists, or believers in some variety of a "mixed economy." They may be Democrats, Republicans, or independents. They may believe that virtue resides only in the breast of the farmer or that culture is only to be found in big cities such as New York. They may speak English, Spanish, or other languages. They may strongly differ on policies involving abortion, taxation, or disarmament. Yet despite these difference, they may still be able to work out successful patterns of accommodation because they agree on the basic principles of the American Constitution: government based on the consent of the governed; free elections; freedom of speech, press, assembly, and religion;

equal justice under the law; and majority rule. Diversity, then, need not lead to failure in coping with the struggle for power. However, learning to cope with diversity is the key to successful accommodation.

Different nations have different conceptions of what is fundamental. We will spell out one model, the Western democratic model, which has been called **polyarchy** (rule by the many). Numerous countries in what is left of the communist world and in the developing world exhibit a political culture quite different from the polyarchy that exists in the countries of North America and Western Europe. The democratic, or polyarchal, framework has the following characteristics:

1. Citizens and governments agree to strive for the common good. Although preached more than practiced, this fundamental principle (as understood in terms of security, liberty, justice, and welfare) clarifies the purposes of politics. It requires citizens and the government to cooperate to achieve these purposes. Conflicts must respect these values, safeguard vital human needs, and protect fundamental interests.

2. Citizens and governments agree on certain bounds for political maneuvers, ruling out patterns of politics such as slavery, genocide, eradication of economic classes, and religious persecution—practices considered evil by most civilized people. Accommodation must be based on an open, not closed, society.

3. Citizens and governments agree that an important area for accommodation lies outside the public sphere. They must agree, therefore, on a private sphere in which individuals and groups may work out their problems by themselves, so long as life, liberty, and law are respected and so long as private accommodation does not violate the common good.

4. Citizens and governments agree on the reality of human diversity and human fallibility as well as on the imperative of searching for patterns of accommodation that are helpful if not perfect. To avoid the imposition of tyrannical or totalitarian truths, people must insist on free expression of ideas and beliefs.

5. Citizens and governments agree about the need for judicious balance. Often, sensible accommodation calls for striking a balance between contending claims, interests, and units of government—the claims, for example, of producers and consumers; the interests of workers, farmers, and industrialists; and the actions of central and local government.

6. Citizens and governments agree that balancing, harmonizing, and adjusting the purposes and powers of political actors call for various skills and functions at many levels. This process requires diverse contributions to successful accommodation—hence, pluralism and polyarchy.

7. Finally, citizens and governments agree on how to secure willing obedience to the process of accommodation. This ensures legitimacy—acceptance of key decisions and public policies. In polyarchies legitimacy is enhanced by widely accepted ideas

such as free and competitive elections, the protection of basic rights, opposition political parties, due process of law, and limited government.

Although countries following the polyarchal, or Western democratic, model may agree on fundamentals, they do not have to have identical political systems. For example, both the British and U.S. systems are democratic. Yet the British have chosen parliamentary supremacy, cabinet government, strong party government, and quasi-unitary government (terms that will be clarified shortly), whereas Americans have opted for separation of powers, presidential government, weak party government, and federalism.

CONSTITUTIONAL FEATURES

This section presents some constitutional features that are especially relevant to conflict and accommodation in politics. While political culture provides the backdrop against which politics is played, every society has certain rules for the political game. These rules are spelled out in the **constitution** of a country. In some cases, the constitution is a clearly written document, such as the U.S. Constitution. In other cases, it is a collection of documents written over many years, such as the British Constitution.

Limited or Unlimited Government

One of the first questions we must ask about any political system is how limited or unlimited government is. For instance, at one extreme, Joseph Stalin's Soviet and Adolf Hitler's German governments exercised almost unlimited domestic power in every sector of society—education, the economy, the arts, and the private lives of citizens. Today, very repressive governments are found in Burma (Myanamar) and North Korea. As noted in chapters 6 and 7, liberal democratic and democratic socialist governments (which follow the polyarchal pattern) insist that governmental power be limited. One of the great examples of how government can be limited is found in the U.S. Constitution's Bill of Rights. In that document, various personal freedoms and rights (such as freedom of speech and religion and the right to a fair trial) are clearly protected from government interference. While there can be spirited disagreements between liberal democrats and democratic socialists about the role of government, both groups agree that there must be some clear limits to what a government can do. Without those limits the specter of tyranny haunts a society.

Representative Government or Direct Democracy

Although governments in the highly developed industrial countries usually depend on the consent of the governed, the people exercise their power through elected representatives—for example, through a president and members of Congress in the United States.

Direct democracy—in which the people make laws firsthand—is rare in the United States. It exists primarily at the state or local level, as in the New England town meeting or when the people vote to amend a state constitution or vote on other cardinal issues of public policy. Other developed systems occasionally permit the whole nation to vote on a major issue—for example, in 1973 the British people voted on whether to join the European Common Market. Though exceptions such as these exist, most democracies primarily rely on some form of representative government.

One of the most important political questions of the twenty-first century is: To what extent the former communist countries will be able to create representative governments? A related question is: To what extent will countries that remain formally communist, such as China, be able to adapt certain features of representative government to their own? It is true that in places such as Russia the form of government is democratic. Yet recent actions by President Putin, such as growing censorship of the media and centralizing of power, makes the movement toward democratic reform seem less clear. We can ask whether this is simply the appearance of representative democracy masking a more fundamental authoritarian regime dominated by authoritarian-minded rulers. This is a classic example of how culture can influence politics. Although the official laws of a country may be democratic and representative, the actual practice of politics, affected by centuries of tradition and custom, can remain stubbornly undemocratic.

Many developing countries have effective representative institutions, but there is a predominance of authoritarianism in the developing world. This authoritarianism may stem from several factors, depending on the region, history, and culture. Power in a number of developing nations is held by a military or political elite that seized control by force and rules without benefit of electoral legitimacy. It is difficult to generalize about so many different countries and regions; however, a few examples will suffice to illustrate the hopes and fears of those who champion democracy. For instance, there is ample evidence that the peoples of Central America aspire to democratic forms of government. One long-standing democracy is Costa Rica. But for long periods, powerful families, such as the Somozas in Nicaragua from 1937 to 1979, and military strong men, such as Manuel Noriega in Panama from 1983 to 1989, dominated the political life of many Central American countries. Patterns of imposed authority left over from Spanish colonial rule and a long history of military involvement in politics sustain these trends.

Democracy has had a difficult time in many Asian countries. Even highly developed countries such as South Korea have, until very recently, been authoritarian. Singapore, one of the most dynamic economic actors in Asia, remains politically authoritarian. Parliamentary democracy has had a very rocky, unstable, and limited existence in Indonesia. According to Nathan Keyfitz of Harvard, one must understand the various strains of Asian culture—the value placed on order, on unity, and on concentration of power, as well as the fear of chaos—to understand these difficulties.[1]

Separation or Connection of Powers

To ensure greater safety amid the struggle for power, a nation's constitutional framework may, in addition to limiting power, also require that power be held by different hands. Thus in the United States power is divided among three branches of government—legislative, executive, and judicial—according to the principle of **separation of powers**. Constitutionally, Congress must enact all legislation. The president may sign or veto the legislation, but Congress may, by a two-thirds vote, override the president's veto. For good measure, the U.S. Congress consists of a Senate and a House of Representatives, and both houses must agree on legislation before it can be enacted. Moreover, the U.S. Supreme Court is independent of both the legislative and executive branches and may declare an act of Congress unconstitutional or hold that a presidential action violates a valid law.

Of course, the Founders did not intend for separation of powers to paralyze government. They expected separation of powers to ensure wise governance. The American system thus rests on the premise of cooperation and accommodation. Deadlocks may occur, however, when the president and Congress favor different political philosophies. Such deadlocks make either for sensible compromise or for ineffectual government. The possibilities of conflict in a system of separation of powers have increased the importance of strong and responsible parties to unite Congress and the president in a common program endorsed by the people. Yet even when government is unified under one-party rule, change can come slowly, if at all. President George W. Bush's efforts to reform Social Security at the beginning of his second term were largely thwarted by opposition from the Democrats—the minority party in Congress—and a lack of strong support from his fellow Republicans.

By way of contrast, political power in the British government rests in a prime minister and a cabinet responsible to a majority in the House of Commons. Here we have a **connection of powers**—not a separation. Unlike the American president, who is elected for a four-year term independently of members of Congress, the British prime minister is usually the person who commands a majority of votes in the House of Commons. With that majority, the prime minister and key leaders of his or her party organize a cabinet that runs the British government. The House of Commons and the cabinet are thus connected. British prime ministers lead the government because they have been empowered by a majority in Commons. Losing that majority seriously jeopardizes their ability to remain in power. The British Parliament must formally enact legislation, but such legislation usually originates in the cabinet.

Theoretically, the British Parliament consists of two branches: the House of Commons and the House of Lords. Constitutionally, however, all effective power resides in Commons. The British also have an independent system of courts; but British courts, in contrast to their American counterparts, have no power to declare an act of Parliament unconstitutional. Consequently, deadlock between the executive and the legislature is impossible in the British system. If the prime minister and the cabinet do not command a majority in the Commons, the prime minister must either resign in favor of someone who will command such a majority or call for new elections that will produce a new majority in Commons and a prime minister who has the confidence of that majority.

In 1997, Tony Blair was voted in as prime minister of England, the first Labour Party member to win since 1979. Here Blair speaks before the House of Commons.

The late twentieth century brought a wave of democratic experiments in the developing world. But many of those governments do not incorporate the American principle of separation of powers. Some (such as India) are close to the British principle of connection of powers, with a prime minister responsible to a majority in the legislature. Others (for example, Mexico) have an independently elected president who rules without effective interference from an elected legislature or an independent judiciary. Nigeria has a long tradition of an independent judiciary, even through periods of military rule. But these examples appear more the exception than the rule. Regarding the Asian cultural emphasis on unity and order, Keyfitz observes, "A division of constitutional responsibility between government, parliament, and the courts would be a dispersal of power, a sign that the community was breaking up." [2]

The American Founders favored separation of powers because they believed (as James Madison wrote in *Federalist* No. 47) that the "accumulation of all powers, legislative, executive, and judiciary, in the same hands, whether of one, a few, or many, and whether hereditary, self-appointed, or elective, may justly be pronounced the very definition of tyranny." Similarly, the British have understood that a connection of powers—with the prime minister responsible to a majority in Commons and a loyal opposition party monitoring the party in power—can advance effective and responsible government without sacrificing freedom.

Federalism or Unitary Government

Every large and complicated political community must include cooperation between the national political community and its component parts. There also must be accommoda-

Figure 11.1 U.S. Federal System (simplified)

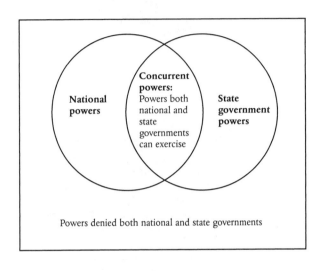

Source: Compiled by authors.

tion between the central government and local governments. And conflicts that arise between various levels of government must be handled sagaciously. How does a federal system contribute to successful accommodation? How is the problem of decentralization handled in a unitary political system as compared with a federal system? How is it possible to keep government close to the people?

Federalism is one attempt to reconcile local liberty and national authority. Federalism allows people living in certain localities (in America think of the fifty states) to handle their local problems while giving the central government (in which they also have a voice) power to handle nationwide concerns. A federal system achieves this accommodation by demarcating national and state jurisdictions and powers, by indicating which powers the national government and the state governments may exercise concurrently, and by denying them certain other powers (see Figure 11.1). Federalism is generally a response to the size and diversity of countries such as Canada, India, and the United States. It is designed to balance necessary central authority on behalf of the nation with local liberty and self-government.

A classic federal system exists in the United States. The central, or national, government holds broad but carefully enumerated powers: powers to handle matters of national concern such as defense, foreign relations, taxation, spending for the general welfare, and regulation of interstate and foreign commerce. Some powers (foreign relations and interstate and foreign commerce) are exclusive powers that only the central government can exercise. Other powers (for example, taxation and spending) may also be exercised by the states. All powers neither delegated to the central government nor logically implied as belonging to it come under the jurisdiction of the states (for example, provisions for local schools and police and fire protection). Certain powers are denied to both the central government and state governments (for example, the power to deprive a person of life, liberty, or property without due process of law).

Theoretically, federalism makes it possible for political actors in state and local government to express their needs and interests. They can determine their local priorities—for example, where they want to locate their schools, or what speed limit to impose on traffic. In this way citizens can keep a closer eye on their local government and make sure that it is acceptable to them and effective in addressing their concerns. In addition, a federal system keeps the central government from absorbing all power.

Of course, there are continuing debates about what should be a state matter and what should be a federal matter. Frequently, this pits local demands to protect certain customary practices against national concerns about justice. A classic example of this in the United States was the decades-long history of state governments discriminating against African Americans. This injustice led to the call for national action that resulted in Congress, under the leadership of President Lyndon B. Johnson, taking action in the 1960s to protect civil rights and voting rights for minorities.

The successes of state (and local) government must, however, also be acknowledged. State and local governments enhance democracy by keeping government close to the people. People can more easily participate in such governments; they can take initiatives and exercise greater local responsibility. They can respond more quickly to problems. In general, the federal division of powers encourages experimentation, with the opportunity to cancel bad experiments without great losses and to duplicate good experiments nationwide after success at the state level. Thus a great deal of reform legislation—involving, for example, wages and hours, collective bargaining, unemployment compensation, and welfare reform—has been pioneered in progressive states.

By way of contrast with federalism in the United States, France and Japan have a **unitary government**. In unitary governments all power emanates from the center—from Paris or Tokyo in these cases. National power includes not only the power to make war or regulate the economy, but also the power to shape the educational curriculum of all public schools, so that in France, for example, on any given day in the public school system, all children are reading the same books. In France the prefect is the national government's chief administrator in each of the country's ninety-five departments (geographic and administrative units). Elected assemblies in the departments and communes (local governmental units) lack significant power. The national government thus carries out policy at the local level; locally elected officials are pretty much restricted to municipal questions and to bargaining with Paris and the prefect.

Great Britain, or the United Kingdom (England, Scotland, Wales, and Northern Ireland), illustrates a pattern between a federal and a unitary form of government, although leaning toward the unitary. Traditionally, all power emanated from London—and the British Parliament. But Northern Ireland had its own parliament before the bloody conflict between Irish Catholics seeking union with Ireland and Protestants insisting on keeping their tie with the British Crown. Moreover, the Scots and the Welsh have been given opportunities to vote on having their own governments within the framework of the British Constitution. Thus because of the unique historical composition of the United Kingdom, the centuries-old tradition of local government, and the complexities of the modern welfare state, Britain has seen a great deal of **devolution** (the surrendering of powers to local authorities by a central government). For example, many national policies are carried out by local units of government. British municipalities govern themselves in local matters, much as American municipalities do. And efforts have been made to maximize the voice that the Scots, Welsh, and Irish have in their own geographic domains.

Not all large countries are federal; China, for example, is not. And a number of small countries (such as Switzerland and Austria) are federal. Nevertheless, three characteristics of states make them good candidates for federalism: large size, diverse ethnic and linguistic groups, and a historical tradition of local self-government. In responding to these factors, federal systems can provide ways to reconcile central authority and local liberty. Successful reconciliation may, however, depend on combining a sense of nationalism with a respect for diversity—a combination difficult to work out at any time.

Majority Rule

Space does not permit a more definitive treatment of all constitutional techniques of accommodation in politics. Yet it is important to treat at least one additional method, one that has figured prominently in the developed countries, is partially employed in communist countries, and plays absolutely no role in purely authoritarian systems: **majority rule**. We define majority rule as the power of one-half of the members, plus one, of any decision-making group to bind the remainder of that group to a decision. This ideal demands that political actors rely on discourse and votes, rather than on edicts and force, in dealing with the struggle for purpose and power. But how many heads are to be counted? In reaching decisions, what percentage of ballots is relied on to identify the winning candidate or policy?

Historically, majority rule has facilitated orderly decision making. Winners have been able to act; losers have abided by the results of the ballot box. Decisions made by majority rule—whether in elections or in the legislative body—have been accepted as legitimate. Majority rule ensures popular and effective government. It avoids the difficulty of having to achieve unanimity on all issues, a difficulty that could lead to a dangerous breakdown in government—and thus to either impotence or anarchy. Majority rule also avoids the unrepublican consequences of relying on a minority whose power is based on force, birth, or wealth. Such minority power lacks legitimacy—the consent of the governed. Minority decisions do not command the will, respect, and peaceful obedience of a population. Instead they engender popular disrespect for the law and undermine the resolution of conflicts by peaceful and orderly processes, thus threatening political stability and governmental effectiveness. Minorities might resort to force to execute their decisions or to make them stick, but they often lack the means to do so. Furthermore, the difficulty of ascertaining which minority is to rule would produce troublesome conflicts among rich and poor, educated and ignorant, white and black.

The functioning of majority rule in the United States and Britain has not, however, produced "majority tyranny." One discerning historian, Henry Steele Commager, has written, apropos of the United States, that there is no "persuasive evidence from our own long and complex historical experience that majorities are given to contempt for constitutional limitations or minority rights. . . . They have not taxed wealth out of existence; they have not been hostile to education or to science. The pulpit, the press, the school, the forum, are as free here as anywhere in the world—with the possible exception of that other great majority-rule country—Britain." [3] This is true largely because the constitutional rules of the game in the highly developed nations also require protection of basic rights for all. In the process of resolving disputes by majority rule, a great deal of accommodation goes on. To achieve a majority, conflicting demands must be adjusted to work out sane compromises. This process makes for helpful moderation and desirable reconciliation. The widespread use of majority rule can be illustrated in runoff elections. In France a runoff election is held when a candidate for president does not receive a majority of votes in the first election. The same is true for the gubernatorial races in some U.S. states. This practice guards against having an official elected by a plurality of votes—that is, the highest number cast but below 50 percent. The second election ensures that the winner has the electoral support of a majority of those voting.

In assessing majority rule as an accommodating technique in countries such as the United States, we should note several qualifications or reservations. Majorities do not necessarily decide all elections. Frequently, a plurality of votes (that is, the highest number cast for a given candidate) rules rather than a majority. This may happen when there are more than two candidates for an office. Even more interesting is that, in certain circumstances, a minority can actually rule. In the 2000 U.S. presidential election, Vice President Al Gore received 500,000 more votes than George W. Bush; however, because of the Electoral College Bush was the winner. (See Map 11.1.) The Electoral College is a unique system for deciding the U.S. presidency, one that does not take into account majority rule. Instead, each state has a number of Electoral College votes equal to the number of representatives and senators it has in Washington. (The District of Columbia, although it has no voting representatives or senators in Congress, does have three Electoral College votes.) In most cases when a candidate wins a state, even if by just one vote, that candidate

Map 11.1 U.S. Presidential Election, 2000

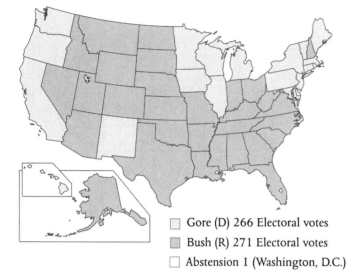

☐ Gore (D) 266 Electoral votes

▨ Bush (R) 271 Electoral votes

☐ Abstension 1 (Washington, D.C.)

Source: J. Clark Archer and others, *Atlas of American Politics 1996–2000* (Washington, D.C.: CQ Press, 2002), 77.

Note: The 2000 presidential election was the closest presidential election in U.S. history. Although Al Gore received more popular votes, George W. Bush received more electoral votes and therefore won the election.

Map 11.2 U.S. Presidential Election, 2004

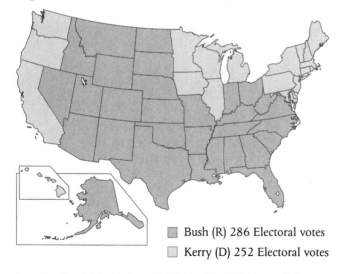

▨ Bush (R) 286 Electoral votes

☐ Kerry (D) 252 Electoral votes

Source: Data from Michael Nelson, *The Elections of 2004* (Washington, D.C.: CQ Press, 2004).

receives all the state's electoral votes. Thus a candidate can win enough states to win the presidency but fail to receive a majority, or even a plurality, of the nationwide vote (because an opponent wins states by many more votes but not enough states to get a majority in the Electoral College). This does not usually happen, but it obviously did occur in the 2000 election, as it did in 1824, 1876, and 1888. Although this did not happen in the 2004 election—George Bush won clear, if narrow, majorities in both the Electoral College and the popular vote—close elections in the United States always leave this possibility. (See Map 11.2.)

Another qualification to majority rule is that a simple majority is not always enough to win. In the United States the Constitution dictates a two-thirds vote or a three-fourths vote on certain matters. For example, Congress needs a two-thirds vote to overturn a presidential veto. Options available for proposing a constitutional amendment are by two-thirds vote in both houses of the U.S. Congress or the call for a constitutional convention by two-thirds of the state legislatures. Proposed amendments are ratified by a three-fourths vote of state legislatures.

Majority rule, like all political ideals, has its critics. Looking beyond the facade of formal decision making (for example, in a specific election or a specific vote by a legislative body), some students of politics question whether it is the majority that really rules in a democracy. They see instead different varieties of rule by minorities. The strongest criticism leveled against majority rule is from those who posit the existence of what is called the power elite—a cohesive and dominant minority that in reality controls policy. A more subtle attack on the ideal of majority rule is that, although majorities formally control politics, different, shifting minorities control the outcome of specific policy issues.[4] For instance, though it may not be true that the oil companies run the United States, they may have undue influence over energy policy.

Majority rule faces difficulties in the developing countries because it presupposes trust among citizens, respect for elections, and a leadership responsive to the popular will. When these are lacking, as they are in many developing countries, majority rule cannot function. Citizens will fight each other; elections will be set aside; military leaders will rule by force. Yet some developing countries have successfully employed majority rule in their elections. The late twentieth century saw remarkable advances in the propensity of places as diverse as Eastern Europe and Latin America to use majority rule.

THE ROLE OF NONGOVERNMENTAL ACTORS

Although political culture and constitutional rules have a great influence on politics, nongovernmental actors also are important to the political process. In this section we will consider the following nongovernmental actors—citizens, interest groups, political parties, and the media.

Citizens

In the older democracies, such as the United States and Great Britain, citizens express vital needs and interests in many ways. They worry about crime, drugs, and the safety of air travel. They complain about high taxes. They attend meetings, write to government officials, and sign petitions. They may also join interest groups that support their positions or participate actively in a political party.

There are three key ways in which citizens can influence government. First, they can exercise significant control over government by their right to vote. Political scientists often debate to what extent citizens can influence the day-to-day actions of any government official; however, what is clear is that citizens have the ability to decide who runs government. In this way, they influence what goes on in government. They register disapproval when they vote to kick the "bums" out. They also can offer their support of government policy by returning officeholders to power. The second way that citizens can affect government is through the power of public opinion. Public opinion cautions government when it seeks to overturn a popular policy or when it oversteps its bounds. For example, public opinion polls, by indicating the popularity of key features of the welfare state, may dissuade a conservative government from tampering with the Social Security system. Polls may also indicate support for "welfare reform" or fiscal responsibility, thus encouraging a government to reduce the federal deficit or crack down on "welfare chiselers." The third way citizens can influence government is through civil disobedience. Their refusal to pay taxes, to support an unpopular war, or to abide by a hated policy could cripple government. In the United States, for example, the Prohibition amendment of 1919 failed because many people—whether a real majority or a very large minority—wanted to drink beer and liquor.

In these varying ways, then, citizens act to further (or deny) cooperation with the government. They may facilitate (or resist) the resolution of conflicts. We should neither exaggerate nor deprecate the role of citizens in a system based on the consent of the governed. Most nations would undoubtedly prefer a cooperative citizenry. Even authoritarian nations cannot deny that there are limits to the use of force and terror to mandate cooperation. Communist regimes have, from time to time, faced intense public pressure from average citizens. One famous case occurred in Poland in the 1980s. There was strong citizen support for Solidarity, an independent Polish labor union. Despite government-imposed martial law, which weakened the union, eventually Lech Walesa, a leader of the union, was elected president of Poland.

We should be cautious, though, in making generalizations about what public opinion can do. Frequently, regimes simply ignore public opinion and hope that intense opposition will wither away. Furthermore, even when public opinion triumphs, this does not mean that democracy and freedom prevail. "People power" was instrumental in helping the Ayatollah Khomeini topple the shah of Iran. However, the Islamic Republic that replaced the old regime is hardly democratic and can be quite oppressive.

Interest Groups

All political communities include interest groups. (See Table 11.1 for a classification.) Such groups, however, are more numerous and more powerful in advanced democracies such as the United States and Britain than in communist countries. These groups' contribution to political accommodation is a source of controversy. What is an interest group? An interest group is a public group that organizes in an attempt to shape public policy of special concern to its members.

In the United States and Britain interest groups clearly express their own needs and concerns by providing information, tendering advice, and exerting pressure. They operate through the media, within political parties, before legislative committees, and in the offices of the bureaucracy. They are not bashful in speaking up on behalf of their constituencies or about spending money to advance their concerns. They represent industrialists, farmers, trade unionists, and a wide range of other professional, ethnic, religious, and reform groups. Unquestionably, they constitute a major source of demands on government.

For example, workers in the U.S. electronic industry would like to limit the number of Japanese television sets and stereos entering the American market. Furniture workers

Table 11.1   Classification of Interest Groups

Type	Types of Interests Represented
I. Cultural	Friends of architecture, music, opera
II. Economic	Farmers, manufacturers, retailers, workers
III. Ethnic	Basques, French Canadians, Kurds, Welsh
IV. Professional	Doctors, educators, journalists, lawyers
V. Racial	African Americans, Asians, Hispanics, whites
VI. Reform	abortion rights advocates and opponents, environmentalists, gun control advocates and opponents, pacifists, prohibitionists
VII. Religious	Catholics, Jews, Muslims, Protestants

in North and South Carolina want to limit the importation of finished furniture. Ranchers oppose the importation of foreign beef. Environmentalists would like the government to impose tighter controls on air-polluting factories and cars, on strip mining, on clear cutting of timber, and on offshore oil drilling. Industries and unions oppose "overly strict" regulations that threaten profits and jobs.

By the very nature of their self-interested concerns, most interest groups do not hold the broad public good as a high priority. They are not normally in business to unite interests or to reconcile a wide range of claims. In pluralist theory, the public good is furthered by the clash of different interest groups, not by the actions of any particular interest group. They do serve a valuable role in providing information to political actors. However, critics charge that powerful interests are able to buy undue power and thwart popular opinion because of their ability to influence political parties and elected officials who need money for campaigns.

Interest groups often are better able to prevent action than to accomplish it. For example, in 1969, by withholding their approval of a Labour government proposal for a new industrial relations act, British trade unions effectively vetoed the proposal in the British cabinet.[5] In the United States, the National Rifle Association has prevented meaningful national gun control legislation for decades, and AARP (formerly the American Association of Retired Persons) has thwarted efforts by budget-minded legislators to limit or cut Social Security and Medicare benefits. Powerful interest groups cannot always utilize the political "veto" to block legislation that would adversely affect them, however. Sometimes when governments take actions that are disliked by key interest groups, the actions are nonetheless effective, particularly if there is widespread support within the country as a whole. For example, in the United States, the National Labor Relations Act of 1935 (the Wagner Act, which required employers to recognize as collective bargaining agents unions that had the support of a majority of workers) was unpopular with many industrialists and their major organizations (such as the National Association of Manufacturers). Yet the public supported the principle of giving a majority of workers, through their unions, the opportunity to bargain collectively and peacefully with their employers. Despite management's opposition to the Wagner Act and its legal actions to nullify the act's administration, the law was passed.

This analysis suggests how interest groups can influence government by seeking to protect their own interests. They do so by watching for "ill-advised" use of government power—that is, anything that will affect them negatively. They naturally scream about any policy that has an adverse impact on their profits, wages, prices, and benefits. Reform groups, in particular, play a watchdog role. They are on the alert for what they see as violations of civil liberties (the American Civil Liberties Union), good ecological principles (the Sierra Club), and public morality (the Christian Coalition). They may challenge government—legally, in the courts; politically, in Congress; or administratively, in the bureaucracy. At their best, interest groups provide valid criticisms of any policy, and the ongoing debate about what a government should do is often helped by the continuing clash of opinion represented by the organized interests.

Outside the established democracies, interest groups play a much weaker and less developed role in politics. In communist countries political dissent groups often exist; however, these are less well organized and powerful than interest groups as we know them in the United States. In much of the developing world, authoritarian regimes severely limit the ability of groups of citizens to organize effectively. However, in democratic developing countries, interest groups do play an important role in politics. For example, in India industrial and business groups that help to fund the Congress Party (until recently the country's dominant party) keep it from moving too far to the left. Student and labor strikes and religious campaigns have been used to oppose unpopular government policies or authoritarian tendencies. On the negative side, such actions have several times required the government to rule by emergency decree—not the most desirable or successful pattern of accommodation in a democratic society.

Political Parties

Political parties—as they respond to public opinion, help educate the electorate, manage interest groups, and carry on the business of government—are the unsung heroes in the process of furthering cooperation, advancing accommodation, and handling conflicts. Modern democratic politics is impossible without political parties. What is a political party? A **political party** is an organized group that seeks to elect candidates to government office. In so doing, political parties represent "teams" that seek to collectively control government.[6] To some observers party organization is the key to success for developing nations. They maintain that the lack of such organization accounts, to a large extent, for the difficulties facing many developing countries: absence of cohesion; disorder; inadequate integration of people, interests, and government; and ineffective and uncontrolled government.

Here a comparison of a major political party and an interest group may be illuminating. Like the political party, the interest group wants to obtain, wield, and enjoy the fruits of power. But the interest group desires power not usually for the sake of mastery or prestige, but for the sake of advancing its group, economic, and social purpose. The interest group tends, therefore, to be concerned with more specific matters than the political party. For example, the interest group may favor or oppose higher prices for domestic oil, higher wages, or farm price supports. It may oppose or support gun control. The interest group generally does not put up candidates for public office as does the party. In contrast to political parties, most interest groups do not usually have a permanent organization concerned primarily with electing or defeating candidates for public office and with marshaling support in the legislature on a wide range of issues. Unlike the political party, the interest group has little or no responsibility to the electorate for the victory or defeat of its favored candidate.

Political parties serve two key roles in making democracies work. First, they provide a context in which citizens can understand a complex political world. In the United States, for instance, which has a two-party system, the two political parties unite numerous social and political groups into either the Democratic or the Republican Party. Furthermore, in the process of selecting their candidates, the parties narrow the field down to two candidates. (Of course, there are frequently more than two candidates; however, the two major parties dominate politics.) In doing this, the parties encourage accommodation between disparate groups—think of all the different groups that make up the Republican Party, such as economic libertarians and social conservatives such as the Christian Coalition. Furthermore, at times, political parties offer clear and distinct policy options to the voters. The second role parties play is in translating these election results into government action. When a party wins an election, a team of officeholders can work together to achieve the goals they promised to deliver. Despite a great deal of cynicism about politicians and parties, recent research has shown that most politicians work hard to keep their campaign promises.[7]

Political party conventions in the United States have lost much of their original purpose: to select presidential candidates. Today the primary election system determines the party nominees long before the actual conventions take place. Conventions do, however, permit parties to showcase rising political figures. Above, Arnold Schwarzenegger, governor of California, addresses the Republican National Convention on August 31, 2004.

The function of political parties can be dramatically illustrated in Great Britain and the United States. For example, Margaret Thatcher became prime minister in 1979, when her Conservative Party won a parliamentary majority. In contrast to her Labour Party counterparts, Thatcher promised to pursue a policy of nonintervention in industry and encouragement of private enterprise while reducing expenditures in central and local government. Over the next eight years, the Conservatives made good on their promises. By 1988 the government had sold to private interests all or part of its holdings in petroleum, gas, civil aviation, airports, shipbuilding, aircraft engine manufacturing, weapons, buses, telecommunications, and seed development and plant breeding, and had privatized the Trustee Savings Banks. The steel industry also became private, as did the water and electric industries and the bus network in Scotland.

American parties, although not as disciplined and coherent as British parties because of separation of powers and federalism, can serve a similar role. For example, the election of Franklin D. Roosevelt and large Democratic majorities in the House of Representatives and the Senate resulted in a flood of important legislation: the Agricultural Adjustment Act (1933), the National Labor Relations Act (1933), the Tennessee Valley Authority Act (1933), the Social Security Act (1935), and the Fair Labor Standards Act (1938). These measures responded to farmers' calls for stable farm prices; to advocates' calls for better electrical power, flood control, and recreation; to labor unions' appeal for collective bargaining; and to workers' demands for unemployment compensation, old-age pensions, a floor under wages, and a forty-hour work week.

Years later Republican president Ronald Reagan (1981–1989) introduced a significant conservative movement away from the tradition of government activism. Reagan based his presidential campaign on a promise of deregulation, cuts in spending on social programs, and significant increases in defense spending. The Reagan administration oversaw deregulation of several key industries, most notably the commercial airline system. Social welfare programs such as Head Start, a preschool program for inner-city children, were limited. Tough, uncompromising stands were taken against federal employees, such as the federally supervised air traffic controllers, who tried to organize and strike. And consistent with his Republican Party platform, President Reagan proposed and supervised an enormous military buildup, the largest peacetime military strengthening in U.S. history. More recently, the George W. Bush administration's first term witnessed a disciplined Republican Party that strongly backed Bush's decision to go to war in Iraq and enacted three major tax cuts championed by the president.

Political parties provide a mechanism for building coalitions. They rally divergent groups on behalf of common programs. In so doing, they work against narrow and extremist positions. They tie sometimes differing interests together on unifying issues. Thus they build support for proposals that the party, if successful in elections, may then transform into legislation.

However, the ability to translate election results into coherent government actions is often difficult. In the United States the principles of separation of powers and of federalism make for a very loosely structured two-party system and, often, deadlock in the national government. Federalism contributes to such a system by creating a number of independent power sources—national, state, and local. Separation of powers reinforces the loose party structure by affirming the independence of the president and members of Congress in their respective spheres. The two major American parties thus emerge as coalitions built around presidential candidates, national party committees, Democratic and Republican members of Congress (or aspirants to congressional seats), state and local parties, officeholders, candidates, rank-and-file partisans, and other key interests seeking a payoff for their support.

Nationally, each party coalition attempts to forge some unity every four years to elect a president, gain majority control in Congress, and enact a party program. It is, however, difficult to achieve unity and carry out a national party program because national interests (most often addressed by the presidential candidates) do not always coincide with regional, state, and local interests. Members of Congress, those seeking election to Congress, and state and local politicians (such as governors and mayors) are often preoccupied with their own elections and with state and local concerns. They are not passionately committed to a national party program. Moreover, our electoral system—rooted in federalism—does not ensure that the president and a majority in Congress will be of the same political party. Additionally, separation of powers ensures the independence of members of Congress in their own sphere of power, which often translates into conflict with the president. Thus the absence of a cohesive and responsible national party system—with deep and disciplined roots in the country—and the constitutional independence of nationally elected officials frequently create governmental deadlock in Washington.

This deadlock may exist even when the president's party controls both houses of Congress. There is no danger of the government falling in the United States if the executive (president) and legislature (Congress) disagree. Representatives and presidents are elected for fixed terms. The president is not responsible to a majority in the Congress, as the British cabinet is responsible to a majority in the House of Commons. In the United States deadlock does not threaten new elections—and thus encourage agreement between members of Congress and the president.

Nonetheless, the loose coalitions known as the Democratic and Republican Parties in the United States may still make government effective. Under the leadership of inspired presidents such as Franklin D. Roosevelt and Ronald Reagan, American parties have achieved many policy innovations. Furthermore, the loyal opposition (as the opposing party is called in Britain) is, without doubt, a marvelous contribution to responsible and peaceful accommodation. Opposition parties can voice strenuous criticisms of the ruling party and thus contribute to the political debate in a democracy; however, a mature party system rests on the ideal of accommodation and encourages a humane and civilized politics. This pattern of accommodation ensures a smooth and peaceful transition from one government to the next and, in this way, enormously enhances effective governance and responsible control of government.

In the developing world and the communist world the role of parties is somewhat different. In communist countries the party is not really a nongovernmental institution; rather, for all intents and purposes, the Communist Party is the government. In such a system, parties are not truly instruments for democracy; rather, they are institutions designed to control politics and limit freedom and democracy.

In the developing world political parties play widely varied roles. Some parties—for example, the Congress Party in India—operate in the same ways as strong parties in the industrial nations. In a number of developing systems, a single party dominates the political scene. In Mexico, for instance, the PRI (Partido Revolucionario Institucional, or Institutional Revolutionary Party) has, until recently, fully dominated the political system. Despite its power, the PRI accepts opposition political parties, and under the party's rule Mexico has protected basic freedoms and preserved private property.[8] Furthermore, in 2000 the PRI, which had controlled Mexican politics since 1929, lost the presidential election to the Partido de Acción Nacional, or People's Action Party, and President Vicente Fox was swept to power. This is a healthy sign that Mexico is developing a competitive party system—although we should note that Fox's administration is dogged by charges of corruption, placing the ability of the People's Action Party to win another term in doubt.

However, in other developing systems such as Syria and Libya, the governing party functions as the instrument of a dominant, often authoritarian, leader. In such countries civil liberties for an opposition party are minimal or nonexistent. Former president Ferdinand E. Marcos of the Philippines was another illustration of an authoritarian ruler who used a political party, called the New Society Movement, to maintain his power. Marcos came to power in 1966 and imposed martial law in 1972—to save the republic, he said. Marcos and his party were ousted from power in 1986 through a broad-based popular movement led by Corazon Aquino.

If a country lacks a competitive party system, the task of political accommoda-

Prime Minister Manmoham Singh of India (right) shakes hands with President General Pervez Musharraf of Pakistan. A member of the Indian National Congress Party and a Sikh by faith, Singh is the first prime minister not from the majority Hindu community. He was elected in May 2004.

tion is inadequately performed: integration does not take place, priorities are not articulated, legitimate legislation and administration are not accomplished. Democracy needs
institutions such as political parties to offer choices to its citizens; without political parties democracies usually founder and fail.

The Media

By the media we mean agencies of communication such as newspapers, magazines, radio,
television, and, more recently, the Internet. Depending on the country involved, the media
play an important role in expressing needs and interests, in sharpening priorities, in legitimating government and strengthening its effectiveness, and in guarding against the abuse
of power. Where the media are independent, as in developed, democratic countries, their
capacity for expression and their ability to influence government is greater than in the
communist world or in many developing countries, where the media are often under party
or government control.

In the United States and Great Britain, for example, the agencies of mass communication attempt, with varying degrees of success, to give citizens "an account of the day's
events in a context which gives them meaning"; to provide "a forum for the exchange of
comment and criticism"; to project "the opinions and attitudes of the groups in the society"; and in general, to reach "every member of the society by the currents of information,
thought and feeling" that the media supply.[9] Through editorials the media can offer judgments about what is happening and urge certain policy outcomes.

Sometimes the media can contribute to the enactment of policy. Such may have been
the case in the American humanitarian intervention into Somalia in 1992. Many analysts
believe that a major factor in the decision to intervene was the constant barrage of images
of war-torn Somalia projected on American television screens—starving children, bodies
in the streets of Mogadishu, harried and frightened international relief workers. Dubbed
the "CNN effect," these images generated considerable sympathy for the plight of innocent Somalis and contributed to the pressure brought on President George Bush to do
something to relieve the situation.[10]

The media have also played a vital role in guarding against the abuse of governmental power. They have protected freedom of the press against censorship and other violations. They have stood strong on behalf of freedom of speech, assembly, and religion.
They have sought to make government, especially in the United States, function in "day-
light" by opposing government secrecy (except in very limited cases). They have exposed
what happened in important matters—as in the Pentagon Papers case—even at the risk
of challenging government contentions that national security mandated such secrecy.[11]
But this might have come with a price: some in recent years have questioned whether the
24/7 quality of news coverage and the quickness of the news cycle have contributed to
a shallowness and coarseness in American politics.

Constantly on the lookout for government illegalities (as in the Watergate case during the Nixon administration, the Iran-contra affair and the Housing and Urban Development scandal during the Reagan years, the "filegate" and Whitewater controversies during Clinton's first term, and a CIA agent's outing during George W. Bush's second term), wasteful spending, and shady government transactions, the media play an important role in keeping government honest. But sometimes the price paid for a free and independent press in Western democratic countries is distortion, narrowness, and sensationalism, which the best members of the press deplore.

In the communist political systems, the media have generally functioned as organs of the party or government to test party and governmental priorities, legitimate policies, and enhance the government's effectiveness. They do not generally function as watchdogs in the Western democratic sense. They do, however, inform the people of the party line, reprimand individuals who deviate from this line, and exhort the people to support party and government. They are instruments in achieving accommodation.

In developing countries, the role of the media, especially the printed press, is mixed. In some countries, such as India, the press functions pretty much as does the press in developed nations. In other countries, the press serves as an organ of the government, ruling party, or ruling military junta, much as the press in traditional communist nations. In still other developing countries, the press occasionally plays a courageous and dangerous role: expressing needs, interests, and criticism—in news stories or editorials—contrary to the approved line of the dominant government. The newspaper *La Prensa* in Nicaragua is a good example of this kind of courage. For years it criticized the ruling Somoza family for its policies. After the Sandinista revolution (which *La Prensa* supported) succeeded, the paper continued to criticize what it perceived to be the ill-advised and sometimes authoritarian policies of the Sandinista ruling council.

CONCLUSION

Our analysis in this chapter focused on three key factors that affect politics. First, we investigated the role of political culture in providing a backdrop against which a country's politics takes place. What is the ethos of a place? Second, we considered the major constitutional questions that must be decided as the "rules of the game" in a society. Finally, we discussed the various nongovernmental actors who play an important role in politics.

Before we can more fully assess our tentative hypothesis about patterns of accommodation, we must consider the role of governmental actors, especially legislatures, executives, bureaucracies, courts, and other political elites. In chapter 12 we will turn to that examination and to questions about who governs, how, to what ends, and with what results.

SUGGESTED READINGS

Almond, Gabriel, G. Bingham Powell Jr., Kaare Strom, and Russell J. Dalton, eds. *Comparative Politics Today: A World View.* 8th ed. New York: Longman, 2004. Examines Britain, France, Germany, Japan, Russia, China, Mexico, Brazil, Egypt, India, and Nigeria within a framework of system, process, and policy. Focuses on political socialization, political recruitment, interest articulation, interest aggregation, and policymaking.

Brown, Bernard E., ed. *Comparative Politics: Notes and Readings.* 10th ed. New York: Wadsworth, 2005. This superb reader touches on virtually all the important issues in comparative politics, including methodology, democracy, authoritarianism, the concept of the state, communism, institutions, political change, and much more.

Cigler, Allan J., and Burdett A. Loomis, eds. *Interest Group Politics.* 6th ed. Washington, D.C.: CQ Press, 2002. An informative and varied group of up-to-date essays on various kinds of interest groups, including both domestic and foreign lobbying efforts.

Clapham, Christopher. *Third World Politics: An Introduction.* Madison: University of Wisconsin Press, 1985. A lucid and informative overview of developing world politics. Places particular emphasis on the fragility of Western political institutions and processes as applied in developing countries.

Coleman, Fred. *The Decline and Fall of the Soviet Empire: Forty Years That Shook the World, from Stalin to Yeltsin.* New York: St. Martin's Press, 1996. Fourteen years of journalistic experience in Moscow is put to good use in this volume. The primary assertion seems to be that the Soviet Union was always much weaker and more insecure than U.S. officials ever knew.

Dahl, Robert. *Polyarchy.* New Haven: Yale University Press, 1971. A classic explanation of the theory of polyarchy.

Elazar, Daniel J. *Federal Systems of the World.* 2nd ed. New York: Stockton Press, 1994. Fine comparative study by one who is sympathetic to federalism and its contributions.

Miller, Judith. *God Has Ninety-Nine Names: Reporting from a Militant Middle East.* New York: Simon and Schuster, 1996. A very fine analysis of the Islamization of politics in the Middle East by the former Cairo bureau chief of the *New York Times.*

Norton, Philip. *The British Polity.* 4th ed. New York: Longman, 2000. A lucid, thorough, and highly praised book on the British political system, including both governmental and nongovernmental actors in the British political fabric. First rate.

Pomper, Gerald. *Passions and Interests: Political Party Concepts of American Democracy.* Lawrence: University Press of Kansas, 1992. A thorough and theoretically rich account of the different types of parties. The focus is on the United States, but the concepts are broadly applicable.

Rothberg, Robert I., and Thomas G. Weiss, eds. *From Massacres to Genocide: The Media, Public Policy, and Humanitarian Crises.* Washington, D.C.: Brookings, 1996. A series of essays on how media coverage shapes foreign policy and distorts perceptions of the developing world.

Weatherby, Joseph, et al. *The Other World: Issues and Politics of the Developing World.* 4th ed. New York: Longman, 2000. An extraordinary, comprehensive text on major issues confronting the developing world, political and economic.

GLOSSARY TERMS

connection of powers (p. 244)
constitution (p. 242)
devolution (p. 248)
federalism (p. 246)
interest aggregation (p. 237)
interest articulation (p. 237)
majority rule (p. 248)
political culture (p. 238)
political party (p. 254)
polyarchy (p. 241)
separation of powers (p. 244)
unitary government (p. 247)

Chapter 12

NATIONAL POLITICS: GOVERNMENTAL ACTORS

This chapter focuses on the role of governmental actors in working out political patterns of cooperation and accommodation and in handling conflicts. Our analysis still rests on the premise that unanimity rarely, if ever, exists in the political community. Citizens often disagree; interests frequently conflict. In many countries the media are not of one mind and parties compete. No invisible hand functions to ensure that the organs of government—legislatures, executives, courts, and bureaucratic departments—work in perfect harmony. This chapter will consider the following questions: *How, then, do governmental actors function in the struggle for power that is politics? How voluntary, humane, and peaceful are the patterns they work out? Can this cooperation among political elites contribute to security, liberty, justice, and the welfare of the nation?*

THE ROLE OF GOVERNMENTAL ACTORS

Governmental actors perform their roles within a constitutional framework of politics, which establishes the rules of the political game. Our guiding hypothesis is that governmental patterns will succeed if they rest on (1) agreement on certain constitutional fundamentals; (2) meaningful opportunities for the expression of needs, interests, and desires; (3) sound mechanisms for the selection of priorities; (4) acceptable ways for legitimating public policy choices; (5) effective governance; and (6) regular and effective controls on government.

The political constitution is concerned with who rules, how, to what ends, and with what results. All of us who think critically about politics must not only investigate these matters but also pointedly ask who benefits and who suffers as political actors cooperate and compete. Governmental actors are in business to manage the struggle for power. Successful patterns must be neither so severe that they destroy the freedom of conflicting interests and parties nor so ineffectual that they are unable to prevent the ultimate terror within a political community—civil war. In our exploration we will focus on how governments function in two advanced democracies—the United States and Great Britain; however, we also investigate examples taken from parts of the developing world and from communist countries.

Legislatures

Legislatures in developed democratic countries have four main, but interrelated, functions: **representative, deliberative, legislative**, and **supervisory**. In performing these functions, legislatures fulfill most conditions of successful accommodation—although we should note that there are significant differences between the way legislatures function in Western democracies such as the United States and Britain and the way they function in communist countries and in the developing world.

The Representative Function. Legislatures give voice to the political, economic, social, and geographic interests of the political community. However, the typical legislator must balance many different considerations in making political decisions. Legislators feel pressure from their party leadership and the people they represent; at the same time they must consider their own beliefs and conscience in deciding how to act politically. American legislators typically attempt to balance the interests of constituency, interest group, party, and nation. British legislators are likely to be more overtly partisan, hewing to the party line on key issues. But because voters are generally interested in only a few subjects, congressional representatives are often freed from their role as "delegates" who do what the dominant interests in the constituency want done. They can function as "trustees" instead, deciding issues by judging what they think is best for the nation. Similarly, members of Parliament (MPs) may vote as delegates on nonparty issues and as trustees on fairly rare matters of conscience. In general, legislators translate key segments of public opinion—and the interests of majority voters, interest groups, and parties—into tangible public policy.

Terms of office vary from country to country in the developed regions of the world. In determining term length for various offices, the architects of a government have to balance the need for politicians to stay close to the people (leading to a brief term) with the need to insulate them from the vagaries of fickle public opinion (leading to a longer term). In the United States, that balancing act can be seen in the different terms of office for members of the House of Representatives and members of the Senate, terms fixed by the Founders in the Constitution. Members of the House are elected by voters in congressional districts for a term of two years. Members of the Senate are elected by a statewide constituency for a term of six years. As we noted earlier, one-third of the Senate is elected at a time. The types of constituency also matter a great deal in the United States. House members represent relatively homogeneous districts, whereas senators typically represent diverse states.

In Great Britain, members of the House of Commons may serve for five years, if an election is not called earlier. Parliament cannot sit longer than five years without a new election. More often than not, however, new elections are called before the end of the five-year period. If the prime minister and cabinet lose their majority in the House of Commons, they can resign or call for new elections.

The second house of the British Parliament, the House of Lords, provides an interesting contrast to the U.S. Senate, one of the most powerful second legislative organs in the world. Its influence, in both domestic and foreign affairs, is significant. No law can be enacted without its approval, and it has often provided leadership on legislative programs. The Senate must **advise and consent** on treaties and major government appointments sought by the president. In comparison, the British House of Lords is an unelected body of lords—an aristocracy of intellect, experience, and accomplishment—appointed by the government. (Until recently, the Lords included hereditary members of the British aristocracy; however, reforms by Prime Minister Tony Blair significantly changed the makeup of the chamber.) Freed of electoral pressures, the House of Lords is theoretically able to represent the interests of the British nation as a whole. The powers of the House of Lords, however, are minimal; for example, it may delay legislation that the British cabinet and the House of Commons wish to enact for one year but not permanently defeat it. Interestingly, the highest judicial body in the British legal system comprises of members of the House of Lords with legal or judicial experience, who are known as the "law lords." The law lords constitute a kind of British supreme court, but they lack power to declare an act of Parliament unconstitutional. Though the hereditary criterion for membership has been largely eliminated, the House of Lords remains a controversial part of British politics, even with recent reforms, because it is still not a directly elected body.

The Deliberative Function. Legislatures provide a forum for debate and formal decision making, thus facilitating the examination of the views of contending parties. Because important decisions in Britain are made in the cabinet, debate in the House of Commons rarely alters the outcome of legislation. Debate may, however, clarify the parties' positions on key issues and thereby educate the public to some extent. In the United States—given the greater independence of Congress—the House and the Senate provide a hearing for the folks back home and for a host of economic, religious, and social interests. This largely occurs through the committee structure in order to facilitate the articulation of grievances and ideas. This offers an opportunity to measure the intensity of the feelings of voters and interests. In addition, the committee structure provides the opportunity for members of the executive branch to meet with members of the legislature.

The Legislative Function. Legislatures also have the formal responsibility for making law. In passing laws legislatures not only express interests and shape priorities but also place the stamp of legitimacy on public policy. In the United States the president's signature is required before a bill can become a law. If the president chooses not to sign—vetoing a bill—a two-thirds vote in both the House and the Senate can override the veto. (Figure 12.1 illustrates the cooperation required to enact a bill into law in the United States.) Duly enacted legislation constitutes formal **legitimacy**—the general acceptance by political actors and citizens that government actions are appropriate and fully accepted. Such legitimacy makes for effective governance. Although in Britain the cabinet shapes basic policy, Parliament must still officially enact legislation. Parliamentary approval embodies the final act of sovereign legitimacy.

Figure 12.1 How a Bill Becomes Law (simplified)

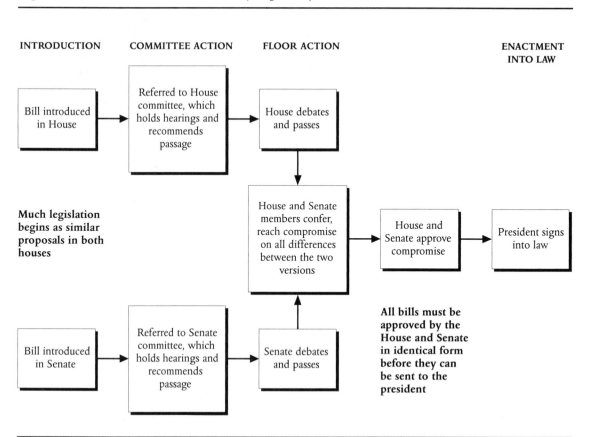

Source: Roger H. Davidson and Walter J. Oleszek, *Congress and Its Members,* 10th ed. (Washington, D.C.: CQ Press, 2006), 238.

Historically, in both the United States and Britain, legislative control of the purse—the power to provide money for the support of government—has given legislators a major means of controlling government. Here, the legislative and supervisory functions overlap. In the United States the power of Congress to raise and spend money exerts a powerful control over the executive. Money, which must be lawfully raised and spent, crucially affects the exercise of political power.

Today in Britain, because the cabinet is really the executive arm of a parliamentary majority, legislative control of the purse is no longer a real safeguard against the executive, the way it was when the British monarch was the executive and when government was not responsible to a parliamentary majority. Nevertheless, the budget, which the House of Commons must formally approve, remains a powerful instrument to control the content and direction of public policy.

The Supervisory Function. Legislatures also supervise the work of the executive and the bureaucracy. Congressional committees have an extensive investigatory power that they often use to evaluate, and thus control, the functioning of the bureaucracy. Debates in the House and the Senate also provide opportunities for the people's representatives—particularly members of the opposition party—to criticize governmental policy. The Senate's agency in giving advice and consent on treaties and other key appointments enables senators to scrutinize policy and personnel. Moreover, the House may impeach (bring charges against) and the Senate may try government officials, even the president of the United States, for "treason, bribery, or other high crimes and misdemeanors."

In Britain the watchdog role falls primarily to the opposition party—Her Majesty's **loyal opposition**—whose task it is to criticize, expose weaknesses, and insist on good performance from the party in power. This job is often performed during the question hour in the House of Commons when the prime minister, or other cabinet

The supervisory function of legislatures can touch upon many walks of life. Above, baseball stars Sammy Sosa of the Chicago Cubs, Mark McGwire of the St. Louis Cardinals, Rafael Palmeiro of the Baltimore Orioles, and Curt Schilling of the Boston Red Sox testify before the U.S. Senate in 2005 on the use of steroids in major league baseball.

officers, may be queried about the conduct of British policy. Parliament may also investigate key problems or government scandals. Often this is done through royal commissions, which are really investigatory committees.

Communist Systems and the Developing World. The prominence of the four functions is different in communist systems and in the developing world. In communist systems, legislatures historically have played a modest role. Representation is formal but ineffective. The primary purpose for the existence of legislative bodies is to rubber-stamp policies as they emanate from the Politburo (the Communist Party's principal policymaking and executive committee). Real supervision of government by the legislature is unheard of. Nevertheless, elaborate procedures are followed to elect representatives and hold endless meetings. In the People's Republic of China the key legislative unit is the National People's Congress, consisting of 2,970 deputies. Deputies are indirectly elected for five years by the provincial congresses, autonomous regions, municipalities directly under the central government, and the People's Liberation Army (PLA). The standing committee elected by the Congress is in permanent session. But again, real legislative as well as executive power resides with the Communist Party.

Legislatures in the developing world vary widely. Some of them are ineffective; others have modest powers. The legislature in India behaves in a parliamentary fashion. Legislatures in other developing countries are dominated by a single party (as was true in Mexico until 1988) or by an authoritarian leader (as in Indonesia). In many developing countries the representative, deliberative, legislative, and supervisory functions remain relatively weak.

Executives

Modern executives in developed countries frequently dominate the political process. (The United States is an exception: the executive and legislative branches share power at a kind of rough parity.) They plan, initiate, and implement overall governmental policy. They are indispensable in the process of articulating vital national needs and fundamental interests. Without executive leadership, developed nations would lack both a national vision and the ability to pull the country together on behalf of national priorities. Executives serve to enunciate and gain approval for policies. Their resourcefulness and vigor enable modern governments to do their jobs. Executives also act to control the very bureaucracy they head. In performing their tasks they must obtain widespread cooperation from legislators, key interests, and citizens in general. Before examining the important roles of executives, let us recall the way they are chosen and their relation to their respective legislatures, again using the United States and Great Britain to illustrate presidential and parliamentary patterns of cooperation, accommodation, and conflict.

In the United States, the Democratic and Republican Parties choose their presidential candidates. The people of the states then choose the president (indirectly, through the Electoral College—see chapter 11), who will serve for a four-year term. Similarly, but independently, the parties choose and the people elect (directly this time) members of Congress, who also serve for fixed terms. Congress must formally enact legislation. The president's signature is required for legislation, unless Congress can override a presidential veto. Constitutionally, presidents cannot force Congress to follow their will; by the same token, if a two-thirds vote to override a presidential veto cannot be mustered in both the Senate and the House, Congress cannot enact vetoed legislation. The president and Congress must cooperate to avoid deadlock. However, politics is frequently dominated by continuing conflict between Congress and the president, as each institution seeks to control the political agenda. This may be true even if the same party controls both branches.

In the British parliamentary scheme, the executive is the cabinet, headed by a prime minister. The prime minister is a member of Parliament who has been elected as party leader by the majority party's caucus in the House of Commons. Other members of the cabinet are leaders of the majority party (generally members of the House of Commons) selected by the prime minister and reflecting support within the dominant party. In 1981 the Labour Party changed its traditional way of electing its leader. Now Labour Party MPs share this power with trade unions and local party organizations. Whichever way he or she is chosen, the prime minister is first among equals in the cabinet. Although in U.S. cabinet sessions the president's decision prevails (since cabinet members have no authority to override the president as chief executive), in the British cabinet the principle of collective responsibility prevails. The prime minister is powerful and often decisive, yet he or she must have the cabinet's support (or at least that of its majority) to continue functioning. Many politicians in Great Britain are constantly on the lookout for a prime minister who acts overly presidential and ignores the collective will of the cabinet.

The British cabinet as a group bears responsibility for key decisions. Cabinet members hold major ministerial posts and are responsible for the day-to-day operation of the government. Members may, of course, resign to take the heat for bad decisions, as British foreign secretary Lord Carrington did in 1982 after the Argentine invasion of the Falkland (Malvinas) Islands. They may also resign if they are unable to support a decision favored by a majority of the cabinet; this happened most recently in 2003, when Robin Cook resigned in protest of Tony Blair's decision to support the war in Iraq. Conflict between the cabinet and the majority party in Parliament is impossible insofar as the cabinet is the majority party's instrument to plan, initiate, and implement policy. The cabinet is thus a forceful and cohesive executive, depending on majority support in Commons to govern responsibly and vigorously. Yet the cabinet leads Parliament. If the cabinet should lose a majority in the House of Commons, the prime minister can ask for new elections to permit the British electorate to speak and return a new Parliament with a clear party majority (and thus a prime minister and a cabinet with authority).

American presidents have a more difficult job of achieving cooperation with the legislature than do their British counterparts. The fact that the president and members of the House and Senate are independently elected makes it possible for the president to be of one party and for one or both branches of Congress to be dominated by another party. During President Bill Clinton's first term, the Republicans won control of both the House and the Senate in 1994. Two years later Clinton was reelected, but both houses of Congress remained in Republican hands. In 2000 Republicans initially controlled both Congress and the presidency; however, after Sen. James M. Jeffords of Vermont left the Republican Party and became an independent, control of the Senate switched to the Democrats. One-party-rule was restored in the 2002 elections and reaffirmed in the 2004 elections, when the Republicans won clear, if narrow, majorities.

If deadlock occurs between the president and Congress, the American people cannot immediately resolve the conflict in new elections. The president remains in office for the full four years, House members the full two, and senators the full six. It is also possible for the president's party to lose, as evidenced by Clinton's presidency, or to gain control of the House and the Senate during the president's tenure in office. Because of separation of powers, there is no effective constitutional reason forcing a president and Congress to agree on a common program. And America's relatively weak party system does not build a strong bridge between the legislative and executive branches. Thus conflict between the U.S. president and Congress is frequent, stormy, and often disruptive. This was evident in 1995 when disagreements over the federal budget between President Clinton and the House of Representatives, led by Speaker of the House Newt Gingrich, resulted in a temporary shutdown of the federal government. A strong and resourceful president is needed to work out patterns of cooperation. We will shortly examine the resources on which the president may draw to achieve cooperation and leadership.

The Roles of the President. Box 12.1 calls attention to the multiple roles the U.S. president plays. In many countries, however, the role of ceremonial chief of state (such as the British monarch and the president of the Republic of Italy or Germany) is separate from the real head of government. The sources of the U.S. president's powers are to be found in the Constitution, historical custom and tradition, and court decisions. For example, the president's role as party chief is not laid down in the Constitution; it emerged in the course of American history.

The U.S. president's powers have evolved largely in response to national problems that called for strong executive leadership—most particularly war and economic crises. To preserve the Union, President Abraham Lincoln had to take extraordinary actions. Without congressional sanction he called for troops; suspended the **writ of habeas corpus**—the fundamental right, found in the Constitution, that protects people against illegal

Box 12.1 U.S. President's Multiple Roles

Chief Executive and Administrator
"The executive Power shall be vested in a President of the United States of America."

"He. . . . shall take care that the Laws be faithfully executed." (U.S. Constitution, Article II, Sections 1 and 3)

Commander in Chief
"The President shall be Commander in Chief to the Army and Navy of the United States." (U.S. Constitution, Article II, Section 2)

Party Chief
Based on historical custom and tradition.

Chief Legislative Brain Truster
"He shall from time to time give the Congress Information of the State of the Union, and recommend to their Consideration such Measures as he shall judge necessary and expedient." (U.S. Constitution, Article II, Section 3)

Power to veto legislation. (U.S. Constitution, Article I, Section 7)

Power of patronage. (U S. Constitution, Article II, Section 2)

Historical custom and tradition.

Chief National Spokesperson
Spokesperson on the "State of the Union."

Historical custom and tradition.

Chief Diplomat
Chief Diplomat. (U.S. Constitution, Article II, Section 1)

"He shall have Power, by and with the Advice and Consent of the Senate, to make treaties, provided two-thirds of the Senators present concur." (U.S. Constitution, Article II, Section 1)

Leader of cabinet—including the Department of State. (U.S. Constitution, Article II, Section 2)

Power to appoint ambassadors. (U.S. Constitution, Article II, Section 2)

Chief Popular Leader
Election, indirectly through the electoral college, by the people. (U.S. Constitution, Article II, Section 1)

Historical custom and tradition.

Ceremonial Chief of State
U.S. Constitution (implied).

Historical custom and tradition.

Source: Compiled by authors.

detention or imprisonment—in parts of Maryland; and imposed martial law on a wide range of civilians. Similarly, to prosecute World Wars I and II, Presidents Woodrow Wilson and Franklin D. Roosevelt expanded the powers of the presidency within the broad framework of legislation passed by Congress. During the Great Depression of the 1930s, President Roosevelt boldly assumed a leadership role in initiating legislation and a host of programs to create jobs, lift prices, protect bank depositors, and stimulate the economy.

The problems of the welfare state, which expanded significantly during Franklin Roosevelt's time, remain today. They are, moreover, worldwide problems that underscore the demand for strong leadership to advance security, liberty, justice, and welfare. Indeed, modern executives all over the world, whose powers also have grown to permit them to cope with the increased demands of the modern world, face what some scholars have called "the statesman's dilemma," which they define as the "dilemma of rising demands and insufficient resources."[1] These problems challenge modern executives and require the critical student of politics to ask if executives can (without abusing their power) plan, initiate, and implement governmental policy successfully.

Planning Public Policy. Modern executives plan on behalf of the nation. Much more so than legislatures, executives possess and use those resources that permit them to plan effectively. These resources include the following:

1. comprehensiveness, or an ability to see the whole problem as a national problem;
2. foresight, or the ability to look ahead and anticipate dangers and opportunities for proposed policies;
3. access to relevant and significant information made available by a command of the bureaucracy;
4. the capacity for broad coordination, or the ability to pull together diverse interests on behalf of common programs; and
5. the ability to act with speed and energy.

These ingredients of successful planning do not belong simply to the person who is the U.S. president, the British prime minister, or the German premier; they belong, rather, to the executive office. Moreover, these resources do not inevitably lead to decisions that enhance security, liberty, justice, and welfare. They do, however, increase the chances for sensible planning.

Initiating Public Policy. Modern executives also have been called on to use their formidable powers to initiate governmental policy. The president of the United States, for example, has become the nation's chief initiator of legislation as well as its chief executive. Presidents can base legislative initiative on their constitutional power to recommend "necessary and expedient" measures to Congress. Presidents can also use numerous other powers to mobilize support for legislative priorities. For example, veto power can be used to oppose and defeat legislation that a president does not favor, assuming that the veto will not be overridden by a two-thirds vote in Congress. Even the threat of the veto can influence what actions Congress might take. Presidents can also use the power to make appointments—the power of patronage—to encourage legislators to support presidential policies. Moreover, as head of the party, presidents can draw on party support on behalf of programs. Party regulars know that loyalty can bring them money and support in their reelection campaigns. In addition, both as popular leaders and as figures who can command television and radio to address the nation, presidents can mobilize public opinion on behalf of their policies. In all these ways, then, presidents can push for legislation.

Policy also arises within the governmental bureaucracy. Because legislation cannot possibly cover all detailed matters, power increasingly is given to the president as head of the administration to interpret general legislation. Thus, as chief administrator, the president initiates policy in the course of administering the law.

In performing this role as initiator of public policy, the president is in a strategic position to accommodate a wide range of political actors—voters, interest groups, party members, legislators, and bureaucrats. A skillful president who has sound policies makes U.S. democracy work well. When a president is inept and has flawed policies, the nation suffers. Sympathetic observers of President Lyndon B. Johnson's domestic programs point to his successes in promoting three civil rights bills, inaugurating the War on Poverty, and improving health legislation. But critics of his foreign policy fault him for involving the nation in a disastrous war in Vietnam and for contributing to inflation by refusing to raise taxes while fighting that war. President Richard Nixon was hailed for his progressive policy in establishing links to the People's Republic of China after twenty-one years of hostility and virtually no contact between the two nations. Within three years of these policies, the Watergate scandal forced Nixon from office.

President Ronald Reagan is given much credit for lifting the morale of the American public and controlling spiraling inflation. During his later presidency and after he left office, however, he came under severe criticism for allowing the national deficit to grow to enormous levels, partly through gigantic military expenditures; failing to monitor and stop a disgraceful scandal at the Department of Housing and Urban Development; failing to recognize and prevent the savings and loan scandal that has cost American taxpayers billions of dollars; and allowing the Iran-contra affair to occur. We might note that many political observers gave Reagan's immediate successor, George H. W. Bush, high marks for the skill with which he built the Desert Storm political and military coalition to retake Kuwait after Iraq's invasion in 1990. Yet in 1992 Bush was denied reelection primarily because Americans believed he had mishandled the nation's economy. Conversely, the public gave President Clinton a vote of confidence through his reelection in 1996. After a disastrous attempt to completely redesign the nation's health care system during his first two years in office, Clinton rallied and achieved a number of successes—passage of the Brady bill controlling handguns, family leave legislation, a deficit-reduction bill, a modest increase in the minimum wage, and a peace accord ending the Bosnian conflict. After the attacks on September 11, 2001, President George W. Bush won strong initial support for his war on terrorism that help propel him to reelection in 2004. But by the end of 2005, the president was under increasing criticism for his initiation of the war in Iraq.

The British cabinet, headed by a strong prime minister, carries the initiative by making policy. Conflicts between divergent interests in the governing party are usually hammered out within or between governmental ministries and then brought to the cabinet for discussion and decision. The cabinet assumes responsibility for enactment of agreed-on policy in the House of Commons.

The British prime minister, like the U.S. president, also uses a number of powers—prestige, ability to influence public opinion, patronage, leadership in the party, and bestowal of benefits—to sustain policy initiatives. In contrast to the U.S. president, the British prime minister can rely on strong party discipline and the threat of new elections to carry policy initiatives. As noted previously, if the majority party does not support the prime minister, the cabinet may fall and a new election may be required; majority members of Parliament may lose in the new elections. Thus there is pressure for party members to stick together in support of their party and the prime minister. Pressures work both ways. The cabinet cannot be out of tune with either the majority party or with popular sentiment. In using the office's powers, the prime minister has enormous opportunities to achieve cooperation, advance accommodation, and deal with conflicts in the struggle for power. Again, however, a weak prime minister with feeble, defective policies may squander any opportunities.

Implementing Public Policy. Executives, traditionally, are in charge of implementing policy and managing the great bureaucracy. The U.S. Constitution requires the president to take care that the laws be faithfully executed. The president also functions as the nation's number one diplomat and as commander in chief of the armed forces. In performing these tasks, the president cannot assume that things will get done automatically. Legislation is not self-executing; orders do not necessarily get carried out. Inevitably, politics impinges on administration. The president, through cabinet members and aides, must follow up on policy; forces within the cabinet or the administration may not see eye to eye on key issues. In Congress, members are especially concerned with policies that affect their home districts or states. In view of these considerations, the president must enlist the support of cabinet members, key aides and bureaucrats, public opinion, affected interests, and members of Congress to carry out administrative duties. In this process—in building and maintaining support, in putting out fires—the president achieves accommodation and also facilitates government performance.

A comparable concern for political support and accommodation can be seen in the British cabinet as it carries out public policy. The cabinet is in trouble, for example, if inflation and unemployment rise too high, public opinion turns against the European Union, or an unpopular tax is proposed. The cabinet must look to the interests whose votes and money sustain it. Thus a Labour Party cabinet cannot neglect the trade unions and the policies they favor, and a Conservative Party cabinet cannot neglect industrial, business, and farming interests. The party in power must look to its parliamentary majority, paying attention not only to its leading figures but also to its backbenchers, or lesser-known members. Without the support of this majority, the cabinet falls and, consequently, loses the ability to deliver on its policies. And, of course, when the party in power has a slim parliamentary majority—and depends for that majority on one or more splinter parties—it must accommodate the members of those parties on vital matters or lose power. Indeed, the 2005 elections returned the Labour Party to power, but with a considerably reduced majority. Speculation immediately arose about how long Tony Blair would last as prime minister.

Despite the resourcefulness of the U.S. president and the British prime minister, it is not clear that they are always equal to the tremendous responsibilities that they are asked to shoulder. Striking the right balance remains the challenge. If these executives do too much, they may be accused of being "imperial"; if they do too little, they may be derided as impotent. British prime ministers and U.S. presidents do demonstrate, however, the value of peaceful succession based on broad electoral support.

In discussing any communist system, we must distinguish between the formal government executive, specifically the prime minister and Council of Ministers, and the real executive that resides in the Communist Party general secretary and the Politburo, a small group of high-ranking party officials drawn from a larger group, the Central Committee. The distinction can be tempered with the knowledge that more often than not there is a high degree of "interlocking membership" in the Council and the Politburo. In other words, many of the highest-ranking government executive officials are also members of the party hierarchy.

A further consideration in analyzing executive power in communist systems is the fact that historically they have been vulnerable to what might be called "personalist" tendencies—one person's rise to extraordinary power, often transcending the highest party organs. Certainly, Joseph Stalin epitomized this tendency in the Soviet Union from 1924 until his death in 1953. In the People's Republic of China, Mao Zedong wielded tremendous power for more than two decades after the Communists came to power in 1949. Though not as charismatic, Mao's successor, Deng Xiaoping, wielded enormous personal power for many years, even without holding any official government position. In North Korea, a highly personalist regime came to power with the rise of Kim Il Sung after World War II and continues with his son Kim Jong Il, in power since 1994.

In general, leaders of developing countries play enormously important roles in implementing public policy. For a variety of reasons, the executive branch of government has tended to be even more important than in the developed world. Planning and implementing public policy has commonly been in the hands of a strong leader (Saddam Hussein of Iraq, 1979–2003; Muammar al-Qaddafi of Libya, 1969–present), a military junta (Argentina, 1976–1983), or a civilian authoritarian figure (François "Papa Doc" Duvalier of Haiti, 1957–1971). This has been particularly true in developing regions that do not have strong legislative traditions or where political and economic circumstances have required

Under Premier and President Fidel Castro, Cuba is another example of a communist regime that has become closely identified with the personality of its leader.

a particularly strong hand, such as Zimbabwe, where Robert Mugabe became prime minister in 1980, became president in 1987, and remains in power.

Even in more democratic nations, such as Mexico, the president has enormous powers.[2] Mexican presidents are close to being popularly elected dictators, but their power vanishes when their six-year term of office is ended. They cannot be reelected. In office, however, they are extraordinarily powerful. This may be changing, to a degree, because the once-dominant party, the Partido Revolucionario Institucional (PRI), or Institutional Revolutionary Party, no longer controls the presidency. The last election resulted in a victory by Vicente Fox of the Partido de Acción Nacional (PAN), or People's Action Party. This may herald a new era of party competition that could change the nature of the Mexican presidency; the next presidential election will show whether Mexico continues to develop as a mature democracy or reverts to the less-promising practices of years ago. Mexico's presidents are also limited by revolutionary tradition. They cannot antagonize key interests in the party and in the country: peasant farmers, workers, business, and industry. They cannot too flagrantly offend intellectuals, students, and the church. The recent tradition of civilian leadership inhibits military dictatorship, and the limited power and size of the armed forces further discourage military rule by an ambitious president or military junta.

Although increasing numbers of developing countries, particularly in South America, have adopted free elections to select their leadership, an unfortunately large number of executives in developing states are authoritarian or military dictatorships. Conflict is often handled by jailing opponents, and cooperation proceeds on the executive's terms only. Accommodation consists in going along with the dominant ruler or junta.

Bureaucracies

Max Weber, an influential German social scientist and perceptive student of bureaucracy, was one of the first political observers to note the importance of **bureaucracy** and to delineate the characteristics of the bureaucratic style—rational, efficient, and impartial.[3] Such governance, contrary to our common, pejorative understanding of bureaucracy, was a great advance over government that was often irrational (having no coherent rhyme or reason for policies), inefficient (unable to keep accurate records, collect taxes, and perform services), and based on favoritism and bribes rather than on merit and honesty. Rational, efficient, and impartial treatment of citizens—based on sensible procedures, good record keeping and follow-up, and evenhanded behavior—contributes to successful accommodation in the political community.

Of course, government bureaucrats can also be impersonal, inflexible, tangled in red tape, overbearing, inconsiderate, and unhelpful. This type of behavior—all too frequent in every bureaucracy—gives the term its bad name. It is thus easy to associate bureaucracy with government out of control—with abuses of power, rude and offensive behavior, waste, and overregulation. The greater the power of government over our lives, the greater the chance there is for bureaucratic abuse of that power. And there is considerable evidence, in all governments, to support charges against the bureaucracy.

Despite frequent and often disturbing complaints about how bureaucrats interfere with security, liberty, justice, and welfare, it would be a mistake to ignore their important role in enabling legislatures, and even more so executives, to carry out governmental responsibilities. Indeed, some observers see the top civil servants (often nameless and faceless) as the key policymakers in government. Clearly, government would come to a standstill without a responsible and capable bureaucracy.

Carrying Out Public Policy. The bureaucracy is government in action; it consists of all the departments or ministries, agencies, officials, and commissions required to carry out public policy. It plans, initiates, and implements on behalf of presidents, prime ministers, and premiers. In doing so the bureaucracy responds to interest groups affected by legislation and regulation, often working out compromises between different interests and the general public. The bureaucracy provides information to executives and legislatures, to the press, and to the public. Lower-level officials may inform senior officials of what is workable. In administering the law honestly and competently, civil servants contribute to approved and effective governance. They may also check on, and work to control, the abuse of power within their domain. There can be little doubt that a well-trained, well-organized, and honest bureaucracy makes an invaluable contribution to modern government. On the other hand, a defective bureaucracy is a prime source of political malaise. Thus the training and quality of the bureaucracy are vitally important.

In Great Britain, Japan, France, and the United States, for example, top civil servants (another name for bureaucrats) usually receive their training at the best universities. Their entrance into government service is usually based on examination, so they constitute a **meritocracy**. Top civil servants are usually highly intelligent, competent, and honest, and some often spend years considering how to solve problems and implement policy. Clearly, the advantage of this civil service is expertise and knowledge. The disadvantage is that civil servants can become committed to certain established ways of doing things and might be unwilling to think creatively about new solutions to old problems.

Ensuring Governmental Stability and Continuity. A nation's dependence on its bureaucracy may be more readily understood if we look to countries where government at the top level is unstable, where prime ministers and cabinets come and go. For instance, this was very characteristic of post–World War II France, from 1945 to 1958, as well as Italy, which has a long history of frequent changes in government but enjoys a stable bureaucracy. Despite frequent changes of top leadership, the business of government goes on largely because the permanent civil service remains stable. The bureaucracy continues to collect taxes, dispense benefits, and maintain law and order. This stability characterizes the civil service in almost all the developed world—in countries where the top leadership is stable and those where it is not—and is crucial to effective government. New administrations in Britain, for example, can count on knowledgeable civil servants to carry on while the new cabinet is "tooling up," and on impartial civil servants to assist cabinet members in devising and executing new programs. By thus ensuring continuity of administration, the permanent bureaucracy makes a most valuable contribution to the transition from one government to the next and also to public trust in orderly government. In the United States, the number of top administrators who come and go is greater when the party in power changes; even so, a core of permanent civil servants near the top remains to provide vital help.

Communist bureaucracies are, in essential respects, similar to those in the developed world. They have, however, greater power than civil servants in the Western world simply because the powers of the government embrace more areas. Government managers control all major economic enterprises (coal mines and steel mills, automobile plants, collective farms, hospitals, and department stores), in addition to collecting taxes, issuing passports, and regulating foreign trade. As systems such as those in the People's Republic of China and Vietnam move toward a free market economy while trying to maintain Communist Party control, we might expect a weakening of the traditionally strong communist bureaucracy.

Communist bureaucracies seem more pragmatic and less ideological than the Communist Parties. This trait often enhances their accommodating dispositions and willingness to face facts and to be guided by scientific rather than ideological considerations. But Communist Party control of top-level bureaucrats has historically inhibited the ability of professionals in governmental posts—economists, engineers, agronomists, and biologists—to take an independent line, even when they think a policy is wrong.

With a few exceptions, bureaucracies in most developing countries are weak. A weak bureaucracy means a weak and ineffective government. Such a government in a developing country often means that tasks vitally affecting the lives of citizens are not performed or are performed poorly. Children may not receive schooling. Pure water may not be available in villages. Peace and order may be nonexistent. Corruption, by no means absent from developed and communist countries, plagues many bureaucracies in the developing world. Two key factors in determining how strong the bureaucracy will be are the numbers of years of independence the country has enjoyed and the extent to which colonial powers left a bureaucratic infrastructure when independence was achieved. The number of qualified personnel—at both the top and bottom of the system—varies tremendously from one nation to another.

India inherited a reasonably good civil service from British rule, and this has undoubtedly strengthened the Indian government's ability to cope with its serious problems. Without such a well-trained administrative structure in place at the time of independence, India would have had much more difficulty carrying on the business of government. Zaire—the former Belgian Congo—did not fare as well, largely because Belgian rulers did little to train native civil servants and to prepare Zaire for independence and self-rule. One dreadful result, partly attributable to the lack of a strong bureaucracy able to hold the nation together and govern it effectively, was the devastating civil war that followed independence in 1960.

The Courts

The role of the courts in the political process varies greatly from nation to nation. Although the variety of developing countries makes generalization hazardous, overall courts are more powerful in developing nations than in communist countries but weaker in developing nations than in developed nations. When they function at their best, courts clearly advance politics as a civilizing process by protecting human rights against the abuses of power and by safeguarding other key constitutional rules. Courts uphold valid law when it is challenged and provide a peaceful forum in which citizens can settle innumerable disputes. Thus the courts enable political actors to express their needs and interests; they affirm priorities; they legitimate legislation and administration; they advance effective governance; and they control the abuse of power.

Safeguarding Rights and Liberties. U.S. federal courts, for example, protect against federal or state government violation of the basic political and nonpolitical freedoms that ensure the proper functioning of the democratic and constitutional process. The federal courts safeguard a host of crucial rights. Some of them—such as the "privilege of the Writ of Habeas Corpus"—are found in the body of the U.S. Constitution. This famous right protects the people against illegal detention or imprisonment. A prisoner must be brought before a court at a stated time and place so that the court may determine whether the prisoner is being lawfully held in jail. Other rights are found in the Constitution's first ten amendments, popularly known as the **Bill of Rights**—a great source of protection of the vital needs and fundamental interests of citizens and groups—and in other crucial amendments. For example:

Amendment I: Congress shall make no law respecting an establishment of religion, or prohibiting the free exercise thereof; or abridging the freedom of speech, or of the press; or the right of the people peaceably to assemble, and to petition the Government for a redress of grievances.

Amendment IV: The right of the people to be secure in their persons, houses, papers, and effects, against unreasonable searches and seizures, shall not be violated, and no Warrants shall issue, but upon probable cause, supported by Oath or affirmation, and particularly describing the place to be searched, and the persons or things to be seized.

Amendment V: No person shall be . . . deprived of life, liberty, or property, without due process of law; nor shall private property be taken for public use, without just compensation.

Amendment VI: In all criminal prosecutions, the accused shall enjoy the right to a speedy and public trial, by an impartial jury of the State and district wherein the crime shall have been committed, which district shall have been previously ascertained by law, and to be informed of the nature and cause of the accusation; to be confronted with the witnesses against him; to have compulsory process for obtaining witnesses in his favor, and to have the Assistance of Counsel for his defense.

Amendment VIII: Excessive bail shall not be required, nor excessive fines imposed, nor cruel and unusual punishments inflicted.

Amendment XIV: All persons born or naturalized in the United States, and subject to the jurisdiction thereof, are citizens of the United States and of the State wherein they reside. No State shall make or enforce any law which shall abridge the privileges or immunities of citizens of the United States; nor shall any State deprive any person of life, liberty, or property, without due process of law; nor deny to any person within its jurisdiction the equal protection of the laws.

Amendment XV: The right of citizens of the United States to vote shall not be denied or abridged by the United States or by any State on account of race, color, or previous condition of servitude.

Other important amendments include the Thirteenth, which eliminated slavery, the Nineteenth, which extended the vote to women, and the Twenty-sixth, which extended the vote to everyone age eighteen years or older.

Both federal and state courts protect these rights as well as other rights enacted by Congress and state legislatures. It is difficult to overestimate the value of such protections for democratic and peaceful accommodation. Citizens know that they need not resort to force and violence to ensure their rights. They know, too, that the electoral process is available as a way to protect their interests. In safeguarding civil liberties and other basic constitutional rules, the courts ensure agreement on fundamentals essential to the success of democratic and constitutional government.

The U.S. Supreme Court holds a unique position in the developed world because of the American principles of separation of powers, **judicial review**, and federalism. These principles make the Supreme Court one of the most powerful judicial bodies in the world. Under the principle of the separation of powers, the Supreme Court may thus protect its own independent and separate status—its own powers and integrity under the Constitution. Under the principle of judicial review, the Supreme Court may declare an act of government unconstitutional. And finally, under the principle of federalism, the Supreme Court also maintains the federal division of powers between the national government and the fifty state governments.

The Supreme Court and the other federal courts umpire the federal system. They do so under rules established in the Constitution and interpreted by Congress, the president, and the courts. Such umpiring is designed to maintain, as Chief Justice Salmon Portland Chase noted in *Texas v. White* in 1869, "a harmonious and indestructible union of cooperative and indestructible states." The federal courts guard against state encroachment on federal power by declaring acts of state legislators and governors unconstitutional or unlawful when they violate the Constitution or federal law. Similarly, if the federal government encroaches on state governments—particularly in ways that threaten their very existence—the Supreme Court has the power, exercised only rarely, to invalidate national legislation that violates the rights and powers given to states. In umpiring the federal system, the federal courts guard against serious conflicts between the nation and the states or among the states. When this umpiring is successful, cooperation and accommodation occur. When rulings are ignored, serious troubles befall American federalism, the most serious and calamitous of which was the Civil War.

British courts also protect civil liberties and the rules of the British Constitution. They do so under Parliament's legislation, which is the supreme law, and no court can declare otherwise. The highest British

Chief Justice John Roberts poses for an official portrait in October 2005. He replaced the late chief justice William Rehnquist, who died in early September.

court—composed of the law lords of the House of Lords—has no power to declare an act of Parliament unconstitutional. This, however, does not mean that civil liberties are violated at will in Britain. The largely unwritten British Constitution, acts of Parliament, and the British legal tradition ensure that basic human rights are protected. It would be unthinkable for the British Parliament to violate the privilege of the writ of habeas corpus (which had its origin in British history) or to deny British citizens the freedoms of religion, speech, press, assembly, or due process of law. British courts thus operate to maintain basic liberties under law. They do not hesitate to rule against British officials who act beyond the law.

Upholding Valid Law and Administration. In the United States, for example, the courts also play a vital role in legitimating economic and social public policy under challenge. In a government of limited powers the Supreme Court serves as a court of last resort in legal actions to test whether Congress has exceeded its powers in passing certain legislation or whether the president has overreached the chief executive's authority in executing duties. In upholding national policy the Supreme Court gives it a stamp of final constitutional approval. This clearly enhances effective governance by definitively ruling on whether the government can, for example, enact Social Security legislation, regulate labor management relations, control the banking system, and subsidize farmers.

In an earlier period, the Supreme Court struck down this kind of legislation at both the state and federal levels—for example, those laws designed to cope with child labor, business monopolies, unfair trade practices, depressed agricultural prices, and lower wages and industrial prices. Most observers of the Supreme Court now generally agree that these Court actions prevented state legislatures and Congress from attending to problems that needed to be addressed. These actions hurt the nation's ability to adjust to the realities of an increasingly industrial, urban, and interdependent society, and to achieve social reforms essential to a healthy life in modern society. The Court interfered with the power of voters—acting through their elected representatives—to satisfy basic needs and address fundamental interests.

In the 1930s, however, the Court began to change its views about economic and social policy. Increasingly, it gave state legislatures greater freedom to address their problems. Only in the field of civil liberties does the Supreme Court maintain its more activist role. The courts may still keep an eye on bureaucratic actions in the economic and social fields that are **ultra vires**, that is, beyond the law. In other words the courts may uphold national policy but insist that government stay within the law in administrating such policy. In this fashion, the Supreme Court enables the president and Congress to respond to national needs and interests, yet still controls overzealous administration. However, the late twentieth century and early twenty-first century began to witness a slight change in the Court's attitude toward government regulation of the economy and social life. Although it is far too early to tell whether this change will mark a new era in constitutional law, Justices Antonin Scalia and Clarence Thomas both seemed disposed to returning to an older, more skeptical approach to government regulations, particularly actions of the federal government.

British courts may also scrutinize governmental actions in appropriate cases to ensure that governmental action follows the law. They may also raise questions about the meaning of a law passed by Parliament. But once Parliament's position on a law is clear, British courts must respect that law. Thus they also function to legitimate legislation and to guard against overzealous administration.

Adjudicating Disputes under the Law. Just as elections enable citizens to decide contests by counting heads instead of breaking them, so the courts enable individuals, groups, corporations, states, and local units of government to rely on judicial procedures instead of force and violence to resolve conflicts. Here we concentrate not on disputes between the individual or group and government, but on those quarrels involving private citizens, groups, or corporations. Unquestionably, these disputes account for most of the work of U.S. state, county, and municipal courts. These conflicts may involve, for example, the law of contracts or the law of torts. A **tort** is a wrongful act, injury, or damage (not involving a breach of contract) for which a civil action can be brought. A **contract** is an agreement— usually written and enforceable by law—between two or more people to do something. We call attention to the courts' role in handling these disputes to underscore both the existence of a mechanism to deal with conflicts and the cultural habit of resort to the law. Although it is not without its weaknesses, the legal system (when it functions at its best and is respected) provides a valuable means for furthering cooperation, advancing accommodation, and peacefully resolving disputes. Effective judicial systems exist in virtually all developed countries.

Courts in communist and developing countries do not generally contribute as significantly to political accommodation as they do in developed countries. Communist courts, in contrast to U.S. courts, have no power to invalidate legislative acts. They function to see that the law is obeyed, not to safeguard human rights as they are understood in Western democracies.

Like legislatures, executives, and bureaucracies, the judicial systems of the developing world vary considerably. In some countries, they are strong enough to challenge the chief executive. For example, in India in 1973 a lower court found Prime Minister Indira Gandhi guilty of minor electoral offenses and disqualified her from holding office for six years, even though the court's decision, pending appeal to the Indian Supreme Court, was suspended for six months. But in many developing countries, particularly those under authoritarian regimes, the courts are powerless to protect citizens against false arrest, illegal imprisonment, and arbitrary punishment. The courts in many developing countries have a long way to go to advance security, liberty, justice, and welfare for their citizens.

ASSESSMENT OF THE PATTERNS OF GOVERNANCE

What lessons do we want you to take away from chapters 11 and 12? A careful reading of these two chapters should have given you a clearer picture of successful patterns of furthering cooperation, advancing accommodation, and handling conflicts. How voluntary, humane, and peaceful are these patterns? Do they maximize security, liberty, justice, and welfare? Which patterns are most successful, and why? What are their costs and benefits? We will try to answer these questions as we examine how our guiding hypothesis holds up.

According to our guiding hypothesis, successful patterns for dealing with the struggle for power in politics rest on (1) agreement on certain constitutional fundamentals, (2) meaningful opportunities for the expression of needs and fundamental interests, (3) sound mechanisms for selecting priorities from among competing interests, (4) acceptable ways for legitimating public policy choices, (5) effective governance, and (6) regular and effective controls on government.

Our conclusions must be tentative, given that we have been able to review only a very small sample of relevant evidence and given our heavy reliance on evidence from highly developed democratic countries, particularly the United States. Moreover, our conclusions on the relationship between political patterns and cardinal national objectives (security, liberty, justice, and welfare) must be treated cautiously because we did not explore this correlation very fully. Nonetheless, although we focused more on institutions and process than on policy results, we need not feel inhibited in asking some key questions regarding the adequacy of these patterns to advance substantive governmental ends.

It seems reasonably clear that the constitutional frameworks and the nongovernmental actors of most developed countries have been more successful than their communist and developing world counterparts in working out voluntary, humane, and peaceful patterns of accommodation in domestic politics. All countries strive for agreement on fundamentals. In important respects, however, they differ on which fundamentals are crucial. In developed countries such as the United States and Britain, successful agreement rests on a historic consensus on popular, or majority, rule and basic rights. These fundamentals call for free elections, representative government, open discourse, opposition parties, and peaceful change. Although communist systems in places such as China and Vietnam have emphasized fundamentals—the ideas of communist ideology such as public ownership of the means of production and exchange, and the leading role of the Communist Party— it seems reasonable to assume that some of these fundamentals are changing. In the People's Republic of China, for instance, new free market mechanisms continue to alter the traditional communist value of public ownership.

People in the developing world place high value on national freedom, independence, cohesion, economic development, and social advancement. But here, too, the winds of change appear to be blowing in some countries, where individual freedom and internal democracy are acquiring greater appeal. In a number of South American nations, for example, basic democratic values, such as free and open elections, are becoming highly cherished.

The critical student of politics must look beyond the rhetoric of agreement on fundamentals to the reality of their operation. He or she must also ask about the costs as well as the benefits of such agreement. For example, in the United States, although great strides have been made, African Americans, women, and the poor continue to face discrimination and formidable economic challenges. In communist systems, public ownership (understood as true worker control of the means of production) is questionable given the history of party and bureaucratic control of the economy. In the developing world, national cohesion may turn out to be rule by a dictator (as in Iraq under Saddam Hussein and Libya under Col. Muammar al-Qaddafi). Economic development may (as in Brazil) widen the rift between rich and poor. Social advancement may take the form of genocide, as with the Khmer Rouge in Cambodia (Kampuchea) from 1975 to 1978.

The strengths and weaknesses of fundamental principles in all three worlds—developed, communist, and developing—must be critically assessed. Thus American federalism can enhance liberty, democracy, and effective government, particularly when the nation and the fifty states cooperate. But federalism frustrates these objectives when certain U.S. states violate civil liberties or tolerate plutocractic tendencies, or when both the nation and the states fail to respond to problems such as protection of the environment. Anticolonialism in the developing world can mean a sensible endeavor to get out from under the domination of an imperial power, or it can become a blind opposition to all Western influence.

And how do patterns in the three worlds deal with human needs and national priorities? Polyarchy—the rule of the many in a constitutional system—is the prevalent mode of democratic government in virtually all developed nations and tends to offer more meaningful opportunities for the expression of vital needs and fundamental interests than can be found in communist and developing countries. Yet here, too, critical political scientists cannot be complacent. In the United States, for example, a number of minority groups— African Americans, Native Americans, Hispanics—do not yet, despite some significant advances, have a strong voice in U.S. politics. And women are still shut out of many aspects of life. Mechanisms are at hand in developed countries—in elections, parties, legislatures, and executive leadership—to select priorities. But how wise are the priorities? Are we spending enough on security or too much? Is our environment being protected or overprotected? How good is our educational system, and what role should the government play in making it better?

Comparable, perhaps even more severe, criticism can be leveled at the Communist Party of the former Soviet Union. The collapse of the communist system in the Soviet Union tends to support critics' contention that the party's historical dominance prevented it from making wise judgments on priorities that would have more genuinely enhanced security, liberty, justice, and welfare for Soviet citizens. For instance, disproportionately high spending on the military and cold war foreign ventures seriously hampered the government's ability to ensure adequate housing, food, consumer goods, and medical care throughout the Soviet Union.

In many developing countries citizens, interest groups, and the media cannot always articulate their needs and interests effectively. Developing countries also may lack effective means for selecting wise priorities: a stable party system, a functioning legislature, and a responsible executive leadership. Their task is often compounded by factors that militate against effective social and political organization and sound decisions—poverty, illiteracy, and serious class and ethnic divisions. In too many developing nations armaments may win out over education, health care, and housing. Economic growth that benefits an affluent minority may win out over distributive justice—that is, greater equity for the poor.

Next let us consider legitimacy and effective governance. Although by no means perfectly responsive to popular needs, particularly those of the "least free," most developed nations have worked out effective patterns (through electoral and legislative majorities) for legitimating public policy choices. Yet the fuller effectiveness of their governments is mixed. Most developed nations have made considerable progress through the welfare state. Yet in affluent, progressive countries such as the United States, poverty has not been eradicated, women have not achieved full equality in either theory or practice, and often ethnic minorities are still not treated as first-class citizens. Pollution as well remains a major concern in all modern, industrial societies.

Moreover, if a healthy government means a government able to ensure peace abroad, we must take a critical look at the war record of developed nations. Although no world war has occurred since 1945, a number of developed nations have been engaged in armed conflicts. France fought wars in Vietnam and Algeria to try to prevent the breakup of the French colonial empire. The United States fought in Korea and Vietnam to block the spread of communism in Asia. Most of these conflicts have produced considerable domestic turmoil. Ironically, among the major powers, only Japan and Germany—aggressor nations in World War II—have not been involved in war since 1945. And the recent threat of global terrorism has brought new challenges in the quest to create a healthy and peaceful world.

In communist systems, such as that of China, public policy choices have been legitimated through the dominance of the Communist Party and ratification by the National People's Congress. From the Western democratic point of view, this legitimacy would be more convincing if it were clear that the Chinese people truly endorsed the Communist Party's perspective.

The legitimacy and effectiveness of many developing governments is in serious doubt. Governments backed by military rule can claim no popular legitimacy. Those developing countries ruled by strong political leaders or single parties on the basis of questionable elections also may be challenged. Only time will tell if the wave of democratic reform sweeping parts of the developing world (such as South America) can be sustained. Poverty, corruption, disease, famine, excessive military spending, and political instability challenge the critical political scientist to explore why the necessary and sufficient conditions of voluntary, humane, and peaceful accommodation are absent in too many developing countries.

Finally, effective and regular controls on government are strong in most developed nations. Even so, the controls have not always prevented abuse of power. For example, the Watergate scandal involved top officials of the U.S. executive branch; this case led to the jailing of an attorney general and key presidential aides and the resignation of President Nixon. Similarly, rationales provided by presidents for various military interventions have been called into serious question. The U.S. involvement in the Vietnam War was partly rationalized on the basis of an attack on U.S. naval forces in the Gulf of Tonkin. Subsequent analysis revealed that the United States had repeatedly entered the territorial waters of North Vietnam on intelligence missions, a fact that the White House withheld from Congress. In the more recent invasion of Iraq in 2003, the White House justified the action on the basis of the need to disrupt the relationship between the Iraqi government and al Qaeda, as well as to destroy what was claimed to be a thriving weapons of mass destruction (WMD) program. The relationship between Saddam Hussein's regime and al Qaeda proved to be highly questionable, and the alleged WMD program nonexistent. At this point it is unclear whether this latter justification was the result of intelligence failure or deliberate distortion. If it proves to be merely an intelligence failure, then utilizing the existence of a WMD program in Iraq would not be an example of presidential abuse of power.

Other abuses of power—for example, by the FBI and the CIA—also have been documented. Most notorious was that of the Iran-contra affair, which led to convictions of the president's national security adviser and a key member of his staff. Ironically, in the very interest of national security, government can violate liberty and justice.

Effective and regular controls on government are weak in communist systems. Political opposition was routinely crushed in the Soviet Union and continues to be repressed in China, as evidenced by the Tiananmen Square demonstrations in 1989 (see chapter 2) and their aftermath. Controls on government in the developing world vary from country to country. In a few nations, controls are comparable to those in the developed world. At the other extreme, in authoritarian regimes of either the right or the left, peaceful opponents of the regime are killed, imprisoned, tortured, or exiled. In the middle are a number of countries that permit only mild peaceful protest, as voiced by brave dissidents.

CONCLUSION

The challenge to work out successful patterns of accommodation to cope with the struggle for power remains. Even modern developed nations—which have a relatively better record than communist and developing countries—still have to improve a lot. How to make these patterns voluntary, humane, and peaceful is a problem that taxes thoughtful political scientists. How to develop patterns that enhance security, liberty, justice, and welfare is a problem that challenges modern statesmanship. In our next chapter we turn to the patterns that international political actors seek to develop to achieve cooperation, advance accommodation, and handle conflicts in international politics.

SUGGESTED READINGS

Almond, Gabriel, G. Bingham Powell Jr., Kaare Strom, and Russell J. Dalton, eds. *Comparative Politics Today: A World View.* 8th ed. New York: Longman, 2004. Examines Britain, France, Germany, Japan, Russia, China, Mexico, Brazil, Egypt, India, and Nigeria within a framework of system, process, and policy, focusing on political socialization, political recruitment, interest articulation, interest aggregation, and policymaking.

Bessette, Joseph. *The Mild Voice of Reason: Deliberative Democracy and American National Government.* Chicago: University of Chicago Press, 1994. A provocative book arguing that the American system of governance actually does encourage deliberation by lawmakers.

Carp, Robert A., Ronald Stidham, and Kenneth Manning. *Judicial Process in America.* 6th ed. Washington, D.C.: CQ Press, 2004. A detailed, well-written survey of the court system in the United States—federal, state, civil, and criminal.

Davidson, Roger H., and Walter J. Oleszek. *Congress and Its Members.* 10th ed. Washington, D.C.: CQ Press, 2006. Very thorough accounting of virtually all aspects of congressional politics.

Greenstein, Fred. *The Presidential Difference: Leadership Style from Roosevelt to Clinton.* New York: Free Press, 2000. A marvelously readable treatment of America's highest political office by a premier presidential scholar.

Johnson, Haynes, and David Broder. *The System: The American Way of Politics at the Breaking Point.* Boston: Little, Brown, 1996. Using the Clinton health care initiative, the authors suggest the U.S. political system is not operating very well.

Kingdon, John W. *Agendas, Alternatives, and Public Policies.* 2nd ed. New York: HarperCollins, 1995. Winner of the Aaron Wildavsky Award by the American Political Science Association. A first-rate analysis of the public policy process in the United States.

Neustadt, Richard E. *Presidential Power and the Modern Presidents: The Politics of Leadership from Roosevelt to Reagan.* New York: Free Press, 1989. An analysis of the presidency that emphasizes the importance of the president's persuasive powers. A classic.

Ulam, Adam. *The Communists: The Story of Power and Lost Illusions, 1948–1991.* New York: Macmillan, 1992. A sweeping analysis of the decline of communism by a distinguished Soviet and Russian authority.

Wice, Paul. *Judges and Lawyers: The Human Side of Justice.* New York: HarperCollins, 1991. Excellent personal look at those who are in the trenches of the American judicial system. See also Paul Wice, *Chaos in the Courthouse* (New York: Praeger, 1985).

Wilson, James Q. *Bureaucracy: What Governments Do and Why They Do It.* New York: Basic Books, 2000. A classic and interesting work on the politics of bureaucracy.

GLOSSARY TERMS

advise and consent (p. 265)
Bill of Rights (p. 279)
bureaucracy (p. 276)
contract (p. 283)
deliberative function (p. 264)
judicial review (p. 281)
legislative function (p. 264)
legitimacy (p. 266)
loyal opposition (p. 267)
meritocracy (p. 277)
representative function (p. 264)
supervisory function (p. 264)
tort (p. 283)
ultra vires (p. 282)
writ of habeas corpus (p. 270)

Chapter 13

INTERNATIONAL POLITICS AND THE GLOBAL COMMUNITY

In chapters 11 and 12 we argued that successful patterns of domestic accommodation rest on agreement about fundamentals, opportunities for expressing vital needs and interests, sound mechanisms for selecting priorities, acceptable ways for legitimating public policy choices, effective governance, and regular and effective controls on government.

Are these the same conditions required for success in furthering cooperation, humane accommodation, and peaceful resolution of conflicts in international politics? Will these conditions maximize security, liberty, justice, and welfare in the global community? Or are there vital differences between domestic and international politics?

POST–WORLD WAR II AND POST–COLD WAR CHALLENGES

This chapter focuses mostly on the patterns of nation-state behavior evident since the end of World War II in 1945 and the end of the cold war in 1990. The end of the Second World War was an important dividing line in many respects. To a large extent, this war ushered in a new world, characterized by (1) the dominance of two superpowers—the United States and the Soviet Union; (2) the advent of the atomic and hydrogen bombs and the globe-girdling missiles, planes, and submarines that deliver these weapons of mass destruction; (3) the breakup of the great colonial empires and the subsequent emergence of new nation-states; (4) an economically interdependent global community; (5) a revolution of rising expectations in all parts of the world—developing and developed; and (6) a host of disturbing ecological problems, including population growth, deterioration of the earth's ozone layer, global warming, urban blight, and pollution of the world's rivers, lakes, and oceans.

As profound as these developments were, the world continues to change, and in the post–cold war world our focus must extend beyond the characteristics normally associated with the post–World War II international environment. In the years following the end of the cold war, the system has been characterized by (1) a large Russian republic struggling with a drastically reduced military capability, a difficult transformation to a market economy, and maintenance of the basic rudiments of democracy; (2) formerly communist Eastern European countries emerging as new market economies; (3) a predominantly Western-dominated European Union, which has reached unparalleled levels of economic integration and is expanding to the east; (4) the emergence of a militant Islamic fundamentalism, particularly in the Middle East and South Asia; (5) a dramatic shift from historically authoritarian political systems to democratic systems of government in many parts of the world; (6) the prospect of a meaningful reduction in nuclear armaments by the superpowers, concurrent with nuclear proliferation in other parts of the world; (7) an alarming increase in civil wars and regional conflicts, many of them emerging out of long-standing ethnic, tribal, and religious resentments; (8) a globalization of the international economic system built on the twin pillars of capitalism and computer-based communications; and (9) a dramatic increase in the reach and lethality of terrorism, including the specter of biological and chemical weapons.

Earlier we asked whether the present international system could adequately protect the vital needs and interests of nation-states and peoples. What do we mean by "adequately protect"? We believe that patterns of international politics should accomplish at least four objectives:

1. prevent a third catastrophic world war, curtail the spread of terrorism, and guard against devastating regional and civil wars;
2. ensure that people live in freedom under governments of their own choice, enjoy basic rights, and govern their own affairs;
3. guard against political, economic, and social exploitation of one nation by another; and
4. ensure that people everywhere have food, decent housing, good medical care, and basic schooling; are safeguarded against ecological disaster; and can enjoy their own diverse lifestyles and cultures.

Our guiding hypothesis is as follows: *Despite some recent and striking successes in international cooperation, present international patterns do not yet adequately protect the vital needs and fundamental interests of all nations and peoples in the global community.*

CURRENT PATTERNS IN INTERNATIONAL POLITICS

In this chapter we elaborate on our guiding hypothesis by analyzing the strengths and weaknesses of three patterns of foreign policy—balance of power, domination, and multilateralism. Balance of power and domination find their theoretical roots in realist thought, which emphasizes a pragmatic, national self-interest approach to foreign policy. Multilateralism is more closely, though not exclusively, associated with idealist thought, a body of thought that tends to emphasize accommodation, negotiation, and collective responsibility. Before assessing these patterns, two concepts central to relations between countries should be explored: national interest and power.

The Standard of National Interest

Patterns in international politics are significantly influenced by national interest. A nation will choose a policy based on the balance of power, domination, or multilateralism because it offers assurance of protecting the national interest. As noted in chapter 10, the national interest serves as a central concern for leaders in international politics. Leaders must protect the fundamental interests of their nation: its freedom and independence, its safety against foreign aggression or subversion, its prosperity, and the rights and welfare of its people. We have used the four concepts of security, liberty, justice, and welfare to summarize the meaning of the national interest.

However, within and between states, debate rages on the more specific meaning of the national interest. For instance, what is in one nation's interest may not be in another's. U.S. involvement in the Vietnam War between 1960 and 1973 illustrates both aspects of this controversy. Within the United States some students, legislators, opinion makers, and other citizens argued that America's national interest was hardly threatened by North Vietnam's effort to take over the whole of Vietnam and unite the country. Other Americans disagreed, believing national interest was indeed threatened: if South Vietnam fell to the North Vietnamese communists, then—like so many dominoes—every country in Southeast Asia would fall, and the United States would be dealt a grievous blow by "international communism." Of course, the governments of the United States and North Vietnam differed on what was in the best interest of Vietnam. The United States sought to contain the spread of communism; the North Vietnamese sought to unify all of Vietnam under the communist banner and rid the country of foreign interests that had caused problems for centuries. Needless to say, the rulers of South Vietnam and the rulers of North Vietnam also had conflicting views of national interest.

To a large extent, disagreements in international politics involve conflicting concepts of national interest. The standard of the national interest—and not some global standard of the human interest of all peoples—is the primary standard for politicians in international relations.

The Primary Role of Power

Patterns in international politics are also significantly influenced by the distribution and exercise of power. Power means the ability of one political actor (say, a nation-state) to get another (say, another nation-state) to do (or not do) something. Political realists assert that power must be mobilized and used in a balanced system, either to maintain an equilibrium of power between countries or to maintain superiority over an opponent. Similarly, domination cannot be maintained without the threat or employment of power. Finally, true collective security, in which peace-loving states band together against aggressors in a global organization, requires that peace-loving states employ their collective or multilateral power against aggressive nations that violate the peace or international law. Thus, regardless of the policy they pursue, nations will employ power to maintain national conceptions of security, liberty, justice, and welfare.

Power can be exercised in many ways. It can be military or economic might, sometimes referred to as **hard power**. There is also what is termed **soft power**, which involves less-tangible techniques and assets.[1] It can be charismatic persuasion: the personal appeal of a gifted leader. Power can be political skill: that of the experienced diplomat. Power can be public opinion: the views of masses of people, putting pressure on decision makers. Power can be prestige: the influence of the respected. Power can be rooted in law: the influence of legitimate authority. Thus power can be military, legal, political, economic, psychological, sociological, or ethical. It is neutral; only its particular use or abuse makes it good or evil.

But another desire also operates in international politics—a desire for mutual benefit. This frequently leads to cooperation, accommodation, and the peaceful resolution of disputes without any military action, economic threat, or political sanctions. Thus nations cooperate on a wide range of practical matters—global communications, ocean and air safety, health, and international postal service—without the threat of coercive power. Nonetheless, when mutual benefits are not obvious, or when disagreements seriously threaten national interests, the exercise of political, economic, and military muscle will be more likely.

BALANCE OF POWER

For a good share of the post–World War II era, roughly 1945 to 1990, balance of power was the most prominent pattern of international politics among the great powers. This pattern dominated the international scene because conditions were not favorable for other patterns. **Balance of power** has many meanings, although most of them are variations on the same theme. Whatever the specific meaning, at the term's core lies the idea that peace is assured when nations' military powers are distributed so that no one state (or combination of states) is strong enough to threaten other states with its military strength. Simply put, peace is achieved through equilibrium. Classic balance-of-power systems are based on the European experience during the seventeenth, eighteenth, and nineteenth centuries. As depicted in Figure 13.1, the system generally had multiple actors of five, six, or seven states (**multipolarity**). During most of the post–World War II period, balance of power was applied to the cold war relationship between the United States and the

Figure 13.1 International Power Distribution Systems

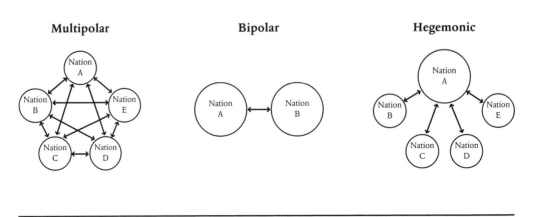

Source: Compiled by authors.

Soviet Union (**bipolarity**). In the post–cold war world, a case can be made that the distribution of power (not really a balance) tends toward **hegemony**, a condition in which one power tends to be an overwhelming, dominating, and perhaps stabilizing force—in this case the United States. Other analysts believe that American domination (or at least near domination) will not last long and that the international system is once again headed for a more multipolar distribution of power.

The Cold War Balance of Power

For forty-five years the United States (and its allies) and the Soviet Union (and its allies) best illustrated the bipolar balance-of-power system. In its own interests, each superpower sought at least equality—and preferably superiority—of power. The United States and the Soviet Union each maintained an arsenal of nuclear weapons designed, so each superpower said, to deter an attack by the other. (These arsenals still exist, but both parties have been reducing their overall nuclear capability considerably.)

The United States and Its Allies. Crucial to the U.S. balance-of-power policy was its alliance system. The heart of the system was the North Atlantic Treaty Organization (NATO, originated in 1949), which affirmed that the "parties agree that an armed attack against one or more of them in Europe or North America shall be considered an attack against them all." [2]

Elsewhere in the world, the United States sought to protect its national interests with other treaties. It extended its protective arm against external aggression over Latin America with the Rio Pact, joined with Australia and New Zealand in the ANZUS Pact, and signed bilateral security treaties with Japan and the Philippines. The Southeast Asia Treaty Organization (SEATO), another cold war security arrangement, dissolved at the end of the Vietnam War in 1975. In 1986 New Zealand objected to American nuclear warships in its ports, thus crippling ANZUS.

The Soviet Union and Its Allies. In the Warsaw Pact, the Soviet Union allied with Eastern European countries as a counterweight to NATO. The relationship between the Soviet Union and its European allies, however, clearly rested on a more coercive basis than that in NATO. The Soviet Union did not hesitate—as its invasions of Hungary (1956) and Czechoslovakia (1968) made clear—to intervene in its allies' internal affairs to ensure the continuation of reliable communist governments. In protecting its own national interests, the Soviet Union (presumably threatened by a united Germany, rearmed and allied with the West) perpetuated the division of Germany and utilized a rearmed East Germany as one of its Warsaw Pact allies, just as the United States, beginning in 1955, utilized a rearmed West Germany as its ally.

By the end of the 1980s the Soviet Union had begun to reorder its priorities. Enormous resources had been expended in cold war efforts around the world at the expense of the Soviet economy. Under Mikhail Gorbachev, the Soviets began to dramatically reduce their commitments. They withdrew their military forces from Afghanistan and cut their military and developmental assistance to Angola, Cuba, Ethiopia, Nicaragua, Vietnam, and other client states in the developing world.

Results of the Cold War

How did the balance-of-power system function after World War II? Did it adequately protect the vital needs and fundamental interests of nation-states and of peoples in the global community? Did it further willing cooperation and peaceful resolution of disputes? Did it enhance security, liberty, justice, and welfare? We have no easy answers to these questions, but some replies are possible.

World War III did not erupt. The Soviet Union did not invade Western Europe or attack the United States. And the United States did not attack the Soviet Union or seek to upset any communist government in Eastern Europe. The mutual fear of a nuclear war, or even a conventional war that might escalate into a nuclear war, preserved the post–World War II settlement in Europe.

American economic aid through the Marshall Plan contributed enormously to Western Europe's recovery. Assisting in this recovery not only made economic sense for the United States but also contributed to building the Western power base squared off against the Communist bloc to the east. Stimulated by the Marshall Plan, Western European countries banded together in the European Economic Community (later to be renamed the European Union) to overcome former disastrous economic and political rivalries (particularly the Franco-German rivalry). Fear of the Soviet Union and the communization of

Eastern Europe served to unite historical enemies (West Germany, France, and Britain) and to keep them in military, political, and economic concert with the United States, primarily through NATO and the European Economic Community. Up to a point, these relationships enhanced security, liberty, justice, and welfare for all the contracting parties.

On the other hand, a heavily armed Western Europe, possessing nuclear weapons, created much anxiety. If deterrence failed and NATO used nuclear weapons to stop a conventional Soviet attack on Western Europe, the outcome would be catastrophic.

As for the Soviet Union, it is now clear that its allies (more accurately, the people of Eastern Europe under communist governments) greatly resented their domination by the Soviet Union in the Warsaw Pact and in Comecon, the communist equivalent of the European Economic Community. Certainly the Hungarian Revolution in 1956, the attempted liberalization of the Czech communist government in 1968, and the Solidarity movement in Poland in the 1980s suggested unhappiness with Soviet domination and no great sympathy with the Brezhnev Doctrine, which asserted the Soviet Union's responsibility to intervene in a communist country to prevent overthrow or liberalization. The dramatic events of 1989, which overturned Communist Party rule in most of Eastern Europe and destroyed the Berlin Wall, confirmed long-held suspicions that most citizens in Eastern Europe were highly dissatisfied with their subjugation.

But what about cooperation, accommodation, and peaceful resolution of disputes between the Soviet Union and the United States? During the late 1960s and early 1970s a policy of **détente** (relaxation of tensions) modestly relieved the worst aspects of the cold war. The United States and the Soviet Union did agree (1) to stop testing nuclear weapons in the atmosphere; (2) to place no nuclear weapons in space; (3) to sign the Nuclear Non-Proliferation Treaty; (4) to limit the arms race as outlined in the Strategic Arms Limitation Talks (SALT) and reduce the number of strategic weapons through the Strategic Arms Reduction Talks (START); (5) to eliminate all intermediate range nuclear forces (INFs), about 4 percent of the nuclear weapons in their combined arsenals; and (6) to limit chemical and biological weapons.

In November 1989, the Berlin Wall crumbled. Dividing the German capital into communist and non-communist zones, it was perhaps the most striking symbol of the cold war.

In addition, the nations of East and West also agreed that some Jews could emigrate from the Soviet Union and that some citizens of East Germany could immigrate to West Berlin and West Germany. In the Helsinki accords on human rights, the West accepted the status quo in Eastern Europe in exchange for human rights concessions from the Soviets. During the 1970s and early 1980s, before Gorbachev's rise to power, the degree of Soviet compliance—or noncompliance—with these agreements aroused considerable controversy in the United States.

Periods of relative calm and progress were, however, interrupted by crisis. Chapter 4 discussed the 1962 Cuban missile crisis, when the Soviets installed nuclear-tipped missiles on an island ninety miles from Florida. Another crisis occurred in late 1979, when the Soviets invaded Afghanistan; the Soviet Union's prolonged military presence there adversely affected détente.

The Costs and Aftermath of the Cold War

Although it appears that the balance of power at least prevented World War III, the cold war also had its costs: huge military expenditures, anxiety and fear over the balance of nuclear terror, harsh domination of peoples in Eastern Europe, an abuse of civil liberties in the 1950s as the United States sought out communists within its borders, costly wars fought in Korea and Vietnam, and the perhaps ill-advised support of right-wing governments by the United States merely because these governments declared themselves anticommunist.

The end of the cold war raised a critical question about the balance of power. Is the international system realigning itself into a new balance-of-power configuration? No crystal ball can answer this question, but several developments in recent years give some clues. First, the cold war bipolar balance of power no longer exists. The Warsaw Pact was disbanded in 1991. NATO has lost its primary reason for existence—the possible invasion of Western Europe by the forces of the Soviet Union and its Warsaw Pact allies. In fact, NATO has expanded its membership to include some Eastern Europe countries. In 2005 NATO's members included Belgium, Bulgaria, Canada, the Czech Republic, Denmark, Estonia, France, Germany, Greece, Hungary, Iceland, Italy, Latvia, Lithuania, Luxembourg, the Netherlands, Norway, Poland, Portugal, Romania, Slovakia, Slovenia, Spain, Turkey, the United Kingdom, and the United States. There are still some unresolved issues concerning NATO's mission, beyond providing for European security. How far east should NATO expand its membership—perhaps someday inviting Russia to become a member? Should NATO concern itself with security issues beyond Europe—for instance, the security of Middle Eastern oil fields?

Second, the United States emerged as the only world superpower, particularly in the ability to project military power beyond its shores for sustained periods of time. Third, although the major powers still maintain enormous nuclear and conventional military establishments, the world increasingly defines power in more economic terms. A new balance between enormous regional economic actors—individual states or regional organizations—may be emerging. This pattern will become clearer later in this chapter. Finally, one can make the argument that the distribution of power among states is diminishing in relevance due to the increase in the power of nonstate actors such as multinational corporations and terrorist groups. Certainly the al Qaeda attacks on New York's World Trade Center and the Pentagon are testament to the growing power of nonstate actors.

DOMINATION

Domination is the policy of exercising direct or indirect control over others. It may be enforced through imperial colonization, conquest, or the exertion of political and economic power. In the nineteenth and twentieth centuries, Great Britain, France, Holland, Belgium, Spain, and Portugal, and to a more limited degree the United States (particularly in Latin America and the Philippines), practiced imperial colonization. During World War II, Germany and Japan made imperial conquests. Another variety of domination is illustrated by Soviet control in Eastern Europe from 1947 to 1989.

During the cold war, observers accused the United States and the Soviet Union—and they accused each other—of wanting to dominate the globe. Critics of the Soviet Union built their arguments on communist rhetoric of worldwide triumph. The Soviet Union would achieve this objective, they claimed, in one or more ways: (1) by direct aggression or takeover (as in the absorption of Latvia, Lithuania, and Estonia in 1939); (2) with the help of local Communists, fortified by the Red Army, as in Eastern Europe; (3) through peaceful means, as in France and Italy, where Communists could poll large numbers of votes; (4) through subversion wherever it was to their advantage; and (5) by encouraging decolonization of the Western imperial regimes, supporting nationalism in the new states and elsewhere, and subsequently taking control in developing countries when communist power and the time were ripe. Similarly, communist and some noncommunist critics of the United States alleged U.S. plans to dominate the world through a capitalist conspiracy, using capitalist puppets to do the bidding of "imperialist" U.S. masters.

Both conspiratorial theories (although grounded here and there in the realities of the Soviet or American struggle for power) are farfetched. In all probability, neither the United States nor the Soviet Union has ever wanted, or has ever had the power, to dominate the world. Global domination by any power is, in fact, a practical impossibility—and is probably even less possible now that the world seems to be moving toward greater nuclear and economic multipolarity.

Charges of regional domination or significant influence, in varying degrees, are somewhat more persuasive and need to be examined more fully. The Soviet Union dominated Eastern Europe for more than forty years. The United States exercised almost overwhelming influence, particularly economic, over Western Europe, Japan, Latin America, South Korea, and Formosa (Taiwan) for nearly fifteen years after World War II.

But even regional domination is increasingly difficult in a world characterized by the rise of new major powers and changing economics. Within the communist world, the Soviet Union reigned supreme until China emerged in the 1950s. In 1989 the Soviets felt that, in view of their collapsing domestic economy, they could no longer afford the high cost of dominating Eastern Europe. Although the United States continues to wield considerable influence in Western Europe, Japan, Latin America, and other countries, it can no longer dominate these nations even if it wants to do so. Indeed, China has recently shown a strong economic interest outside its borders, particularly in Asia, Latin America, and, increasingly, Africa. The United States must cooperate with its partners as equals, even though it can still limit some of their initiatives. But even this limited power is being eroded by the economic integration of Europe, which could create one gigantic economic actor that is far less vulnerable to U.S. influence.

MULTILATERALISM

Multilateralism involves groups of countries collectively solving problems and conflicts, usually through formal international organizations. These organizations may be global, such as the United Nations, or regional, such as the African Union (formerly, the Organization of African Unity) and the Organization of American States. They may be both regional and economic, such as the European Union, or resource based, such as the Organization of Petroleum Exporting Countries. Multilateralism is most often practiced through the day-to-day operations of international organizations. It can also be conducted through special conferences on any number of issues, ranging from arms control to AIDS to pollution of the world's oceans to women's rights to terrorism.

The basic motivation for a strong commitment to multilateralism remains the same, regardless of the problems being dealt with. Decision makers believe that their country's interests will best be protected or advanced through the collective efforts of governments. It is increasingly difficult for individual countries (or even two countries) to deal with the wide range of problems confronting the international system—disease, pollution, global warming, and human rights, to name a few. Most recently, the need for cooperation between states was evidenced in America's concerted efforts to find allies in its global war on terrorism. Although other patterns—balance of power, domination—have not been abandoned in the international system, multilateralism is increasingly seen as a viable technique for advancing the security, liberty, justice, and welfare of states.

We will examine two variations of multilateralism: the work of the United Nations and the economic integration of Europe.

The United Nations in Theory and Practice

It would be a mistake either to overestimate or to ignore the rhetoric, purposes, and principles of the UN Charter, but they cannot substitute for a critical analysis of UN behavior. As we examine the United Nations (founded in 1945), we must consider its aspirations and ideals, but we must also look candidly at the realities of fulfillment—what the United Nations actually does.

The preamble to the charter contains an inspiring vision of peoples in nations determined "to save succeeding generations from the scourge of war . . . to reaffirm faith in fundamental human rights . . . to promote social progress and better standards of life in larger freedom . . . to practice tolerance and live together in peace with one another as good neighbors . . . to unite our strength to maintain international peace and security." [3]

Article 1 elaborates on that vision in spelling out the purposes of the United Nations: "To maintain international peace and security . . . to develop friendly relations among nations based on respect for the principle of equal rights and self-determination of peoples . . . to achieve international cooperation in solving international problems of an economic, social, cultural, or humanitarian character, and in promoting and encouraging respect for human rights . . . to be a centre for harmonizing the actions of nations in the attainment of these common ends."

Article 2 lists some of the important principles that guide the United Nations. These guidelines include "the principle of the sovereign equality of all its Members"; a commitment to "settle their international disputes by peaceful means in such a manner that international peace and security, and justice, are not endangered . . . [and to] refrain in their international relations from the threat or use of force against the territorial integrity or political independence of any state"; and a recognition that "nothing contained in the present Charter shall authorize the United Nations to intervene in matters which are essentially within the domestic jurisdiction of any state." Theoretically, according to Article 4, membership in the United Nations is open to all "peace-loving states."

The major UN organs are the General Assembly, the Security Council, the Economic and Social Council, the Trusteeship Council (no longer very important), the International Court of Justice, and the Secretariat. These organs and their functions are outlined in Box 13.1. The only United Nations body that can pass resolutions with the force of international law is the Security Council. Because of the unique power vested in the Council, each of the five permanent members has the right of veto, which means one negative vote from any of these five states defeats the resolution.

How has the United Nations functioned in practice? The UN has experimented with a number of approaches to peace—its primary concern—and to related concerns such as human rights, economic and social progress, and self-determination of peoples. Seven such approaches can be discerned: (1) collective security, (2) peaceful settlement, (3) disarmament and arms control, (4) preventive diplomacy (peacekeeping), (5) the grand debate, (6) trusteeship and anticolonialism, and (7) functionalism. We use these approaches to explain and illustrate the functioning of the United Nations. [4]

The idea behind **collective security** is that all peace-loving nations, including the most powerful, will band together to maintain international peace and law and that they

Box 13.1 Basic Organization of the United Nations

General Assembly
- Includes all UN members
- Meets annually
- May make recommendations on any matter

International Court of Justice
- Consists of fifteen elected judges representing the world's legal traditions
- May arbitrate any dispute states are willing to submit to it
- Located in The Hague, Netherlands

Trusteeship Council
- Designed to help a number of non-self-governing territories, such as colonies, transition to independence
- In practice, has almost worked itself out of a job (only one trust territory remains—that of the Trust Territories of the Pacific, held by the United States)

Security Council
- Fifteen members, five of whom are permanent: United States, United Kingdom, China, Russia, France
- Does not meet regularly
- Has primary responsibility for maintaining peace

Economic and Social Council
- Fifty-four members
- Produces studies and reports dealing with economic and social issues such as human rights, development, and the environment
- Meets annually

Secretariat
- Administrative arm of the UN
- Headed by the secretary general
- Staffed by international civil servants from around the world

Source: Compiled by authors.

will use their collective strength to deter or punish aggressors who would violate international peace and law. The United Nations was a move in the direction of collective security, but only if the great powers that had banded together to defeat fascism and aggression in World War II could remain united. Given American-Soviet tensions and the veto that the superpowers had in the Security Council, genuine collective security was nearly impossible.

Even the collective action by the United Nations in the early 1950s to prevent a North Korean military takeover of South Korea was less than perfect collective security as envisaged in the UN Charter. The vote was possible only because the Soviet Union was absent from the Security Council and could not cast a veto against UN action on the Korean

U.S. army soldiers in action in the 1991 Desert Storm operation against Iraq. Although the United States provided the preponderance of forces, a coalition of thirty-six nations participated, including a number of Middle East countries—Egypt, Kuwait, Oman, Qatar, Saudi Arabia, Syria, and the United Arab Emirates.

peninsula. When the Soviets returned, action was shifted to the General Assembly, where the Soviets had no veto. Moreover, a powerful police action became possible only because the United States was willing to deploy U.S. personnel and military arms. There is little doubt the United States would have defended South Korea even if the United Nations had done nothing. The outcome of the Korean War was only a partial success for the United Nations. The North Koreans were prevented from taking over South Korea by force of arms, but Korea remains divided.

The Iraqi invasion of Kuwait in 1990 constituted the first major post–cold war international crisis, and for the first time in the history of the United Nations, the collective security machinery operated precisely the way it was designed to. In 1991 twelve Security Council resolutions were passed condemning Iraq for its invasion of Kuwait, establishing a worldwide economic embargo against Iraq, and authorizing military action to enforce the embargo and, if necessary, to force Iraq to withdraw from Kuwait. Many observers considered this operation to be a major watershed for the United Nations, since the sanctions and military action were authorized under chapter 7 of the UN Charter, the document's collective security provision. Under these resolutions, a U.S.-led coalition of military forces successfully forced Iraq to withdraw from Kuwait. Despite these actions directed at Iraq, however, the UN's appeal to collective security for handling breaches of peace has been disappointing overall.

Peaceful settlement employs inherited techniques such as influence, inquiry, mediation, and conciliation. Here the United Nations—whether through the General Assembly, the Security Council, the secretary general, or the International Court of Justice—functions as a third party in the dispute. But success depends on the disputants' willingness to allow the United Nations to work out a peaceful settlement. The techniques may work for unnecessary and essentially avoidable wars but not for the gravest threats to world peace and order.

The United Nations has attempted to facilitate peaceful settlement in a host of cases: Greece, Palestine, Indonesia, Kashmir, Afghanistan, Iran, and Iraq; in the Balkan conflict involving Serbia, Croatia, and Bosnia-Herzegovina; and, most recently, in the Sudan, trying to resolve two conflicts: the first between the northern Islamist government and the Christian southerners, and the second between factions fighting in the Darfur region of the country. The record is mixed. Peace came to Greece in the late 1940s less because of UN actions—aimed at stopping military aid for Greek communists seeking to overthrow the government—than because of U.S. military support for Greece under the Truman Doctrine and because of Yugoslavia's break with Moscow. UN efforts to achieve a peaceful partition of Palestine in 1947 did not succeed. War between Israel and its Arab neighbors broke out, and the region has suffered through a seemingly endless cycle of violence. But the United Nations has facilitated a number of cease-fires and monitored them (as discussed later in this chapter). The United Nations played an important role in ending hostilities between Indonesia and the Netherlands and in gaining Indonesian independence. In Kashmir, where Muslims claiming allegiance to Pakistan and Hindus loyal to India have slaughtered each other for decades, the United Nations has helped restrain more open and serious conflict but has not been able to achieve a definitive solution. The most promising developments took place when the United Nations negotiated the withdrawal of Soviet forces from Afghanistan in 1989 and when it effected a cease-fire in the war between Iran and Iraq (1980–1988); these two efforts are widely considered major successes. In 2002 the United Nations had some success in negotiating a cease-fire and peace framework ending the north/south, Muslim/Christian conflict in Sudan. Similar efforts in the Darfur region of the country had not met with success as of November 2005. In sum, the United Nations has encountered mixed results in its efforts toward peaceful settlement. Still, it has certainly helped make violence less intense and less contagious than it might otherwise have been.

The theory of **arms control** and **disarmament** rests on achieving peace by significantly limiting and ultimately reducing armaments. The United Nations has attempted to advance the cause of arms control and disarmament without major success. Neither the great powers nor the smaller powers have been willing to reduce their propensity to acquire conventional weapons. As mentioned earlier, limited nuclear disarmament has taken place between the United States and the Soviet Union (now the Russian Republic) within the Strategic Arms Reduction Talks (START), but outside the auspices of the United Nations.

Dag Hammarskjöld, secretary general of the United Nations from 1953 to his untimely death in 1961, was a major architect of preventive diplomacy. Hammarskjöld understood **preventive diplomacy** as action by the United Nations to help smaller powers settle disputes peacefully, before they escalated and involved the United States and the Soviet Union in a dangerous confrontation. The primary mechanism used in preventive diplomacy has been peacekeeping, whereby a multinational UN military force intervenes between conflicting parties, usually at the point of cease-fire. Such UN intervention was designed to keep the superpowers out of conflicts in areas outside their crucial spheres of influence.

Preventive diplomacy can work only if the immediate parties to the dispute will accept the UN peacekeeping role and if the major powers on the Security Council go along with this role. Preventive diplomacy will not work, or will not work well, if one of the major powers with a Security Council veto opposes UN action. Current UN peacekeeping operations are shown in Box 13.2. A more extensive discussion of the United Nations' peacekeeping role can be found in chapter 15.

By serving as an international forum for the **grand debate**—where problems can be raised, discussed, and analyzed; where diplomats can meet and test ideas; and where the strength of policies can be measured—the United Nations can modestly advance the cause of peace and other UN objectives. Through the constitutional processes of debate and voting, major issues facing the global community can be aired: the danger of nuclear holocaust; the struggle for national independence; ways to overcome poverty, ill health, and illiteracy; and ways to address violations of human rights. Through discussion, standards of international conduct can be articulated, policy propositions advanced, and education furthered. Global consciousness can be raised.

On the other hand, we should not expect too much from such an international forum. Talk is not always salutary: it may exaggerate and intensify mistrust. And UN resolutions are no substitute for peaceful settlement. Some states that find themselves politically isolated may feel beleaguered by the barrage of hostile UN resolutions (Israel is a good case in point), whereas developing nations (a big majority in the UN General Assembly) may decline to censure a favored nation for its aggression, domination, or violation of human rights.

Trusteeship involves the idea that a developed nation, most often a colonial power, should look after dependent people and prepare them for independence and self-governance. The United Nations was entrusted with supervising the system of trusteeship and other non–self-governing territories that, a few years after the close of World War II, involved only eleven territories in Africa and some Pacific islands. The United Nations fulfilled its supervisory responsibility reasonably well. The only remaining trust territory is that of the Trust Territories of the Pacific held by the United States.

Anticolonialism involves the movement of the colonies or former colonies to become and remain independent nation-states able to govern themselves and achieve economic, social, and political progress. After World War II the United Nations consistently tried to protect dependent peoples in their battles with colonial powers. During the 1950s, 1960s, and 1970s the United Nations functioned as a powerful force in the process of anticolonialism. With the adoption of the 1960 Declaration on the Granting of Independence to Colonial Countries and Peoples, the General Assembly emphatically declared that all peoples have a supreme right to national self-determination. The United Nations

Box 13.2   United Nations Peacekeeping Operations, 2005

UN Mission of Observers in Burundi
(Since 2004)

UN Mission in Sierra Leone
(Since 1999)

UN Interim Administration Mission in
Kosovo
(Since June 1999)

UN Mission in Liberia
(Since 2003)

UN Interim Force in Lebanon
(Since 1978)

UN Peacekeeping Force in Cyprus
(Since 1964)

UN Observer Mission in Georgia
(Since 1993)

UN Organization Mission in the
Democratic Republic of the Congo
(Since 1999)

UN Operation in Côte d'Ivoire
(Since 2004)

UN Mission in Ethiopia and Eritrea
(Since 2000)

UN Mission for Referendum in Western
Sahara
(Since 1991)

UN Truce Supervision Organization
(Since 1948)

UN Military Observer Group in India
and Pakistan
(Since 1949)

UN Disengagement Observer Force,
Golan Heights, Syria
(Since 1974)

UN Stabilization Mission in Haiti
(Since 2004)

UN Mission in Sudan
(Since 2005)

Source: United Nations, 2005, www.un.org/dpts/dpko/index.asp.

was an important, though not primary, cause of the gradual elimination of European empires in what we now call the developing world.

Functionalism is based on the premise that the barriers to cooperation and peaceful resolution of disputes can best be overcome when peoples and nations work together to meet common needs and advance mutual interests. These needs and interests involve practical problems such as trade and shipping, health and literacy, agriculture and fishing, aviation and broadcasting, and nuclear research and development, and are primarily

---

Box 13.3 Specialized Agencies of the United Nations

Food and Agriculture Organization
(FAO)

International Bank for Reconstruction
and Development (IBRD or World
Bank)

International Civil Aviation
Organization (ICAO)

International Fund for Agricultural
Development (IFAD)

International Labor Organization
(ILO)

International Maritime Organization
(IMO)

International Monetary Fund (IMF)

International Telegraphic Union (ITU)

UN Educational, Scientific, and
Cultural Organization (UNESCO)

UN Industrial Development Organization (UNIDO)

Universal Postal Union (UPU)

World Health Organization (WHO)

World Intellectual Property
Organization (WIPO)

World Meteorological Organization
(WTO)

---

nonpolitical.[5] Specialized agencies (actually intergovernmental organizations) have been established to address various functional issues. (See Box 13.3.)

Through the General Assembly and the Economic and Social Council, the United Nations has created a number of additional programs and organizations that report directly to the Assembly or the Economic and Social Council. These organizations include the United Nations Development Programme, the United Nations Children's Emergency Fund (UNICEF), the World Food Council, and the United Nations Environmental Programme.

All these organizations contribute to peace by addressing what some people consider the root causes of war: poverty, illiteracy, disease, and distrust. Some of the work of these agencies and programs is very impressive. The United Nations has eradicated smallpox, immunized millions of children, and funded more than four thousand projects, including schools, health clinics, communications systems, and food preservation and processing facilities. The organization has played an important role in world weather forecasting and has cut illegal opium production by 50 percent in Southeast Asia. It has taken the lead in the global fight against AIDS and in efforts to preserve the earth's ozone layer. The successes are heartening, but it is by no means clear that these programs have dealt with the real political problems that create national rivalry, conflict, and war. Still, without the work of the United Nations and its agencies, distress among peoples would probably be greater and tensions more likely to erupt into conflict.

How do we assess the UN's contribution to security, liberty, justice, and welfare for the peoples of the globe? Although the balance of terror between the United States and the Soviet Union has probably been most responsible for preventing a nuclear World War III, the United Nations was able, under extraordinary circumstances, to prevent North Korea from conquering South Korea, but it was unable to bring peace to Vietnam. The United Nations has not been able to prevent war in a number of cases (for example, in the Israeli-Arab, India-Pakistan, and Bosnian conflicts), but its peacekeeping activities have sometimes helped mitigate a grave crisis. In some instances, as in Indonesia and Kashmir, the UN's good offices have either brought peace or cooled off an actual conflict.

The United Nations has probably spurred movements for national independence in the developing world, but it was ineffective in preventing Soviet domination of Eastern Europe or U.S. interference in Chile and elsewhere. The United Nations has raised a standard of human rights throughout the world, but this did not prevent violations in Argentina, Cambodia (Kampuchea), South Africa, the Soviet Union, and elsewhere.

Through its functional agencies, the United Nations has greatly contributed to the battle against poverty, disease, and illiteracy, particularly in many developing countries. These activities are promising but still inadequate, and they have not yet grappled with or dissolved the political rivalries that have led to war.

Regional Integration

Space does not permit us to explore the many and varied regional organizations in the world today. But special attention must be given to at least one that illustrates the functional approach to peace and economic prosperity, and perhaps ultimately to political union: the **European Union (EU)**.

The European Union was built on a foundation created after World War II by the Marshall Plan, an operation that required Europe to organize for economic cooperation and development. The EU was also built on the European Coal and Steel Community of 1952, designed to tie France and West Germany together economically. In the Treaty of Rome (1957) six nations of Western Europe (Belgium, France, Italy, Luxembourg, the Netherlands, and West Germany) established the European Economic Community (EEC) and the European Atomic Energy Community (EUROTOM). These six nations sought to establish a common market among themselves and a common tariff toward other countries. They sought to abolish "obstacles to the free movement of persons, services and capital." They sought to inaugurate common agricultural and transport policies and hoped to improve employment and raise the standard of living in the member nations.

In 1986 twelve countries of Western Europe (Belgium, Denmark, France, Greece, Ireland, Italy, Luxembourg, the Netherlands, Portugal, Spain, the United Kingdom, and West Germany), building on the success of the EEC, signed the Single European Act (SEA). In doing so, they committed themselves to complete economic integration by the end

Map 13.1 European Union, 2005

Source: Data from European Union Web site, http://europa.eu.int/abc/governments/index_en.htm.

of 1992. If the unification had been successful by the target date, the collective market would have had a gross national product exceeding that of Japan, South Korea, Taiwan, Hong Kong, and Singapore combined.

Although full integration was not reached by 1992, enormous progress was nevertheless made by that time. In 1994 the three original organs of the movement—the European Coal and Steel Community, the European Atomic Energy Community, and the European Economic Community—collectively adopted the designation of the European Union. The EU (whose membership as of 2005 is depicted in Map 13.1) has not entirely overcome important nationalistic suspicions and rivalries, but it has enhanced economic strength and relative prosperity in Western Europe. Even though the dream of full European economic integration has yet to be fully met, it is very close. The most recent accomplishment is the official adoption of the European currency (the euro) in 2001 and its general circulation in 2002.

Aside from the European Union's enormous economic implications, an intriguing issue is the extent to which it will contribute to Europe's political integration. Over the years, the political arm of the EU, the European Parliament, has increased in prestige. This alarms those who cherish their national sovereignty. Indeed, in June 2005 the citizens of France and Denmark rejected a new European constitution, effectively slowing down the political integration of Europe at least for the foreseeable future.

Globalization

Globalization is a term that has risen to great prominence in recent years. While it describes a phenomenon based more in economics and communications than politics, it nevertheless warrants some comment given its impact on the world of politics. At its heart, globalization is built on the twin pillars of capitalism and high-tech communications. Perhaps its most notable characteristic is the enormous increase in international economic integration and interdependence—in trade, banking, transportation, and investment—that has characterized the past ten to fifteen years. The trade figures alone are staggering. The volume of international trade as measured by world merchandise exports has gone through a stunning increase in the period since World War II (see Figure 13.2).

Figure 13.2 World Merchandise Exports, 1953–2002

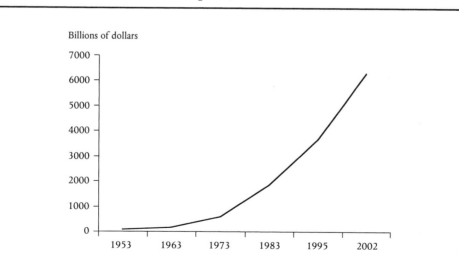

Source: World Trade Organization, *International Trade Statistics, 2003,* www.wto.org.

The globalization movement has engendered considerable protest from those who believe that it contributes to economic disparity between rich and poor countries as well as being detrimental to the global environment. Here, protesters march in Richmond, California, in November 2001.

As Thomas Friedman notes in *The Lexus and the Olive Tree,* this is not the first era of globalization. "From the mid 1800s to the late 1920s, the world experienced a similar era of globalization. . . . [W]hat is new today is the degree and intensity with which the world is being tied together into a single globalized marketplace. What is also new is the sheer number of people and countries able to partake of this process and be affected by it." Friedman goes on to note that a second element differentiating modern globalization from its predecessor is computer-based rapid telecommunications.[6] The Internet, cellular phones, satellite-based relays—these are the tools that facilitate the enormous increase in global economic integration.

What impact does globalization have on the relations between countries of the world? Time and space do not permit an exhaustive examination of this question. But a number of observations made by students of globalization are worthy of thought:

1. *A challenge to sovereignty.* Globalization may constitute a threat to sovereignty, that is, the independence of countries. A globalized world is one in which countries become increasingly interdependent, and the more you depend on others, the less freedom of movement you have. Furthermore, a globalized world facilitates the rise of powerful independent nonstate economic actors such as multinational corporations (discussed in the next section). Finally, the enormously complex, high-speed, computer-based, global communications network is leading to greater transparency. In other words, it is becoming increasingly difficult for countries to hide their behavior, to isolate themselves from the international system. All of these forces associated with globalization tend to erode sovereignty.

2. *Political instability.* Globalization is a high-speed phenomenon, and some people, countries, perhaps even regions of the world may be left behind. The "have nots" of globalization, those that do not benefit from the enormous profits and increase in standard of living that it can generate, become resentful, angry, perhaps violent, and lash out at forces they have little control over. This kind of backlash movement has the potential to foment various forms of political instability—riots, rebellions, revolution, terrorism, even war.

3. *Environmental degradation and the plight of labor.* While globalization in one sense can lead to a greater sense of order in the world, there is no central authority governing its policies and practices. Excesses are inevitable. One area of great concern is environmental degradation brought on by the rapid, unregulated growth in manufacturing facilities, such as those in Mexico along the border with Texas. Another concern has been for the treatment of laborers in various parts of the world. One aspect of this problem is that manufacturing companies enjoy a mobility that labor forces do not have. Entire groups of workers in a country can be left high and dry if companies move from country to country in the never-ending search for lower costs and higher profits.

OTHER FORMS OF BEHAVIOR: NEUTRALITY, NONALIGNMENT, AND ISOLATION

Neutrality, nonalignment, and isolation are state policies not widely practiced in today's world. While we will not engage in a lengthy assessment of their efficacy, they are nevertheless worth defining. **Neutrality** is a legal doctrine that has particular meaning during times of war. States that practice neutrality remain nonaligned with adversaries for the duration of the war, as Switzerland did during World War II. **Isolation** is an extremely difficult policy to maintain, particularly in an age of globalization. It is basically a policy of withdrawal and nonparticipation in the affairs of the rest of the world. Myanmar (Burma) is one example of a country that has attempted to maintain a high degree of isolation for several decades. **Nonalignment** was a policy adopted by many nation-states in the developing world during the cold war. The heart of nonalignment is a refusal to participate in the struggle between major powers or superpowers. Unlike isolation, it is not necessarily a policy of abstention from world affairs. Nor does it mean, as does the concept of neutrality, that these countries refuse to express preferences in conflict situations. Quite the contrary: nonaligned nations feel a positive responsibility to protect their national freedom and independence, to guard against the dangers of a hot war that will engulf them, and to actively fight for economic and social advancement.

NONSTATE ACTORS

Our treatment of the patterns of international behavior has focused on nation-states and their organizations. But students of politics must be aware of other actors in the international system who are playing increasingly important roles.

Nongovernmental Organizations

Nongovernmental organizations (NGOs) are private, international actors whose purposes and activities parallel those of what in domestic politics we call interest groups. Many are small, grassroots organizations working in the countrysides, small towns, and villages of poor, developing countries. Others find themselves in crowded, poverty-ridden urban centers. Others are spread across continents with hundreds of thousands of members and a variety of elaborate organizational structures. Their interests are incredibly broad: cultural preservation, human rights, trade, labor conditions, education, women's rights, health, social services, children's rights, disaster relief, economic development, environment, law, and public advocacy. NGOs attempt to raise public awareness, impact public opinion, and influence the policies of states.

Some of these groups, like those fighting slavery, promoting women's suffrage, and aiding in disaster relief, have been around for more than a century. But until recently their numbers have been small. Roughly a century ago they numbered perhaps four hundred. The growth in the number of NGOs in recent years has been staggering. In the early 1990s they numbered perhaps eight thousand. Today there are at least twenty-six thousand, and some estimates put the number as high as thirty-seven thousand, with individual membership running well into the millions. No doubt, the work of the NGOs, as well as the increase in their number, has been facilitated by the revolution in computer-based communications.

The NGO community has been particularly effective in a number of areas. Certainly in the protection of human rights, organizations like Amnesty International and Human Rights Watch have made an enormous impact. Nongovernmental organizations were instrumental in pushing for the establishment of the International Criminal Court in 2000. They have also had a large presence at some of the better-known global conferences, such as the 1995 World Conference on Women held in Beijing and the 1992 Earth Summit held in Río de Janeiro, where some 1,500 NGOs were present. Organizations like Oxfam that specialize in development have begun to forge working relationships with the World Bank. Finally, the NGO relief organizations played a critical role in relieving the suffering caused by the tsunami that devastated Southeast Asia in 2005.[7]

Terrorist Organizations

The U.S. State Department lists some forty-two fully active terrorist organizations around the world, with an additional forty groups deemed relevant in the global war on terrorism. These range in size from very small, regionally based organizations to groups such as Osama bin Laden's al Qaeda, which may have several thousand followers working in cells all over the world.[8]

It is difficult to make a case that these groups in any way advance international security, liberty, justice, and welfare. As the September 11, 2001, attacks on New York's World Trade Center and the Pentagon outside Washington, D.C., and the subsequent anthrax attacks through the U.S. mail system so aptly illustrate, terrorism is enormously destructive in many ways. The cost in human and economic terms can be enormous, not to mention terrorism's potential as a politically destabilizing force. And although terrorism was brought home to the people of the United States by the 9/11 attacks, it has been an ongoing problem elsewhere. This was dramatically illustrated by the major bombings against the Madrid transit system in 2004, the London transit system in 2005, and the Egyptian resort complex at Sharm el-Sheikh, also in 2005. Because terrorism is such a destructive and destabilizing force, the student of politics would do well to try to understand its origins.[9]

Multinational Corporations

Over the past several decades, perhaps the most powerful nonstate actor has been the large **multinational corporation (MNC)**, a private company such as General Motors, Exxon, SONY, Royal Dutch Shell, or IBM operating in more than one country. Of the hundred largest

While a majority of the casualties resulting from the September 11, 2001, attack on the World Trade Center were Americans, the citizens of 109 additional countries either died or suffered injuries.

economies in the world, more than half are multinational corporations.[10] The multinational corporation has been both extravagantly praised and blamed. It has been commended for its vision of a global market, its recognition of international economic interdependence, its ability to get things done, and its contribution to profits and economic development. On the other hand, it has been censured for exploiting peoples and nations, interfering in the internal affairs of nations, and holding back human development.

How does the multinational corporation affect security, liberty, justice, and welfare around the globe? Does it contribute to voluntary cooperation, humane accommodation, and peaceful resolution of conflicts? Despite its global economic perspective, the multinational corporation lacks the political vision and power to resolve political conflicts or to promote security, liberty, justice, or welfare in the global community. Its primary business is, after all, to make profits for its stockholders. To the extent that profit making is compatible with the security, liberty, justice, and welfare of the peoples in the communities in which it does business, the multinational corporation may enhance these objectives, but they are not its primary objectives. Indeed, profit making may, in fact, lead the MNC to act contrary to those goals. In addition, the multinational corporation is not a political organ; it is a private, elitist organization. And MNCs have often meddled in countries to the detriment of their independence and integrity and to the detriment of their poorer people. Chile is a good case in point. There is reliable evidence to support the charge that U.S. corporate actions (those of International Telephone and Telegraph, to be specific), in league with the CIA, tried to prevent the democratic election of Salvador Allende Gossens in 1970.

Multinational corporations may play an important role in enhancing global prosperity, but nations will have to pass laws to guard against MNC abuses. Their activities will also have to be coordinated with larger developmental purposes and their vision broadened to include the creation of a global mass market based on the fulfillment of human needs. Because multinational corporations are not philanthropic organizations and are not responsible political organizations, it may be asking too much to expect that these qualifications be fulfilled without government mandate.

CONCLUSION

And so we return to our tentative guiding hypothesis that, despite some successes, present international patterns do not yet adequately protect the vital needs and fundamental interests of all nations and peoples. The global community lacks agreement on fundamentals, except perhaps about the horrors of an all-out nuclear war. Although the United Nations has emerged as a forum for addressing vital needs and interests, establishing priorities, and legitimizing decisions, it was not intended to be, and does not function as, a global government. Other patterns of politics—such as working through alliances in the balance of power—have achieved only partial success.

The balance of power, understood as the balance of terror, probably prevented an American–Soviet war—a mutually devastating World War III fought with nuclear weapons. Yet the peace so secured for forty-five years was fragile and purchased at a heavy price. This was the price of armaments, the domination of Eastern Europe for virtually that entire period, and conflicts in Berlin and Cuba that threatened to escalate into World War III. There was also the price of a worldwide struggle for power that was intertwined with drives for national independence and unity and that turned much of the developing world into a violent battleground. Thus it cannot be said that the vital needs and fundamental interests of Americans or Russians—or of other peoples and nations—were protected without enormous cost and risk. With the end of the cold war, the world may have taken a step back from the nuclear abyss. But although the United States and the former Soviet Union have stepped back, there is still the disturbing possibility of widespread proliferation of these terrible weapons of mass destruction.

So our assessment of balance of power does not offer great hope. Does multilateralism offer more hope—and less risk? Our answer is a qualified yes. The United Nations has set laudable standards for peace, liberty, and economic and social justice and, through its varied approaches to peace, has achieved modest success in a number of cases. It defeated military aggression in two important instances (Korea and Iraq's invasion of Kuwait). The United Nations has promoted peace in Indonesia and Kashmir and has kept the superpowers from confronting each other in the Congo, Cyprus, the Middle East, and parts of South Asia. The United Nations has helped dozens of developing world countries advance from colonies to independent nations and has helped them fight disease, illiteracy, and famine. It has aided the economic development of many new states. It has provided a valuable forum for airing global problems and has played an increasingly important role in places such as Afghanistan, Angola, Cambodia, Central America, Iran, Iraq, Namibia, and Sudan. Despite these modest successes, the United Nations did not deal effectively with East-West tensions or prevent dozens of countries from descending into vicious cycles of civil war based on ethnic and religious differences. Nor did the United Nations facilitate political accommodation that might have led to real peace and disarmament in the world.

The European Union has taken significant steps to overcome historic military struggles among its members and to advance economic and political integration. It remains to be seen if its very promising results can be successfully extended to the rest of Europe.

With the qualification that some forces of multilateralism—an enhanced United Nations, greater economic integration—have had salutary consequences, we must nevertheless conclude that present international patterns do not adequately protect the vital needs and fundamental interests of all peoples and nations. Can we do better? We will return to this question in part 4. In the meantime, we can benefit from a fuller consideration of models and patterns of political decision making.

SUGGESTED READINGS

Dougherty, James E., and Robert I. Pfaltzgraff. *Contending Theories of International Relations.* 5th ed. Addison-Wesley Longman, 2001. One of the most comprehensive, well-organized, and lucid surveys of the major theories of international relations.

Hoffman, Stanley. *World Disorders: Troubled Peace in the Post Cold War.* Lanham, Md.: Rowman and Littlefield, 1998. A thoughtful treatise by a giant in the field of international relations.

Kaplan, Robert D. *The Coming Anarchy: Shattering the Dreams of the Post Cold War.* New York: Random House, Vintage Books, 2000. A grim yet fascinating view of global political environment now and in the future.

Kissinger, Henry. *Diplomacy.* New York: Simon and Schuster, 1994. Former U.S. secretary of state and national security adviser lucidly relays the history of diplomacy with special emphasis on the role of power.

Mingst, Karen A., and Margaret P. Karns. *The United Nations in the Post–Cold War Era.* 2nd ed. Boulder: Westview Press, 2000. Timely and well-received discussion on the problems plaguing the United Nations in the 1990s and recommendations for addressing those concerns.

Morgenthau, Hans J. *Politics among Nations: The Struggle for Power and Peace.* 6th ed. Revised by Kenneth Thompson. New York: McGraw, 1985. Classic text that articulates the position of the most influential "realist" in international politics. Morgenthau strongly defended the standard of an enlightened national interest.

National Commission on Terrorist Attacks Upon the United States. *The 9/11 Commission Report.* New York: W. W. Norton & Company, 2005. Extremely readable and gripping account of the 9/11 attacks on the World Trade Center and the Pentagon. Penetrating analysis leads to a serious of major recommendations for strengthening the nation's security infrastructure and intelligence community.

Reid, T. R. *The United States of Europe: The New Superpower and the End of American Supremacy.* New York: Penguin Press, 2005. Former *Washington Post* European bureau chief makes the case for an economic and political powerhouse emerging out of the European integration movement. Whether or not his thesis proves valid in the long run, the book makes for an interesting read on future balance-of-power relationships.

Shawcross, William. *Deliver Us from Evil: Peacekeepers, Warlords, and a World of Endless Conflict.* New York: Simon and Schuster, 2000. A gripping firsthand account of the international community, particularly the UN's struggle to confront a post–cold war world characterized by ethnic conflict, massacres, and endless streams of refugees.

Shenkar, Oded. *The Chinese Century: The Rising Chinese Economy and Its Impact on the Global Economy, the Balance of Power and Your Job.* Philadelphia: Wharton School Publishing, 2004. China's rise over the next twenty years will alter the global economy and balance of power.

Stoessinger, John G. *Nations in Darkness: China, Russia, and America.* 9th ed. New York: Wadsworth Publishing, 2004. Highly readable analysis of how perception has influenced relations among the United States, China, and Russia.

Waltz, Kenneth. *Man, the State, and War: A Theoretical Analysis.* New York: Columbia University Press, 1959. A classic statement on the cause of war.

GLOSSARY TERMS

anticolonialism (p. 304)

arms control (p. 303)

balance of power (p. 293)

bipolarity (p. 294)

collective security (p. 300)

détente (p. 296)

disarmament (p. 303)

domination (p. 298)

European Union (EU) (p. 307)

functionalism (p. 305)

globalization (p. 309)

grand debate (p. 304)

hard power (p. 293)
hegemony (p. 294)
isolation (p. 311)
multilateralism (p. 299)
multinational corporation (MNC) (p. 313)
multipolarity (p. 293)
neutrality (p. 311)
nonalignment (p. 311)
nongovernmental organization (NGO) (p. 311)
peaceful settlement (p. 302)
preventive diplomacy (p. 303)
soft power (p. 293)
trusteeship (p. 304)

Chapter 14

DECISION MAKING IN POLITICS

So far in our search for a science of politics we have explored (1) the political values of political actors and (2) domestic and international patterns of cooperation, accommodation, and conflict. We can now attempt, somewhat more systematically, to organize our understanding of decision making in politics.

We are searching for a science of decision making in politics—a most difficult task. As social scientists, we are intrigued by significant empirical problems in the domain of decision making. For example, at varying levels, and in varying political contexts, what values, what understanding of political phenomena, and what grasp of public policy alternatives actually influence decision making? How adequate is the machinery available to decision makers? What are the consequences of our public policy decisions? Ultimately, how is power wielded, and how are political conflicts resolved?

In this chapter we may not be able to deal with all these questions, but we can make a start. We will leave a fuller treatment of some of the great public policy issues to part 4. Here, however, we can address this question: *Which guiding model best illuminates our exploration of decision making in politics?*

To do justice to our examination we consider five decision-making models. A **model** is a simplified version of what goes on in the real world—it highlights the important elements in the subject of interest. The first part of this chapter focuses on the following models: (1) the rational actor, (2) the political actor, (3) the organizational actor, (4) the elitist actor, and (5) the idiosyncratic actor. These models are not mutually exclusive. Some elements may be found in more than one model. But the models emphasize the importance of different factors in, and different approaches to, decision making.

The final section in this chapter will address several important queries: Is one model more helpful than another in explaining decision making? Does one model make more sense in domestic politics and another in international politics? Does one model do a better job of explaining decision making in democratic and developed countries, another in communist countries and postcommunist countries, still a third in developing countries? And is it possible to integrate all five models in one masterful synthesis?

THE RATIONAL ACTOR MODEL

In the rational actor model of decision making, decision makers seek to accomplish four tasks:

1. accurately identify the problem that confronts them;
2. take into account the key factors in the political (and general) environment that bear on the problem—factors that may facilitate or limit the decision makers' efforts to fulfill their goals;
3. critically examine alternative courses of action designed, in the light of political realities, to address the problem; and
4. make a choice that will wisely maximize benefits and minimize costs.

Problem Identification

Problems often can best be identified if they are put in question form. Thus in the U.S. presidential election of 2004 the key problem facing voters was, Which presidential candidate should I vote for and why? Or, Which candidate, supporting which set of policies, will best advance the national interest? A rational president and rational members of Congress must ask, Which policies will enable the nation to protect its vital interests? To obtain an adequate defense? To combat terrorism? To reduce budget and trade deficits? To secure full employment? To achieve more comprehensive health coverage? To encourage economic investment and enterprise? To enhance education, fight crime, and protect Social Security?

How are conflicting interests to be balanced? Are both budget and tax cuts an option? Cutting the budget may help the nation balance income and expenditures, but it reduces governmental income and may harm people who depend on expenditures for social services. A big defense budget may conflict with a balanced budget. How far should arms reduction go? Must revenues be increased through taxes? If so, which taxes? As a champion of liberty, should the United States vigorously safeguard international human rights? Even if it might mean—as in Somalia, Bosnia-Herzegovina, Kosovo, and Iraq—getting involved in an uncertain and costly military conflict? How does the government balance respect for environmental standards against the adverse effect these standards may have on profitability and jobs?

Other countries face comparable problems that tax their decision-making ability. Can Russia balance the introduction of free market practices with adequate protection of social services? How can a host of countries—France, Germany, and Sweden, to name a few—retain generous welfare benefit systems and still balance their budgets? How can India handle Hindu-Muslim religious controversies and clashes? What policies will bring peace to Israel and its neighbors?

In all such matters, rational decision makers pose the general problem and then seek to refine it. As they identify the relevant issues, conflicts, and difficulties, they are better able to formulate the exact problem. Political conflicts—involving, as they always do, people, power, and passion—are innumerable, disturbing, and challenging. They are intimately related to such values as national security, human liberty, social justice, and economic welfare. The task is to understand the problem clearly in terms of the values that decision makers deem most worthy.

The Environment of Politics

Problems do not occur in a vacuum. They emerge out of a troublesome environment that shapes their character. What do people or interests or nations want? Which factors influence what political actors can do or get? These factors—including military, economic, and political power and information, money, support, time, and geography—may either facilitate or limit responses to political problems.

It is hard to make decisions when not all the facts are known and when future consequences of current actions cannot be accurately measured. For instance, assuring the physical security of U.S. citizens and property is difficult in the face of a terrorist threat when the exact number and location of terrorist cells is unknown. Furthermore, the consequences of any vigorous policy to counteract terrorism within the United States are not entirely clear. The government cannot be 100 percent sure what the impact of such a policy will be on the legal system and on civil liberties.

How to deal with an enormous deficit has also perplexed U.S. presidents. Excessive deficits penalize future generations. They harm the economy by siphoning money away from capital markets. Some combination of budget cuts and increased revenue should be instituted, but as a president addresses this complicated issue, it becomes obvious that there are no easy answers. How much should the federal budget be cut? How much of the defense budget can be cut without causing serious economic dislocation or endangering national security? What are the long-term consequences of eliminating major social welfare programs?

A variety of factors complicate the ability to answer these kinds of questions. Clearly, then, leaders will be better equipped to pose alternatives and make wise choices as they increase their understanding of the decision-making environment.

Alternative Possibilities

Rational political actors attempt to state, and critically examine, the strengths and weaknesses of alternative courses of action. Thus in the U.S. presidential election of 2004 rational voters sought to assess the pros and cons of the policies of Republican president George W. Bush and Democratic senator John Kerry. Presumably, by weighing favorable and unfavorable arguments on an ethical, personal, and political scale, they could arrive at a sensible judgment.

In 2004 Democratic senator John Kerry (left) challenged incumbent president George W. Bush.

Comparable calculations enter into the decision-making process within the national government. According to some decision makers, the U.S. government can fight slow economic growth by encouraging investment in infrastructure and productivity; it can reduce the federal deficit by cutting the defense budget, certain entitlement programs, and bureaucratic fat, and by raising certain taxes (for example, on the wealthy and on gasoline). Other members of the government, however, have a different view of how to achieve economic prosperity, increase employment, and achieve a leaner government. They want to leave the economy largely unregulated; they are loath to cut the military budget or sacred entitlement programs; and they forthrightly oppose new taxes.

On international issues, such as the protection of human rights, presidents may rely primarily on quiet diplomacy, publicity, or economic sanctions, reserving military action for rare and carefully selected cases. In choosing their course of action, presidents consider the likely consequences of the policy as it relates to their values—protecting national security, safeguarding human rights, and enhancing the moral reputation of the United States. They will, of course, also consider the costs and benefits of their course of action.

Other nations and decision makers presumably act in a comparably rational manner as they examine the strengths and weaknesses of alternative policies.

Wise Judgment

According to the rational actor model, choices will be reached after careful balancing of costs and benefits to ensure that preferred values will be maximized. Thus the voter decides that, on balance, Candidate X is preferable to Candidate Y. Congress concludes that Policy A is preferable to Policy B in dealing with economic growth, unemployment, the deficit, health care, the environment, or civil rights.

The U.S. government's response to Katrina, the hurricane that devastated the Gulf Coast in August 2005, illustrated failed decision making on all levels—city, state, and federal. Bureaucratic bungling, communications failures, fear of making the wrong decision, inability to accurately assess the magnitude of the problem, and general failures of leadership led to a tardy and inadequate response to the disaster. Above, citizens of New Orleans, unable to evacuate the city, wait for days at the city's Superdome to be rescued.

The rational actor model assumes that decision makers are conscious, careful, calculating people who face problems sensibly. They know exactly what their values, purposes, and goals are and what is at stake in the problem that confronts them. Rational decision makers are, or try to become, cognizant of the key environmental factors that bear on their problem. They are able to set forth and debate alternative courses of action. And they have the ability, after careful analysis of costs and benefits, to make a wise judgment that, in light of their values, will maximize benefits and minimize costs.

But is this the way decisions are really made? Or do other models suggest a different answer?

THE POLITICAL ACTOR MODEL

According to the political actor model:

1. Decision makers are involved in a struggle for power, and decisions emerge from that struggle.
2. Decision making involves political actors with diverse values, purposes, and goals; diverse interests; and diverse perceptions of relevant political realities, alternatives, costs, and benefits.
3. Decision making necessitates bargaining, accommodation, and consensus—and controversy, conflict, bluff, threat, and even deceit.
4. Reaching the key decision in politics is most often the result of bargaining among political interests.

Politics as a Struggle for Power

According to the political actor model, decision making is not essentially rational deliberation, as depicted in the preceding model. It does not involve well-thought-out values, careful understanding of environmental factors, orderly presentation of selected alternatives, and deliberate choices best designed to maximize preferred values or advance the national interest. Rather, decision making involves a struggle for purpose and power among a number of political actors, some more powerful, influential, or strategically placed than others. This struggle calls for bargaining, negotiating, and compromising. The great Greek political philosophers Plato and Aristotle saw politics as a struggle for power. So did later thinkers such as Niccolò Machiavelli and Karl Marx. Twentieth-century students of American politics have also seen politics in this light. Thus a keen student of congressional decision making, Bertram Gross, titled one of his books *The Legislative Struggle,*[1] and another student of politics, Hans J. Morgenthau, titled his book *Politics among Nations: The Struggle for Power and Peace.*[2]

The Plurality and Diversity of Players, Values, and Interests

According to Graham T. Allison, one of the foremost public policy analysts in the United States, in the political actor model, decisions are made not by a single actor but by many, who "focus not on a single strategic issue but on many diverse intranational problems." They "act in terms of no consistent set of strategic objectives but rather according to various conceptions of national, organizational, and personal goals." They "make government decisions not by a single, rational choice but by the pulling and hauling that is politics."[3]

Not even the president of the United States is a monolithic commander who can simply order an action and see it effectively carried out. President Harry S. Truman's comment in contemplating Dwight D. Eisenhower's taking over the presidency is apt: "He'll sit here and he'll say 'Do this! Do that!' And nothing will happen. Poor Ike—it won't be a bit like the army."

Allison gives us a helpful summary of the many players involved in what he calls "the national security game":

> For example, in the U.S. government the players include *Chiefs:* The President, the Secretaries of State, Defense, and Treasury, the Director of the CIA, the Joint Chiefs of Staff, and since 1961, the Special Assistant for National Security Affairs; *Staffers:* the immediate staff of each Chief; *Indians:* the political appointees and permanent government officials within each of the departments and agencies; and *Ad Hoc Players:* actors in the wider governmental game (especially "congressional influentials"), members of the press, spokesmen for important interest groups (especially the "bipartisan foreign policy establishment" in and out of Congress), and surrogates for each of these groups. Other members of the Congress, press, interest groups, and public form concentric circles around the central arena—circles that demarcate limits within which the game is played.[4]

This model emphasizes the many diverse goals and values that must be reconciled in decision making, the many competing people associated with key alternatives, and the power of key actors. Advocates of this model maintain that the power of key political actors is as important to the final decision as the attractiveness of their goals or the persuasiveness of their arguments.

The Crucial Role of Bargaining

Decisions are not made calmly by isolated, rational players pursuing a priestlike dedication to a clear-cut national interest. Rather, they are made amid conflict and controversy by political actors who bargain and negotiate, bluff and threaten. Political actors may compromise, sidestep, or paper over conflicts. They may iron out or ignore disagreements. They may threaten or seek to seduce their opponents.

Moreover, decision making in politics is characterized much more by incremental (step-by-step) "muddling through" than by deliberate, rational choices in accord with a well-thought-out plan or grand design. What seems a coherent policy may really be hundreds of diverse bargains. According to advocates of this model, bargaining characterizes all of politics. Within the United States government, we may be able to recognize bargaining more clearly in the Congress, but it also characterizes the presidency. And bargaining is also a prominent, if neglected, feature of the Supreme Court. Moreover, bargaining goes on among voters and, certainly, among interest groups.

THE ORGANIZATIONAL ACTOR MODEL

The organizational model affirms the organization's crucial role in decision making:

1. The model stresses the importance of the organization's vital interests, standard operating procedures, and capabilities.
2. It emphasizes how the organization sees problems, obtains information, shapes alternatives, assesses costs and benefits, and makes choices.
3. Finally, it stresses the organization's important role in political bargaining, accommodation, and consensus.

These three points are interrelated. We analyze them separately below to underscore their importance.

Organizational Interests, Procedures, and Capabilities

Organizations, both inside and outside government, seek to protect their vital interests. Inevitably, they favor decisions that enhance those interests. For example, almost all governmental agencies—whether the Department of Defense or the Department of Health and Human Services—seek adequate budgets; without adequate budgets, agencies say, they cannot fulfill their missions. They argue vigorously that they need money to defend the nation, improve education, increase good housing, and the like. Similarly, they oppose policies that adversely affect their interests. This same logic of self-protection holds for groups outside government (such as organizations of industrialists, farmers, or workers) that are vitally interested in certain policies and decisions.

Governmental organizations make decisions in the very process of carrying out decisions; their operating procedures are therefore highly important. **Standard operating procedures (SOPs)** are an organization's regulations and guidelines. They specify priorities, speed of response, and how services are delivered. For example, these procedures may determine whose income tax return is audited and how thoroughly, whose safety regulations are inspected and how carefully, whose civil rights are protected, and in what way the military responds to suspicious "hostile" missiles, planes, and ships.

The capability of governmental organizations also affects decision making and public policy. Their perspective is most often partial and incomplete, their approach limited and cautious. They seek solutions that are "good enough" rather than solutions that maximize benefits. They do best in handling familiar routines. Bureaucracies, in general, find safety in familiar processes; they avoid uncertainty. Consequently, they often lack imagination, the ability to deal with new circumstances, and the courage to break through to new choices. It is said, for example, that armies are always better at fighting the last war than the next war.

How Organizational Life Affects Decision Making

Organizations view problems from their own special angle. For example, officials in the military worry less about the impact of the arms race on social priorities and the deficit than about the military's ability to defend the nation against actual and potential dangers. The Treasury Department is concerned about inflation, the Labor Department about unemployment. These limited perspectives inevitably affect organizations' understanding of problems.

These perspectives also clearly influence an organization's understanding of relevant information and significant alternatives, its assessment of costs and benefits, and therefore its final decision. Depending on one's perspective, this may be helpful or harmful. Thus even within an organization such as the State Department, the section concerned with human rights will see things differently from that concerned with safeguarding national security.

In general, organizations are not farsighted, creative, or flexible. America's failure to be prepared for the Japanese attack on Pearl Harbor on December 7, 1941, is a case in point. The U.S. Navy did not carry out long-distance reconnaissance of Japanese activities around Pearl Harbor. The U.S. Army, which had focused on the threat of subversive activity, was woefully unprepared for the actual Japanese air attack. Central coordination of navy and army intelligence did not exist. Similarly, it would appear that there was an enormous intelligence lapse prior to the September 11, 2001, terrorist attacks on New York City's World Trade Center and the Pentagon outside Washington, D.C.

An organization's lack of creative long-term planning, and even imaginative short-term problem solving, is often explained by its dedication to its own "life"—its concern for its own budget, personnel, and territory. The struggle of organizations to protect their central concern leads to our next point.

Organizational Bargaining

Organizations are important actors in political bargaining. They are concerned with who gets what (money), who does what (leadership and personnel), and where power is exercised (territory). Thus monetary, leadership, and territorial imperatives drive organizations. Conflicts over these matters within and between organizations significantly influence decisions about dealing with other countries, fighting illegal drugs, coping with the AIDS epidemic, fighting terrorism, and handling a host of other issues. Here, of course, the political actor model and the organizational actor model overlap.

The State Department and the Defense Department may not see eye to eye on disarmament. The Coast Guard, the FBI, the Drug Enforcement Agency, the U.S. Air Force, and the U.S. Navy may disagree on how to handle the war on drugs. The Department of Health and Human Services may have a different strategy on AIDS from that of the Centers for Disease Control in Atlanta or the Office of Management and Budget. Federal intelligence agencies may not only squabble among themselves, but they also may be less than helpful when dealing with state and local law enforcement as the nation struggles with its war on terrorism. In the wake of the attacks on the World Trade Center and the Pentagon in September 2001, President Bush created the Office of Homeland Security, charged with the daunting task of gathering information and coordinating policy emanating from no fewer than twelve major departments. Later, in response to recommendations from the *9/11 Commission Report,* the president created the Office of the Director of National Intelligence. Figure 14.1 demonstrates that governmental structure can be very complex, with a lot of room for bureaucratic infighting.

THE ELITIST ACTOR MODEL

The elitist actor model affirms that

1. very powerful individuals or limited groups of influential people known as elites make the really significant decisions in politics; and
2. they do so to protect their own self-interest and power.

Figure 14.1 Office of the Director of National Intelligence

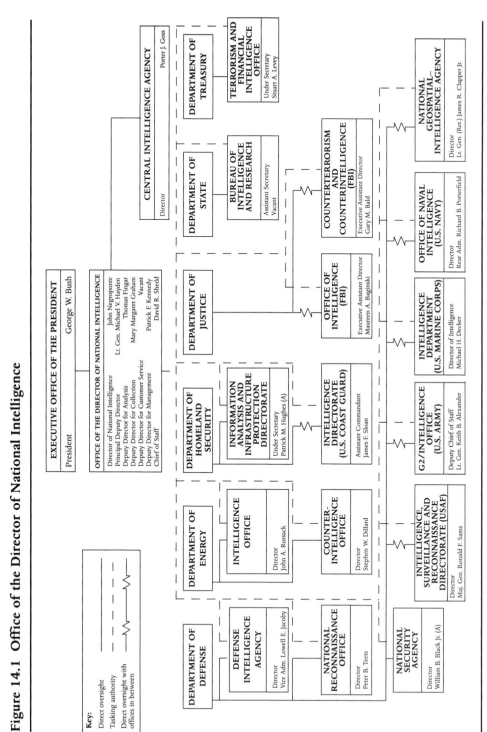

Source: Carroll Publishing, www.carrollpub.com/NationalIntelligence.asp, 2005.

This model asserts that to understand political decision making, we must identify the key individuals, the so-called movers and shakers as well as the vested interests and economic, political, and social power they seek to guard. Students of the elitist actor model believe they are more realistic than political scientists who are tuned in to the other models. Elite model theorists are persuaded that they are asking the really important questions in politics: Who really rules? Who really benefits?

The Pervasiveness of Elite Rule

Proponents of this model maintain that basic decisions in politics and government—as in all large organizations—are always made by a small, self-interested, knowledgeable, and active group of insiders: the **elite**. Proponents recognize an iron law of oligarchy,[5] meaning that the very nature of large organizations—and government is certainly a large organization—makes this law of elite rule inevitable. There may, of course, be a rotation of such elites—that is, leadership may change from time to time or even from issue to issue—but there will always be an elite in charge of decision making.

This view further asserts that decision making cannot really be democratic. It takes interest, intelligence, money, skill, and time to make decisions, and these qualities are to be found only in a tiny minority—the governing elite. Such elite rule is not restricted to authoritarian or totalitarian regimes—left or right, communist or fascist—or to military regimes or old-fashioned aristocratic regimes. It characterizes all governments, no matter how democratic they say they are. The United States is no exception.

As Thomas R. Dye and L. Harmon Zeigler point out in their well-known book *The Irony of Democracy,* in the United States "a small number of persons allocates values for society." These people—the members of the elite—are "drawn disproportionately from the upper socioeconomic strata of society." Nonelite individuals move only slowly into the governing circle and only after they have "accepted the basic elite consensus." Public policy reflects "the prevailing values of the elite." In the United States, these values include belief in private property, free enterprise, limited government, and individual liberty.[6]

Historically—in authoritarian regimes of the far left or far right—a communist or fascist elite has clearly been in charge. In the old Soviet Union or in China today, this elite has been made up of top leaders of the Communist Party. In Nazi Germany, the leaders of the Nazi Party constituted this elite. In many developing countries, a similar pattern of elite rule takes the form of a military junta, a small group of extraordinarily wealthy and powerful families, or a dictator.

Self-Interested Rule

It is important to know not only who rules (and how) but also who benefits (and how). Here scientific judgment among students of elitism is strained, and the student of elitism becomes more a judge of values. Some are hostile to elite rule as being undemocratic and pro-capitalist; others see elite rule as efficient and wisely aristocratic, even favorable to civil rights and economic well-being.

Marxists argue that a bourgeois elite rules in capitalist countries. This elite does not represent the interests of the overwhelming majority of people, who are workers. Rather, the governing elite—reflecting the dominant influence of capitalism in all aspects of life—represents a highly integrated group of industrialists, bankers, corporate lawyers, politicians, and high military officers working hand in glove with the active or passive support of educational, religious, and media leaders. Key policy decisions are designed to protect capitalism, private property, and corporate profits. Those who benefit from government decisions are the capitalist "haves." Those who suffer under such regimes are the proletarian "have nots." The exploitation of workers and peasants in most developing countries, Marxists argue, is understood in terms of imperialism, colonialism, domination, and dependence.[7]

Other students of elite rule argue that such governance characterizes all authoritarian regimes. Historically, the Politburo—the top leadership of the now defunct Communist Party in what was the Soviet Union—may have claimed to rule as representative of the people, but it was actually ruling on behalf of the Communist Party elite. Such rule, moreover, perpetuated undemocratic domination, violations of human rights, flawed economic policies (guns instead of butter), and foreign policies contrary to the wishes of the people (such as the interventions in Hungary in 1956, Czechoslovakia in 1968, and Afghanistan in 1979). A similar critique applies to the Communist Party in China, Vietnam, and Cuba.

Many theorists of elite rule also sharply criticize other forms of authoritarian regimes as perpetuating military dictatorships and as being contemptuous of human rights. Such regimes may benefit a wealthy minority of the native elite and their foreign friends, but they do little or nothing for most of the people—a frequent criticism leveled at regimes like those in North Korea under Kim Jong Il, Zimbabwe under Robert Mugabe, and Iraq under Saddam Hussein.

Still other students of elite rule note that not all elites are intellectually or morally backward. They cite the positive, humanitarian, and modernizing role played by many elites. For instance, some observers argue that a highly elitist institution such as the U.S. Supreme Court is the best protector of civil liberties and rights. These groups would be Thomas Jefferson's "natural aristocrats," prominent, for example, in shaping a democratic future for the new American Republic. These natural aristocrats have carried Europe forward in a wide range of activities, including the rebirth of democratic institutions in post–World War II Germany, the growth of the European Economic Community, and the end of colonialism. They are also the leaders in modern America who are more responsive than the general public to civil rights for African Americans and greater freedom for women. The motivation of such leaders may spring from genuine humanitarian considerations or from the calculated, broadly self-interested view that the liberal establishment must consistently pursue the principle of freedom in order to stay in power.

The leadership role of such enlightened elites, which some scholars consider atypical, leads us to consider yet another form of decision making, the idiosyncratic actor model.

THE IDIOSYNCRATIC ACTOR MODEL

Given the tremendous impact of leaders such as V. I. Lenin, Joseph Stalin, Adolf Hitler, Franklin Delano Roosevelt, Winston Churchill, Mao Zedong, Charles de Gaulle, Harry S. Truman, Mohandas Gandhi, Martin Luther King Jr., and Mikhail Gorbachev, the political scientist must pay careful attention to the role of personality in politics. Such qualities may be neutral (intuition, critical acumen, and speech), positive (charisma and compassion), or negative (demagoguery, ruthlessness, and dogmatism). The idiosyncratic actor model stresses the crucial role of the decision maker's unique personality, emphasizing leadership's dual role in decision making: destructive and creative.

The Destructive Decision Maker

Stalin, Hitler, and Saddam Hussein are three frightful examples of destructive decision makers. A destructive leader can have a tremendous impact on his country. Determining how much that impact has to do with leadership and personality and how much with other forces is not always easy. Under Stalin's leadership, millions of Soviet citizens suffered. His continuous purges of enemies on the communist left and right, his liquidation of the kulaks (prosperous peasants), his decimation of military leaders, and his savage treatment of millions of rank-and-file citizens exhausted Soviet society and made efforts such as repelling the Nazi invasion of June 1941 infinitely more difficult. How many of these brutal policies can be directly traced to Stalin's personality is an open question. Perhaps some of them can be explained as practical, albeit barbarous, politics. But the historical record is clear that Stalin was extraordinarily crafty, incredibly ruthless, and possessed by acute paranoia. It is hard to accept the idea that these well-documented traits had no impact on his destructive policies.

Hitler is another case in point. Would the Nazi state have done what it did—barbarically destroy Europe's Jews and brutally attack its European neighbors—even if Hitler had died in 1933? Would Germany's fate have been different if Hitler had trusted his generals more and his intuition less? If Hitler had not been driven by a megalomanic passion? Again, these questions cannot be answered decisively. But Hitler's personality—his sick mind, dogmatic convictions, political and military intuitions, and oratorical gifts—made a vital difference.

Saddam Hussein also must be considered a destructive decision maker. His brutal murders of those he suspected of domestic disloyalty or political opposition, his repression of

Kurds and Shiites in Iraq, his seven-year war against Iran, and his aggression against neighboring Kuwait in 1990 certainly suggest megalomania, paranoia, cruelty, and irrationality of a terribly destructive kind.

The Creative Decision Maker

Leaders may, however, be charismatic in a positive way. They may possess unique gifts of grace, appeal, and talent that inspire allegiance and are used to further peace, freedom, and justice. Gandhi and Martin Luther King Jr. illustrate these qualities. Although India's fight for independence and African Americans' struggle for civil rights were complicated, Gandhi's and King's decisions to use nonviolence made an important difference in their campaigns.

Saddam Hussein, the brutal dictator of Iraq, was placed on trial in October 2005 for crimes against his own people, accused of causing the deaths of hundreds of thousands of his fellow Iraqis during his twenty-four-year rule.

Similarly, the eloquent leadership of Franklin Delano Roosevelt and Winston Churchill made a difference. Roosevelt's buoyant personality, pragmatic temper, and sagacious political skills helped the United States cope with its worst economic depression. Churchill's stubborn courage, memorable words, and special relationship with Roosevelt sustained Britain during its greatest peril in World War II and prepared the way for Allied triumph. Churchill was one of the twentieth century's most eloquent masters of the English language. A sample of his great skill with language is the following passage from his famous speech on Dunkirk, delivered to the House of Commons on June 4, 1940:

> We shall not flag or fail. We shall go on to the end. We shall fight in France, we shall fight on the seas and oceans, we shall fight with growing confidence and growing strength in the air, we shall defend our island, whatever the cost may be, we shall fight on the beaches, we shall fight on the landing grounds, we shall fight in the fields and streets, we shall fight in the hills; we shall never surrender.

A more recent example of remarkable leadership under enormous stress can be found in the person of New York mayor Rudolf Giuliani following the September 11 terrorist attacks on the World Trade Center. His courage, calm, resolve, and communication skills were lauded and admired across the nation and around the world.

The idiosyncratic actor model thus points to important personality factors that may sometimes run counter to the rational, political, organizational, and elitist assumptions of

Rudy Giuliani's behavior after the World Trade Center tragedy inspired New Yorkers to band together and help one another. Here he greets firefighters working through the rubble on October 16, 2001.

the other models. Highlighting the unexpected, which may either be creative or demonic, better equips political scientists to deal with novel elements in decision making. Whether these varying models can be integrated into one coherent model remains a challenging question for students of politics. Before reflecting on that possibility, we will explore the five models as they apply to a single political system. Of course, nations vary in decision-making style, but we believe that it is important to explore the application of these models in some depth. This dictates that we examine only one country—in this case, the United States.

DECISION MAKING AT VARIOUS LEVELS IN AMERICAN POLITICS

Let us now consider the role played by the voter, the legislative representative, the president, and the Supreme Court justice in American politics. How do the five models help explain the way they vote?

The Voter

Why do American voters vote the way they do? Do they make rational choices based on enlightened self-interest? Do they follow a party line? Do they go along with the organization—corporation, labor union, or farm bureau—that represents their vital interests? Do they follow an elitist leader? Or are their choices idiosyncratic—stemming from their own personality quirks?

Studies of American voting behavior show that voters are not fully informed, keenly discriminating, totally rational, or supremely dedicated to the public interest. Neither, on the other hand, are they vastly ignorant, utterly lacking in powers of analysis, completely irrational, or unaware of how their self-interest relates to the common good. Let us examine some generalizations about voters in presidential elections and try to discern which model of decision making these generalizations sustain.

Studies suggest that, from the mid-1970s to the early 1990s, Democratic presidential candidates tended to be supported by a loose coalition of working-class voters, African Americans, and Hispanics. They were predominantly urban residents, with high school degrees, who considered themselves liberal.[8] Republican presidential candidates, on the other hand, tended to draw voters who were college-educated, business or professional people, in the upper-income brackets, white, and Protestant. They tended to live in small towns or rural areas and/or considered themselves conservatives.[9]

These correlations could support the rational actor model. For example, working-class, grade school–educated, African American, urban, and lower-income voters could logically perceive that their interests in jobs, housing, medical care, education, and mass transportation are better served by a Democratic president. Similarly, professional, college-educated, white, Protestant, small-town, and upper-income voters could believe that their interests in lower taxes, less regulation, and budget cuts are best served by a Republican president. These conclusions assume that a Democratic president would favor more liberal policies and a Republican president more conservative policies. Moreover, voters who consider the family's financial situation worse at the time of the election tend to vote against the incumbent president.

Other evidence, however, supports other hypotheses. Despite a general weakening of political allegiances, party identification still accounts for a large percentage of the U.S. presidential vote. After heated and sometimes bitter party primary battles, the faithful return to the fold and vote for the party's candidate in the final election.[10]

Nonparty organizational loyalty also plays a role in how people vote. This is true particularly when the organization's single issue achieves great importance: for example, abortion, the environment, gun control, Social Security, or Israel. Although workers did not overwhelmingly follow the recommendations of trade union leaders in the past couple of decades, many workers who had voted Republican in earlier elections supported their organizational leaders and voted Democratic in 1992.[11]

Even the elitist actor model may affect the voter's decision. The voter may be influenced by the leadership qualities of the presidential candidate: character, personality, strength, eloquence, and "class." Candidates may be helped or harmed by perceptions that they are safe or radical—sympathetic or hostile to the operative ideals of the establishment. For example, in 1964 Sen. Barry Goldwater was perceived as too radical on the right, and in 1972 Sen. George McGovern was perceived as too radical on the left. Both lost by large margins. Elitist influence may also be manifested in voters' support for candidates endorsed by an elite voice they respect, such as the *New York Times*.

Finally, voters may make their decisions on idiosyncratic grounds: on the basis of a personal handshake, a candidate's smile, or sex appeal, or a candidate's stand on a single—sometimes odd—issue. Thus a number of factors—rational, political, organizational, elitist, and idiosyncratic—help explain a voter's decision.

The Representative

Why do our representatives in Congress vote the way they do? Five hypotheses can be entertained. Three correspond to single decision-making models; the other two overlap several models.

The Representative as Trustee. According to this hypothesis, the representative actually matches Edmund Burke's famous portrait: although the representative lives in "the closest correspondence . . . with his constituents," he does not "sacrifice . . . his unbiased opinion, his mature judgment, his enlightened conscience" to any person. His judgment is "a trust from Providence," exercised after reasonable discussion and deliberation and on behalf of the common good.[12] The representative does not blindly follow the constituents' wishes as an unthinking delegate or the party's dictates as a robotlike partisan. Here we can detect the rational actor model at work.

Support for this hypothesis has come from a number of sources. In *Profiles in Courage*, John F. Kennedy noted that a number of brave senators did in fact act as trustees in the Burkean sense. They bucked party and constituent pressures and even risked their careers to follow their consciences. They acted on the assumption that they had been elected because their judgment—and their ability "to exercise that judgment from a position" where they "could determine what were their own best interests, as part of the nation's interests"—was respected by the voters.[13]

Despite the skepticism of "realistic" political scientists who tend to scoff at the reality of the trustee (or Burkean) role, political scientists have found empirical support for this hypothesis. For example, in a 1959 study of four states—California, New Jersey, Ohio, and Tennessee—John C. Wahlke, Heinz Eulau, and their colleagues found that 63 percent of the state's legislators defined themselves as trustees. This was in contrast to 14 percent who saw themselves as delegates—following the majority will of their constituents—and to 23 percent who saw themselves as "politicos"—attempting to balance the pressures of party, constituents, and conscience. Wahlke and his colleagues concluded that "the role orientation of trustee may be one of necessity." They argued that legislators have greater access to facts and information, have difficulty knowing what constituents want, and must wrestle with the conflicting desires of constituents and constituents' lack of interest in key matters. These points, they noted, emphasize the actual discretion representatives have in following their own good, rational judgment as trustees.[14]

More recent studies, like that of Roger H. Davidson and Walter J. Oleszek in 2005, also support the conclusion that the representative functions as a trustee. These scholars note that the influence of interest groups is exaggerated and emphasize that legislators respect the expertise of colleagues—concerned with the common good—whose grasp of issues may exceed their own.[15]

The Representative as Delegate. According to this hypothesis, representatives are delegates who express the will, and speak the opinion, of the constituents (especially the powerful ones) who elected them to office. This hypothesis is supported in such early studies as James MacGregor Burns's *Congress on Trial* (1949), by polls indicating that the public expects their congressional representatives to vote the way the majority in the district feel, and by more rigorously empirical studies of representatives.[16]

Burns, a perceptive observer of American politics, contended that the typical congressional representative is a diplomatic agent for his or her constituency. Members of Congress are realists who vote in harmony with the home folks—especially the well-organized home folks. Always aware of the next election, members avoid or straddle national issues that seriously divide their supporters, while being sure to protect local rights. When their party's national platform conflicts with the strongly held interests of their constituents, they do not hesitate to disagree with their party.

Is Burns's assertion about the constituency's importance still valid? Most studies indicate that constituencies are still critical. One indicator is found in data collected by Glenn R. Parker about the time senators and representatives spend with their constituents. His study reveals that the average number of days spent with constituents increased dramatically from approximately 11 days per year for both types of legislators in 1959 to more than 140 days for senators and nearly 250 days for representatives in 1990, a rate that has been maintained to this day.[17] This makes sense for a number of reasons, among them advancements in technology and transportation allowing representatives to return home to meet with constituents more easily, and promises by the leadership in both houses to schedule proceedings in ways permitting members long weekends in their districts and states. Not only do legislators spend a great deal of time with constituents, the overall volume of constituent communications has increased dramatically in recent years. Communications quadrupled between 1995 and 2004 almost exclusively due to Internet messaging. This has forced congressional offices to devote more resources to managing the growing volume of constituent contacts.[18]

The Representative as Partisan. Students of politics who advance this hypothesis maintain that the representative is a **partisan** who, more often than not, votes with the party on key issues. In strong party systems such Britain's, this hypothesis is supported by rather overwhelming evidence. But how does it fare in the supposedly weaker party system of the United States? The reality is that despite legislators' tendency to define themselves as trustees, party affiliation is the strongest predictor of voting preference.

In his brilliant 1952 study, *Party and Constituency: Pressure on Congress*, Julius Turner addressed this question, although his study was more an attempt to measure party cohesion in Congress than to determine if members are, or see themselves as, party persons. Turner's study underscores the significant partisan role of the representative.[19] Are Turner's

Figure 14.2 Party Voting in Congress

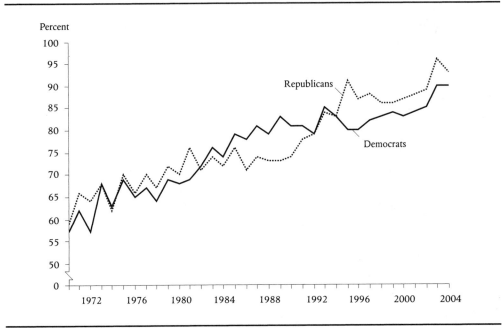

Source: Roger H. Davidson and Walter J. Oleszek, *Congress and Its Members,* 10th ed. (Washington, D.C.: CQ Press, 2006), 285.

Note: The graph shows the percentage of times the average Republican or Democrat in Congress voted with his or her party majority in partisan votes for the years listed. These composite party unity scores are based on votes that split the parties in the House and Senate—a majority of voting Republicans opposing a majority of voting Democrats. We have recomputed the scores to correct for absences.

conclusions valid today? Data drawn from the past thirty years strongly support the correlations between voting and party affiliation. Davidson and Oleszek, in their book *Congress and Its Members,* note:

> Party voting levels in both houses, which were relatively high in the 1950s, fell in the 1960s and rose again perceptibly after the 1970s. Sharpened partisanship has marked congressional politics since then, to the point that "partisan gridlock" has become a buzzword in recent campaigns.[20]

Figure 14.2 shows the pattern of levels of party voting in Congress from 1970 to 2004.

The Representative as Politician. This hypothesis illustrates well the political actor model. Supporters of this hypothesis argue that the representative is, in fact, a politician who, depending on political circumstances, juggles several roles in response to diverse and shifting interests and pressures. Representatives are sometimes trustees, sometimes delegates, sometimes partisans—depending on the political conditions that affect their decisions; but always they are politicians, sensitive to the bargaining and balancing that is central to political decision making.

George B. Galloway, a keen and knowledgeable student of Congress, insisted that a member of Congress is neither purely the spineless agent of constituents nor the godlike trustee of the public interest. Members lead and follow. On most issues they legitimately compromise with party and constituency because they are political animals with an eye on the next election. As Galloway put it:

> The desires of [the congressman's] constituents, of his party, and of this or that pressure group all enter into his decision on matters of major importance. The influence of these factors varies from member to member and measure to measure.[21]

Frank J. Sorauf, in his prize-winning study *Party and Representation* (involving the Pennsylvania legislature), concluded that the average legislator balances constituency, party, and personal judgment and makes tentative and cautious choices on the issues in light of these demands:

> The average legislator appears, then, to make no firm commitment to constituency, party, or self. Their demands on him and their sanctions over him shift from issue to issue. Both the shifting political demands and the finely balanced equities of choice force him to choose only tentatively and cautiously, one issue at a time.[22]

Other students of the legislative process, such as journalist Elizabeth Drew, have a more cynical view of the legislator as politician.[23] Interest groups can generate enormous amounts of money to support ever more expensive election campaigns. This situation seems to have become worse during the 1980s, leading to the assertion that U.S. legislators are captives of special interests and not responsive to the people or their political parties.

The Representative as Idiosyncratic Legislator. There is also a view that representatives often vote on a purely personal basis, which may reflect their own preferences, biases, institutions, or quirks. They may support a personal friend or oppose a foe. They may, as in Sen. Edward Kennedy's case, strongly favor gun control because of the tragic loss of family members. They may support disarmament because of a loved one's death in war or human rights because of a memory of the Holocaust or environmental controls because of a love of nature.

These views on representation address the "why" question—why representatives reach the decisions they do. Rational and elitist factors enter into the trustee role. Political and rational factors influence the delegate role. The interests, procedures, and capabilities of the party—as an organization—shape the representative's role as a partisan. The political actor model almost completely explains the role of the representative as a politician. And idiosyncratic elements do enter into the representative's judgment on at least some issues. In turning next to consider decision making in the White House and on the Supreme Court, we will explore the "how" (as well as the "why") of decision making.

The Chief Executive

How do presidents make decisions and why? A pluralist interpretation—drawing on all five of our models—may be the most helpful. We take our leading example from *Essence of Decision,* Graham T. Allison and Philip Zelikow's in-depth study of the Cuban missile crisis.[24] Superficially, presidential decision making appears to illustrate splendidly all the elements of the rational actor model: problem, environmental factors, alternatives, and choice. The 1962 Cuban missile crisis seems to offer a textbook example.

1. The problem: how—safely—to get the Russian missiles out of Cuba.
2. The environmental factors: the proximity of the missiles (ninety miles from Florida) and their range, destructive capability, and effect on the balance of power.
3. The alternatives: an invasion of Cuba, a "surgical" air strike, a quarantine (blockade), negotiations with the Russians, an approach to Castro, or doing nothing.
4. The choice: the quarantine, plus contact with the Russians and support in the Organization of American States (OAS) and at the United Nations (UN).

As we saw in chapter 2, President Kennedy and his team of advisers (ExCom) addressed the problem carefully and prudently. They were disturbed by the military, political, and psychological consequences of the Soviet missiles because they believed the missiles threatened America's national security. The team considered a number of alternatives for safely putting pressure on the Soviet Union to remove the missiles, and they held in reserve the possibility of more drastic military action. ExCom gave the Russians time to respond and to save face (withdraw the missiles in return for a "no invasion of Cuba" promise) while building support for the U.S. position with allies in Europe, members of the OAS, and other nations.

Yet, as Allison demonstrates, the complete dominance of the rational actor model is open to challenge. A good deal of political bargaining went on. The hawks on ExCom pressed for a strong military response: a "surgical" air strike to take out the missiles, if not an invasion; they were also open to a surprise attack. UN ambassador Adlai Stevenson's arguments to rely on diplomacy at the United Nations were not well received by anyone. Defense Secretary Robert McNamara's idea of a quarantine (blockade) was not strongly endorsed at first by the hawks. Attorney General Robert Kennedy took a strong stand against a surprise attack. The do-nothing option was not seriously entertained. Only slowly did judgment crystallize around the idea of the quarantine as a firm but prudent response, buttressed by the threat of stronger measures, contact with the Russians, and diplomacy at the OAS and the United Nations to obtain support for the U.S. position.

The Cuban missile crisis also underscores the elitist character of decision making. There was no public referendum on the president's decision. A very small group of men advised him. And the final decision was made by the president himself.

Finally, idiosyncratic elements are also apparent in the president's decision. For example, John Kennedy's tendency to reject a do-nothing approach was probably reinforced by his need to demonstrate toughness (especially in light of a presumed Russian impression of him as weak, after an earlier meeting with Nikita Khrushchev in Vienna). Robert Kennedy's opposition to a surprise attack on Cuba was based on his strong conviction that—after Pearl Harbor—the world would not forgive such an attack.

As with the Cuban missile crisis, in-depth examination of other presidential decisions would also support a pluralist interpretation. Presidents rationally seek to maximize goals, but they often have to accept something less than ideal. They engage in negotiating, bargaining, and compromising. They strive for consensus among divergent political actors. They are influenced by the bureaucratic organizations on which they rely for an understanding of key problems, relevant information, selected alternatives, and recommended choices—choices with the greatest benefits and the least costs. Very few people may actually participate in key decisions designed to protect the national interest as understood by the establishment. And idiosyncratic factors play a role. The ingredients of these models are not neatly isolated from one another; they often interweave and overlap each other.

We will now turn to the decision-making process in the U.S. Supreme Court to test the five models of decision making.

The Supreme Court Justice

Superficially, the judicial process seems to be a model of rational decision making:

1. Justices begin with a legal problem that calls for a resolution.
2. They seek to understand the problem in its context, which means that they must understand both the facts of the case and the relevant precedents (previous court decisions and the text of the Constitution).
3. They then argue alternative approaches to the problem.
4. Finally, they vote and by majority decision reach a choice, with one justice being selected to write the majority opinion (and set forth the reasoning that led to that opinion) and with opportunity for concurring or dissenting justices to set forth their differing logic.

As a result of the Brown v. Board of Education *case in 1954, public schools in the American South were integrated, sometimes forcefully. Here, troops of the 101st Airborne Division escort black American students into Central High School in Little Rock, Arkansas, in September 1957.*

Let us examine one case as indicative of the issues justices must face: Did "separate but equal" education in Topeka, Kansas (and other states), violate the equal protection clause of the Fourteenth Amendment to the U.S. Constitution, which declares that no state shall deprive a citizen of the equal protection of the laws? The facts proved that African Americans were being educated in separate schools. The key legal precedent, in *Plessy v. Ferguson* (1896), held that separate but equal education does not inherently violate the equal protection clause. Arguments in *Brown v. Board of Education of Topeka, Kansas* centered on whether the Court should reverse that precedent. Finally, in 1954 the Court unanimously decided that separate schools are inherently unequal and constitute a violation of the equal protection clause of the Fourteenth Amendment.[25]

Thus justices, in a highly rational manner, attempt to consider problems, facts, precedents, alternatives, and choices. They seek to maximize the values enshrined in the Constitution. They address the relevant factors in the judicial environment. They seriously consider the pros and cons of alternative arguments. And they finally arrive at a reasoned judgment that balances, as necessary, costs and benefits.

But is the judicial process quite as neat and pat as the preceding paragraphs suggest? Most observers of the Supreme Court think not. The Court's problem is not always so clear-cut; often several formulations of the key problem compete for selection. Similarly, the facts and the meaning of the pertinent precedents can be ambiguous; different justices often interpret the facts and precedents differently. They may quarrel about the relevance of precedents. Moreover, different justices will find differing responses to the agreed-on problem logical and compelling. Thus there may be concurring opinions that set forth different reasons for the same conclusion or dissenting opinions that set forth reasons for different conclusions.

Do our other decision-making models help explain these differences among well-educated, intelligent, and rational justices who are dedicated to the values of the Constitution? Students of politics would be naive indeed if they ignored the fact that justices are often appointed because they reflect a particular political ideology. To put it bluntly, liberal presidents normally appoint liberal judges to the Court, and conservative presidents usually appoint conservative judges. Although justices may be remarkably independent once they accept their lifetime posts, they usually bring to the Court a socioeconomic background and political and judicial ideology that influence their judicial opinions. For example, they may be more or less sympathetic to the power of the president, of Congress, or of the states or to civil rights, business, labor, or the environment.

Perhaps the most controversial action of the Supreme Court in decades came amid the turmoil of the 2000 presidential election, when the Court ruled against hand recounts of ballots in the state of Florida. In doing so, the Court reversed a Florida Supreme Court order to recount votes in several Democratic parts of the state, thereby all but assuring a victory for Republican George W. Bush over Democrat Al Gore. Although the decision was accepted by Vice President Gore, critics noted that the decision, which slapped down the Florida Supreme Court ruling, was made by what many consider to be the five most "conservative" members of the Court, led by Chief Justice William Rehnquist and Justices Antonin Scalia and Clarence Thomas. Dissenting minority opinions by the more "liberal" or "moderate" side of the Court centered on whether the case should be sent back to the state for more work or whether the Supreme Court should even be second-guessing state court justices in Florida. Countering these criticisms, the Republicans noted that every one of the Florida Supreme Court justices was a Democratic appointee. What the decisions of both courts raised, of course, was the possibility that America's most revered court system was politicized.

Justices cannot be oblivious to the struggle for power in politics and of the Court's role in that struggle. They cannot overlook the diverse values and interests of those who battle for power—labor and management; the president and Congress; the federal government and the states; farmers, consumers, Hispanics, African Americans, and women. Justices cannot be removed from the bargaining, accommodation, and consensus of politics.

For instance, in unanimously declaring that "separate but equal" was unconstitutional in 1954, the Court made an important political statement against racial discrimination. Over the course of the Supreme Court's history, majorities on the Court have reflected diverse views on key political questions in the struggle for power. They have at different times, for example, upheld states' rights and then defended national power, protected slavery and later advanced the civil rights of African Americans, and vigorously supported corporate interests and subsequently secured labor's rights to organize and bargain collectively. In these diverse matters, justices have also made political statements and participated in the struggle for power in American politics. Given the diversity and complexity of this struggle, concurring and dissenting opinions on the Court should not be a surprise.

But it would be a mistake to think of the Court as the same kind of political actor as Congress or the president. The Court, as an organization, has a life and logic of its own. Here the organization process model may throw additional light on judicial decision making.

The Court has its own vital interests to protect. These are clearly spelled out in the "Judicial Power" statement of Article III, Section 2, of the Constitution, and are evident

in its historically affirmed and sanctioned power to declare an act of Congress unconstitutional. The Court will protect its independence and integrity against congressional or
presidential onslaughts. It will try to avoid "mistakes" or "self-inflicted wounds" that
weaken its prestige, such as upholding slavery, striking down an income tax, limiting
the ability of either Congress or the states to regulate corporations, or upholding racial
discrimination. Chief Justice Charles Evans Hughes, in the midst of the nation's efforts to
cope with the Great Depression of the 1930s and to adjust to the realities of what later
would be called the welfare state, worked very hard (especially on Justice Owen Roberts,
a "swing" member of the Court) to build a bare majority of at least five to sustain key New
Deal legislation. Roberts's switch in 1937 from the conservative to the liberal side of
the Court has facetiously been called "the switch in time that saved nine." The Court
might have lost some of its powers if it had persisted in striking down vital New Deal legislation. Roosevelt's general frustration with earlier Court decisions led him to propose
a fundamental reform of the Court. His plan, commonly called the "Court-packing plan,"
would have allowed him to appoint more justices, ones more sympathetic to his views.

The Court's standard operating procedures also significantly influence its decision making. These procedures, or rules, greatly influence which cases the Court will or will not take.
For example, the Court will not take a case unless a real controversy between real adversaries exists under the Constitution. The Court will not take a case unless it involves "the
protection or enforcement of valuable legal rights, or the punishment, prevention, or redress
of wrongs directly concerning the party or parties bringing the justiciable suit," to quote
Henry Abraham, a longtime Court observer.[26] Legal procedure requires the party or parties in a suit to have "standing," that is, the right to be recognized in a court of law.

The Court's standard operating procedures also dictate that it not render advisory opinions—that is, opinions rendered in the absence of a real legal controversy properly before
the Court. Decisions can be made only on live issues. The Court also insists that all remedies in lower courts be exhausted before review by the Supreme Court. The Court normally avoids clearly political questions by insisting that these are properly handled by legislative bodies. In dealing with an act of Congress, the Court normally presumes that
the act is constitutional; this means that challengers will have to demonstrate very clearly
why they think the act is unconstitutional. The Court normally will also decide cases
before it on the narrowest basis—avoiding, for example, constitutional questions if the
case can be decided on other grounds. The Court generally avoids passing judgment on
the wisdom of governmental action. In many ways, then, the Court's operating procedures
condition its decision making.

The elitist actor model may also throw light on judicial decision making. Members
of the Supreme Court are clearly an elitist group of nine persons. In a split decision the
majority may comprise only five justices. Before Sandra Day O'Connor was appointed
in 1981, no woman had served on the Supreme Court. As of early 2005, only two African

Americans, Thurgood Marshall and Clarence Thomas, and two women, O'Connor and Ruth Bader Ginsburg, had ever been so appointed, while no Hispanic had. Does the Court go its independent way, regardless of legislative, executive, and public opinion? Or do the Court's decisions reflect the views of voters and their representatives? The historical record is mixed. For example, in the post–Civil War period, the Court's defense of corporate interests was often not in tune with majority sentiment as reflected in state and federal legislation. In the 1950s the Court's record on civil rights was perhaps in advance of national sentiment as measured by state and federal legislatures. In general, the Court has protected the prevailing values of the elite: private property, free enterprise, limited government, and individual liberty.

Idiosyncratic factors may also influence judicial decisions.[27] Justices are not bloodless, emotionless creatures; they are not legal computers. They love and hate with passion. They may be judicial activists, open to governmental reform and judicial initiatives in politics, the economy, and society, and vigorously committed to civil rights and environmental protection. Or, despite their personal liberal or conservative views, they may be committed to a philosophy of judicial restraint, allowing Congress to take the initiative in matters of social policy. The justices may be pragmatic or dogmatic—as well as liberal or conservative—in their decision making. The personality of the chief justice is particularly important because it is his or her task to keep the Court together, to assign justices to write decisions, and in general to ensure the Court's healthy functioning. Powerful chief justices, such as John Marshall, have made a difference. Political and ideological leadership—whether from a Charles Evans Hughes or an Earl Warren or a William Rehnquist—has been important.

TOWARD A THEORY OF COMPARATIVE DECISION MAKING

Let us now reflect on the five decision-making models and our brief explanation of some decision makers in American politics. We will be particularly interested in how widely these models apply to decision making in other countries and in international organizations such as the United Nations. We are also curious about whether these five models can be combined into a coherent and helpful synthesis. We would like to know how decision-making patterns can help satisfy human needs.

Some tentative, exploratory propositions may help the critical student move toward a more substantial theory of worldwide decision making. First, all political decisions contain rational, political, organizational, elitist, and idiosyncratic elements. The political scientist's task is to precisely identify these elements and to assess their actual influence in decision making. Second, although a pluralist decision-making model is more helpful than any one of the models outlined in this chapter, a synthesis of all five models is too difficult to obtain at this time. Third, only more modest generalizations about aspects of decision making are possible at this stage in the history of political science. For example:

- The rational actor model is an ideal that is rarely approximated in the real world of politics.
- The political struggle for power is universal, and bargaining is widespread in all political communities. Political bargaining is more prominent in the countries lacking strong party systems or effective legislative majorities. For instance, constituents have more influence in the United States than in Britain and more influence in Britain than in China.
- Organizational influences are worldwide, but they are potent in liberal democracies such as the United States and in the social democracies of the industrial world. Organizations are also potent in the communist world and in some developing countries because of the power of bureaucracy and the primacy of party in communist countries and because of the prominence of the military in many developing countries. In developing countries where the bureaucracy, party, and military are weak, such impact is lacking.
- Elite rule is worldwide, but the elites may be authoritarian or subject to varying degrees of democratic control. Elites normally seek to protect the status quo (whether capitalism, communism, democracy, or authoritarianism), but there may also be revolutionary, reactionary, and reform elite groups seeking to alter the status quo.
- Idiosyncratic actors do make a difference in politics. We have just barely begun to understand the role of the creative (or destructive) idiosyncratic decision makers.

Finally, certain decision-making models are more helpful in explaining foreign policy decisions than domestic decisions. In most countries, the foreign policy decision-making process tends to be concentrated in the executive. There are several reasons for this: (1) executives tend to control the instruments of foreign policy; (2) they tend to have more resources for gathering and processing information about foreign affairs; and (3) because countries must "speak with one voice," executives—whether prime ministers, presidents, dictators, or kings—speak for the country as a whole. For these reasons, rational actor, organizational, elitist, and idiosyncratic models tend to be more influential. Domestic decision making is a bit more diffuse, and more political factors affect the process.

CONCLUSION

Thus we see how decision making in politics may be illuminated by exploring a number of key empirical models—rational actor, political actor, organizational actor, elitist actor, and idiosyncratic actor. These five models enable us to profitably examine actual decision-making processes in American politics and to ask about the relevance of these models in decision making in other countries and in international politics. With more empirical work in this vital area of decision making, it may be possible to move beyond modest generalizations to a more ambitious synthesis of key models.

Beyond decision-making models, however, other important questions must be asked. Who benefits, and who suffers, as a result of policy decisions? Is there any relationship between certain decision-making processes and values such as peace, liberty, justice, and economic well-being? Can the decision-making process be improved to enhance these values?

The four chapters of part 4—"Political Judgment and Public Policy"—provide a fuller opportunity to discuss these questions. We will pose and explore some of the big issues of public policy—troublesome problems that engage our capacity for prudent judgment. We will set forth key aspects of the record on these problems and explore policies relevant to war and peace in the modern world, the battle on behalf of the "least free," the struggle for economic well-being, and the imperative of ecological health.

SUGGESTED READINGS

Allison, Graham T., and Philip Zelikow. *Essence of Decision: Explaining the Cuban Missile Crisis.* 2nd ed. New York: Addison-Wesley Longman, 1999. Uses three models (rational actor, organizational process, and governmental politics) to throw light on decision making in general and the Cuban missile crisis in particular. Brilliant!

Barber, James D. *The Presidential Character: Predicting Performance in the White House.* 4th ed. Englewood Cliffs, N.J.: Prentice Hall, 1992. A classic treatise on how the personality types of various leaders are reflected in their presidencies.

Davidson, Roger H., and Walter J. Oleszek. *Congress and Its Members.* 10th ed. Washington, D.C.: CQ Press, 2006. Readable, thorough, and well-regarded text on the American legislative system.

Irons, Peter H. *A People's History of the Supreme Court.* New York: Viking Penguin, 2000. An excellent history with emphasis on how ordinary citizens attempted to attain their rights through appeal to the Court.

Janis, Irving. *Groupthink: Psychological Studies of Policy Decisions.* 2nd ed. New York: Houghton Mifflin, 1986. Fine study of how advisers can fall all over each other to please the decision maker and achieve consensus without genuine debate. Both good and bad decisions are reviewed: Bay of Pigs, Marshall Plan, Vietnam, and more. See also Janis's *Crucial Decisions: Leadership in Policymaking and Crisis Management.* (New York: Free Press, 1988).

Kingdon, John. *Congressmen's Voting Decisions.* 3rd ed. New York: Harper and Row, 1989. A critical weighing and blending of statistical data and information generated by personal interviews.

McCullough, David. *Truman.* New York: Simon and Schuster, 1992. Considered one of the finest and most popular biographies of the last half of the twentieth century. The remarkable story of how the responsibility for reshaping the post–World War II world befell a very common man.

Mills, C. Wright. *The Power Elite.* New ed. New York: Oxford University Press, 2000. Classic study that first appeared in the 1950s suggesting that a narrow elite controls politics in America.

Nelson, Michael, ed. *The Elections of 2004.* Washington, D.C.: CQ Press, 2005. A very helpful summary and analysis of the Bush-Kerry race.

Neustadt, Richard E. *Presidential Power and the Modern President: The Politics of Leadership from Roosevelt to Reagan.* New York: Free Press, 1990. Underscores the importance of presidential personality and the constraints on, as well as opportunities for, presidential leadership. Full of valuable insights.

Parenti, Michael. *Democracy for the Few.* 7th ed. New York: St. Martin's Press, 2001. Sees decision making in the United States as dominated by capitalist values, institutions, and political actors. Sharp criticism of the dominant liberal democratic elite.

GLOSSARY TERMS

elite (p. 328)
model (p. 318)
partisan (p. 335)
standard operating procedures (SOPs) (p. 325)

POLITICAL JUDGMENT AND PUBLIC POLICY

In part 4 we turn to our third major concern in political science: the development of political wisdom in the public policy arena. The overall problem that we shall address is: How can we sharpen our prudent judgment on key issues of public policy?

We shall attempt, by critically examining key issues of public policy, to explore the prudential component of political science, the component concerned with wise judgment. In dealing with such issues as war and peace in the modern world (chapter 15), the battle on behalf of human rights (chapter 16), the struggle for economic well-being (chapter 17), and the imperative of ecological health (chapter 18), we encourage you to study political judgment and public policy in light of what you have learned about political philosophy in part 2 and about the real world of politics in part 3.

You will be encouraged to articulate and examine the guiding ethical values that are so crucial to political philosophy and ideology. You will also be asked to assess empirical findings relevant to a science of politics. Prudent judgments—wise judgments—draw on such critically understood ethical values and empirical realities. They demand that political actors clearly understand their purposes and the possibilities of the real world. Prudent judgments also demand that political actors balance a number of principles—competing values such as how to maintain freedom and equality—in deciding issues of public policy.

Chapters 15, 16, 17, and 18 should thus engage your judgment on a number of controversial problems of the present and the future. These are some of the real challenges of politics: war, violations of human rights, the persistence of poverty, and the environmental degradation of the planet. In addressing momentous issues of public policy, we first explore ethical and empirical factors helping to define each problem. Secondly, we identify alternative approaches to the problems and the strengths and weaknesses of those approaches. In setting forth alternative approaches, we are ever alert to the possibility of what we call **creative breakthroughs**, innovations generally prompted by tough problems that conventional wisdom says cannot be solved. We do not offer these potential creative breakthroughs in order to advance a political agenda. They are designed to stimulate your thinking as to the possible solutions to difficult problems.

Creative political breakthroughs are rare in history. Roger Williams's concepts of religious tolerance and liberty might be thought of as a creative breakthrough, as well as James Madison's formula for the design of a republic with a strong central government while maintaining liberty, self-government, and justice at the local level of state government.[1] Harry Truman's adoption of the Marshall Plan at the end of World War II demonstrated incredible foresight for the advancement of economic welfare as well as the security of Europe and the United States. Under excruciating pressure, President John Kennedy's use of a quarantine as an alternative to a potentially disastrous military strike in the Cuban missile crisis might also be considered a creative breakthrough. In addition, many believe that the European integration movement epitomized by the formation of the European Union will prove to be an incredible breakthrough, considering the centuries of warfare that have plagued that region of the world. Students of politics have a major contribution to make in advancing such breakthroughs. In this section of the book, we invite and encourage you to set forth your own solutions to some of the most difficult problems facing humanity.

Chapter 15

WAR AND PEACE IN THE MODERN AGE

The specific question to be explored in chapter 15 is, *What creative breakthroughs can help us achieve a more peaceful world order?* To begin, we need to define war, peace, and creative breakthrough as they apply to our question.

By **war** we mean military activity—armed violence—carried out in a systematic and organized way by nation-states (or organized groups that aspire to become nation-states) seeking to impose their will on other nation-states. With this definition we include not only wars between states but also domestic wars, such as civil wars, revolutions, and intercommunal fighting based on ethnic, tribal, or religious identity.[1] For most of this chapter we do not include the war on terrorism begun by President George W. Bush after the September 11, 2001, attacks on the World Trade Center and the Pentagon. This is a new form of war, a war against a movement. Because of its unprecedented nature, it will be treated in a separate section of this chapter.

By **peace** we mean the absence of war. Positively, peace is a condition of harmony between nation-states (or organized groups that aspire to become nation-states) that enables them to cooperatively, lawfully, and voluntarily (through discussion, voting, mediation, conciliation, and arbitration) work out conflicts and deal with disputes.[2] Peace does not mean the end of all conflict, competition, and tension. Rather, we mean eliminating catastrophic world wars, regional wars, civil wars, and wars of national liberation. We mean minimizing the level of armed conflict. We also mean making significant arms control and disarmament possible. In essence, we envision a world in which major disputes (between and within nations) are settled without resort to violence and bloodshed, in which dangerous international tensions are considerably reduced, and in which world energies and monies are used to meet human needs for food, housing, medical care, education, community, and social and cultural development.

By creative breakthroughs we mean ethical, empirical, and prudential changes to promote a more peaceful world order: a higher ethical consciousness of global community, a new or more penetrating scientific understanding of the causes of war, and wiser judgments about how to overcome war and its disastrous consequences.

ETHICAL AND EMPIRICAL FACTORS

This section presents several important factors that affect war and peace in the modern world: the threat of nuclear war, the consequences of conventional war, the arms race, the sovereign nation-state system, and the new war on terrorism.

The Mortal Threat of Nuclear War

With the end of the cold war in 1990, the world seemed to have stepped back from the edge of the nuclear abyss. The immediate threat of a major nuclear exchange between the United States and the former Soviet Union has lessened. The Strategic Arms Reduction Talks (START) and the resulting START I and START II agreements have resulted in reductions of nuclear weapons in both the United States and Russia (see Figure 15.1). Thus the cold war tension that fueled the nuclear arms race has subsided.

But these bilateral steps between the United States and Russia are tempered by other grim realities. The threat of nuclear war is far from over. The American and Russian arsenals still contain thousands of strategic nuclear warheads. China, France, India, Israel, Pakistan, and the United Kingdom are also capable of making nuclear war. And several developing countries such as Iran and North Korea are actively pursuing the means to produce nuclear warheads. With the collapse of the Soviet Union, there is great concern over the disposition of thousands of short-range tactical nuclear weapons spread throughout the former republics of the USSR. There is also a fear that fissionable material and nuclear know-how could be sold to countries or terrorist groups outside the former Soviet Union. These realities raise the disturbing possibility of a regional nuclear exchange as opposed to global nuclear war.

In a worst-case scenario, all-out nuclear war could destroy most of the globe. The biological destruction of the species *Homo sapiens* would be a real possibility. But even if humanity is not literally wiped out in the event of a nuclear war, the devastation wrought by a more limited nuclear exchange of several hundred large warheads in a regional or global war is almost too horrible to contemplate. Assuming urban centers would be prime targets, nuclear warheads would burn everyone—and everything—within a radius of ten to twenty miles. Millions more would suffer grave wounds and would, subsequently and rapidly, perish. Additional millions—burned or mutilated—would suffer a lingering death from their wounds or radiation sickness. The wounded would overrun hospitals, and doctors would be unable to care for them. The networks of modern life—communication,

Figure 15.1 Deployed Nuclear Warheads

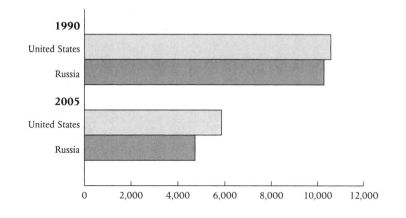

Source: U.S. Arms Control Association, Fact Sheets, www.armscontrol.org/factsheets.

business, factories, agriculture, government, and social life—would unravel. Survivors would face the psychological trauma of loss of loved ones, the dangers to unborn children, and unknown genetic mutations.

The Consequences of Conventional Wars

The record of conventional wars in the twentieth century tells of massive deaths, injuries, and dreadful human suffering. The human, monetary, and political costs of these wars have been devastating.

Human Costs. World Wars I and II alone killed more than 60 million people. The following statistics from World War II offer a unique perspective on war's immense human costs: 1 of every 22 Soviet citizens was killed, 1 of every 25 Germans, 1 of every 46 Japanese, 1 of every 150 Britons, and 1 of every 500 Americans. For a more graphic image of the number of soldiers killed or missing in World War II, picture a parade lasting eighty-nine days (almost thirteen weeks), with a row of ten soldiers passing the reviewing stand every five seconds, day and night.

In addition, more than 21 million soldiers and civilians have been killed in conventional wars since the end of World War II. Civil wars have contributed to these totals. For

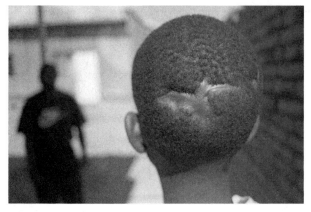

The Rwandan genocide of 1994 took a terrible toll with roughly 900,000 people killed. Here, a fourteen-year-old Rwandan boy bears the scars resulting from a machete attack by Hutu militia.

example, between 1960 and 1989, internal wars killed an estimated 700,000 Chinese; 500,000 Indonesians; 2,000,000 Nigerians; 600,000 Ugandans; 500,000 Ethiopians; 415,000 Mozambicans; 105,000 Iraqis; and 138,000 Guatemalans.[3] In the decade following the end of the cold war, internal wars in places such as Rwanda, Congo, Burundi, Somalia, Sierra Leone, Bosnia-Herzegovina, Croatia, and Sri Lanka claimed 3.6 million more lives.[4] As war progressed through the twentieth century, armed combatants drew less of a distinction between soldier and civilian.

As well as directly killing and wounding people, wars also bring death, injury, and suffering from starvation or malnutrition; the ravages of disease; violations of liberty and justice; the plight of refugees; and ecological damage. For example, the Holocaust—the Nazi murder of six million Jews and thousands more of other minorities—could not have happened without World War II. The creation of "slave laborers," forced to work for the Nazi war machine, would have been impossible in peacetime. The displacement and dislocation of whole peoples (by the Nazis, the Russians, and also the Americans, in the case of Japanese Americans) were another consequence of World War II.

Monetary Costs. War does not come cheap. Reliable estimates put the monetary costs of World War II alone at more than $1.3 trillion. To conceive the war's astronomical cost, imagine a person spending approximately $12 million a week, year in and year out, from the birth of Jesus to 1980.[5] Estimates on the 2003 Iraq War, which as of November 2005 was still going strong, run as high as $176.4 billion.[6]

Political Costs. War also produces unsettling political effects. For example, it seems quite likely that World War I opened the door to communism in tsarist Russia—to V. I. Lenin and then to Joseph Stalin. World War I also weakened Germany (as it had weakened Russia) and opened the way to Nazism and the triumph of Adolf Hitler. Similarly, World War II enabled Stalin to establish communist regimes in most Eastern European countries and to dominate them. America's tragic involvement in Vietnam not only led to terrible devastation in that land, but also contributed to a sequence of events resulting in the rise of the murderous Pol Pot regime in neighboring Cambodia (Kampuchea), years of wrenching political division in the United States accompanied by a level of civil violence unprecedented since the Civil War, and the decision of a president (Lyndon Johnson) not to run for a second term.

Despite the end of the cold war, the 1990 Iraqi invasion of Kuwait proved that states are still capable of aggression against each other. In addition, many of today's conflicts originated in bitter and long-standing ethnic tensions (see Map 15.1). Tribal and clan rivalries in Africa have led to devastating wars in Angola, Burundi, Ethiopia, Liberia, Mozambique, Nigeria, Uganda, and Rwanda. South Asia has been wracked by ethnic, tribal, and religious violence in India, Iran, and Sri Lanka. In the Middle East, terrible ethnic violence has plagued Iraq and Syria. And Southeast Asia has not been immune from the plague as evidenced by conflict in places such as Myanmar (Burma) and the Philippines. These kinds of conflicts and tensions are not confined to the developing world. In Europe as well, especially in multicultural societies such as Yugoslavia and the former Soviet Union, the potential for widespread violence is ever present. The former Soviet Union has recently been shaken by protests and violent conflict, most notably in the Nagorno-Karabakh Republic, where the struggle has been between Christian Armenians and Muslim Azerbaijanis. And finally, a particularly brutal civil conflict has broken out in Chechnya, within the Russian Republic itself.

The Burden of Arms Expenditures

Another oppressive reality is the high levels of global expenditures on armaments. Economically, politically, and socially, the global quest for weapons is expensive. Global expenditures for arms declined in the years immediately following the end of the cold war, but during the latter half of the 1990s, they began to rise once again, reaching nearly $800 billion by the end of the decade.[7] By 2004 they had reached a staggering $1,035 billion, or roughly $160 for every man, woman, and child on the planet. The United States accounts for 47 percent of the world total.[8] The costs of weapons—both nuclear and conventional—are staggering. During the 1960s and 1970s America's frontline fighter planes cost between $2 million and $4 million each. By the 1990s a mainstay fighter plane in the American inventory such as the F-16 Falcon cost between $18 million and $31 million, depending on the model and various modification packages. The Lockheed Martin F-117 Nighthawk stealth attack aircraft runs an astounding $435 million a copy.[9] Nor are strategic weapons systems exactly cheap. The estimated cost of producing a B-2 bomber runs $1.16 billion per plane.[10] And according to the Brookings Institution's Nuclear Weapons Cost Project, the *Trident* submarine runs $1.9 billion and each of its Trident II D5 missiles $89.7 million.[11]

Perhaps the most distressing aspect of the arms race is that everywhere it drains resources away from basic human needs: for constructive jobs; for food, clothing, housing, education, and medical care; and for social and cultural development. As Ruth Sivard

Map 15.1 Areas of Ongoing Conflict and High Tension, 2005

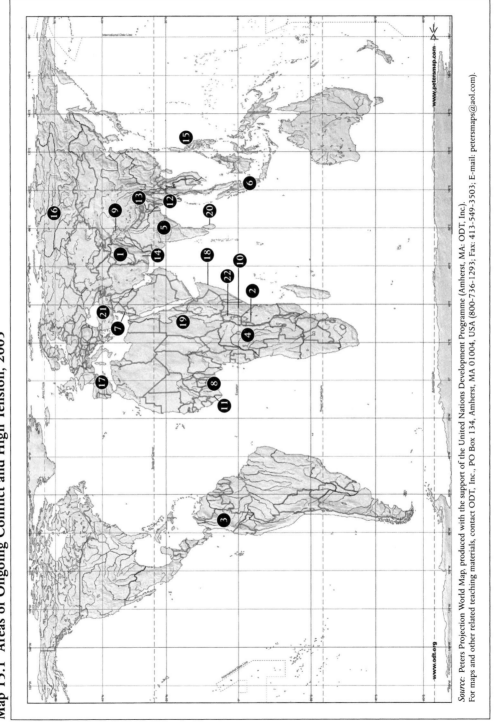

Source: Peters Projection World Map, produced with the support of the United Nations Development Programme (Amherst, MA: ODT, Inc).
For maps and other related teaching materials, contact ODT, Inc., PO Box 134, Amherst, MA 01004, USA (800-736-1293; Fax: 413-549-3503; E-mail: petersmaps@aol.com).

Map Reference	Country	Type of Conflict	Primary Participants
1	Afghanistan	civil war/factionalism	Afghanistan government, multiple warlord-led factions Taliban attempting to regain power
2	Burundi	ethnic conflict	Hutu, Tutsi tribal groups
3	Colombia	civil war/narcotics war	Columbian government, drug cartels, National Liberation Army (ELN), Revolution Forces of Colombia (FARC)
4	Congo	civil war	Multiple tribal and political factions supported by rebels from Rwanda, Uganda, and Burundi as well as armies from Congo, Zimbabwe, and Namibia
5	India	ethnic/sectarian violence	Hindu, Muslim, and Sikh factions
6	Indonesia	terrorism	Dissident Muslim groups
7	Israel	political/territorial war	Israeli government, various Palestinian groups
8	Ivory Coast (Côte d'Ivoire)	civil war	Ivory Coast government, rebel forces
9	Kashmir	territorial dispute	India and Pakistan governments, liberation movements
10	Kenya	ethnic violence	Kenyan government, Kikuyu separatists
11	Liberia	insurgency	Liberian government, National Patriotic Front
12	Myanmar (Burma)	political/ethnic struggle	Myanmar government, National League for Democracy
13	Nepal	insurgency	Nepalese government, Maoist insurgents
14	Pakistan	civil unrest/factionalism	Pakistani government, Islamic extremists
15	Philippines	separatist war	Philippine government, New People's Army
16	Russia	separatist war	Russian government, Chechnya
17	Spain	separatist movement	Spanish government, Basque separatists (ETA)
18	Somalia	clan conflict	multiple clans
19	Sudan (Darfur region)	ethnic cleansing, genocide	Darfur rebels, Sudanese government, Jajaweed rebels
20	Sri Lanka	civil war	Tamil and Sinhalese ethnic groups
21	Turkey	ethnic tension/separatists	Turkish government, indigenous Kurds
22	Uganda	ethnic violence	Ugandan government, Lord's Resistance Army (LRA)

Source: Compiled by authors.

Note: The comprehensiveness of this and similar lists will vary depending on the definition of conflict. This list is not designed to be inclusive but to provide a reasonable representation of the range of conflicts throughout the world.

noted when commenting about the cold war years, "In the 1980s, two governments in three . . . spent more to defend their citizens against military attack than against the everyday hazards of disease, accidents, and ill health; one in three has spent more on military power than on education and health care combined." [12]

Spending in the arms race hurts the battle against inflation and national debt; militates against healthy economic growth; and wastes valuable money, personnel, and resources. In rich and poor countries throughout the world, governments neglect basic human needs in favor of military might and the technology of destruction.

Dangers of the Sovereign Nation-State System

The threat of nuclear war, the disastrous consequences of conventional wars, and the burden of arms expenditures are all intimately tied up with the sovereign nation-state system. As Robert L. Holmes so eloquently states in his highly regarded book *On War and Morality*:

> The threat of nuclear annihilation grows out of the workings of an international system in which, if many realists are correct, the promotion of national interest is the governing norm. And if, as many of them would also have it, national interest ought to be the guiding norm (either of some or of all nations), then we need some accounting of how such a judgment is justified in light of the apparent consequences of its implementation. If one places the highest value upon the survival of the state, and if that survival is jeopardized by the pursuit of national interest, it would seem that pursuit should be abandoned.[13]

The nation-state system requires countries—for example, the United States, the People's Republic of China, and Israel—to protect their national interests by relying on their own arms. No peaceful appeal to a supranational authority or global law is required in the event of serious conflicts between nations. Nothing prohibits a nation's ultimate resort to war to protect its vital interests. The United States, Russia, Britain, France, China, Israel, India, and Pakistan have interpreted their own vital national interests as requiring stockpiles of nuclear weapons and the capability to deliver them.

National rivalries have also played a major role in triggering conventional wars. Wars existed before the modern nation-state system took shape with the Peace of Westphalia in 1648. (The treaty, which ended the Thirty Years' War, recognized the independence of the Netherlands and Switzerland and the autonomy of the German principalities.) But wars have become broader and more savage with the development of modern nationalism—and, paradoxically, with the advance of democracy, science, and socialism. Nationalistic rivalries had devastating consequences in the twentieth century. Nationalistic conflicts helped produce World War I. The nationalistic and militaristic ambitions of Germany and Japan primarily caused World War II.

Since World War II, wars for national liberation have also been fought. The great nation-states of Western Europe usually did not peacefully relinquish their colonial empires in Asia and Africa. They often fought to protect what they considered their vital national interests in preserving their empires—whether in India, Malaysia, Indonesia, Indochina, Algeria, or the Congo. Sometimes the colonial powers granted independence with reasonable speed and grace, as the British did India after partitioning the subcontinent between Pakistan and India in 1947. In other instances—the French in Indochina and Algeria, for instance—European colonial countries fought bitter and bloody battles against indigenous peoples, who felt justified in resorting to arms to gain national independence and freedom.

The great Western nation-states are not the only ones to go to war because of rivalry. Wars between India and Pakistan, between Israel and its Arab neighbors, between Iran and Iraq, between Ethiopia and Somalia, between Vietnam and Cambodia (Kampuchea), and between Peru and Chile indicate that nationalistic rivalries also cause war among less powerful countries. Whether small or large, weak or powerful, the sovereign nation-state defers to no higher law or court to settle disputes affecting its vital national interests.

The imperative of self-defense leads nation-states to arm themselves, and thus begins the spiral of the arms race. Nation after nation seeks protection in more arms and more sophisticated (and expensive) weapons—and, if they can manage, even nuclear arms. So the war system seems locked in a deadly embrace with the sovereign nation-state system, which is not going to be abandoned any time soon.

The War on Terrorism

Although this chapter is devoted to a better understanding of war between and within countries and considers how the international community might deal with these conflicts, a brief look at the war on terrorism is appropriate. After the terrorist attacks on the World Trade Center and the Pentagon on September 11, 2001, President Bush declared that the United States was going to wage a "war on terror." Perpetrators of terror, beginning with Osama bin Laden's network, al Qaeda, would be hunted down, and countries that aided or harbored terrorists would be held accountable. There are a number of characteristics of this war as it unfolds that together make it unprecedented.

First, it is not a war between states. It is a war against a number of nonstate actors—terrorist groups—that are part of a series of movements with a variety of purposes. They may seek to drive the United States out of Saudi Arabia, to force the United States to cease its support of Israel, or to bring down governments or establish new ones.

Second, the very transnational nature of the adversary makes the scope of the war less than clear. Even if al Qaeda is crushed or severely damaged, how many other terrorist groups do the United States and its allies go after? True, many of the terrorist groups have some affiliation with al Qaeda, but not all of them do.

America's war on terrorism included major military operations in Afghanistan to displace the Taliban government and destroy al Qaeda forces. Beyond military actions, however, Operation Enduring Freedom also incorporated nation building. Here U.S. Marines distribute food to villagers outside Kandahar in December 2001.

Third, because the September 11 attacks were on American soil and a domestic catastrophe, waging the war involves a major new domestic security component. The creation of the Department of Homeland Security and appointment of the director of homeland security are indications of that reality. Although domestic security concerns were present during World War II, nothing exceeds the efforts of law enforcement and intelligence arms to root out terrorist cells in the continental United States and to protect the country's infrastructure, including airlines and nuclear power plants.

ALTERNATIVE APPROACHES TO A MORE PEACEFUL WORLD

In this section we consider six approaches to a more peaceful world order: (1) a new balance of power, (2) an invigorated United Nations, (3) collective security, (4) global economic integration, (5) functionalism, and (6) nonviolence. These alternatives do not exhaust all the possibilities, and they may sometimes overlap. They do illustrate the strengths and weaknesses of key approaches. While reading this section, consider whether they are truly creative breakthroughs.

A New Balance of Power

The new-balance-of-power position is based on the assumption that foreign policy must realistically accept the struggle for power in world affairs generally and between great powers specifically. Great powers will seek to exert and extend their influence on behalf of their vital national interests. Only power can balance power; only strength can deter or defeat aggression. Current trends in the international system indicate that a **new balance of power**, while based on the power-versus-power equation, would differ in some ways from the system that characterized the cold war.

First, a new balance of power would probably be multipolar rather than bipolar. (See chapter 13 for a discussion of various power configurations.) The United States, Japan,

Germany, Russia, China, and perhaps some regional units such as Western Europe, Latin America, or Southeast Asia might constitute a new balance-of-power system. Not all of these powers need be equal in strength, and whether all of these actors would have nuclear weapons is uncertain. No doubt all would be capable of arming themselves with such weapons if they chose.

Second, it is likely that a new balance would place greater emphasis on economic power (though military might would certainly not be abandoned). Apropos of this new power configuration is a comment by former British prime minister Margaret Thatcher at the end of the 1990 Economic Summit in Houston, Texas. She noted that a new balance of power had been formed in the world—one created with dollars, yen, pounds, and marks rather than based on bullets and bombs.

Creative Breakthrough? A new, multipolar balance of power might preserve the peace if three conditions were to prevail: (1) all members of the system had sufficient countervailing military power (in nuclear or conventional arms) to deter attack by any other member of the system; (2) all members of the system had adequate economic and political power to defeat nonmilitary threats by any other member of the system; and (3) all members had the political skill, through the use of the diplomacy of accommodation and creative statesmanship, to avoid mistaken judgments about vital interests, to pursue détente (relaxation of tensions), and to build the conditions of international security, human rights, economic prosperity, and social justice that will make free peoples immune to authoritarian rule.

Such a policy is both desirable and feasible, but it will call for strong, astute, and far-sighted statesmanship. It is desirable because it guards the member nations' vital interests, particularly peace and national freedom. The policy provides time to work, step-by-step, toward arms control, real disarmament, worldwide democracy and constitutionalism, and economic well-being. Peace through a new balance of power is feasible because this policy did work at the bipolar level to prevent World War III. It safeguarded the freedom of Western Europe and West Berlin. It made the United States and the Soviet Union careful about taking actions that would threaten each other's vital interests. It restrained aspects of Soviet-American rivalry that might have gotten out of hand and escalated into a nuclear war that neither party wanted.

The weaknesses of this policy must, however, be recognized. First, a policy of strength calls for armaments, which figured in the arms race during the cold war years. Second, even overwhelming strength does not always enable major actors in the system to deter aggression. For example, the old cold war bipolar balance did not dissuade a less powerful actor such as North Korea from attempting to seize South Korea. Nor were the North Vietnamese deterred from attempting to unify Vietnam—first through peaceful means (nationwide elections) and then through internal subversion, guerrilla warfare, and military intervention. In Vietnam (in contrast to Korea, where the United States intervened with the blessing of

At two million ground troops, the People's Republic of China maintains the largest infantry in the world. In recent years it has invested substantially in high-tech weaponry in its pursuit of world-power status.

the United Nations), American arms did not prevent the communists from taking over the whole country. Third, it is not always easy to identify vital national interests. Was U.S. involvement in Vietnam dictated by vital U.S. interests? Would a communist Vietnam really have upset the American-Soviet balance of power? Fourth, following the old adage, "Those who possess a gun will eventually use it," a balance-of-power policy based to any degree on military strength increases the probability that at some point power will be used for purposes other than deterrence. Fifth, the balance-of-power mentality may make it extremely difficult to avoid the paranoia that, for example, sometimes characterized the cold war in the 1950s. Sixth, a multipolar balance system is more complex than a bipolar balance system; because there are more major actors, assessing the power of each relative to the others is far more difficult. Seventh, a new emphasis on economic power does not guarantee a lower probability of military confrontation. An economic balance of power can get out of hand. Rather than an arms race, member states might engage in trade wars, using protectionist methods (such as high tariffs and quotas) to counteract the economic power of actors they view as threatening. Of course, economic warfare can lead to military warfare if decision makers believe that vital national interests are threatened.

The United Nations' Third-Party Activities

The ending of the cold war has profoundly affected the United Nations. This is most evident in the UN Security Council's ability to agree on a variety of issues that previously sustained frequent vetoes by either the United States or the Soviet Union. The effect is also reflected in the propensity of the major powers to give the organization more genuine power. This raises the possibility of a more vigorous and effective role for the United Nations as a third-party actor or a counterforce to aggression in international conflicts. **Third-party activities** cover "a wide range of essentially ad hoc techniques, good offices, conciliation, investigation, mediation, arbitration, observation, truce supervision, interposition [in the case of the United Nations, placing UN forces between the fighting parties]." [14] The third party does not participate directly in the conflict but seeks to help both sides resolve a situation. The third party does not coerce; it persuades.

The third-party approach thus relies on the essentially persuasive means of Chapter VI of the UN Charter, "Pacific Settlement of Disputes," rather than on the essentially coercive means of Chapter VII, "Action with Respect to Threats to the Peace, Breaches of the Peace, and Acts of Aggression." That is, third-party intervention looks to such means as "negotiation, enquiry, mediation, conciliation, arbitration, judicial settlement, resort to regional agencies or arrangements, or other peaceful means." [15] It does not rely on economic, diplomatic, and military sanctions. The third party helps opponents work out their disputes peacefully or extricate themselves from military conflicts. For example, the third party may simply help opponents talk to each other. It may dramatize the dangers in failing to reach an accord. The third party may dissolve fears by inspecting danger spots and verifying the absence of aggressive forces. It may provide a neutral buffer between military forces.

This approach to peace recognizes the realities of current international politics. It acknowledges that the United Nations is not, and was not intended to be, a true collective security organization, in which the overwhelmingly powerful peaceful nations use their collective strength (through diplomatic boycott, economic pressure, or military force) to deter and punish an aggressive state that dares violate the peace. The third-party approach recognizes that during the cold war years, veto power made it impossible for the Security Council to act coercively against a great power accused of or guilty of aggression and made it extremely difficult—if not impossible—to act against an aggressive ally of a great power. This approach recognizes that even with the end of the cold war, it may be difficult for UN members to agree that collective action against aggression should be taken. The UN's failure to halt ethnic cleansing in the former Yugoslavia is a case in point. The best the Security Council could muster was a rather ineffective peacekeeping force, UNPROFOR (United Nations Protection Force), which operated from 1992 to 1995. The "ethnic cleansing" and warfare were not really brought under control until the fall of 1995, when a powerful non-UN force, IFOR (NATO's implementation force), led by the United States and NATO (North

Ghanaian peacekeepers highlight the United Nations' third-party role as they observe activities at an outpost along the Lebanese-Israeli border in 2001.

Atlantic Treaty Organization), was deployed in Bosnia to oversee implementation of the Dayton accords, which had been brokered by the United States, not the United Nations.

Creative Breakthrough? The United Nations' third-party efforts at the end of the cold war and beginning of the post–cold war era were impressive, at least in terms of numbers. Between 1988 and 1994 the UN established missions in Afghanistan, Angola, Cambodia (Kampuchea), Croatia-Bosnia-Macedonia, El Salvador, Georgia, Iran-Iraq, Iraq-Kuwait, Haiti, Liberia, Mozambique, Namibia, Nicaragua, Pakistan, Somalia, Uganda-Rwanda, and Western Sahara. In all, there were twenty new missions, involving seventy thousand personnel from sixty-six countries.[16]

But the third-party process has not been without problems. For instance, in Angola, after successful UN-supervised elections in 1992, the country plunged into renewed civil war. Moreover, as indicated earlier, the United Nations was incapable of stopping Serbian aggression and ethnic cleansing in Bosnia-Herzegovina. Perhaps the most serious shortcoming was the UN's total lack of meaningful response to the slaughter of nearly a million people in Rwanda in 1994, when members of the Hutu tribe killed Tutsi tribe members by the tens of thousands.

So, despite some success, this third-party approach is not a panacea. In appraising the UN's third-party role as a creative breakthrough, we can identify at least eight weaknesses. First, third-party intervention will not work if the parties to the dispute do not consent to such intervention, and in some cases they will not. Second, the veto of a Security Council resolution on third-party activity may weaken the secretary general's role. Third, the secretary general and the Security Council may disagree. Fourth, because of the time it takes for the Security Council (or the General Assembly) to act, the secretary general may have to risk speedy action in a controversial case, and this may create difficulties. Fifth, a creative, resourceful, and sagacious person may not always hold the office of secretary general. Sixth, even with the best intentions, and the fullest support in the Security Council or General Assembly, third-party activities may not work. Seventh, adequate financial and other resources (including a crisis center, a crisis staff, and a UN police force) may not be available. Eighth, third-party peacekeeping usually attacks the symptoms, not the causes, of conflicts; it does not address the fundamental causes of war.

In addition, it should be noted that the United Nations is having difficulty wrestling with conflicts that some observers have referred to as being in the "gray" area, where neither traditional peacekeeping nor collective security measures seem appropriate. These conflicts—such as those in Bosnia, Haiti, and Rwanda—found initial UN intervention occurring while the violence still raged. Furthermore, these conflicts were basically internal in nature, not classic cases of aggression by one nation against another. In these cases, the secretary general's neutrality was highly susceptible to compromise since he was forced, almost by the nature of the conflict, to take sides. Whether the United Nations becomes more adept at dealing with these kinds of conflagrations remains to be seen. At the very least, a great deal will depend on the support of the major powers on the Security Council.[17]

Collective Security

Collective security is an agreement among member states, usually within the context of an international organization, to protect each other from aggression by any state that is a party to the agreement. In other words, collective security offers protection from "inside" threats. (This differs from a *mutual defense* agreement, in which the member states agree to protect each other from threats by nonmember states—that is, "outside" threats. A prime example is NATO, which was set up during the cold war primarily as a defense against the Soviet Union and the Warsaw Pact nations.) Chapter VII of the UN Charter is the collective security provision and the heart of the organization's stated peace and security mechanism. The use of this device requires a two-thirds vote of the UN Security Council and no negative votes (vetoes) from any of the five permanent members—China, France, Russia, the United Kingdom, and the United States.

Creative Breakthrough? The inability of the United Nations to make full use of collective security during the cold war was treated extensively in chapter 13. But the end of the cold war may have made the collective punishment of aggressors under Chapter VII of the UN Charter more feasible. After all, two superpowers are no longer squared off against each other in the Security Council. But two recent conflicts indicate that it is far too early for a definitive prediction about the future of collective security.

Iraq's invasion of Kuwait in 1991 led to more than a dozen Security Council resolutions condemning the aggressor and levying sanctions. A worldwide economic embargo against Iraq was established, with military force authorized to enforce it. Ultimately, direct military force was authorized to expel Iraq from Kuwait. Desert Storm was carried out under these resolutions. Later, authorization was granted for UN teams to enter Iraq to find and destroy its stockpiles of and production facilities for weapons of mass destruction—nuclear, chemical, and biological. But it should also be noted that few conflicts in the international arena so clearly threaten the national security interests of so many countries as the Iraqi actions did. For the United States, the European community, and Japan, Iraq's seizure of the Kuwaiti oil fields and the threat to the Saudi oil fields were unacceptable. For many of the Arab states, Saddam Hussein's actions were a clear sign that he was a potential threat to their security.

Still, the collective actions against Iraq might be a cause for optimism, although it remains a serious regional problem after the United States' 2003 invasion to displace Saddam Hussein. As noted earlier, the United Nations' response to the tragedy in the former state of Yugoslavia was anything but heartening. Serbian aggression against the people of Croatia and Bosnia-Herzegovina remained unchecked until U.S.-NATO action in 1995. In this case, the threat to national security interests was not so clear.

At best it is doubtful whether United Nations collective security will be an effective instrument for peace on any consistent basis, even with the end of the cold war. The major obstacle to collective security is no longer an ideologically based veto in the Security Council. The main obstacle now appears to be the international community's lack of will and resources to use the instrument with any degree of consistency, particularly when no clear self-interest of the major powers is evident.

Global Economic Integration

Both regional and global **integration** (globalization) were covered in chapter 13. By way of brief review, recall that we are talking about groups of states, either at the regional or even on a more global level, dramatically increasing their economic interaction—trade, finance, transportation, communication—to the point where the separate national economies become increasingly interdependent. We cited the European Union as perhaps the most advanced example of economic integration in the contemporary world. Some scholars contend that global economic integration, which is well under way, works powerfully against the divisive norms of the nation-state system. The more integrated and interdependent economies become, the higher the cost to be paid for engaging in violent conflict.

Creative Breakthrough? The question, however, is not whether powerful economic integrative forces are operating in the international system and leading to greater interdependence. Obviously they are. The question is, Do they constitute a basis for a new world order that is better equipped to mitigate violent conflict, ensure adequate standards of living for the world's population, and guarantee fundamental human rights?

A certain logic argues that economic integration helps reduce international conflict. In its simplest (indeed, probably oversimplified) form, widespread economic integration means that many countries have economic investments in other countries. Therefore, it is in the interest of all countries to ensure that each other's economies thrive. To injure or destroy another economy is to risk injuring or perhaps destroying one's own economy. If economic integration becomes elaborate enough, warfare will be perceived as benefiting no one. As Charles W. Kegley Jr. and Eugene R. Wittkopf put it:

> [G]lobal interdependence may draw the world's diverse components together in pursuit of mutual survival and welfare. Awareness of the common destiny of all, alongside the inability of sovereign states to address many shared problems through unilateral national action, may energize efforts to put aside national competition. Conflict will recede,

according to this reasoning, as few states can afford to disentangle themselves from the interdependent ties that bind them together in the common fate on which their welfare depends. From this perspective, then, we should welcome the continued tightening of interstate linkages, for they strengthen the seams that bind together the fragile tapestry of international relations.[18]

Finally, as the integrative process becomes more complex, the need for multilateral diplomacy increases. Group deliberation and decision making about how to manage this complex system become imperative. Most international relations scholars and practitioners would probably agree that economic integration is a positive force in international affairs. But it is not without its problems.

First, it is not at all clear that economic integration can either confront or overcome some of the most intractable problems in international affairs—ethnic, religious, cultural, and territorial tensions and disputes. Second, multinational corporations and financial institutions provide much of the impetus behind economic integration, and despite international efforts to establish guidelines of behavior, there are still serious questions about their accountability. Third, despite the promise of such dramatic patterns as the European Union (which holds out the hope of genuine global integration), critics worry about the limited perspective of such regional organizations. The critics contend that in periods of scarce resources or generally bad economic times, these trade zones could adopt some of the less desirable traits of nation-states, such as protectionism and self-righteousness. Regional associations could be characterized by the same blind loyalties that we have seen in nation-states. Moreover, globally oriented integrationists, such as the functionalists (discussed in the next section), contend that regional associations still do not address humanity's fundamental problems—disease, food production and distribution, shelter, poverty, and environmental quality—from the necessary global perspective.

Peace through Functionalism

Functionalism is a theory positing that the world would be better off if it were organized around the fulfillment of basic human needs such as food, water, shelter, health care delivery, environmental concerns, and communications. These are the "functional" areas of human endeavor. Functionalism stands as an alternative to the nation-state system.

Those who endorse this approach maintain that human beings will move toward world peace if functional organizations can better meet common needs and advance mutual interests. With increased powers, funds, and activities, and by grappling with common problems, these organizations can build a trusting global community. The common problems involve providing decent jobs and increased productivity for workers, farmers, and fishers; furnishing better health care for children, mothers, and workers; building decent housing; developing effective transportation; supplying good schools; developing freer trade; maintaining access to raw materials, credit, and markets; performing scientific research; curtailing crime; limiting pollution; and encouraging cultural development and creative uses of leisure. As such basic problems are resolved, some of the underlying causes of war—distrust, fear, poverty, illiteracy, and disease—will be dealt with. In dealing pragmatically with these problems, humanity can transcend the limitations of national sovereignty and build a workable global system.

David Mitrany made one of the most cogent arguments on behalf of the functional approach. Here we present and, as necessary, modify and update the analysis in his influential book *A Working Peace System: An Argument for the Functional Development of International Organization.*[19]

The fundamental problem of the present age, according to Mitrany's initial formulation, is to determine how to achieve a new international system. This system must be able to prevent aggression and to organize peace and peaceful change. Without destroying the valuable diversity and freedom of nations, the system must be able to unify a badly divided world. The new world order must also successfully address the world's mounting insistence on social and economic betterment. National loyalties have tended to divide people politically in the modern world, even if they have frequently increased human freedom within the nation-state. On the other hand, the demand for social and economic betterment and the fact of economic interdependence have increasingly bound people together, even if they have also created tensions between the rich and the poor within countries and between countries.

Logically, unity could be obtained by conquest or consent. It could be achieved immediately or over a long period, by revolution or reform. The new world order could result in a centralized world state or a federal state or a global order. The new world order could be pursued according to a formal, constitutional blueprint or by informal, practical pursuit of urgent needs.

On the basis of these considerations, Mitrany reformulates the problem as follows: How is it possible to stimulate a voluntary and progressive evolution of world society that will preserve the valuable aspects of nationality and yet satisfy the legitimate needs of humankind? Mitrany is impressed by the difficulties of the formal, constitutional approach to peace through a new kind of international system. He does not believe that current nations, divided as they are and functioning within the framework of a balance-of-power system, will put aside their differences and agree at some constitutional convention to establish a global world order.

Similarly, he does not believe that the United Nations can do the job required because it leaves untouched the identity and policy of the sovereign nation-states that compose it; the United Nations is too loose an organization to achieve unity in diversity. Theoretically, a federal system of international organization provides the cohesion lacking in a league of sovereign nations, but in Mitrany's opinion, the basic community of interest needed for such a federal state does not yet exist worldwide (a condition that appears as true today as when Mitrany first advanced his theory). A federal system would have to operate within the limits of a region or within the framework of an ideological union. However, such a regional or ideological union would be defective because it could divide the world into several potentially competing units.

Creative Breakthrough? The primary advantage of the functional approach, according to Mitrany, is that it would "overlay political divisions with a spreading web of international activities and agencies, in which and through which the interests and life of all nations would be gradually integrated." [20] International government, he argues, can be effective only when it coexists with practical international activities. The starting point for a system of peace must be common needs, with momentary disregard for the presence of jealously sovereign nation-states and the absence of a larger political or ideological unity. The proper approach must be experimental and practical, free of insistence on formal blueprints and constitutional requirements.

Mitrany uses the functional approach to deal with the problem of national sovereignty and the insistence of nations on protecting their vital interests through military power. As peoples and nations work together to meet practical and pressing problems—involving trade and shipping, health and literacy, agriculture and fishing, aviation and broadcasting, scientific research and development—sovereignty would be gradually transferred, in the work involved, from the participating nations to the agencies performing the agreed-on job. "By entrusting an authority with a certain task," Mitrany writes, "carrying with it command over the requisite powers and means, a slice of sovereignty is transferred from the old authority to the new; and the accumulation of such partial transfers in time brings about a translation of the true seat of authority." [21] In this way, too, Mitrany maintains, the tough questions of peaceful change, sovereign borders, and vital national interests would be given a new perspective. Peaceful change must come about internationally as it does nationally. We can make changes of frontiers unnecessary by making frontiers meaningless through the continuous development of common activities and interests across them. [22]

Mitrany believes that, in addition to developing the conditions that must underpin the eventual world community, functional agencies could play an important role in advancing the crucial function of security. For example, they could watch over and check activities that lead to aggressive warfare, whether nuclear or conventional, including mobilization of soldiers, deployment of armaments, uses of transport, and accumulation of strategic materials. In conventional wars these agencies might even check those elements threatening aggression by withholding vital services from the potential aggressors.

What are the weaknesses in the purely functional approach to a more peaceful world order? First, functionalism does not deal with the immediately pressing problems of nation-state rivalry that threaten to break out into armed conflict. Second, it does not move the world immediately away from the mortal threat of nuclear war. Third, it has not yet been demonstrated that the functional approach will lead nations to slowly give up dangerous aspects of their sovereign power. Fourth, it is not clear how the functional approach, further down the road, will help transfer national means of defense to a common global authority. Fifth, it is not clear that economic, social, and scientific successes in dealing with poverty, disease, ignorance, and other problems are strong enough to overcome nations' sovereign pride, parochialism, and prejudice or elites' desire to maintain their privileges.

On this final note of criticism, we should mention a vision in the intellectual tradition of functionalism yet different in one important respect. This is **neofunctionalism**.[23] Mitrany's vision of functionalism was essentially nonpolitical; the world must work around the political flashpoints that divide the human race. The neofunctionalists believe that human beings cannot avoid the political problems that divide them. Nor can they ignore the power of nationalism and of national elites. In recognition of these realities, cooperation and integration must take place at the political level and not be confined to merely economic, technical, and humanitarian levels. Political union is as important as nonpolitical union.

Nonviolent Civilian Defense

Advocates of peace through **nonviolent civilian defense** maintain that a breakthrough to a more peaceful world order can be achieved only if nonviolence is seriously considered. "Now, more than ever, we need to question some of our basic assumptions about defense, security and peace, and to examine possible new policies that might help achieve those goals." So writes Gene Sharp in his book *Exploring Nonviolent Alternatives.*[24] Sharp is critical of the modern military and traditional solutions to political conflict. Military power does not adequately defend a people. Indeed, taken to its extreme—nuclear weapons—military power threatens mutual annihilation.

Another proponent of nonviolent defense, Robert Holmes, questions the basic function and efficiency of violence. He writes:

> Destructive force does not automatically add up to social power. . . . Moreover, beyond a certain point increments in the capacity for violence cease to yield increases in power. Beyond that point, in fact, power may decrease, however much destructive force one commands. The United States discovered this in Vietnam. . . . The Soviets did the same in Afghanistan.[25]

Sharp notes that conflict is unavoidable and traditional means of dealing with conflict are inadequate and may be disastrous. These traditional means, according to Sharp, include (1) removal of causes; (2) increased understanding of the opponent; (3) compromise; (4) negotiation, conciliation, and arbitration; (5) democratic institutions; (6) world government; (7) violent revolution; (8) war; (9) avoidance of provocation; and (10) apathy and impotence. Although some of these means may have merit, they are still insufficient. For example, there is not always time to remove the causes of conflict; present conflicts must be dealt with immediately. Understanding does not automatically reduce conflicts; indeed, it may sometimes heighten them. Some compromises are morally and politically dangerous; they may not achieve acceptable results. Democratic institutions are frequently nonexistent, incomplete, or inadequate. World government is, at best, a long way off; it may not be achieved peacefully, and even if it is, it may turn out to be dangerous.

So, Sharp maintains, nonviolence must be examined seriously. He defines nonviolent action as various forms of protest and noncooperation without

Mohandas Gandhi, a powerful proponent of nonviolent resistance, led India to independence from British rule. For a man of such enormous influence, Gandhi led a simple life. He would sit for hours spinning cotton at his wooden wheel and was known to receive world leaders as he practiced this ordinary task.

physical violence. But can nonviolent action, as a substitute for military armaments, ensure defense, security, and peace? Sharp believes that nonviolent civilian defense is not only desirable but feasible. He maintains that nonviolent action can both deter and defeat aggressors.

Creative Breakthrough? Sharp argues that nonviolent civilian defense would actually discourage nuclear attack by eliminating the national lightning rod of nuclear weapons. The very fear that one's opponent might launch a nuclear attack, or perhaps even the fear of a conventional military defeat, might provide the reason for launching a nuclear attack. Civilian defense, which can only be used for defensive purposes, would remove that motive, and hence, if not cancel out the danger, at least greatly reduce it. Moreover, nonviolent civilian defense would deter conventional aggression because the aggressor would know that resistance would take the form of effective nonviolent protest, noncooperation, and intervention.

If aggression did occur, nonviolent civilian defense would defeat it. The invader would have to deal with a population prepared to resist nonviolently. For example, the population could resist the entry of enemy troops by obstructing the docks, refusing to operate railroads, and blocking highways and airports with thousands of abandoned automobiles. Strikes, boycotts, empty streets, shuttered windows, and noncooperation in general would give the aggressor an empty victory.

According to Sharp's philosophy of nonviolent civilian defense, police would refuse to arrest patriotic opponents of the invader. Teachers would refuse to use invader propaganda in the schools. Workers and managers would strike to prevent the enemy from exploiting the country. Clergy would encourage refusal to help the invader. Politicians, civil servants, and judges would defy the enemy's orders, thus denying the use of the community's legal machinery. Underground newspapers and radio stations would support the cause of nonviolent resistance and report only the truth. In these ways, Sharp maintains, nonviolent action would deny the aggressor the obedience needed to make aggression successful.

Nonviolent civilian defense, Sharp concedes, involves risks, dangers, costs, and discipline. It is not easy and takes considerable training and commitment. Robert Holmes elaborates on this point by noting that "nonviolence is no guarantee against bloodshed. No system has such a guarantee. But the use of violence not only allows situations to develop in which bloodshed is inevitable; it entails the shedding of blood." [26]

At its best, then, nonviolent civilian defense would deter and defeat aggression—reducing the level of violence, inhibiting invaders, resisting tyrants, and enhancing peace and freedom. Although not inexpensive, it would permit significant savings. Developed and, especially, developing countries would have more money to deal with unmet human needs. Civilian defense "would very likely become a potent force around the world for liberalizing or overthrowing tyrannical regimes." It would give people greater control over their own destinies. Indeed, "increased confidence in civilian defense and liberation by nonviolent action could produce a chain reaction in the progressive abolition of both war and tyranny." [27]

Critics point to a number of weaknesses in the nonviolent approach. First, given the nature of people and nations, critics say, it is utopian to assume that the nonviolent option can be relied on. Unless there is a miraculous transformation of human nature and of nations, the adoption of nonviolence invites surrender and domination by one's rivals. Second, although nonviolent civilian defense might make a nuclear attack unnecessary, it is not at all clear that nonviolent civilian defense can prevent hostile domination. Third, the notion that it is better to live under an authoritarian regime than not to live at all is cowardly and unacceptable. Fourth, although nonviolent civilian defense might work with humane, civilized, and reasonable opponents, there is no certainty that it would work, at acceptable costs, with brutal barbarians or ideological fanatics.

CONCLUSION

We can now see more clearly the importance—and difficulty—of judging wisely on issues of war and peace. A mere dedication to peace does not produce wise judgments on how to achieve it. Similarly, recognition of the dangers of war does not automatically offer a wise choice about how to secure peace. Costs and benefits are often perceived differently by political scientists, citizens, and policymakers. Yet people must make judgments. They must choose. The failure to judge and choose is itself a judgment and a choice.

Judgment and choice are creative acts. They call for critical acumen; for powers of analysis and synthesis; and for balancing and weighing values, facts, and alternatives. Judgment and choice call for courage because they are not free of doubts, difficulties, ambiguities, and uncertainties.

The widely varying policy options considered in this chapter were chosen to stimulate the imagination and to make choices more ethical, more realistic, and more prudential. The radical alternatives were introduced to provoke thought and to make readers reconsider ethical priorities, reexamine "realities," and reassess wise choices. Only this kind of intellectual endeavor can lead to genuinely creative breakthroughs.

We turn next, in chapter 16, to the possibility of creative breakthroughs in the battle for the "least free."

SUGGESTED READINGS

Biddle, Stephen. *Military Power: Explaining Victory and Defeat in Modern Battle.* Princeton: Princeton University Press, 2004. Intriguing book on how to win battles in warfare with less emphasis on numbers and technology and more on the manner in which forces are deployed and employed.

Dallaire, Roméo. *Shake Hands with the Devil.* New York: Carroll & Graf Publishers, 2004. Gripping and heart-wrenching story of Lieutenant General Dallaire, the United Nations force commander in Rwanda during the 1994 genocide.

Findlay, Trevor, ed. *Challenges for the New Peacekeepers.* SIPRI Research Report No. 12. New York: Oxford University Press, 1995. A unique analysis of United Nations peacekeeping from the perspective of nations that have chosen to participate in these kinds of operations.

Gurr, Ted Robert, and Barbara Harff. *Ethnic Conflict in World Politics.* Boulder: Westview Press, 1994. First-rate study on the wave of ethnic conflict emerging after the end of the cold war. Central thesis is that ethnic hostilities are often triggered as much by international factors as by domestic influences.

Holbrooke, Richard. *To End a War.* New York: Random House, 1998. A career diplomat tells the remarkable story of how he and others brokered a deal to try to end the 1990s war in the Balkans. Superb description of how hard-nosed diplomatic negotiations are carried out.

Holmes, Robert L. *On War and Morality.* Princeton: Princeton University Press, 1989. One of the finest books in years on the ethics of war. Contains a powerful argument against the realist school and against the "just war" theory, as well as an equally compelling argument for nonviolence.

Lund, Michael S. *Preventing Violent Conflicts: A Strategy for Preventive Diplomacy.* Washington, D.C.: U.S. Institute of Peace Press, 1996. A State Department commission task force explores the role of "preventive diplomacy," which attempts to head off conflicts before they start.

Mitrany, David. *A Working Peace System: An Argument for the Functional Development of International Organization.* 4th ed. London: National Peace Council, 1946. Still one of the most persuasive arguments for developing an international organization and a functional approach to peace.

Nye, Joseph. *Understanding International Conflict*. 3rd ed. New York: Longman, 2000. Excellent survey and analysis of twentieth-century international conflicts.

Sharp, Gene. *Exploring Nonviolent Alternatives*. Boston: Porter Sargent, 1971. Sets forth the nonviolent approach that makes the hair on the realist's head stand up straight. Is the world ready for this approach? Can the world endure without it? Also see Sharp's *Civilian-Based Defense: A Post–Military Weapon Defense* (Princeton: Princeton University Press, 1990).

Shawcross, William. *Deliver Us from Evil: Peacekeepers, Warlords, and a World of Endless Conflict*. New York: Simon and Schuster, 2000. Superb analysis of many of the regional ethnic-based conflicts of the post–cold war decade and the difficulties of the international community, particularly the United Nations, in dealing with them.

Stiglitz, Joseph. *Globalizations and Its Discontents*. New York: Norton, 2002. Discussion on globalization, its principle functions and powers, and its primary institutions. Stiglitz addresses what works and what doesn't in current global policy.

Stoessinger, John. *Why Nations Go to War*. 9th ed. New York: Wadsworth, 2004. Extraordinarily readable treatise on the causes of war, with excellent case studies.

Waltz, Kenneth. *Man, the State, and War: A Theoretical Analysis*. New York: Columbia University Press, 1959. A classic statement on the causes of war.

GLOSSARY TERMS

integration (p. 364)
neofunctionalism (p. 368)
new balance of power (p. 358)
nonviolent civilian defense (p. 368)
peace (p. 349)
third-party activities (p. 360)
war (p. 349)

Chapter 16

THE BATTLE ON BEHALF OF HUMAN RIGHTS

In the battle on behalf of human rights, significant progress has been made in recent years in certain respects. Major political actors (the United Nations, many nations, and dedicated nongovernmental organizations) are on record in support of a wide array of human rights. Constitutional democracy, which is built on a crucial respect of human rights, has become an ethical norm for many nations around the globe. Increasingly, evidence of violations of human rights is brought to the world's attention. And slowly, if not always effectively, **sanctions** (political, economic, and military penalties) are being employed to combat the worst violations of human rights.

Both ad hoc and permanent international courts have been established to hold the perpetrators of crimes against humanity accountable for their actions. Yet, as the reports of the United Nations (UN), the United States, and nongovernmental organizations such as Amnesty International and Human Rights Watch make clear, much remains to be done with regard to the protection of human rights. Needless to say, daunting problems confront any student of politics dealing with this issue.

This chapter focuses on a crucial question: *What wise and effective policies can help in the continuing, and difficult, battle to protect human rights around the globe?* In our investigation in this chapter, we will focus on the **least free**—the powerless, the deprived, and the maltreated, who are often the politically oppressed, such as racial or religious minorities and women—because their status challenges our commitment to democratic, constitutional, and humane values.

Our format will be similar to that adopted in the preceding chapter. After clarifying the problem, we will set forth some factors that prompt a fuller exploration of it. We will then present and evaluate alternative approaches to securing greater freedom for the least free.

CLARIFYING THE PROBLEM

By freedom we mean power over one's own destiny. Freedom is often viewed in different ways, commonly referred to as "negative freedom" and "positive freedom." Negative freedom means the absence of arbitrary restraints that limit the power to pursue one's destiny. Positive freedom is the presence of opportunities that enable individuals and groups to fulfill their own peaceful and creative potentialities.

Because we feature **human rights**, a concept closely allied to freedom and sometimes used as a synonym for it, let us define this term as well. What do human rights include? As Cyrus R. Vance, secretary of state in Jimmy Carter's administration, put it:

> *First, there is the right to be free of violations of the integrity of the person.* Such violations include torture; cruel, inhuman, or degrading treatment or punishment; and arbitrary arrest or imprisonment. And they include denial of fair public trial, and invasion of the home.
>
> *Second, there is the right to the fulfillment of such vital needs as food, shelter, health care, and education.*
>
> *Third, there is the right to enjoy civil and political liberties—freedom of thought, of religion, of assembly; freedom of speech; freedom of the press; freedom of movement both within and outside one's country; freedom to take part in government.*[1]

Other definitions of human rights would also explicitly include the right to be free of racial or sexual discrimination.

These are working definitions only; there is no universal agreement on the exact meaning of the term. Some scholars interpret human rights narrowly, limiting them to civil and political rights understood as *legal claims,* which, if violated, can be upheld by legal remedies. Thus, for example, if the government deprives an American citizen of freedom of speech, through the courts he or she can stop such a violation. Other scholars prefer to interpret human rights more broadly to include economic (and even social and cultural) rights understood as *moral, political,* and *legal obligations* that governments are pledged to advance. Thus in many countries government has a moral obligation to help the destitute, a political obligation to find jobs for the unemployed, and a legal obligation to educate children. A government's capacity to fulfill its legal, political, and moral obligations, however, may depend on the nation's economic development. And, of course, a government's capacity to fulfill legal claims will depend on its constitutional commitments and its political state of health.[2]

Historically, liberal democracies in the West have been primarily concerned with civil and political rights. But with the advent of the welfare state and the advance of democratic socialism, economic, social, and cultural rights have also become prominent. Governments in communist countries and in some developing countries have also emphasized economic, social, and cultural rights. However, whether such rights are actually protected remains a troubling question. Arguments over priorities—and the relationship of one right to another—are central to the battle for human rights.

Other questions are also important. What should and what can the international community do when nations, which should be primarily responsible for protecting the human rights of their own people, fail to safeguard such rights? What should and what can human rights advocates within such delinquent nations do? What should and what can sympathetic nations do to advance the cause of human rights in other countries? What should be and what can be the role of the United Nations? Of nongovernmental organizations concerned with human rights? Should persuasive or coercive strategies be relied on? This chapter seeks to address such vital questions.

Before we can sensibly explore alternative approaches to protecting human rights, we will set forth some key factors that have led to awareness of human rights problems.

ETHICAL AND EMPIRICAL FACTORS

The least free have always needed protection. In the twentieth century, however, ethical consciousness was raised to a new level of sensitivity because of widespread and flagrant violations of human rights. The existence of human rights violations on a massive scale seized public attention when Allied troops overran Adolf Hitler's concentration camps and discovered the horrifying crimes that had been committed there. Other outrageous violations of human rights became public knowledge after Nikita Khrushchev, the Soviet premier, delivered to the Communist Party Congress the now-famous secret 1956 speech in which he exposed Joseph Stalin's crimes. After World War II, the struggle of peoples of the developing world for freedom from colonial masters called attention to imperial exploitation and racism. Until 1989 the Soviet Union's domination of adjacent countries in Eastern Europe illustrated another pattern of imperial control. Racial discrimination in the United States, long a troubling problem, became even more so in a post–World War II America that had just defeated a racist Nazi regime and subsequently sought to assume political and moral leadership in a world more nonwhite than white. The feminist movement exposed the reality of sexism—in the United States and the world. And authoritarian governments of the right and left continued to persecute, imprison, and degrade peaceful dissidents.

We will now investigate in greater detail some of the realities, both historical and contemporary, that have made the problem of human rights so pressing in world politics.

Genocide

The dreadful reality of the **Holocaust**—the systematic persecution and murder of millions of Jews as well as of other minorities—strongly influenced the writing of the UN's Uni-

Table 16.1 Jews Killed in the Holocaust

Country	Estimated Number Killed
Austria	50,000
Belgium	25,000
Belorussia	245,000
Bohemia/Moravia	80,000
Bulgaria	11,400
Denmark	60
Estonia	1,500
Finland	7
France	90,000
Germany	130,000
Greece	65,000
Hungary	450,000
Italy	7,500
Latvia	70,000
Lithuania	220,000
Luxembourg	1,950
Netherlands	106,000
Norway	870
Poland	2,900,000
Romania	270,000
Russia	107,000
Slovakia	71,000
Ukraine	900,000
Yugoslavia	60,000

Source: *The Holocaust Chronicle: A History in Words and Pictures* (Lincolnwood, Ill.: Publications International, 2000), 702.

versal Declaration of Human Rights in 1948. The Nazis' shocking actions were dramatically revealed when Allied armies entered Germany and the countries it had dominated and liberated the survivors of the concentration camps, the death factories that were the ultimate step in what the Nazis called "The Final Solution of the Jewish Question." At Auschwitz, 2,000,000 had been murdered; at Majdanek, 1,380,000; at Treblinka, 800,000; at Belzec, 600,000; at Chelmno, 340,000; at Sobibor, 250,000.[3] (See Table 16.1 for estimates of the number of Jews killed in each country.) The full extent of the slaughter—and of the systematic campaign of mass murder—was not immediately apparent but emerged at the post–World War II Nuremberg trials of war criminals and in subsequent investigations. The evidence—in confessions, eyewitness accounts, Nazi records, and pictures of tyranny and terror—of crimes against innocent civilians is incontrovertible and led world opinion to resolve, "Never again!"

The crimes of Hitler and his supporters against Jews started with prejudice; were stimulated by propaganda; advanced through political, social, and economic persecution; and finally ended in mass murder. World opinion came to realize that the crimes against Jews by the Nazis and their supporters were inextricably connected with Nazi violations of the human rights of civilian Germans, Poles, Czechs, French, Russians, and other Europeans.

It is difficult to grasp the campaign of extermination carried out by many ordinary Germans in "police battalions" in Nazi-occupied lands. It is impossible to comprehend the living hell-on-earth of the Nazi concentration camps—the horror, brutality, starvation, degradation, and murder. Again and again, survivors could only say, unless you have lived through it yourself, you can never understand. All the photographs and documents in the world will never explain what it was like. Even if you had seen the piles of corpses with your own eyes you would not know.

In 1948, in response to these Nazi crimes, the UN General Assembly adopted the Convention on the Prevention and Punishment of the Crime of Genocide, which went into force in 1951. **Genocide** is defined as any of the following acts committed with the intent to destroy, in whole or in part, a national, ethnic, racial, or religious group as such:

1. killing members of the group;
2. causing either bodily or mental harm to members of the group;
3. deliberately inflicting on the group conditions of life calculated to bring about its physical destruction in whole or in part;
4. imposing measures intended to prevent births within the group; or
5. forcibly transferring children of the group to another group.[4]

The Genocide Convention makes a number of actions punishable: genocide itself, the conspiracy to commit it, incitement to

Buchenwald concentration camp in Germany was the scene of more than 56,000 deaths at the hands of Nazi officials. The primary objective was to kill prisoners by work, but thousands also perished through torture, beatings, starvation, and lack of hygiene. This picture was taken as the camp was liberated by the United States 80th Army Division in April 1945.

commit it, the attempt to commit it, and complicity in it. Genocide is held to be a matter of international concern, a crime under international law. Moreover, by interpretation or amendment, the antigenocide convention should also clearly protect political groups or economic classes from genocidal killing.[5]

Has genocide occurred since World War II? Although nothing quite comparable, at least in sheer numbers, to the Holocaust has occurred, the actions of Pol Pot's Khmer Rouge regime in Cambodia (Kampuchea) can be described as genocidal. "While in power from 1975–1979, the Khmer Rouge (Cambodian communists) compiled one of the worst records of human rights violations in history as a result of a thorough and brutal attempt at restructuring Cambodian society. More than 1 million people, out of a total population of 7 million, were killed or died under the Khmer Rouge's genocidal regime." [6]

Other massive and egregious violations of human rights have also occurred. The 1990s saw dreadful genocidal attacks in the central African country of Rwanda and in the Balkan countries of Bosnia and Kosovo. "The immediate consequences of the genocide [in Rwanda in 1993 and 1994] were that about 500,000 Tutsi were killed, 10,000 to 30,000 Hutus (also targeted by the *genocidaires*) were killed and substantial number of Tutsi women were raped, tortured and sexually mutilated." [7] Genocide in Bosnia, in 1992–1995, called **ethnic cleansing,** was "the process whereby Muslims were forced from their homes; [whereby] thousands were placed in compounds reminiscent of concentration camps; [whereby] hundreds, perhaps thousands, of women were raped; and [whereby] tens of thousands of cit-

Refugees attempt to survive ethnic cleansing and geno-cide in the Darfur region of Sudan—victims of leaders who, facing threatened international action and claiming the country could break apart under outside pressure, encourage tribal warfare and a resurgence of the fundamentalists who once let Osama bin Laden make Sudan his home.

izens were murdered. . . . Before the violence was ended in 1995 as many as 200,000 Bosnian Muslims had perished, and the number of refugees had reached nearly three million."[8] In 1999 a comparable pattern of ethnic cleansing of Kosovar Albanians produced deplorable human rights violations. "Up to 10,000 or so died at Serb hands, mostly innocent civilians; thousands more were raped or otherwise brutalized. Some 800,000 people were forcefully expelled from Kosovo, and hundreds of thousands more were displaced within the territory."[9] Other egregious violations of human rights include, for example, the Indonesian army's brutal assault on the inhabitants of East Timor, on Timor island, and the savage suppression and murder of Kurds in Saddam Hussein's Iraq. Most recently, the Darfur region of Sudan has been plagued by what President George W. Bush in 2005 labeled a genocide as thousands of black Sudanese have fled the region and nearly four hundred thousand perished at the hands of government forces or the nomadic Arab militias known as the Janjaweed.

The Persistence of Racism

Racism has been an ugly reality in the history of humankind. It is rooted in the idea that some races are superior or inferior to others. This judgment becomes a basis for discrimination against the race alleged to be inferior. Such discrimination may be legal, political, economic, or social. Racism has promoted human slavery, separate treatment, and prejudice in the United States and around the globe. From the late 1940s to the early 1990s the separation of and discrimination against black South Africans was embedded not only in daily life but also in the legal system, in a policy known as **apartheid**.

Americans who feel self-righteous about the history of apartheid in South Africa should remember that slavery in the United States ended only in 1865. Moreover, despite the Thirteenth, Fourteenth, and Fifteenth Amendments to the Constitution (amendments passed after the Civil War to protect the civil rights of African Americans), African Americans suffered notorious discrimination. As noted in chapter 14, the **separate but equal** doctrine—which held that equality was not violated if African Americans were required to use separate vehicles for transportation and separate facilities for education and other public services—remained an approved constitutional doctrine from 1896 to 1954. After 1938 the U.S. Supreme Court did begin to look realistically at so-called separate but equal facilities for African Americans and struck down separate treatment in a number of cases. Yet only in the sweeping decision *Brown v. Board of Education* (1954) did the Court declare that "in the field of public education the doctrine of 'separate but equal' has no place because separate educational facilities are inherently unequal." The *Brown* decision set up a series of decisions that fundamentally changed a variety of aspects of American life, such as access to public spaces and criminal rights. All these legal changes occurred against the backdrop of an emerging civil rights movement. Effective constitutional and legislative reform went hand in hand with the political actions of average Americans of all colors. Among the most important of those reforms was the Voting Rights Act of 1965: a century after the end of the Civil War, African Americans finally received real legal protection for their voting rights. Unfortunately, despite these advances racial prejudice continues to mar American society today—although its extent and what to do about it are hotly debated.

Though the United States did not eliminate slavery until 1865, other countries were even slower to outlaw it. Ethiopia did so only in 1942, Kuwait in 1949, and Qatar in 1952. More disturbing, however, is the fact that slavery, involuntary servitude, and forced labor continue to exist in the twenty-first century. Two to four million people may still live in slavery or involuntary servitude. "Some are plain chattel slaves. Some are serfs, doomed to remain in that status for life. Some are in debt bondage. Some are, in a formal sense, adopted children. Some are wives, bought by their husbands and classified as property." [10]

The Charter of the United Nations, the Universal Declaration of Human Rights, and the two international covenants on human rights (discussed later in this chapter) prohibit discrimination on the grounds of race or color. In other conventions the United Nations has ruled against discrimination in employment (1958) and in education (1960). And in 1965 the General Assembly adopted the International Convention on the Elimination of All Forms of Racial Discrimination. Parties to the convention not only condemn racial discrimination but also agree to eliminate it in all its forms. Parties to the convention also declare that disseminating ideas based on racial superiority or hatred or inciting racial discrimination is punishable by law. They also agree to "declare illegal and prohibit organizations" that "promote and incite racial discrimination" and to "recognize participation in such organizations . . . as an offense punishable by law." [11]

Left-Wing and Right-Wing Violations

Some people might argue that horrors such as the Nazis' genocide and Stalin's destruction of the kulaks (well-to-do peasants) and other real or imagined opponents are things

Aung San Suu Kyi of Myanmar, formerly Burma, is renowned for her work on behalf of human rights and democracy in opposition to repression in her country. Over several decades, she has been subject to periodic house arrest by the military regime of Myanmar. In 1991 she was awarded the Nobel Peace Prize.

of the past. Stalin in the Soviet Union, Hitler in Germany, Benito Mussolini in Italy, and Francisco Franco in Spain—the dictators of the left or right, communist or fascist, in the 1920s, 1930s, and 1940s—are dead. The worst of Western imperialism and colonialism is behind us. Even racism, which lingers in a number of countries around the globe, has few public defenders.

Unfortunately, although the world has come a long way in articulating standards of human rights, persistent and flagrant violations are still widespread. They occur in communist countries such as China, Cuba, North Korea, and Vietnam, as well as in a number of right-wing authoritarian regimes in Africa, Asia, Latin America, and the Middle East. Even nations that are considered more democratic—Israel, the United States, and nations of Western Europe, for example—are not entirely immune. These violations (documented in the annual reports of Amnesty International, Freedom House, and Human Rights Watch, and in the U.S. State Department's annual *Country Reports on Human Rights Practices*) include systematic torture, imprisonment, and killing of political opponents, as well as denial of freedom of speech, press, and association. (For a list of countries rated by degree of freedom, see chapter 10, Table 10.1.)

The war on terror in the United States has led to two controversies of note. The first deals with the **Patriot Act**, signed by President Bush shortly after the September 11 attacks on the World Trade Center and the Pentagon. The act was basically designed to enhance the tools available to law enforcement for detecting, tracking down, and prosecuting terrorists and those who aid them. The act, as critics often fail to point out, actually strengthens protection of certain civil liberties and immigrant groups and constrains some of the new government powers.[12] But there is a great deal of controversy over a series of provisions that confer new and broaden old surveillance powers of the government. For instance, the act permits the government to investigate material that people check out of libraries. In addition, some of the new powers granted the government are, according to critics, lacking in transparency and accountability. For champions of civil liberties in the United States, these are serious defects in the act and run counter to some of the most fundamental rights upon which the nation was founded. For these critics, reform is desperately needed and efforts to that end are currently underway in Congress.[13]

The second controversy has to do with the treatment of prisoners held by the U.S. government seized in the war on terror. As the American intervention into Afghanistan unfolded in 2002 in order to destroy al Qaeda training camps as well as bring down the Taliban regime in Kabul, hundreds of enemy fighters were captured and brought to the Guantánamo Bay naval base in Cuba. The United States contended that detention and interrogation of these prisoners were critical for success in the war on terror. Further, the government argued, the prisoners at Guantánamo were outside the United States and therefore not subject to constitutional rights—an argument rejected by the U.S. Supreme Court in 2004. The government also contended that the prisoners were "illegal enemy combatants." But in November 2004 a U.S. district court judge ruled that the Bush administration had exceeded its authority in its stated intention to try the enemy combatants in military tribunals, denying them access to evidence used against them. In July 2005 a three-judge panel of the United States Court of Appeals for the District of Columbia Circuit yet again reversed the district court decision, ruling that the military could conduct war-crimes trials of terrorism suspects. In addition to the judicial wrangling over the conditions under which the detainees could be tried, there were reports of prisoner abuse and, most specifically, mistreatment of the *Koran,* the sacred book of Islam. The controversy over the Guantánamo prisoners moved to a new level in June 2005, when Amnesty International's secretary general, Irene Khan, labeled the U.S. detention center "the gulag of our times," evoking images of the deplorable prison/labor camps of the former Soviet Union. Many Americans were offended by the charge, including the president of the United States, who countered that it was "absurd."

It is also important to emphasize the reciprocal connection between freedom and human development (understood in terms of life expectancy, educational attainment, and income). Economically better-off countries generally have a large measure of freedom as well. According to the *Human Development Report 1992:* "There appears to be a link between a country's per capita income and the extent of its democratic freedom," even though some rich nations may not rank high on a freedom index, and some poor nations may enjoy a high level of political freedom.[14] The report went on to point out that "[p]eople now see freedom as an essential element in human development, not as an optional extra. Political freedom and human development do seem to move in tandem."[15]

Following the war in Afghanistan, hundreds of enemy combatants and suspected al Qaeda members have been flown to the U.S. naval base at Guantánamo Bay, Cuba. The conditions of their detention and their legal rights have become subjects of considerable controversy.

What is frequently debated, though, is whether freedom leads to economic development or economic development leads to the desire for greater freedom. This is an issue debated hotly by students of politics, and it significantly affects how we view U.S. foreign policy. For instance, how do we treat a country such as China, an authoritarian communist country undergoing an economic conversion to a market economy?

Although violations are widespread and flagrant, there is a positive side to the human rights record in the past few years. Mikhail Gorbachev's decision to allow the countries of Eastern Europe to pursue their own destinies, free of Soviet domination, signaled the end of the human rights violations that had kept these countries among the least free. The decline of a number of authoritarian regimes in South America in the 1980s signaled another triumph of human rights. Similarly, the end of apartheid in South Africa constituted a significant advance for human rights.

Offenses against Women

The rights of half the human race continue to be violated on a massive scale around the globe. This is true despite the pronouncements of national constitutions in developed and developing nations and despite the eloquent prohibitions against sexual discrimination in key UN documents. The preamble of the UN Charter endorses the principle of "equal rights of men and women." Article 1, Paragraph 3, declares that one purpose of the United Nations is to promote "respect for human rights and for fundamental freedoms for all without distinction as to race, sex, language, or religion." The same language—"without distinction as to . . . sex"—appears again in Articles 13, 55, and 62. Similar, and even more explicit, guarantees are found in the International Covenant on Civil and Political Rights. These rights relate to such matters as marriage, voting, and public affairs and to protection against sexual discrimination. Both documents affirm that marriage must be entered into with the free "consent of the intending spouses." The International Covenant on Economic, Social and Cultural Rights affirms the principle of "equal remuneration for work of equal value" and equal opportunity in promotion (Article 7), the "right of everyone to education" (Article 13), and the "right of everyone to take part in cultural life" (Article 15). These provisions built on earlier agreements on the rights of women and anticipated the 1967 Declaration on the Elimination of Discrimination against Women.

The 1967 declaration holds that discrimination against women—sexism—is fundamentally unjust and an offense to human dignity. It calls for appropriate measures to abolish discriminatory laws and customs. The document contains several provisions to protect women's status in the family; women's right to acquire, use, and inherit property; and women's right to legal equality. It calls for measures to end prostitution and to give women equal rights with men in education and in economic and social life. It also proposes measures to prevent women from losing their jobs in the event of marriage and supports paid maternity leave and necessary childcare facilities.

The language of the 1967 declaration—and of subsequent conferences—is impressive. But what about the reality? The reality of equal rights for women around the globe shows some progress but remains disappointing. Some women are still enslaved or bought by their husbands and classified as property. Certain marriages—including child marriages—are still arranged in Southeast Asia. The traffic in women for purposes of prostitution still exists.

People who see the persistence of sexism often link the problem to the idea of patriarchy. **Patriarchy**—the belief in male superiority (and female inferiority)—is a powerful cultural norm around the world. Since it is a societal norm, embedded in the heritage of many cultures, it leads to a disturbing set of practices. Such practices often seem nor-

Gertrude Mongella (center) of Tanzania was secretary general of the fourth United Nations World Conference on Women, held in Beijing, China, in 1995. In recognition of her work on behalf of women around the world, the International Federation of Business and Professional Women established an award in her name.

mal and are unquestioned by many people. Not only does discriminatory behavior persist in many parts of the world; it is often supported by archaic laws that dictate women's subordinate position in family and society.[16] The double standard of morality (one moral code for men, another for women) that the patriarchal heritage often perpetuates is revealed by the following list of practices:

- adultery (for men only)
- prostitution (most often for women only)
- infanticide (girl children only)
- child marriage (brides even younger than grooms)
- arranged marriages (veto power to men)
- illegitimacy (children as property of men)
- wife selling and wife beating
- slavery in marriage (divorce available only to men)
- prohibitions against birth control and abortion[17]

Other practices—emphasizing the double standard actually at work in the world—can be identified:

- double duty (women work outside the home and care for the children and home as well)

- unequal pay for equal work
- greater number of illiterate women than illiterate men in the world
- male dominance in policymaking in politics, the corporate world, labor unions, the mass media, and universities
- no pay for wives for housework
- female workers in lower-level jobs

Women in every country, Western and non-Western, industrialized and rural, modern and premodern, are underutilized in terms of their numbers, denied access to positions of prestige and power, and expected to find their primary fulfillment as mothers and wives. Women generally are poorer than men. Minority women often bear the twin burdens of race and sex discrimination. The 1977 Declaration of American Women, drawn up at the National Women's Conference, states that women have had "only minor and insignificant roles in making, interpreting and enforcing our laws, in running our political parties, unions, schools and institutions, in directing the media, in governing our country, in deciding issues of war or peace." [18]

More disturbing still is the fact that women are far too often the victims of crimes of violence, especially in cultures that treat them as sex objects and promote pornography for profit.

ALTERNATIVE APPROACHES TO SECURING HUMAN RIGHTS

This section is concerned with who does what and how in the realm of human rights. We focus primarily on the United States, the United Nations, important nongovernmental organizations, and the least free themselves. Some of the questions that the alternative approaches will explore are the following: Should policy emphasize persuasion; political, economic, and legal redress; or military coercion? What mixture of persuasion and more forceful sanctions makes most sense? How quickly or slowly can actors move? Will significant protection require moderate reform or drastic revolution? What political, economic, and social considerations influence what key actors should or can do? What are the strengths and weaknesses of alternative policies, strategies, and tactics?

Efforts of Powerful States

Jack Donnelly, an astute student of human rights, argues convincingly that "the fate of human rights—their implementation, abridgement, protection, violation, enforcement, denial, or enjoyment—is largely a matter of national, not international, action." Although Donnelly is persuaded of the "moral universality of human rights" and of the importance of authoritative international norms, he maintains that human rights can best be realized through national action.[19] With this perspective in mind, let us consider how one nation, the United States, might act to protect and promote human rights.

The United States can play its role domestically (by respecting human rights at home) and internationally (by promoting the cause of human rights abroad). But what policies should the United States employ to protect international human rights?

Sound international policy begins with a sound commitment. Before World War II, the United States and the other major Allied powers did not do what needed to be done to prevent Hitler's aggressions, particularly his genocidal actions against European Jewry. In 1948, in what one might view as a belated reaction to these horrors, the Allied countries and other members of the United Nations signed the Universal Declaration of Human Rights. It was a significant response to the war's horrible human rights violations. Yet the advent of the cold war—U.S.-Soviet rivalry—cast a cloud over American efforts to protect human rights. A forthright policy to protect these rights consistently took a backseat to national security.

In the early 1970s, fed by evidence of substantial violations all over the world, especially in South America, the U.S. Congress did pass important human rights legislation. For instance, laws were passed to prohibit economic and military aid to governments brutalizing their populations. Country reports on human rights practices were required from the State Department. Countries that denied or restricted their citizens' right to emigrate were denied most-favored-nation (MFN) treatment, meaning that a country's right to be granted the lowest possible tariffs in trade relations would be withheld. American representatives on international lending agencies were also required to vote against loans for countries that grossly violated internationally recognized human rights.

In his 1977 inaugural address, President Jimmy Carter declared that the U.S. commitment to human rights must be "absolute" and a "central concern" of American foreign policy. He supported the establishment of human rights machinery in the executive branch as well as congressional initiatives to interpret that commitment and concern. But what fuller philosophy and policies should guide that U.S. commitment to human rights? How does an American president balance the central need to protect vital national interests with the need to enhance the protection of human rights around the globe? If the U.S. commitment to human rights should be a "central concern" of American foreign policy, how "absolute" can that commitment wisely be? Here we can identify two general philosophies.

Prudent realists such as Henry Kissinger, former secretary of state under Richard Nixon and perhaps the most powerful person to ever hold that office, argue that the United States does, indeed, have an interest in protecting human rights, but this interest must be balanced by the primary need in foreign policy to protect vital U.S. national interests.[20] *Prudent idealists* such as William F. Schulz, executive director of Amnesty International USA (who advocates a "new realism" for our "interconnected age"), argue that defending human rights "benefits us all" and is "in our best own interest." [21]

Ironically, both prudent realists and prudent idealists could find support in the perspective outlined by Carter's secretary of state, Cyrus Vance. Vance suggested that the United States could act on its own or with and through the United Nations. The United States could also work through regional organizations such as the Inter-American Commission on Human Rights. Vance contended that there is a range of policy initiatives available to the United States, including quiet diplomacy, public pronouncements, and the withholding of foreign assistance. He further stated: "Whenever possible, we will use positive steps of encouragement and inducement. Our strong support will go to countries that are working to improve the human condition. We will always try to act in concert with other countries through international bodies." [22]

According to Vance, "We seek these goals because they are right, and because we too will benefit. Our own well-being, and even our security, are enhanced in a world that shares common freedoms and in which prosperity and economic justice create the conditions for peace. And let us remember that we always risk paying a serious price when we become identified with repression." [23] Vance insisted that it was possible to act forthrightly, yet realistically, on human rights. A realistic position would explore violations carefully, consider the prospects of effective action, and avoid self-righteousness.

Vance's prudential guidelines can be endorsed by prudent realists or prudent idealists. Although the Carter administration's position was closer to an idealistic policy of publicity and sanctions than to a realistic diplomacy, liberal critics have, nevertheless, argued that there was more rhetoric than reality in the Carter years. They point out that U.S. policy singled out the Soviet Union and left-wing regimes for criticism. They note that although during the Carter years the United States did cut aid to repressive regimes in Argentina, Ethiopia, and Uruguay, it did not recommend cuts for Iran under the shah, the Philippines, or South Korea—all human rights violators at the time.

Tough-minded realistic diplomacy was the preferred option of the Reagan and first Bush administrations, as it has been of the second Bush administration. Critics note that Reagan's and George H. W. Bush's administrations did not cut off aid to El Salvador or Iraq—countries with dreadful records on human rights. In those authoritarian regimes, America's alleged security interests conflicted with its human rights concerns. Prudent idealists would avoid the hypocrisy of going easy on national security friends while leaning heavily on national security foes and on little countries that can be scolded with impunity.

Bill Clinton's administration, too, was not without critics on this issue. Although characterized by good intentions and by positive actions in such countries as Haiti, the American government proved inadequate in Rwanda and distressfully slow in responding to dreadful violations of human rights in Bosnia and Kosovo. Belatedly, the United States did move to bring a halt to the fighting in Bosnia with the diplomatic settlement of the Dayton accords in 1995. And after diplomatic efforts failed with regard to Serbia's actions in Kosovo, the United States joined in NATO's air campaign to end Serbia's ethnic cleansing in Kosovo.[24] However, the Clinton administration eventually backed off on any meaningful action on human rights in China, apparently deferring to the importance of good trade relations with the People's Republic of China and asserting that this policy would help, over time, in "liberalizing" China's human rights record. Moreover, although Clinton in his last days in office did sign the treaty for a new Permanent International Criminal Court, he did not push energetically for Senate ratification. Of course, it is by no means clear that the U.S. Senate would have approved the treaty even if Clinton had campaigned for its acceptance. In any case, President George W. Bush withdrew the U.S. signature from the Rome treaty (which founded the court) in May 2002.

Not unlike many of his predecessors, President George W. Bush actively supported democracy and human rights around the world but was also subject to criticism for his relations with countries with questionable human rights records such as Pakistan, Russia, Saudi Arabia, Tajikistan, Turkmenistan, and Uzbekistan, all of varying importance in the war on terror.

Both prudent realists and prudent idealists may agree that wise judgment is called for in articulating and implementing policy. It is relatively easy to say that decisions call for informed and careful judgment. It is much more difficult to articulate in concrete cases what constitutes wise policy that both protects human rights and is in the national interest.

Creative Breakthrough? Prudent idealists argue that the protection and advancement of human rights are a moral imperative. Powerful countries such as the United States should pursue policies that are consistent with their professed values. To do otherwise not only is hypocritical but also serves to undermine the state's moral legitimacy in the eyes of the international community.

Prudent realists, on the other hand, argue for a more proactive policy on behalf of human rights based on the premise that the United States has a vital security interest in protecting human rights. Genocide, especially, is a threat to the security of the international system, and the United States, as a major power, has a responsibility to protect the security of the international system. Moreover, respect for human rights advances the cause of constitutional democracy; it is clear that constitutional democracies do not make war on each other. Put simply, U.S. national security interests, and not abstract morality, must guide foreign policy, including human rights policy. The United States, of course, has an interest in advancing human rights. But the United States must always ask how its actions on behalf of protecting human rights relate to its basic vital interests. Moreover, the United States government must always ask about domestic support for its actions on behalf of human rights abroad and about the human and monetary costs and consequences of those actions. When costs are too high and consequences dangerous, and domestic support is absent, actions on behalf of protecting human rights may not be prudent. One can argue that the failure of the Clinton administration with regard to Rwanda was tied to a belief that there was little domestic support for such action.

In both cases, prudent idealism and prudent realism, there is always the risk that human rights policies will be perceived as, or in reality will become, heavy-handed attempts to impose American values on others.

The United Nations

Another approach to protecting human rights, not necessarily in conflict with national policy, would emphasize working through the United Nations. This argument builds on the United Nations' forthright commitment to human rights. The United Nations exemplifies what is called an international human rights regime.[25]

In many respects the United Nations has done a remarkable job of articulating common principles—and thus a common standard—for human rights worldwide. Wise and effective implementation is now the United Nations' major problem. A host of UN organizations and offices are actively concerned with human rights. These include the General Assembly, which, according to the UN Charter, is to assist "in the realization of human rights and fundamental freedom for all without distinction as to race, sex, language, or religion"; the Security Council, which may be involved if human rights violations endanger international peace and security; the secretary general; and the Economic and Social Council, which can "make recommendations for the purpose of promoting respect for, and observance of, human rights and fundamental freedoms for all." Most recently, in 1993, the United Nations established a high commissioner for human rights to work with the UN Commission on Human Rights and other UN groups. But what can these organizations and offices do now to advance human rights principles? What powers do they have to fulfill the UN standard? Which policy options might become open in the future?

In general, the United Nations has articulated standards and convinced nations to endorse them. The United Nations invites compliance reports from parties to its human rights conventions. It receives complaints about violations of human rights from governments, nongovernmental organizations, and at times individuals. The United Nations may investigate complaints

From left, Swiss Federal Councilor Pascal Couchepin and Alvaro Gil-Robles, the Council of Europe's Commissioner for Human Rights, listen to Doudou Diene of Senegal, Special Reporter of the United Nations for Human Rights, during the closing conference of the fund "Projects against Racism for Human Rights" in Bern, Switzerland, in November 2005.

and report on violations—specifically those revealing a gross and consistent pattern of violations of human rights. It may exercise quiet diplomacy or invoke sanctions of one kind or another.

In the first two decades of its existence, "the only systematic activities of the United Nations with regard to the monitoring and protection of individual human rights" related to the trust territories and non-self-governing territories.[26] Beginning in 1967, however, UN organs became more active. They investigated violations in Argentina, Cambodia (Kampuchea), Chile (after the coup that overthrew Salvador Allende Gossens in 1973), Cyprus, El Salvador, Rhodesia (Zimbabwe), South Africa, and Southwest Africa (Namibia). Today the UN is involved in monitoring human rights all over the world, in places like Afghanistan, Eritrea, Haiti, Kazakhstan, Kyrgystan, Nepal, Sudan, and Uzbekistan. Yet its power to safeguard human rights is constrained—by its limited authority, its reluctance to interfere in the internal affairs of its members (particularly powerful members), the absence of a police force to protect human rights, the veto in the Security Council, and the stubborn defiance of nations that violate human rights.

In view of these considerations, which policy options are available to the United Nations? One course of action would be to strengthen the processes of articulation of standards and the use of quiet diplomacy to gain adherence to those standards. A second course of action would be to focus more sharply on verifying consistent patterns of gross violations through independent UN investigation and on exposing those violations to the glare of public scrutiny. A third course of action would be to place primary emphasis on developing effective political, economic, judicial, and military sanctions to protect human rights.

Each of these courses of action has strengths and weaknesses. Clearly, it is important to move toward a global consensus on human rights standards. But what does consensus mean? Agreement on words? Or fulfillment of principles? Furthermore, rhetorical consensus on standards is one thing; operative respect is another. Nations may pay lip service to rights but ignore them in practice. Quiet diplomacy is certainly a legitimate means and may work, but often it is a code for procrastination. Tact and tactful publicity are often sensible, but sometimes they enable nations to give precedence to alleged national security interests over ethical human rights obligations. Thus in the past nations have soft-pedaled human rights violations by their friends. And the United Nations has been reluctant, or unable, to take action against powerful nations.

Verification through UN investigation and subsequent publicity also run into problems. Nations object to interference in their internal affairs and cite the UN Charter in their defense. Investigative visits depend on the consent of the alleged violator of human rights. Public embarrassment may be counterproductive; it may anger the nation whose practices the United Nations is seeking to alter. Compliance reports depend on the good faith of the nation submitting them; no nation guilty of gross human rights violations would willingly incriminate itself.

Given the persistence of the sovereign nation-state system, UN member states will often resist the use of more powerful sanctions to protect human rights. The United Nations has generally been loath, or unable, to invoke sanctions, a matter that falls within the powers of the Security Council, where each permanent member can veto action. In one important exception—Rhodesia (now Zimbabwe)—the great powers agreed to invoke economic sanctions. The 1966 agreement rested not on the issue of human rights but on the fact that the situation there threatened peace. Majorities in the General Assembly can be more easily mustered for resolutions against unpopular members—South Africa, with its former practice of apartheid, has been the best example—but these resolutions lack the teeth of the Security Council's diplomatic, political, economic, and military sanctions. Now that the end of the cold war has made great power agreement easier, the Security Council may be more likely to invoke sanctions in clear-cut cases, especially when aggressors seek to wipe out the very existence of a previously independent nation (as in the Iraqi invasion and attempted annexation of Kuwait).

In more difficult cases—the protection of human rights in Bosnia-Herzegovina or Kosovo or Rwanda—action is more complicated. UN policy in Rwanda did not stop genocide there. UN military action in Kosovo would probably have been blocked by a Russian or Chinese veto in the Security Council. Nonetheless, the organization has been modestly successful in establishing ad hoc international criminal tribunals for Rwanda and Bosnia, in prosecuting some of those individuals guilty of crimes against humanity, war crimes, and genocide, and even in indicting and bringing to justice a former head of state, Slobodan Milosevic of Yugoslavia.[27] **Crimes against humanity** refers to acts of murderous persecution against a group of people and are considered criminal offenses above all others. Genocide is a crime against humanity. **War crimes** consist of violations of the laws of war as spelled out by various international covenants and include such things as atrocities committed against civilians and the mistreatment of prisoners of war.

Given these difficulties, how should and can the United Nations best proceed in protecting human rights, particularly from the scourge of genocide? One bold thought experiment envisages the establishment of a global human rights regime, under the auspices of the United Nations, that would (1) significantly strengthen global human rights institutions, (2) be guided by a

Former Yugoslav president Slobodan Milosevic, on trial at the war crimes tribunal in The Hague, the Netherlands, in 2002. Created by the United Nations in 1993 in the aftermath of massive killing and ethnic cleansing in the Balkans, the tribunal is the first such court established since the Nuremberg trials of Nazi leaders after World War II.

cogent theory of prudent prevention, (3) utilize an operative theory of effective staged implementation, and (4) employ a wise theory of just humanitarian intervention.[28]

The strengthened institutions would include, for example, an invigorated UN Security Council, the recently established UN high commissioner for human rights, a more proactive UN Commission on Human Rights, and the newly established Permanent International Criminal Court. Additional institutions would include, for example, a UN human rights monitoring agency and a UN human rights protection force, to provide, respectively, watchful eyes and really effective muscle in cases of potential or actual genocide. A cogent theory of prudent prevention (designed to prevent genocide rather than cope with it retroactively) would rest on three cardinal principles: the need to develop mature constitutional democracies worldwide, the need to develop the philosophy and practice of deterrence of genocide, and the need to develop the philosophy and practice of preemptive action in the event that deterrence does not work.

A workable theory of wisely staged implementation is also imperative. First, such a policy would call for really effective machinery for monitoring, investigating, and reporting on potential or actual genocide. Second, such a policy would require that the power of publicity be employed to deter genocidal violations—where there is a clear and present danger of the eruption of genocide—and to solidify global support for just humanitarian intercession to stop genocide in progress. Third, effective remedies—political, judicial, economic, and military sanctions—must be on hand, to be prudently chosen and employed to stop genocide. To have any chance of success, such remedies must have the support of UN members willing and able to implement decisions of the UN Security Council. Finally, there is a crucial need to work out the problem of what might be called "human rights consolidation," namely, what it takes to ensure that human rights will continue to be respected after initial efforts at prevention or intervention have been successful.

There is, additionally, a need to articulate and employ a cogent theory of just humanitarian intervention. Such a guiding theory might include the following principles: intervention only by an appropriate authority (such as the UN Security Council); just cause; timely military intervention when other pacific means—political, economic, judicial sanctions—have been tried and found wanting; prudent appraisal of benefits and costs of intervention; expectation of reasonable chance of success in the short term; employment of humane and proportionate means; careful calculation of the reasonable chance of success for the long run. A tall order? Yes. Impossible? No. But how probable?

Creative Breakthrough? One school of thought argues that the United Nations has an important job to do in articulating standards for the global community. These standards shape the consensus that will make international freedom a reality. At this time, the United Nations cannot go beyond this important task without meddling in the internal affairs of nations. Perhaps in the future the United Nations will acquire real power to investigate violations of human rights and to fashion effective remedies.

Another school of thought favors developing wise and effective remedies now. Proponents of this school would not only strengthen UN power to investigate complaints, but also establish effective machinery to protect human rights after persistent and gross violations have been verified. Interpretation of the UN Charter should clearly allow humanitarian intervention in such cases as genocide.

Political realists are particularly skeptical of the grand thought experiment outlined above—a global human rights regime. They argue that little can be done; that the world lacks adequate policy, machinery, and particularly will—and that these deficiencies will not be overcome in the foreseeable future; that the costs of intervention and protection are too high; that the United Nations is ill-equipped to handle the tasks outlined; that even well-intentioned nations (looking to their own vital interests) will not cooperate with the United Nations; and that it is unwise, dangerous, and unlawful to meddle in the internal, domestic affairs of sovereign nation-states. The reasons for this skepticism must be understood; but it would be tragic, indeed, if the United Nations were to prove unable to bring a halt to genocide and other serious human rights violations.

Nongovernmental Organizations

Numerous nongovernmental organizations (NGOs) have done splendid work to protect human rights. They include Amnesty International, Human Rights Watch, Freedom House, the International League for Human Rights, and the International Commission of Jurists. Amnesty International works to secure the release of prisoners of conscience and, in recent years, to abolish torture and capital punishment. Human Rights Watch is also dedicated to the protection of a wide range of human rights. Freedom House monitors human rights worldwide and reports annually on its findings. The International League for Human Rights drafts human rights standards for the United Nations, forms civil liberties unions around the globe, protects political dissidents and religious minorities, and guards against the extermination of South American Indians. The International Commission of Jurists seeks to preserve the worldwide rule of law, particularly the right to a fair trial.

Other nongovernmental organizations also crusade for human rights. Church, scientific, and professional groups have been involved. The Roman Catholic Church has been in the forefront of the battle for human rights in Latin America, stimulated by the Vatican II meetings of the Catholic leadership to discuss key religious and social issues and the establishment of the Pontifical Commission on Justice and Peace.[29] For Protestants, the World Council of Churches and the American National Council of Churches have also made human rights a priority. In 1976 the American Association for the Advancement of Science formed a human rights clearinghouse to look after scientific freedom and responsibility. P.E.N. International, a global association of writers, works on behalf of freedom of expression and champions writers, artists, and other intellectuals whose work arouses hostility. Jewish organizations have also worked hard for human rights.

In their strategy and tactics, the NGOs take a threefold approach. First, many work to influence the United Nations to draft international human rights standards. Second, some NGOs target for investigation those governments that have allegedly practiced human rights violations, and the organizations publicize the violations. Third, other NGOs, such as Amnesty International, attempt to put direct pressure on governments to obtain legal representation for political prisoners, improve the conditions of prisoners, or stop specific practices such as capital punishment. Some NGOs, of course, adopt all three approaches.

The NGOs are quite strong, particularly in their current roles. They can often obtain reliable information about human rights violations and bring it before the United Nations or a national government. They have made publicity a powerful weapon in the battle for human rights. Because NGOs have no vested national, political, or economic interests to protect, their reports have a degree of credibility that other reports may not. Given their single-minded devotion to human rights, they are not compromised by questions of politics or by the balancing of security and rights in their efforts to report on, and obtain relief for, those who suffer human rights violations. The NGO activities often involve hundreds of thousands of people directly. Their consultative status with the United Nations allows NGOs to engage in private diplomacy, and they can directly approach offending governments to seek information about and redress for violations of human rights. Their activities have raised global consciousness, made governments more hesitant to violate rights, secured the release of persons unjustly imprisoned, and mitigated the punishment of others.

Creative Breakthrough? Political scientists who are impressed by the NGOs argue that the organizations' careful work in documenting and publicizing violations has helped protect human rights by making violating governments take notice. The NGOs cannot perform miracles, but they can make actual or potential offenders think carefully about their practices. In fact, these organizations may have prevented violations that would otherwise have occurred, and they have secured the release of at least some victims.

Other scholars, who applaud the limited good that NGOs do, nevertheless are quick to emphasize their weaknesses. These critics note, for example, that although the NGOs can organize influential and even mass memberships in the United States and Western Europe, they cannot do so in China, Iran, Iraq, Libya, or North Korea. Unlike states, they cannot invoke political, economic, or military sanctions.

Efforts of the Least Free

What role will the least free play in their own emancipation? Some scholars are persuaded that human rights for the least free cannot be achieved without significant transformation in the global community or without major reform or radical revolution within the countries that now violate their own people's human rights. The victims of genocide, colonialism, racism, political repression, and sexism themselves have to be involved in the changes essential to securing their rights. For example, to guard against another Holocaust, Jews needed a nation-state of their own (Israel) as a homeland for persecuted Jews everywhere, a strong haven against genocide. They needed a nation with the power to make "Never again!" a reality. So, in 1948, Jews already in Palestine joined forces with refugees from Europe to found the modern state of Israel. Jews who prefer to remain citizens of other countries must actively defend their constitutional rights and vigorously support the freedom of their coreligionists in Israel and elsewhere in the world.

Efforts on the part of citizens in authoritarian regimes to advance freedom are never easy. It takes courage, personal sacrifice, and oftentimes the suffering of physical abuse to effect change. In places where freedom was curtailed for certain periods of time, such as El Salvador, Argentina, and South Korea, indigenous challenges were not entirely futile. Through the use of civil disobedience, public demonstrations, or outright revolt, significant changes in these countries improved protection of human rights. In countries much more authoritarian, such as Burma (Myanmar), Iraq, North Korea, Sudan, and Syria, it is far more difficult for citizens to effect significant change in pursuit of human rights protection.

Specifically, what can the people in these countries do to protect their human rights? Will strategies vary for different regimes, depending on whether they are totalitarian or authoritarian? Will tactics that enable U.S. citizens to cope with violations of civil liberties work in China, Iraq, or Vietnam? These questions are not easily answered, but they call attention to the important and difficult work of the least free and their allies around the globe. A process of liberalization did overturn an authoritarian Soviet Union; most countries in South America are now free of military rule; and some repressive regimes (such as that of Ferdinand Marcos in the Philippines in 1986) have been overthrown with the help of "people power," massive nationwide protests.

It is also important to realize that philosophies such as liberation theology—rooted in a particular interpretation of Christianity and drawing on Marxist social analysis—can help people struggling to improve their human rights. Liberation theology interprets Christianity as a gospel of freedom and justice for the oppressed. It also uses a Marxist analysis to highlight capitalism and imperialism as sources of economic, political, and social oppression. Critics still ask which understanding of liberation theology is to be chosen by the least free with this religious commitment. They also wonder how effective liberation theology will be in both theory and practice.[30]

For all the oppressed, one basic policy choice is between peaceful and violent means of change. Another fundamental choice is between incremental, constitutional reform and radical, extralegal revolution. Combinations of these choices are, of course, theoretically possible. In making their choices, the least free have to face the most difficult task of judgment—the balancing of costs and benefits. Violence, for example, may lead to the loss of life, and a militant revolution often calls for a sacrifice of liberty. It is extraordinarily difficult to balance the human rights sacrificed and the lives lost under a repressive regime against the human rights and lives potentially saved by a revolutionary regime of the least free. And there is always the danger that a revolution will simply replace one repressive regime with another. Similarly, it is unusually difficult to balance the sacrifices in human rights of slower, incremental, constitutional, peaceful reform against the gains of speedy, wholesale, extra-legal, violent revolution. The choices are agonizing. Perhaps a top priority of any strategy by the least free should be to avoid, or minimize, any sacrifices of human rights or lives.

Other tasks in the battle of the least free are less agonizing. For example, the least free have to realize their plight and position. They must achieve self-identity and self-reliance. They must also organize to enhance their collective strength. They need to reach out to allies and form coalitions to maximize their strength. And they need to realistically assess the strengths and weaknesses of the institutions that oppress them. At the right time, they must focus their power to extend their freedom.

This is easier said than done. Yet there are success stories to juxtapose against the failures and the incomplete successes. Racism is by no means completely absent in the United States; yet, as we noted earlier, in a remarkable civil rights "revolution" in the 1950s and 1960s, the separate but equal doctrine, which was an integral part of the American South, was defeated. While this revolution involved the actions of tens of thousands, it was sparked by courageous African Americans such as Martin Luther King Jr., head of the Southern Christian Leadership Conference; Thurgood Marshall, the lead attorney arguing the *Brown v. Board of Education* case of 1954; and Rosa Parks, the seamstress who in 1955, in segregated Montgomery, Alabama, refused to give up her seat in the middle section of a bus so that a white man could sit there.

The Holocaust was a dreadful reality; yet the state of Israel was reborn and lives through the efforts of the Jewish people. Apartheid, the government-sanctioned separation of races in South Africa, no longer exists—in no small measure because of the work of people such as Archbishop Desmond Tutu and Nelson Mandela. Through the protests and other political activities of people such as Lech Walesa in Poland, Andrei Sakharov in Russia, and Vaclav Havel in Czechoslovakia, the groundwork was laid for the eventual elimination of communist rule and establishment of democracies in Eastern Europe and the Soviet Union.

Sexism pervades the modern world, with women enslaved, prostituted, battered, and denied education, the vote, and equal pay for equal work. But in some countries women have made significant gains in education, politics, and social life. In the United States, for example, Elizabeth Cady Stanton and Susan B. Anthony led the nineteenth- and early-twentieth-century movement to gain legal rights for women, including the vote (achieved in 1920). The U.S. women's movement of the 1960s and 1970s went further, demanding economic, political, and personal equality. Internationally, four global conferences on women's issues were held in the last three decades of the twentieth century: in Mexico City, Mexico (1974); Copenhagen, Denmark (1980); Nairobi, Kenya (1985); and Beijing,

China (1995). These conferences have been instrumental in facilitating communication between women around the world and in developing strategies to obtain basic rights.

Creative Breakthrough? Supporters of peaceful incremental reform believe that it is important to establish, and then build on, institutions of freedom in all countries. They concede that the battle will be easier in countries having a constitutional tradition than in authoritarian nations. Still, whatever the form of government, supporters of this approach believe reform will be less costly and more beneficial if it is achieved by peaceful means rather than violent revolution.

Supporters of a more militant policy point out that those who keep the least free powerless will not easily permit peaceful, constitutional change. Repression will continue until power is mobilized to overturn it. Because those who now oppress the least free use explicit violence, violence may be necessary to defeat them. The degree of militancy will depend on the character of the oppressor, and different strategies may be required for different categories of the least free—for example, blacks or women or political dissidents—as they confront different types of repressive regimes.

CONCLUSION

If politics is viewed as a civilizing process, creative breakthroughs to policies that can enhance the freedom and human rights of the least free must be explored. Thus students of politics must understand the values, behavior, and judgments that make such breakthroughs possible. Ethically, a civilizing politics must give top priority to helping the least free and to opposing the worst evils: nuclear war, genocide, brutalizing racism, savage torture, and inhumane sexism. Systematic, persistent, and gross violations of human rights must be opposed and ended. A civilizing politics should prefer lawful, constitutional, nonviolent means to protect human rights.

The next chapter focuses on economic well-being, an important ingredient of human rights that merits a separate chapter.

SUGGESTED READINGS

Donnelly, Jack. *Universal Human Rights in Theory and Practice*. Ithaca: Cornell University Press, 1989. Argues on behalf of human rights as universal moral rights. Emphasizes the connection between human rights and Western liberalism. Rebuts various relativist challenges. Favors priority of national action in implementing human rights. A very persuasive analysis.

Felice, William F. *Taking Rights Seriously: The Importance of Collective Human Rights*. Albany: State University of New York Press, 1996. Maintains that the protection of human dignity calls for expanding our understanding of human rights to include rights of groups, peoples, and collectivities.

Formicola, Jo Renee. *The Catholic Church and Human Rights: Its Role in the Formulation of U.S. Policy, 1945–1980*. New York: Garland, 1988. An illuminating study of the movement of the American

Catholic Church from complacency and a limited concern for human rights to renewed concern and effective involvement in helping shape a more humane and moral American foreign policy, especially in Latin America.

Freedom House. *Freedom in the World: The Annual Survey of Political Rights and Civil Liberties, 2002–2003.* New York: Freedom House, 2004. Ranks countries on a scale of 1–7, with 1 meaning most free and 7 least free.

Howard, Rhoda E. *Human Rights and the Search for Community.* Boulder: Westview, 1995. Favors a conception of rights that embraces economic as well as civil and political rights.

Human Rights Watch. *Human Rights Watch World Report 2004.* New York: Human Rights Watch, 2004. Annual publication that describes and analyzes significant human rights developments in sixty-five nations.

Morsink, Hans. *The Universal Declaration of Human Rights: Origins, Drafting, and Intent.* Philadelphia: University of Pennsylvania Press, 1999. Award-winning historical and philosophical account of the development of the declaration.

Power, Samantha. *A Problem from Hell: America and the Age of Genocide.* New York: Basic Books, 2002. Award-winning account of twentieth-century genocide and the American response.

Riemer, Neal. *Protection against Genocide: Mission Impossible?* Westport, Conn.: Praeger, 2000. Contains articles on the case for a Global Human Rights Regime, crucial changes in the international system, Rwanda, economic sanctions, the Permanent International Criminal Court, a proposed UN constabulary, and humanitarian intervention.

Schulz, William F. *In Our Own Best Interest: How Defending Human Rights Benefits Us All.* Boston: Beacon Press, 2001. A persuasive argument on behalf of a "new realism" by the executive director of Amnesty International.

U.S. Department of State. *Country Reports on Human Rights Practices.* Washington, D.C.: U.S. Government Printing Office, annual. The State Department's yearly report to Congress. Informative, measured. Should be supplemented by reports of nongovernmental organizations such as Amnesty International.

GLOSSARY TERMS

apartheid (p. 378)
crimes against humanity (p. 390)
ethnic cleansing (p. 377)
genocide (p. 377)
Holocaust (p. 375)
human rights (p. 374)
least free (p. 373)
patriarchy (p. 383)
Patriot Act (p. 360)
sanctions (p. 373)
separate but equal (p. 379)
war crimes (p. 390)

Chapter 17

THE STRUGGLE
FOR ECONOMIC
WELL-BEING

As noted in chapter 16, many people consider economic well-being to be a basic human right—the right to fulfill vital needs for food, shelter, health care, and education—one so important it deserves its own chapter. Economic well-being is closely related not only to human rights and freedom but also to peace. War can harm or destroy economic well-being. Nations attack each other's soldiers (and, too often, civilians) and each other's economic systems—factories, transportation, and sources of strategic raw materials. Modern wars destroy food and housing along with guns, tanks, planes, ships, and munitions. Even the mere threat of war is damaging. The arms race consumes valuable resources (such as capital, labor, scientific skill, and organizational ability) that could be better used to fight poverty, disease, illiteracy, and inadequate housing. Many scholars also believe that economic well-being and war are connected in another way: the frustration of economic deprivation facilitates war.

Economic well-being and ecological health are also closely connected. For example, economic well-being calls for a sensible balance between population and resources, and both pollution and the imprudent use of resources affect the quality of economic and social life. We will touch on these ecological problems in this chapter, but we defer a fuller discussion to chapter 18.

This chapter focuses on the following problem: *What creative breakthroughs can promote greater economic well-being?* In responding to this problem, we focus primarily on the world's poor, especially those who live in developing nations—the least developed ones in particular. But we cannot forget the pockets of poverty and the problems of unemployment, homelessness, inflation, and industrial stagnation that continue to plague the developed world. Given the interrelatedness of the world economy, unhealthy economies in the industrial North (Northern Hemisphere) adversely affect the developing areas as well. For similar reasons, we cannot close our eyes to economic performance and social well-being in the communist world. The post–World War II record of China, Cuba, the Soviet Union, Vietnam, and the communist countries of Eastern Europe was at best mixed and at worst disastrous. The repercussions of failed communist systems are still being felt in places such as the Russian Republic, where more than a decade after the fall of the Soviet Union, the economy continues to struggle.

DEFINING ECONOMIC WELL-BEING

By economic well-being we mean a level of income, food, health care, education, shelter, and quality of life that satisfies minimum standards of life and decency and permits full growth and development. In contrast, **poverty** is that level of income, food, health care, education, shelter, and quality of life below minimum standards of life and decency. Poverty usually precludes full growth and development. People living in poverty—as we will see more clearly in the second section of the chapter—are undernourished. They may die in periods of famine. They are vulnerable to disease. They are often illiterate. They live in substandard housing, are ill clad, and are poorly equipped to move up the economic and social ladder. They are most often unemployed or underemployed and poorly paid. They usually do not participate in politics.

Geographically, a large percentage of the poor live in the South—that is, in the Southern Hemisphere and the southern part of the Northern Hemisphere. Collectively, they are known as developing countries; in 2004, 135 states were designated as such. Within those 135, approximately 49 are known as **least developed countries (LDCs)**. These are the world's poorest countries, a high percentage of which are found in Africa. Most of the world's affluent nations, the **developed countries**, are in the Northern Hemisphere. Hence our use of the terms *North* and *South* to designate developed and undeveloped nations, respectively. The poorest nations and peoples are in sub-Saharan Africa and South Asia. The richest nations tend to be in North America and Europe and also include Japan and Australia. In addition, there are several dynamic and relatively prosperous Asian economies, known as the **newly industrialized economies (NIEs)**: they include Singapore, South Korea, Taiwan, and increasingly Thailand. Finally, in Eastern Europe there are what are now called **emerging economies**, countries such as the Czech Republic, Hungary, and Poland that were formerly members of the Soviet bloc.

In exploring the struggle for economic well-being, we will set forth the ethical and empirical factors that prompt exploration of the problem. These factors are grim and sobering. They underscore the absence of political, economic, and social resources that people need in order to cope with economic malaise. They pose troubling ethical and prudential questions—involving the calculus of costs and benefits—for policymakers seeking wise and humane choices.

After examining these ethical and empirical factors, we will consider some major alternatives facing policymakers in the United States and elsewhere in the West, in the developing countries, and in communist China as they deal with economic challenges. These alternatives present a number of broad options that involve varieties of capitalism, communism, and democratic socialism. We will consider options that favor the nation-state and the current economic world order as well as options that look toward a different world order. Finally, we will challenge readers to devise their own solutions on the basis of their critical analysis.

ETHICAL AND EMPIRICAL FACTORS

The sense of urgency that will guide our analysis here was summed up by UN Secretary-General Kofi Annan in his *Millennium Report of the Secretary-General of the United Nations* in 2000:

> How can we call human beings free and equal in dignity when over a billion of them are struggling to survive on less than one dollar a day, without safe drinking water, and when half of all humanity lacks adequate sanitation? Some of us are worrying about whether the stock market will crash, or struggling to master our latest computer, while more than half our fellow men and women have much more basic worries, such as where their children's next meal is coming from.
>
> Unless we redouble and concert our efforts, poverty and inequality will get worse still, since the world population will grow by a further two billion in the next quarter-century, with almost all the increases in the poorest countries.[1]

The Persistence of Poverty

There is no question that, over the past several decades, enormous progress has been made in terms of eradicating poverty in many regions of the world. Mortality rates have been drastically reduced in a number of developing countries. Between 1960 and 2000, life expectancy increased from forty-six to sixty-three years in developing countries. Access to education has opened up for millions in the developing world. Illiteracy was nearly halved between 1975 and 2000, and real per capita income more than doubled from $2,000 to $4,300.[2]

But it must also be recognized that the distribution of gains has been anything but even. In a grim summary statement, the *United Nations Human Development Report 2004* noted:

> Despite . . . impressive progress, massive human deprivation remains. More than 800 million people suffer from undernourishment. Some 100 million children who should

Table 17.1   Comparison of Poor and Affluent Countries, 2004

Nation (ranked by GDP/capita)	Per Capita[1] GDP (US $)	Infant Mortality (per 1000)	Life Expectancy (years)	Telephone Mainlines (per 1000 people)
Switzerland	36,687	5	79.1	734
United States	36,006	7	77.0	646
Spain	15,961	4	79.4	506
Greece	12,494	5	78.2	491
Philippines	975	29	69.8	42
Mexico	905	24	73.3	147
Indonesia	817	33	66.6	37
Kenya	393	78	45.2	10
Bangladesh	351	51	61.1	34
Malawi	177	114	37.8	7

Source: United Nations Development Program, *Human Development Report 2004* (New York: Oxford University Press, 2004).

[1] GDP (Gross Domestic Product) is the sum of value added by all resident producers in the economy.

be in school are not, 60 million of them girls. More than a billion people live in countries where regimes do not fully accommodate democratic, political and civil freedoms. And about 900 million people belong to ethnic, religious, racial or linguistic groups that face discrimination.[3]

Compounding the problem of poverty in the developing world, the gap in economic welfare between the richest and poorest regions is a wide one, as demonstrated in Table 17.1.

Where do the poor live? Using the $1 per day income as a measure of extreme poverty, Figure 17.1 indicates that the largest concentrations of poverty are in South Asia, sub-Saharan Africa, and East Asia and the Pacific.

This picture of poverty is made even more disturbing when we realize there are significant pockets of poverty in affluent countries. In the United States, significant numbers of poor can be found in the inner cities, the Appalachian region, and rural areas of the South. Of course, many of these people seem, in relative terms, better off than many of the destitute in developing countries. Yet poverty in the midst of affluence, like affluence in the midst of the developing world's terrible poverty, should sensitize critical students to probe for reasons and solutions.

Figure 17.1   Distribution of World's Poor, 2004

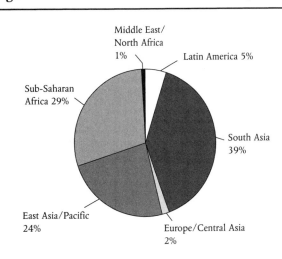

Middle East/
North Africa
1%

Latin America 5%

Sub-Saharan
Africa 29%

South Asia
39%

East Asia/Pacific
24%

Europe/Central Asia
2%

Source: Graph created by authors based on data from *United Nations, Human Development Report 2004* (New York: Oxford University Press, 2004), 129.

The poor frequently lack money because they are unemployed, underemployed, or not receiving fair pay for their labor. Unemployment is particularly acute in many developing countries (see Table 17.2 for stark contrasts between developed and developing countries). Yet in both worlds, unemployment remains a chronic problem, mirroring economic ill-health. That ill-health is reflected in industrial stagnation, sectional depression, economic recession, low agricultural productivity and rates of growth, and inadequate use of human and material resources. Economic troubles in the developed world hinder economic well-being in the developing world.

The plight of women in the poorest countries is particularly distressing. In poor households women often shoulder a much greater workload than do men and have considerably fewer chances to earn money. The latter problem has, ironically, become worse in developing areas where modern technology—such as computer-based mass production—has led to even lower female employment. Furthermore, the relative lack of educational opportunities for women hinders their ability to gain managerial positions.

Poor housing—inadequate space, sanitation, and protection—is the lot of millions, particularly in poor developing nations. Reliable statistics are difficult to obtain, but the plight of the world's poor in rural areas and urban slums is familiar to experienced world travelers. In many crowded cities in the developing world (and even in developed world cities such as Chicago, Los Angeles, and New York), some poor people sleep on the streets. The loans that the World Bank has made to rehabilitate slums and build low-cost housing testify to the inadequacy of, and need for, housing.

Hunger remains an agonizing problem for the world's poor, despite the fact that world food stocks are reasonably high. The food problem is largely one of inadequate purchasing power and inadequate and inequitable distribution. Whatever the reason, the problem is gigantic: over eight hundred million people in the developing world do not get enough food. Hunger and malnutrition, however, are not absent from rich, developed countries. For example, malnourishment has been particularly severe among the elderly in the United States, although great progress has recently been made in dealing with this problem. Unemployed women with dependent children also seem to suffer inordinately from malnourishment.

People need either money to buy food or the ability to produce their own food. Poorer nations unable to grow food must be able to import it for reasonable prices. To increase their own production, they require fertilizers and appropriate farm equipment. Most experts agree that many developing countries would benefit significantly from agrarian reform, understood as more equitable distribution of land and income. They would also benefit from adequate transportation and educational services to ensure that nutritional food is locally available at reasonable cost. Finally, in periods of famine, many developing nations desperately need shipments of food from richer, food-exporting countries.

Malnutrition and starvation lead to serious health problems and death, as does disease. Perhaps the greatest health scourge facing the developing countries of the world is HIV/AIDS. Worldwide there are about 39.4 million people with HIV/AIDS, with 4.9 million new infections in 2004 and 3.1 million deaths the same year. The preponderance of cases are in the poorer regions. Also in 2004, sub-Saharan Africa was by far the hardest-hit region, with 25.4 million cases.[4]

Table 17.2 Comparative Unemployment in Developed and Developing Countries, 2004 Estimates (in percentages)

Nation	Unemployed
Switzerland	3.4%
New Zealand	4.2
United States	5.5
Denmark	6.2
Germany	10.6
Ghana	20.0
Honduras	28.5
Bangladesh	40.0
Djibouti	50.0
Turkmenistan	60.0

Source: CIA, *The World Factbook*, www.odci.gov/cia/publications/factbook.

In the developing world, poverty and hunger, the lack of clean water and effective sanitation, the absence of immunization programs, and the shortage of trained health workers all contribute to high infant and child mortality, to a host of debilitating diseases, and to shorter life expectancy. Statistics reflecting the grim reality of poverty are disturbing. In sub-Saharan Africa infant mortality is more than 100 per 1,000 births, and more than 170 children out of 1,000 die before they reach the age of five.[5]

One area in which significant progress has been made is in wiping out illiteracy. Between 1970 and 2002 the literacy rate in developing countries increased from 47 percent to 76.7 percent. But there are still disquieting figures, such as those in sub-Saharan Africa, where there is only a 63.2 percent literacy rate among people fifteen years and older. Collectively, the forty LDCs have a discouraging literacy rate of 54.3 percent.[6] Further, as Figure 17.2 demonstrates, throughout the developing world troubling percentages of school-age youths (especially so in comparison with percentages in the developed countries) are not enrolled in schools. Another disturbing fact is that females in the developing countries receive only about half the higher education that males receive.

Figure 17.2   Enrollment Ratio for Primary, Secondary, and Tertiary Schools, 2001–2002

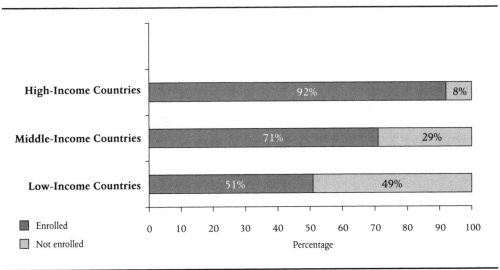

Source: United Nations Development Program, *Human Development Report 2004* (New York: Oxford University Press, 2004) 142.

The Causes and Consequences of Poverty

There are numerous explanations offered for the persistence of poverty in the developing world. Some analysts point to the vagaries of geography and demography, a major thesis of Jared Diamond in his widely read book *Guns, Germs, and Steel: The Fates of Human Society*.[7] For Diamond, the geography and general environment of Eurasia made it more conducive (than the more tropical southern regions) to efficient food production via the domestication of plants and animals, the evolution of populations more resistant to disease, and ultimately the development of complex communication and political systems.

Other writers point out that adverse trade and financial conditions also affect most developing regions of the world. Many developing nations suffer economically because they are so dependent on the export of commodities—coffee, tea, rubber, or copper—whose prices fluctuate and thus may not produce steady, reliable income. Compounding the problem, prices for raw materials such as wood, minerals, petroleum, and grains generally increase more slowly than prices for processed or manufactured goods. At the same time, developed nations, seeking to protect domestic sectors of their economies, frequently place extraordinarily high tariffs on manufactured or processed goods from developing countries, which makes these products noncompetitive. Because of these adverse trade conditions and the net outflow of capital, most developing countries carry alarmingly high debt levels, making it difficult to find new capital for investment and expansion of their economies.

Many people, particularly in the developing world, believe that these conditions are merely carryovers from European colonialism during the nineteenth and twentieth centuries. The European colonial powers—Belgium, Britain, France, Germany, Holland, and Italy—did not have the economic well-being of the native people as a prime objective. Colonial powers were interested in profits and their own national security, not in developing balanced economies. Because colonial powers did not care about social justice, they perpetuated patterns of domination and dependence. In the eyes of many scholars, those same patterns exist today in the form of **neoimperialism**, whereby large multinational corporations owned and controlled by powerful forces in the developed North take unfair advantage of the poor

Characteristic of many poor countries is the use of sweatshops, manufacturing facilities where the workers labor for long hours for little pay and often under unsafe working conditions. Some multinational corporations have been accused of exploiting the poor in developing nations for cheap labor to increase their own profits.

developing countries in the South. The large corporations exploit cheap labor in the developing countries, squander natural resources there, and reap incredible profits, but they reinvest little of those profits in the infrastructure of the developing countries.

Regardless of the cause, chronic poverty has consequences that go beyond the kind of human suffering we have already chronicled. Political instability has characterized many of the developing nations, and we cannot discount the probable relationship between deprivation and political turmoil. Burundi, Congo, Liberia, Nigeria, Rwanda, Sierra Leone, Sri Lanka, and Sudan, among others, have been plagued by civil war in recent years. Many countries have been affected by coups, revolutions, and wars with their neighboring states. As Figure 17.3 illustrates, violent conflict is overwhelmingly concentrated in regions of the world with the highest number of poor countries.

A high percentage of developing countries lack stable, cohesive, and responsible political leadership. A number of them have struggled to establish democratic political systems, but many have been and continue to be ruled by an army strongman, a military junta, or a powerful single political party with low tolerance for dissent.

The Calculus of Costs and Benefits

The benefits in the struggle for economic well-being are reasonably clear: ending degrading poverty, providing jobs and decent income, ensuring adequate food and good health,

Figure 17.3 Major Armed Conflicts, 1990–2003

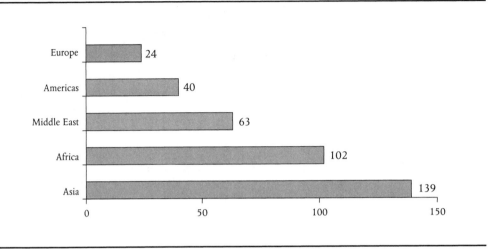

Source: Stockholm International Peace Research Institute, 2004, http://www.sipri.org/contents/conflict/MAC_patterns.html

Note: A "major armed conflict" is defined as a use of armed force between the military forces of two or more governments, or of one government and at least one organized armed group, that results in the battle-related deaths of at least 1,000 people in a single year and concerns control of government and/or territory.

advancing literacy, and sharing the common wealth more fairly. But at what costs—as reflected in which policies—might those benefits be obtained?

Debate rages about whether the poor developing nations can lift themselves, with enough speed, and at acceptable costs. How dependent will the developing countries be on the richer nations to assist them in conquering poverty? Will the richer nations be willing to provide significant enough resources to wage an effective war on poverty?

Controversy has also surrounded the role of various political and economic models in the struggle to achieve greater economic well-being. Developing nations might follow a communist, totalitarian, and egalitarian model. They might also opt for a capitalist, authoritarian, and nonegalitarian model such as the one Brazil used for most of the 1970s and 1980s. Or they might ask whether a liberal capitalist or democratic socialist path is possible. We now turn to some approaches and assess their potential for a creative breakthrough in mitigating poverty.

ALTERNATIVE APPROACHES TO ECONOMIC WELL-BEING

Which policies adopted by which political actors will bring about economic well-being? First, we will examine a liberal capitalist and liberal democratic option characteristic of the United States. Next we will present the strengths and weaknesses of the Chinese communist and Brazilian capitalist models of development. Then we will consider a democratic socialist model. We present these models to stimulate thought about how to achieve economic well-being, particularly for the poor in developing countries. Numerous variations on each model are possible.

Liberal Capitalism and Liberal Democracy

It is impossible in a few pages to present a definitive statement on the liberal capitalistic and democratic approach because there is no universal agreement on all aspects of that model. There are, however, a few common basic elements. In general, supporters of this model maintain that the way to overcome poverty and related ills is to increase the size of the economic "pie" (agricultural and industrial production) and to encourage a more equitable distribution of income and services. Robert S. McNamara, former president of the World Bank, held that "the basic problem of poverty and growth in the developing world can be stated very simply. . . . The growth is not equitably reaching the poor. And the poor are not significantly contributing to growth. Development strategies, therefore, need to be reshaped in order to help the poor become more productive." [8]

A threefold strategy is required. First, poor people and nations must help themselves. Second, richer nations such as the United States must help developing nations in a variety of ways. Third, private enterprise (including multinational or transnational corporations) must assist in crucial ways. Working together, these forces can contribute to balanced growth and equitable distribution within a framework of freedom.

Developing nations need a stable and reasonably efficient political and administrative structure that can encourage greater agricultural and industrial productivity and thus increase profits, jobs, and income. They require a social, educational, and medical infrastructure (transport, communications, schools, and health services) to deliver basic services (decent housing, clean water, and literacy) in the interest of basic human needs. As necessary, these nations also have to undertake agrarian or social reform to give poor people a greater stake in their productivity and a decent share in the common wealth. Such reform must include conscious decisions to bring population and resources into a better balance and to avoid spending valuable money and resources on excessive military armaments.

The United States and other rich Western nations can play an important role by extending credit and aid, stabilizing prices of commodities from developing nations at a reasonably remunerative level, relieving some of the crushing international debt levels of poorer countries, and allowing trade to flow freely. They can also help by ensuring lower food prices and by working toward a global energy policy to make oil (or energy substitutes) available at fair prices. These wealthy nations must encourage the kind of self-help outlined in the preceding paragraph. These acts are not mere kindness. In the long run, it is essential for the United States and the other affluent countries to assist in the developing world's economic improvement because their vital interests cannot really be secure in a world containing so much poverty and discontent.

Private enterprise, by adopting a more enlightened view of economic well-being in developing nations, can see that sensible profits and the battle against poverty are not incompatible. Increased productivity and trade and a vast new army of consumers can be linked to reasonable profits and to the satisfaction of basic human needs. Thus wise private investment and credit can aid in the struggle for economic well-being. Multinational (or transnational) corporations, operating under sensible rules to ensure that productivity, technology, and profits redound to benefit the poor in the host country, can also help overcome poverty.

Creative Breakthrough? The strengths of this option are considerable. It emphasizes peaceful, evolutionary development within a democratic and constitutional framework, and it emphasizes the value of political, economic, and social freedom. This model taps people's interest in their own improvement. It connects the self-interest in reasonable profits to the satisfaction of human needs. Historically, it has also proven to be the most powerful engine of economic growth. And economic success, some scholars believe, attacks one of the most serious problems now plaguing the developing world—enormous population growth. The **demographic transition theory**, as it is known, basically posits that as societies grow economically and become more industrialized, more modern, population growth begins to subside as it did in Europe and North America when the Industrial Revolution took hold.

With the end of the cold war, the world has witnessed an enormous effort to encourage variations of this model within the developing world as part of the whole globalization movement. Actually, the movement started long before the 1990s, with the rejection of a protectionist trade system and the push to establish a system of free trade after World War II. The problem was that for decades the primary participants in this system were the developed countries of the noncommunist world—only a very limited number of developing states participated. When the Soviet empire collapsed, Eastern European states and a preponderance of the developing countries that were run on some variation of the socialist model almost immediately began the shift toward free market capitalist systems. At the same time, more than one hundred developing countries ended military or one-party rule and moved toward more democratic political systems.[9] How have they fared? For the Eastern European countries, the so-called emerging economies, the shift has been successful. For the developing world, the results are mixed. Developing countries in East Asia along the Pacific Rim, such as Indonesia, Malaysia, the Philippines, and Thailand, are good examples of limited to outstanding success. In this part of the world, trade is up, jobs have been created, significant amounts of direct investment by multinational corporations have taken place, burgeoning indigenous manufacturing has taken root, and standards of living have generally improved.

Other parts of the developing world have not fared so well, despite the adoption of capitalist and democratic models. This is particularly true of Africa, which not only lags far behind the developed countries of the world but also significantly behind other regions of the developing world. In addition to the disappointing performance of the liberal capitalist experiments, democratic reform has also been problematic at best.

So while there have been successes, failures in other regions of the world dictate that the weaknesses of a liberal capitalism and liberal democracy model must also be seriously considered. The most fundamental criticism is that capitalists are motivated by profits, not economic and social justice. Since capitalists have a tendency to stress short-run payoff rather than long-run development, they are, and will be, unwilling to adopt those policies necessary to overcome poverty. Critics contend that liberal democratic capitalists are financially too tied into the dominant system of exploitation to respond to the claims of the least developed.

Even putting aside or rejecting this criticism, we are left with other points of contention. Liberal capitalism, the critics claim, may not overcome the economic and social inequities of the developing country. Indeed, many observers assert that by its very nature, liberal capitalism increases socioeconomic divisions within countries. Moreover, this option may presume too much wisdom and self-control on the part of the people and leadership of developing nations. It may also presume too much enlightened self-interest and long-range perspective on the part of affluent nations. This option may overestimate the intelligence of capitalist entrepreneurs, both inside and outside the developing country. Finally, its critics say, this option fails to come to grips with old-fashioned capitalistic exploitation or economic imperialism. Despite the lowering of trade barriers, other unfair trade practices have retarded economic development that would benefit the poor people of the developing countries.

How desirable and how feasible is the liberal capitalistic and democratic alternative? How do we assess, more exactly, its costs and benefits? Without actual testing of this model, it is difficult to judge. But we may look to the past performance of the United States, of other liberal capitalistic and democratic nations, and of countries in the developing world for clues. Past behavior does not dictate the future, but it may help the prudent policymaker to judge the chance for significant change.

Egalitarian Communism

One might assume that with the end of the cold war, communism is "dead" as a viable economic or political model. Perhaps. But it would appear that not all countries are faring well under a new capitalist experiment, and as frustration grows, the temptation to seek out other models could be powerful. It is not beyond the realm of possibility that various communist models might guide the struggle for economic well-being in developing nations. There are a number of real-life case studies to pick from: Chinese, Cuban,

Soviet, and Vietnamese. Because conditions in most developing countries are closer to those in China than to those in the former Soviet Union, we will examine the case of China. In doing so, however, we must recognize that China, like several other communist countries, is a nation in transition. From about 1949 to 1976 China's political and economic system was what might be termed a Maoist version of communism. After Mao's death in 1976, China began to institute very limited and tightly controlled changes in the economic system, with emphasis on free market reforms. The following analysis will take these changes into account.

In the periods before the major market reforms, again roughly 1949 to 1976, the Chinese egalitarian model had several fundamental elements. The economic system was characterized by virtually no (or very little) private property. The major means of production were owned by the state. The regulation and management of virtually the entire economy—industry, agriculture, transportation, communications, and finance—were by the state. Finally, there was an underlying premise that society was a collective, and maintaining the welfare of the entire community is the fairest, most equitable, and most just means of running the economy. The political system, of course, was under the complete control of a single party, the Communist Party.

In the early years, from about 1949 to 1957, China followed the conventional Soviet model of development, emphasizing heavy industry and rapid industrialization. Beginning in 1958 Mao began to put his imprint on China's development policies, which—as we noted in chapter 8—featured the terribly disruptive and costly Great Leap Forward and the Cultural Revolution. This Maoist period, which ran from 1958 to 1976, emphasized all-around industrial and agricultural development: self-reliance and communes in the countryside; mass mobilization of the people and heroic, if not brutal, labor policies to increase productivity; the primacy of politics and party to guide the revolution; and decentralization to stimulate local initiatives.

The post-Mao model, which began with the Chinese leader's death in 1976 and continues to the present, is attempting to achieve what are known as the "four modernizations": in agriculture, industry, national defense, and science and technology. It is a mixture of communist doctrine and free market reform requiring a number of crucial balances—specifically five.

First, the post-Mao model seeks to balance egalitarianism and excellence. That is, without giving up the effort to satisfy the basic needs of all, the Chinese are attempting to enable those individuals with expertise to address specialized problems in industry, agriculture, science, and education. Second, the post-Mao model attempts to balance central direction and local initiative. Here, without squelching local originality and effort, the Chinese are trying to follow a national plan of development. Third, China today seeks to balance party control and order on one hand with greater freedom and legality on the other. Without party control, the Chinese leadership believes, there can be no coherent development, yet people need to be free of oppressive control if they are to contribute their best to national development.[10] Fourth, the current Chinese model strives to balance the old Maoist emphasis on self-reliance with a modern reliance on foreign trade, credits, and investment. The present leadership recognizes that China needs scientific, technological, and economic help from countries such as the United States and Japan, yet China strives to be as self-reliant as possible as it develops modern capability in a number of fields. Finally, the Chinese are attempting to balance public ownership of land with small private agricultural plots. They recognize that the small plots can significantly enhance agricultural productivity, yet they do not want to completely relinquish the principle of communal ownership and operation.[11]

In 1980 the Chinese leadership decided to slow down the four modernizations but not abandon them. In 1986 priority was given to reform and expansion of the open-door policy, that is, the encouragement of foreign investment. This involved decentralizing the economic system and relinquishing the state monopoly on foreign trade. In addition, six "special economic zones" were established to encourage foreign investment and trade. Finally, major reforms were begun in banking, pricing, labor law, and agriculture.

Creative Breakthrough? As implemented in China, egalitarian communism at least holds out the hope (if not the promise) of significantly improving the economic well-being of the developing nations that choose it. If China is at all typical, the basic human needs of most of the world's people might be met. Between 1975 and 2003 China's per capita growth rate, as measured by its gross domestic product (GDP), ran a superb 8.1 percent; between 1990 and 1999 the growth rate was an astounding 9.5 percent. By comparison, the average for high-income countries between 1975 and 2003 was 2.5 percent. The welfare of a majority of Chinese living today has progressed significantly. China's literacy rate is 97 percent. Life expectancy went from 47.1 years in 1960 to 70 years in 2002, and the infant mortality rate (below 5 years) dropped from 150 per 1,000 births in 1960 to 38 per 1,000 in 2002.[12]

On the subject of population growth, it must be noted that China's has been enormous. China had 570 million people in 1952 and 983 million in 1977; today there are 1.28 billion people. However, with the help of family planning, easily accessible abortion, and bonuses for small families, the rate of growth has been slowed. Between 1975 and 2003 the annual population growth rate was a low 1.0 percent.[13] Yet that reduction in population growth rate was at least in part made possible by the implementation in 1980 of policies restricting the number of children that couples could have. In 1982, when census figures revealed that China's population had topped one billion, a rather ruthless enforcement policy was enacted: a national standard of one child per couple was established. Grim stories of forced late-term abortions, infanticide, and child abandonment began to appear. In recent years, there have been some signs that the strict quota system is being softened.

The strengths of the communist model are appealing. In China life has improved for the vast majority. The worst ravages of starvation have been overcome. Abject poverty has sub-

While tremendous increases in standards in living have been achieved in China, particularly along the coastal regions, interior provinces still suffer from considerable poverty.

sided. People have better nutrition, health, and housing. Literacy continues to spread. The economy—especially industry—grows rapidly and holds out hope for larger slices of a bigger pie. Income is distributed more fairly. *But this rosy picture must be tempered with the understanding that the economy, while certainly not 100 percent capitalist, has been shifting increasingly toward major free market reforms.* Although great progress in human welfare was made during China's more pure communist phase of development, our assessment of the strengths of the communist economic model are severely affected by the spread of free market mechanisms. One disturbing trend has emerged. Parts of China, in particular the coastal provinces of Fujian, Guangdong, Jiangsu, and Zhejiang, have benefited enormously by a shift away from embracing a strict communist economic system to becoming free enterprise market economies. The benefits for these regions have been remarkable, but that success has caused economic disparity with the poorer, interior provinces of China. Recently, China has seen signs of unemployment, something that is not supposed to happen in a communist system.

In sum, advocates of the egalitarian communist model maintain that the benefits outweigh the costs. Improving the economic well-being of the overwhelming majority of people in a developing nation is well worth the loss of freedom to exploiting capitalists and their friends. Proponents also suggest that a more humane communism than that of the former Soviet Union or China is possible.

Yet despite what appear to be some successes (or at least potential successes), critics contend that the grave weaknesses of the communist regime itself must be faced. One weakness is the continuing high cost of the communist revolution, which includes destruction of the regime's opponents; the terrorization of those who do not follow the leaders' or party's current line; and authoritarian control of speech, press, and culture. These costs include the regime's willingness to sacrifice millions in one generation for gains to be achieved in the next. Communist regimes also have to worry about bureaucratic centralization of power and failures of the master plan. Above all, communist systems do not rely on individual incentives as a prime motivator, and some critics argue there are few if any other incentives to work harder, produce more, or innovate. Without individual incentives, people tend to do only what is necessary, to play it safe, to be more concerned with security than production. The most graphic example of the limitations of this kind of system can be seen in the Soviet economy, which by 1990 was near collapse. Similarly, the Cuban communist system has not fared well since the end of the cold war, when the Soviet Union ended its enormous economic aid program in Cuba.

Illiberal Capitalism and Right-Wing Authoritarianism

There are many varieties of what we call illiberal capitalism. This form of capitalism emphasizes capital growth at the expense of, or in disregard of, economic and social justice. Variations on this model may be found in Chile (under Augusto Pinochet from 1973 to 1989), the Philippines (under Ferdinand Marcos from 1972 to 1986), South Korea (under a variety of military strongmen during the post–World War II period), Indonesia (under military strongman General Suharto from 1966 to 1998), and Singapore (under Lee Kuan Yew, who, though elected the country's first prime minister in 1965, nevertheless ruled the island country for decades with an iron hand). This option rests on the assumption that economic growth, an enlarged gross national product (GNP), and capitalist profitability precede, and create the conditions for, greater economic and social justice. Wealth must be created before it can be equitably distributed. And there must be a favorable environment for those who can create it—the capitalist entrepreneurs.

Right-wing authoritarianism complements illiberal capitalism in the sense that economic growth requires political, economic, and social stability. Left-wing agitation is not allowed to get out of hand. Strikes are not permitted in essential industries. Adverse criticism of the nation's rulers, if it goes too far, may be subject to punishment. When "national security" is at issue, civil liberties may be jeopardized by the intervention of the military, as was the case in countries such as Brazil, Chile, the Philippines, and South Korea.

In illiberal capitalist and right-wing authoritarian systems, the government encourages a high rate of growth in the GNP. The state plans, regulates, and directs the economy to accomplish this purpose. It may even own and operate basic industries crucial to capitalistic growth.

Individuals in this Russian village of Mymrino have seen little betterment in their lives after the fall of communism and the rise of capitalist reform. They still depend on a few animals and small plots of land to get by.

The state must be willing, if necessary, to impose wage controls in the fight against inflation. It must be willing to make the poor wait, to defer the satisfaction of basic economic
needs. Leaders of the regime seek to advance the nation's economic growth, military
strength, and security. They will cooperate with, but try to avoid overdependence on, rich
capitalistic countries and multinational corporations. This variety of illiberal capitalism
seeks a big enough pie to ensure, in time, larger slices for all. Then, presumably, the people's basic need for greater economic well-being can be satisfied.

Brazil's record from 1964 to 1985 illustrates the illiberal capitalism and right-wing
authoritarianism model's pattern, its key results, and its continuing problems. In recent
Brazilian history, for example, a military coup ousted the democratically elected government of President João Goulart in 1964. In 1979 Gen. João Baptista de Oliveira Figueiredo
was sworn in as president after winning a two-party contest in late 1978 and promising
a return to liberalization and democracy. In 1985 General Figueiredo's government was
replaced by an elected civilian government, which ruled with a fragile coalition. In 1988
a new, substantially liberalized constitution was approved. During the essentially authoritarian regime from 1964 to 1985, the military or military-backed civilian leadership
worked closely with capitalist entrepreneurs, the upper-urban bourgeoisie, and technocratic
civil servants. The Brazilian leadership sought to maintain economic and political order
and thus make possible the "economic miracle."

From 1967 to 1974 Brazil's economy grew at impressively high rates. For example,
Brazil's gross domestic product rose an average of 11.3 percent per year during this
period. Between 1975 and 1980 the annual growth rate was 6.5 percent, the slowdown
partly due to the OPEC oil crisis. Investment poured into Brazil.[14] The country's gross
national product (in U.S. dollars) climbed from $125,600,000,000 in 1976 to
$250,568,000,000 in 1986. And per capita GNP rose from $1,088 in 1976 to $1,809
in 1986.[15]

There is little doubt Brazil did achieve significant aggregate economic growth. But how
this growth affected human welfare is debatable. At the end of this period of illiberal capitalism, were the people of Brazil any better off than the people of Latin America in general? Not really. Using 1986 as the base year for comparison, we note the following. Only
78 percent of Brazil's people were literate, compared with 80 percent for all of Latin
America. Life expectancy in Brazil was sixty-five years; for all of Latin America it stood
at sixty-six years. Brazil's annual infant mortality rate was 63 deaths per 1,000 live births;
for Latin America it was 56 deaths per 1,000 live births. GNP per capita for Brazil was
$1,809; for Latin America overall it was $1,872.[16] In 1986 a substantial percentage of
the Brazilian population still lived in poverty in both country and city. Finally, there was
a severe maldistribution of wealth. In 1984, twenty years after the beginning of the illiberal capitalist period, 10 percent of the population controlled nearly 50 percent of Brazil's
household income.[17]

As noted above, the Brazilian experience helps explain the strengths and weaknesses of this model. Rapid economic growth can occur, particularly in capital-intensive industries. As a result of the groundwork laid during the period of illiberal capitalism, Brazil now produces consumer products—automobiles, refrigerators, and television sets—for its affluent minority. The hope is that sooner or later the larger economic pie—the increased gross national product—will benefit more people, including the poor.

The Brazilian model, like the Chinese one, requires present sacrifice for future gain. Economic and social justice—especially for the poor—is postponed. Although a new Brazilian constitution has been adopted to reduce the power of the president, abolish censorship, and generally expand civil liberties, it remains to be seen whether wealth can be more fairly distributed. Brazil's twenty-one-year authoritarian experience was relatively mild in comparison with the illegal arrests, imprisonment, and torture that characterize other right-wing regimes. In Brazil's case, as in other right-wing regimes, the ruling elite maintained that its economic and political policies were necessary but temporary. But one must ask, How necessary? How temporary?

Creative Breakthrough? Defenders of this model are firmly convinced that the economic pie must be enlarged considerably before the basic human needs of the poor can be satisfied. They believe that postponing political, social, and economic justice is a necessary, but temporary, sacrifice. They concede that capitalist economic growth may immediately favor the affluent minority, but they emphasize that all citizens benefit a little from a larger gross national product and that eventually those who are less well off will benefit much more than they would have under communism. Proponents also maintain that right-wing regimes offer greater opportunity for eventual political liberalization than do left-wing regimes.

Democratic Socialism

This option rejects communism, liberal democratic capitalism, and right-wing authoritarian capitalism. The possibility of public ownership of key economic and social services is assumed. Agriculture may be communal and genuinely democratic (say, on the model of the Israeli kibbutz), or it may be private. Other aspects of the economy—small businesses and service industries—remain in private hands. This option assumes, moreover, a two-party or multiparty system, political competition, and civil liberties. It assumes central guidance in areas essential for satisfying human needs (such as education, health, or housing) that will not be met by the private sector.

Consequently, the democratic socialist state will not hesitate to nationalize monopolies or regulate fundamental industries (banking, railroads, and key services) to ensure sensible growth, equitable distribution, and key services in the interest of the majority. Top priority is given to employment, minimal levels of income, literacy, health care, and housing.

Because of widespread rural poverty in the developing world, there will be substantial agrarian reform, development of cooperatives, attention to labor-intensive production, and balanced industrial growth. Better urban planning is also necessary to ensure decent housing, sanitation, and transportation. Education is crucial to both rural and urban development.

The democratic socialist model for the developing world requires family planning and population control to prevent imbalance between population and resources. Balanced agricultural and industrial growth is also important. Low or modest expenditures for national security are most helpful; resources can thus be used for healthy economic growth and attendance to basic human needs.

Democratic socialist governments seek to maintain both freedom and equality. The difficulties most developing nations face hamper these attempts. Those on the right complain that freedom and egalitarianism breed disorder. Those on the left complain that excessive concern for freedom inhibits egalitarian policy. There are few, if any, genuinely successful democratic socialist governments in the developing world. The post–cold war emphasis on free market systems and privatization in much of the developing world has resulted in significant movement away from democratic socialist (and communist) models.

Creative Breakthrough? The strengths of the democratic socialist option lie in its commitment to meeting basic human needs as quickly as possible and within a framework of freedom. Supporters argue that this model is the only one that makes sense in developing countries. They state that democratic socialism is the only policy that can strike the right balance between liberty and equality and between economic growth and satisfaction of basic needs. A certain amount of central planning is required to direct a nation's resources, increase production, and tackle problems such as hunger, disease, and illiteracy. Moreover, only a government truly respectful of people's liberties and needs can enlist their energies in a successful program of development.

Democratic socialism may be vulnerable to attacks from the left or the right. The extreme left believes that democratic socialist governments fail to achieve a truly egalitarian society. The extreme right is frightened by socialism and democracy, by the commitment to more equitable distribution and to freedom. These two types of opposition were dramatically demonstrated in the early 1970s. In 1971 extreme leftists mounted an unsuccessful armed rebellion against the democratic socialist government of Sirimavo Bandaranaike (the world's first elected female prime minister) in Sri Lanka. Two years later a right-wing military coup overthrew the democratic socialist government of Salvador Allende Gossens in Chile. Both left and right believe (for different reasons) that democratic socialist governments lack strength and are too easy on rightists and leftists, respectively. The left holds that democratic socialist governments lack the courage to wipe out capitalistic domination. The right maintains that democratic socialist governments frighten away private investment by threatening profits and are too soft on communists.

THE CRITICAL ROLE OF THE INTERNATIONAL COMMUNITY

This chapter has concentrated on presenting and evaluating fundamental economic-political models to be employed by developing states to overcome the problems of poverty. We would be remiss, however, if we did not discuss the role of some actors in the broader international community who are key to the development process, regardless of which model is adopted. Efforts toward development are very complex, and there is no way that any discussion included here can be comprehensive. So a few brief comments about three key actors will be useful to help flesh out the picture: international organizations, non-governmental organizations (NGOs), and state-based foreign aid programs.

International Organizations

Multilateral assistance plays a vital role in today's development process. Although some foreign assistance is channeled through regional organizations, by far the most critical activities in this area are to be found in the efforts of various organs within the United Nations system. Several of the specialized agencies, such as the Food and Agricultural Organization (FAO) and the World Health Organization (WHO), are instrumental in development efforts. But the following three organs are absolutely central to development efforts and are particularly worth noting.

The **World Bank** (also known as the International Bank for Reconstruction and Development, or IBRD) is headquartered in Washington, D.C., and is in the business of making loans to countries for development purposes. In fiscal 2004 it loaned out more than $20.4 billion and had operations in more than one hundred developing countries. Its strategic priority is to meet the Millennium Development Goals outlined later in this section.

The **International Monetary Fund (IMF)**, also headquartered in Washington, D.C., is comprised of 183 member countries. Its activities are concentrated on stabilizing financial systems, promoting international monetary cooperation and exchange stability, and helping to manage excessive debt load. The IMF's efforts to wrestle with enormous debt loads assumed by many developing countries in the mid- to late 1980s have been controversial over the past three decades. In order to provide debt relief by rescheduling loans under more favorable conditions (such as lower interest rates over a longer payback period), the IMF has insisted on certain fiscal conditions being met by the debtor country, concerning, for instance, how much can be spent by the government and on what. Designed to impose fiscal discipline on these countries to increase the probability that the loans will be paid back, the conditions, in some cases, have been characterized by critics as repressive and injurious to economic growth. The IMF has reviewed a number of cases and in some instances has eased conditions. The controversy continues, however.[18]

The **United Nations Development Program (UNDP)** provides development advice and grant support. Its advisory role is concentrated in assisting countries to draft development reports and adopt development programs that integrate both public and private programs and projects. One of the principle coordinating mechanisms is the UNDP resident representative, stationed in each recipient country, who acts as an onsite coordinator of development activities.[19]

At the United Nations Millennium Summit held in 2000, 189 governments adopted the Millennium Declaration, which established a set of eight goals. The **Millennium Development Goals**, designed to drastically reduce, if not eliminate, global poverty in the twenty-first century, were as follows:

Goal 1. Eradicate extreme poverty and hunger by halving the proportion of people whose income is less than $1 per day by 2015;

Goal 2. Achieve universal primary education by 2015;

Goal 3. Promote gender equality and empower women by eliminating gender disparity in primary and secondary education, preferably by 2005, and to all levels of education no later than 2015;

Goal 4. Reduce child mortality (the under-five mortality rate) by two thirds between 1990 and 2015;

Goal 5. Improve maternal health (the maternal mortality ratio) by reducing by three quarters between 1990 and 2015;

Goal 6. Halt and reverse the spread of HIV/AIDS by 2015 as well as the incidence of malaria;

Goal 7. Integrate the principles of sustainable development into country policies and programs and reverse the loss of environmental resources and halve the proportion of people without sustainable access to safe drinking water and sanitation by 2015. Also to significantly improve the lives of at least 100 million slum dwellers. [For a discussion of the concept of sustainable development, see chapter 18];

Goal 8. Develop a partnership for development between international organizations, countries, and the private sector.[20]

Though it is still early in the program, indications are that the international community is achieving mixed results, with some developing countries benefiting substantially and others being left behind, particularly in sub-Saharan Africa.

Nongovernmental Organizations

Nongovernmental organizations have become a major part of the efforts to promote development and combat poverty in the developing world, and their number has increased dramatically over the past thirty years. The range of development concerns of these organizations is almost limitless. A few examples include:

- Arab Council for Childhood and Development
- Asian Women in Cooperative Development
- Care International
- Center for Development Services
- Egyptian AIDS Society
- Habitat for Humanity International
- Human Rights Watch
- International Association of Planned Parenthood
- International Cartographic Association

One of the keys to successful development efforts in poor countries is the use of appropriate technology. In this photograph, Oxfam development workers and villagers sink a well for a Cambodian village.

- International Centre for Human Rights and Democratic Development
- International Rural Housing Association
- International Save the Children Alliance
- Maryknoll Sisters of St. Dominic, Inc.
- Mercy Corps International
- Oxfam
- Population Council
- United Methodist Church—General Board of Global Ministries
- World Energy Council

There are now more than 2,600 NGOs officially credited with consultative status with the Economic and Social Council (ECOSOC) of the United Nations.

State-Based Foreign Aid Programs

There are a number of myths, or at least misperceptions, about foreign aid given from the developed countries of the North to the developing countries of the South. To be sure, the aid has been generous, approximately $78.5 billion in 2004 and over a trillion dollars since the end of World War II. But several points must be considered.

First, not all foreign assistance is in the form of grants, or outright gifts. A significant percentage is in the form of loans, which lenders expect to be paid back. Second, a significant amount of foreign aid is in the form of military aid. Third, some of the major aid programs, such as those of the United States, tend to be highly concentrated. For instance, Israel and Egypt receive an enormously disproportionate percentage of American bilateral foreign assistance. Nevertheless, this constitutes a very small percentage of the U.S. budget.

Fourth, while attacking poverty and promoting development are part of major aid programs, there are other significant considerations. Foreign aid is an instrument of influence, and donor countries by and large want something in return—political allegiance, military basing rights, support in international organizations, and friendship. Donors may also demand changes in behavior, such as improvements in human rights or democratic reforms. Not that any of these conditions are necessarily bad, but one should remember that more often than not, foreign aid comes with a price.

Finally, it should be noted that the end of the cold war has had a significant impact on foreign aid programs. Within the developing world, the shift toward free market capitalist models has caused donor states to reconsider their aid programs and to question whether, with the increases in trade and the influx of foreign investment into developing countries, aid programs are still necessary, at least at the levels of the past.

CONCLUSION

The need for a creative breakthrough to greater economic well-being, particularly for the world's poor, is clear and present. The persistence of poverty, unemployment, hunger, ill health, illiteracy, poor housing, and inequality is well documented. What is not clear is how to overcome these agonizing problems and how to deal with the troublesome task of balancing costs and benefits in proposed policies. All of the alternatives that we have examined contain difficulties. The challenge facing the decision maker is to select the alternative that will quickly maximize benefits for the world's poor at acceptable costs to those in developing and developed countries.

Policies for economic well-being must be worked out by most developing nations (where most of the poor live) in the face of severe problems. Most developing nations lack the prerequisites for significant and humane development. They often have no democratic and constitutional consensus. They do not enjoy political stability. They are short on effective party and administrative organization, trained personnel, good transportation, and schools. They face enormous obstacles in the very evils they seek to overcome: low incomes, malnutrition, disease, illiteracy, and inadequate housing.

Scholars concerned with advancing global economic well-being must also question the foresight, will, and judgment of the richer nations of the developed world. Too often such nations seem unable to adopt a long-range policy to help the world's poor; too often their policies are foolishly motivated by short-range interests that are frequently identified with national security. The richer nations seem unable to speed up the process of economic development for the poorer developing nations. Their assistance is not always in tune with freedom and humane treatment for the poor. Moreover, the domestic policies of rich nations such as the United States do not offer attractive models for economic well-being. Indeed, while the standard of living in the United States remains high for most people, there are indications that the gap between the "haves" and the "have nots" within the country is widening.

Minimal economic well-being in a totalitarian state is not appealing either. Nor is lopsided and unjust economic growth in a right-wing authoritarian regime. Both models call for present sacrifices to achieve future gains. A democratic socialist model and a more genuinely liberal capitalist and democratic option are more attractive, as is the world order option, but how attractive, and how feasible, are they?

Ethically, political scientists recognize the need for sane and humane policies to deal with the empirical realities of economic malaise, but we find it hard to make prudent decisions that can help balance acceptable costs and clear-cut benefits on the road to greater economic well-being. Ethically, our consciences compel us to search for creative breakthroughs. Empirically, we appreciate the difficulties of achieving greater economic well-being, particularly for the world's poor, but we have not yet developed empirical explanations to help us, prudentially, overcome economic malaise rapidly and satisfactorily.

In our next chapter we will concentrate on the imperative of ecological health, an issue vitally related to economic well-being.

SUGGESTED READINGS

Bhagwati, Jaquati. *In Defense of Globalization*. New York: Oxford University Press, 2004. An eminent economist lays out a powerful case on behalf of globalization, particularly its positive impact on some developing countries.

Hulme, David, and Michael Edwards, eds. *NGOs, States, and Donors: Too Close for Comfort*. New York: St. Martin's Press in association with Save the Children, 1997. An enormously informative set of essays exploring the ways in which nongovernmental organizations are engaged in the development process.

Judd, Ellen, and Marilyn Porter, eds. *Feminists Doing Development: A Practical Critique*. New York: Zed Books, 1999. Includes both theoretical and applied work of women in the field of development.

Mittelman, James, and Mustapha Kamal Pashi. *Out from Underdevelopment Revisited: Changing Global Structures and the Remaking of the Third World*. New York: St. Martin's Press, 1997. A thoughtful treatise on modern development. Perhaps the most interesting question raised is, "Where have all the modernization thinkers gone?"

Roberts, J. Timmons, and Amy White, eds. *From Modernization to Globalization*. Malden, Mass.: Blackwell, 2000. Very fine edited textbook of readings on a wide range of development theories: classical, modern, dependency, world-system, and globalization.

Sachs, Jeffrey. *The End of Poverty: Economic Possibilities for Our Time*. New York: Penguin Press, 2005. One of the most anticipated and important books on the problem of poverty. Makes a strong case for putting critical infrastructure in place to facilitate the growth of market-economy mechanisms.

United Nations Development Program. *Human Development Report*. New York: Oxford University Press. A valuable annual analysis of the human condition in the world. Combines economic indicators and assessment of political welfare.

Weatherby, Joseph W., et al. *The Other World: Issues and Politics of the Developing World*. 4th ed. New York: Longman, 2000. An interdisciplinary approach to the most fundamental issues and problems of development. Includes regional briefings on Asia, Latin America, the Middle East, North Africa, and sub-Saharan Africa.

White, Gordon. *Riding the Tiger: The Politics of Economic Reform in Post-Mao China*. Stanford: Stanford University Press, 1993. A first-rate analysis of those forces that brought about the remarkable economic changes in China since the late 1970s.

World Bank. *World Development Report*. New York: Oxford University Press. Excellent and authoritative annual world development picture. Statistical tables are invaluable.

GLOSSARY TERMS

developed countries (p. 399)

demographic transition theory (p. 408)

emerging economies (p. 399)

International Monetary Fund (IMF) (p. 417)

least developed countries (LDCs) (p. 399)

Millennium Development Goals (p. 418)

neoimperialism (p. 405)

newly industrialized economies (NIEs) (p. 399)

poverty (p. 399)

United Nations Development Program (UNDP) (p. 418)

World Bank (p. 417)

Chapter 18

THE IMPERATIVE
OF ECOLOGICAL
HEALTH

Ecological malaise, or environmental illness, has emerged as a major concern in world politics. Granted, it is perhaps less dramatic than the possibility of catastrophic nuclear war, and the harmful consequences of ecological illness may seem far more remote than the deaths through starvation or torture that result from poverty or tyranny. Yet ecological degradation has consequences as bad as those of poverty or human rights violations; indeed, it may be even more dangerous than modern warfare.

At its worst, ecological ill health threatens humankind's biological existence. It affects both developed and developing nations. The depletion and waste of resources; population growth wildly in excess of food, land, water, and energy; and global warming—these are all real threats to hopes for a better tomorrow. In particular, ecological dangers may prevent developing nations from overcoming poverty and threaten the prosperity of developed nations.

In examining the imperative of ecological health, we see again the linkage between the values of peace, human rights, and economic well-being that we have been considering in part 4 of this book. For example, war not only destroys human beings; it also destroys the countryside, poisons the air, and wastes vital resources. Economic well-being is vitally related to a stable population, adequate resources, and clean air and water. Human rights are violated if people starve to death because population outruns food supply or if they have no clean air to breathe or clean water to drink. In the interests of biological existence, societal growth and development, and the cultural quality of life, political actors must understand and respond to threats to ecological health. Hence our question for this chapter: *What creative breakthroughs can help humanity achieve ecological health?*

Ecological problems cannot be considered apart from political philosophy and practical politics. The ideologies of liberal democracy, democratic socialism, communism, and right-wing regimes are based on ideas of growth and abundance intimately related to the world's ecological difficulties. Thus the ecological challenge is also a challenge to the world's prominent political philosophies and to the ideas and institutions that stem from them. In brief, the ecological crisis suggests (at least to some critics) that both capitalism and communism may have fatal flaws. Liberal democracy and democratic socialism may also be in trouble because some of their key ideas (individualism, freedom, social justice) may be jeopardized by the ecological crisis and responses to it. Thus a number of political problems may have to be rethought as the world examines and responds to the ecological crisis.

Before proceeding, we need to determine the meaning of **ecology**, particularly of human ecology. Ecology is concerned with the relationship between organisms and their environment. Human ecology deals with the relationship between people and their larger physical, biological, social, economic, and political environment. For human beings, ecological health is the relationship between people and their larger environment that eases their biological existence and permits a superior quality of life. Ecological health means clean air, pure water, the prudent use of natural resources, and a sensible balance between population and resources. It means respect for the planet, a partnership between people and resources. Ecological health calls for people to manage their "household"—the household of the human race—in a caring way.

Let us now consider some of the key factors that prompt our critical exploration of ecological health. Then we will examine some leading approaches to ecological health. Finally, we will encourage the reader to make wise judgments that may move us toward creative policy breakthroughs on ecological health.

ETHICAL AND EMPIRICAL FACTORS

Our search for key factors is part of a search for a sound ecological philosophy to guide humankind toward sane public policy judgments. We have to reconsider whether, and to what extent, traditional political and economic philosophies are adequate. We have to ask how we can respond to factors that bear upon ecological health. Although controversy rages between ecological pessimists and optimists about responses to these factors, the challenges are generally recognized by all.

Many people see the depletion of the earth's ozone layer, global warming, depletion and misuse of scarce and nonrenewable resources, air and water pollution, and the imbalance of population and resources as the five major threats to quality of life and life itself. They threaten those now living as well as future generations. They constitute direct ecological threats, present and future, to the biosphere and indirect political threats to human freedom. Humankind could be overwhelmed by an ecological catastrophe brought on by the slow degradation of the planet caused by poisoned water and air; it could be rendered poverty-stricken by the disappearance of vital nonrenewable resources; or it could be dehumanized by populations wildly in excess of the resources necessary to sustain adequate living conditions. Efforts to cope with these ecological difficulties could accentuate selfish nationalism and international tensions between "have" and "have not" nations or could intensify class conflicts between rich and poor within both developed and developing nations.

Depletion of the Ozone Layer

In the mid-1980s scientists confirmed long-held suspicions that something ominous was happening to the thin **ozone layer** that encircles the earth's stratosphere: the planet's ozone shield was dissipating. The most observable phenomenon was a 1.2 million-square-mile hole above Antarctica. Ozone is important because it protects the earth from the full force of the sun's ultraviolet rays. As Will Steger and Jon Bowermaster put it in their book *Saving the Earth:*

> The problem with ozone loss is that it increases the amount of one form of ultraviolet light—UV-B—that reaches the Earth. Each 1 percent drop of ozone allows 2 percent more UV-B to reach the ground. This, in turn, increases the potential for skin cancer by 3 to 6 percent. If ozone depletion continues at the current rate, and if CFC [chlorofluorocarbon] usage continues unabated, the EPA [Environmental Protection Agency] predicts more than 60 million additional cases of skin cancer and about one million additional deaths among Americans born by the year 2075.[1]

Loss of ozone increases people's vulnerability to infectious diseases through suppression of the immune response system. Furthermore, ozone depletion will disrupt the food chain. Field studies of soybeans have demonstrated that ozone depletion of up to 25 percent could decrease crop yields by more than 20 percent.[2] The death of microscopic organisms in the world's oceans—another danger with ozone depletion—will seriously endanger other marine life. Finally, climate will be dramatically affected. Ozone depletion will cause a cooling of the stratosphere, perhaps altering global wind patterns.[3]

The cause for this potential ecological disaster is the continuing release of chlorofluorocarbons (CFCs) and bromine from gases called halons (fire-extinguishing agents). The CFCs are used as sterilizing agents in the production of plastic foam products and as propellants in aerosols. Roughly forty-two tons of CFCs were released into the world's atmosphere in 1950. By 1988 that figure had increased to an astounding and dangerous 1,260 tons.[4] Then over the following eight years the amount of CFCs released fell to 141 tons.[5] How did this change come about?

Because the threat to life on earth was so great, the international community moved quickly in its attempt to rectify the problem. In 1987 twenty-four nations and the European Economic Community signed the Montreal Protocol on Substances That Deplete the Ozone Layer. Most of the major producers and consumers of CFCs and halons signed the agreement, which froze world CFC production and called for overall consumption to be reduced 50 percent by 1999. The agreement further called for a freeze on halon production beginning in 1992—the freeze to be effective at the 1986 level of production.

Even before the Montreal meeting, however, the ozone layer was found to be disappearing at a rate far faster than expected. In response to this development, parties to the Montreal Protocol met in London in May 1992 and agreed to a 100 percent ban for developed nations by the year 2000, with a ten-year time lag for developing nations. This agreement included new chemicals, such as carbon tetrachloride, that had only recently been recognized as contributors to ozone depletion.[6] Through this remarkable act of international cooperation in the face of powerful scientific realities, as of 2005 the goals of the Montreal Protocol have largely been achieved.

The greatest responsibility for reversing the ozone crisis clearly rests with the world's developed nations, which produce roughly 70 percent of the world's total. Not all international environmental problems generate responsible international political action. The depletion of the ozone layer may be an exception.

Global Warming

Perhaps the most serious environmental problem facing the planet is **global warming**, caused by the **greenhouse effect**. The greenhouse effect is the trapping of the earth's heat in the atmosphere by such heat-absorbing gases as carbon dioxide, CFCs, methane, nitrous oxide, and ozone. Coal burning, vehicle emissions, and large-scale clearing of tropical forests each add to increased carbon dioxide levels in the atmosphere. Carbon emissions rose from 1,624 million tons in 1950 to more than 7,000 million tons in 2004.[7] (See Figure 18.1).

The response of the international community to global warming has been mixed and certainly cautious. At the **Earth Summit** held in Rio de Janeiro, Brazil, in June 1992, a Convention on Climate Change was drafted that proposed international action to prevent carbon dioxide and other greenhouse gases from building up in the atmosphere to levels that could cause damaging climate changes. It established financial aid for developing countries, as well as institutions to review and update commitments. However, after thirteen years, the impact of the convention has been negligible. The major problem with the treaty is that it contains no specific emission targets, and carbon dioxide concentrations as measured by parts per million have increased steadily from a low of 356.2 in 1992 to 377.4 in 2004.[8]

In December 1997, some 160 nations met in Kyoto, Japan, and drew up the Kyoto Protocol to the Framework Convention on Climate Changes. And by 2000, emissions had fallen slightly, to 6,299 million tons, thanks to efforts spearheaded primarily by the emerging economies of the former eastern bloc nations. In contrast, during the same time

Figure 18.1 Carbon Emissions Worldwide, 1950–2004

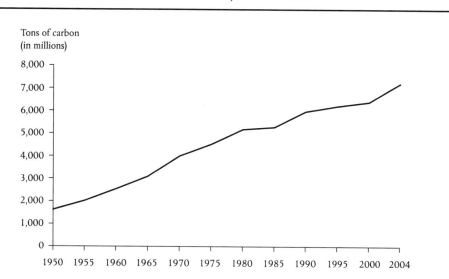

Source: Janet L. Sawin, Worldwatch Institute, "Climate Change Indicators on the Rise," *Vital Signs 2005: The Trends That Are Shaping Our Future* (Boston: W. W. Norton, 2005) 40–41.

frame the industrial nations of the West, including the United States, failed to reduce carbon emissions. About ten countries share responsibility for roughly two thirds of the world's carbon emissions—led by the United States and China, which combined are responsible for 39 percent.[9] Furthermore, although more than thirty nations have ratified the Kyoto Protocol, it takes fifty-five nations to bring it into force. The United States is one of several countries that as of mid-2005 had yet to ratify the agreement.

Although there is a growing consensus in the scientific community that the greenhouse effect is real, there is by no means unanimity. One reason is that the greenhouse effect, unlike the hole in the ozone layer, is not clearly observable. Many of the greenhouse predictions come from complex computer models. Additionally, there is disagreement on whether a global disaster will result; some scientists believe nature will intervene and compensate for the abuse of the planet.

Believers in the greenhouse effect have little doubt about what is happening and what the impact will be. Steger and Bowermaster note: "Current models predict that the average global temperatures will rise by several degrees Fahrenheit within the next century. By comparison, world temperatures rose just 1 degree in the past 100 years."[10] Figure 18.2 records the variations in temperature from a 1960–1990 average and clearly reflects the upward trend of global temperature over the past quarter century. It is thought that this overall rise is at least partially due to greenhouse warming.

Many scientists believe that the impact of global warming can be readily observed in the dramatic reduction in the size of glaciers. These photos taken of the Riggs glacier in 1941 and 2004, respectively, dramatically illustrate this phenomenon.

Such global warming could dramatically affect climate patterns. It would alter crop yields and water supplies, raise sea levels, and flood coastal and low-lying cities. If temperatures were to experience an increase of three degrees to sixteen degrees Fahrenheit (two degrees to nine degrees Celsius) by the middle of the twenty-first century, sea levels could rise an average of two inches per decade.[11] Freshwater supplies could be threatened. Fishing yields might decline because of slower ocean currents. Warmer oceans might cause stronger hurricanes and typhoons.

The greenhouse effect raises serious questions for policymakers throughout the world. How much longer can fossil fuels be relied on as the primary source of energy in the industrialized world? Will developing nations, as they become more industrialized, use more fossil fuels? Are such energy sources as hydropower, wind power, geothermal power, solar power, and biomass power realistic alternatives? How would a drastic reduction in the use of fossil fuels affect the world economy? Can the destruction of the world's great rainforests in places such as Brazil be allowed to continue?

Pollution

Modern warfare, especially nuclear weapons, has had a devastating effect on ecological health. Radiation poisoning, which killed one of every five people who ultimately died at Hiroshima, has also taken lives in the peacetime testing of nuclear weapons, and it remains a hazard in all nuclear plants and waste dumps. Herbicides used in Vietnam to defoliate jungle cover not only devastated millions of acres of natural foliage and farmland but also caused severe medical problems for soldiers and civilians alike.

As contaminating to the environment as war is, massive pollution over extended periods of time has mostly been caused by modern industrialization and agriculture. Indus-

Figure 18.2 Global Temperature Variations

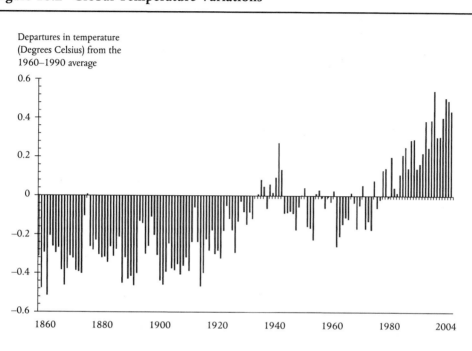

Departures in temperature (Degrees Celsius) from the 1960–1990 average

Source: The Hadley Centre for Climate Prediction and Research, Government of the United Kingdom, 2005, www.met-office.gov.uk/research/hadleycentre/index.html.

trial cities suffer from smog. Acid rain may fall hundreds or thousands of miles from a factory or coal-burning energy plant and injure lakes, streams, buildings, and antiquities. Automobiles are among the worst polluters, filling the air with noxious fumes, including lead. The pollution of rivers and oceans and air by factory smoke, industrial chemicals, and agricultural pesticides threatens people, animals, and fish. Shorelines are desecrated when millions of gallons of oil spill from tankers that run aground. How long can the earth sustain this kind of injury? How long will people tolerate it?

Insults to the environment are found in every industrial society. Europe, which is densely populated and highly industrial, faces pollution problems even worse than those in the United States. The Baltic and Mediterranean Seas and the Rhine River are heavily contaminated. Oil spills have plagued European shores. Acid rain falls on Scandinavia. Ironically, Japan's very economic success in the second half of the twentieth century contributed to its severe pollution problem. An illustration of this problem was the tragedy in Minamata Bay in the early 1950s. Mercury poisoning from industrial sources is believed to have caused the death of more than 600 people and the severe illnesses, including

In Vietnam during the 1960s, Operation Ranch Hand planes delivered the defoliant Agent Orange over dense vegetation in order to deny the enemy cover. Today, alternative herbicides, Roundup and Ultra Roundup, are being used in Colombia in the war on drugs in order to destroy cocoa and poppy fields. The use of these defoliants has been subject to criticism by some environmentalists for causing health problems for the local population.

paralysis, of approximately 1,300 more. In 1989, as the cloak of secrecy surrounding much of Eastern Europe was lifted, it became painfully clear that the industrialized communist countries had not been immune to ecological problems and damage. Areas of Bulgaria, Poland, and Romania turned out to be ecological disaster zones. Communist Soviet Union had been no better able to deal with insults to the environment than the United States or other capitalistic countries. Indeed, some of the most treasured natural assets of the former Soviet Union, such as Lake Baikal, may be irredeemably polluted.

Depletion of Valuable Resources

For much of humanity's time on earth, scarcity, not abundance, was the rule. The idea of endless abundance is relatively new, associated with the discovery (dated to 1492) by Western peoples of "virgin" and abundant lands and resources in Africa, the Americas, and Asia. Until quite recently, science and technology seemed to hold out the hope of limitless development of resources.

The impression of limitless clean air and water nourished the impression of bountiful lands and resources. Given abundant nature and scientific genius, many Westerners concluded that they could overcome scarcity throughout the world. With hard work and the opportunity to accumulate capital, human beings could produce abundantly and overcome the traditional hardships of nature. Per capita income could grow enormously. Abundant energy sources—whether human labor, hydroelectric power, coal, or oil—could make production and growth zoom. It seemed as though the Malthusian fears of population growing in excess of food supply unless checked by war, disease, famine, or birth control had finally been laid to rest. Liberals and capitalists shared these high hopes with democratic socialists and communists. All of them assumed that the economy—rightly directed—could produce abundantly and (given the right political and social direction) enhance freedom and justice. In this period dominated by the idea of growth and progress, few people saw that the earth was finite and limited, that exponential growth—unless checked or controlled—might seriously threaten the carrying capacity of the globe.[12]

Today the idea of scarcity as a problem is widely accepted. Humanity may be producing too many people, whose increasing appetites may mean running out of the resources necessary to sustain their lives. Some natural resources, such as oil, are **nonrenewable resources**; once used up, they are gone forever. Indeed, some oil analysts believe we may soon reach peak production and less and less oil will be extracted after that point. Certain nonrenewable resources, such as coal, may be plentiful at present, but even they will not last forever. Moreover, these types of resources will be depleted even faster if present practices of consumption continue. And these are the practices on which current economic growth and lifestyle depend. Thus the supplies of key nonrenewable resources can be exhausted at exponential rates. As nonrenewable resources decline, their prices increase. When key energy sources become excessively expensive and are depleted, a major ingredient of modern growth and life will be denied. Which energy source will then run the modern industrial plant? What fuel will automobiles use? What about the jobs of automakers? What will happen to the world's system of highways?

Wasteful and imprudent use of **renewable resources**, such as land and trees, could also produce terrible consequences. The land could become exhausted, wasted, and ruthlessly exploited. Trees could be recklessly cut down and not replanted. Water and air could be poisoned.

This picture of the imprudent use of renewable resources has been dramatically captured by Garrett Hardin's metaphor of the **tragedy of the commons**.[13] The commons is the communal grazing plot. If all farmers seek to exploit the free grazing of their herds on the communal plot, the grass will soon be gone and will be incapable of renewal, and all the farmers will lose. Tragically, individual farmers are unable to abstain from overgrazing because while they abstain, selfish competitors graze. In this case, immediate self-interest triumphs over long-range concern. In the end the grass is destroyed, the commons cease to benefit anyone, and all farmers and animals suffer.

The global degradation of land is alarmingly illustrated by what has become known as deforestation, brought on by humanity's seemingly unquenchable need for wood and wood products and for new arable land. Global forests are roughly half of what they were eight thousand years ago. Modern rates of deforestation are jaw dropping. During the 1990s, there was a net loss of 9.4 million hectares, an annual loss roughly the size of Portugal. Deforestation remains a problem in the early years of the twenty-first century. For instance, Brazil lost more than 2.3 million hectares of Amazon forest between August 2002 and August 2003. This is an area about half the size of Switzerland.[14]

In the Mexican town of Tlaxiaco, two women pass through a field of pine logs cut for lumber. Despite Mexico's strong laws against deforestation, many of the country's forests have been decimated.

Oceanic and freshwater fish are also overexploited; in time this could significantly reduce catches, and nets may come back to the boat empty. Other renewable sources, such as clean air and water, are threatened just as the commons are.

"The tragedy of the commons" is now a global tragedy. So unless the global community can discover new resources or employ science to find substitutes for current resources, the earth faces ecological scarcity. As shortages loom, prices are bound to inflate, living standards are bound to suffer, and inequalities are bound to worsen. The waste of scarce resources hurts the present generation but may deal an even more devastating blow to posterity. The present recklessness may doom future generations to a lack of adequate food, clothing, shelter, energy, clean air, and pure water. Poverty may be intensified; the hope of overcoming it in developing areas may be dashed. Tension between the relatively rich and poor may increase and with it, perhaps, conflict and repressive measures to perpetuate the inequalities no longer relieved by a bigger "pie."

The Danger of Population Imbalance

Our mania for growth is also reflected in the population explosion. As we saw in chapter 5, world population began a steep climb with the onset of the Industrial Revolution (at the end of the eighteenth century) and continued that climb during the revolutions in transportation, medicine, and agriculture in the nineteenth and twentieth centuries. The world's population doubled between 1850 and 1950, moving up from about 1 billion to 2 billion, and now stands at roughly 6.5 billion.

Even though population growth has slowed in many developed and industrial countries (to an average annual increase of 1.3 percent), the overall picture remains disturbing, largely because of the increasing birth rates in poor, mostly undeveloped countries. By 2050, Pakistan's population is expected to rise to 348 million from 142.6 million in 2000, Nigeria's to 258.5 million from 114 million, and India's to 1.5 billion from 1 billion.[15]

We must keep in mind that the trouble comes from population growth in excess of resources—food, energy, water, nonrenewable resources, space, and heat.[16] Globally, there

Table 18.1 Hunger in Developing Countries, 1995–2002

Country	Underweight Children 1995–2002 (% of those under 5 years)	Undernourished People 2001 (% of population)
Bangladesh	48	32
Burundi	45	70
Ethiopia	47	42
India	47	21
Mali	33	21
Niger	40	34
Pakistan	38	19

Source: United Nations Development Program, *Human Development Report 2004* (New York: Oxford University Press, 2004), 162–163.

may not be enough food to sustain the growing population. Countries with high growth rates may also have to double industrial and agricultural production to keep up with population—an almost impossible feat and a further strain on an already damaged environment.

Since 1980 agricultural output in East Asia and Latin America, particularly the production of grains, has substantially increased, and the percentages of their populations that are hungry have been reduced. The same cannot be said for two other regions of the developing world—the Indian subcontinent and sub-Saharan Africa.[17] Table 18.1 lists some of the most severely affected countries.

This grim picture raises critical questions. What will happen in 2015, when world population has reached seven billion, with nearly six billion of these people in the less developed regions? The task of feeding so many (particularly in poorer countries) may not be impossible but will be difficult. And if population does not stabilize, there may be as many as nine or ten billion people on earth by the middle of the twenty-first century. Feeding these people will be even more difficult. Earth's population is likely to put enormous strain on the planet's carrying capacity. And clearly, scarce resources accentuate the problem.

Of course, it may be possible to expand necessary resources and to limit population through family planning. The prospects here are bleakest in the most vulnerable segments of the globe: the poorest regions of South Asia and Africa. The greatest successes will probably occur in countries with richer resources and the lowest birthrates. Other "solutions" for the imbalance of population and resources—war, famine, and disease—are possible, of course, although none are appealing.

The Challenges of Ecological Politics

The challenges that face policymakers depend on the fundamental diagnosis of the ecological plight. If ozone depletion, global warming, pollution, ecological scarcity, and the imbalance of population and resources are realities—and if they cannot be offset by a natural leveling-off process or by science and technology—then a number of questions must be faced.

Can peoples and nations adjust to the idea of (at least relative) scarcity, which undercuts modern belief in growth and requires a new lifestyle of prudent ecological balance? Can we adjust to the idea that population growth must slow or stop because it imperils resources? Can we accept the idea that pollution threatens the quality of life on earth?

These ecological challenges are also political challenges. They challenge liberalism and socialism, capitalism and communism, nationalism and internationalism. They challenge democratic and constitutional government.

Is laissez-faire economics—with individuals, businesses, and corporations relatively free to produce, consume, and trade as they please—tolerable any longer? Or must government—in recognition of the dangers of scarcity, of the population explosion, and of pollution and in pursuit of a common ecological good—act to safeguard the globe? Will ecological philosopher-kings have to coerce selfish and thoughtless people to save them and the planet? Can democracy endure under these conditions?

Socialists and communists have also built a political, economic, and social philosophy on the premise of productive growth and abundance. But even if the people own the means of production and exchange, can they avoid the consequences of scarcity, population growth, and pollution? Will communist regimes have to be more coercive in order to ration scarce resources, control population, and curtail pollution?

Can developing nations fulfill their dreams of overcoming poverty and achieving democratic development if they cannot fulfill plans for economic growth? Will the need to adopt some form of ecological balance—to husband resources, to limit population growth—doom their aspirations for a better life? And what setbacks will occur if richer nations cannot extend needed help to developing nations?

These questions point toward difficult judgments on public policy. If the ecological optimists are correct, these questions will not be so troubling. If a world of abundance can still be counted on, if population growth will stabilize, if pollution can be overcome, the ecological future will be brighter. There may still be some worries, but given the genius of modern science and technology and sound political decisions, perhaps the scenario of the doomsday prophets can be avoided.

ALTERNATIVE APPROACHES TO ECOLOGICAL HEALTH

It is, of course, entirely possible to adopt a do-nothing, hedonistic, or piggish approach to ecological health. One could ignore ecological problems, assuming they will go away.

One could also embrace the hedonistic philosophy of "eat, drink, and be merry, for tomorrow we die." Or the leaders of currently rich and powerful nations could try to perpetuate their dominance by continuing to exploit the poor. They could try to isolate themselves from growing scarcities, booming populations, and growing pollution. Although all these responses are possible—and, indeed, are likely in some nations—we shall presuppose a more rational and ethical response.

Liberal Conservation

Those who adopt the liberal approach to conservation maintain that modest reform can do the job. They emphasize the feasibility of conserving scarce resources, limiting family size, and safeguarding the environment. They point to actual policies and developments in countries such as the United States to highlight the possibilities of reform.

During the 1970s and 1980s a number of steps were taken to conserve energy in the United States: for example, a fifty-five-mile-per-hour speed limit; smaller, gas-efficient cars; lower temperatures in heated buildings; less joyriding. Unfortunately, the mid-1990s witnessed a reversal of several of these steps. On a more positive note, efforts to recycle paper, aluminum, glass, and other valuable resources enjoy considerable popularity, although recycling could be increased still further.

Much more can be done. Water and land can be used more prudently. Educational programs can successfully encourage water conservation. Better farming practices, food control, and reforestation can save soil and trees. The conservation of nonrenewable resources and the prudent care and replacement of renewable resources can go a long way toward achieving ecological balance. Most of these actions can be done voluntarily, but in some instances democratic government may have to intervene on behalf of the common good.

Family planning is easier in the developed world, where the higher level of well-being reduces the pressure for large families and where education, literacy, and the relative emancipation of women encourage birth control. But the industrialized nations can encourage family planning in other nations through education about birth control, better programs of health and welfare, and efforts to improve economic well-being. Such measures may reduce the need for more radical and controversial means of limiting population, including vasectomy (the operation that prevents passage of sperm from the testes to the penis), tubal ligation (the cutting and tying off of the Fallopian tubes), and free abortions on demand.

Environmental protection can also work. Sensible legislation to protect against flagrant polluters already exists. Resources must be protected against those who would pollute the air, water, and land. It is not too much to ask of chemical companies to safely dispose of contaminating wastes. It is not too much to insist that factories and power plants release fewer pollutants through their smokestacks. It is not too much to require strip miners to restore the earth after they have removed the coal.

Creative Breakthrough?   The strengths of this reform alternative are many. There can be little argument about the need for conservation, family planning, and environmental protection—especially when they are undertaken voluntarily. When good habits are widespread, they contribute enormously to ecological health. Democratically agreed-on, wise regulation on behalf of these objectives is desirable. And sometimes, especially where the common good is involved, people may legitimately be "forced to be free."

But are reforms that build on existing policies enough? Here we uncover some of the weaknesses of this alternative. Critics maintain that these reforms do not come to grips with the true scarcity, overpopulation, and pollution. These critics believe that current conservation only postpones the day of reckoning. They hold that present reforms have not seriously addressed the problem of useless, wasteful, destructive production. They say that these reforms do not address the scandalous fact that the developed countries use a disproportionate share of the world's resources to maintain their high standard of living. Moreover, these reforms cannot balance population and resources in the poorer countries or cut pollution in any significant way. The critics gravely doubt that present measures can work fast enough to ensure the planet's continued ecological health. They believe that the reformist approach makes too many compromises, such as accepting pollution to avoid the loss of industrial jobs and succumbing to the mania for growth to maintain prosperity. These considerations suggest to some that bolder and more radical policies are in order.

Guarded Optimism and Economic Growth

Scholars such as Herman Kahn, Julian L. Simon, Dennis T. Avery, and Bjorn Lomborg take a guardedly optimistic approach toward ecological health.[18] Kahn and two of his colleagues at the Hudson Institute, Leon Martel and William Brown, set forth their views in a widely read book, *The Next 200 Years: A Scenario for America and the World.* Although published almost thirty years ago, it remains perhaps the most compelling work of the guarded optimists. First, these scholars believe that many of the pessimistic environmental projections are exaggerated, temporary in nature, or patently false. Additionally, they maintain that to the degree some of these problems do exist they can be overcome. Table 18.2 summarizes the way these guarded optimists see themselves and their ecological opponents.

Guarded optimists argue that to the extent they exist, the problems of population, hunger, energy, disappearing raw materials, and pollution are solvable in the future and that the principal means to their solution is cutting-edge technology and economic growth. Indeed, many of these problems are the temporary problems of a world in transition from poverty to prosperity. Guarded optimists further maintain that neither the world nor the United States must suffer from long-term shortages of energy or resources.

The guarded optimists and growth enthusiasts do not accept conventional wisdom about patterns of population growth. For Avery, currently a senior fellow at the Hudson Institute, the world's population is "not spiraling out of control. What we are seeing is

Table 18.2 Ecological Health: Four Views

Ecological Health Issue	Convinced Neo-Malthusian	Guarded Pessimist	Guarded Optimist	Technology and Growth Enthusiast
Basic world model	Finite pie	Uncertain pie	Growing pie	Unlimited pie
Technology and growth	Largely illusory and counterproductive	Mostly diminishing return	Required for progress	Solves almost all problems
Management and decision making	Failure almost certain	Likely failure	Moderately successful	Not a serious problem
Resources	Steady depletion	Continued difficulties	Generally sufficient	Economics and technology can provide superb solutions
Current growth	Carcinogenic	Large potential for disaster	Probable transition to stability	Desirable and healthy
Innovation and discovery	A trap	Increasingly ineffective	Usually effective	Humankind's greatest hope
Income gaps and poverty	Destined to tragic conclusions	Increasing and threatening	Declining absolute poverty	Not a real problem
Industrial development	A disaster	A step backward	Should continue	Necessary for wealth and progress
Quality of life	Ruined	In conflict with much growth	More gains than losses	A meaningless phrase and issue
Long-range outlook	Bleak and desperate	Contingent disaster	Contingent success	High optimism and confidence

Source: Adaptation of table, pp. 10–16 in *The Next 200 Years: A Scenario for America and the World*, by Herman Kahn, Leon Martel, and William Brown (New York: Morrow, 1976).

a one-time surge. In fact, the world is in the final stages of the third—and probably last—human population surge." [19] Avery notes that the first surge began ten thousand years ago with the invention of farming. The second surge occurred with the Industrial Revolution and was associated with increases in human wealth. We are now in the final surge, which is linked to vast improvements in medical science and public health systems. He concludes:

> The current population surge is expected to be over before the year 2050. Total fertility rates in the poorest countries have already come more than 60 percent of the way to stability, essentially in one generation! [20]

As the population stabilizes, hunger will be drastically reduced and ultimately eliminated. The optimists do not see a growing gap between demand and supply. Rather, they see abundant food in the future. Poor weather, natural disasters, bad policies, and inadequate distribution have led to malnutrition, hunger, and famine in some areas of the world, but there is enough land, water, and fertilizer to sustain the present and future populations, particularly as we continue to make advances in high-yield crops and sophisticated irrigation techniques.

In the eyes of the guarded optimists, global energy problems are to a large extent attributable to bad luck, poor management, and general waste. Future energy is not dependent on an endless supply of fossil fuel. Given scientific breakthroughs, there is every reason to believe that the world will have an inexhaustible supply of energy, including solar, wind, hydroelectric, geothermal, and nuclear. Many optimists believe that a milestone was reached with University of Houston professor Paul Chu's discovery of a compound that is a near-perfect conductor of electricity at high temperatures—the superconductor. Superconductivity is the process of transmitting energy with limited or no loss of energy. The potential of this technology is revolutionary. As Robert M. Hazen describes it:

> Powerful and efficient lightweight magnets and motors, compact computers faster than any now in existence, magnetically levitated bullet trains able to travel hundreds of miles per hour, money-saving power transmission cables linked to safe, remote nuclear and solar generators, long-term energy storage systems, and a multitude of other devices are all possible in theory through the utilization of superconductivity. [21]

Hazen continues:

> Superconducting motors could be smaller and more powerful than conventional designs. Battery-powered automobiles with light, efficient superconducting electric motors could revolutionize society and its dependence on fossil fuels. [22]

There is also optimism about other raw materials, which guarded optimists believe will be abundant for future generations. They reject the idea of exhausted vital resources and emphasize the potential of mining the oceans and even of extraterrestrial mining. Recycling, conservation, and substitution can secure vital materials now in short supply.

As far as pollution is concerned, the guarded optimists hold that short-term problems can be solved. They place their faith in technology, money, time, and intelligent self-restraint. They believe that in the not too distant future, human beings will look back proudly on ecological achievements. The enormous progress made over the past twenty years in reducing air pollution in U.S. cities and in the nation's waterways is proof of what can be done to improve the environment.

Finally, the guarded optimists and growth enthusiasts are obviously committed to economic growth, but they believe such growth will taper off somewhat over time. Despite some stubborn pockets of poverty, continuing overall economic growth will benefit all.

Creative Breakthrough? The strengths of this philosophy of guarded optimism and economic growth are considerable. If true, this orientation provides hope for a future wherein science and technology, prudently joined with wise public policies, can cope with scarce natural resources, balance population and resources, and provide a clean environment. Growth and prosperity can continue to progress.

The weaknesses of this alternative are found in its assumptions: that population growth will level off fast enough and be in balance with abundant and deliverable food supplies; that resources, especially energy, will be available at reasonable costs to keep industrial and agricultural machinery operating; and that pollution can be overcome. But if population does not level off; if food supplies do not reach hungry people; if no new natural resources can be found; if the sun, the wind, the rivers and oceans, and the earth cannot be tapped for energy; and if pollution continues and is too expensive to curtail, then we human beings would be in deep trouble. Will we have the scientific genius or political will to do all that Kahn and his associates see as essential?

Critics of technological solutions point to alarming costs involved in scientific efforts to cope with scarcity, population, and pollution. For example, nuclear power, science's answer to fossil fuel use, is expensive and potentially dangerous. The partial meltdown at the Three Mile Island reactor in Pennsylvania in 1979 and the reactor explosion at Chernobyl in the Soviet Union in 1986 clearly demonstrate that serious accidents at nuclear power plants can happen and can release harmful radiation. The disposal of radioactive waste remains a troubling problem. The widespread use of nuclear power complicates the problem of the proliferation of nuclear weapons.

Alternative sources of "clean" energy, such as solar power, are not easily or inexpensively obtained. Hydroelectric power is a possibility only for countries fortunate enough to be able to tap the potential of falling water. Geothermal power, which is comparatively benign

Wind-powered generators near Tehachapi, California, are an example of alternative energy sources favored by the guarded optimists who believe that the earth's supply of fossil fuel is not infinite.

but not entirely pollution free, is by no means universally available. Only wild optimists predict that geothermal energy will constitute more than 20 percent of the world's future energy supply. The loss of cheap, abundant energy is particularly damaging to the dream of a technological solution to the ecological crisis, since so much industrial and agricultural productivity relies on such energy. Cheap energy, for example, has fueled growth and affluence in many industrial, developed nations. The green revolution that significantly increased the food supply now requires increasingly expensive fertilizer (itself dependent on oil) for success. Even with remarkable discoveries such as superconductivity, skeptics conclude that there are decided limits on how far science and technology can go in overcoming the fundamental problems of scarcity, the imbalance of population and resources, and pollution.

A Sustainable Development Model

In 1987, under the auspices of the United Nations, the World Commission on Environment and Development published *Our Common Future*.[23] The report lays out several clear theses. First, the world is under severe environmental stress. Second, sound ecological management is not incompatible with development. In fact, economic growth can and must continue. The question is, "What kind of growth leads to ecological problems and what kind of growth is compatible with sound environmental management?" Third, there is linkage between environmental protection and world peace. Environmental crises present a threat to national security in two ways. Obviously, the threats to the biosphere, oceans, fresh water, and other resources are a danger to human welfare. Beyond this, arms expenditures siphon off valuable resources that could be used for environmental protection.

The strategy that *Our Common Future* proposes for both development and environmental management is called **sustainable development**. The concept has been widely accepted in UN circles and the wider environmental community.[24] As the report notes, sustainable growth contains two key concepts: "the concept of 'needs,' in particular the essential needs of the world's poor, to which overriding priority should be given"; and "the idea of limitations imposed by the state of technology and social organization on the environment's ability to meet present and future needs." [25]

Sustainable development is really a call for what the commission sees as a more rational and equitable approach to development. Growth in the more industrial regions of the world has been highly material and energy intensive, putting enormous strain on the environment. Similarly, but for different reasons, poverty, as found in the developing regions of the world, "reduces people's capacity to use resources in a sustainable manner; it intensifies pressure on the environment." [26] High birthrates along with seemingly desperate overuse of land are but two manifestations of this.

Sustainable development depends on a two-pronged management approach. First, there must be a high degree of responsible and rational management of growth at the national level. Educating people to the damage done by short-term, irrational development is crucial for this to be possible, let alone successful. Second, "sustainable development can be secured only through international cooperation and agreed regimes for surveillance, development, and management in the common interest. . . . Without agreed [upon], equitable, and enforceable rules governing the rights and duties of states in respect to global commons, the pressure of demands on finite resources will destroy their ecological integrity over time." [27]

Numerous international efforts at different stages of development highlight the possibilities of international cooperation. The oceans are governed under the Law of the Sea Treaty, the International Whaling Commission, and the 1985 Convention on Prevention of Marine Pollution by Dumping of Wastes and Other Matter. Space is regulated by the UN Global Environmental Monitoring System and by an outer space treaty that states that outer space is not subject to national appropriation. Antarctica has been the subject of several agreements, including a 1959 treaty that confined the continent to peaceful uses; the 1964 Agreed Measures for Conservation of Antarctic Fauna and Flora; the 1972 Convention of Conservation of Antarctic Seals; and the 1980 Convention on the Conservation of Antarctic Marine Living Resources. These efforts to build effective regimes for managing earth's ecological welfare are only a start. The future is clearly a multilateral one, and much needs to be done to expand and strengthen these regimes as well as to create new ones.

In keeping with the tone set by *Our Common Future,* former U.S. vice president Al Gore proposed a global Marshall Plan. In his 1992 book *Earth in the Balance,* Gore calls for the United States to lead a dramatic multilateral effort to reestablish global ecological balance.[28] The objectives he advocates, while formidable, parallel the concept of sustainable development:

1. stabilization of world population;
2. rapid creation and development of environmentally appropriate technologies;
3. economic accounting that assigns appropriate values to the ecological consequences of marketplace choices made by individuals, companies, and nations;

4. negotiation and approval of a new generation of international agreements;

5. a cooperative plan for educating the world's citizens about our global environment; and

6. establishment, especially in the developing world, of the social and political conditions most likely to build sustainable societies.[29]

More recently, Maurice Strong, former undersecretary general of the United Nations, laid out a similar sustainable development model in a book published in 2001, *Where on Earth Are We Going?* Strong makes a powerful plea when he states:

The basic principles of environmental protection and sustainability must be fully absorbed into the ethos of our industrial civilization and into every aspect of our economic life and behavior.[30]

Creative Breakthrough? The sustainable development argument is appealing. It does not reject the notion of growth. Advocates of sustainable growth claim that development in the poorer parts of the world must proceed and that economic growth in the developed world cannot be halted but must be more environmentally sound. Sound national policy must be combined with more international programs committed to planetary management. To fund national and international efforts, resources now devoted to other priorities, such as the military, must be reallocated.

Critics of sustainable development have serious doubts about the model. Is there not an element of "having one's cake and eating it too" in this philosophy? Are developed countries willing to drastically change their energy-intensive and materially driven economies if such change means they must lower their standards of living? Will the countries that compose the international community be willing to grant international organizations and programs the power necessary to effectively manage the earth's ecological systems? Can governments realistically reach practical accords on the environment? These critical questions raise the possibility that the problems of planet management may require even more radical solutions.

A Steady-State Philosophy

The concept of a steady state is closely related to that of sustainable growth, but the emphasis is different. Clearly, economic growth and development are more important to sustainable growth than to a steady state. Advocates of a steady state are convinced that the present ecological crisis is a deep-seated, ongoing reality and cannot be dealt with through superficial reform and democratic muddling or by relying on a scientific and technological fix. Adopting the minimum, frugal steady state will require radical ecological, political, and economic changes. William Ophuls forcefully advanced this argument in

Figure 18.3   Environmental Demand Versus Carrying Capacity

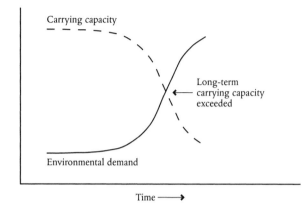

Source: William Ophuls and A. Stephen Boyan Jr., *Ecology and the Politics of Scarcity Revisited: The Unraveling of the American Dream* (New York: W. H. Freeman and Company, 1992), 181.

Note: What this figure depicts is how growth and the carrying capacity of the planet may interact. If growth in such areas as population and industrialization results in environmental degradation, carrying capacity is progressively reduced.

his 1977 book, *Ecology and the Politics of Scarcity: Prologue to a Political Theory of the Steady State,* and again in his 1992 follow-up volume, *Ecology and the Politics of Scarcity Revisited: The Unraveling of the American Dream,* coauthored with A. Stephen Boyan Jr.[31]

Ophuls argues that ecological scarcity adversely affects the political system. It seriously challenges policies of liberal reform. Such liberal policies, he argues, can only briefly postpone the day of reckoning. Our planet's finite character, set against humanity's unchecked exponential growth, materialistic appetites, and indifference to pollution, presages a severe and alarming crisis, for which there is no scientific and technological fix. Figure 18.3 illustrates the crisis in terms of environmental demand versus **carrying capacity**—that is, the ability of the planet to support human and other forms of life. Ophuls estimates that the saturation point will be reached by 2036. Ecological scarcity involves shortages of food and of mineral and energy resources. Our ability to use technology to increase resources is limited. Earth is a finite planet with finite and increasingly costly resources and technology.

The only sane response to the ecological crisis, according to Ophuls, is a steady-state philosophy. He defines a steady-state society as "one that has achieved a basic long-term balance between the demands of a population and the environment that supplies its wants."[32] Such a society calls for a healthy biosphere, careful use of resources, wise limitations on consumption, long-term goals to guide short-term choices, and a respect for future generations. Human beings must learn to live within their annual incomes and thus avoid eating up the world's capital. They must manage the planet prudently so that it continues to nourish this generation and future generations.

Ophuls believes that swift action in the right way can achieve transition to a high-level steady state. Otherwise, a lower-level steady state may result, or people may even be forced back to a premodern, agrarian way of life. The philosophy of the steady state requires that we physically tune into the cycle of nature, that we try to replenish what we withdraw. It is vital that we maintain population within our planet's ecological carrying capacity.

We must also consider the sociopolitical characteristics of the steady-state society. Politically, Ophuls favors the Jeffersonian ideal: small, self-governing communities associated with a federal government pursuing clearly defined national purposes. As people turn away from the rape of the globe, from mindless growth, they will find economic, social, and political satisfaction and personal fulfillment. Humanity will have to move away from rampant individualism to place a higher priority on community and the common good. The community will need authority to enforce its demands on individuals. Although authority need not be remote, arbitrary, and capricious, and although basic rights will have to be retained in a constitutional system, the right to ecological destruction will have to be curbed. Ophuls anticipates a shift from egalitarian democracy toward political competence and stratification. He looks to agreed-on governmental values—"aristocratic principles"—favoring the common interests of the steady state. Ideally, a class of elites, under constitutional restraints, would govern in accord with a steady-state philosophy of virtuous restraint. Liberal, laissez-faire, muddling-through politics will no longer do. Courageous political decisions will have to be made on behalf of ecological health. Such health will not result from the free play of market forces; such free play has only produced "the tragedy of the commons."

Ophuls also sees diversity as a characteristic of the steady state society. He looks forward to a greater role for small-scale enterprise. He anticipates great opportunities for people at the local level.

The steady-state society will more genuinely embrace the principle of holism—the interrelationship of the whole global system. A new, more virtuous and spiritual morality will characterize the steady-state philosophy. Ophuls believes that people will cultivate a more mature economy to protect precious resources and the quality of life. Care for the earth will reward humanity with beauty and amenity as well as ample sustenance. The modern age of thoughtless growth will come to an end.

Ophuls's steady state offers a happy mean between degrading poverty and wasteful abundance. He insists that the steady state is not stagnation, that it does not oppose all forms of growth. Rather, it seeks a dynamic equilibrium affording ample opportunity for ethical, cultural, and scientific growth. Ophuls is sympathetic to small-scale and self-sufficient enterprises that help individuals control their own economic lives.

Creative Breakthrough? What can we say of the strengths and weaknesses of this philosophy of the steady state? The vision of a harmonious balance between people and resources is most attractive. So, too, is a world of ample sufficiency that provides generous scope for artistic, intellectual, moral, scientific, and spiritual fulfillment. A philosophical review of materialistic and aggressive appetites (toward other peoples and nations as well as toward the planet) has long been in order. The philosophy of growth and progress needs critical analysis, as does our often unthinking reliance on science and technology. **Metanoia**—a fundamental transformation of our worldview—may be required to meet the ecological challenge.

But are the steady-state philosophers correct in their empirical analysis of the ecological crisis? And if they are right, is their prescription desirable and feasible? These questions call attention to possible weaknesses. The guarded optimists, in particular, disagree with Ophuls's empirical analysis. They see population stabilizing, hence no exhaustion of resources; and they believe pollution can be controlled. They insist that Ophuls's extrapolations about exponential growth are misleading and, furthermore, believe that economic growth will slow in ample time to avert disaster. Above all, science and technology will ensure abundance and defeat pollution.

Even if Ophuls's analysis is correct, and assuming that the steady-state society is desirable, can such a society be achieved? Critics maintain that people lack the will to cut back to a more frugal economics. People are simply not willing to pay the costs of the steady state: reduced economic growth, more modest lifestyles, and the expenses of pollution control. Furthermore, it is not clear that ecological health on the model of the steady state can be achieved without coercive governmental decisions to limit population, direct economic production, avert the tragedy of the commons, and stop pollution. Other critics find Ophuls's preference for "small is beautiful," "aristocratic principles," decentralization, and less government to be reactionary, authoritarian, and contradictory. These critics insist that the clock cannot be turned back on larger economic and political organizations. A central government is needed to ensure the common good; we may need more governmental powers acting on behalf of ecological health rather than fewer.

Benevolent Authoritarianism

Some contemporary critics are convinced that the dangers of ecological ill-health cannot be met in a democratic and constitutional way. They maintain that only benevolent authoritarianism can prevent disaster.[33] They argue that the masses cannot understand the dangers of ecological disorder and that even if they could, neither they nor the governing elites would be willing to adopt steady-state measures to curb population, protect resources, and stop pollution. Consequently, a benevolent elite (which understands the ecological dangers, has the common good and posterity in mind, and has the courage and will to act) must use coercive, authoritarian means to rescue humankind. Such "medicine" will not be pleasant, but it must be taken. If education and propaganda succeed, people will take the medicine voluntarily. If not, the benevolent authoritarian elite must step in.

Thus if people can voluntarily—with the aid of bonuses for small families—limit family size through late marriage, abstinence, contraception, sterilization, and sensible abortion, then stronger compulsory measures may not be necessary. But if population growth threatens the carrying capacity of the planet, then sheer survival may dictate harsher measures. Some worried observers even raise the prospect of triage. According to this concept, the peoples of the world would be divided into thirds: those who can survive with no help; those who can survive with reasonable help; and those considered to be beyond help no matter what is done for them and so will be left to die.

Compulsion will be required to conserve the planet's resources and to overcome pollution. Wasteful production will be prohibited. Government will have to allocate scarce resources equitably. Recycling will be compulsory. Automobile travel will be severely curtailed in favor of mass transportation and bicycles, and will be heavily taxed. Polluters will face significant tax burdens or, in the worst cases, be put out of business.

The benevolent authoritarian government will seek to lower birthrates by lifting the level of economic well-being, education, and social security. And it will go all out to obtain relatively pollution-free energy (such as solar power) and to use the best scientific and economic knowledge in the interest of ecological health.

Creative Breakthrough?   This approach appeals to those who believe that a "strong doctor" is needed to restore ecological health. Proponents maintain that certain democratic freedoms may have to be abandoned in order to deal with the ecological crisis. A kind of ecological constitutional dictatorship may have to be instituted to handle the coming period of great peril. Strong measures may have to be taken to curb population growth, curtail the reckless use of resources, and develop a new set of ecological habits. The alternative may be mass starvation, an increasing gulf between rich and poor, and other social explosions.

Opponents of benevolent authoritarian government feel that the medicine is worse than the disease, that ecological health can be regained in ways more compatible with democratic and constitutional government. They worry about the ecological philosopher-kings who would be in charge. They wonder if people have to be "forced to be free" in quite this way. And, of course, those who doubt that there really is such deep ecological trouble are even less inclined to opt for benevolent authoritarianism.

CONCLUSION

In June 1992 more than 20,000 people representing 172 governments, 1,400 nongovernmental organizations, and hundreds of news media gathered in Rio de Janeiro,

Brazil, for the UN Conference on Environment and Development, otherwise known as the Earth Summit. Attempts to evaluate this conference illustrate the enormous complexity of global ecological problems and related political difficulties. Some people see the conference as a new beginning, a cause for hope. These people base their optimism on the unprecedented level of participation and the growing scientific consensus on the seriousness of our environmental problems. Other observers do not assess the conference so charitably. True, there was a good deal of consciousness raising. But the fine print of the documents produced—the Rio Declaration, Agenda 21, the Convention on Climate Change, the Convention on Biological Diversity, and the Forests Charter—contains no specific targets or timetables. The documents are filled with good intentions but little more. Can the world's nations find the political will and funding to go beyond Rio to address the ecological dilemmas outlined in this chapter?

Another conference, Earth Summit 2002, took place in Johannesburg, South Africa. It remains to be seen whether more meaningful progress toward effective management of the planet's ecological systems took place in comparison with the disappointments of the Rio conference ten years earlier.

Few observers deny the imperative of ecological health. But, as we have seen, many do disagree about the urgency of our short-term problems and the accuracy of long-term predictions. Some of these disagreements may fade as the future confirms or denies trends and forecasts. There can be little doubt, however, that we must work to preserve our home—planet Earth—on which we all live. The form this care must take arouses political dispute. As we have seen, our ecological problems require a momentous political response that taxes the human capacity for wise judgment. In responding to the imperative of ecological health, we must rethink our political values; study the empirical realities of ecology, economics, and politics; consider alternatives and their costs and benefits; and ultimately choose a prudent course of action.

SUGGESTED READINGS

Brown, Lester R., Christopher Flavin, Hilary F. French et al. *State of the World: A Worldwatch Institute Report on Progress toward a Sustainable Society.* Edited by Linda Starke. New York: Norton in association with Worldwatch Institute, annual. Brown and his researchers cover a variety of global environmental problems in this increasingly influential publication.

Brown, Lester R., et al. *Vital Signs: The Trends That Are Shaping Our Future.* New York: Norton in association with Worldwatch Institute. Published annually, this is an excellent companion to Brown's *State of the World* series. Examines key indicators—environmental, economic, military, and social—over periods running from forty to forty-five years, that have major impact on the condition of the planet. Extremely valuable use of statistical data, graphs, and charts.

French, Hilary F. *Vanishing Borders: Protecting the Planet in the Age of Globalization.* Washington, D.C.: Worldwatch Institute, 2001. Thoughtful treatment of the impact of increased global integration on the planet's ecological system.

Hardin, Garrett E. *Exploring New Ethics for Survival.* New York: Viking, 1972. The philosophy of the author of "The Tragedy of the Commons." Will we have to move toward the benevolent authoritarianism that Hardin sees as necessary to cope with harsh ecological realities?

Kahn, Herman. *The Next 200 Years: A Scenario for America and the World.* New York: Morrow, 1976. Articulates the argument of the guarded optimist, who is sympathetic to the technology-and-growth enthusiast and opposed to the guarded pessimist and the convinced neo-Malthusian. Who is right? And what is the price of being wrong? See also Julian L. Simon, and Herman Kahn, eds. *The Resourceful Earth: A Response to Global 2000* (New York: Blackwell, 1984).

Lomborg, Bjorn. *The Skeptical Environmentalist.* New York: Cambridge University Press, 2001. Another optimistic view of our environmental future. See also Lomborg's *Global Crises, Global Solutions* (New York: Cambridge University Press, 2004).

Ophuls, William, and A. Stephen Boyan Jr. *Ecology and the Politics of Scarcity Revisited: The Unraveling of the American Dream.* New York: Freeman, 1992. This follow-up to Ophuls' initial volume, *Ecology and the Politics of Scarcity: Prologue to a Political Theory of the Steady State,* argues that American and democratic values and institutions are "grossly maladapted" to the era of ecological scarcity. Hope for the United States lies in moving toward a politics of the steady state.

Simon, Julian L. *The Ultimate Resource.* Princeton: Princeton University Press, 1981. Reinforces the anti-doomsday position. People working (producing wealth) and creating knowledge are the ultimate resource. Vast natural resources remain to be tapped by science and technology. Will, technique, and money can cope with pollution. We can overcome famine. Population alarmists are wrong. See also Simon's *Population and Development in Poor Countries* (Princeton: Princeton University Press, 1992), and his *The State of Humanity* (Oxford, UK: Blackwell Publishing, 1996).

Strong, Maurice. *Where on Earth Are We Going?* New York: Texere, 2001. A superb treatise on the state of the world and a powerful case for sustainable development by a highly respected former undersecretary general of the United Nations.

United Nations Environment Program. *Global Environment Outlook 3.* London: Earthscan, 2002. As the title indicates, an update on the major environmental problems facing the world.

GLOSSARY TERMS

carrying capacity (p. 443)
Earth Summit (p. 426)
ecology (p. 424)
global warming (p. 426)
greenhouse effect (p. 426)
metanoia (p. 445)
nonrenewable resources (p. 431)
ozone layer (p. 425)
renewable resources (p. 431)
sustainable development (p. 440)
tragedy of the commons (p. 431)

Conclusion

We come, finally, to our last question: *How will the study of politics as a civilizing enterprise be carried on in the twenty-first century?* To answer this question, we may find it helpful to recall the four key concerns we posed in our Introduction, which highlight the features of our approach to the study of politics and political science. Concern for these features must be central to the challenging study of politics in the twenty-first century.

1. Can we as citizens, as well as students of politics, articulate and defend a view of the good political life and its guiding political *values*? At the level of political ethics, we must continue to explore values, institutions, behavior, and policies that maximize life, growth, and fulfillment. We must continue to define such civilizing values as peace, liberty, democracy, human rights, justice, economic well-being, welfare, and ecological balance. Moreover, we must investigate those institutions and behavior patterns that advance voluntary cooperation and accommodation and that resolve conflicts in peaceful and constitutional ways.

2. Can we develop a *science* of politics to help us understand significant political phenomena—the empirical realities of politics? In the twenty-first century, we remain concerned with what advances the good political life and politics as a civilizing process. We seek to understand conflict and cooperation, force and reason, and the interests of key political actors, including nations, interest groups, regional organizations, and the United Nations. We pursue a better empirical understanding of what promotes peace, freedom, justice, and welfare—and what encourages war, tyranny, poverty, and ecological malaise. Students of politics must be cognizant of both the bright and the dark sides of the powerful—and challenging—forces that have shaped modern civilization and that will continue to do so.

3. Can we bring a high level of political *prudence*, or *wisdom*, to bear on judgments about politics and public issues? A wide range of political actors can benefit from an increased capacity for such prudence as they strive to make ethical and rational

choices about war and peace, economic welfare, human rights, and environmental degradation. Exercising restraint and asking the difficult questions underscore the difficult tasks of prudent judgment.

4. Finally, can the student of politics creatively address the *future of politics*? Our concern with political breakthroughs calls attention to a concern for the future of politics as a whole. Political scientists try to learn from the past and attempt to deal with present problems. But they are shortsighted indeed if they do not look into both the immediate and the long-range future. This requires an appreciation of the future effect of values and a knowledge of emerging realities that will transform politics. It also requires an awareness of the need for wise judgments about potential problems and choices. For our final thoughts on the challenge of politics, it is to this task of future projection that we now direct our attention.

Some problems may require students of politics to venture beyond mere wisdom and prudence and search for *creative breakthroughs* that address the most intractable of political problems. Such breakthroughs, as we know, are rare; nevertheless, they do occur. James Madison's breakthrough to the federal republic in the United States or Roger Williams's breakthrough to religious liberty are two historic examples. A present-day example is the founding and continuing evolution of the European Union. Are future creative breakthroughs possible? Breakthroughs that would allow us to confront our demons, including war, genocide, poverty, and environmental degradation?

No one can predict the exact character of future politics. But we are certainly deficient as political scientists and as citizens if we do not think about the future. If politics is to remain a civilizing enterprise, we need to be concerned about how future developments will affect key values and people's vision of the good political life. We must be prepared for whatever unfolds—good or bad. By thinking about the future, we are reminded that politics is about what is possible. As Robert Kennedy, the former U.S. attorney general repeatedly said during his 1968 presidential campaign prior to his assassination: "Some men see things as they are and say why. I dream things that never were and say why not."

Let us consider some scenarios that evolve from current developments. Then, in the interest of stimulating the creative imagination in politics, we will move on to a prophetic planetary scenario. We will view these scenarios as "thought experiments" designed to prepare people for the future.

A Best-Case Scenario

A best-case scenario, based on current developments, presents the fullest consequences of the end of the cold war. Significant disarmament would occur. The burden of the arms race would be lifted. Humane, democratic, and prosperous regimes would emerge in Russia and the other republics of the former Soviet Union. Effective constitutional democracies would triumph in Eastern Europe. The component states and peoples of the former Yugoslavia would learn to live together peacefully and in mutual respect and would also become members of European Union. All of Europe would profit from a common, mutually beneficial market. China's market-based economy would continue to expand, and perhaps a transformation from communism to democracy would begin. North and South Korea would achieve a peaceful reunification under a democratic and constitutional government. Israel and the Palestinians would achieve peace and freedom, fostering a renewed sense of security and prosperity that may lead to a general peace throughout the Middle East. New democracies would replace old autocracies in that region. Peace would also come to troubled Northern Ireland. The countries of the African continent would know peace. A settlement would be arranged between India and Pakistan over the province of Kashmir.

On the broader global canvas, there would be an easing of tensions between cultural groups, and the scourge of terrorism would become little more than a bad memory. Nations would reap the benefits of a "peace and justice" dividend. The United States would achieve a strong and prosperous full-employment economy, usher in a sensible national health care plan, revitalize its educational system, and free the country of crime and drugs. Violent revolution or aggressive war as a means of effecting political change would disappear. An invigorated United Nations would fulfill the objectives of its charter. Debilitating diseases, such as AIDS, would be brought under control. Developing nations would overcome economic malaise and political authoritarianism.

This would be a better, but not a perfect, world. It would still contain sovereign nation-states. There would still be some political and economic rivalry among great and small powers. People of sincere conviction might disagree about the means used to achieve a humane world, but the debate would presume the existence of common ground concerning the ultimate goals. Countries would debate the extent of arms reduction and the character of the peace-and-justice dividend. Discussion would continue about the best way to achieve nuclear disarmament. The developing world would still struggle to overcome poverty and to deal with the persistent gap between rich and poor nations. People would still argue about how to deal with continuing, if somewhat diminished, human rights violations. Disturbing ecological conditions would most likely remain. In the United States, debate would continue on how to make the new economic, health, educational, and social policies work even better.

We, the authors of this book, cannot confidently predict that this best-case scenario will be fulfilled. The end of the cold war did bring about many positive results, but it is by no means clear that all aspects of this rosy scenario will come to pass as the future unfolds. Russia faces a difficult battle in achieving a democratic and constitutional polity and a prosperous free-market economy. Not all nations of Eastern Europe will quickly achieve politically successful and economically productive societies. A measure of arms reduction did take place in the 1990s, but major powers appear once again to be significantly increasing their defense budgets and more countries seek to add nuclear weapons to their arsenals. Despite current stumbling, the long-range economic unification of Western Europe progresses, although fuller political unification still lags far behind. China's path toward a greater measure of domestic freedom will be halting. The displacement of other authoritarian regimes will not occur easily. The Israelis and Palestinians may hammer out a peace of sorts, but a fully harmonious and prosperous Middle East will still have to withstand resistant hardliners. Revolution in the developing world may diminish, but violence, poverty, and authoritarian rule will probably still characterize many of these nations. Civil wars—such as those in Afghanistan, Chechnya, and the Democratic Republic of the Congo—will continue. Although taking its first baby steps toward democratic rule, Iraq could still easily slip into civil war and fall back into rule under another dictator like Saddam Hussein.

For the United States, economic prosperity will be maintained, but full employment will not be achieved. Entitlement programs, such as Social Security and Medicare, will face limited resources and rising costs. More modest proposals for universal health care will evolve, but efforts at full coverage and cost containment will still trouble the health care industry. The nation will continue to struggle to improve its educational system and to combat crime and drugs. Internationally, the United Nations will modestly strengthen its war prevention, peacekeeping, and rights protection capabilities. But it may still have trouble moving from rhetorical resolutions and modest actions to more complete fulfillment of the laudable objectives of its charter.

A Worst-Case Scenario

As they face the future, resourceful students of politics would be wise also to anticipate worst-case scenarios that could develop from present realities. A worst-case scenario would envisage a resumption of great-power rivalry among developed nations and all of its debilitating consequences. Authoritarian rule would resurface in Russia as its democratic experiment collapses. Tensions between the People's Republic of China and the Nationalist government on Taiwan would escalate into a full-blown conflict, drawing the United States into a violent conflict with mainland China in the Taiwan Straits. North Korea, seeking to take advantage of the chaos, would launch a military attack on South Korea.

The arms race would accelerate. Horizontal proliferation of nuclear weapons would transform limited nuclear powers, such as India, Iran, Israel, North Korea, and Pakistan, into major players. The probability of weapon deployment would increase significantly.

European tensions would once again resurface as some of the countries in Eastern Europe face economic failure. The Balkan region would once again erupt in a vicious cycle of ethno-nationalistic violence. Economic depression would sweep through Europe, fracturing the carefully constructed European Union.

The hope for peace and justice following the end of the cold war would evaporate. Poverty and authoritarian rule would sweep through large parts of the developing world, reversing much of the progress of the years since the end of the cold war. AIDS and a new strain of influenza would become pandemic. Violent revolution, civil war, and aggressive war would return to many areas of the globe. Iran would ultimately dominate the Middle East, control world oil prices, and dominate the Islamic world. Because of a failure by major economic powers to collectively plan for their energy needs, including the development of alternative fuels, tensions over access to fossil fuels would turn into a violent war for natural resources. The moderate governments of Algeria, Egypt, Saudi Arabia, and other Islamic countries would topple to Islamic religious fundamentalism.

The United States would fail to get its economic, political, and social act together. Its budget and trade deficits would grow menacingly larger. The nation would slide into a persistent recession. Unemployment would rise to 15 to 20 percent. Racial unrest would explode in the nation's cities. Health care would decline, and housing would deteriorate. Educational reform would fail. Drugs and crime would be rampant.

The United Nations would be incapable of dealing with the difficult issues dividing the great powers. The financial strains on the organization would be so great that it would, in effect, declare bankruptcy and collapse.

Will such a worst-case scenario really materialize? Probably not. But it would be foolish to ignore the underlying realities that might produce such a scenario or at least its key parts. These realities include the persistence of great-power rivalries and the rivalries of other nations. They also include Russia's difficulties in achieving economic and political reform and, as a result, a stable society; the comparable difficulties facing some Eastern European nations trying to overcome a legacy of political and economic authoritarianism; mainland Chinese aspirations to regain control of Taiwan; and the festering violence between Israel and the Palestinians. Meanwhile, a number of countries continue their efforts to build nuclear or chemical and biological warfare capabilities. And the global society continues to consume natural resources at an alarming rate.

In sum, the world is filled with the realities of frustrated nationalistic and ethnic aspirations and ambitions, weapons acquisition, chronic poverty, and authoritarianism in many developing countries; environmental degradation on a planetary level; and the very limited capabilities of even the best-intentioned nations to address these problems.

A more balanced assessment of the realities of the U.S. political experience suggests that the United States will probably not slide into economic, political, and social disaster. It remains strong economically. Historically, the nation has demonstrated a pragmatic ability to deal with problems once it perceives that they must be faced. The odds are highly favorable that the United States will control its finances, shore up its social and health care infrastructures, revitalize its economy, improve its educational system, and in all other respects avert a worst-case scenario. So, too, a worst-case scenario will probably not see the United Nations disintegrate in economic ruin.

A Prophetic Planetary Scenario

It is also possible to move beyond the best-case scenario presented here. It is possible to envisage a transition to a twenty-first century characterized by planetary prophetic politics. Here we come to the greatest challenge confronting political scientists as they approach the future: Can ethical, scientific, and prudential resources really be used to usher in a world without catastrophic war, flagrant violations of human rights, egregious poverty, or dangerous ecological malaise? This scenario envisages a world in which conflicts are handled in a genuinely constitutional way; in which prevention would make political, legal, and military remedies for violations of human rights unnecessary; in which peoples and communities work together for economic well-being; and in which the steps necessary to ensure ecological health have been taken. This scenario imagines a world in which nations and regional, functional, and global communities cooperate fully and generously to advance the creative situations outlined in our discussion of a best-case scenario.

The steps necessary to move toward these goals call for numerous creative breakthroughs in politics. Although political scientists would not be the only ones involved in such breakthroughs (humanists, physical and biological scientists, and social scientists from other disciplines would also participate), they would play a leading role. And as creative breakthroughs to a more prophetic politics occurred, individuals all over the globe would be able to cultivate that excellent quality of life that is the supreme mark of politics as a civilizing enterprise.

Is such a scenario possible? Yes, because we can envision it. Is it probable? Given our current understanding of political realities, it is not highly probable. Nonetheless, we may be able to take significant strides toward fulfilling key features of this scenario. How far we can go will depend on the creative steps we take now and in the future.

It is possible to be both bold and prudent in politics. The possibilities of creative human endeavor encourage people to be bold. The limits to human endeavor—the dangers of pride—encourage us to be prudent. Sometimes, however, the prudent course is the bold course, and the bold course is the prudent course. Genuine and effective worldwide arms reduction is both bold and prudent. Establishing global constitutional machinery to protect human rights is also bold and prudent. Similarly, it is both audacious and wise to adopt policies and develop programs to advance economic well-being, particularly for poor people in developing countries. It is both courageous and sensible to move globally toward some version of a balanced ecological order. Our success in these creative endeavors is a test for a creative political science in the twenty-first century.

SUGGESTED READING

Barber, Benjamin R. *Jihad vs. McWorld: How Globalism and Tribalism Are Reshaping the World.* New York: Ballantine Books, 1996. Argues that vices of parochial tribalism and commercial globalism are threats to a democratic future. Suggests combining the virtues of a healthier, wealthier world with a sense of democratic community that respects liberty, variety, and difference.

Falk, Richard. *On Humane Governance: Toward a New Global Politics.* University Park: Pennsylvania State University Press, 1995. Articulates the views of one of the most perceptive advocates of a global politics that can overcome key weaknesses of the present sovereign nation-state system.

Friedman, Thomas. *The Lexus and the Olive Tree: Understanding Globalization.* Revised edition. New York: Farrar, Straus & Giroux, 2000. Eminently readable and basically optimistic description of the globalization process and its potential problems. See also Friedman's *The World is Flat* (New York: Farrar, Straus & Giroux, 2005).

Galbraith, John Kenneth. *The Good Society: The Humane Agenda.* Boston: Houghton Mifflin, 1996. A seasoned economist's assessment of past, present, and future.

Kaplan, Robert. *The Coming Anarchy: Shattering the Dreams of the Post Cold War.* New York: Random House, 2000. A very grim yet fascinating view of the global political environment now and in the future.

Strong, Maurice. *Where on Earth Are We Going?* New York: Texere, 2000. A superb treatise on the state of the world and a powerful case for sustainable development by a highly respected former undersecretary general of the United Nations.

Notes

CHAPTER 1

1. The description here and in the following paragraphs is derived from *The Complete Writings of Thucydides: The Peloponnesian War,* trans. Richard Crowley (New York: Random House, Modern Library Edition, 1951), 330–337.
2. U.S. State Department, *Country Reports on Human Rights Practices for 1989* (Washington, D.C.: U.S. Government Printing Office, 1990), 792.
3. Mark Burgess, "A Brief History of Terrorism," Center for Defense Information, July 2, 2003, http://cide.org/friendlyversion/printversion.cfm?documented=1502.
4. The following discussion is based on Niccolò Machiavelli, *The Prince,* trans. Luigi Ricci, rev. by E. R. P. Vincent, and *The Discourses,* trans. Christian Detmold, in *The Prince and the Discourses* (New York: Random House, Modern Library Edition, 1940).
5. See Aristophanes, *Lysistrata: An English Version by Dudley Fitts* (New York: Harcourt Brace, 1954).
6. See "On Civil Disobedience" in *Walden and Other Writings of Henry David Thoreau* (New York: Random House, Modern Library Edition, 1937).
7. Karl Marx illuminates the game of "class conflict"; Alexander Hamilton, that of "stake-in-society"; Fyodor Dostoevsky, that of "miracle, mystery, and authority." See, for example, Marx's *The Communist Manifesto;* Hamilton's state papers; and Dostoevsky's "Legend of the Grand Inquisitor," book 5, chap. 5, of *The Brothers Karamozov.* On Dostoevsky, see also Neal Riemer, "Some Reflections on the Grand Inquisitor and Modern Democratic Theory," *Ethics* 14, no. 4 (1954–1955): 458–470.

CHAPTER 2

1. The quotations in this paragraph and the following are from *Apology, The Republic, and Other Works by Plato,* trans. Benjamin Jowett (Garden City, N.Y.: Doubleday, Anchor Books, 1973), 460–484.
2. In *Federalist* No. 10, Madison defined *faction* as "a number of citizens, whether amounting to a majority or minority of the whole, who are united and actuated by some common impulse of passion, or of interest, adversed to the rights of other citizens, or to the permanent and aggregate interests of the community." *The Federalist (1787–1788)* (Cleveland: World, 1961), 57.

3. This section draws freely from Neal Riemer's *James Madison: Creating the American Constitution* (Washington, D.C.: Congressional Quarterly, 1986). For a fuller exploration of creative breakthroughs, see Riemer, *Creative Breakthroughs in Politics* (Westport, Conn.: Praeger, 1996).

4. Franz L. Neumann, *Behemoth* (New York: Oxford University Press, 1942), 30.

5. For the electoral statistics, see Seymour Martin Lipset, *Political Man: The Social Bases of Politics* (1960; reprint, Garden City, N.Y.: Doubleday, Anchor Books, 1962), 139; and Jeremy Noakes and Geoffrey Pridham, eds., *Documents of Nazism, 1919–1945* (London: Jonathan Cape, 1974), 126.

6. Neumann, *Behemoth,* 30.

7. Lipset, *Political Man,* 138–148. See also David Schoenbaum, *Hitler's Social Revolution: Class and Status in Nazi Germany, 1933–1939* (New York: W. W. Norton, 1997); and Noakes and Pridham, *Documents of Nazism.*

8. Seymour Martin Lipset, *Revolution and Counterrevolution* (1968; reprint, Garden City, N.Y.: Doubleday, Anchor Books, 1970), 234.

9 Lipset, *Revolution and Counterrevolution,* 234.

10. Schoenbaum, *Hitler's Social Revolution.*

11. Graham T. Allison, *Essence of Decision: Explaining the Cuban Missile Crisis* (Boston: Little, Brown, 1971), 193. See also Graham T. Allison and Philip Zelikow, *The Essence of Decision: Explaining the Cuban Missile Crisis,* 2nd ed. (New York: Longman, 1999). The following presentation draws generously on Allison's study and also on the account by Arthur M. Schlesinger Jr., *A Thousand Days: John F. Kennedy in the White House* (1965; reprint, Greenwich, Conn.: Fawcett Crest, 1967).

12. Schlesinger, *Thousand Days,* 805–806.

13. As it appears in Michael R. Beschloss, *The Crisis Years: Kennedy and Khrushchev, 1960–1963* (New York: HarperCollins, 1991), 505–506.

14. Laurence Change and Peter Kornbluh, eds., *The Cuban Missile Crisis, 1962: A National Security Archive Documents Reader* (New York: New Press, 1998), 198.

CHAPTER 3

1. The word *empirical* may be unfamiliar to some readers. As used here, it means "that which is based on experience and observation." The word *behavioral* refers to those actions, or forms of behavior, that can be observed.

2. The concept of prudence was first treated systematically in book 6 of Aristotle's *Nichomachean Ethics.* The concept figures prominently in the writings of St. Thomas Aquinas (particularly I–II, Q. 21, A4, 5, 6 of his *Summa Theologica*), Edmund Burke, and James Madison. Charles Merriam, an outstanding American political scientist, devoted a section to "Political Prudence" in his *New Aspects of Political Science* (Chicago: University of Chicago Press, 1939), 163–180. Merriam defined political prudence as: "the conclusions of experience and reflection regarding the problems of politics—wisdom that does not reach the state of science, yet has its own significance" (p. 163). Leo Strauss was well aware of the concept; see his *What Is Political Philosophy?* (Glencoe, Ill.: Free Press, 1959), especially pp. 81–82 and 86–87. The concept is also treated prominently in Neal Riemer's *The Revival of Democratic Theory* (New York: Appleton-Century-Crofts, 1962).

3. For an illustrative reassessment of welfare policy in the United States (as it bears on equality, poverty, and unemployment), see the excellent study by David Raphael Riemer, *The Prisoners of Welfare: Liberating America's Poor from Unemployment and Low Wages* (New York: Praeger, 1988).

4. Karl Deutsch, *The Nerves of Government* (New York: Free Press, 1963), 178. For a provocative, sharply adverse critique of American political science's obsession with a narrow view of science and its attachment to, yet ironic neglect of, classic wisdom and democratic ideals, see David M. Ricci, *The Tragedy of Political Science: Politics, Scholarship, and Democracy* (New Haven: Yale University Press, 1984). For a more balanced view, see Gabriel Almond, "Separate Tables: Schools and Sects in Political Science," *PS: Political Science and Politics* 21 (fall 1988): 838–842. Almond contends that mainstream "political science is open to all methods that illuminate the world of politics and public policy."

5. Leo Strauss, "What Is Political Philosophy?" *Journal of Politics* 19, no. 3 (1957): 100–107, especially p. 101.

6. Robert Dahl, *Modern Political Analysis* (Englewood Cliffs, N.J.: Prentice Hall, 1964), 100–107.

7. John H. Hallowell, "Political Science Today," *Social Order* 11, no. 2 (1961): 109, 113, 120, 121.

8. Alfred Cobban, "The Decline of Political Theory," *Political Science Quarterly* 68, no. 3 (1963): 321–337, especially pp. 330, 335.

9. David Easton, *A Framework for Political Analysis* (Englewood Cliffs, N.J.: Prentice Hall, 1965), especially pp. 7, 8, 13ff.

10. Albert Somit and Joseph Tanenhous, *The Development of American Political Sciences* (Boston: Allyn and Bacon, 1967), especially pp. 177–179.

11. Two excellent works in the area of rational choice are Anthony Downs, *An Economic Theory of Democracy* (New York: Longman, 1997); and Kenneth A. Shepsle and Mark S. Bonchek, *Analyzing Politics: Rationality, Behavior, and Institutions* (New York: Norton, 1997).

12. Hans J. Morgenthau, *The Decline of Democratic Politics*, vol. 1 of *Politics in the Twentieth Century* (Chicago: University of Chicago Press, 1962), especially pp. 41, 43, 45, 48, 49.

13. See David Riemer, *Prisoners of Welfare*.

14. Neal Riemer, *Revival of Democratic Theory*, especially pp. 60–65. On prudence and political judgment, see also the fine book by Ronald Beiner, *Political Judgment* (Chicago: University of Chicago Press, 1983).

15. Bertrand de Jouvenal, "Political Science and Prevision," *American Political Science Review* 59, no. 1 (1965): 29–38, especially p. 29.

16. Harold Lasswell, *The Future of Political Science* (New York: Atherton Press, 1963), especially pp. 1, 17–26.

17. David Easton, "The New Revolution in Political Science," *American Political Science Review* 63, no. 4 (1969): 1051–1061, especially p. 1052.

18. See Neal Riemer, *The Future of the Democratic Revolution: Toward a More Prophetic Politics* (New York: Praeger, 1984), especially pp. 236–237; and Riemer, "Political Health as an Integration Model in Political Systems Theory," *Systems Research* 3, no. 2 (1986): 85–88.

CHAPTER 4

1. Jacob Bronowski, *The Common Sense of Science* (New York: Vintage Books, 1960), 100, 130.
2. Irving M. Copi, *Introduction to Logic,* 2nd ed. (New York: Macmillan, 1961), 418.
3. Karl R. Popper, *The Logic of Scientific Discovery* (London: Hutchinson, 1968), 281.
4. Ibid., 280.
5. David Easton, *The Political System: An Inquiry into the State of Political Science* (New York: Knopf, 1953), 66–78.
6. Abraham Kaplan, *The Conduct of Inquiry: Methodology for Behavioral Science* (San Francisco: Chandler, 1964), 308.

CHAPTER 5

1. Population data from the Population Division, Department of Economic and Social Affairs, United Nations, *World Population Prospects: The 2004 Revision* (February 2005).
2. Sandra L. Postel and Aaron T. Wolf, "Dehydrating Conflict," *Foreign Policy* (September–October 2001): 60–67.
3. This discussion follows Abraham Maslow's analysis in *Motivation and Personality,* 3rd ed. (New York: Addison-Wesley, 1987).
4. Konrad Lorenz, *On Aggression* (New York: Harcourt, Brace, and World, 1966); Robert Ardrey, *The Territorial Imperative* (New York: Dell, 1966).
5. Leonard Berkowitz, *Aggression: Social Psychological Analysis* (New York: McGraw-Hill, 1962).
6. Julian S. Huxley, *On Living in a Revolution* (New York: Harper, 1944), 114.
7. Ibid.
8. This paragraph and the following two cite Erich Fromm, *The Anatomy of Human Destructiveness* (New York: Holt, Rinehart, and Winston, 1973), 230–232.
9. R. Scott Appleby, *Religious Fundamentalism and Global Conflict,* Headline Series (New York: Foreign Policy Association, 1994), ii.
10. Grant Wacker, "The Christian Right," Teacher Serve, National Humanities Center, October 2000, http://www.nhc.rtp.nc.us:8080/tserve/twenty/tkeyinfo/chrrght.htm.
11. Crane Brinton, *Anatomy of Revolution* (New York: Vintage, 1972).
12. Gabriel A. Almond and Sidney Verba, *The Civic Culture: Political Attitudes and Democracy in Five Nations* (Boston: Little, Brown, 1965), 312–313.
13. David P. Conradt, "Changing German Political Culture," in *The Civic Culture Revisited,* ed. Gabriel A. Almond and Sidney Verba (Boston: Little, Brown, 1980), 246, 256, 264–265.

CHAPTER 6

1. Plato, *The Republic,* trans. Benjamin Jowett (Garden City, N.Y.: Doubleday, Anchor, 1973).
2. Aristotle, *Politics,* trans. Benjamin Jowett (New York: Random House, Modern Library, 1943), 168–169.

3. Augustine, *The City of God,* in *Readings in Political Philosophy,* ed. Francis W. Coker (New York: Macmillan, 1946), 159.

4. Thomas Aquinas, *Commentary on the Nicomachean Ethics,* in *Theories of the Political System,* ed. William T. Bluhm (Englewood Cliffs, N.J.: Prentice Hall, 1965), 196.

5. *Summa Theologica* (1265–1273), I–II, 90.4, in *The Basic Writings of St. Thomas Aquinas,* ed. Anton C. Pegis (New York: Macmillan, 1946), 200.

6. Thomas Aquinas, *Of the Rule of Princes (1266),* quoted in Coker, *Readings,* 200.

7. See Niccolò Machiavelli, *The Discourses,* trans. Luigi Ricci and rev. E. R. P. Vincent, in *The Prince and the Discourses* (New York: Random House, Modern Library, 1940).

8. Thomas Hobbes, *Leviathan* (New York: Dutton, 1943), 64–65.

9. John Locke, *Second Treatise on Civil Government* (1690). A good critical edition is Peter Laslett's *John Locke: Two Treatises of Government* (Cambridge: Cambridge University Press, 1960).

10. Jean-Jacques Rousseau, *The Social Contract* (1762; reprint, New York: Dutton, 1946), 1.

11. See, for example, Edmund Burke, *Reform of Representation in the House of Commons, 1782,* in *Burke's Politics: Selected Writings and Speeches on Reform, Revolution, and War,* ed. Ross J. S. Hoffman and Paul Levack (New York: Knopf, 1949). See also Burke, *Reflections on the Revolution in France* (1790) in *The Works of the Right Honorable Edmund Burke* (Boston: Little, Brown, 1869), vol. 3; and *An Appeal from the New to the Old Whigs* (1791) and *On Conciliation with the American Colonies* (1787), in *Orations and Essays* (New York: Appleton, 1900).

12. Burke, *Reflections,* 359.

13. John Stuart Mill, *Utilitarianism* (New York: Liberal Arts Press, 1957), 10.

14. John Stuart Mill, *Considerations on Representative Government* (1861), in *On Liberty, Representative Government, the Subjection of Women* (London: Oxford University Press, 1946), 198.

15. Mill, *The Subjection of Women,* in *On Liberty,* 427.

16. Of particular value here is Robert C. Tucker, ed., *The Marx-Engels Reader* (New York: Norton, 1971).

17. William T. Bluhm, *Theories of the Political System* (Englewood Cliffs, N.J.: Prentice-Hall, 1965), preface, vi.

CHAPTER 7

1. In this and succeeding sections, the senior author drew from his work in the field of democratic theory: Riemer, "Democracy: Merits and Prospects," in *World Affairs: Problems and Prospects,* by Elton Atwater et al. (New York: Appleton-Century-Crofts, 1958); *The Revival of Democratic Theory* (New York: Appleton-Century-Crofts, 1962); *The Democratic Experiment* (Princeton: Van Nostrand, 1967); *The Future of the Democratic Revolution: Toward a More Prophetic Politics* (New York: Praeger, 1984); *James Madison: Creating the American Constitution* (Washington, D.C.: Congressional Quarterly, 1986); *Let Justice Roll: Prophetic Challenges in Religion, Politics, and Society* (Lanham, Md.: Rowman and Littlefield, 1996); and *Creative Breakthroughs in Politics* (Westport, Conn.: Praeger, 1996).

2. See Neal Riemer, ed., *The Representative: Trustee? Delegate? Partisan? Politico?* (Boston: Heath, 1967).

3. See William S. Maddox and Stuart A. Lilie, *Beyond Liberal and Conservative: Reassessing the Political Spectrum* (Washington, D.C.: Cato Institute, 1984). For Theodore Lowi's classification of the traditions of American political thought, see Table 1.3 in his *End of the Republican Era* (Norman: University of Oklahoma Press, 1995), 19.

4. For a recent assessment of liberalism, see Riemer, *Future of the Democratic Revolution,* chap. 4, "Liberal Democratic Politics: The Conservative Politics of Pluralistic Balance."

5. The idea of "possessive individualism" was developed by C. B. Macpherson in his seminal work, *The Political Theory of Possessive Liberalism: Hobbes to Locke* (New York: Oxford University Press, 1962).

6. David Halberstam, *The Best and the Brightest,* 20th anniversary ed. (New York: Fawcett Books, 1993).

CHAPTER 8

1. For help in understanding the remarkable changes that have occurred in the communist world, see Zbigniew Brzezinski, *The Grand Failure: The Birth and Death of Communism in the Twentieth Century* (New York: Scribner's, 1989); and Adam B. Ulam, *The Communist: The Story of Power and Lost Illusion, 1948–1991* (New York: Scribner's, 1992).

2. Frank E. Manuel, *The New World of Henri Saint-Simon* (Notre Dame: University of Notre Dame Press, 1963), 5. On utopian thought in general, see the splendid study by Frank E. Manuel and Fritzie P. Manuel, *Utopian Thought in the Western World* (Cambridge: Harvard University Press, 1979).

3. See Robert Owen's *New View of Society* (1813), quoted in George Lichtheim, *The Origins of Socialism* (New York: Praeger, 1969), 114.

4. Lichtheim, *Origins of Socialism,* 34.

5. This account draws on Peter Gay, *The Dilemma of Democratic Socialism: Eduard Bernstein's Challenge to Marx* (New York: Collier-Macmillan, 1962). See Eduard Bernstein, *Evolutionary Socialism* (New York: Schocken, 1961); and Leszek Kolakowski's account of "Bernstein and Revisionism," in *The Breakdown,* vol. 3 of *Main Currents of Marxism* (New York: Oxford University Press, 1978).

6. Anthony Crosland, *Socialism Now and Other Essays by Anthony Crosland,* ed. Dick Leonard (London: Cape, 1974).

7. Karl Marx, *Critique of the Gotha Program,* in *The Marx-Engels Reader,* 2nd ed., ed. Robert C. Tucker (New York: Norton, 1978), 531.

8. Karl Marx, "The German Ideology: Part 1," in *Marx-Engels Reader,* 155–156.

9. Karl Marx and Friedrich Engels, *Manifesto of the Communist Party,* in *Marx-Engels Reader,* 473–474. For definitions of *bourgeoisie* and *proletariat,* see the footnote added by Engels in 1888 in *Marx-Engels Reader,* 473.

10. V. I. Lenin, *Imperialism: The Highest Stage of Capitalism,* in *The Lenin Anthology,* ed. Robert Tucker (New York: Norton, 1975), 244.

11. Karl Marx, "The Possibility of Non-Violent Revolution," in *Marx-Engels Reader,* 523.

12. V. I. Lenin, "The Three Sources and Three Component Parts of Marxism," in *Lenin Anthology,* 640–644.

13. Karl Marx, "Theses on Feuerbach," in *Marx-Engels Reader,* 145.

14. John Plamenatz, *German Marxism and Russian Communism* (London: Longman, 1954), 308. On Marx and the utopian tradition, see Manuel and Manuel, *Utopian Thought.*

15. See Tucker, *Lenin Anthology;* and Alfred G. Meyer, *Leninism* (New York: Praeger, 1962).

16. The February date is the date according to the Russian calendar, which, until changed by Lenin not long after the Russian Revolution, was about a half month behind the Western calendar.

17. See V. I. Lenin, *The State and Revolution,* in *Lenin Anthology.*

18. Joseph Stalin, *Problems of Leninism* (Moscow: Foreign Language, 1940). See also Kolakowski, *Breakdown.*

19. On Mao, see Stuart R. Schram, *The Thought of Mao Tse-tung* (Cambridge: Cambridge University Press, 1989); John Bryan Starr, *Continuing the Revolution: The Political Thought of Mao* (Princeton: Princeton University Press, 1979); and Ross Terrill, *China in Our Time* (New York: Simon and Schuster, 1992).

20. James R. Townsend and Brantly Womack, *Politics in China* (Boston: Little Brown, 1986).

21. Some defenders of communism hold that it is a liberating philosophy and that the Soviet Union never truly practiced communism. This raises the question of the relation of Marx's Marxism to the Soviet Union. Kolakowski, in *Breakdown,* 226, writes: "It would be absurd to maintain that Marxism was, so to speak, the efficient cause of present-day Communism; on the other hand, Communism is not a mere 'degeneration' of Marxism but a possible interpretation of it, and even a well-founded one, though primitive and partial in some respects."

22. Mikhail Gorbachev, *Perestroika: New Thinking for Our Country and the World* (New York: Harper and Row, 1988).

23. See Terrill, *China in Our Time;* and (for the quotation) Roderick MacFarquhar, "Deng's Last Campaign," *New York Review of Books,* December 17, 1992, 22.

CHAPTER 9

1. Guy Hermet, "Dictatorship/dictator" in *The Blackwell Encyclopedia of Political Science,* ed. Vernon Bogdanor, (Oxford: Basil Blackwood, 1991) , 174–175.

2. See S. E. Finer, *The History of Government,* vol. 1 (Oxford: Oxford University Press, 1999), 76–77.

3. Hermet, "Dictatorship/dictator," 174–175.

4. See Finer, *History of Government,* vol. 1, book 2, chap. 4.

5. See S. E. Finer, "Authoritarianism," in *The Blackwell Encyclopedia of Political Science,* 34–35.

6. Joseph de Maistre, *"The Works of Joseph de Maistre,"* trans and ed. Jack Lively (New York: Macmillan, 1965), 207.

7. Paul M. Hayes, *Fascism* (New York: Free Press, 1973), 23. In our presentation of Nazi roots we follow, with modifications, Hayes's presentation of eight fascist ideas, 2–119. See also Walter Laquer, *Fascism: Past, Present, and Future* (New York: Oxford University Press, 1996).

8. For a record of Nazi imperialism, war, and destruction, see Karl D. Bracher, *The German Dictatorship* (New York: Praeger, 1970); William L. Shirer, *The Rise and Fall of the Third Reich* (New York:

Simon and Schuster, 1960); Lucy S. Dawidowicz, *The War against the Jews, 1933–1945* (New York: Holt, Rinehart, and Winston, 1975); Daniel J. Goldhagen, *Hitler's Willing Executioners: Ordinary Germans and the Holocaust* (New York: Knopf, 1996). For a comparative study of totalitarianism, see Bruce F. Pauley, *Hitler, Stalin, and Mussolini: Totalitarianism in the Twentieth Century* (Wheeling, Ill.: Harlan Davidson, 1997).

9. Hayes, *Fascism,* 66.

10. For a brief analysis of Bodin's definition of *sovereignty* ("supreme power over citizens and subjects, unrestrained by law"), see George H. Sabine, *A History of Political Theory* (New York: Holt, 1937), 405–411. See also Jean Bodin, *The Six Bookes of a Commonweale,* trans. and ed. Richard Knolles, with an introduction by Douglas McRae (Cambridge: Harvard University Press, 1962).

11. Hayes, *Fascism,* 106.

12. Heinrich von Treitschke, *Politics,* abridged and ed., with introduction, Hans Kohn, and trans. Blanche Dugdale and Torebende Bille (New York: Harcourt, Brace, and World, 1963).

13. Frederich Nietzsche, *The Genealogy of Morals,* trans. Walter Kaufmann (New York: Vintage Books, 1989); and Nietzsche, *The Will to Power,* trans. R. Hollingdale and Walter Kaufmann (New York: Random House, 1987).

14. Oswald Spengler, *The Decline of the West,* ed. Helmut Werner and trans. Charles F. Atkinson (New York: Oxford University Press, 1991).

CHAPTER 10

1. J. David Singer, "The Level-of-Analysis Problem in International Relations," in *The International System: Theoretical Essays,* ed. Klaus Knorr and Sidney Verba (Princeton: Princeton University Press, 1961), 77–92.

2. See Hans J. Morgenthau, *Politics among Nations,* 2nd ed. (New York: Knopf, 1954). See also Charles A. Beard, *The Idea of National Interest* (Chicago: Quadrangle Books, 1966). Beard writes that "it may be said that national interest—its maintenance, advancement, and defense by the various means and instrumentalities of political power—is the prime consideration of diplomacy" (p. 21).

3. For clarification of the concept of public interest, see Richard E. Flathman, *The Public Interest: An Essay Concerning the Normative Discourse of Politics* (New York: Wiley, 1966).

4. Some of the better-known efforts in this area include the work of (a) the Correlates of War Project, directed by J. David Singer, at the University of Michigan; (b) the Stockholm International Peace Research Institute (SIPRI); and (c) the Conflict Data Project at the Department of Peace and Conflict Research, Uppsala University, Sweden.

5. Zbigniew Brzezinski, *Out of Control: Global Turmoil on the Eve of the Twenty-First Century* (New York: Scribner's, 1993), 9–10.

6. Samuel P. Huntington, *The Clash of Civilizations and the Remaking of World Order* (New York: Simon and Schuster, 1996).

7. See Robert Dahl, *On Democracy* (New Haven: Yale University Press, 1998), appendix C.

8. On the CIA, for example, see Senate Committee on Foreign Relations, *CIA Foreign and Domestic Activities,* 94th Cong., 1st sess. (Washington, D.C.: U.S. Government Printing Office, 1974). On Chile, see Robert C. Johansen, *The National Interest and the Human Interest: An Analysis of U.S. Foreign Policy* (Princeton: Princeton University Press, 1980), chap. 4, "The United States and Human Rights in Chile," 196–281. On the FBI, see Senate Committee to Study Government Operations with Respect to Intelligence, *Intelligence Activities and the Rights of Americans,* Book II, 94th Cong., 2nd sess. (Washington, D.C.: U.S. Government Printing Office, 1976).

9. Information for these two paragraphs extracted from: Stockholm International Peace Research Institute (SIPRI), "Recent Trends in Military Expenditures," 2004, www.sipri.org ; id21 Insights, "Military Spending and Development," 2005, www.id21.org/insights ; United Nations Development Program, *Human Development Report 2004* (New York: Oxford University Press, 2004).

10. Ronald Inglehart, *The Silent Revolution: Changing Values and Political Styles among Western Publics* (Princeton: Princeton University Press, 1977). For Maslow's own position, see Abraham H. Maslow, *Toward a Psychology of Being,* 3rd ed. (New York: Wiley, 1998); and Maslow, *Motivation and Personality,* 3rd ed. (New York: Addison-Wesley, 1987).

11. See Hadley Cantril, *The Pattern of Human Concerns* (New Brunswick: Rutgers University Press, 1965).

12. Ronald Inglehart, "The Nature of Value Change in Post-Industrial Societies," in *Politics and the Future of Industrial Societies,* ed. Leon N. Lindberg (New York: McKay, 1976), 38, 84–85.

13. Morris P. Fiorina, Samuel J. Abrams, and Jeremy C. Pope, *Culture War? The Myth of a Polarized America* (New York: Longman, 2004).

14. See Benjamin Page and Robert Shapiro, *The Rational Public* (Chicago: University of Chicago Press, 1992), 10–11.

15. Ibid., chap. 2.

16. On interest groups, see Allan J. Cigler and Burdett A. Loomis, eds., *Interest Group Politics,* 6th ed. (Washington, D.C.: CQ Press, 2002); and Philip Mundo, *Interest Groups: Cases and Characteristics* (Chicago: Nelson-Hall, 1992). See also David B. Truman, *The Governmental Process* (New York: Knopf, 1951); and H. Gordon Skilling and Franklyn Griffiths, eds., *Interest Groups in Soviet Politics* (Princeton: Princeton University Press, 1971).

17. Skilling and Griffiths, *Interest Groups in Soviet Politics,* 383.

18. See Gabriel A. Almond and G. Bingham Powell Jr., eds., *Comparative Politics Today,* 2nd ed. (Boston: Little, Brown, 1980), 46, 48, 49.

CHAPTER 11

1. Nathan Keyfitz, "The Asian Road to Democracy," in *Comparative Politics: Notes and Readings,* 7th ed., ed. Roy C. Macridis and Bernard B. Brown (Pacific Grove, Calif.: Brooks-Cole, 1990), 111–117.

2. Ibid., 113.

3. Henry Steele Commager, *Majority Rule and Minority Rights* (New York: Oxford University Press, 1943), 80–81.

4. See Robert Dahl, *A Preface to Democratic Theory* (Chicago: University of Chicago Press, 1956).

5. See Richard Rose, "Politics in England," in *Comparative Politics Today: A World View*, ed. Gabriel A. Almond and G. Bingham Powell Jr. (Boston: Little, Brown, 1980), 177.

6. See Gerald Pomper, *Passions and Interests: Political Party Concepts of American Democracy* (Lawrence: University Press of Kansas, 1992). See especially chaps. 3, 5, and 6.

7. See Gerald Pomper, *Voters, Elections, and Parties: The Practice of Democratic Theory* (New Brunswick, N.J.: Transaction Books, 1988), chap. 9.

8. See Robert G. Wesson, *Modern Governments: Three Worlds of Politics* (Englewood Cliffs, N.J.: Prentice Hall, 1981), 277.

9. Commission on Freedom of the Press, *A Free and Responsible Press* (Chicago: University of Chicago Press, 1947).

10. See Stephen Hess, *International News and Foreign Correspondents* (Washington, D.C.: Brookings Institution, 1996); Johanna Neumann, *Lights, Camera, War: Is Media Technology Driving International Politics?* (New York: St. Martin's Press, 1996); Robert I. Rotberg and Thomas G. Weiss, eds., *From Massacres to Genocide: The Media, Public Policy, and Humanitarian Crises* (Washington, D.C.: Brookings Institution, 1996).

11. The Pentagon Papers were a secret history of the Vietnam War commissioned by Secretary of Defense Robert McNamara. They were extremely candid in telling the story of how the United States became involved in the war and fought it, including distortions and lies told to the American public to justify various Vietnam policies. In 1972 Daniel Ellsberg, a Defense Department employee who helped to write the papers, secretly began feeding them to the *New York Times*. They were also published by the *Washington Post*.

CHAPTER 12

1. See Harold and Margaret Sprout, "The Dilemma of Rising Demands and Insufficient Resources," *World Politics* 20, no. 4 (1968): 660–693.

2. See Robert G. Wesson, *Modern Governments: Three Worlds of Politics,* 2nd ed. (Englewood Cliffs, N.J.: Prentice Hall, 1985), chap. 10.

3. H. H. Gerth and C. Wright Mills, eds. and trans., *From Max Weber: Essays in Sociology* (New York: Oxford University Press, 1958), 196–244.

CHAPTER 13

1. Joseph Nye offers an extensive discussion of soft and hard power in his thoughtful book *Bound to Lead: The Changing Nature of American Power* (New York: Basic Books, 1990).

2. Article 5, North Atlantic Charter, Washington, D.C., April 4, 1949.

3. The Charter of the United Nations, United Nations, www.un.org/Overview/Charter/contents.html.

4. Here we follow the excellent analysis of Inis Claude Jr., *Swords into Plowshares: The Problems and Progress of International Organizations,* 4th ed. (New York: Random House, 1984), 236–365. We draw, too, from Claude's equally keen analysis in *Power and International Relations* (New York: Random House, 1962). The analysis has been historically updated with the help of such fine texts as A. Leroy Bennett, *International Organizations: Principles and Issues,* 7th ed. (Englewood Cliffs, N.J.: Prentice Hall, 2001).

5. Two classic works on functionalism are David Mitrany, *A Working Peace System* (Chicago: Quadrangle Books, 1966); and Ernst B. Haas, *Beyond the Nation-State* (Stanford: Stanford University Press, 1964).

6. Thomas L. Friedman, *The Lexus and the Olive Tree: Understanding Globalization* (New York: Farrar, Straus, Giroux, 1999), xiv.

7. See Brad Knickerbocker, "Nongovernmental Organizations Are Fighting and Winning Social, Political Battles," *Christian Science Monitor* Web site, February 6, 2000; James A Paul, "NGOs and Global Policy-Making," Global Policy Forum, June 2000, http:www.globalpolicy.org/ngos/analysis/anal100.htm; Michael Hill, "The NGO Phenomenon," *Baltimore Sun,* January 9, 2005.

8. U.S. Department of State, *2001 Report on Foreign Terrorist Organizations,* www.state.gov/s/ct/rls/fto/2001/index.ctm?decid=5258.

9. U.S. Department of State, *Country Reports on Terrorism, 2004,* April 2005, 92–129.

10. CorpWatch, www.corpwatch.org/issues/PID.jsp?articleid=378, 2002, 2.

CHAPTER 14

1. Bertram Gross, *The Legislative Struggle* (Westport, Conn.: Greenwood, 1978).

2. Hans J. Morgenthau, *Politics among Nations: The Struggle for Power and Peace,* 6th ed., rev. Kenneth Thompson (New York: McGraw, 1985).

3. Graham T. Allison and Philip Zelikow, *Essence of Decision: Explaining the Cuban Missile Crisis,* 2nd ed. (New York: Addison-Wesley Longman, 1999), 255.

4. Ibid., 296.

5. See the work of Robert Michels, *Political Parties* (1915; reprint, New York: Free Press, 1966), who articulated the concept of an "iron law of oligarchy"; C. Wright Mills, *The Power Elite* (New York: Galaxy, 1959); David Spitz, *Patterns of Anti-Democratic Thought* (New York: Macmillan, 1949); Peter Bachrach, *The Theory of Democratic Elitism* (Boston: Little, Brown, 1967); David Ricci, *Community Power and Democratic Theory: The Logic of Political Analysis* (New York: Random House, 1971); and Michael Parenti, *Democracy for the Few* (New York: St. Martin's Press, 1994).

6. Thomas R. Dye and L. Harmon Zeigler, *The Irony of Democracy* (Belmont, Calif.: Wadsworth, 1970), 6.

7. For the appeal of Marxist analysis to the clergy in Latin America, see José Miguez Bonino, *Doing Theology in a Revolutionary Situation* (Philadelphia: Fortress, 1973).

8. For an excellent breakdown of voting patterns from 1976 to 2000, see Marjorie Connelly, "Who Voted: Portrait of American Politics, 1976–2000," *New York Times,* Nov. 12, 2000, Sec. 4.

9. Ibid.

10. Ibid.

11. Ibid.

12. Edmund Burke, "Speech to the Electors of Bristol," *The Works of Edmund Burke,* 3rd ed. (Boston: Little, Brown, 1869), vol. 2, 95. Also quoted in Neal Riemer, ed., *The Representative: Trustee? Delegate? Partisan? Politico?* (Lexington, Mass.: D. C. Heath, 1967), 2–3.

13. John Fitzgerald Kennedy, *Profiles in Courage* (New York: Harper, 1956).

14. John C. Wahlke et al., *The Legislative System* (New York: Wiley, 1962).

15. For an excellent summary of recent findings about the voting characteristics of legislators, see Roger H. Davidson and Walter J. Oleszek, *Congress and Its Members,* 10th ed. (Washington, D.C.: CQ Press, 2006).

16. James MacGregor Burns, *Congress on Trial: The Legislative Process and the Administrative State* (1949; New York: Gordian Press Incorporated, 1966).

17. Glenn R. Parker, *Homeward Bound: Explaining Changes in Congressional Behavior* (Pittsburgh: University of Pittsburgh Press, 1986), 74–75, 78–79. As reported in Glenn R. Parker, "Home Styles—Then and Now," in *Congressional Politics,* ed. Christopher J. Deering (Chicago: Dorsey Press, 1989), 40–61; Steven S. Smith, Jason Robert, and Ryan Vander Wielen, *The American Congress,* 3rd ed. (St. Louis: Washington University, 2004), 11. Also see R. Douglas Arnold, *The Logic of Congressional Action* (New Haven: Yale University Press, 1990), 64–65.

18. Brad Fitch and Kathy Goldschmidt, *Communicating with Congress: How Capitol Hill Is Coping with the Surge in Citizen Advocacy* (Washington, D.C.: Congressional Management Foundation, 2005), 4.

19. Julius Turner, *Party and Constituency: Pressure on Congress* (Baltimore: Johns Hopkins University Press, 1952).

20. Davidson and Oleszek, *Congress and Its Members,* 274.

21. George B. Galloway, *Congress at the Crossroads* (New York: Crowell, 1946), 320.

22. Frank J. Sorauf, *Party and Representation: Legislative Politics in Pennsylvania* (New York: Atherton Press, 1963), 126.

23. Elizabeth Drew, *Whatever It Takes: The Real Struggle for Political Power in America* (New York: Penguin, 1998); and Drew, *The Corruption of American Politics: What Went Wrong and Why* (New York: Overlook Press, 1999). Also see Frank J. Sorauf, *Money in American Elections* (Glenview, Ill.: Scott, Foresman, 1988).

24. Allison and Zelikow, *Essence of Decision.*

25. *Brown v. Board of Education of Topeka, Kansas,* 347 U.S. 483 (1954).

26. Henry Abraham, *The Judicial Process,* 3rd ed. (New York: Oxford University Press, 1975).

27. An excellent study of the challenging decisions justices make is Lee Epstein and Jack Knight's, *Choices Justices Make* (Washington, D.C.: CQ Press, 2002).

PART 4

1. See Neal Riemer, *Creative Breakthroughs in Politics* (New York: Praeger, 1996).

CHAPTER 15

1. Our definition, in contrast to narrower definitions, includes civil wars and revolutionary wars of national liberation. Compare with Francis A. Beer's more traditional definition, in which a clear distinction is made between interstate warfare and domestic violence, in *Peace against War: The Ecology of International Violence* (San Francisco: Freeman, 1981), 6.

2. Again, our conception of peace speaks to the issue of civil wars and revolutionary wars of national liberation. In linking war and peace and the nation-state, we do not ignore criminal violence involving individuals or groups within a nation-state, or troublesome race or class relations. Such violence is not, however, carried on in a systematic and organized way by the political community that has a lawful monopoly on the use of force and violence or by those who aspire to achieve such a monopoly.

3. Beer, *Peace against War,* 36; Ruth Sivard, *World Military and Social Expenditures, 1989* (Washington, D.C.: World Priorities, 1989), 14; Kevin Merida, "Wreckage in Forgotten Lands," *Dallas Morning News,* Aug. 6, 1989, 3M–4M.

4. United Nations Development Program, *Human Development Report 2002* (New York: Oxford University Press, 2003).

5. U.S. war costs for World War II came to $664 billion; for the Korean conflict, $164 billion; for the Vietnam conflict, $352 billion. See Beer, *Peace against War,* 122.

6. National Priorities Project, "The War in Iraq Costs," http://costofwar.com.

7. Stockhom International Peace Research Institute (SIPRI), *Recent Trends in Military Expenditure,* January 2002.

8. U.S. Air Force, http://www.af.mil/factsheets/factsheet.asp?fsID=104.

9. *Jane's All the World's Aircraft, 2004–2005* (Surrey, United Kingdom: Jane's Information Group, 2004).

10. Sivard, *World Military and Social Expenditures, 1991* (Washington, D.C.: World Priorities, 1991), 54; and Sivard, *World Military and Social Expenditures, 1993* (Washington, D.C.: World Priorities, 1993), 56.

11. The Brookings Institution, *The U.S. Nuclear Weapons Cost Study Project.*

12. Sivard, *World Military and Social Expenditures, 1989,* 7.

13. Robert L. Holmes, *On War and Morality* (Princeton: Princeton University Press, 1989), 89–90.

14. For our theoretical observations in this section, we have relied heavily on Oran R. Young, *The Intermediaries: Third Parties in International Crises* (Princeton: Princeton University Press, 1967). See also Richard Rhone, "What You See Is Not Necessarily What You Get: The Role of the United Nations Security Council" (Paper presented at annual conference of the New Jersey Political Science Association, Jersey City, spring 1981); and Douglas W. Simon and Richard Rhone, "United Nations and Conflict Management in the Post–Cold War World," *Harvard Journal of World Affairs* (fall 1995): 1–12.

15. Rhone, "What You See Is Not Necessarily What You Get," 13.

16. United Nations, *United Nations Peacekeeping Update.* Peace and Security Programmes Sector, Department of Public Information, PS/DPI/6/Rev5-May 1994. See also Simon and Rhone, "United Nations and Conflict Management," 3.

17. For a full analysis of this problem, see Simon and Rhone, "United Nations and Conflict Management."

18. Charles W. Kegley Jr. and Eugene R. Wittkopf, *World Politics: Trends and Transformation,* 5th ed. (New York: St. Martin's Press, 1995), 553.

19. David Mitrany, *A Working Peace System: An Argument for the Functional Development of International Organization* (Chicago: Quadrangle Books, 1966).

20. Ibid., 14.

21. Ibid., 9.

22. Ibid., 34–35.

23. Perhaps the leading figure in neofunctionalist thinking is Ernst Haas. See his books: *Beyond the Nation-State: Functionalism and International Organization* (Stanford: Stanford University Press, 1964); *The Uniting of Europe: Political, Social, and Economic Forces, 1950–1957* (Stanford: Stanford University Press, 1958); and *Why We Still Need the United Nations: The Collective Management of International Conflict, 1945–1984* (Berkeley: Institute of International Studies, University of California at Berkeley, 1986).

24. Gene Sharp, *Exploring Nonviolent Alternatives* (Boston: Porter Sargent, 1971). Also see Sharp, *Social Power and Political Freedom* (Boston: Porter Sargent, 1980).

25. Holmes, *On War and Morality,* 272.

26. Ibid., 274.

27. Sharp, *Exploring Nonviolent Alternatives,* 70–72.

CHAPTER 16

1. Cyrus R. Vance, "Law Day Address on Human Rights," in *Human Rights and American Foreign Policy,* ed. Donald P. Kommers and Gilburt D. Loescher (Notre Dame: University of Notre Dame Press, 1979), 310.

2. For an excellent, balanced, and critical discussion of this issue, see Jack Donnelly, *Universal Human Rights in Theory and Practice* (Ithaca: Cornell University Press, 1989).

3. For estimates of those murdered in Nazi concentration camps and elsewhere, see Lucy S. Dawidowicz, *The War against the Jews, 1933–1945* (New York: Holt, Rinehart, and Winston, 1975), 149. See also Martin Gilbert, *The Holocaust: A History of the Jews of Europe during the Second World War* (New York: Holt, Rinehart, and Winston, 1985); Daniel J. Goldhagen, *Hitler's Willing Executioners: Ordinary Germans and the Holocaust* (New York: Knopf, 1996); and Eric A. Johnson, *Nazi Terror: The Gestapo, Jews, and Ordinary Germans* (New York: Basic Books, 1999).

4. See the text of the United Nations Convention on the Prevention and Punishment of the Crime of Genocide, in Neal Riemer, *Protection against Genocide: Mission Impossible?* (Westport, Conn.: Praeger, 2000), appendix 1, 161–164.

5. On this point, see Leo Kuper, *Genocide: Its Political Use in the Twentieth Century* (New Haven: Yale University Press, 1982), especially 9–10 and chap. 8, "Related Atrocities," 138–160.

6. U.S. Department of State, *Country Reports on Human Rights Practices for 1989* (Washington, D.C.: U.S. Government Printing Office, 1990), 792.

7. See Helen Fein, "The Three P's of Genocide Prevention: With Application to a Genocide Fore-told—Rwanda," in Riemer, *Protection against Genocide,* 57.

8. Douglas W. Simon, "The Evolution of the International System and Its Impact on Protection against Genocide," in Riemer, *Protection against Genocide,* 23.

9. Ivo H. Daalder and Michael E. O'Hanlon, *Winning Ugly: NATO's War to Save Kosovo* (Washington, D.C.: Brookings Institution Press, 2000), 3.

10. Vernon Van Dyke, *Human Rights, the United States, and World Community* (New York: Oxford University Press, 1970), 25. Also see Paula Dobriansky, Under Secretary of State for Global Affairs, "Ending Modern Day Slavery: U.S. Effects to Combat Trafficking in Persons," remarks to the Northern California World Affairs Council, San Francisco, March 30, 2004.

11. Moshe Y. Sachs, *The United Nations: A Handbook of the United Nations, Its Structure, History, Purposes, Activities, and Agencies* (New York: Worldmark Press, 1977), 101.

12. Stephen J. Schulhofer, *Rethinking the Patriot Act: Keeping America Safe and Free* (New York: The Century Fund Press, 2005), 2.

13. Ibid., 6.

14. United Nations Development Programme, *Human Development Report 1992* (New York: Oxford University Press, 1992), 27.

15. Ibid., 32.

16. See Lynne B. Iglitzin, "The Patriarchal Heritage," in *Women in the World,* ed. Lynne B. Iglitzin and Ruth Ross (Santa Barbara, Calif.: Clio Books, 1976), 7–8. For updates that substantially confirm these conclusions, see Kelley D. Askin and Dorean M. Koenig, eds., *Women and International Human Rights Law,* 3 vols. (Ardsley, N.Y.: Transnational, 1999–2001); and United Nations Department of International and Economic Affairs et al., *The World's Women, 1970–1990: Trends and Statistics* (New York: United Nations, 1991). See also *The Human Rights Watch Global Report on Women's Human Rights* (New York: Human Rights Watch, 1995).

17. Iglitzin, "Patriarchal Heritage," 14. Here Iglitzin is quoting or citing Carol Andreas, *Sex and Caste in America* (Englewood Cliffs, N.J.: Prentice Hall, 1971), 74.

18. 1977 Declaration of American Women in *The Spirit of Houston: The First National Women's Conference (An Official Report to the President)* (Washington, D.C.: National Commission on the Observance of International Women's Year, 1978).

19. Donnelly, *Universal Human Rights,* 250, 269.

20. Henry Kissinger, *Does America Need a Foreign Policy? Toward a Diplomacy for the 21st Century* (New York: Simon and Schuster, 2001).

21. William F. Schultz, *In Our Own Best Interest: How Defending Human Rights Benefits Us All* (Boston: Beacon Press, 2001).

22. Vance, "Law Day Address on Human Rights," 314.

23. Ibid.

24. On Rwanda, see Fein, "Three P's of Genocide Prevention." On the Dayton accords, see Richard Holbrooke, *To End A War* (New York: Random House, 1998). On NATO intervention in Kosovo, see Daalder and O'Hanlon, *Winning Ugly.*

25. The Universal Declaration of Human Rights and various covenants associated with the declaration provide the norms of what Jack Donnelly terms a "global human rights regime," a system of rules and implementation procedures centered on the United Nations. The principal organs of this regime are the UN Commission on Human Rights and the various human rights committees. See Donnelly, *Universal Human Rights,* 206.

26. As Nigel S. Rodley noted in "Monitoring Human Rights by the U.N. System and Nongovernmental Organizations," in Kommers and Loescher, *Human Rights and American Foreign Policy.*

27. See Michael P. Scharf, *Balkan Justice: The Story behind the First International War Crimes Trial Since Nuremberg* (Durham, N.C.: Carolina Academic Press, 1997). Scharf deals with a key early case handled by the International Tribunal for the former Yugoslavia. Subsequently, more prominent individuals involved in crimes in the Bosnian conflict have been indicted, including Milosevic.

28. See Neal Riemer, *Creative Breakthroughs in Politics* (Westport, Conn.: Praeger,1996); and Riemer, *Protection against Genocide,* chaps. 1 and 8. In addition to the United Nations (a global regime), there are regional human rights regimes: for example, a European regime and an inter-American regime. There are also single-issue regimes, which concern themselves with such issues as workers' rights, racial discrimination, torture, or women's rights. See Donnelly, *Universal Human Rights,* 213–223.

29. See Jo Renee Formicola, *The Catholic Church and Human Rights: Its Role in the Formulation of U.S. Policy, 1945–1980* (New York: Garland, 1988).

30. On interpretations of liberation theology, see José Miguez Bonino, *Doing Theology in a Revolutionary Situation* (Philadelphia: Fortress Press, 1975); Philip Berryman, *Liberation Theology: The Essential Facts about the Revolutionary Movement in Latin America and Beyond* (New York: Beyer, Stone, 1987); Gustavo Gutierrez, *A Theology of Liberation* (New York: Orbis Books, 1973); and John R. Pottenger, "Liberation Theology, Political Realism, and Prophetic Politics," in *Let Justice Roll: Prophetic Challenges in Religion, Politics, and Society,* ed. Neal Riemer (Lanham, Md.: Rowman and Littlefield, 1996).

CHAPTER 17

1. Kofi Annan, *Millennium Report of the Secretary-General of the United Nations* (New York: United Nations, March 2000).

2. United Nations Development Program, *Human Development Report 2004* (New York: Oxford University Press, 2004), 129.

3. Ibid., 129.

4. UNAIDS/WHO, *AIDS Epidemic Update, December 2004* (2004), 1.

5. UN Development Program, *Human Development Report 2004,* 171.

6. Ibid., 142.

7. Jared Diamond, *Guns, Germs, and Steel: The Fates of Human Society* (New York: Norton, 1997).

8. Robert S. McNamara, *The Assault on World Poverty* (Baltimore: Johns Hopkins University Press for the World Bank, 1975), v.

9. UN Development Program, *Human Development Report 2004,* 10.

10. In recent years the Chinese leadership has leaned toward party control and order, as the massacre at Tiananmen Square demonstrated (see chapter 8).

11. Our discussion of China has benefited from the keen analysis of James R. Townsend and Brantly Womack, *Politics in China,* 3rd ed. (Boston: Little, Brown, 1986); Gabriel Almond, G. Bingham Powell Jr., Kaare Strom, and Russell J. Dalton, eds., *Comparative Politics Today: A World View,* 7th ed. (New York: Longman, 2000); and Gordon White, *Riding the Tiger: The Politics of Economic Reform in Post-Mao China* (Stanford: Stanford University Press, 1993). Also of great value was the *Europa Yearbook* (London: Europa Publications, annual).

12. UN Development Program, *Human Development Report 2004,* statistical tables.

13. Ibid.

14. Peter L. Berger, *Pyramids of Sacrifice: Political Ethics and Social Change* (Garden City, N.Y.: Anchor Books, 1976), 155.

15. Ruth Leger Sivard, *World Military and Social Expenditures, 1981* (Leesburg, Va.: World Priorities, 1981), 25; Sivard, *World Military and Social Expenditures, 1989* (Washington, D.C.: World Priorities, 1989), 50.

16. See Sivard, *World Military and Social Expenditures, 1989,* 47–55.

17. World Bank, *World Development Report 1990: Poverty* (New York: Oxford University Press, 1990), 127.

18. For more information, go to the International Monetary Fund's Web site: http://imf.org.

19. For more information, go to the UN Development Program Web site: http://undp.org.

20. UN Development Program, *Human Development Report 2004,* 135–136.

CHAPTER 18

1. Will Steger and Jon Bowermaster, *Saving the Earth: A Citizen's Guide to Environmental Action* (New York: Knopf, 1990), 31.

2. Environmental Protection Agency, "CFCs and Stratospheric Ozone," briefing paper, Office of Public Affairs (Washington, D.C., December 1987).

3. Steger and Bowermaster, *Saving the Earth,* 31–32.

4. Molly O'Meara, "CFC Production Continues to Plummet," in *Vital Signs 1998: The Environmental Trends That Are Shaping Our Future,* by Lester R. Brown et al., ed. Linda Starke (New York: Norton in association with Worldwatch Institute, 1998), 70–71.

5. Ibid.

6. Beatrice Lacoste, "Saving Our Ozone Shield," *Our Planet* 4, no. 4 (1992): 5.

7. Janet L. Sawin, Worldwatch Institute, "Climate Change Indicators on the Rise," *Vital Signs 2005: The Trends That Are Shaping Our Future* (Boston: W.W. Norton, 2005), 41.

8. Ibid, 40.

9. Ibid.

10. Steger and Bowermaster, *Saving the Earth,* 3.

11. Robert Morrison, "Global Climate Change," CRS Research Report (Washington, D.C.: Congressional Research Service, Library of Congress, 1989).

12. Much of this discussion is based on William Ophuls, *Ecology and the Politics of Scarcity: Prologue to a Political Theory of the Steady State* (San Francisco: Freeman, 1977); and William Ophuls and A. Stephen Boyan Jr., *Ecology and the Politics of Scarcity Revisited: The Unraveling of the American Dream* (New York: Freeman, 1992).

13. Garrett E. Hardin, "The Tragedy of the Commons," *Science,* December 13, 1968, 1243–1248.

14. Gary Gardener, "Forest Loss Continues," *Vital Signs 2005* (Washington, D.C.: The Worldwatch Institute, 2005), 92.

15. United Nations, Economic and Social Affairs, *World Population to 2300,* ST/ESH.A236, 2004, 199–200.

16. These are the six types of resources that Paul Ehrlich and Anne Ehrlich deem essential to the survival of human populations. See their *Population, Resources, Environment* (San Francisco: Freeman, 1972), 59. See also Dennis Pirages, *Global Ecopolitics: The New Context for International Relations* (North Scituate, Mass.: Duxbury Press, 1978), especially 14–23.

17. Lester R. Brown, "Eradicating Hunger: A Growing Challenge," in *State of the World 2001,* by Lester R. Brown (New York: Norton, 2001), 44.

18. Herman Kahn, Leon Martel, and William Brown, *The Next 200 Years: A Scenario for America and the World* (New York: Morrow, 1976); Julian L. Simon, *The Ultimate Resource* (Princeton: Princeton University Press, 1981); Simon, *Population and Development in Poor Countries* (Princeton: Princeton University Press, 1992); Simon, *The State of Humanity* (Oxford, UK: Blackwell Publishing, 1996); Dennis T. Avery, *Saving the Planet with Pesticides and Plastic,* 2d ed. (Indianapolis: Hudson Institute, 2000); Bjorn Lomborg, *The Skeptical Environmentalist* (New York: Cambridge University Press, 2001); and Lomborg, *Global Crises, Global Solutions* (New York: Cambridge University Press, 2004).

19. Avery, *Saving the Planet,* 50.

20. Ibid., 52.

21. Robert M. Hazen, *The Breakthrough: The Race for the Superconductor* (New York: Summit Books, 1988), 8.

22. Ibid., 257.

23. World Commission on Environment and Development, *Our Common Future* (New York: Oxford University Press, 1987).

24. Four examples of environmental studies adopting a sustainable development model are the following: World Bank, *World Development Report 1992: Development and the Environment* (New York: Oxford University Press, 1992); Lester R. Brown, Christopher Flavin, and Hilary F. French et al., *State of the World 1993: A Worldwatch Institute Report on Progress toward a Sustainable Society,* ed. Linda Starke (New York: Norton in association with Worldwatch Institute, 1993); Al Gore, *Earth in the Balance: Ecology and the Human Spirit* (New York: Houghton Mifflin, 1992); Maurice Strong, *Where on Earth Are We Going?* (New York: Texere, 2001).

25. World Commission on Environment and Development, *Our Common Future,* 43.

26. Ibid., 49.

27. Ibid., 261.

28. Gore, *Earth in the Balance.*

29. Ibid., 306–307.

30. Strong, *Where on Earth Are We Going?* 372.

31. Ophuls, *Ecology and the Politics of Scarcity;* and Ophuls and Boyan, *Ecology and the Politics of Scarcity Revisited.*

32. Ophuls, *Ecology and the Politics of Scarcity,* 113.

33. Writers who express the need for such an alternative include Hardin, "Tragedy of the Commons," 1243–1248; Hardin, *Exploring New Ethics for Survival* (New York: Viking, 1972); Robert L. Heilbroner, *An Inquiry into the Human Prospect: Updated and Reconsidered for the 1990s* (New York: Norton, 1991); Buckminster R. Fuller, "An Operating Manual for Spaceship Earth," in *Environment and Change: The Next Fifty Years,* ed. William R. Ewald Jr. (Bloomington: Indiana University Press, 1968); B. F. Skinner, *Walden Two* (New York: Macmillan, 1948); and Skinner, *Beyond Freedom and Dignity* (New York: Knopf, 1971). For an analysis of the ecological problem that favors benevolent authoritarianism, see Ophuls, chap. 4, "The Politics of Scarcity," in *Ecology and the Politics of Scarcity.*

Glossary

accommodation   Political behavior that seeks a compromise between competing interests and is marked by cooperation, bargaining, and balloting.

advise and consent   Process by which the U.S. Senate provides advice to the president on treaties and key appointments through the mechanism of hearings and approves these items with a vote requiring a two-thirds majority.

anticolonialism   Political movement seeking to achieve independence for colonies, thus permitting countries to govern themselves.

anti-Semitism   Prejudice against, or dislike of, Jews often leading to discrimination or persecution.

apartheid   Former South African legal system of racial discrimination—separate political, economic, and social life for blacks and whites—designed to perpetuate white supremacy.

aristocracy   A privileged, educated, and powerful upper class that rules society. Interpreted by Plato and Aristotle as government by the best.

arms control   Negotiations and agreements that limit the production of weapons by nations.

autarky   Doctrine of self-sufficiency that calls for protecting a nation against interfering economic activity by other nations.

authoritarian   Anti-democratic political stance that favors placing political power in the hands of an elite group or a dictator.

balance of power   The maintenance of peace through the even distribution of power among competing nations so that no single state or combination of states is dominant.

balance of principles   Edmund Burke's view of the British constitution as a monarchy directed by laws, balanced by an aristocracy, and controlled by the democracy.

behavioralism   Approach to social science that emphasizes empirically observable, discoverable, and explicable patterns of behavior.

behavioral revolution   Influential post–World War II movement in the social sciences promoting the application of scientific methodology to the study of complex human behavior.

Bill of Rights   The first ten amendments to the U.S. Constitution, which establish such individual rights as freedom of speech and religion.

bipolarity   The distribution of power between two nation-states.

bourgeoisie   For Marx, the social class composed of modern capitalists, owners of the means of social production, and employers of wage-labor. In general, the middle class in a capitalist society.

bureaucracy   Governmental departments, ministries, agencies, and officials that carry out public policy, ideally in a rational, efficient, impartial, and stable manner.

capitalism   Economic system marked by private ownership of the means of production and exchange, a market economy, economic competition, free trade, and consumer sovereignty.

carrying capacity   Ability of the earth to support life without suffering deterioration.

civic culture   Set of attitudes toward citizenship and politics held by those in a particular nation.

civil disobedience   Doctrine advocating that an individual may peacefully, publicly, and selectively disobey a morally outrageous government policy, although the individual must be prepared to face the consequences for such disobedience.

civil liberties   Rights that allow citizens to evaluate how the government operates and to assess the character and performance of parties and political leaders.

class   Division of people by their economic, social, and political standing, such as upper class, middle class, and lower class.

class struggle   In the modern period, conflict between the bourgeoisie (capitalist oppressors) and the proletariat (working oppressed).

class values   Political interests shaped by social classes, such as worker or capitalist.

collective security   Joining of countries into an organization to maintain international peace and law. Their collective strength deters or punishes aggression by member nations. The United Nations is one such organization.

communism   Ideology that upholds equality by demanding an end to private wealth and insisting on public ownership of property and the means of production.

connection of powers   Connection of political power among governmental bodies, as opposed to the separation of powers.

conservative/conservatism   In the American context, an ideology that is respectful of traditional values and institutions, including private property, enterprise, and family. Generally favors liberty over equality.

constitution   Founding document or documents that spell out the structure and rules of a political system and reflect the political culture.

contract   An agreement, usually written, and enforceable by law, between two or more people to do something.

conversion   The peaceful transformation of a political opponent through voluntary agreement and free choice. The instruments of conversion include love, conscience, and reason.

creative breakthrough   The significantly fruitful resolution of a problem that conventional wisdom deems insoluble.

crimes against humanity   Acts of persecution, including genocide, against a group of people; considered criminal offenses above all others.

culture wars   Term that came into use during the first decade of the twenty-first century to describe sharp divisions within the American public over fundamental values as reflected in disagreements over such issues as abortion, gay marriage, prayer in public schools, euthanasia, genetic research, and sex education.

deliberative function   That part of the legislative process consisting of discussion and debate on issues.

democracy   Rule by the people, usually via elected representatives, under a constitution that provides for the protection of basic rights and majority rule.

democratic socialism   Ideology committed to popular, constitutional rule and the protection of basic rights while maintaining that key aspects of economic life must be publicly owned, or socially controlled, to ensure an equitable distribution of the community's wealth.

demographic transition theory   Theory that posits that as societies economically grow and become more industrialized, population growth begins to subside. This occurred in Europe and the United States after the advent of the Industrial Revolution.

destruction Political game in which violence and other instruments of force are used to annihilate one's opponent.

détente A relaxation of tensions between nation-states.

developed countries Affluent, highly industrialized, and technologically advanced nations located predominantly in the Northern Hemisphere.

devolution Surrendering of powers to local authorities by a central government.

dialectical change Major societal change arising from the clash of two opposing ideas, forces, or social contradictions.

dictatorship Form of government in which power is centralized under the control of a single person or possibly a small group of people.

dictatorship of the proletariat Rule, sometimes coercive, by the overwhelming majority of workers in their own self-interest.

direct democracy Form of democracy in which citizens vote directly on matters of public policy instead of electing representatives.

disarmament Negotiations and agreements whereby countries agree to reduce or eliminate weapons.

divine law Law revealed by God and found in scripture that helps humans understand natural law while guiding them toward their supernatural end.

domination Policy of exercising direct or indirect control, sometimes despotic, over others.

due process Right that forbids such governmental action as the systematic destruction of a religious group, race, or class, or such spuriously legal action as a trial based on false evidence or coerced confession.

Earth Summit Global environmental conference held in June 1972 in Rio de Janeiro, Brazil. A number of other world environmental conferences have since taken place.

ecology The relationship between organisms and their environments.

economic well-being Level of income, food, health care, and education that satisfies minimum quality-of-life standards and permits full growth and development.

egalitarianism Political goal, stressing equality, that unites socialists and traditional communists.

elite Select group, often characterized by superior political, economic, social, or cultural skills or power.

emerging economies Economies of former communist bloc countries that began shifting to a free market system with the end of the cold war. Hungary, Poland, and the Czech Republic are examples of emerging economies.

empiricism Approach to social science concerned with political phenomena—what has been, what is, and what will be. Methods of empirical science include observation, description, and reasoning.

Enlightenment Eighteenth-century, Western-dominated movement that believed in reason, freedom, and progress.

equality Concept that emphasizes equal political and social rights or the condition of being neither superior nor inferior.

eternal law The reason of God ("God's grand design") by which all things are governed.

ethics The study of the nature of moral standards and choices of judgment and behavior.

ethnic cleansing Forceful displacement of a group from a given territory based on their religion, ethnicity, race, or nationality. May involve a variety of methods, including mass murder, military force, or intimidation through torture or rape.

European Union   Regional organization built on the foundation of free trade. Seeks total European economic integration.

explanation   Process of fitting the pieces of a scientific puzzle together.

extensive republic   Madison's term for a federal republic governing a large territory.

Fabians   Group of British intellectuals in the nineteenth and twentieth centuries committed to the gradual achievement of socialism.

faction   Self-interested group that acts in ways inconsistent with the common good.

fascism   Authoritarian political ideology characterized by dictatorial leadership, an oppressive one-party system, strong nationalism, and aggressive militarism.

federalism   Governmental system that combines central authority for nationwide concerns with state, provincial, or regional authority for local concerns, with certain powers shared by, and certain powers denied to, both levels of government.

finite resources   Resources, such as minerals, petroleum, and safe drinking water, whose quantities are believed to be limited.

freedom   Power over one's destiny, interpreted negatively as the absence of restraints and positively as the ability to fulfill peaceful and creative potentialities.

functionalism   Concept in international politics that asserts that the barriers to cooperation and peaceful conflict resolution can best be overcome when peoples and nations work together to meet common needs and advance mutual interests. Emphasis is on such functional areas as trade, health, agriculture, transportation, and environment.

general will   The constant will of the sovereign people; the public good or public interest that is always right.

genocide   Systematic mass destruction of a national, ethnic, racial, or religious group.

globalization   Rapid and explosive increase in integrative international economic activity—trade, investment, and banking. Built on the twin pillars of capitalism and high-tech communications.

global warming   Theory that posits that because of the emission and trapping of heat-absorbing gases, such as carbon dioxide, CFCs, methane, nitrous oxide, and ozone, the planet's temperature is rising.

goal   An objective.

grand debate   Function of the United Nations whereby problems can be presented, discussed, and analyzed, ideas can be tested, and the strength of policies can be measured.

greenhouse effect   The trapping of heat-absorbing gases within the earth's atmosphere, which increases the temperature of the planet. See also global warming.

hard power   Military or economic influence, as opposed to soft power, which involves less tangible elements such as persuasion, political skill, and public opinion.

hegemony   When one nation-state has overwhelming, dominating power.

Holocaust   Systematic extermination of six million Jews in World War II by the Nazis and their supporters.

human law   Application, in specific circumstances, of natural law in our earthly affairs.

human rights   Freedom—legal, political, or moral—from government violations of people's integrity; civil and political liberties; and satisfaction of vital human needs such as food, shelter, clothing, health care, and education.

hypothesis   Tentative assertion—usually attempting to explain a cause and effect—made in order to guide the empirical and logical investigation of a problem.

integration   Groups of states, at the regional or global level, expanding their economic interaction to the point where the separate national economies become increasingly interdependent.

interest aggregation   Means of selecting priorities in which political actors build support for certain proposals and not for others, usually by working with other like-minded individuals or groups.

interest articulation   Expression of political actors' needs, interests, and desires, as by voting, speaking at public forums, or joining political parties or interest groups.

interest group   Members of the public who organize in an attempt to shape public policy on issues of concern to them.

International Monetary Fund (IMF)   Specialized agency of the United Nations whose concerns include stabilizing national financial systems, promoting international monetary cooperation and exchange stability, and managing debt.

isolation   Policy of withdrawal from, and nonparticipation in, world affairs.

judicial review   The ability of the U.S. Supreme Court to declare an act of Congress or a state legislature unconstitutional.

justice   Variously defined as fairness, rightfulness, giving persons their due, and a balancing of liberty, equality, and fraternity.

laissez-faire   Economic policy in which commerce receives minimum interference from government.

law   Rule established by authority or custom; according to Thomas Aquinas, "an ordinance of reason for the common good, promulgated by him who has the care of the community."

least developed countries (LDCs)   World's economically poorest nations.

least free   The powerless, the deprived, and the maltreated; often the poor, racial minorities, women, and the politically oppressed.

legislative function   Formal responsibility of legislatures to make laws.

legitimacy   The general acceptance by political actors and citizens that government actions are appropriate and fully accepted.

liberal/liberalism   Modern political ideology that favors government intervention in the interest of public welfare, social justice, and fair play.

liberal democracy   Constitutional government characterized by popular rule, protection of basic rights, and political and economic competition.

libertarian   A person with strong beliefs that oppose government intervention in economic and personal affairs; believes in the maximization of personal freedom.

libertarianism   In the American context, an ideology that consistently opposes government intervention in economic affairs and favors expansion of personal freedoms.

liberty   Freedom from slavery, imprisonment, captivity, or any form of unlawful or arbitrary control; the sum of rights of a free individual or group.

lion and fox   Game of politics as understood by Machiavelli, in which a state's vital interests are at stake and must be protected by the use of both force and craft.

loyal opposition   Name given to the opposing, or minority, party in the United Kingdom.

majority rule   Power of one-half of the members, plus one, of any decision-making group to bind the remainder of that group to a decision.

materialism   Belief that a society's economic structure is the underlying force behind all societal institutions, including law, politics, ethics, religion, philosophy, ideology, and art.

meritocracy   Achievement of employment and advancement by merit as opposed to other means, such as patronage or personal favor. Often applies to systems of personnel recruitment in government by civil service examination.

metanoia   Fundamental transformation of a world view.

Millennium Development Goals A set of eight development goals to drastically reduce global poverty in the twenty-first century; adopted by the United Nations in 2000.

mixed economy An economy that is both privately and publicly controlled.

model Simplified version of what occurs in reality; highlights the important elements in the subject of interest.

modified laissez-faire political economy Economy without government intervention; compatible with liberty, the satisfaction of human needs, and the advancement of individual and social happiness.

multilateralism Groups of countries operating through international organizations and engaged in collective problem solving and problem resolution.

multinational corporation (MNC) Private company operating in more than one country.

multipolarity When power is distributed among several nation-states.

national interests Fundamental needs and interests of nations, such as security, liberty, justice, and welfare, essential for independence, prosperity, and power.

nationalism Strong sense of cultural belonging and group loyalty generally used to achieve political, economic, and social freedom.

nation-state Term used by political scientists to label countries. Combines the legal term "state" with the more psychological term "nation," which is a strong sense of group identity.

natural law That part of the eternal law known through reason, such as the ability to discern good from evil.

Nazism Particularly racist, anti-Semitic, and militantly aggressive variety of fascism that characterized German politics under Adolf Hitler's dictatorship.

neofunctionalism Theory that argues that integration must take place at the political level as well as at the economic, technical, and humanitarian levels. Working within traditional international organizations, neofunctionalists, unlike traditional functionalists, do not avoid political problems or nationalism.

neoimperialism Body of thought that asserts that multinational corporations, owned and controlled by powerful forces in the developed Northern Hemisphere, take advantage of poor, developing countries in the Southern Hemisphere by exploiting cheap labor, squandering natural resources, and reaping enormous profits.

neutrality Legally based policy of remaining nonaligned with adversaries for the duration of a war. Can also be practiced in times of peace by the taking of an officially neutral position on a variety of international issues.

new balance of power New multipolar balance of power that may include a number of major nation-states as well as regional organizations. While military might would be retained, greater emphasis would be placed on economic might. See also balance of power.

newly industrialized economies (NIEs) Several of the dynamic and relatively prosperous Asian economies along the Pacific Rim, exclusive of Japan. They include South Korea, Taiwan, Singapore, and Thailand.

nonalignment Policy whereby states refuse to participate in the struggle between major powers or superpowers.

nongovernmental organization (NGO) Private international actors whose purposes and activities parallel those of interest groups.

nonrenewable resources Irreplaceable resources, such as fossil fuels.

nonviolent civilian defense Body of thought that maintains that a breakthrough to a more peaceful world can be achieved if nonviolence is seriously considered. Espouses the notion that traditional means of dealing with conflict are inadequate and in some cases have proved disastrous.

oligarchy   Generally understood as government by the few, especially for corrupt and selfish purposes. According to Plato, it meant government by the rich and money loving.

ozone layer   Thin layer of ozone that encircles the earth's stratosphere and protects the planet from the full force of the sun's ultraviolet rays.

partisan   One who, more often than not, votes with his or her party on key issues.

patriarchy   Belief in, or practice of, male superiority or domination.

Patriot Act   Legislation passed in the wake of the September 11, 2001, attacks on the World Trade Center and the Pentagon that is designed to enhance the tools available to law enforcement for detecting, tracking, and prosecuting terrorists and those who aid them.

peace   The absence of war. A condition of harmony between nation-states that enables them to cooperatively, lawfully, and voluntarily work out conflicts and deal with disputes.

peaceful settlement   Resolution of disputes through nonviolent means, such as influence, inquiry, mediation, and conciliation.

players   Contestants in the game of politics who win or lose, who compete or cooperate in pursuit of certain goals, who exercise power or will, who enjoy or suffer.

pluralist school/pluralism   Political school maintaining that balance in diverse political communities is best achieved through a representative democracy acting in accord with policies that advance the general welfare, while still recognizing that a rough approximation of the public interest emerges from the clash of contending interests.

policy   In the context of political science, a government course or general plan of action designed to solve problems or achieve specified goals.

polis   Greek city-state.

political actor   Individual or group that expresses and shapes public values, struggles for power, and decides issues of public policy.

political creativity   Achievement, in both theory and practice, of a more fruitful, ethical, empirical, and prudential understanding of politics.

political culture   The distinguishing attitudes, habits, and behavior patterns of a political community.

political health   The political, economic, and social well-being of the political community judged in terms of peace and peaceful constitutional change, security, liberty, democratic governance, justice, economic prosperity, and ecological balance.

political ideologies   Beliefs and practices that guide political actors in real political communities.

political obligation   Concept that examines why people obey or disobey those who demand their political allegiance, such as a government, a law, or a state.

political party   Organized group that seeks to elect candidates to government office. It represents a "team" that seeks to control government.

political science   Field of study characterized by a search for critical understanding of the good political life, significant empirical understanding, and wise political and policy judgments.

political values   Important beliefs about the goals, principles, and policies that are worthwhile in public affairs.

politics   Process whereby public values are debated, political actors cooperate and struggle for power, and policy judgments are made and implemented.

polity   Constitutional government—a mixture of democracy and oligarchy. Form of government believed by Aristotle to provide the best practicable good life.

polyarchy   Rule by the many in a democratic and constitutional system.

popular sovereignty   Constitutional rule by the many. Also known as republican rule.

populist/populism   In the American context, an ideology that favors government intervention in economic affairs and may oppose expansion of some "liberal" personal freedoms. See also liberal/liberalism.

positivism   Philosophy stating that humans can know only what is based on observable, scientific facts or on data derived from experience.

poverty   Level of income, food, health care, education, or shelter that is below minimum quality-of-life standards; may preclude full growth and development.

power   Political, legal, economic, military, social, or moral ability of one political actor to get another to do or not to do something.

power politics   Political pattern characterized by the acquisition, preservation, and balancing of power. Most often used to describe the competitive-conflictive behavior of the United States and Soviet Union during the cold war.

prescriptive constitution   Successful and proven ways of conducting social, economic, and political business that originate in a community's history.

preventive diplomacy   Action by such groups as the United Nations to help states, often smaller ones, settle disputes peacefully, before the disputes escalate and involve major powers.

principle   Basic truth or doctrine used as a basis of reasoning or a guide to behavior.

proletariat   Class of modern wage laborers.

prudence   Wise judgment about the practical tasks of politics, respectful both of sound values and the limitations and opportunities of social reality.

public interest   Community interest that transcends the personal interests of individuals or groups and expresses the best long-range interests of the nation.

racism   Belief in the superiority or inferiority of a given race resulting in discrimination against, or maltreatment of, the supposed inferior.

realism   Position advocated by Reinhold Niebuhr that states, in part, that there can be no perfect justice and that in politics there are only proximate solutions to insoluble problems. Despite this, Niebuhr urged people to fight for reform.

renewable resources   Resources, such as forests, that can be replaced.

representative function   One of the roles performed by legislative bodies. Legislators represent and look out for the interests of their constituents who elected them to office.

representative government   Constitutional system in which government leadership is determined, directly or indirectly, by decisions of the electorate.

republicanism   Constitutional rule by the many.

responsible citizenship   The sensible response of citizens to social, economic, and political tasks and problems.

revisionists   Adherents to this intellectual tradition, led by Eduard Bernstein, who agreed with Marx's outlook but opted for a peaceful, evolutionary path to socialism. See also Marxism, socialism.

revolution of rising expectations   Phrase characterizing the hopes for a better way of life, especially among peoples in the developing world.

rule of law   Idea of regularized and consistent laws that are not changed by the whim of leaders or by circumstances like anarchy.

rules   Agreed-on procedures that regulate the conduct of the political game.

sanctions   Penalties, often economic, imposed on states that violate human rights or international law.

science   The critical and systematic search for knowledge.

scientific method   Pattern of reasoning used in the systematic search for knowledge. It involves identifying the problem, articulating a guiding hypothesis, obtaining evidence to test the hypothesis, and validating and explaining the significance of the hypothesis and the findings that support it.

separate but equal   Constitutional doctrine in the United States from 1896 to 1954 that held that equality was not violated if blacks were required to use separate facilities in transportation, education, and other public areas, as long as the services were equal.

separation of powers   Division of powers into legislative, executive, and judicial in the U.S. government.

sexism   Discrimination based on gender.

social contract   Agreement in which a number of people unite for a common purpose.

soft power   Influence exercised by less tangible means than raw power, such as persuasion, public opinion, and political skill. Stands in contrast to hard power, which is the application of military or economic power.

stakes   That which can be gained in victory or lost in defeat.

standard operating procedures (SOPs)   Guidelines and procedures used by government organizations in carrying out policy.

state   Legal term for the entity commonly known as a country; requires people, territory, government, and acceptance by the international community.

strategies and tactics   Plans of action, schemes of attack or defense, and judgments that bring about victory or defeat.

strike   Withdrawal of important services by one party from another in order to advance its own objectives.

supervisory function   The legislative responsibility to monitor and oversee the work of the executive and the bureaucracy.

sustainable development   Rational and equitable approach to development that attempts to balance societal needs against environmental limitations.

terrorism   The use of violence against civilians to achieve political goals.

theory   Larger body of principles offered to explain phenomena.

third-party activities   Conflict resolution techniques used by the United Nations and other international actors not involved in a given dispute. They include good offices, conciliation, investigation, mediation, arbitration, observation, truce supervision, and interposition.

timocracy   Government by people of honor and ambition.

tort   A wrongful act, injury, or damage (not involving a breach of contract) for which a civil action can be brought.

totalitarian/totalitarianism   Ideology that espouses the complete political, economic, and social control of people and institutions by a dictatorial, single-party regime.

tragedy of the commons   Ecological metaphor calling attention to the overuse and eventual destruction of commonly held and used resources.

trusteeship   Commission from the United Nations to a country to look after a region, territory, or colony until the people of that land are believed ready for independence and self-government.

tyranny   Lawless rule by one leader.

ultra vires   Beyond the law.

unitary government   Form of government in which all major power and policy emanates from the central government.

United Nations Development Program (UNDP)   Provides development advice, planning, and grant support to countries of the developing world.

utilitarianism   Creed that accepts utility and the search for happiness as its foundation.

utopia   Perfect political and social order.

utopian socialists   Nineteenth-century writers who stressed cooperation and the possibilities of using education to change the social and economic environments.

validation   Corroboration to determine a fit between a hypothesis and evidence.

war   Military activity, or armed violence, carried out in a systematic and organized way by nation-states (or organized groups that aspire to become nation-states) against other nation-states (or organized groups with nationalistic aspirations).

war crimes   Violations of the laws of war as spelled out by international covenants; include atrocities committed against civilians and the mistreatment of prisoners of war.

welfare   Government provisions for, or contributions to, individual needs for employment, income, food, housing, health, and literacy.

welfare state   Society that provides social services to ensure better family life, health care, and housing; protection against unemployment; and security in old age.

wipeout   Pattern of politics in which one player, insisting on total domination, encounters resistance and employs brute physical force to destroy an opponent.

World Bank   Specialized agency of the United Nations, also known as the International Bank for Reconstruction and Development (IBRD), that makes loans to countries for development purposes.

writ of habeas corpus   Literally, "produce the body"; legal document requiring that a prisoner be brought before a court to determine whether he or she is lawfully being held in jail.

Index

Author Citations